ERATUM:

Page 411, footnote 122: The word "sociology"
should read "sociobiology."

ACTION THEORY
AND THE
HUMAN CONDITION

ACTION THEORY
AND THE
HUMAN CONDITION

Talcott Parsons

THE FREE PRESS
A Division of Macmillan Publishing Co., Inc.
NEW YORK
Collier Macmillan Publishers
LONDON

The Free Press
A Division of Macmillan Publishing Co., Inc.
866 Third Avenue, New York, N.Y. 10022

Collier Macmillan Canada, Ltd.

Library of Congress Catalog Card Number: 77–94084

Printed in the United States of America

printing number

1 2 3 4 5 6 7 8 9 10

Library of Congress Cataloging in Publication Data

Parsons, Talcott
    Action theory and the human condition.

    Bibliography: p.
    Includes index.
    1. Sociology--Addresses, essays, lectures.
2. Social medicine--Addresses, essays, lectures.
3. Educational sociology--Addresses, essays,
lectures. I. Title.
HM24.P283   301   77-94084
ISBN 0-02-923990-7

To my fellow
members of the Faculty Seminar
on the Human Condition

University of Pennsylvania, 1974–1976

in appreciation of their
contribution to a memorable experience
of intellectual effervescence

Contents

Preface

The present volume is the promised sequel to *Social Systems and the Evolution of Action Theory,* published by The Free Press in the summer of 1977. As a sequel it is, relative to the promises made in its predecessor, only a few months late, which seems to me to be a creditable performance, especially since a substantial part of the extra time was taken by the author for last minute revisions, especially of Chapter 15, which is here published for the first time.

As compared with its predecessor this volume, though the bulk of it also consists of previously published essays, has a different emphasis. The preceding collection, it may be said, in a relative sense looked more toward the past. This is true above all of Part I of it, which dealt especially with matters significant to my intellectual career and its development. In a somewhat different sense, it was true of Part II, which presented four papers that may be said to have been particularly significant in consolidating my theoretical position as an analyst of the social system, and very tentatively looking toward further systematization of the analysis of the general system of action (Chapter 10).

Though the difference is relative, the present volume looks more to the future—not, of course, primarily from the personal point of view of the author, who has already exhausted most of his career time span, but along the lines of theoretical development that I hope I will be remembered as having done something to initiate and stimulate.

Concern with the idea of evolution permeates both volumes, and this applies not only to the evolution of theory but also of action systems in an empirical sense. Readers of both will, however, note that the present volume is first concerned substantially more with the general system of action as compared with the stress, in the case of its predecessor, on the social system. Thus all of the sections into which the essays of this volume are divided concern boundaries of the general system of action. This is relatively obvious for the groups dealing with health, in its relation to the organic world, and religion, in relation to what we call the "telic" world. However, it is also true of the treatment of higher education in its relations to cognitive culture and to science generally, including the physical and biological sciences and, of course, certain aspects of philosophy.

Indeed, the analysis of this book may be said to head up to its concluding chapter, "A Paradigm of the Human Condition," which, as noted, is here published for the first time. I think its genesis is adequately explained in the introductory materials. Here it is sufficient to say that the logic of the line of theoretical development that I have been following throughout my intellectual career has for some time been pointing to the necessity of going, in systematic terms, beyond even the general system of action, to attempt to work out something at a still more general level—namely, that which is here called the human condition.

The boundary of the general system of action that is most prominently involved is the one vis-à-vis the organic system, a theme which figured prominently in the last collection of essays. We should not, however, neglect the importance of much further exploration of the boundary relations between the system of action and the physical world, starting perhaps from the recently developing subdiscipline of the sociology of science. And, not least, just possibly there are new opportunities for intellectual progress in understanding the critically important boundary problems between the action system and the "telic grounding," as we have chosen to call it, of action in the human condition.

This particular way of "looking toward the future" is, among the possibilities available, highly selective. Nonetheless, this avenue has caught not only my own imagination, but also that of a small group of collaborators. It may not prove to be the least important of the possibilities with which the complex intellectual culture of our time has come to be concerned. This is, however, in no way meant to disparage other lines of concentration on the intellectual future, notably the more technical developments internal to the established disciplines. For persons defined as sociologists, this clearly includes not only the further development of empirical knowledge in our field, but also the more technical theoretical development, specifically of the theory of the social system. My venturing beyond that area—in a sense of level of generalization—by no means implies that I feel that all the problems within it have been solved. Quite the contrary! I do feel, however, that putting such problems in a more general framework can contribute importantly to making progress in their solution. Perhaps the final section of Chapter 15, dealing with the articulation of human biology with kinship structure at the social level, can serve as an example of this potential.

I should like to take this occasion to express my appreciation to The Free Press for being willing to include in the present volume an updated version of the bibliography of my personal publications. After an interval of nearly a decade, this should prove useful to various interested people. Then this is the occasion to express very special thanks to Ms. Mounira

Charrad. As my research assistant through the period of preparing both the present volume and its predecessor for the press, she has contributed much faithful, detailed, and imaginative work, without which neither book could have been successfully completed.

Talcott Parsons
October 1977

General Introduction

As the latest in a series of my collected essays published by The Free Press, the present volume should be considered in close relation to its very recent predecessor, *Social Systems and the Evolution of Action Theory*.[1] Taken together, the two collections document certain main trends of interest and thinking in my theoretical work that have been salient during approximately the last decade.

The two volumes are organized about two aspects of the same general theme, which was discussed in the General Introduction to *Social Systems and the Evolution of Action Theory*. This is the attempt to help solve problems inherent at a given system level, by systematic consideration of their relations to theory at the next more general level. There had been an earlier history of trying to move from the economy as a subsystem of the society to the societal system as a whole and to relate these two levels to each other.

After various preliminary attempts, *Social Systems and the Evolution of Action Theory* documents, more fully than before, the effort to deal seriously with the problems of the relations between the social system and the general system of action; it was a renewed attempt after the earlier one documented in *Toward a General Theory of Action*.[2] Although the implications of this venture are still very incompletely worked out, the present volume is organized mainly about the step of theory development that seeks to go beyond even the general system of action. Thus, the essays in this book seek to place the general system of action in a still broader setting, that which we have called the "human condition" considered as a system.

An explicit treatment of the problem of dealing with the human condition level in terms of technical and formal theory is made in Part IV of this collection. As I hope will be made clear, the chapter included

---

[1] Talcott Parsons, *Social Systems and the Evolution of Action Theory* (New York: Free Press, 1977).

[2] Talcott Parsons and Edward A. Shils (eds.), *Toward a General Theory of Action* (Cambridge, Mass.: Harvard University Press, 1951).

1

therein represent a tentative attempt, which I and a group of collaborators hope to improve upon in later publications. However, for the first time we make this problem area explicit and try to *do* something about it in a formal theoretical sense rather than engaging only in programmatic discussion of what needs to be done. I do not think that more has to be said either about the preliminary nature of this effort or about my indebtedness to the group with whom I have worked on these problems at the University of Pennsylvania since 1974.

Social Systems and the Evolution of Action Theory paved the way for this volume in two particularly important respects. Most notably, it brought to light, especially in Part I, further developments of thinking about the central problem of the relations between the theoretical concerns and structure of the theory of action, on the one hand, and of theory concerning biological systems in the organic sense, on the other. Starting with the General Introduction and Chapter 1 of that volume, there are several treatments of a new level of concern with the relevance to the social scientist of biological theory, as well as examples of the channels through which this relevance has become salient and fruitful. Accordingly, the first three parts of the present volume include essays, to be interpreted against this background, that are concerned with what are at least boundary problems of the traditionally conceived action system vis-à-vis that of the human condition.

Part I consists of four essays that deal, from different perspectives, with problems of health and illness and their setting in modern societies. Appropriate details about the occasions for their writing appear in the Introduction to Part I. (For purposes of the present General Introduction, however, the main point is to make clear the place of this set in the larger outline just sketched.)

The interest in problems of health and illness grew, for me personally, out of my interest in the professions, which in turn arose from my concern with the nature of the modern industrial economy, referred to as "capitalistic." The focus of my initial interest lay in the problem of the role of what, especially in the utilitarian tradition,[3] is called "self-interest." By contrast with the usual depiction of the businessman, the professional has tended to be characterized as repudiating the imputation of primary actuation by self-interest in the relevant sense.

Pursuing my undergraduate concern with biology, I choose medicine as the first profession to study.[4] In the course of this study, I became very much interested in the problem of self-interest in the sense associated with economics and the utilitarian tradition, as well as in the problems pre-

---

[3] For a discussion of this tradition see Talcott Parsons, *The Structure of Social Action* (1937); reprint ed., New York; Free Press, 1949), chaps. 2 and 3.

[4] Talcott Parsons, *The Social System* (New York: Free Press, 1951), chap. 10, "Social Structure and Dynamic Process: "The Case of Modern Medical Practice."

sented by what was then called the "psychic factor" in disease and its relation to the rise of psychiatry as a branch of the medical profession. If nothing else, the prominence of such phenomena clearly established the importance of a subtle set of connections between social structure, on the one hand, and the state of human organisms and personalities, on the other.

Part I of the present volume begins with what I called a "reconsideration" of my approach to the problem of the "sick role" and that of the physician as these had been set forth in my most general statement in the field more than twenty years earlier.[5] In the light of justified criticisms and further consideration, a number of qualifications of the earlier statements were introduced, but I think it is fair to say that the essentials of the earlier position are reaffirmed in Chapter 1. Perhaps the most succinct way of making this point is to express my conviction that the states we define in our culture as illness, and the social structures in which sick people are placed, constitute a subtle and complex set of articulations between structures and processes at the level of action in our technical sense (including personality and behavioral systems and the states and vicissitudes of human organisms.)[6]

Chapter 2 shifts the focus of attention to a development in the health complex that had become much more conspicuous in the period between my original study and the recent concern, namely, biomedical research. The latter area has in critical ways to deal with human "subjects" in order to carry out its functions. My main concern in the article reprinted as Chapter 2 of this volume was to show that the social structures in terms of which this extension of function had been accommodated to were above all understandable against the background of development in the "professional complex" analyzed in earlier studies.

Chapter 3 is written on a more general level. It deals with the problems of defining health and its negative, illness (or, as the editors preferred to say, "disease"), as a human—that is, action—concern in general and in the context of our theoretical interests in particular. It was in this connection that, for the first time, it seemed appropriate and feasible in examining such a problem to invoke the formal paradigm of the human condition, which is explicated in Chapter 15 of this volume. The problem of defining health and illness has proved to be a difficult one in the framework of our culture. Most conspicuously, there has been a strong tendency toward ambivalence and ambiguity with reference to the category of "mental" health and/or illness. This has frequently been associated with a tendency to give up on the problem and to settle for defining health and

---

[5] Ibid.

[6] Renée C. Fox, "The Medicalization and Demedicalization of American Society," *Daedalus*, vol. 106, no. 1 (1977): 9–22.

illness as "physical" conditions, which must be taken to mean "organic" in the sense of drastically downplaying the "mental" component.[7]

Needless to say, this so-called solution is radicaly unsatisfactory from the present point of view in that it constitutes a rather crude case of reductionism in a field of paramount concern in the current human bioethical context. I think that the alternative presented in Chapter 3 is greatly preferable to the reductionist position. The notable feature of this alternative, theoretically speaking, is precisely that in dealing with mental health, it does *not* invoke considerations *internal* either to the action system or to the organic but steps to a level of generality higher than either, namely, that of the human condition. The important point is that this level embraces *both* the organic and the action level and defines their relations in terms of a third level that is still higher than either in the scale of generality. I agree in advance with skeptical commentators that this is a "radical" solution of the problem, but is anything less radical of sufficient promise to merit serious consideration?

Chapter 4 is on a different theme. It presents some considerations relevant to relating psychoanalytic theory to that of action. There seemed, in spite of its brevity, good reason to include it in this collection, but the question was where? The decisive criterion was the intimate relation of Freud's theoretical work generally to problems of mental health and illness. Since, as has just been noted, in dealing with problems of heath and illness in the present context, I was concerned with emphasizing strongly the importance of a positive theoretical treatment of problems of mental health, it seemed useful to include an indication of the lines of theoretical work that are available to give a sound theoretical underpinning to that endeavor.

In the revisit to Freud's *The Interpretation of Dreams,*[8] which is documented in this chapter, I was in particular impressed with how strongly Freud, in this his first major theoretical work, emphasized that he was dealing with the structures and processes of a "psychic" system, the term he himself used, and was not treating neurosis primarily as disturbance of the organism in the sense of somatic medicine. Insights based in considerable part on this revisit to Freud's work figure prominently in the discussions in Part IV of the modes of articulation of the individual's personality and the organism, that is, his own body. Without insight going well beyond the level common in our generation, long after Freud's own works, the essential articulation could not be worked out.

The selections included in Part II turn to an area that is peripheral to the system of action in one sense, especially to the social system within it.

---

[7] The Concept of Health," *Hastings Center Report,* vol. 1 no. 3 (1973). The issue contains five essays on health and illness; see especially the paper by Daniel Callahan.

[8] Sigmund Freud, *The Interpretation of Dreams,* in vols. 4 and 5 of *The Standard Edition of Complete Psychological Works of Sigmund Freud* (London: Hogarth Press and the Institute of Psychoanalysis, 1953; first published in German in 1900).

The focus of this section is higher education. Higher education in this respect is part of both the modern type of social system and the cultural system within the action system. However, the aspect of the cultural system that is most directly relevant to Part II is that which we have previously called "cognitive symbolization." This in turn of course has ramified articulations with aspects of the human condition other than the action system itself. In the first instance both the physical world and the organic are the objects of ramified clusters of scientific disciplines. Yet they also consist of objects that are of a variety of other types of significance to human beings. Since the modern phase of the development of higher education, the physical and biological sciences have constituted a major, and perhaps until recently, growing part of its curriculum and research concern.

More recently there has been a notable growth of a third set of intellectual disciplines, often called the social sciences. Because this group includes psychology, I prefer to use the term "sciences of action." These sciences have developed especially closely in connection with the system of higher education. Substantial development has also occurred in a fourth area—that which is ordinarily called the "humanities" in the sense of a set of disciplines that in German are grouped with what English speakers call the "sciences" under the concept *Wissenschaft*.

Not only are the intellectual disciplines characterized as clearly including three of the four primary subsystems as objects (and I think in a slightly modified sense the fourth) but also *knowledge* of all three categories must clearly be grounded in considerations deriving from sources other than the relevant externalities themselves. Whatever other philosophical positions may be possible, I have explicitly taken one in the Kantian tradition. Starting with the objects of science in the strictest sense, this position maintains that the sense data that constitute the empirical components of knowledge (for example, of the physical and organic worlds) must be articulated with the categories of the understanding that are independent of the raw data. My collaborators and myself further maintain that this consideration applies also to knowledge of the phenomena of action. The relevance of the Kantian epistemology to our treatment of the human condition and, in articulation with that, of higher education, is explored in Chapter 15.[9]

The relation of the action system to the telic system, the fourth primary subsystem of the human condition that we have postulated, is the subject matter of the essays in Part III. That this relation is in some respects subject to "objectification" is indicated by the fact that not only have such problems been treated philosophically ever since men have philosophized but also that there are important scientific treatments of problems in this area, such as those in the history, sociology, and psychology of religion. When examined in these ways, the phenomena of religion—

[9] Figure 1, Chapter 15 of this volume.

or, to quote William James's title, "the varieties of religious experience" [10] —must be treated as involving nonempirical objects of some sort unless such experience is held to be totally "internal" (not experience "of" anything). This, therefore, is not to imply that there is no input to the action system from the telic, and that there is "nothing" beyond the boundary of the action system in this direction. It is not my present concern to discuss the complex philosophical problems of this area but only to indicate that this is an area that the action scientist, who takes seriously the importance of the action system's relation to the larger human condition, cannot afford to neglect. We would contend that structuring the problem of the nature of appropriate cognitive orientation in this area sets the stage for consideration of some of what in the light of Western cultural tradition are still subtler problems of the nature of the noncognitive components.

The nature of and occasions for writing the essays included in Part II are explained in the Introduction to that part. However, it should be remembered that all these selections come from a period in which I was very much concerned in general with problems of the nature and status, in modern societies, of the phenomenon of higher education and its emergence as a salient feature of such societies. The most important documentation of this interest for me is *The American University*.[11] The present set of essays, however, explore some of the important aspects of the subject such as the conditions of the growth of the system in American Society, an aspect of the relation of its structure to that of the larger society (Chapter 7),[12] and the question of stability and change in the system.

Just as dealing with the social status of biomedical research in Chapter 2 formed something of a bridge to the treatment of higher education as an essential part of the cognitive complex in Part II, so dealing with the relations of the cognitive complex [13] especially the intellectual disciplines treated as a system and particularly as incuding the intellectual treatment of religion, forms a bridge between the subject matter of Part II and that of Part III. The latter section deals with a variety of problems in the sociology of religion.

As I have frequently noted, the sociology of religion has been a central concern of my work, starting forty years ago with *The Structure of Social Action*,[14] indeed earlier with exposure to the teaching of Bronislaw Malinowski. The first intensive work I did in the field, however, was aimed at understanding the contributions of Emile Durkheim and Max Weber, and

[10] William James, *The Varieties of Religious Experience* (New York: Longmans, Green, 1902).

[11] Talcott Parsons and Gerald M. Platt, in collaboration with Neil J. Smelser, *The American University* (Cambridge, Mass.: Harvard University Press, 1973).

[12] Ibid., chap. 7.

[13] Ibid., chap. 2.

[14] Parsons, *Structure of Social Action*.

the first major stage of this inquiry was documented in *The Structure of Social Action.*

It does not seem to be too much to say that in this as in other aspects of my theoretical work a new phase began about 1965. The essays presented in Part III all prepare the way for the intellectual venture of systematic exploration of the human condition. Thus, Chapter 9, "Christianity" (which appeared in the *International Encyclopedia of the Social Sciences*), served greatly to clarify my historical perspective on the role of religion in Western society. Chapter 10 was based on a revisit to Durkheim's work in this field. Perhaps the most important result of that reconsideration was the clear conception that what Durkheim meant by the social environment (*milieu social*) can be interpreted to define the *internal environment* of the general system of action. That the distinction between an external and an internal environment should apply to the action system as well as to organic systems has proved to be an immensely illuminating idea. Not only has it served to unify theoretical conceptions of the field of action and of organic systems but also it has served greatly to clarify a whole series of problems at the action level. To cite only one of these clarifications, this distinction makes it possible to integrate, in the same theoretical analysis, Durkheim's famous discussion of "social facts" as exterior and constraining and his later analysis of the nature and sources of "constraint by moral authority," which was based on a theory of the internalization of moral norms in individual personalities.

The final theoretical interest that is documented in Part III is the interpretation of the religious situation in contemporary "secularized" society. This theme is central to Chapters 11 and 13 and is prominent in Chapter 12. The latter selection, however, also is connected with the themes of Part I in its concern with the relation of death to what has come to be thought of as the bioethical complex. Chapter 12 also bears on themes of evaluation of the significance of the cultural history of the contemporary situation. Indeed, how relevant is the symbolic structure of the Christian tradition to the formation of attitudes in very "practical" situations in the modern world? My own view, and that of my collaborators in that paper, is "much more than is usually thought."

The theoretical climax of the present volume, indeed of both it and its predecessor, is Chapter 15, "A Paradigm of the Human Condition." Chapter 14, "Death in the Western World," was written immediately after completion of the first draft of the essay preceding it. Essentially, Chapter 14 builds on the theoretical analysis of the more general treatment, "A Paradigm of the Human Condition," and attempts to relate that analysis to a theme clearly associated with both the biomedical complex and religion.

From my point of view today, more important than the substantive problems and contributions toward their solution that may result from this theoretical attempt (namely, Chapter 15) is the promise that such a venture will in the long run prove to work precisely at the*theoretical* level—by this I mean its potential contribution to the cognitive ordering of areas of human experience, which has attracted an immense amount of attention from many sorts of observers of the human situation over the centuries.

The intention of this venture is in no sense to derogate the insights of these various interpreters of things human. Indeed, without many of them the present attempt would not have been possible at all. What is distinctive about our approach here to the problems of the human condition, however, is not the substantive insight it may immediately provide but rather the question of the adaptability and usefulness, in cognitively "looking at" it, of a particular theoretical scheme that has served well in the analysis of a number of aspects of the enormous subject matter of relevance.

Analysis of the system of action itself in terms of a unified theoretical scheme has proved complicated and difficult enough; indeed to many it has seemed a vain and hopeless undertaking. As I have, however, suggested at a number of points in this General Introduction and in the introductory materials in *Social Systems and the Evolution of Action Theory,* there seems to be a built-in cognitive pressure to attempt to improve understanding of one sector of the subject matter of action by seeking better understanding of the framework in which it is located in a more comprehensive system. Witness the incentives for supplementing the study of social systems by paying systematic attention to psychological and cultural problems. The logic that accounts for this long experienced cognitive pressure, as I am calling it, is what underlies the present attempt to go a major step further in trying systematically to place the general system of action in a paradigm of the human condition.

PART I
SOCIOLOGY OF HEALTH AND ILLNESS AND RELATED TOPICS

Introduction to Part I

PART I IS CONCERNED with the first of the three more empirical areas mentioned in the General Introduction, namely, health and illness, higher education, and religion. As noted in the General Introduction, health and illness were for me an object of substantial study in an examination of certain aspects of modern medical practice in the period immediately following the completion of *The Structure of Social Action.*[1] A number of publications appeared in this period, the most important of which was Chapter 10 of *The Social System,*[2] entitled "Social Structure and Dynamic Process: The Case of Modern Medical Practice." A group of other papers, though not all on this topic, were collected in the considerably later volume *Social Structure and Personality*[3] and in *Family, Socialization, and Interaction Process* (with Robert F. Bales and others).[4]

Two themes were dominant in this phase of concern with problems of health and illness. The first of these was centered on the relevant role structure in the social system; primary focus was placed on the roles of physician and patient, the latter greatly overlapping with what I called the "sick role." (The two are not coterminous since many sick people are not patients and a few patients are not sick.) This role complex was treated as a salient example of the larger category of the profession role complex, which above all was contrasted with that of the business proprietor and his customer, which has been so prominent in modern society and so important in debates over capitalism versus socialism. This phenomenon clearly belonged in the context of problems of the relation between economic and sociological theory. One of my theses has been that the heavily

---

[1] Talcott Parsons, *The Structure of Social Action* (1937; reprint ed., New York, Free Press, 1949).

[2] Talcott Parsons, *The Social System* (New York: Free Press, 1951).

[3] Talcott Parsons, *Social Structure and Personality* (New York: Free Press, 1964).

[4] Talcott Parsons and Robert F. Bales, in collaboration with J. Olds, M. Zelditch, and P. E. Slater, *Family, Socialization, and Interaction Process* (New York: Free Press, 1955).

economic tradition of our social sciences has not done justice to the importance of the professional complex in modern society.

The second primary theme concerned the relation of social structure to the personality of the individual, with special reference to the health and illness of individuals. Not only was my first careful reading of Freud's works associated with this area of inquiry but so was my emphasis, derived from my field experience, on what many practitioners I observed stressed—the "psychic factor in disease"—and in part by extension on the problem of the nature of "mental" illness and of course health and the reasons for the salience in modern (especially American) society of these problems.

The revisit to these two sets of themes in the essays included in the present volume does not repudiate my previous positions but puts them in a broader perspective, adding certain important insights to them. The four essays in Part I may be characterized as follows. Chapter 1, "The Sick Role and the Role of the Physician Reconsidered," is strictly a revisit, formulated in the light of discussion subsequent to my earlier proposals about the roles of the physician and patient and the sick role. It is a summary, interpretive comment on problems presented to me in a session on the sick role (organized by Andrew C. Twaddle) at the 1974 Toronto meeting of the International Sociological Association. My role was to comment on four papers that were made available to me in advance. Chapter 1 was written after the Toronto meeting at the request of the editors of the *Milbank Memorial Fund Quarterly;* still, it was very much oriented to that meeting and its discussions.

The three other papers explore some of the peripheries—in sociological terms—of this central core. Chapter 2, "Research with Human Subjects and the 'Professional Complex,' " was written at a time (1968–69) when the ethical issue of such experimentation was coming to occupy a leading position in the debate over public policy. In this situation, *Daedalus,* at the request of the Surgeon General of the United States, convened a high level conference of various medical people, a few social scientists, and others, chaired by Paul A. Freund, a professor of law. Being invited to present a paper, I chose to try to relate the topic of the conference to the professional complex considered at the sociological level. This approach drew very much on my background of study of medical practice but also reflected my enhanced awareness of the fact that since my earlier studies teaching in hospitals attached to medical schools increased as a major focus for the medical world and that there had been in addition an efflorescence of the research function, especially in what are still called teaching hospitals. Patients, therefore, had become "subjects" not only for the teaching of medical students but also for "utilization" by research personnel, a large proportion of whom were not physicians. What were the implications of this new situation for the role in particular of the patient? I tried to link this problem to that of the structure of the intellectually prominent world in the university and the place of research in it. Indeed, by that time I had begun to be engaged in special study of the system of higher education.[5]

This phenomenon in the medical world is one of the most important examples of a much broader one; namely, the penetration of the professional complex beyond the more academic parts of the university into many branches of the organization of the society. Thus, biomedical research is carried on in the teaching hospitals of medical schools, as well as in a variety of government agencies, pharmaceutical firms, and elsewhere. Most of the large industrial firms in our society have research agencies, and so it goes. The higher level staffs of these organizations almost uniformly include considerable numbers of technically trained professional personnel, many of whom have or have had a choice between academic and non-academic careers and sometimes have pursued both. I deliberately include here not only natural scientists and engineers but also social scientists, especially economists and psychologists, and lawyers.

The phenomenon of professional penetration may be regarded as an important aspect of a principal structural change in modern society. It seems to me at least that we have been in the midst of a major example of the process of adaptive upgrading, which is discussed in the Introduction to Part III of *Social Systems and the Evolution of Action Theory*.[6] The central process has been the emergence of what Gerald M. Platt and I have called the "cognitive complex" [7] into a new position of structural salience in Western societies, in part superseding the previous position of the economy. For this reason (among others) a predominantly economic interpretation of the course of development of modern societies is unacceptable to me. This article also serves to link Part I of the present collection with Part II, which deals with higher education.

Chapter 3, "Health and Disease: A Sociological and Action Perspective," is one of the most recent I have written. It was requested by the editor of the new *Encyclopedia of Bioethics* (1978). I was asked to treat the sociological aspects of the problem, but at my request the word "action" was included in the title. I sought this rephrasing because I believed that the subject could not be adequately covered without explicit consideration of the other parts of the general system of action, especially the personality system.

This article constitutes a renewed probing into the foundations of the health-disease complex, which must in my opinion be pursued to the level of the human condition. Moreover, this level must be linked with the sociological, cultural, and psychological levels because among other things,

---

[5] See the Introduction to Part II of this volume.

[6] Talcott Parsons, *Social Systems and the Evolution of Action Theory* (New York: Free Press, 1977).

[7] Talcott Parsons and Gerald M. Platt, in collaboration with Neil J. Smelser, *The American University* (Cambridge, Mass.: Harvard University Press, 1973).

of the involvement of the phenomena of health and disease with the organic level of the human condition. It seems that an adequate articulation between these levels is essential to clarifying the meaning of health and disease and that most attempts to do so fail to provide this clarification.

Chapter 4, *"The Interpretation of Dreams* by Sigmund Freud," is a very brief and quite recent paper. It is another invited contribution—an interesting case in which I allowed myself to be influenced by an editor and am glad to have accepted his advice. Stephen Graubard, the editor of *Daedalus,* was planning an issue on key books of the twentieth century reconsidered and asked me to discuss one of them. I proposed Durkheim's *The Division of Labor in Society,*[8] stretching a point because it was first published in 1893. Graubard, however, countered with, "Why not Freud?" leaving to me which work to discuss. On reflection, I accepted the suggestion and chose *The Interpretation of Dreams,*[9] which barely falls within the limits because it was originally published in 1900. I completely reread the book *in German,* which some perhaps tend to forget was Freud's native tongue and the language in which he wrote.

I chose *The Interpretation of Dreams* because I knew it was Freud's earliest major book-length publication, a rather late effort since he was forty-four when it was published. Clearly, it is the first mature statement of the foundations of psychoanalytic theory. My revisit of this work many years after my initial reading left me enormously impressed with its quality. Let me mention only two major themes. The first is the clarity with which Freud thought in terms of the conception of the human personality as a *system* in the scientific sense of that word. It was almost as if, which obviously could not have been the case, he had been brought up on the writings of Lawrence J. Henderson [10] and Alfred N. Whitehead,[11] as I was. The second impression is the clarity and consistency with which Freud stuck to his last in insisting that he was dealing with, to use his own term, a "psychic" system. Freud has very generally been interpreted, especially because of the prominence of the term "instinct" in English translations of his work, to be a "biological reductionist." To me this is an egregious misinterpretation.

One of the most important corollaries, we may almost call it, of Freud's strict adherence to the conception of the personality as a psychic

[8] Emile Durkheim, *The Division of Labor in Society,* trans. George Simpson (New York: Free Press, 1964); first published in French in 1893).

[9] Sigmund Freud, *The Interpretation of Dreams,* in vols. 4 and 5 of *The Standard Edition of the Complete Psychological Works of Sigmund Freud* (London: Hogarth Press and the Institute of Psychoanalysis, 1953; first published in German in 1900).

[10] Lawrence J. Henderson, *Pareto's General Sociology: A Physiologist's Interpretation* (Cambridge, Mass.: Harvard University Press, 1935); and idem, *The Order of Nature: An Essay* (Cambridge, Mass.: Harvard University Press, 1917).

[11] Alfred N. Whitehead, *Science and the Modern World* (New York: Macmillan, 1935).

system is that a central theme of his analysis of dreams is that of the role of *symbols* in the dream process. This of course is a theme on which Freud concentrated much attention throughout the rest of his career. It is of particular significance to us because its importance to Freud clearly points to the interpretation that his theory of personality is basically a part of the *theory of action* not a part of what has come to be known as *physiological psychology*.

To carry this point one step further. When Freud refered to the human mouth ("orality"), anus, penis, and vagina as symbols, he was of course referring, for the manifest content of the symbols, to anatomical features of the human body. The psychological *meanings* of these symbols, however, are not organic but are phenomena in what Freud himself would have called the "intrapsychic" realm. I call these meanings "motivational." They have to do with the *directions* and types of commitment in which, in Freud's own term, the individual is brought, in the course of his/her life history, to "invest" the libidinal energy available. This level of psychological symbolization is in turn articulated with that of cognitive-behaviorial systems and that of social and cultural systems.

In a later statement, Freud wrote about instincts as the "psychical representations of an endosomatic, continuously flowing source of stimulation." [12] They are thus psychic entities that operate on the boundary of what we call the personality system vis-à-vis the organism. They are, then, indispensable, as factors in the generation of libido, to the cathexis of objects through which the structure of the personality of the individual comes to be built. In a still later statement,[13] Freud asserted that *verbal* meanings also are essential component's of libido.

It seems that a main source of the difficulty over reductionism in the interpretation of Freud's work is the fact that although he was—as a medical man—exceedingly well versed in the biology of his time there is not a comparably firm grounding in theory of the action aspect of his work. Freud was himself one of the few greatest builders of the theory of what he called the psychic system of the human individual. As we have seen, however, this human individual must be regarded as intricately embedded in a larger action matrix, to the cognitive aspects of which Freud made few contributions and in regard to which he took available resources only partly into account. More important, he had little *theoretical* understanding of the social system and the cultural aspects of the action system even though, empirically, he was very sensitive to these fields.

This lack is understandable since the disciplines dealing with action were substantially less developed in Freud's formative days than they have

[12] Sigmund Freud, *Three Essays on the theory of Sexuality,* vol. 8 of *Standard Edition* (1953; first published in German in 1905), p. 168.

[13] Sigmund Freud, *Beyond the Pleasure Principle,* vol. 18 of *Standard Edition* sect. 4, (1955; first published in German in 1920).

since become. A very recent revisit to some of these themes in these discussions is reported on (as the main part of Part IV of the present volume) in Chapter 15, "A Paradigm of the Human Condition." I hope the reader will agree that the advance over earlier considerations of these problems is heavily dependent on further theoretical development of the theory of action, which in turn has cleared the way for a better analysis of the boundary relations between the action system and the system of human biology, both as individual organism and as species.

1. The Sick Role and the Role of the Physician Reconsidered

THIS PAPER WILL ATTEMPT a restatement of certain aspects of the so-called sick role, and its relation to the performances and functions of physicians, or more generally therapeutically oriented health service agencies.[1]

The papers and oral discussion presented at the ISA session, in their discussions of my own previous contributions to the field, stressed the extent to which I had emphasized the ways in which sick role could be considered a form of social deviance. There was also a tendency on the part of authors and commentators to suggest that this analysis was applicable only to the case of acute illness, and neither to chronic illness nor to matters having to do with a preventive orientation. Especially in the oral discussion, however, another note became particularly prominent. In my own earlier work I had stressed the asymmetry of the role patterns of patient on the one side, physician on the other. The quite incorrect implication was made by some of the participants that I had claimed the role of patients to be purely passive, as objects of manipulation, and not as, in any important sense, participative. However, there was a good deal of criticism of this position, and a certain tendency to allege that any fundamental structural asymmetry in this role complex should be regarded as anomalous and pathological. The present paper is oriented to a reconsideration of some of these issues, I hope in a somewhat more extended theoretical context than either my own earlier work took advantage of or the work of the authors of papers or oral comments.

First, may I say something about the relevance of the concept of social deviance. I do not think it was ever my intention to attempt to make this

[1] Its primary reference is to the papers and discussion which were presented at a session on the sick role at the meeting of the International Sociological Association in Toronto, Ontario, in August 1974. The session was organized and chaired by Professor Andrew Twaddle, of the University of Missouri.

From *Milbank Memorial Fund Quarterly,* vol. 53, no. 3 (Summer 1975). Reprinted by permission.

concept cover the whole range of phenomena associated with the sick role on the one hand, the roles of therapeutic agents on the other. My own earlier thinking was heavily influenced by a concern which was widely prevalent in medical circles at the time the work was done, namely the 1930s. This was true not only of psychiatry and psychoanalysis but, with respect to conditions where the symptomatology was mainly somatic, of the so-called "psychic" factor in disease. I found this in my field investigations to figure very prominently in the thinking of internists, and by no means only of phychiatrists.

These considerations suggested that, on the part of the sick person himself, there might be, more generally than had been believed, an element of "motivatedness" not merely in the etiology of the pathological condition, but also in the maintenance of it, a context which included resistance to therapeutic efforts on the part of various agencies. Seen in this perspective then, one primary aspect of therapeutic roles came to be their functions as mechanisms of social control.

It was on this basis that I built up an analysis of some of the functionally significant features of the role of the sick person, attempting to distinguish between the state of illness as such and the role of patient in interaction with therapeutic agents. In complementary fashion, then, the role of the therapeutic agent was analyzed, stressing the functions of social control. It was emphasized throughout that the prevailing attitude toward illness was that it was an inherently undesirable state, and that the role of therapeutic agencies should be "the recovery of the sick person." This concept has been particularly closely related to capacity for full and satisfactory functioning in a system of social relationships.

In this connection, a particularly valuable contribution seems to me to have been made by Eugene Gallagher (1974) in his paper presented to the session. This was Gallagher's conception of health, which he suggested should be regarded as a category of the capacity of the human individual. From this point of view, illness would be a state of affairs which would impair, in varying ways and degrees, the capacity of the sick person to function, as the saying has been, "normally." We can think of a variety of aspects of this impairment of capacity. The privilege of exemption from ordinary day-to-day occupations which has gone with the institutionalization of the sick role is a kind of institutional measure of incapacity when it is combined with the fundamental tenet that being ill, if it is genuine and not malingering, cannot reasonably be regarded as the sick person's "fault."

Gallagher's conception of health as capacity seems to me to help show the relevance to this analysis, not merely of acute illness, but of chronic, even terminal, illness. There are many conditions which are, in any given state of the art of medicine, incurable. For them the goal of complete recovery becomes impractical. However, recovery is the obverse of the process of deterioration of health, that is, a level of capacities, and in many of these chronic situations tendencies to such deterioration can be held in check by the proper medically prescribed measures based on sound diagnostic knowledge. An outstanding example is diabetes, where diabetics, by such measures as a modest regulation of diet, and stimulation in the milder cases by oral medication, in the more severe ones by the use of insulin, can maintain a relatively normal pattern of physiological functioning and the many activities of life which depend on normal physiological functioning. To be sure, there is a cost involved in this. The cost consists, above all, on the diabetic's part, of adhering to a proper regimen and of deferring to a competent professional authority in defining what it should be. The fact then, that diabetes is not, in the sense of pneumonia, "curable," does not put it in a totally different category from that of acute illness.

The other most important issue at this level seems to me to be that of the concept of the "motivatedness" of illness, looked at either in the etiological or maintenance context or both. It seems to me quite clear that modern knowledge of unconscious motivation makes a much more extended scope of the concept of motivatedness entirely acceptable than older common sense, including that of the medical profession, has allowed for. I would not, however, at all claim that this covers the whole ground. Certainly human beings, like other categories of organism, are subject to pathogenic influences of many sorts which are altogether independent of the processes we call motivational. Thus, doubtless, most cases of bacterial or viral infection or of degenerative processes may be so regarded, as can some of the traumatic consequences of accidents.

It is, however, important to note that the interweaving of motivated and non-motivated factors at both conscious and unconscious levels is complex indeed and any simple formula about these matters is likely to prove misleading. We can, thus, speak of accident-prone people even though the physical consequences of an accident, once it has occurred, are clearly not analyzable in motivational terms. Such people, however, may unnecessarily expose themselves to the risk of such accidents. Probably somewhat similar considerations apply to such fields as infections, and indeed, to the degenerative diseases like cancer. In sum, then, the relevance of the category deviance from the point of view of the sick role itself should be confined to the impact of motivated components in, on the one hand, etiology and therapy, and, on the other hand, maintenance of states categorized as constituting illness. Our conception is that the motivated and hence potentially deviant element shades without specific breaks into those areas where motivation is not a relevant interpretative category.

Some of the papers submitted to Professor Twaddle's session made the suggestion, which had already been made independently by Twaddle himself, that adaptation was a more general and more appropriate category of characterizing the functions of the sick role than was deviance. I should like to conclude the present section of the paper with a brief comment on this issue. I should regard deviance and social control as phenomena concerned with the integrative problems of a social system. Illness we may speak of as, at least in one primary aspect, an impairment of the sick person's integration in solidary relationships with others, in family, job, and many other contexts. Seen in this perspective, therapy may be interpreted to be predominantly a reintegrative process. To be successful, such a process must take account of adaptive considerations, notably the pathological state of the organism and/or personality and the nature of the patient's adaptive problems in various aspects of his or her life.

The most important consideration I wish to put forward, however, is one that is not commonly taken into account in sociological analyses. This concerns an underlying relativity as between the concepts and functions of integration on the one hand, adaptation on the other. Certain concrete problems and phenomena may belong in one of the other category according to the system reference in terms of which they are treated. Just to take an organic case, the circulating body fluids, notably blood, from the point of view of the functioning of internal cells and tissues, constitute an environment. What is or is not available in the bloodstream in what concentrations and the like, constitutes a fundamental set of conditions under which the physiological processes of cells, tissues, and organs operate. Thus, in the example of diabetes I gave above, a deficiency of insulin in the blood will lead to an excessively high level of blood-sugar concentration in the blood with pathological consequences. From the point of view of the organism as a whole, however, the bloodstream constitutes an aspect of the internal environment which must be distinguished from the environment external to the organism as such, for example, the physical environment, and indeed, most of what Durkheim and others have called the social environment. From the point of view of the relation of the organism as a whole to its external environment, the problem of maintenance of the circulation of the blood and of its biochemical composition is to be regarded as primarily an integrative problem not an adaptive problem, though there may well be adaptive repercussions relative to the external environment. It therefore seems to me that the proposals to supplant the emphasis on deviance with one on adaptation is not very helpful unless it pays very careful attention to the relativities and complex interrelations between integration and adaptation.

The main concern of the present paper, however, is not with the problem of the relation between illness and deviance but rather with the problem of the symmetry and/or asymmetry in the role relations between sick people and therapeutic agencies. I should now like to address myself to this topic as such.

I start, as I have for many years, with the proposition that illness is not merely a state of the organism and/or personality, but comes to be an institutionalized role. There is not such thing, of course, as perfect coincidence in that people, who from a medical point of view are more or less sick, may refuse to acknowledge that this is the case, and behave as if nothing were the matter. I have, on occasion, used the neologism "hyperchondriac" to designate the type of person who, rather than exaggerating states of illness, takes the opposite tack and minimizes them. There are a great many such people.

There are, however, three primary criteria of accepting the social role of being sick. The first of these is the assertion with the view of its acceptance by both self and others, that being in a state of illness is not the sick person's own fault, and that he should be regarded as the victim of forces beyond his control. A second social-structural feature of the sick role is the claim of exemption from ordinary daily obligations and expectations, for example, staying at home in bed instead of going to school or office. The third is the expectation, if the case is sufficiently severe, of seeking help from some kind of institutionalized health service agency. This seeking of help further includes the admission that being sick is undesirable and that measures should be taken to maximize the chances to facilitate recovery or, if the condition is chronic, as noted above, to subject it to proper "management." It is true that in my earlier work I noted the physician as a particularly central health service agent. Of course, at the time that work was done, the physician by no means stood alone, and, for example, I did a great deal of my own observation in hospitals which were very complex organizations involving staff personnel way beyond that composed of physicians. This, however, is not the place to enter a complex analysis of the social structure of complex health service agencies, an exceedingly important subject in its own right. For convenience, therefore, I shall continue to focus on the physician.

In order to approach the problem of symmetry and asymmetry, I think it best to build up a certain context in the form of a typology of social structure. First it seems to me that there are at least two main types of which the especially salient characteristic is a presumption of symmetrcal equality, though perhaps the list should be extended to three. An historic example has been that of the relations between participants in a competitive economic market. Participation in market translations is held to be basically voluntary, and the doctrine of economic rationality suggests that people participate only so long as they can see it to be to their economic interests to do so. Much publicity, of course, has been given to many different sources of inequality in market relationships, such as some kind of monopoly power on one side, various kinds of coercion more on one side than on the other, or the pressure of need on the part of certain participants which reduces the range of their alternatives and makes it difficult for them to withdraw. These considerations, however, do not invalidate the pattern of the potentially equal and free competitive market nexus.

Closely related to the market is what is sometimes called a communications network, where what is transmitted from one participant to another is not rights of possession in goods and services but in some sense information, that is, access to symbolically meaningful representations; particularly important cases are to be found where such information is "broadcast" whether through the printed word as in publication or through electronic media like radio and television. With certain exceptions there is no institutionalized obligation to transmit information, especially when one considers this at a particularized level; though, for example, a member of the faculty of a high-standing university may have an obligation to publish the results of research, it is not inherent in his role that he is obliged in advance to publish any particular content. One has a certain choice as to what newspapers to read and what parts of any given issue of a newspaper, what periodicals to read, what books to read, and what radio or television programs to tune in on or to shut off. Similar considerations about factors of inequality apply to communication networks as do to markets, but this is not to say that a communication network is inherently unequal.

Finally, the third case is that of the voluntary association or at least the association in which the status of participants or members is declared to be formally equal. There is a sense in which the status of citizen is not altogether voluntary, but in modern democratic societies a fundamental equality as between citizens is typically institutionalized, for example, in the principle, one citizen, one vote. I think probably the best designation for the presumptively egalitarian type of association is the term "democratic" association. This, of course, is by no means confined to citizenship.

Equality in these respects is closely related to what, in Anglo-American tradition, is often referred to as "equality before the law." I do not think that this conception is in need of extended discussion on this occasion, but this case exemplifies a very important type of complication of the equality problem. This is to say that administration of a legal system not infrequently brings citizens into some kind of legal complication where they are in the need of advice of lawyers and may be participants in proceedings before courts of law. Presumably in a court of law in the role of plaintiff or of defendant a citizen enjoys the rights we sum up in the phrase "equality before the law." It does not follow, however, that with respect to the procedure of the court, every participant in such a proceeding is an equal. Litigants before a court are not the equals of judges who are conducting the procedure of the court. If there happens to be a jury, in certain respects members of the jury occupy a special status which is carefully separated from that of litigants or for that matter their counsel. Litigants, that is, are not permitted nor required to issue legally binding verdicts of guilty or not guilty, which jurors are. Similarly, litigants cannot make procedural rulings about the conduct of a court case as a judge can. It is notable here, however, that some courts involve more than one judge. In such cases, the judges are ordinarily equals of each other. Where decisions of the court are arrived at, it is on the principle, one member, one vote. Thus, in the case of the United States Supreme Court, though the Chief Justice has certain executive privileges and functions, in the Court's decision of cases, he has only one vote, not a heavier weight because of his position as Chief Justice.

It seems best to introduce a discussion of the problem of asymmetry of health care role structure by reviewing the principal types of social structure where asymmetrical structures are involved. I confine this consideration of asymmetry to the cases that involve a hierarchical component of authority, power, prestige, and the like. It is a somewhat different question, whether, for example, the role in marriage of the partners, by virtue of the fact that they belong to opposite sex categories is or is not asymmetrical. I think it is in certain respects. This issue, however, will not be involved in the present discussion.

Subject to these limitations, then, I think it is important to distinguish three principal types of hierarchically asymmetrical roles. The first concerns the relation between the incumbent of elective office in the democratic association as that concept was reviewed above, including of course, governmental office, and other members. The incumbent of an office in this sense, for the period of his incumbency, stands in certain relations of superiority to the ordinary constituent who is "only a member" of the association. We are exceedingly familiar with this situation with respect to democratic government, and of course similar principles are operative in the institutionalization of office in a wide variety of different types of private associations.

The second type is almost equally familiar. This is what may be called administrative-bureaucratic authority in organizations. Such authority in modern cases is ordinarily legitimized primarily by the powers of appointment of superordinate elected bodies, in limiting cases constituents as a whole. Within the limits defined by the organizational roles the incumbent of this type of office enjoys a status superior to that of those connected with the organization over whom his office gives him jurisdiction. Thus appointees of the Internal Revenue Service in the United States may call in taxpayers to review the adequacy of the tax returns they have submitted, and, within a set of rules, revise the obligations they have made or agreed to make under those returns. Similarly, administrative officials of a hospital may make many and complex decisions about the admissions of patients, the financial charges to be assessed against them, and various other aspects of the behavior of participants in the hospital social system, including physicians, nurses, and other health service personnel.

The third primary type is of a different order from either of these two. It is what I have been referring to in a variety of publications as the exercise of fiduciary responsibility in the context of what it has often been convenient to call "collegial association." A striking type case of such a collegial association is a multijudge court of law; another is a university department or faculty. A wide variety of boards or other such collectivities may also be included.

In the collegial association members of a given stratum are typically treated as equals of each other, as was noted in the case mentioned above of the United States Supreme Court. By no means all people who participate in relevant interaction in such a system, however, are treated as the equals of each other. As I noted above, only judges can vote as participants in the decisions of an appelate court. Only members of an elective body in democratic politics like a legislature or one house of a legislature can vote in contributing to the binding decisions made on behalf of that body. Clearly only members of a department can vote on matters of the educational or appointment policy of that department in the academic world.

I suggested above that litigants before a court of law stand in a status very different from that of judges of the court or, in another context, members of a jury. Similarly, it is clear, in an academic type of organization, faculty members within their own departments, or more generally within the faculty, stand in a status different from that of students on the one hand and administrative personnel of the academic organization on the other. On occasion, and for certain purposes, of course, all members of a professional group may be collegial equals, as would be the case for licensed physicians, vis-a-vis government, in enjoying a common right to engage in the practice of medicine. Similarly, all members of the faculty of a complex university may have common rights in that capacity independent of what subdivisions of the organization they are attached to.

I should now like to suggest that social organization of health care, overwhelmingly in modern societies, but particularly in North America, has come to be organized in terms of an asymmetrical hierarchy with respect to the functions of this particular system, of which the two polar aspects are the role of physician as the highest grade of publicly certified expert in health care and the role of sick person independent of the latter's status in other respects. As I have suggested, the health care agency may include a number of different role types other than that of physician, but there is as yet little tendency to challenge the basic position of the physician as having the highest order of professional—as distinguished from administrative—status in such an agency. The sick person, of course, may himself be a physician, but in his role as a patient he stands, relative to non-sick physicians, very much as do patients who medically speaking are lay people.

The most general basis of that superiority of health agency personnel generally, and physicians in particular, seems to me to rest in their having been endowed with special responsibilities for the health of persons defined as ill or as suffering threats to their future health who have come under their jurisdiction, that is, who have become in some sense patients of the individual physician or of the health care organization in which he performs a role. This is to say in very general terms that the physician has been institutionally certified to be worthy of entrusting responsibility to in the field of the care of health, the prevention of illness, the mitigation of its severity and disabling consequences, and its cure insofar as this is feasible.

I hasten to add that this fiduciary responsibility for the health of participants in the health care system not only need not be confined to physicians but need not be confined to members of a health care agency as such. It most definitely should be regarded as shared by sick persons. Indeed, the acceptance of the role of patient, that is, participation in interaction with the health care agency, may be said to impose a definite responsibility on the patient in working toward the common goals of the system as a whole. The first of the obligations thereby assumed, seems to me to consist in the commitment to cooperation in the health care therapeutic or management functions of the system. This commitment may, in certain cases, be confined to the patient exposing himself as a passive object to the manipulations of the health care personnel. It may not, however, be confined to this passive level. In many different degrees and respects, patients are asked to, and they often do, take the initiative in assuming the responsibility for a more active role in the care of their own health. The case of diabetics, cited above, is very much to the point. It should not be forgotten that other known sick people, who medically speaking are lay people, may often be involved as well. A striking case is that of family members, particularly a spouse, in the case of the very demanding techniques of home dialysis for patients with severe cases of renal failure.

The implementation in concrete action of what I have just called the fiduciary responsibility of the health care agent, particularly the physician, seems to me to work out in three principal contexts, which I should now like to review.

The first of these may be called the presumptive competence of the health care agent to deal with the kind of health-threatening or health-impairment situations that the relevant category of sick or potentially sick people face. Competence in this sense seems to me to rest on three principal grounds or base. One of these is the level of capacity independent of personal experience of the health care agent himself. In other words, a good physician requires high intelligence and moral probity of an order which is probably higher than that required at least by many other occupational roles in modern society.

Building on the innate aspect of ability, or capacity however, there must be a development of technical knowledge and skill which is acquired typically through two closely interrelated processes, namely, formal training and experience. The modern physician is subjected to a very elaborate formal training, starting with the basic sciences which underly effective medical practice, a very large branch of physical and biological science, such as biophysics, biochemistry, physiology, bacteriology, and the like, and gradually increasing. I think, behavioral science—in the first instance psychology, but sometimes extending even into the non-individual-oriented sciences of behavior and action, like sociology.

This knowledge at more general scientific levels is then articulated with the exigencies of the health care roles through the device of clinical activity and orientation. Thus the medical student is rather early exposed to the processes of the actual going care of concrete sick people, learning the rudiments of physical examination and diagnosis, of history taking, of the interpretation of all manner of pathological symptoms presented by concrete cases. There seems to be a very fundamental consensus that both what in medical parlance is called "basic science" training and clinical training are the central ingredients of the competence of a physician. In detail, of course, the ramifications are exceedingly broad and various.

I should like, however, to add a third component essential to the implementation of fiduciary responsibility in this field. This essentially is the willingness of the person assuming such a role in fact to exercise such responsibility and to act within the limits of his prerogatives as a genuine trustee of the health interests of the patient population relative to whom he assumes responsibility. This is a component which goes beyond competence in the more narrowly technical sense. It involves an important component of moral authority, grounded in the common assumption of health care agents and sick people that health is a good thing and illness by and large a bad thing, and that the balance should, insofar as it is indeed feasible, be altered in the direction of maximizing the levels of health and minimizing the incidence of illness. It is in this connection that the health care agent performs functions of social control in the sense in which that concept is relevant to the emphasis on deviance and social control as part of the health care complex.

Indeed, I should insist that this last circumstance extends the relevance of the deviance concept well beyond the range within which illness, particularly in the etiological context, may be regarded as motivated. Here, the relevant point is that the health care agent, notably the physician, is conceived as reinforcing his patient's motivation to minimize illness and its disabilities. In the case of relatively acute illness, the meaning of this is relatively simple: it is the physician's obligation to reinforce the patient's motivations to recover. In the case of chronic illness, like diabetes, the corresponding obligation is to reinforce the patient's motivation to minimize the curtailment of his capacities because of his pathological condition, even though that condition cannot be eliminated in the sense of total cure. The case of clearly terminal illness, where death is regarded as not merely inevitable but likely to occur relatively soon, raises a few special problems, which, however, probably need not be entered into here.

Let me reiterate the importance of the fact that the health care agent, and, very notably, the physician, is typically caring for sick people as a full-time occupation. Day in and day out his or her work is concerned with this order of problems. Of course, the occupation need not be totally confined to patient care, since many physicians, especially those attached to important organizations like high-level hospitals and medical schools typically devote a substantial amount of their time and effort to non-therapeutic functions. Of these the most important clearly are, on the one hand, research, regarded as relatively independent of treatment of the individual sick patient, and, on the other hand, what broadly may be characterized as administrative functions, as in the case of a physician who acts for the time being as chief of service in his hospital situation.

There is a sense in which the sick role sometimes matches the full-time occupation of the physician in the case of acute illness. The patient who is sufficiently sick to be bedridden is, in a sense, devoting his whole attention for the time being to coping with the state of illness and to goals of facilitating recovery. These circumstances, however, do not apply literally to the whole range of illness. Many of the cases of chronic illness require only a very partial attention on the part of the patient as well as the physician to take the appropriate measures which a management regimen requires. Thus, in the case of diabetes, for the relatively mild case, sufficient care to take the medication prescribed according to the regimen, some attention to testing of sugar level in urine, and some attention to diet are daily routine obligations of the patient. Usually, if he is under medical supervision, there will be, in addition to that, periodic checks on his condition by the physician in question. Outside of performance of these obligations, however, in cases of this sort, the "sick person" goes about his business in other concerns of life than participating in a health agency–illness interaction. He presumably engages in occupational work, in family and friendship relations, and the rest of the normal concerns of people who are not defined as ill.

It is particularly important for the health care agent, again notably the physician, that his concern with problems of illness is typically a career occupation which, following the completion of training, can be expected to go on throughout his more active life. In the type case of acute illness, the state of being sick is, for the sick person, however, a temporary episode, such that every effort will be made, both by himself and by his physician, to limit its duration as much as possible. Once "recovered" he relinquishes the sick role, but even in cases of chronic illness of the sort discussed, though the role of being sick is not temporary, it becomes a part-time but not totally absorbing role, except in very severe cases, which of course are by no means of negligible importance.

I have already noted that it is erroneous, as some interpreters of my previous work in this area have maintained, to consider the role of the sick person, notably in the capacity of patient, who is positively related to health care agencies, as that of a purely passive object of manipulation or "treatment." Indeed, I should regard even the acceptance of such treatment as one type of active participation of the sick person. However, his activity very generally goes well beyond this. We might suggest that the level of activity is minimized for acutely ill patients, particularly when they are hospitalized and subject to the ministrations not only of physicians but of nurses and other hospital personnel. Even in these cases, however, some active participation in addition to merely accepting hospital treatment is generally involved. And, the less acute the mediate situation, the more likely it is that this participation will be substantial. Such as it is, it may concentrate on a role complementary to that of the health care agent in furthering the goal of either recovery or minimization of the curtailment of the capacities of the healthy person. It may, however, extend into functionally different areas. A notable example has been described by Dr. Renee Fox in her Experiment Perilous (1959) with respect to the way in which the patients on Ward F12 actually participated in substantial ways in the research program to which the ward was committed. They served in a very real sense as research assistants of the investigating medical team. This assistance above all focused on self-observation and reporting to the medical team on what had, in fact, been observed about their own conditions.

This topic of the sick person's active participation shades over into another very important one. This concerns the fact that lay people, as a consequence of their education and experience, have a certain amount of knowledge and understanding in matters of illness. At the very minimum, this should concern decisions about when professional help is indicated and when it can safely be dispensed with. Of course the matter of the concern is not only with the decision maker's own state of health or illness but of others close to him, in particular, members of his family. There is a considerable range of situations in which self-care or non-professional care in the household is not only undertaken but not infrequently proves to be adequate. Lay judgments in these matters are, of course, notoriously fallible. Thus, how many women have died because of failure to seek professional investigation of a lump in a breast which might be a symptom of cancer of the breast? The woman in question may have observed this herself for a long period without seeking professional judgment. But surely, no ordinary medically untrained woman would be able to deliver a competent judgment, simply from feeling her own breast, whether a lump which was present was malignant or not.

I do not mean to contend that lay opinion and decision making are infallible. For example, various kinds of health examinations and checkups may be extremely important. (I might simply report that my own mild diabetic condition came to light as a result of a general medical checkup. At the time I underwent that checkup I had no intimation of being a diabetic, but the routine urine tests conducted in connection with the general checkup revealed sugar in the urine.)

It has been my intention in the above discussion to set forth the most important reasons why the professional-lay relationship in the field of illness and health care cannot be treated as a fully symmetrical relationship in the hierarchical dimension. This is to say that, with respect to the inherent functions of effective care and amelioration of conditions of illness, there must be a built-in institutionalized superiority of the professional roles, grounded in responsibility, competence, and occupational concern. This is not for a moment to say that the exact ways in which the lines should be drawn can be neatly deduced from such general considerations as my discussion has advanced. These matters are inherently extremely complex, and the situation is far from being static. Hence, it is entirely reasonable to suppose that the lines should be shifted from time to time in the light of new knowledge and changing conditions. I fail, however, to see how it is at all possible to eliminate the element of inequality. To go too far in attempting to do so would surely jeopardize the therapeutic benefits of the vast accumulation of medical knowledge and competence which our culture has painfully built up over a very long period.

Perhaps the health-illness case can be somewhat clarified by a relatively extended comparison with the academic example. This, probably even more conspicuously than the health-illness case, has recently been a subject of passionate polemical disagreement, with one school virtually taking the position that the relation between teacher and student, notably at the level of higher education, must be a fully egalitarian one with no special authority or privileges on the professional side. It seems to me that this position is basically wrong and rests on inadequate understanding of the nature of the functions of teaching and its conditions.

I should suggest that the academic role, to ignore for our purposes considerations touching teaching at more elementary levels than higher education, has in common with the commitment to health care interests the element of fiduciary responsibility. Just as we may assume that in the institutionalized value system of our culture health is better than illness, we may also assume that knowledge and competence are better than ignorance and related degrees and modes of incompetence. As it has worked out in modern societies, responsibility for implementation of this fiduciary function with respect to knowledge and competence has come to be institutionalized in differentiated social structures which we generally refer to as institutions of higher education, a conception in which I should like most emphatically to include the function of research, that is, pursuit of the advancement of knowledge as a goal, relatively independently of its practical applications.

The note just sounded in relation to the health-illness complex is completely relevant in the present context. The fiduciary responsibility of members of the academic profession rests in their role of trusteeship for the preservation, development, and utilization of a major tradition of very obviously transgenerational significance. This is the tradition of significant and valid knowledge, which has been built over many centuries by extremely complicated processes, but has been preserved as available to many current generations in, for example, externalized symbolic form, books and other publication and the like, and in the competence of persons whose training and experience have exposed them to the essential characteristics of aspects of this tradition, including their history. What I refer to, of course, is the cultural aspect, the cognitive aspect, of what more generally we call the cultural tradition.

Seen in this light, the teaching function is essentially a matter of responsible contact between those who are specially trained in the relevant matters and members of oncoming generations or age cohorts who, for the first time in their particular lives, are becoming engaged in the problems of mastery of relevant aspects of this tradition and developing capacities to use it in their own lives and to contribute to its further development.

If we accept the value premise that where the choice is given, ignorance is always inferior to knowedge, just as illness is inferior to health, it seems to follow that alleviation of the condition of ignorance, which is to say the acquisition of knowledge about and mastery of the great cognitive tradition of our culture, can more effectively be promoted by people who exercise a special competence in these matters than by non-selective interaction among people who, from this point of view, are lay people.

Taking account of appropriate differences and also of the very substantial overlap, the analysis applied in the health-illness case seems to me to be fully applicable here. Of course, the technical character of knowledge varies enormously from elements where only very high-level experts can presume to have competent opinions, such as some of the central issues of the advanced sciences, to elements where professional expertise shades into the kind of competence which lay people can fairly readily acquire. Even, however, with respect to the sector of the spectrum of which the latter propositions are true, it should not be assumed that professional levels of competence are irrelevant to effective performance of what seems to be fairly generally agreed are the relevant functions. Thus, most students exposed to programs of general education will not be technical experts in any particular cognitive central field.

Stress should be laid on the importance of the exposure in programs of general education of the student to the disciplines and procedures which have gradually come to be institutionalized in the great cognitive traditions of the culture. Indeed, as the cognitive culture has advanced, differentiated, and proliferated, stress has been placed decreasingly on direct mastery of specific content of knowledge and has shifted in the direction of emphasis on the importance of command of general principle, methods of mobilizing the necessary detailed knowledge, and the like.[2]

It seems to me to be an essential defining characteristic of the educated citizen, in the sense that Gerald Platt and I use that concept in *The American University* (1973; see especially Chapter 4), that such persons should, as part of their socialization experience, have acquired a high level of internalization of these more general characteristics of cognitive culture.

As also seems to me to be true of socialization in general, the fully egalitarian pattern of interaction between socializing agents and persons in the process of coming to be socialized would be inherently ineffective. Its ineffectiveness would rest above all on the fact that the socializing agent was deprived of any significant basis of leverage to exert an influence on his interaction partner which would lead to such internalization.

We would maintain that the teacher has a primary function in his capacity as a socializing agent of exerting such leverage to motivate the subject to learn and above all to acquire cognitive habits of orientation which will facilitate both new learning of cognitively relevant matters and their utilization in an indefinitely wide variety of practical affairs.

We would hold that the grounds of the capacity of the teacher are directly comparable with those of the expertise of the physician. That is, they rest on three primary factors; namely, the special, we hope on the average, above-average level of inborn ability in the relevant respects enjoyed by teachers at levels of higher education relative to the general lay population of non-teachers. The second concerns the efforts of formal training extending back into the elementary grades of education, but culminating at the higher-education levels, of persons who specialize in roles which involve assumption of the fiduciary responsibility to which we are referring. The third factor is that of experience with respect to which

---

[2] It seems to me that this is above all what Daniel Bell has in mind in his references to the increasing importance as modern society has developed of *theoretical* knowledge, as distinguished from discrete empirical items of information.

it is particularly relevant that teaching in higher education is generally conceived to be a lifelong career commitment.

There is, in our opinion, a notable parallel between the asymmetry just reviewed for the health-illness case and the situation in the educational area. This is essentially the asymmetry of role status as between professional components in the relevant interaction system and "lay components." Even though analysis of the health-illness situation is not to be narrowly restricted to the case of acute illness, we still have presented an analysis which strongly suggests that the fact that the typical physician as a career committed full-time occupational person presents a very sharp contrast to the role of the average patient, who is presumably not making a life career out of being sick. In the academic case, the typical teacher in the field of higher education is comparably committed to a life career. The role is that of a full-time occupation extending over many years. The teaching function is a central function in this occupational role, even though, as is very clear for the academic world, teaching is not the only function expected of and performed by academic professionals. Research has a particularly important part in the structure of the academic role as it has evolved in the more recent period, and so do administrative functions. Nevertheless, the function of teacher over long periods of time and in an occupational context is clearly central to the academic situation.

The student, however, is comparable to the sick person in one crucial respect. One is not, except in certain chronic cases, permanently ill, but rather is ill because of occasions which will normally be expected to be temporary. The type case is, of course, in the episode of specific, acute illness. The student role is different; however, one may speak perhaps, of a comparable state of "acute" ignorance. If a person is to progress beyond that state, he or she must be exposed to formal educational procedures. These, however, are not typically of lifelong duration, but are rather concentrated in relatively brief periods which are sectors of a more comprehensive life course. Thus, the perennial student who, let us say, after twenty years is still a student, has a certain parallel to the sick person who enjoys high levels of "secondary gain" in his illness and is highly resistant to pressures to recover. It is for this reason that students cannot qualify in, for example, presumptively revolutionary neo-Marxist thinking as a "social class," since social class is a status to which its members are in a typical case allocated for life. To be a student is not that kind of categorization any more than to be a sick person is typically such. Clearly, therefore, the population of the "ignorant," that is people who are under pressure to study, is no more a categorization of a permanent, lifelong group of human individuals than is that of the sick as a permanent category vis-à-vis the well, to say nothing of vis-à-vis the professional personnel whose services are relevant to the control of their conditions and the consequences of such conditions.

I therefore conclude that there is an inherent built-in asymmetry in the teacher-student interaction system which rather closely parallels the asymmetry of the physician-patient system.

Conclusion

I very much hope that the above embodies an adequate explanation of the fact, so it seems to me, that except in cases which are clearly marginal to the phenomena of illness and its care, the relation of sick person and health care agency is inherently asymmetrical on the hierarchical axis. It should be made very clear, however, that this hierarchical difference is relatively speaking functionally specific and not diffuse. Relative to sick people, physicians do not constitute an aristocracy occupying a diffusely superior status. Their superiority is focused on the specific functions of handling people who have impairments of health, that is, who in some specific sense or some respect are sick. Though the status of physician in our general scale of stratification is rather a high one, it is not at all infrequent that physicians will have patients who in general social status are their superiors, not their inferiors. This, for example, would be the case when very high officials of government become ill, including presidents and prime ministers. With respect, however, to the complex of health and illness, there can be no doubt of the institutionalized superiority of the health care agent, notably the physician. I have contended that this feature holds not only for the health care field but also all of those where professional groups occupy roles characterized by what above has been called fiduciary responsibility.

This goes back to the role of parenthood. Where children are small, it is clearly out of the question that in every relevant respect they should be treated as the complete equals of their parents. Indeed, attaining a stage when such equality makes sense is normally the signal for ceasing to be in the role of child in the family orientation. The typical "grown" child tends to leave the parental household and live independently, often or rather in the majority of cases setting up with a marriage partner an independent household. I hope that sufficient evidence has been presented to make it clear that a similar asymmetry is to be found in the teacher-student relationship with special reference to functions of higher education. Of course, this patterning extends far beyond the two or three cases just mentioned. Brief mention was made above of the legal situation where an ordinary lay person who has sufficiently complex legal problems to require the services of professional lawyers is, with respect to the performance of the function of advocating or protecting the lay person's legal rights, definitely not to be considered the equal of the attorney. Just as we do find cases of self-medication or the calling on other medically speaking lay people to deal with some kinds of illness, so we find cases where lay individuals act as their own lawyers and, indeed, cases were people who are initially ignorant do not resort to the professional services of regular teachers but undertake to teach themselves. These marginal cases, however, cannot be legitimately used as a model for the institutionalization of these types of functions, all of which in different ways involve the assumption of fiduciary responsibility.

References

BELL, DANIEL
   1973   The Coming of Post-Industrial Society. New York: Basic Books.
FOX, RENÉE C.
   1959   Experiment Perilous. Glencoe, Ill.: Free Press.
GALLAGHER, EUGENE
   1974   "Lines of reconstruction and extension in the Parsonian sociology of illness." Paper presented at World Congress of Sociology, Toronto, August.
PARSONS, TALCOTT
   1974   "The sick role revisited a response to critics and an updating in terms of the theory of action." Paper presented at World Congress of Sociology, Toronto, August.
PARSON, TALCOTT, AND GERALD PLATT
   1973   The American University. Cambridge: Harvard University Press.

2. Research with Human Subjects and the "Professional Complex"

THE ETHICAL PROBLEMS INVOLVED in research that makes use of human subjects are by no means new, but they have become intensified in recent years through a number of circumstances. In the medical field, which has stood at the center of the discussions leading to this issue of *Dædalus,* the rapid technical advances have raised many ethical issues. Not only new but more daring and, presumptively at least until fully tested, riskier procedures are increasingly being employed. Organ transplants are, of course, the most commonly discussed example today.

Another reason for the increasing concern with these problem is the rapid growth of research in the behavioral and social sciences. Almost in the nature of the case, such research makes use of human subjects over a wide range. For example, the concern with child development and various aspects of education involves very sensitive areas. Survey research and various forms of participant observation have been expanding rapidly, and these matters will undoubtedly call for careful scrutiny in the future.

This paper will not be concerned specifically with the medical problem, but will stress the continuity of the impingement of medical research on human subjects with that of research in other areas. There is a sense in which our tendency to underplay such ethical problems arises from the early predominance in research of the physical sciences, where injury to the chemical substances in the test tube does not raise ethical issues, though the cost of the substances may be relevant, as may also be the possibility of an explosion that would injure persons or property.

Medical research, on the other hand, has a direct and obvious impact on persons. Also, the ethical problems involved in medical research are close to those raised in the therapeutic care of patients. Indeed, a large

Reprinted by permission of *Daedalus,* Journal of the American Academy of Arts and Sciences, Boston, Massachusetts. Spring 1969 (vol. 98, no. 2), *Ethical Aspects of Experimentation with Human Subjects.*

proportion of research subjects is drawn from patient populations. The ethical problems of therapy are very old indeed, and tradition provides a frame of reference from which to consider new aspects of medical involving human subjects. There is also an important continuity with other professional fields. The legal profession, for example, has a long tradition dealing with the relations between lawyers and their clients.

Research and practice are two principal functions of what I shall call the "professional complex" in modern society: The first is concerned primarily with the creation of new knowledge and the second with the utilization of knowledge in the service of practical human interests. Since, however, this complex is grounded in important ways in various forms of competence, there is a third salient function—namely, that of teaching, or the transmission of knowledge to those classes of persons with an interest in its acquisition,

It is significant that a large proportion of medical research clusters around medical schools. Though, of course, oriented to research and to practice (for example, through their teaching hospitals), medical schools are primarily concerned with the training of future physicians. At the same time, the central locus of "pure" research in the modern intellectual disciplines is in the "academic" world, notably the faculties of arts and sciences where research is typically combined with teaching, but where there is much less emphasis on practice than in the professional school or those organizations specifically oriented to practice.

I suggest that the ethical problems of research with human subjects possess important continuities not only with the relations of professional personnel to patients and clients in the realm of practice, but also with the relations of teachers to the "subjects" on whom they perform certain kinds of "operations"—namely, their students. Just as patients often serve as research subject, so do students, particularly in the behavioral sciences.

This paper will attempt to deal with the ethical problems of human experimentation in research in the context of the professional complex as a whole. The discussion will focus on the interdependencies of the three principal professional functions of practice, research, and teaching. In modern systems, the interrelations among the institutional provisions for these functions are complex. They overlap to a great extent, however, since the same organizations and the same personnel are frequently involved in at least two, if not three, of the functions. In all three cases, a "professional" element must etablish an appropriate pattern of relationship to a "lay" element—whether the latter consists of patients, clients, students, or research subjects, and the former of practitioners, professors, or investigators.

By some kind of informal consensus, two focal points of this relationship have crystallized: the problem of "voluntary informed consent" and that of "protection of privacy." I suggest that these problems are continuous between the three principal functional contexts of the professional complex, and that none is altogether new. In my analysis, I shall interpret the two "standards" in terms of their bearing on the functioning of the professional complex as a whole.

I shall treat the question of ethics here as essentially one of *social* responsibility—that is, responsibility to promote or at least do no harm to the values and welfare of the societal system and the various classes of its members. The investigative activities in question are part of this system, and I conceive this social reference in sufficiently broad terms to include protection of rights more or less fully institutionalized. (Violation of the rights of individual or collective units is not usually the result of the implementation of a value or interest of the society.) Allowances must be made, of course, because legitimate values and interests are often difficult to interpret, and conflicts of values and interests are exceedingly pervasive in all complex and rapidly changing societies.

For the sociologist, the desirability of "enforcing" high levels of responsibility immediately raises the question of the "mechanisms" of "social control" by which relative conformity with normative expectations is or can be achieved. A brief outline of a classification of such mechanisms may serve as a useful introduction to a more detailed analysis of the mechanisms of particular interest here.

Mechanisms for Favoring Accountability

In one sense, the most elementary mechanism is the "discipline" of the market. This device maximizes the chances that participating units will act responsibly by following the dictates of their own self-interest, as measured in terms of monetary gain or loss. Generally speaking, this balance cannot hold unless markets are normatively regulated at least at two levels. The first is the framework of legal institutions and moral sanctions in such matters as property, contracts, and honesty; the other is the more specific level of regulation, which often attaches particular monetary consequences to certain classes of acts. (Guido Calabresi has analyzed such regulation in accident control through traffic laws and insurance systems.[1])

Legal sanctions and mechanisms, defining rights and obligations as well as enforcing them, back up systems of market control. These mechanisms operate in many fields other than the market, but in the present context they appear first at this point. An interest of a person—or a collectivity—can be protected if he has both the right and the realistic opportunity to

[1] cf. G. Calabresi, "Reflections on Medical Experimentation in Humans," in Paul Freund (ed.), *Experimentation with Human Subjects* (New York: Braziller, 1970), pp. 178–196.

seek "remedy" in the courts and thereby hold accountable those who have injured or might injure his interests. Both these modes of control have serious limitations for many classes of cases, but they are, nevertheless, of great importance in establishing a broad framework within which expectations of accountability are established. Thus, the importance of the adjudicatory system is by no means confined to the cases in which formal court decisions are made, since anticipation of such decisions serves as an exceedingly important guide to action.

A second set of mechanisms concerns the more direct use of collectively sanctioned authority (in principle, that of any collectivity, but especially public authority).[2] The first level of this process involves the operation of administrative or executive agencies that implement policies or other decisions binding on the members of a collectivity. Here, of course, responsible administrators or executives have authority, according to established rules, to "enforce" the agency's policies either on non-members (for example, taxpayers in the case of the Bureau of Internal Revenue) or on its own members.

The question is bound to arise as to who holds the administrators accountable. The most important mechanism for such a check is the authority of elective office, whereby executive implementers are responsible to elected officials who, in turn, are responsible to an electorate. This set of institutions is particularly conspicuous in the field of private organizations within the limits of the latter's jurisdiction.

Just as the first pair of mechanisms leaves important gaps in necessary or desirable controls because it is difficult to insure that the self-interest of acting units will effectively coordinate with the objectives of such control, so the second pair just mentioned leaves gaps in the "enforceability" of controls through the exercise of authority. One of these of special interest to us concerns the "competence" of untrained persons, whatever their position of authority to evaluate either the individual or the collective interest in a mode of action, in the sense that only medically trained people can competently judge the therapeutic effects or dangers of certain procedures.

Within the gaps left open by all the control mechanisms so far discussed, but still in the category of institutionalized mechanisms rather than movements of revolt against the institutionalized order, we may speak of still a third pair. Both of its members operate through *persuasion,* mobilizing "opinion" in favor of or in opposition to courses of action, but without invoking either inducements for self-interested compliance or coercive or compulsory sanctions.

---

[2] I am thinking of "legal" accountability, as just sketched, as involving an indirect rather than direct use of public authority. Put in sociologically functional terms, the system of courts and the processes of adjudication perform more integrative than executive functions in the operation of a society.

For the first, the mass media constitute the most tangible as well as largest scale example. They "broadcast" to indefinitely general publics, most of whose members do not claim any special expertise in judging the content of the communication. This mechanism undoubtedly exerts important pressure in bringing to bear sanctions of approval and disapproval with respect to many kinds of action. Thus it has been claimed that the immediacy of experience of televised actions involving violence has introduced a new factor into the evaluation of the role of violence in modern society.

The second of the currently relevant pair narrows the "public" within which persuasion is attempted. There are many bases of qualification, such as commitment to a specific religious or ideological position, but that of special interest here is some order of technical competence importantly, if loosely, validated by status in a professional group. Such a group is defined by qualifications for membership that combine functions in and on behalf of the society with levels of technical competence to perform them which require grounding in some phase of the general intellectual tradition.

Competence is conceived to be an essential condition of effective performance of this combination of functions. In addition, however, there must be integrity of institutionalized responsibility of a fiduciary sort. To some extent, this integrity insures that such competence will be used in the interest not only of the societal "clients" to whom these functions are important, but also of the wider collective systems. This combination of criteria implies, of course, that technical functions, are to some degree specialized. Most of the interests on which their performance impinges lack, to a greater or lesser degree, the competence not only to perform these functions, but to evaluate the way in which they are being performed. Thus, the ultimate responsibility for standards both of competence and of integrity must rest with the professional complex itself.

To use the medical case for reference, the principle of *caveat emptor* for the purchaser of health services will scarcely be adequate as a basis for accountability. Nor will legal liability be sufficient, if this must be enforced by judges and attorneys who are not technically competent at professional levels in anything but the law, and if the initiative is left to litigants who conceive themselves to be injured and are willing and financially able to assume the burden of litigation. Nor can accountability reside with administrators who are not themselves professionally competent in the subject matter in question, nor with grievance procedures, nor, finally, with the "decent opinion of mankind" as expressed through the mass communication system. Professional groups must, to some essential degree, be self-regulating, taking responsibility for the technical standards of their profession and for their integrity in serving societal functions.

In concluding this sketch of mechanisms for implementing account-

ability, two points must still be made. First, the six mechanisms just outlined should be regarded as ideal types. In reality, several—if not all—
are involved in most concrete situations. My central purposes here are,
namely, to focus on the indispensability of fiduciary professional responsibility in insuring accountability in the ethical contexts that involve professional function in important degrees and, secondly, to give a rough
frame of reference for characterizing the alternative, complementary, and
supplementary mechanisms for the concrete cases where professional responsibility alone will not suffice.[3]

All such mechanisms—being attempts to "control," to enforce compliance with norms—imply some common background of legitimation, which
will be differently structured in the different cases. Where a division of
labor is involved, as is true of our interest— this will always have to include the legitimation of the functions of the groups and types of activity
in question, of the ways in which the standards of performance of those
functions arc upheld, and of the protection or enhancement of the rights
and interests of those outside the groups of performers of the functions on
whom the actions of such groups impinge. The paramount question in this
context, of course, is that of the basis of legitimation of the *function* itself.

The Professional Complex

In modern societies generally, and rather especially in the United
States, the research function has, as we have suggested, come to be institutionalized as part of what we have called the professional complex. This is
a complex of occupational groups that perform certain rather specialized
functions for others ("laymen") in the society on the basis of high-level
and specialized competence, with the attendant fiduciary responsibility.
Since the competence of their members, along with components of special
skill and "know-how," is grounded in mastery of some part of the society's
generalized (intellectual) cultural tradition, the acquisition of professional
status is almost uniformly contingent on undergoing training of a relatively formally approved type. In our society, such training has come increasingly to be acquired in the university, whatever special provisions for
practicum experience there may also be (for example, in hospitals).

---

[3] An interesting development in recent years combines the factor of fiduciary
responsibility on the part of members of the profession with that of certain important lay elements. This is the system of review boards which in hospitals and various
other institutions that engage in research with human subjects pass on the ethical
admissibility of research projects undertaken within their organization. Often, in
somewhat the manner of boards of trustees, lay citizens of important standing are
enlisted along with the professional contingent. It is significant that among these laymen two groups figure prominently, namely lawyers and clergymen, who in general
have a rather high reputation for readiness to assume such responsibility.

These specialized functions range widely—from dealing with the spiritual welfare of persons by the clergy (the original contrast with "laymen"), through the ordering by law of the relations of people to one another and to public authority, the management of conditions of health and illness, and the control of the physical environment through technology. On another and crosscutting basis, professional functions (besides participation in the government of professional organizations) may be classified in three categories: *practice* (for example, the provision of services to predominantly lay groups who are ill or threatened with illness); *teaching* of the knowledge and skills important to the practice of one's own profession; and *contributing* to the advancement of knowledge, or research. Since professionals are trained in the general cultural tradition, specialized teaching of future professionals is closely articulated with the more general function of teaching, especially what is often called "general education."

In American society, the center of the professional complex has come to be the university—"flanked" by other components of the system of higher education. The university is the focal center of the research function, especially in its most prestigious sector. Graduate schools of arts and sciences are the main training organ for the academic profession itself, including that sector primarily concerned with the teaching of undergraduates. University professional schools are now the primary locus of the training of members of the "applied" professions, including not only practitioners in the narrower senses, but future teachers in such schools and many future research workers.

One of the main bases of this clustering of professional functions around the university lies in the crisscross relation between the pure intellectual disciplines and the fields of their application in practice. So far as one can speak of a "science of medicine," it is not a discipline, but a mobilization of the relevant parts of a whole group of sciences (in the discipline sense) in terms of their bearing on problems of health and illness. The teachers of and researchers in the "basic sciences" in medical schools, and indeed increasingly in teaching hospitals, are not in the practitioner sense "medical men." They are scientists whose expertise is similar to that of their brethren in arts and sciences departments. Concentration in the university facilitates the cultivation and explotation of such linkages.

The university is not simply a congeries of discrete individuals, departments, and schools, but an interwoven nexus of relationships. The great majority of its members at professional—faculty—levels perform in varying combinations all three of the principal substantive functions of the professional complex. That most of them are teachers almost goes without saying, since teaching is historically the primary "academic" function. Nevertheless, an increasing proportion are at the same time engaged in research. At university levels, such people are now the overwhelming majority. Furthermore, not only are many of the members of professional faculties engaged in the practice of their professions, but members of faculties of arts and sciences are generally engaged in performing a variety of services for laymen, such as "consulting," writing, or lecturing for lay audiences.

Since there is such concentration of multiple functions among university faculties, it would seem likely that there should be some important common themes in the social organization of the settings in which these functions are carried out. These common themes should include both the relational systems in which such members are related to one another in their work and the discharge of their common responsibilities as well as their relations to the classes of laymen with whom they are—in their specialties, in professional terms—brought into contact.

It is fairly well known that the structure of faculties and their constituent departments is of a relatively distinctive sociological type, which some of us have called *collegial*. This is a subtype of the associational pattern of structure and stands in strongest contrast to the hierarchy of authority characteristic of administrative bureaucracies. It is distinguished from other associational types, above all, because its membership is typically determined by occupational role, the performance of which is a "full-time job." On the other hand, the members constitute, in ideal type, a "company of equals." Power tends to be widely distributed within such a group, and each member has relatively protected spheres of autonomy—a major aspect of what we call "academic freedom." Corporate action is typically taken by the "democratic" procedure of one member, one vote. Such decision is, moreover, generally preceded by discussion conducted according to "rules of order." In both cases, there is sharp contrast with "executive" decision-making.

The collegial pattern of organization of professional groups is, in turn, linked with another common structural theme permeating the complex. This involves the professional individual in membership in a common solidary collectivity. This is most obvious in the case of the teaching function. The student is "admitted" to the college or school. To continue to function as a student, he must retain his membership "in good standing" until graduation. Similarly, however, patients are "admitted" to hospitals in what is, in some sense, a membership status. The case of the private patients of "individual" physicians is not so different as it seems on the surface; physician and patient join together for a common therapeutic task.[4] Hence we suggest that the research subject is also "selected," perhaps because he has characteristics of technical interest that are presup-

[4] For the argument in favor of this point of view, see Talcott Parsons, "Some Theoretical Considerations Bearing on the Field of Medical Sociology," in *Social Structure and Personality* (New York: Free Press, 1964).

posed; but he also participates in a solidary relationship with the investigators.

Thus if this feature of inclusion of the "client" in a relation of common collective solidarity with the professional person or agency applies to the roles of practitioner and of teacher, it should also apply to that of researcher whose "client" is the human research subject. This possibility has probably been obscured by at least three factors. First, we have tended to treat research in the physical sciences as the prototype, but there the objects of investigation are not human beings with whom the investigator has to establish *any* kind of social relationship. Second, on the whole, the research function has received less attention from social scientists than have the other two primary professional functions. Third, there are deep-seated tendencies in our cultural tradition to define the relation in other ways. To many students, including for long the present writer, it seemed only "natural' 'to conceive the practitioner-client relationship as a special case of the market relationship, especially where it is performed on an individual fee-for-service basis. The professional offers his services on a market, and they are purchased by the client. This account of the process highlights certain aspects of a complex relationship while underplaying others. In particular, perhaps, it makes elucidation of the role of the research subject difficult. The typical client, including the medical patient, expects relatively immediate "value received" from the services of his physician, whereas there is usually no comparable *quid pro quo* in the case of the research subject. Thus, it is more difficult to see how the latter is in any sense assuming obligations by serving as a subject.

Again, a certain suspicion about the adequacy of this point of view might be aroused by various features of the market for professional services. But one factor in particular stands out. Though some professional services are given on a contingent fee basis (notably in law), the rule applying both to medicine and to teaching is, rather, that fees are due regardless of the success of the endeavors. Even though the patient dies, his medical bills must be paid; even though the student "flunks out," his tuition is not reimbursed. Failure in the common endeavor does not absolve either party from making a fair contribution on the basis of *capacity to contribute* and not value personally received. In this respect, the relationship is more like marriage with the definition of obligations in terms of "for better, for worse," and not of specific benefits received from the relationship, which is the guiding principle of the commercial market relationship.

As we have suggested, the market perspective tends to dissociate the client role from that of the research subject and, indeed, to treat that of the student as a case altogether separate from either of the two. A striking empirical fact, however, is the extent to which there has actually been a coincidence of two or more of these roles on the "lay" side, as there has been on the professional function side. In medical research, where subjects are humans rather than animals, they are *also* patients in a very large proportion of cases. I suggest that more than considerations of pragmatic convenience underlie this state of affairs. If patients are conceived as "cooperating" with their physicians or therapeutic "teams" in a common enterprise within a framework of solidarity, and if, furthermore, the therapeutic agency is engaged in the distinct but closely related function of research, then it would seem positively appropriate that there be a presumption of willingness to cooperate in the research enterprise as well. The basic principle is that fellow members of solidary groups are disposed, and in some sense obligated, to help one another whenever they can, subject to their basic rights and the possibility of conflict with other obligations, usually in other solidary contexts.

The problem of "what each gets out of it" involves certain complexities. Uncertainty is a fundamental feature of the medical situation generally. Careful diagnostic investigation in particular cases aims to reduce this uncertainty to a minimum, but it remains considerable in a large proportion of cases, especially the more "serious" ones. In addition, of course, many therapeutic procedures impose other burdens on the patient, such as suffering and disability, in the hope that these burdens will eventually prove to be the cost of favorable outcomes. Uncertainty, then, is a particularly prominent feature of research. If it were fully known in advance what the consequences of research procedures would be, there would be no point in instituting them—except, in the medical case, for therapeutic reasons. Hence the primary problem of justifying use as research subjects concerns the positive benefits to be gained, rather than the costs and burdens.[5]

Before entering into this, however, a word should be said about the coincidence of student and research roles. Certainly this coincidence is relatively common in the case of medical students, but it has also been much practiced in psychology and the social sciences, where many researchers have drawn their subjects from their own college classes. There

[5] Dr. Renée Fox has made particularly illuminating contributions to the sociological understanding of the combination of the roles of patient and research subject. See her book *Experiment Perilous* (New York: Free Press, 1959) which reports a study of a metabolic research ward, where the patients had been subjected to especially drastic and risky procedures. (See especially pp. 85–109 and 243.) She has generalized this analysis, with much additional material, in the article "Some Social and Cultural Factors in American Society Conducive to Medical Research on Human Subjects," *Symposium on the Study of Drugs and Man,* Part IV. In a personal communication Dr. Fox has suggested the following paradigm of types of subjects as a function of lessening degrees of uncertainty: 1) research on animal subjects, where uncertainty and risk are at a maximum; 2) research on moribund, terminally ill subjects, who have "little to lose"; 3) research on patients somewhat less desperately ill, in degrees to those with more or less "normal" expectations of health and longevity.

is, of course, an important sense in which both patients and students constitute "captive audiences," a circumstance that introduces certain constraints on the more absolute versions of the standard of "informed voluntary consent." I shall postpone more general discussion of such constraints, but perhaps the direction the discussion will take is evident from the above argument.

Solidarity and the Problem of Trust

We have suggested that social control in the professional complex cannot rest mainly on the common sanctions of economic inducement as this operates in market systems, nor on authority and power in the ordinary administrative sense. The discussion of solidarity was meant to suggest that the most important mechanisms of social control in this area are to be found in the operation of solidary groups relatively independent of the above classes of sanctions. Commitment to values on the basis of a sense of moral obligation is an indispensable basis of control, but—though a central one—this is *one* factor in the disposition of members of solidary groups to *trust* one another. A somewhat further analysis of the nature and bases of such trust, as it operates in the professional complex, should bring us closer to a useful interpretation of the principal current discussions of ethics in this field.

Relative to its relevant "laity," the professional relation is by its nature asymmetrical and thereby drastically different from the democratic associational relationship among "peers." In one essential aspect, the primary axis of this asymmetry lies in the superior competence of the professional, without which there would be no legitimizing sense for a layman to enter into any one of the three basic types of relationship we have discussed. The process of learning "with" peers (in ignorance) is different from that of learning "from" a teacher who has superior competence in the subject matter. Seeking the services of a competent physician or lawyer is different from peers "agreeing" about what should be done in a distressing situation. And "cooperating in the research plan of a trained investigator is different from a group of (non-expert) peers in the subject discussing what would be interesting to "find out."

In all three of these basic respects, there exists a "competence gap" between professional and lay persons. The variations in the specific nature of this gap are endless in different relations, but this is pervasive. *If* the necessary lay cooperation with the professional is to be assured, it cannot rest on the layman's full understanding of "what the professional is doing" in a sense presupposed by the slogan *caveat emptor* in the market field. There must be bases of trusted validation of competence other than the typical layman's personal competence to evaluate it. But this issue also raises the fundamental question of integrity—namely, not only whether the pretension of competence is justified, but whether, if it exists, it will be used to exploit or benefit the participating lay elements or, as I much prefer to put it, be used in a higher-order *common* interest.

Such a competence gap must be bridged by something like what we call trust. We suggest the following principal factors on which the generation of such trust depends: First, it must be believed on both sides of the gap and, of course, by a sufficient proportion of the participants that the enterprise in question is in the service of *common* values. This is generally the case with respect to the valuation not only of good health but also of education. Second, this sharing of common values must, within the requisite ranges, be translatable into common *goals,* such as the curing of a particular form of ailment in an individual patient or in a class of patients. In the achievement of such common goals, patients are more likely to be asked positively to cooperate than passively to "submit" to the ministrations of their physicians.[6]

A third condition is the successful fitting of the expectations engaged on both sides of the relationship into the balance of the plural set of solidary involvements in which all actors, individual and collective, are involved. Just as it is scarcely possible for a concrete individual to be "only" a sick person and thus a patient—except in extreme conditions and temporarily—so it is not possible to be only a student or only a research subject, to say nothing of the corresponding conditions on the other side. This, as we shall argue below, is the focus of the "privacy" issue. A fourth condition is that the acceptance of a relation of trust should not be grossly incompatible with known facts and conditions of feasibility. A physician who had been known to be guilty of various kinds of malpractice would certainly forfeit a good deal of trust, as would a teacher who had grossly misinformed his students about the subject in question. Thus, there must be some adequate "symbolization" of both competence and integrity.

In the favorable case, these four factors mutually reinforce one another. Sharing values makes agreement on common goals easier, and "confidence" in competence and integrity makes commitment to mutual involvement in such goals easier. Integrity includes respect for the interests

---

[6] In a striking oral statement, the head of a pediatric service in a major hospital once said in my presence that in his opinion fully one half of the therapeutic failures on that service were attributable not to the lack of available knowledge and therapeutic measures adequate for success in the case, but to failure of the staff to secure the *cooperation* of "patients"—that is, children and members of their families—which was necessary for the successful implementation of a therapeutic program. Such noncooperation is grounded in deficiency of trust in the present sense. It can, of course, reach into unconscious psychodynamic levels.

of the layman outside the technical concerns of the professional context. All these considerations focus mutual trust in the conception or "feeling" of the solidarity of collective groups.[7] However dependent this "feeling" may be on "input" factors, once established, it acquires a certain autonomy of its own. People defined as sharing one's values or concrete goals and in whose competence and integrity one has "confidence" come to be thought of as "trustworthy individuals" or "types." Because of these aspects of belonging together, such people can be relied on, within limits of course, not only to respect one another's interests, but more critically to give certain benefits of the doubt to the importance of a common interest that transcends the interest of the individual unit members. Thus, we mean by the solidarity of a collectivity the "pull" of a common interest that can motivate actions which, while not necessarily in conflict with unit interests, at least are not fully "dictated" by them.

Beyond this, we suggest that solidary groups exert "pressure"— through leadership, ideology, norms, and the like—on their units to play the expected role in the process of interaction. They exert such pressure by means of sanctions that come to focus in appeals to loyalty to the values, goals, and collective solidarity of the group in question. Such a sanction system depends, of course, on participants in some sense defining themselves as belonging to the group: hence the importance of the concept of membership and the voluntary principle.

The "interests" that are served in the professional functioning of the three categories may be classified under three rubrics. The first has been the main point of reference of much general discussion—namely, each participant receives in a short run a *quo* for the *quid* that he contributes. The usual model here is that of the market. The patient pays for the value of the services he receives from his physician. We are, however, all aware that there are important sources of "satisfaction" other than monetary gain or the relief of a particular distressing condition.

This exchange of relatively immediate benefits, however, merges into broader contexts primarily in two ways. The first is the extension of the set of collective interests that are involved on both sides. Thus a patient's recovery benefits not only himself, but his family and the organization that employs him. A physician's record of therapeutic success not only brings him income from practice and personal satisfaction, but it redounds to the benefit of the reputation of his profession and the subunits of it that he is associated with. Certainly in the teacher role, what the individual student has specifically learned is not the only aspect of the successful performance of the function. The class, the department, the college, or the

---

[7] See Fox, *Experiment Perilous* and "Some Social and Cultural Factors in American Society Conducive to Medical Research on Human Subjects," for the way in which Dr. Fox has analyzed these relationships in a concrete case of medical research.

school all have genuine interests in successful teaching. Indeed, morale in a class is enhanced when some of its members learn effectively. In outstanding cases, people treasure the experience of having been a member of an unusually effective teaching-learning system. Indeed, the ramifications of this "Chinese box" of increasingly extensive collective inclusions go far to provide an essential base of operations for performance of the various kinds of professional functions.

One major indication that such institutionalization is important is the persistent ambivalence that exists in public attitudes toward all the main professional groups. The medical profession, in general, enjoys a high level of public confidence. Nevertheless, a persistent minority regards the whole system as a pious fraud that exists only to line the pockets of its practitioners at the expense of helpless and gullible people. To take another example, the wave of radical student protest in our universities expresses profound distrust of that part of "the system." This protest is partly significant precisely because of the high esteem in which higher education is *generally* held.

The second direction of the extension of the "interest base" of professional function is temporal. Generally speaking all but the more trivial benefits of professional function take time to materialize. Many therapeutic regimes are of long duration, and the course of learning is proverbially not only hard but long. "Instant education" is deservedly felt to be unlikely to be worth much. Research, however, is at the extreme of a range in this respect. Indeed, the values of the scientific world make it clear that research oriented to relatively immediate and specific practical goals is likely to be less "fundamental" and less productive of practical benefits in the long run than is more "basic" research concerned with general and often largely theoretical problems of science.

The "logic" of investment in the economic sense is the most familiar example of the general principles involved in the use of resources without reference to short-run utility and in the interest of larger benefits in the long run. Education is, of course, such a process of "investment" of present resources in the interest of a future. Research is simply a further step along the same path. Instead of imparting what he now knows to students, the investigator himself assumes the "student" role and attempts to learn things which nobody yet knows, but which, when known, could subsequently be taught to others. The dissociation between the research function and the two other primary professional functions obscures these continuities.

If we accept the general proposition that the research subject, like the client or the student, is in a fundamental sense included in the professional system, then the question posed above—"what does the research subject get out of it?"—can immediately be answered in principle. According to his status in the system, he gets the same *kinds* of rewards that all other participants get and, in particular, that the investigators get. The highest order of reward is the prestige and satisfaction of having made a "contribution to the advancement of knowledge."

We refer to this reward as the highest, but by no means the only one. Thus, investigators are generally also paid in money, essentially because they are performing more or less full-time jobs and must make their living that way. Research subjects are sometimes paid, sometimes not. In the other sectors of the professional system, clients are generally not paid, but themselves pay. Some students or their parents pay tuition, but it is not too farfetched to say that many, especially the more advanced students, are paid through various kinds of fellowships and stipends. Nevertheless, the pay, where it exists, is not conceived primarily as matching the economic value of the contribution, as a commercial price is. It is thought of as an "honorarium," itself a contribution to getting the primary contribution made.

"Bracketed," in a sense, between this highest motive of the sense of contribution to knowledge and the "lowest" of financial remuneration is a whole series of other motives that are relevant. In the medical field, the research interest in the advancement of knowledge is, of course, closely linked to the valuation of health and hence to the interest in the conquest of preventable and curable disease and of premature death, though eventual death is surely recognized to be inevitable and even in some sense desirable.[8] Another important cluster of motives concerns the fact that the sick person is, in the nature of his position in society, relatively isolated and deprived of the opportunity for normal functioning. Thus, if the sick person has the opportunity through an active contribution to be more than the passive "object" of treatment or investigation, he may gain a sense of meaningfulness that would not otherwise be available to him.

Interaction with respect to professional function is not nearly so one-sided as it is often held to be. Clients are not, in general, simply passive recipients of service; they are contributors to the common output of the cooperative system. Indeed, students are rather loudly insisting that they be considered active participants in the learning process, not just "receptacles" into whom information is poured by their teachers. Research subjects must be thought of in the same way, as has been particularly vividly brought out by Renée Fox. In all three categories, there are, of course, cases where the role of the nonprofessional is overwhelmingly passive, but it is legitimate to regard such cases as relatively marginal rather than definite instances of the main structural relationship. Thus, the role of active par-

---

[8] See Talcott Parsons and Victor M. Lidz, "Death in American Society," *Essays in Self-Destruction,* ed. Edwin Shneidman (New York, 1967).

ticipant seems to us clearly to presuppose a positive bond of solidarity across the professional-lay line.[9]

Voluntary Informed Consent and the Protection of Privacy

The two formulae included in the title of this section have come, by a kind of informal consensus, to be the main foci of the discussion of the ethical problems of human experimentation. I should now like to attempt to show how the considerations advanced above throw light on the problems involved in these two formulae, singling out the elements of legitimacy in them as well as showing some of the limits on their too-sweeping use.

We have suggested that the professional complex belongs basically in the associational sector of the structure of modern societies. In this connection, we have stressed that inclusion in some sort of membership status is important for the "lay" contingent in the system. Certainly, then, the voluntary principle is much involved with this complex, as is indicated by the key term "voluntary association." But voluntariness involves two-way consent. Certain associational structures impose no qualifications for inclusion, but such qualifications are of central importance in the professional complex. Thus we have emphasized, on the professional side, validation of competence through training and certification. On the lay side, for example, one cannot ordinarily be a patient without being defined as ill or potentially so; nor can one be a lawyer's client without having a "legal problem." Otherwise, the professional may simply refuse to spend time and effort over that person.[10] To enter various courses of study, a student often has to meet qualifications independent of his mere desire to pursue those courses, as well as to be "motivated" to learn in them. Finally, a research subject must be evaluated as to whether he is a suitable source for the information that would contribute to the success of the investigation.

The reciprocal of professional consent to inclusion, often phrased as

[9] Often, even where it is not clearly intended, reflection and analysis can bring out the appeal to values and solidarity. If a personal example may be permitted, Dr. Gerald Platt and I have been engaged in a rather large-scale study of members of the American academic profession. Our basic data are derived from a long questionnaire which was mailed to over 4,500 individuals. Sixty-six per cent, slightly over 3,000, of them responded at the expense of about 2½ hours of time and effort each. No honorarium was offered, but the covering letter appealed explicitly not only to the valuation of research, but to long-run professional interests. Also prestige symbols such as the location of the investigators at Harvard University and the blessing of the American Association of University Professors on the project were explicitly used. Our basic apeal could be phrased "Fellow academic men. . . ."

[10] This is very different from a relation of friendship in which such specific qualifications are not essential criteria of a claim to "help" or, more generally, participation.

"admission" to a program, is "lay" consent to participate. Clearly, by no means all potential students consent at various levels—for example, to accept an offer of admission to a college, to undertake a program of study, or to "take" a particular course. So far as the client relationship is concerned, the most salient case is the strong medical emphasis on the importance of the patient's right to choose his physician. The voluntary aspect of participation in the capicity of research subject should be placed in essentially the same framework.

In this framework, however, there is both the stress on the desirability of voluntary consent and the problem of defining certain limitations on it. The framework of admissions to institutions of higher education and those to hospitals and clinics implies that the collective entity the layman is "joining" can, in part, define the new member's range of choice and thereby limit it in certain respects. A first-year medical student simply cannot impose his conception of a good medical education, including a perfectly free choice among the teachers currently functioning at his school. He must somehow fit into a program. The same is true of the patient in a clinic or hospital. If he entrusts his interests to the collective entity, he must "adapt"—within limits, of course—to the exigencies of the organization, though he can refuse to accept service or even leave against medical advice. The clinic or college is in command of scarce resources that cannot be made indiscriminately available simply on "demand." Thus, to take one familiar case, a particularly popular teacher cannot pay equal attention to all students who might like to receive his attention.

Research subjects, like the other two classes of laymen, are both selected and select, and the voluntary principle has its applications on *both* sides of the relationship. Not infrequently there is an element of conflict between the two sets of interests. Thus students who desire admission are sometimes rejected, and clients who desire the services of particular practitioners cannot obtain them. Although it is not yet common, it is relevant that potential subjects are often denied opportunity to participate in important research because of selective procedures. Similarly the right of students, clients, and subjects to refuse opportunities of participation often imposes frustrations on the professional element who would like to secure their participation.

Conflicts at the threshold of participation and involving a membership status are complicated because constraints of other elements in the relational nexus restrict the voluntary principle. Thus, we have suggested that neither patients nor students are wholly free to refuse reasonable requests to serve as research subjects. They tend to retain a "formal" right to refuse, but seldom exercise that right in normal circumstances.[11] Scarcity factors

[11] There is a particularly important parallel here in the relation of bank depositors to the lending operations of banks. The "contract of deposit" leaves the depositor full rights to withdraw his total deposit on demand at any time. But the function of the

also play a part, as in shortages of hospital beds or places in the "better" colleges.

The standard of voluntary consent should rightly be regarded as a decision on *both* sides of the relationship to "admit" to and to accept a membership status, but certain circumstances impose legitimate exceptions. The standard usually makes explicit only part of the relational complex discussed—namely, the voluntariness on the part of the research subject. On the professional side, there is selectivity, and certain presumptions may be created by multifunctional role relations or the distinction between formal rights and informally legitimate expectations. In any case, the maximization of voluntariness may be said to apply at the point of decision as to whether or not to participate.

It can be fairly said that our society strongly values rationality of action, and that we wish to create conditions of action where people know, so far as possible, what they are doing when they make commitments. I can see no general objection to the obligation to inform subjects, as well as members of the other two relevant categories of laymen, as fully as possible in advance about "what they are letting themselves in for" in deciding to participate. To modify too naïve and literalistic interpretations of "being informed," however, three sets of considerations need to be kept in mind: uncertainty, cost, and relative competence.

We generally use the term "risk" where uncertainty is calculable to some fair degree of approximation. Where risks in this sense are rather clearly known, certainly prospective participants should be informed of them, though this obligation can easily be overformalized. Admissions officers do not usually give applicants precise statistical estimates of the probabilities of their successfully completing a course of study, nor do physicians overformalize the risk of treatment. There is a cost factor involved here in which the expenditure of time and effort by the professional should certainly figure prominently, but there may be a similar expenditure on the other side.

There is, however, more to uncertainty than risk in the above sense. Student performance can only be predicted within considerable margins of error; the same is true of decisions of courts as well as of the course of various forms of illness and research. The essential point is that *nobody* in the system can be *fully* informed about what participants "may be in for," except in the more trivial kinds of situation—which is one of the primary

_____

bank as a creator of credit in the interest of economic efficiency depends on the probability that the large proportion of depositors will "trust" the bank and leave considerable balances in it. Indeed, if most of them exercise their legal rights, the "good" bank which is doing its job is necessarily insolvent. We are suggesting that both students and clients, and of course research subjects, are in the role analogous to depositors, and that they in a similar sense are under a kind of obligation to trust the professional elements with whom they associate. This obligation is a kind of "citizenship" of the collective system in question, not a "formal" obligation.

reasons why mutual trust is so important in such relational systems. Thus, there is the danger that the criterion of being informed may introduce undesirable constraints on the performance of the professional function if it is too strictly construed.

The importance of the cost factor should also not be underestimated. When Gerald Platt and I sent out questionnaires to members of the American academic profession, we certainly did not in any sense "fully" inform our prospective academic respondents in detail, question by question, about our reasons for asking them what we did. Even to approximate such a standard, we would have had to prepare a long and complex document that they would have had to read carefully before deciding whether or not to accede to our request. Such a measure would probably at least have doubled, in both time and trouble, the burden imposed on the respondent and would have reduced greatly the rate of return. Hence, the cost factor applies on both sides of the relationship and is far from trivial.

In this and many other cases, the factor of cost merges into that of competence. In a short time and at relatively low cost, it is often impossible for the professional to inform the layman fully, if by that is meant giving him as good an understanding of what is involved as he, the professional, has. Being informed, like the voluntary component, cannot be absolutized without imposing severe impediments on all three of the primary professional functions. *What* it is important for the student, the client, or the research subject to know must be selectively defined in terms of the function he performs in the system and the ways in which the activities of the others impinge on his role and functions. Only in limiting cases does sufficient knowledge constitute in any absolute sense *full* information about everything involved.

To return to the standard of voluntariness: Once a decision to participate in an associational collectivity has been made, the participant becomes entitled to the rights of membership in the collectivity, but he also becomes subject to the corresponding obligations. Perhaps the most important single protection of his rights is his freedom to resign his membership status at any time or to use the threat of doing so as a source of leverage for protection of his rights—individually or in concert with others. This is indeed the actual case of the bank depositor; withdrawal of all deposits comes close to being a form of "resignation."

On the other side of the coin, however, no complex collective system can operate unless there is a relative concentration of authority and power by virtue of which many decisions binding on the collectivity as a whole are taken without the full consent of *all* participant members. However many problems there may be today about the authority systems impinging on students, there would seem to be little serious defense of the view that *no* authority system whatever needs to be involved in the teacher-student relationship, a position that would be tantamount to eliminating all "requirements" from courses of study. The same clearly holds true for the professional-client relationship—whether the use of authority be rather nakedly stated in such a phrase as "doctor's orders" or more subtly as "legal advice." Surely if we are correct about the parallelism of the three professional subsystems, the role of research subject, once assumed, cannot be totally immune from authority and power.

Thus, there must be constraints on the voluntariness of cooperation from moment to moment as the process unfolds, except in the important sense of freedom to "resign." The research program, like the program of study and the therapeutic regimen, has "requirements" that someone is authorized to enforce.[12] Put a little differently, the status of membership in a collectivity is not compatible with an act-by-act reservation of rights. The member cannot refuse to comply with the requests of legitimate leadership and authority within the collective system of reference—except, again, in the sense of his right to withdraw. Such authority, of course, should be exercised sparingly and with an understanding of sensitivities, but it cannot be dispensed with altogether.

Thus, the voluntary principle in associative relationships is of truly fundamental importance. At the same time, however, it cannot operate effectively if it is not balanced in the *same* collective system by a system of obligations that are enforced by authority. Compliance with this authority —in the *ad hoc,* act-by-act sense—cannot be wholly voluntary.[13] In professional collective systems, the need for this involuntary aspect stems primarily from two sources. The first is the role of special technical competence in such systems and the presence of a competence gap. The second, however, is the simple exigency that effective action in complex collective systems necessitates differentiation on an axis of leadership and followership, or relative concentration of authority and power. Associational *collectivities* on the whole, relative to other types, minimize this concentration, but do not eliminate it.

In this "dialectic" situation, by stressing one side to the total exclusion of the other, the operation of the factors on the other side may be impeded even though they are essential to the functioning of the system. There should, in my opinion, be *no* total burden of proof on either side— either that *any* limitation on voluntary informed consent, as judged by the strictest criteria, is presumptively illegitimate, or that *any* limitation on the exercise of professional prerogative or authority in the interests of the autonomy and freedoms of the "lay" element is presumptively illegitimate.

---

[12] The right to resign is, of course, restricted in a few cases—such as legal commitment of patients to mental hospitals—but these cases are not of central significance to this analysis.

[13] In the sense that *every* participant's desire to have it done "my way" has no claim equal to that of legitimate leadership in determining collective decisions.

There is a similar "dialectic" in the professional complex between the rights of privacy and the obligations to sacrifice privacy—most obviously, but by no means exclusively, through the disclosure of information.[14] It is, of course, well known that a doctrine of privileged communication is deeply embedded in the tradition of the practicing professions. It is one of the principal features of the Hippocratic Oath and is also central to the legal profession. The privileged communication between attorney and client, however, is connected with an institution of obligatory disclosure as one of the fundamentals of procedure in systems of adjudication. Admissible evidence is restricted to what has been *publicly* stated under oath and subject to cross-examination. Witnesses, usually including litigants themselves, are obliged to answer counsel's questions in public.[15]

This relation surely obtains in medicine, where "case records" available publicly *within* the professional system constitute an essential part of the professional decision-making system. The relationship also applies within the teaching system, but is a little more difficult to see there. But on the disclosure side, a teacher is surely not entitled to withhold from students "personal" opinions touching on the subject matter of his teaching; he is obligated to answer to the best of his ability any legitimate questions put to him by his students, often exposing thereby his "shameful" ignorance, bias, or prejudice. On the other hand, the privacy of his "personal" life is protected. A sociologist teaching a course in marriage and the family may legitimately refuse to answer students' questions about his *own* marriage situation on the ground that they are "too personal." The teacher also enjoys an area of privacy in his professional capacity. An obvious example concerns the preparation of materials for use in teaching. He may retire to his study "free from interruptions," as we often say, consult such books and other sources as *he* deems appropriate, organize his thoughts in the manner he considers best, and then "present" the subject in the way he thinks most satisfactory. Student "participation" could not reach the point where the teacher could not prepare a lecture without securing student consent to every decision on what was to be presented, what sources were to be used, or how the material was to be presented. This clearly would be "invasion of privacy." Students, of course, enjoy similar prerogatives of privacy when they are writing a term paper or preparing for an examination.

Both teacher and student, however, eventually come to the "moment of truth" when they *must* perform "in public." The teacher must actually

[14] In the medical case, access to the body is an exceedingly important "privilege" of the physician that "invades" otherwise operative privacies.

[15] I am especially indebted to Lon L. Fuller for insight into this set of connections. See his book *The Morality of Law*, rev. ed. (New Haven: Yale University Press, 1969).

present the subject to his class, if only in the concealed sense of "setting the tone" for an ostensibly free discussion, and the student must submit the paper or write the examination.

It would, indeed, be strange were the research function totally outside this general pattern. There has been so much talk about the rights to privacy of research subjects that a word needs to be said about the rights of investigators. Clearly the research process itself is in some respects privileged in that the laboratory or the office in which research operations are being carried out is certainly not open to any wanderer who might be "curious."

There is, however, a particularly telling example on the professional side of this process. The researcher is exposed to a stringent test of *public* evaluation, the most important aspect of which follows the publication of the results of his work. Especially in the more rigorous of the sciences, this evaluation usually takes place in journals that have a special fiduciary relation to the professional group in question. Publication, in this sense, may be regarded as a particularly prominent case of "obligatory disclosure" of professionally relevant information. Like the witness in court, the author will be evaluated almost ruthlessly, in terms of what he "reveals" in the article he publishes. Interestingly enough, however, not only are the earlier phases of the investigative process relatively free from "invasions of privacy," but in general the privacy of the decision to publish is elaborately protected by professional institutions. The core of this protective process is the "referee" system whereby manuscripts submitted to technical journals are "entrusted" to the editor and then anonymously evaluated by referees of the editor's choice. The editor or sometimes a board takes sole responsibility for the decision.

This process very frequently does not result in an either-or decision— to publish or not—but in a decision as to the "form" in which material should be published. Thus articles usually undergo extensive revision in the editorial process, in which anonymous referees play a considerable part. We suggest that the "privileged" process of preparation for publication— including, of course, reaching negative decisions—is analogous to the preparation of a legal case, in which the "ordeal" of presentation in open court is not undertaken without an important process of preparation in private.

These examples occur on the professional side of the relationship. In accord, however, with our general principle that the patterns should be basically reciprocal, we can say in general that research subjects, as selected members of the professional community, undertake obligations to "disclose" information that would not be disclosed in the ordinary course of daily life. Of course, the rule of anonymity frequently protects their privacy by limiting the "personal" repercussions of this disclosure, but the more important point is that the rights of privacy are dynamically linked to an obligation to disclose things which, apart from the professional nexus, would not be disclosed.

For the clinical practice of medicine, in addition to confidential information, access to the body presents an especially important aspect of the problem of privacy. It is merely necessary to recall that not much more than a century ago in most of the Western world the notion of a male obstetrician dealing with cases of pregnancy and childbirth was at least frowned upon, if not widely forbidden. The concept of privacy also extends to information about people's medical conditions, so far as they are not fully evident. Hence, the doctrine of privileged communication applies even where these conditions are in no sense shameful.

A particularly interesting point, however, concerns the extension of the concept of privacy, and in a related form of consent, to the situation of death. Renée Fox, in her illuminating analysis of the autopsy situation, has emphasized the ways in which the corpse is treated as a sacred object.[16] Permission to dissect it is a special privilege, one which for long was totally forbidden in official religious doctrine, forcing medical teachers and students to raid cemeteries to procure cadavers for the study of anatomy.

A new phase of this problem has, however, developed recently with the technical possibilities or organ transplants in cases where removal from the "donor" would be fatal. There is consensus that consent, in this case consent of the next of kin, must be given. But the problem of the medical definition of death has arisen in a new form because of the relation of timing to the condition of the organ to be transplanted. There seems to have been a strong movement to the conception put forward, especially by Dr. Beecher, that "brain death is death indeed," which justifies earlier intervention than the older conceptions emphasizing heart action and respiration would have permitted. This possibility of earlier intervention presents a particularly important ethical problem in the American setting where the desirability of the conquest of disease is so strongly emphasized.

Thus, like voluntary consent, the protection of privacy is not an absolute, but is linked with a complementary obligation of otherwise "unusual" disclosure. "Privileged communication" commonly applies to relatively early stages in the genesis of results that in turn must, for various reasons, be placed in what is in some sense a legitimate public domain.

The common factor between the voluntary consent context and that of protection of privacy thus appears to be concerned with the outcome of the temporal genesis of values. The granting of consent, in this sense, may be taken to mean a "commitment" to participate in a specially important kind of professionally collective enterprise. On the "lay" side, protection of privacy defines certain limits to the claims that participation in the enterprise may impose on individuals. But the reciprocal is that such par-

[16] Dr. Renée C. Fox, "The Autopsy: Its Place in the Attitude-Learning of Second-Year Medical Students," unpublished paper.

ticipants also have their privileges of privacy in being free to "work on" their contributions without unnecessary interference.

Voluntary consent is in its most important aspect a grant of freedom to the professional complex to advance those interests that are most central to that complex. The privacy issue, on the other hand, concerns the definition of the limits of the legitimacy of such commitments to the professional enterprise—but, be it noted, defining the privileges not only of the lay, but also of the professional elements involved.

Summary and Conclusion

Ethics is, in one primary aspect, a system of control of human behavior in the interest of maintaining and implementing values. For this reason, we began the substantive analysis of this paper with a sketchy classification of the principal types of mechanisms of social control on which ethical considerations may impinge. The emphasis was on social control because this paper has been primarily concerned with the social level of the problem.

Although our classification of six types is a description of components —all of which may, in principle, operate in every situation of social control—their combinations vary greatly in different kinds of social context. To the sociologist, the present problem belongs in the distinctive sector of modern social organization that we have called the "professional complex." The emphases in the field of social control distinguishing this sector differ especially from commercial markets and bureaucratic-administrative organizations, which depend much more directly on economic inducements or on authority and power, rather than on persuasion.

We therefore turned next to an outline of the professional complex with an attempt to locate the research function and some of the forms it takes within this complex as a whole. From one perspective, this complex is the main point of articulation between the primarily cognitive aspect of the cultural tradition and the concrete organization of modern societies. Its structural core lies in systems of higher education understood in a broad sense. This core has become much more highly differentiated in recent times, both internally and from other sectors of the society. Not only has it incorporated the extended range of the modern intellectual disciplines, but it has differentiated the functions of teaching—both of "educated citizens" and of professional practitioners—establishing an important relation to practice in the application of knowledge itself and, most important for us, developing an extended and highly differentiated research function.

All of these functions necessitate structured relations between members of professional groups and "laymen," the difference being defined in terms of the special competence of the former gained through training and experience. Corresponding to the classification of professional functions is a categorization, again in ideal type, of the lay personnel involved— clients (including the patients of medical practice), students, and research subjects. We have noted, however, that the categories often overlap, and that, for example, patients often serve as research subjects.[17]

Our general suggestion with respect to these three categories of lay-men is that they must, by and large, be brought into some kind of mem-bership status with the professional personnel, in common solidary collec-tive structures. Although this membership status is highly tenuous in some cases, it dominates the social structure of the relational systems involved. Thus, the sociological nature of these relational systems becomes of vital importance.

We have further suggested that the predominant structural type of in-ternal professional relationships is a special form of the collegial. This associational category stands in sharp contrast with both the market type and that of administrative bureaucracy, especially in its egalitarian em-phases. Though clients, students, and research subjects are not "colleagues" of the professionals they deal with, the relationship still belongs em-phatically in the associational category. This is true despite the element of inequality deriving from differences of competence. This factor does, how-ever, draw a crucially important line between such relational systems and those in which the members are strictly peers—as colleagues, members of many voluntary associations, and indeed citizens generally are.

It is in this setting that we raise the question of the importance of mu-tual trust, its conditions, and its relations to associational solidarity. That such trust is problematical is indicated by the general ambivalence toward professional function present in the undercurrent of hostility to medicine and in student distrust of the educational "establishment." Trust in the presently relevant sense is the attitudinal ground—in affectively motivated loyalty—for acceptance of solidary relationships. These confer not only the enjoyment of the rights of participating membership, but also the cor-responding obligations. We suggested, as one major implication of this

---

[17] It should, of course, be noted that there are other important categories of laymen with whom members of the professional complex must establish relations. These are not categories in relation to whom the professional functions are per-formed, but those who in different ways undertake responsibility for the support of the professional function—shading into tolerating its performance in the face of actual or potential disturbances by it or opposition to it. These include persons and collective agencies involved in financial and political support outside professional organizations as such, trustees and other members of professional organizations with fiduciary functions on their behalf, administrative personnel whose functions are facilitative of the professional, and, not least, many kinds of subprofessional sup-portive personnel such as secretaries, technicians, orderlies, and simple caretakers of physical facilities.

point of view, that the rewards enjoyed by research subjects are, qualitatively, essentially the same as those of investigators. The most important, though by no means the only, reward is the satisfaction of having helped in making a "contribution to the advancement of knowledge," with the corresponding recognition of this contribution.

We have suggested that the achievements of the professional complex are essentially collective achievements, including the contributions of both professional and lay elements. For the latter, however, given both the presumptively voluntary basis of participation (especially marked since the typical layman does not have a career stake in the function) and the competence gap, there is a particularly important problem of the legitimation of the process as a whole and of the professional element's role in it. One primary focus of this legitimation problem we have called the context of the integrity of the professional element and, assuming its leadership, of the collective organization as a whole, including lay contribution. It is in this context that we consider the ethical problem to focus and the problems of voluntary informed consent and of protection of privacy to center as two primary foci of the ethical problem.

It is particularly important to be clear that this ethical problem does not focus on the most general levels of acting in terms of the values of "common honesty" or elementary "good will." The standards worked out must take full account of two further factors. The first is the technical nature and complexity of the issues at stake. Thus, there is no commonsense solution to the question of *when* a person has died, for the ethical purposes of a decision to remove his heart. The second is the *social* problem of the balancing—by the same units that bear ethical responsibilities—among plural, partly conflicting, and potentially competing ethical obligations.

This moral complexity, which goes beyond common sense, can be handled only insofar as it is grounded in an ethic of the professional complex. This ethic goes beyond the levels of differentiation of the more general ethic of the society. What is often referred to as "professional ethics" is part of what is needed. It is insufficient, however, because it does not take adequate account of the role of the laity in all three of the respects discussed in this paper. There is consideration of the ethical obligations of professionals, especially toward clients but also toward students, yet there is relatively little discussion of the reciprocal obligations of the lay components—not only toward the professionals, but toward the effective performance of the functions of the relevant part of the professional complex as a whole.

The problem is, perhaps, particularly acute with respect to the research function for two reasons. The first is its relative newness, at least on anything like the recent scale. The second is the relative absence or secondary significance of tangible, immediate rewards for participation in the role of subject. In any case, the two contexts of consent and of privacy clearly relate to the associational pattern, since the participation for which consent is sought and given implies a membership status. Further, the requirement of being informed is of a piece with the role of information in the research function. What the investigator requires of his subject is always, in some sense, information, though the techniques of acquiring it may go far beyond simply asking the subject questions or passively observing his behavior; much of the relevant information the subject himself may not know, as in the case of states of his internal organs.

The dynamic connection between consent and privacy may be brought out at one level by pointing out that consent to participate actually constitutes consent to relinquish certain areas of privacy that might otherwise have been enjoyed and protected. Indeed, this is patently true in many kinds of research with human subjects such as eliciting intimate details of personal history.[18] Hence, the canon of protection of privacy is thereby importantly relativized. It is not *all* privacy that has to be protected, but those areas that are not included in the relinquishment to which explicit or implied consent has been given. One example of such protection is the anonymity device, by which confidential information is kept within a small, responsible professional group and diffusion takes place only in forms that eliminate identifiability of individuals. Another device is the exercise of care not to invade areas of privacy not germane to the program of research.

We have insistently argued that both the consent and the privacy criteria not only apply to ethical standards for the protection of research subjects, but also define important rights of *both* professional and lay participants in *all three* of the primary professional functions. Thus, we noted "admission" as the counterpart of consent and also the professional's right to privacy in certain phases of his work as a counterpart of the subject's right of privacy.

Similarly, however, neither the right to consent nor the right to the protection of privacy can be considered to be absolute on either side of the professional-lay relationship. Each is one side of a more or less "dialectic" structure that includes elements of its opposite in the *same* structure. Consent applies with maximum salience to the decision whether or not to accept a proposal to participate in any one of the three lay capacities. Even here, however, there may be presumptive obligations, as in the case of patients in a research-oriented medical institution. Once participation has been consented to, however, there is considerably greater constraint to accept collectively legitimized decisions—including those made by legitimate leadership—without having consented to them in advance in detail. This is

---

[18] A good case here would be the Kinsey studies. Cf. Alfred C. Kinsey et al., *Sexual Behavior in the Human Female* (Philadelphia: Saunders, 1953); and *Sexual Behavior in the Human Male* (Philadelphia: Saunders, 1948).

a consequence partly of special exigencies of the professional complex and partly of the nature of effective social organization more generally. Thus, there is an especially important linkage between the protection of privacy and the institutionalization of obligatory disclosure.

In the internal "dialectic" of the consent and the privacy problems as well as in the relation of the two complexes to each other, a temporal order suggests functions that are not readily understandable on common-sense bases. The right to consent is presumptively maximal at the stage of the decision whether or not to participate, which in general means to accept a membership status. After this stage, however, in all three contexts of lay participation, the relative absoluteness of the right to consent becomes modified by the exigencies of effective collective action (subject to the continuing residual right to "resign"). These exigencies include performances of superior competence by professionals, legitimized by standards of integrity as well as of competence and also, where needed, by assertion of authority. This, of course, is one of the most important contexts in which the factor of trust operates. One way of putting it is to say that trust is a necessary basis for the operation of effective leadership, which in turn is an essential ingredient of the success of complex collective enterprises.

Similarly, however, certain protections of privacy seem to constitute prior conditions of the mobilization of information and of other resources through processes that eventually entail various forms of obligatory disclosure. Thus we cited the preparation of legal cases for trial and of academic materials both for teaching purposes and for evaluation of research results.

Further, there is the interesting sense in which the consent complex is "bracketed" within that of privacy. The essential meaning of "invasion of privacy" seems to be "intervention" in the lives of persons and, we add, of collectivities. Consent is a kind of legitimating mechanism that attempts to distinguish the interventions which are legitimate from those which are not. Hence we have spoken of the voluntary relinquishment of privacies under institutionalized conditions that often involve privileged communication, anonymity, and so forth.

Neither privacy nor intervention can reasonably be confined to an informational context. The relevance of information as the core desideratum, however, is deeply grounded in the societal functions of the professional complex, because this complex is the primary "interface" between the cognitively primary component of the cultural tradition and the main structure of modern societies. The professional complex is the primary location of the three primary modes of ordering the relations inherent in this interface—namely, *utilizing* available rational knowledge or information in the interest of a multiplicity of functional needs of the society and its subunits; *transmitting* available knowledge from those who already have mastered it to various classes of people who may need it; and *extending* and *improving* the state of knowledge beyond that given at any specified time.

Thus, the three main professional functions lie on an important continuum that certainly relates to the temporal dimension. The first function —practice—is defined mainly by the utilization of available knowledge and its embodiment in technologies for the solution of *relatively* current and immediate problems. The sick person has a "condition" that calls for remedial action, and he turns to a physician or health agency for help. The time-span may be considerable, but it is far from indefinite. The second function—teaching—is a process of generating resources for the future performance of applied functions. This function may be called the generation of competence, though presumably competence does not exhaust the desired outcome of teaching. The assumption, however, is that the teacher imparts what is known. Hence, the typical contribution is distinguishable from the research function—which is to improve the cognitive base underlying both practice and teaching.

Thus, the continuum runs from utilization of given resources to relatively proximate increase of resources for such utilization to the genesis of still more "ultimate" resources. This continuum is associated with increasing time-spans necessary for the fulfillment of the conditions of societal "payoff." Students, while in a course of training, cannot be fully competent practitioners, and their training requires rather extended periods of time. Programs of research involve, in general, still longer periods of time before significantly usable results can be attained. Often, research processes must take the "detour" of concern with problems of "pure" science without reference to immediately practical results. Moreover, there remains in the research function the inherent factor of uncertainty.

The increasing importance of time along this continuum, however, is connected with that of autonomy. The professional practitioner can only be subjected to detailed accountability through the intervention of lay agencies. At every step, such intervention is made at the expense of sacrificing the benefits of special professional competence. In teaching, this relative immunity from immediate accountability must be extended to the student as well as to the teacher. For many purposes, a half-trained student is less useful than one without any training. Only after the period of "gestation" has been completed is direct accountability appropriate. This situation clearly as even more true of the research function, which requires a longer "moratorium" from payoff accountability and is generally more esoteric than most of the practice and teaching functions. Clearly lay participants in research are also in a relatively difficult position: It is difficult for them to be nearly fully "informed"; tangible and immediate rewards are relatively secondary; and the incidence of uncertainty factors is high.

It seems to follow from these considerations that what we refer to as academic freedom is part of a larger complex of institutionalized autonomy that may be called professional freedom—the institutionalized focusing of the more immediate responsibilities for the upholding of standards of competence and integrity on the individual professional and on various practices and agencies within the professional complex, rather than on the lay groups on whose interests the consequences of these functions impinge.[19]

This freedom complex is characteristic of institutions whose functions are associated with growth and development of societies for the future, with the genesis of new resources rather than the utilization of present resources. In the creation of credit and the stimulation of economic growth, banking operations belong to the same general family of social phenomena and have many of the same basic properties as a system—including the institutionalization of special freedoms based on trust as well as similar vulnerabilities (financial panic, for example).

These considerations, taken together, illustrate why the common-sense level of ethical orientation is not only "inadequate," but potentially dangerous in the conditions of a pluralistic modern society. On the lay side of the relationship, in our particular subject matter, insistence on the more absolute versions of the right to voluntary informed consent and the protection of privacy has the high probability of putting pressure on lay participants to exercise their residual "rights to resign" or to refuse to participate except on terms of the most stringent guarantees that their putative interests will not be injured.

This is a familiar pattern. The rigid insistence on "rights" is essentially a declaration of distrust in the professional complex. Its effect will ordinarily be a "deflationary" or "fundamentalist" restriction of developmental potential.

The inclusion of the "lay" element in the positive functioning of the professional complex is the primary mechanism by which this tendency to withdraw or implement the right to resign is counteracted, and the basis of trust preserved and strengthened. The positive participation of the research subject and its ethical regulation hence are of special salient significance, because research has become the most important single spearhead of the trend of progressive advance of modern societies.

The problems of this study, thus, concern the exceedingly important interface between one main sector of the professional complex and the laity on which it impinges in one direction—that of performance of professional function. It is not surprising that the ethical problems have become acute with respect to the "highest" level of these functions—that of research. It has been our endeavor to go beyond analyzing this interface as

---

[19] Some such qualification as "more immediate responsibilities" is of course essential because the kinds of autonomy and support which are essential to the functioning of the professional complex cannot be taken for granted by its members as a matter of right without *any* corresponding responsibilities or accountability. The latter cannot, however, be immediate and detailed without stultifying effects. It can be seen here again how important the factor of trust is in bridging the gap.

such and to place it in the context of the social organization and functioning of the professional complex as a whole. We have particularly emphasized the continuities of structure between the lay and the professional sides of the relation with respect to both the consent problem and that of privacy. We have also stressed the broad nature of the pattern of social organization into which both sides fit, and which extends, with the appropriate modifications, to all three of the principal professional functions.

In this context, one can see the sense in which the standards of voluntary informed consent and of the protection of privacy may prove to be double-aged swords. The perspective from which the present discussion arose concerned the protection of the lay element against abuses and exploitation emanating from the professional side. Such protection, if carried too far in terms too rigidly defined, however, can easily encroach on the rights of consent and privacy that are essential to the professional's performance of *his* functions and those of the complex as a whole. The operation of the professional complex depends on certain balances, both among its internal components (most emphatically including the lay elements) and in its relation to the nonprofessional social environment. It is my conviction that only by seeing the professional complex as a system can one cope with pressures that are threatening to distort either the internal or the external balances. Society has a profound stake not only in the successful operation of the professional complex, but also in the rights of the laity to minimization of injuries from this operation. Balancing of these interests within a workable and appropriate societal framework is a paramount societal interest.

3. Health and Disease: A Sociological and Action Perspective*

Introduction

HEALTH, AND ITS NEGATIVE, illness, have probably been major human subjects of preoccupation and concern as long as anything like human society has existed. Some kind of illness has been very prevalent in diverse non-literate societies, such as those of Central Africa [1] or the Navaho of the American Southwest. [2] The main tradition of the conception of and concern with health that has dominated Western civilization, however, has its roots more in Greek culture than in any other single source. The earliest connected literary remains of this tradition are usually called the body of the Hippocratic writings, which date from the fifth century B.C.

The Hippocratic writings contained an exceedingly important formula that has survived ever since, mainly in its Latin form. This is what has been called the *vis medicatrix naturae* (i.e., the healing power of nature). This formula seems appropriate to provide a major point of reference for the present analysis. It will be interpreted in terms of possible relevance to the social and action contexts that are stressed in the title of the present article. *Vis medicatrix* may be thought of as a property of living systems, in the first instance, individual organisms, by virtue of which such systems have

* The term "action" in the subtitle of this article does not refer to practical effectiveness, but to the theoretical scheme called the "Theory of Action" with which I and a variety of colleagues have been working for a number of years.

[1] Renée C. Fox and Willy De Craemer, *The Emerging Physician: A Sociological Approach to the Development of a Congolese Medical Profession* (Stanford, Calif.: Hoover Institution on War, Revolution and Peace, 1968).

[2] Clyde Kluckhohn and Dorothea Leighton, *The Navaho* (Cambridge, Mass.: Harvard University Press, 1946).

the capacity to cope, often without outside intervention, with disturbances to health or cases of illness, that is, cases not so severe as to exceed certain limits. It was one of the primary tenets of Hippocratic medicine that the physician should take account of the inbuilt capacity of his patients to recover from illness and work along with such capacities, rather than to intervene arbitrarily without reference to such capacities.[3]

We share the view, which has been prevalent almost throughout the history of Western medical thinking, that the *primary* focus of the problems of health and illness lies in the state of the organism, that is, as a living biological system. The task of the present article, however, is to put this biological aspect of the problem in a somewhat larger setting. Of all living species, man is predominantly characterized by being, to paraphase Aristotle, in the first instance a "social animal" and in the second instance a bearer of symbolically organized cultural traditions. In the usual senses of the history of science, then, man—though very obviously an organism in the biological sense—is more than an organism. He is a behaving system, a personality, a member of structured social systems, and a participant in cultural systems and patterns of meaning of what is sometimes called "the human condition." Though there are obviously many continuities between the problems of health and illness at non-human levels and the human problems, our primary concern is with certain features of the health-illness complex that are most specifically human.

Health as a central feature of the state of the living organism is quite clearly one of the most important aspects of the human condition for problems of bioethics. We shall argue in the next section that problems of health should not be regarded as only organic even though they are "rooted" in the state of the organism; yet, we do not negate the importance of the organic reference. Futrhermore, we wish to stress that we regard health as a state of the human individual, not of collectivities such as populations or species or, in more concretely human terms, groups of societies.

In empirical human experience, after all, the life of the individual is bounded by birth—whatever the interpretation of states between conception and birth—and by death—however organic death be defined. In any case, problems of health are intimately intertwined with those of both birth and death, perhaps especially the latter. It is clearly no accident that birth and death have constituted primary foci of meaning for every known human religion. Such problems seem to be at the very center of the ethical problems of the human condition.

If this be true of the beginning and the end of the life cycle of the human individual, it is clearly also true of what happens to such individuals in between. If we must recognize the existence and importance of mental as well as organic health, as I think we must, the focal religious category

[3] Bernard Barber (ed.), *L. J. Henderson On the Social System: Selected Writings* (Heritage of Sociology Series) (Chicago: University of Chicago Press, 1970).

of suffering can surely have an organic reference—though presumably not in the strict sense physical; a stone presumably does not feel pain when it is hit with a sledgehammer—but there seems to be no reason to limit the concept of suffering to the organic level. Thus, mental or spiritual pain and anguish seem very real as not mere epiphenomena of organic events. Insofar as there is mental health or illness it is clearly intertwined with these.

Finally, another classic field of religio-ethical concern, the "problem of evil," seems to stand on a different level, relatively dissociated from the state of the organism. It articulates with the problem of justice precisely, in the sense of what happens to individuals. Since injustices, objectively suffered or subjectively felt, affect the whole person, they can scarcely fail to interact with the problems of health.

Definition of Health

In seeking the focus of a definition of health, I should like to rely on the work on an eminent contemporary biologist, Ernst Mayr, who has introduced, at least for the American biological world, the concept of *teleonymy*.[4] Teleonymy, a term that Mayr uses to avoid the metaphysical connotations of the old teleology, may be defined as the capacity of an organism, or its propensity, to undertake successful goal-oriented courses of behavior. In the common classification of aspects of organic systems, behavior has a special place that should be distinguished from structure in its anatomical references and from non-behavioral processes such as those involved in metabolism. In one sense, behavior involves the mobilization of the resources and capacities of the organism as a whole in the regulation of its relation to its environment. A prototypical category of behavioral orientation concerns food seeking and securing activities on the part of organisms, which activities become more elaborate and organized as a function of advance in the evolutionary scale. Similar contexts are protection of the organism's integrity from such threats as predators or infectious disease.

Mayr's concept of teleonymy is meant explicitly to link the behavioral category of goal-orientedness with the levels of anatomical structure and physiological process. It is, in a certain fundamental sense, a *functional* concept in that it has to do with understanding the conditions under which certain properties of the requisite types of organisms are possible. For

---

[4] Ernst Mayr, "Teleological and Teleonomic: A New Analysis," in Marx Wartovsky (ed.), *Method and Metaphysics: Methodological and Historical Essays in the Natural and Social Sciences,* Proceedings of the Boston Colloquium for the Philosophy of Science, 1969–1972, Vol. 6 (Holland: Brill, 1974), pp. 78–104.

purposes of the present analysis, however, I should like to extend the conditions, the frame of reference, beyond the internal anatomical-physiological conditions of the organism itself and its physical and organic environments, to include also the action level, in the technical sense of the theory of action, within the framework of the human condition. This notably involves considerations of the personality of the individual as differentiated from both organism and its behavioral system and also includes the levels of social interaction and cultural symbolization and their relation to problems of meaning in Max Weber's sense of that concept.

Against this background, then, I should like to put forward a tentative definition of health. It may, in this broadened sense, be conceived as the teleonomic capacity of an individual living system. The teleonomic capacity that we wish to call health,[5] is the capacity to maintain a favorable, self-regulated state that is a prerequisite of the effective performance of an indefinitely wide range of functions both within the system and in relation to its environments. The very generalization of the concept is one of its most fundamental properties. One centrally important reference of the concept is the capacity to cope with disturbances of such a state that come either from the internal operations of the living system itself or from interaction with one of more of its environments. Again, let it be said that although we accept the focusing of the concept of health at the organic level of the individual, we wish to extend its relevance, on the one hand, into the physical environment and, on the other, into the action environment and the telic [6] system, that is, its psychological and sociocultural environments.

From this point of view, the illness of an individual should be seen as an impairment of his/her teleonomic capacity. It may be grounded in any one or in a complex combination of factors, the effect of which is to interfere with satisfactory and effective functioning. Thus, a state of illness may result from some failure to cope with the exigencies of the physical environ-

---

[5] I should like to confine the concepts of health and illness to states of individuals, human or sub-human. At the organic levels it does not seem to be expedient to refer to species or populations as sick, though the incidence of illness in such species or populations may be particularly high in some cases. With reference to the action aspect of these matters, I do not like the usage that refers to societies as sick or healthy and similarly of cultures. I would like to keep the concepts of health and illness firmly tried to the concept of the individual as living system, but we have tried to make clear that such an individual is not only in the analytical sense, an organism, but also a physical system and an action system.

[6] The term telic, which is obviously related to teleonomic, is used in the present article to refer to one primary aspect of the human condition, that in which the problems of culturally and symbolically defined meanings of the human conditions and its various aspects, come to a head. There is an important sense in which the telic environment is cybernetically superordinate to the general system of action and, by virtue of this fact, to the organic level of the organization of living systems as well.

ment, as in the case of invasion by agents of bacterial infection. It may arise from malorganization of the relations of organic and action level subsystems of the more general human condition or from internal pathological processes such as a malignant tumor.

Though a special point has been made of centering or anchoring the phenomena we denote by the concepts of health and illness in the individual organism, for humans at least we wish quite explicitly not to confine them to the organic level but to speak also of mental health and illness. Making allowance for complex states of interdependence, as in the so-called psychosomatic field, we think of mental health and illness as anchored in the personality of the individual, as part of the action system that must be analytically distinguished from the organism. We think, however, of organism and personality as involved in complex relations of interdependence and interchange that cannot be analyzed here.

Another problem, besides that of the status of the concept of mental health, concerns the respects in which health is to be differentiated from other states of individual well-being, and illness from other varieties of human "ills," as this problem for instance has been posed by the well-known definition of health adopted by the World Health Organization.[7]

In our opinion the most important criterion for drawing the line between health and illness concerns the individual's capacity to *control* the state referred to and some of the conditions on which it depends, especially conditions internal to the individual of reference. Thus, though many persons are "ignorant" in various respects, given opportunity and adequate intelligence, they can, if "motivated," diminish their ignorance by learning. If faced by temptation to commit a crime, they can mobilize their moral standards and abstain, but if afflicted with a bacterial infection they cannot simply "decide" not to be sick. This criterion has the advantage of applying equally to organic and to mental illness.

The essential point concerns the capacities for "voluntary action" on the part of the individual. It is, by consensual definition, undesirable to be ill for both the individual himself and others associated with him. But if "really" ill and not malingering, he cannot be expected simply to "pull himself together" and proceed to get well. Rather, he must seek to gain control of certain conditions normally beyond the range of voluntary action through resort to outside therapeutic agency, through self-care, or simply "letting" the *vis medicatrix* operate. Put in terms of Freud's psychology, therapy is in general beyond the range of direct ego function capacities but requires some kind of management of id functions.

It is above all failure to discriminate these two categories of well-being of the human individual that, in this direction at least, vitiates the famous

[7] See "The Concept of Health," *Hastings Center Report,* I, No. 3 (1973), especially the paper by Daniel Callahan.

World Health Organization definition of health. It is unacceptable to identify health with well-being in general. Of course, it does not follow that the health-illness context is the only one in which the mechanisms of voluntary control prove inadequate. The other principal one historically has been closely associated with that of health but should be clearly differentiated from it, namely, to put it in Christian terms, the religious "state of grace." In that area it has repeatedly been asserted that the human individual cannot attain grace by his own efforts alone but only, again in Christian terms, by divine intervention. This, however, is clearly very different from the boundary between illness and failure or incompetence in the areas normally subject to voluntary control.

Within this latter area, it is also important to make another distinction related to the problem of individual control. Of course, in the spheres of ego function, of voluntary action, the degree of control open to any particular individual is always limited by conditions beyond his control, such as those altogether outside human (certainly individual) control (e.g., the weather) and those in the control of other human agencies (as in the much discussed sphere of power relations). This sphere of uncontrolled factors includes exposure to risk of the genesis of illness. To identify "powerlessness" in this sense with illness is, however, highly confusing. They are quite different aspects of the human predicament.

I should finally like to put forward the concept of health under a rubric that has proved to be of substantial importance in the theory of action. This way of looking at it, however, will certainly be unfamiliar to most people who have been considering the problem of health. The rubric I have in mind is that health should be considered to be a "generalized medium of interchange." [8] The prototype of such a medium is money. In a somewhat different context, language may be treated as such a medium. Finally, a recent attempt has been made to deal similarly with the concept of intelligence; [9] thus, it is treated as a circulating symbolic medium rather than as a trait of the individual.

It seems reasonable at least to experiment with the conception that health can feasibly be fitted into this theoretical context. The attempt to do so, however, raises exceedingly complicated theoretical issues that can only be suggested within the limits of the present brief article. It is hoped that future work will develop these matters substantially further. A very brief outline is presented here.

[8] On media of interchange, see Talcott Parsons, *Politics and Social Structure* (New York: The Free Press, 1969). See chap. 14: "On the Concept of Political Power"; chap. 15: "On the Concept of Influence"; and chap. 16: "On the Concept of Value Commitments."

[9] Talcott Parsons and Gerald Platt, *The American University* (Cambridge, Mass.: Harvard University Press, 1973), especially chap. 2: "The Cognitive Complex," and the "Technical Appendix."

Illness and Life Expectancy

In whatever senses health and illness may be considered problems focusing predominantly at the organic level, there can be little doubt that problems of coping with illness or its threat, as well as of maintaining the levels of health of a population, are paramount concerns at the action level. The background of the problems of health and illness lies in the fact that there is an underlying expectation that a normally participating member of a human community will manifest certain variant, but probably determinable, levels of health defined as teleonomic capacity. There is a long history of the bearing of these problems on the human condition, perhaps most dramatically illustrated by the changing profile of vital statistics. The most significant single figure in this complex has been the expectancy of human life at birth. There are, of course, many different aspects of this story and, in historical perspective, there is a serious lack of evidence. The general impression, however, seems to be that it was not until well into the nineteenth century that really great generalized increases in the expectancy of life began to occur. The figures are uncertain but we might tentatively fasten on thirty years as the norm for a "good" society of earlier periods. In the United States in 1975 the figure had reached seventy-two years, and the American record in this respect is by no means the best among the advanced countries. This enormous increase in the expectancy of life has occurred in spite of the twentieth's having been a century of great wars and many other vicissitudes.

A substantial part of this effect is attributable to the control of life-threatening diseases by measures of medical care and public health. Another major component is improvement in the standard of living such as better nutrition and safer housing. This is not the place to attempt to assess the relative importance of these contributions.

To be sure, many of the individuals of reference have been, as it were, kept alive by "artificial" means. These have covered a wide range, including protection against specific diseases by immunization measures such as vaccination for smallpox and control of diabetes through insulin treatment or other therapies to improve regulation of blood sugar levels. It would, however, be difficult to interpret the term "artificial," which was placed in quotation marks earlier, in a simple pejorative sense. We witnessed severe controversies over the problem of the justification of "interference with natural selection" in an earlier era and there would today be very few defenders of the point of view that the "unfit" should be allowed to die without medical intervention or public health measures. There is, it seems, no generalized basis for believing that susceptibility to particular diseases under so-called natural conditions is an index of general tele-onomic incapacity that would merit such drastic selective policies.

By and large, the evidence indicates that maintenance of the recently acquired long life expectancy and of concomitant improvements in the health of human populations depends on certain kinds of institutionalized interventions in the situations that define the conditions of health and that counteract the incidence of a wide variety of illnesses including the many historic cases in which the consequences of illness have been substantially higher death rates than would otherwise have obtained.

Social Role of Sickness

Perhaps it is at this point that the question of illness as a social role category and the social dynamics of its relation to the problems of health can appropriately be introduced.[10] Surely, in previous stages of both organic and sociocultural evolution, there have evolved numerous improvements in the capacity of organisms and individuals to cope with disturbances in their health, that is, their teleonomic capacity as we have defined it. Equally clearly, however, the modern age introduced a new set of conditions in this respect that may very broadly be characterized as the application of scientific methods and procedures to this problem. Medicine and public health, as professional complexes in modern society, do not have meaning unless they constitute innovations relative to the primordial process of natural selection, though they of course have had many forerunners.

It is in this sense that such concepts as the "sick role" and its counterpart, the therapeutic role, become meaningful in modern society. This sick role clearly includes not only the social status and treatment of individuals who actually are undergoing impairment of the normally expected levels of health but also various possibilities of, and threats to, current states of health, such as those involved in the spread of epidemic disease.[11] The essential point is that the actuality or threat of illness is treated as an explicit problem for more or less rational action on the part of selected elements of the population concerned, including those whose health is impaired or those who stand under threats of such impairments. This population includes, on the one hand, the laity (in a medical frame of refer-

[10] Cf. Talcott Parsons, *The Social System* (New York. Free Press, 1951), chap. 10; Talcott Parsons, "Illness, Therapy and the Modern Urban American Family," in *Patients, Physicians, and Illness,* E. Gartley Jaco (ed.), (New York: Free Press, 1958); and Talcott Parsons, "The Sick Role and the Role of the Physician Reconsidered," *Milbank Memorial Fund Quarterly,* vol. 53, no. 3 (Summer 1975): 275–278, reprinted as Chapter 1 in the present volume.

[11] See Parsons, "The Sick Role . . . Reconsidered"; Chapter 1 of this volume.

ence) and, on the other hand, the most competent specialists who have expertise in coping with complicated, specific problems of illness or its possibility.

Sociologically, the problem is the nature of the institutionalization of the relations between actually or potentially sick people and participants in health care agencies. Very generally, in the modern world, the latter have come to center on members of the medical profession so far as the treatment of sick individuals is concerned. The practice of medicine in this sense should be distinguished from the administration of public health measures such as the attempt to eliminate infectious diseases by mass immunization programs or by controlling sources of infection, which, however, do not operate primarily on particular individuals.

With due allowance for the complexity of the social organizations involved in therapeutic functions in the first sense above, the relation traditionally called that between physician and patient may be taken as central and prototypical for certain broad purposes. The two role types are institutionally defined as complementary to each other in such ways that the meaning of either assumes involvement with the other.

In discussing the problem of institutionalization of both the sick role and that of therapeutic agencies, particularly physicians, a certain background is essential to keep in mind. I should like to stress two sets of background considerations. The first of these concerns the centrality and virtual universality of the positive valuation of health and the correlative, negative valuation of states of illness. Of course, assuming that such valuations concern the state of individuals, I would hold that it is only on certain romantic fringes of modern thinking that exceptions to these statements could be made, exceptions which have something to do with systematic cults of pessimism and anti-worldly values.[12]

Valuations of health, however, cannot be fully institutionalized without a number of other contributions to the outcome. Among possibilities of control of states of illness and threats to health, there must be some sort of selection with respect to criteria of feasibility and possibility of generalization for larger populations. There must be mobilization of the resources essential for coping with the states which do come to be treated as feasibly controllable. Thus, one of the most important chapters in the institutionalization of modern medicine and public health consisted in the achievement of control over a number of infectious diseases. Vaccinations against smallpox and the contributions of Pasteur and Koch are landmark aspects of this story. The mobilization of facilities for effective control generally involves the availability of trained personnel, to say nothing of the grounding of the knowledge of what to do in the requisite branches of

---

[12] I am, however, assured by the Reverend Willy De Craemer, a Jesuit priest, that the monastic orders in general have very strongly insisted on the importance of health.

science. It also involves the institutionalization of relevant modes of contact between the professional personnel involved and the people in need of professional help. This is the context in which we would like to consider the state of illness and that of therapeutic agents defining, as social roles, the sick role and the therapeutic role, respectively.

We may start by suggesting that the core type of role of members of the therapeutic agency, particularly physicians, is an example of what has come to be known as the professional type of role. The physician may be presumed to be committed to the valuation of health in a sense parallel to that in which Gerald M. Platt and I have maintained that the academic professional is typically committed to the valuation of cognitive rationality.[13] The two values, of course, overlap substantially in that scientific knowledge has become a key factor in the control of illness and in the promotion of health.

Like other professional roles, that of physician may be categorized in pattern variable terms. It has a high incidence of universalistic standards, for example, of the generalizability of propositions about diagnosis and probable therapeutic consequences of medical measures. It is functionally specific in that the relations of physicians to their patients are focused on problems of the patients' health rather than on other sorts of personal problems. It is performance oriented in that the task of the physician is to intervene actively in actual cases of illness and its threat, not to sit passively by and "let nature take its course." It is also predominantly affectively neutral, though with the kinds of qualifications that Renée Fox has proposed under her concept of "detached concern." [14] Finally, by contrast with certain other occupational roles, for example, with that of the business entrepreneur or executive, the professional role generally, including that of physician, is governed by an orientation toward collective values. The most central manifestation of this is the professional ideology that puts the welfare of the patient ahead of the self-interest of therapeutic agents, physicians in particular.

Complementary to the role of physician (or more generally of the therapeutic agent) is the social role of the actually or potentially sick person. In this connection, social roles should be clearly distinguished from other aspects of the patient's condition, most notably those that figure prominently in processes of medical diagnosis and plans for therapeutic intervention. This is a framework of expected social relationships normatively defined, conformity with which is not part of the technical discipline of medicine or other health services. We may organize the description of the sick role's four main properties as follows.

[13] See Parsons and Platt, *The American University,* chap. 3: "The Core Sector of the University: Graduate Training and Research."

[14] See Renée C. Fox, *Experiment Perilous: Physicians and Patients Facing the Unknown* (New York. Free Press, 1959).

First, the exemption from normal social responsibilities on account of illness is distinguished from their willful and deliberate avoidance. Where simulating a state of illness can be ascribed to deliberate motivation, medical people speak of malingering.[15] Apart from the phenomenon of malingering, however, to be sick is to be in a state that is institutionally defined as not the sufferer's personal fault. The issue of how far personal responsibility may have been involved in entering such a state, as through unnecessary exposure to sources of infection, should be distinguished from the issue of considering the patient personally responsible for "pulling himself together" by an act of will and simply behaving as though he were not sick. If the sick person is genuinely sick, it is presumed that this is not an efficacious mechanism of social control.

Second, a closely related feature of the role of illness, depending on the character and acuteness of the state of illness, is that the impairment of teleonomic capacity and the risk of future impairments are held to justify exemption from performance expectations that are normally applied to altogether healthy persons. The simplest type of case would be abstention from the performance of both occupational and family obligations and the sanctioning of this abstention by medical authority, such as the medical injunction to stay home in bed for a given period. Of course, many patients afflicted with chronic illnesses may have to accept certain handicaps with respect to the fulfillment of performance expectations or undergo some kind of regimen of management of their condition with perhaps minimal abstention from performance.

Third, there is a sharing of the positive valuation of health and the negative valuation of illness between therapeutic agent and sick persons. For the sick person, of course, such valuation by other persons closely bound up with his daily life, such as members of his family, can be very important. This sharing involves a commitment to the attempt to recover a state of health or in the case of chronic illnesses or threats of illness to accept regimens of management that will minimize the current impairment of teleonomic capacity and future risks that the actual or presumptive illness may entail. In view of certain recent discussions,[16] it is important to emphasize that this commitment is not confined to recovery from states of

---

[15] Mark Field has presented an impressive analysis of the role which "malingering" assumed in the Soviet Union under the pressure of extreme forms of labor discipline. The type case, with which Field was concerned, was the problem raised by tardiness in arrival at work, a serious problem for many workers because of congestions and delays in public transportation systems. A common response, Field found, to the rigor of discipline in this matter, on the part of Soviet production authorities, was to resort to medical excuses for tardiness, saying that this was explained by illness. This is a beautiful example of certain kinds of conflicts engendered in some kinds of social situations. See Mark G. Field, *Doctor and Patient in Soviet Russia* (Cambridge, Mass.: Harvard University Press, 1957).

[16] See Parsons, "The Sick Role . . . Reconsidered"; Chapter 1 of this volume.

acute illness but very definitely extends to medically acceptable management of chronic states and of threats to health.

Fourth, the sick role is characterized by a commitment to cooperate with relevant therapeutic agencies—most notably, for our purposes, with physicians. It should again be made clear that this cooperation is not definable as a one-way relationship in which the patient simply puts himself under the control of the therapeutic agent. It is a far more complex, reciprocal interaction between these role carriers.

Like every other type of professional role and social function of organizations in which professional roles are prominent, those of the physician and other therapeutic agents have important functions that may be characterized as functions of "social control" in a well-established sociological sense. It is this aspect of both the role of illness and the physician-patient relation that in earlier publications I had predominantly in mind in connecting illness with the idea of deviant behavior. This categorization applies best to cases in which the state of illness approximates being "purely mental"; yet the range is far broader than this, extending throughout the field of so-called psychosomatic illness. Deviant behavior and illness are not coextensive, but the fact that there is considerable overlap seems scarcely open to doubt.

To complete this part of the analysis, I would suggest that a certain, relatively definite patterning is characteristic of agencies of social control in their orientation to the objects of such control. In this connection I should treat as limiting cases, social control by an individual agent alone or control by a predominantly rational, bureaucratic type of authority. The kinds of social control I have in mind involve resort to much subtler mechanisms. As was originally worked out in connection with a paradigm of the nature of psychotherapeutic processes, however, I think this is a very widespread organizational phenomenon and that it has an important bearing on health and illness. That it should not be construed to be confined to this context should be made evident by the way in which comparable conceptualization has been employed for the analysis of the socialization process, most recently on my own part in work on the socialization component of higher education, in collaboration with Platt.[17]

The roles that have prominent functions of social control can be characterized by four primary features. The first of these is that the agent of control tends to treat his objects or subjects, whichever way the relationship is formulated, with a certain permissiveness. I would link this with the conception, in the institutionalized version of the sick role, that being ill cannot ordinarily be conceived to be the fault of the sick person and that illness can justify certain exemptions from normal expectations of performance. Permissiveness is an important consequence of the affective

[17] Parsons and Platt, *The American University,* chap. 4.

neutrality of the therapeutic role in that the typical physician is not supposed to react to many manifestations of his patient's sentiments and behavior with the usual value controlled patterns of reaction.

A second component of the social control paradigm is that the agent of control must, at a certain level, be supportive of the sick person in the latter's endeavor to control. This involves a certain acceptance of the state of the individual "in trouble," whether that be illness with its disabilities and incapacities or ignorance on the part of the uneducated. Perhaps the prototype of the supportive relation is parental concern for the welfare of young children who have not yet attained the capacities for autonomous performance in many areas. In the medical context the supportive relation pertains to an aspect of what Renée Fox [18] has called detached concern. It is perhaps most conspicuous where patients are involved in painful and dangerous states and where it is of great importance to them to believe that their physicians deeply "care" about their welfare and are doing everything they can to help.

Linked with permissiveness and support are two other characterizations of the role of agent of social control. One of these is the maintenance of a certain aloofness from the more exigent and imperative preoccupations of the persons to be controlled. In the psychotherapeutic context, this above all takes the form of refusing to respond to various kinds of overtures that patients make toward the therapist, for example, defining the therapist in an unrealistic type of cohesive non-professional relationship as love object or as target of inappropriate hostility and aggression.

Finally, the last of the features of the paradigm of social control concerns the manipulation of rewards, the occasions for actually implementing such rewards, and the occasions for withholding them. In psychotherapy, by far the most common mode of such implementation is to reinforce the patient's own attainment of insight into his condition and the motivational background manifested in such insight. Particularly in psychoanalytic practice, the most powerful instrument of such manipulation of rewards is what has often been called "the psychoanalytic interpretation." [19]

The present section of this essay should be understood as an attempt to delineate in three different context—the professional role, the sick role, and the more general paradigm of social control—the principal structural components of the role complex in which, on the one hand, the handling of sick people and their illnesses and, on the other, the orientations and activities of therapeutic agents, notably physicians, are located.

Illness as impairment of the state of health and the possibilities and threats of its occurrence when in the state of health stand at the very

[18] Fox, *Experiment Perilous.*

[19] See Marshall Edelson, *Language and Interpretation in Psychoanalysis* (New Haven and London: Yale University Press, 1975).

center of the problems of bioethics. In common with other organic species, humans are capable of exposure to possibilities of illness and in fact to the certainty that the misfortune of illness will be inflicted on many in any given generation. This is an essential part of "man's fate." Moreover, it is an essential part of this aspect of the human condition that there is no simple one-to-one correspondence between the incidence of illness, including its severity, its accompanying suffering or the risk of premature death it entails, and the primary ethical concerns of human society, notably those of the relation between the individual's voluntary and presumptively responsible actions and the way in which their consequences impinge upon him.

The "dialectic," if one uses this term, of the relation between health and illness is, of course, bracketed within the still deeper set of dilemmas of the human condition concerning life, coming to the individual through human organic birth, and that channel alone, and the inevitable, though in timing and circumstances very uncertain, fate of individual death. It is surely not without significance that, though pregnancy and the imminence of childbirth can scarcely be called in the usual sense illness from which a woman suffers, in the modern world they have, especially through the role of physicians, come to be drawn into the "health complex," and similarly, though eventual death is as "normal" as any human phenomenon, a very large proportion of expected or potential death situations are also brought into the health complex.

Clearly, birth and death of individuals constitute a principal focus of the problems of bioethics that have become salient (though not for the first time) in modern societies. Surely, then, the intimate connection between birth and death and the problems of evil and suffering is central to bioethics, and back of the inevitable problematics of religious meaning.

In conclusion of this discussion it may be suggested that an addition should be made to the traditional list of dilemmas in the life course between birth and death, namely what have been called the problems of suffering and of evil. It may, indeed, be a particularly important consequence of the emergence of what we here call the health complex in modern society, that a third irresolvable focus of human dilemmas has become salient, namely what may be called the problem of *capacity*. If the problem of suffering comes to focus in human exposure to the impact of deprivation independent of individual agency, and that of evil, in exposure to that of consequences independent of active intentions, that of capacity focuses on the fact that, however much we may *want* to do something, we may be prevented to incapacity from actually doing it, Of course, illness is far from being the only source of human incapacity, but it is a focally prominent and symbolic one, especially in a society with an activistic orientation.

Health as Interaction Medium

At the beginning of this article it was suggested that health might be treated as a symbolic circulating medium regulating human action and other life processes. Since this is an unfamiliar concept, a brief further elucidation seems to be in order. The concept has been worked out with reference to such phenomena as money and political power at the level of human social interaction and, in certain respects, language may be viewed as such a medium. There seem also clearly to be important parallels at the organic level. The best known are, at the macrophysiological level of the individual organism, the hormones such as insulin, adrenaline, or cortisone and, at the microphysiological level, the enzymes in their role in the synthesis of proteins in the cell.[20]

As is most familiarly illustrated by the case of money, a unit in an interacting system—such as an individual or an organ or tissue—must receive an "income" of the medium in question with which to acquire essential means of its functioning; in the latter process, the unit must "expend" this resource. This is what is meant by the "circulation" of the medium. I shall not take the space here to elucidate these complicated processes further.

From this point of view, health may be conceived as circulating, within the organism, within the personality, and between personality and organism. From this point of view, good health is an "endowment" of the individual that can be used to mobilize and acquire essential resources for satisfactory functioning as organism and personality. Health, in this meaning, would function only if it is "used" and not "hoarded."

When conceived as such a medium, health stands midway between the action level media such as money, power, and language and the intraorganic media such as hormones and enzymes. If the general idea of continuity as well as interdependence between such levels is tenable, and it has underlain the whole pattern of analysis of this article, the further development of the implications of this approach to the concept of health

---

[20] The idea should be familiar that at the organic levels, media of the general character we have in mind, play a prominent part as has come to be increasingly well understood through biological studies. One of the most important categories of such media are the hormones that function mainly at a macro-physiological level—for example, insulin or cortisone or theroxin. A second set of examples concerns the enzymes that function at a micro-physiological level, notably in the processes involved in the synthesis of proteins within the cell as these processes have relatively recently been elucidated by micro-biologists. On the hormones, see above all Walter B. Cannon, *The Wisdom of the Body* (New York: W. W. Norton, 1932), and on the enzymes, Salvador E. Luria, *Life: The Unfinished Experiment* (New York: Scribner, 1973).

should prove to be of far-reaching significance for the future. Its working out, however, will require a great amount of analytical effort.

Conclusion: Health and Illness in the Human Condition

This article has endeavored to approach the problem of understanding health and illness by treating them as central aspects of the human condition. Just as man himself is both living organism and human actor, who is a personality and social and cultural being at the same time, so health and illness are conceived, as human phenomena, to be both organic and sociocultural. At the organic level, health is conceived to be one highly generalized underlying capacity, to be distinguished from strength, agility, or intelligence. Similarly, at the action level, the meaning of health is to be carefully distinguished from the relevant aspect of intelligence, from knowledge, from ethical integrity, and from other qualities of the individual. To return to the World Health Organization's conception yet again, health definitely cannot be identified with human welfare in general but must be further specified.

At the same time it cannot be confined to the organic level, to say nothing of the still more narrowly conceived "physical." It must be conceived as bridging both organic and "social" or, more generally still, "action" levels in the sense of symbolic involvements. It is by virtue of this dual involvement, and not simply its organic relevance, that health is a focal center of the problem area of bioethical issues. Health concerns the underlying conditions of the organic life of human beings, their biological births, their ultimate deaths, and the levels of functioning in between, but at the same time it concerns the problem of the meaning of this life and its vicissitudes. To squeeze out either aspect would be to vitiate the significance of the concept as a whole.

4.   The Interpretation of Dreams by Sigmund Freud

FREUD's *The Interpretation of Dreams* seems particularly appropriate for discussion in the present issue of *Dædalus* because it was first published in the opening year of the twentieth century, 1900, when Freud was forty-four years old. It was the first major publication of what came to be known as psychoanalytic theory. This field, if not his unique creation, is overwhelmingly dominated by the figure of Freud. The main outline of psychoanalytic theory is clearly present in *The Interpretation of Dreams* and, indeed, in a surprisingly subtle and fully developed form. In preparation for writing the present article, I entirely reread the book in its seventh German edition, since I had not read it for a good many years.[1] I was more profoundly impressed by it than I was originally, essentially because, on the one hand, I have a much better understanding of psychoanalytic thinking than I did, and secondly, because I now connect Freud's book with a great many theoretical preoccupations of my own which have undergone very substantial development since I first read Freud.

In a great many respects this is a unique book. Although there was a rather extensive literature on dreams in his day, which Freud meticulously reviews in his first chapter, there was surely nothing of a scope and depth comparable to his interpretations. Another unusual aspect of this book is the fact that, as Freud himself points out, many of the theoretical problems it deals with are adaptations of the problems he had encountered in trying to understand his own field of the psychoneuroses over a series of years before writing it. So far as we know, Freud himself was not in

[1] My reading was done, as I noted, in the 7th German edition (Wien: Franz Deuticke, 1945).

Reprinted by permission of *Daedalus*, Journal of the American Academy of Arts and Sciences, Boston, Massachusetts. Winter 1974 (vol. 103, no. 1), *Twentieth Century Classics Revisited.*

any gross or obvious sense a neurotic. Through a variety of channels—notable through his recognition of the phenomenon called *transference*—he became increasingly aware that a person who attempts to treat the neuroses of others through the psychoanalytic procedure must first acquire a very unusual knowledge of himself. This requirement has, within the psychoanalytic movement, been institutionalized in the didactic analysis which is a primary condition of admission to psychoanalytic practice. Freud was the only psychoanalyst, however, who ever carried out the procedure of psychoanalysis on himself. Among its other features, *The Interpretation of Dreams* is the primary documentation of this self-analysis.

The Interpretation of Dreams contains, as far as I know, Freud's first published statement about the Oedipus complex, which was to figure so very prominently in his general theory. It is, I think, highly significant that Freud's father died in 1896, four years prior to the publication of *The Interpretation of Dreams*.[2] Painful and disturbing as it was at the time, there is reason to believe that the death of his father had the long-run effect of freeing Freud from a good many of the inhibitions that had impeded his work of self-analysis. In the book, he recounts and analyzes a considerable number of his own dreams, as well as those recounted to him by his patients then subjected to analysis in the course of a therapeutic program. He also draws, though not so heavily, on dreams from the more general literature.

One might ask why Freud chose, as the primary subject matter of his first major theoretical work in psychoanalysis, the study of dreams rather than the direct study of neurotic symptoms and the conditions of their resolution through therapy. Part of the answer lies in his own convictions concerning the importance of his self-analysis for the furtherance of his work. Through his psychiatric practice, he had come to realize that neurotic symptoms were very generally connected with dreams. Since he was personally, for the most part, free of neurotic symptoms, dreams provided a particularly appropriate vehicle for his self-analysis. At the same time, he surely realized that in the history of science, indirect attacks on fundamental theoretical problems have frequently proven more fruitful than direct ones. In addition, as a responsible physician, Freud may have considered the very fact that the study of dreams was at one remove from the focus of his clinical responsibilities as an argument in its favor since it enabled him to concentrate on psychological problems as such, rather than on the balancing of therapeutic success and failure.

[2] Freud's relation to Wilhelm Fliess was particularly important to Freud. On this and the whole background of Freud's life, see the monumental biography in three volumes by his close English associate and friend Ernest Jones, *The Life and Work of Sigmund Freud* (New York: Basic Books, 1953, 1955, 1957). The relation to Fliess is discussed in Vol. I, ch. 13.

The Nature of Psychoanalytic Theory

There can be no doubt about the tremendous impact of psychoanalytic theory on the culture of the twentieth century, nor about Freud's preponderant creative role in establishing it as part of our culture. The big main outline of the conceptual scheme was already quite fully developed in *The Interpretation of Dreams,* although Freud was clearly not a man to rest content at one stage in the development of his thinking. On the contrary, through the rest of his long life—he died in 1939—he never ceased to extend and modify his theories. He did not, however, turn aside to any radically different line of thinking, and there is a fundamental continuity between *The Interpretation of Dreams* and all of his subsequent writings.

It is often said that Freud's greatest discovery was that of the Unconscious. Seen in the proper perspective, I think this is correct. In more general terms, his great achievement was to have worked out, with considerably greater theoretical sophistication than his predecessors, an account of the structure and functioning of the human person as a psychological entity operating as a self-regulating system. In the formulation of this scheme, the Unconscious was already, in *The Interpretation of Dreams,* one of three subsystems in his total psychological system, the other two being the Conscious system and the Preconscious system. Many years later, he modified this tripartite division, calling the new subsystems the Id, the Ego and the Superego, but the continuity between the two formulations is patent.

Freud's discourse throughout the book deals with the *meaning* of psychic events—meaning that is, in some kind of subjectively rereferable sense, rather than simply as an index of somatic processes. Thus he decisively repudiates any form of somatic reductionism. Freud's concept of the Unconscious is built primarily around his concept of psychic energy, in German, *Triebe,* usually mistranslated into English as "instinctual." This energy is basically a common pool, not irrevocably attached to particular objects of "desire." It is transferable through various processes, one of the most important of which is called, in psychoanalytic vocabulary, *displacement,* or, in later statements, *cathexis.* The tendency of this psychic energy source is unidirectional, tending always toward the achievement of states of gratification. This is the focus of the concept, *wish,* which figures so prominently in *The Interpretation of Dreams,* especially in Freud's dictum that a wish-fulfillment component is present in every dream and, in fact, provides the motive force for dream activity.

Freud attributes the property of *unconsciousness* to things which are not remembered because they are protected by certain mechanisms from gaining access to the conscious components of the personality. The Unconscious is clearly, in his view, not a completely fluid pool, but one distributed in relation to what might be called the unconscious cathexes of a system of objects. Freud adheres rigorously to the psychic character of the Unconscious and strongly emphasizes the importance of childhood experience. My rereading of the book has reinforced my conviction[3] that its primary structure at the object level is the internalized object system of childhood experience, which is, of course, very heavily affected by the social structure of the human family. This is closely connected with Freud's own emphasis on the sexual—or better, perhaps, erotic—component in the motivation of unconscious wishes. In the development of the individual, this has roots in the very special role played by eroticism in childhood, eroticism connected primarily with the child's motivational attachment to human objects in his environment, but transferable to nonhuman objects such as animals and indeed physical objects. Freud's contribution to the understanding of the eroticism of childhood is crucial. Fellow members of the child's family are clearly the most important of these objects, followed by nonfamilial household members. Central to Freud's analysis is the significance of these objects as potential sources of pleasure or fulfillment gratification, and of the blocking of such gratifications. This is the main axis of the famous Freudian concepts of *pleasure* and *unpleasure*. The arousal of an impulse or desire always induces unpleasurable feelings, but in the process of gratification the unpleasure is converted into pleasure; when the cycle is complete, however, with full consummation, the whole *affective tone,* as he calls it, disappears.

In his remarkable final chapter, Freud speaks of the Unconscious as tending to maintain a rather stable equilibrium of energy potential and allocation. Only in rather carefully regulated ways and in relatively small doses is its underlying energy released into the Preconscious and the Conscious sectors of the personality. It can be released through dreams, or through what later came to be called *ego-activity,* or through pathological symptoms. It is important to realize that there is a cognitive component in the structure of the Unconscious.[4] Objects on the one hand, and wishes on the other, clearly fit into the paradigm of goal-orientation, a paradigm familiar in the sciences of human action and behavior and in biology as well. The processes of the Unconscious, however, are not primarily those of cognitive reasoning; rather, they are what Freud calls *affective processes,* essentially those which deal with the "investment of psychic energy" in wishes and the objects through which they can be gratified, and the reallocation of such energy within systems of objects. The relevant system of

[3] Talcott Parsons, *Social Structure and Personality* (New York: The Free Press of Glencoe, 1964).

[4] Marshall Edelson, "Dreams and Language," *Psychoanalytic Study of the Child,* ed. Ruth S. Eissler *et al.* (New York: International Universities Press, 1973).

objects extends past the boundaries of the Unconscious into the Preconscious and eventually into the Conscious subsystems.

The endowment of an object with psychic energy is what has come to be known as *cathexis* (German *Besetzung*). Freud's term for the paths by which energy is transmitted from one object to another is *association*. This kind of association—quite different from the processes of logical inference in conscious thinking and reasoning—connects objects with primarily affective meanings according to their symbolic properties. These may be either resemblances or contrasts, and actual reversal is a very common phenomenon in dream processes. Freud is insistent on the difference between what he ends up calling the *primary* process of the Unconscious and the *secondary* process of the Conscious world. One of his most important propostions in *The Interpretation of Dreams* is that the objects which enter the manifest content of actual dreams should be regarded as the nodes where several complex association paths intersect. By these association paths the dream content is related in turn to the latent "dream thoughts" which he contends are predominantly of preconscious origin—though some are actually conscious, notably references to the previous day's experiences. The main task of dream interpretation is tracing out these paths of association to significant objects and events.

The principles of organization of the Unconscious and the Conscious sectors of the personality are radically different. I think that it is because of this difference that Freud holds that unregulated interchange and interpenetration between them cannot fail to be disorganizing on both sides of the boundary. Since Freud's own approach as therapist and analyst of dreams had necessarily been from the point of view of the consciousness system, he was particularly impressed by the functioning of agencies which prevented components of the Unconscious from crossing the boundaries to the Conscious and vice versa in an unregulated manner. First he formulated the concept of an agency which he called the *cen*sor, which essentially prevented boundary crossings from the Unconscious to the Conscious, then he developed the concept into what he called *repression*. Especially in the field of pathological symptom formation, he was greatly impressed by the amount of conflict which could be generated in this area of boundary relationships. He seems to have felt, however, that, in the relatively integrated and mentally healthy adult personality, the elements of conflict could at least be minimized to the point where they were tolerable. In the dream, he clearly saw a kind of safety valve which, under the protection of sleep, permitted expression of unconscious wishes and thus a kind of gratification of them which would result in minimal disturbances to the conscious life. It is important to realize that there are direct parallels here to the process of psychoanalytic therapy. In the analytic relation the therapist encourages the verbal expression of any and all thoughts, deliberately seeking to stimulate the expression of those which belong primarily in the Unconscious. There is, however, a fundamental distinction in psychoanalytic procedure between verbal expression on the one hand and what is called "acting out" on the other. Thus, to use a familiar example, if a patient has displaced his hotility toward his father onto his analyst, he may express his hostility verbally in very bitter terms without its leading to retaliation. However, a physical attack on the analyst is strictly forbidden and would be promptly suppressed. Sleep seems to provide an analogous situation in that, motor activity having been suspended by sleep, the acting out of dream wishes is precluded.

The Integration of Psychoanalytic Theory in the Sciences Dealing with Living Systems

It is not clear to me how far Freud was aware of the similarity of the theory of the human psyche he developed in *The Interpretation of Dreams* and the parallels which have just been sketched to certain more general movements in the theoretical analysis of living systems, both organic and human, at the psychological, social, and cultural levels. It strikes me quite forcibly that there is an important parallel between Freud's conception of the Unconscious as a relatively stabilized and rather tightly controlled system and the conception of the internal environment of the organism developed in physiology, especially by Freud's contemporary Claude Bernard and Bernard's successor Walter B. Cannon.[5] The forces and mechanisms are different but the main theoretical format is strikingly similar. Both the subsystems which, because of their effective insulation in certain fundamental respects from fluctations in the environment, are able to maintain a higher level of constancy than free interchange with the environment would permit.

Such a parallel throws light on the sharp differences which Freud himself emphasizes between primary and secondary processes—processes which he connects directly with affective process and cognitive process respectively. The cognitive function organizes a set of mechanisms which enhance the individual's chances of coping successfully with the contingencies—dangers as well as the opportunities—inherent in the environment external to his own personality. Though the psychic components of the environment and the internal system may in certain respects be the same, their combinations are quite different. The components we associate with such conceptions as rationality and reasoning are far more pertinent in relation to the environment than they are to the internal system.

This is only one of a number of similarities which suggest themselves

[5] Claude Bernard, *An Introduction to the Study of Experimental Medicine,* transl. H. C. Greene (New York: Dower, 1957; first published in French in 1865); and Walter B. Cannon, *The Wisdom of the Body* (New York: W. W. Norton, 1932).

between Freud's analytical schemes and those developed in a variety of neighboring disciplines. Somewhat similar theoretical constructs have appeared in the fields dealing with human societies and cultures. Particularly prominent beginnings are found in the work of Emile Durkheim, who sees society as a "reality sui generis," functioning as the internal environment of a general system of human action.[6]

Conclusion

Psychoanalytic theory has, of course, been highly controversial ever since its first massive promulgation through *The Interpretation of Dreams*. Indeed, it is still drastically repudiated in some quarters. There can be little doubt, however, that it has been one of the most important intellectual movements of the century. It is my own view that, far more than is generally realized, it is in accord with the main movement of science, extending all the way from sciences on the biological side and psychology to those dealing with human phenomena at the social and cultural levels. In tackling the task of systematically analyzing the individual human personality, Freud stood at a particularly crucial nodal point in this larger intellectual movement. He made advances in theoretical penetration, comprehensiveness, and clarity far beyond the points reached by any of his predecessors. Certainly I regard *The Interpretation of Dreams* as one of the great landmarks in the intellectual development of the twentieth century.

[6] Talcott Parsons, "Durkheim on Religion Revisited: Another Look at the Elementary Forms of the Religious Life," *Beyond the Classics? Essays in the Scientific Study of Religion,* ed. Charles Y. Glock and Phillip E. Hammond (New York: Harper Torchbooks, 1973), pp. 156–180.

PART II
SOCIOLOGY OF HIGHER EDUCATION

Introduction to Part II

PART II DEALS WTH THE SECOND of the broad empirical fields of interest mentioned in the General Introduction: the place and significance of higher education in modern society. More generally this area is interpreted to include not only the teaching of what has been called "higher learning" but also various custodial functions and above all what has come to be called the "research function," or the "advancement of knowledge."

In my own intellectual biography this interest is in the first instance a development from my early interest in the professions in modern societies, particularly medical practice.[1] It soon became clear that a criterion of the standing of an occupational group as a profession is the requirement for its practitioners of technical training, in which the mastery of bodies of knowledge, that is, cognitive competence, has come to play a central part. In modern societies, the acquisition of such training has become an increasingly important part of the professional complex.

Insofar as this tendency has come to be generalized, it was an obvious inference that the university had become institutionalized, as it were, as the "mother" of this institutional complex. That is, abandoning the metaphor, the university became the primary trustee of that phase of the cultural heritage of modern societies that was important for the grounding of professional competence (granted its functions are much broader).

These interests naturally led to a larger investigation of the nature of what we came to call the "cognitive complex" within the system of action. This complex is rooted in the cultural system itself. But it has ramified into the other subsystems of action and into the organic and especially, within action, to the behavioral system and into the telic system. Indeed, this complex of the human action system has become the paramount focus of the differentiation, in action systems, particularly at the cultural and social levels, of the system of higher education and its relations to other complexes such as the political and the religious. In particular, as noted in the Introduction to Part I, in certain ways the cognitive complex has sup-

---

[1] Talcott Parsons, *The Social System* (New York: Free Press, 1951), chap. 10, "Social Structure and Dynamic Process: The Case of Modern Medical Practice."

91

planted the economic complex, as the latter was characteristically emphasized in nineteenth-century thought; in my opinion this emphasis has been shared in common between the utilitarian economists and the Marxist tradition.

For the reader who takes the theoretical issues involved in the papers included in Part II most seriously, it seems particularly important to be acquainted with *The American University* (co-authored with Gerald M. Platt).[2] This book contains extensive discussions of the theoretical framework in terms of which I have attempted to analyze the system of higher education and its place in modern societies. In particular, it contains a full discussion of the nature of the cognitive complex (Chapter 2), of the place and nature of the structural pattern of the collegial association, of the institutionalization of tenure and of academic freedom (Chapter 3), and of the place of inflationary and deflationary movements in the dynamic processes of the academic system (Chapter 7).

Though it was the last to be written, "The Future of the University" opens in Part II because it presents a general outline of the development, growth, and structure of modern higher education. This chapter was first presented as a lecture at the Australian National University at Canberra and was repeated with variations in Melbourne, Brisbane, and Sydney, Australia, in 1975. It was put into final written form after the oral presentations, and is being nearly simultaneously published with the present volume in the Australian Journal *Vestes*.

Whereas Chapter 5 looks toward the future of the modern university, it also attempts to sketch many of the structural features of the university and of its place in modern societies and to give a broad account of some salient features of its historical background. It is for such reasons that it seemed appropriate to use "The Future of the University" as an introduction to the other essays in Part II.

Chapter 6, "Some Considerations on the Growth of the American System of Higher Education and Research" was written for the volume in honor of Edward Shils, edited by Terry N. Clark and Joseph Ben-David, and published by the University of Chicago Press early in 1977. This selection is concerned with a problem in historical sociology, namely, the constellation of social forces in American society, from the end of the Civil War on, that can account for the development in the United States of a massive system of higher education and research. This has been not merely a "mass" system, though it has been that, extending undergraduate education to the unprecedented level of slightly more that half the secondary school graduates of both sexes. At the same time, however, the American system exhibits much qualitative variety, and it has, in its more

[2] Talcott Parsons and Gerald M. Platt, in collaboration with Neil J. Smelser, *The American University* (Cambridge, Mass.: Harvard University Press, 1973).

elite sectors, reached levels of academic excellence comparable with the best anywhere in the world.

Chapter 6 takes the line that this development cannot be explained by an economic interpretation, whether utilitarian or Marxist, even though, of course, without large economic resources, from both private and public sources, it could not have taken place. Over against this, we place the view that it is necessary to invoke as a major factor in such social change the operation of a value complex in which cognitive values, as part of the largest complex of what I have called "instrumental activism," have figured prominently. This is closely related to the famous Protestant ethic, and my insights in this connection owe a great deal to the well-known work of Robert Merton.[3]

Value-commitments, however, do not simply implement themselves; to suppose that they do is the idealistic fallacy. My hypothesis in Chapter 6 is that the main implementers, especially in the early phase of institution-alization, were members of an elite class in American society who looked mainly to Europe for their models of prestige. Particularly since formal aristocratic status was, under American conditions, denied them, they could still assimilate and promote certain cultural interests that at the time were much better represented in Europe. These interests were above all the cognitive and the esthetic values; there was a notable wave of sponsor-ship of the arts, most evident in the founding of museums and symphony orchestras, as well as marked expansion of the intellectual disciplines in colleges and universities, at about the same time (the late nineteenth and twentieth centuries).

Two further conditions seem to have been very important. These were, first, the extension of the range of access to higher education in accord with the democratic values so important in American society and, second, the application of the results of cognitive achievement to the practical in-terests of various members of the society, ranging from the ailments of the sick to the technological concerns of the military, with industrial tech-nology in a sense standing in the middle. Important as these "payoffs" have been, however, I do not think that their anticipation, with all the un-certainties of concrete situations, could account for the main impetus to this institutional development. Without the value-commitments, as I have sketched them, plus the prestige rewards to be gained from their early im-plementation, the prospect of practical payoffs would not have brought about these changes.

Finally, I may note the fact that in the historic socialism-capitalism controversies, very little indeed has been said of the importance in modern society of the cognitive complex and its institutionalization. Moreover, its

[3] Robert K. Merton, *Science, Technology, and Society in Seventeenth Century England* (New York: Fertig, 1970).

reaching the point it has, seems to me to provide strong ground for the contention that the old capitalism versus socialism dilemma has in many respects become obsolete. We have come into a mode of social organization in which factors outside the ken of *both* camps have acquired decisive importance.

Chapter 7, "The University 'Bundle': A Study of the Balance Between Differentiation and Integration," is essentially a theoretical analysis. As noted in its introductory statement, this essay arose out of discussions among Neil J. Smelser, Gerald Platt, and myself about drafts of The American University, in which Smelser referred to a certain "resistance to differentiation," about the "normality" of which he raised questions.[4]

In the background was the often expressed view that the aspect of modern society that we continually discussed as substantially increasing levels of differentiation would lead unrestrictedly to more and more refined specialization. Many have deplored this process as allegedly producing a kind of fragmentation that makes communication across specialties and hence their integration impossible. Such a view seems in conflict with Durkheim's contention that increase in the division of labor is a particularly important source of solidarity.[5] This paper is basically a study in the nature of the balance between trends to increasing differentiation and complementary mechanisms of integration.

Relatively early in our study of the structure of the university, Platt and I noticed certain phenomena that seemed incompatible with the thesis of the rush to specialization. The first of these is the inclusion in the ordinary college or university faculty (of arts and sciences) of the whole range of intellectual disciplines instead of their separation into, for example, schools of natural science, social science, and the humanities, to say nothing of still narrower specialization. To be sure, such faculties are divided into departments, but faculties have not been abandoned as organizations. A second failure to specialize consisted in the fact that undergraduate teaching, graduate teaching, and research are performed within the same faculties and departments and to a large extent by the same people. Again, separate undergraduate colleges have survived; yet there are few purely graduate schools and few institutions devoted specially to research. Finally, schools for applied professional training have for the most part become faculties of the same universities that have undergraduate colleges and academic graduate schools. The reader will note that the features of the professional complex emphasized in Chapter 2 with reference to certain problems of biomedical research are part of this "bundle" phenomenon.

---

[4] Neil J. Smelser, "Epilogue: Social-Structural Dimensions of Higher Education," in Parsons and Platt, American University, pp. 389–422.

[5] Emile Durkheim, *The Division of Labor in Society,* trans. George Simpson (New York: Free Press, 1964; first published in French in 1893).

This paper was written for, and published in, the volume edited by Neil Smelser and Gabriel A. Almond, *Public Higher Education in California,* the main part of which contains Smelser's study of that system, alongside a number of other commentaries on these problems. Smelser, as noted in the Preface to *The American University,* functioned as a kind of house critic to that project and wrote an epilogue that was published as a chapter of that book. There is a sense in which Chapter 7 is, and it was so entitled, a corresponding kind of epilogue to the Smelser study. An attempt to extend the pattern of "clustering" that characterizes the university bundle to analyzing the elite structure of American society is briefly developed in Chapter 9 of *Social Systems and the Evolution of Action Theory,* "Social Structure and the Media of Interchange." [6] This paper was written *after* Chapter 7 of the present volume.

The last selection in Part II is very brief. Chapter 8, "Stability and Change in the American University," was written as part of a symposium to which there were some eighty-one contributors. The symposium, published in *Dædalus* in 1974, was an attempt by the editors to assemble a wide variety of views, after the turmoil had largely subsided, on the consequences of the disturbances in the American university system, which culminated in the later 1960s, with 1970 as the last year of acute disturbance. Written two years later than the last parts of *The American University,* this essay could take advantage of a better perspective on developmental trends than could earlier work. In this contribution I came to the conclusion that although important changes had been and were taking place, the main structure we had outlined and analyzed in *The American University* had remained intact in most universities of the type we had treated. I did not then, and do not now, see the portent of a truly radical swing to a quite different type of university from what had developed prior to the disturbances, as some have. In a sense, Chapter 5 and Chapter 8 serve to bracket Part II's consideration of problems of higher education in modern society.

[6] Talcott Parsons, *Social Systems and the Evolution of Action Theory* (New York: Free Press, 1977).

5. The Future of the University

THE RECENT RAPID DEVELEPMENT of higher education has been one of the most striking processes of social change in all of modernized societies in the world and in many at earlier stages of modernization. In the short time I have been in Australia, I have been greatly impressed by the magnitude and intensity of the process of growth in these respects in your country. This clearly must be construed to include both qualitative and quantitative growth and due regard for the research function, that is the advancement of knowledge, in addition to its transmission through teaching in many fields and at many different levels. I am fortunate in my temporary anchorage at the Australian National University at Canberra to have a direct opportunity to see a relatively new but very high quality academic institution in operation. And my briefer visits to other Australian universities specifically in Melbourne, Brisbane, and Sydney have given me a picture not merely of qualitative status but of the rapid extension of your university system. In the present article however, I shall deal mainly with the United States simply because I know more about it through personal experience and through explicit study than about any other system of higher education.

I

It seems to me that this impressive expansion and upgrading of higher education must be regarded as in a sense the spearhead and culminating aspect of a major change in the nature and structure of modern societies. It is so important a change that I have become accustomed to referring to it as the educational revolution, meaning that phrase in a sense comparable

From *Vestes* (1977). Reprinted with the permission of the Publisher of the journal.

to the industrial revolution which took hold in the Western world in the late eighteenth century and proceeded throughout the nineteenth. If again I may refer to American conditions, before what I am calling the educational revolution, there existed higher education of a sort going back to early colonial days, mainly what were referred to as colleges which were chiefly designed to prepare candidates for the ministry of religion. Thus my own college, Harvard, was founded as early as 1636, though not until after the Civil War could it by and stretch of the imagination be called a university.

The first major change from a relatively stable situation came with the introduction of public elementary education which began on a substantial scale in the 1840's. The movement spread throughout the country so that by about the turn of the nineteenth to the twentieth centuries, an approximation to the universalizing of elementary education had been attained. I think it important to keep in mind the extent to which this was a major innovation, which of course occurred in Europe at about the same time. Previous to that there had not been the attempt to provide even literacy for virtually all members of a large scale population. Only very small scale cases like the more advanced Greek *poleis* and perhaps Calvin's *Geneva* had attempted universal literacy. Even literacy, to say nothing of other features of educated groups, was confined to very small specialized and elite groups. The educational revolution then proceeded to quantitative expansion within the revelant age cohorts to the levels of secondary education. In the United States, the great expansion of public secondary education, in what we have called the high schools, occurred in the first third of the present century so that by about the mid-1930's an approximation to the universalizing of secondary education had been attained.

The transformation of higher education that is beyond the high school (in American terms) began shortly after the Civil War. The appointment of Charles W. Eliot as President of Harvard College in 1869 is a convenient landmark since it was under Eliot's leadership that Harvard was transformed from a college into a university in the modern sense. This process of transformation proceeded at a considerable rate during the rest of the nineteenth century. It involved: the restructuring of quite a number of older colleges in addition to Harvard, Columbia, Yale, Princeton, and Cornell for example; the foundation of a number of notable new ones such as Johns Hopkins and the University of Chicago; and the development of a number of the beginning state universities, such as the University of Wisconsin, of Michigan, and a little latter of California, in a direction comparable to that of the private ones. There is a sense in which by the turn of the cenutry the main outline of the system was established. It is also important to note that this was the period which saw the establishment of graduate schools—notably in the arts and science disciplines—and of professional associations in the principal disciplinary fields. By

1910 most of the currently recognized disciplinary associations had been established.

Down to the first World War however, the newly burgeoning universities remained small and higher education was available only to a very limited proportion of the relevant age cohorts. Thus, even undergraduate education was open to scarcely more than a few percentages of the cohort group, somewhere between 5 and 10 percent, and beyond the undergraduate level was open to a much smaller percentage. The big quantitative expansion began between the two world wars but accelerated at a very rapid pace in the wake of the Second World War.

By the turn of the 1960's to the 70's, this expansion had reached a peak. Slightly over 50 percent of the graduates of secondary schools were going on to some kind of higher education,[1] surely an unprecedented state of affairs for a very large country. This was accomplished not so much by the expansion of existing institutions—though this of course did occur—as it was by the foundation of new ones especially in the public sector. In particular, the state universities, instead of confining themselves to one campus established new ones in different locations throughout the state. Thus, the University of California having first had only the one campus at Berkeley, then a second at Los Angeles, now has nine. Older eastern states which have not gone in for state higher education on a considerable scale, perhaps notably New York and Massachusetts, did so. Then, there was a big spate of foundation of municipal institutions which had a long history in a few places like New York City, but were greatly expanded in this era. Finally, there was a very rapid growth of two year community colleges which furnished both some education beyond the secondary school and an opportunity to transfer to four year colleges.

During the period when this expansion of undergraduate education was going on, there was a very large expansion of graduate study, particularly in the arts and sciences and especially in the natural sciences. This of course was very much stimulated by the demand for teaching personnel in the newly expanded and established institutions of undergraduate study. It was also immensely stimulated by the rapid expansion of the research function which centered in the larger, more elite universities but was also expanding to academic institutions of other sorts and beyond the academic world into governmental agencies and corporate industrial organizations.

Research, of course, and the training of personnel for research functions was immensely stimulated by financial support particularly from governmental sources and particularly, though by no means exclusively, in the natural sciences. This was the era in which for the first time practical payoff in technological connections became a major factor in the decision

[1] *Fact Book on Higher Education* (Washington, D.C.: American Council on Education, 1969), p. 9048; see also Martin Trow, 'Reflections on the Transition from Mass to Universal Higher Education," *Daedalus*, vol. 99, no. 1 (1970); 1–42.

—especially of governmental bodies—to support research and training. The symbol alerting to this possibility indeed urgency was the Soviet success in launching the Sputnik missile into space. As however the reader of Chapter 6 below will become aware, I do not believe that the prospect of such practical payoff furnished the main explanation of the impressive growth of the system of higher education and research more generally. I think much more important has been the prestige of certain European models of the cultural value of these activities; in the American case, these came particularly from German and British sources.

The beginning of the 1970's saw a peak in this process of expansion. The economic recession of the recent period has brought about severe financial stringencies in the academic world as elsewhere, and considerable but by no means drastic reduction of the scale of operations. The growth, however, had gone far enough so that, in a sense which could not remotely be imagined at the beginning of the present century, a system of higher education and research had become not only an integral part but an exceedingly prominent part of the structure of American society as in other modern societies. I will comment on the larger significance of this change at the end of this paper.

II

The American system of higher education involves a wide variety of types of institution which however can be treated as a case of functional differentiation and not merely relatively random variety. A particularly strategic place is occupied within this system by a relatively small group, perhaps a dozen to fifteen, of "elite institutions" which my collaborator Gerald Platt and I in our book *The American University* called the "full" universities.[2] The list of these institutions has been relatively stable throughout most of the present century. It is important that it crosses the private-public line. It includes such institutions as Harvard, Yale, Columbia, University of Chicago, and Stanford on the private side and the University of California, Wisconsin and Michigan on the public side. (This is not meant to be an exhaustive list.)

The rest of this article, like the book *The American University,* will focus on this type of university. Unfortunately, there is not space here to dicuss adequately the other types and their relation to this.

There are certain relative uniformities of structure of this university type which, however, are not without exception. I would like to discuss this structure on two levels. The first of these might be called the macro-

[2] Talcott Parsons and Gerald M. Platt, in collaboration with Neil J. Smelser, *The American University* (Cambridge, Mass.: Harvard University Press, 1973).

sociological level, namely dealing with the university as a total social system, whereas the second is a structural pattern level dealing with the kinds of relational patterns which have come to be institutionalized within it.

Except for new foundations within a recent period, all American universities began as undergraduate colleges (obviously being modeled in the first instance on the colleges of the ancient British universities.) In terms of primary functions, their process of change has introduced new suborganizations which have been the bearers of more of less new functions. Probably the most important single one of these is the development of graduate schools which have concentrated on the core intellectual disciplines, in the sense of emphasis on being "pure" as distinguished from being "applied." These graduate schools have come to be differentiated from the undergraduate college in a sense in which this has not been the case to a comparable degree in either Britain or continental Europe. Their teaching function has been primarily oriented to the training of candidates for an academic career, more than anything else, in what are in the above sense the "pure" academic disciplines. It is notable that graduate schools in this sense have not displaced the undergraduate colleges, but have continued to coexist with them under the same collective structures.

There have been variations from institution to institution in the exact pattern of integration. My own institution, Harvard, has integrated them more closely than most others. There is in most cases a considerable overlap of personal to say nothing of substantive subject matter in the teaching of both graduate and undergraduate students. Of course a smaller proportion of undergraduates are destined to academic careers than of graduate students. Nevertheless, a striking feature of the population of the more elite undergraduate colleges (elite in the sense of academic prestige) have been going on from undergraduate studies to the graduate level.

This coexistence of undergraduate and graduate studies in the same institution is a first example of the pattern of integration which in Chapter 7 below we have called "the university bundle." The sense in which this is a notable phenomenon is that it runs counter to the alleged tendency of the structure of modern societies to maximize specialization wherever that is objectively possible. This is a case where an apparently quite reasonable line of differentiation has tended not to be sharply drawn. At the same level, we should call attention also to another phenomenon of integration: the founding of what are ordinarily called professional schools, that is schools for the training of practitioners of the principal applied professions of which the prototypes are medicine and law. This goes back to a period before the development of the university type in the latter part of the nineteenth century. The new movement of structural change however led to drawing in of existing professional schools into closer integration with the university in general, and the founding of a good many new schools, some of them in the older professional fields but others in new ones such as education, business, public administration, architecture, social work and the like. It is notable that the medical profession has established (embodied for the most part in legislation) that licenses to practice medicine will be granted to graduates of what they call "Class A" medical schools. And the definition of "Class A" medical school is one which is an integral part of a university not an entity independent of universities.

There is one final structural aspect which belongs to the bundle complex which I would like to mention. The much touted trend to specialization has not operated, or only in a modified sense, within the faculties of arts and sciences, as I tend to think of them, which comprise both undergraduate colleges and academic graduate schools. This is to say that in such faculties instruction is offered covering the whole range of what have become the established intellectual disciplines. These tend to be grouped in the United States as elsewhere in the three categories of the natural sciences, the social sciences, and the humanities. There has been a notable absence of the tendency to establish separate faculties in any one of these three clusters of disciplines, to say nothing of still more specialized faculties for example of physical sciences or biological sciences. It is of course true that these faculties have come to be differentiated into departments, which has been a universal tendency. This is important, but it does not negate the importance of the fact that these many departments remain within a single faculty instead of separating to constitute independent organizations. Among many other constraints which this status involves is that they are all subject to the fiscal authority of a central faculty and in some respects university administration and do not command adequate financial resources to operate independently of such fiscal authority.

Finally, let me say a word about the research function. This is another example of the bundle phenomena. From time to time there has been advocacy of the separation of the research function from that of teaching, most recently in connection with the recent wave of student disturbances. By and large, however, this separation has not occurred. Indeed in one conspicuous case, that of what was once the Rockefeller Institute of Medical Research, the trend has run the other way and this institution is now the Rockefeller University which has instituted the teaching of graduate students though not yet of undergraduates. By and large, the primary center of advanced "pure discipline" research in the United States has remained in the universities and has been conducted by faculty members who are also teachers at the same time. There are research professorships, but Dr. Platt and I found in our investigation that the overwhelming sentiment of members of the academic profession is in favor of the combination of research and teaching, not of the abandonment of teaching in favor of an exclusive research function.[3]

---

[3] Ibid.

The American situation as I have sketched it so far has much in common with the university structure in other countries notably in Europe and in the countries overseas of European settlement such as Canada, Australia, and New Zealand. One of the best authorities on the university structure, Professor Joseph Ben-David [4] of the Hebrew University, suggests that in the American case there are two particularly important structural innovations. The first of these is the institution of the department organized about a group of several senior colleagues of essentially equivalent status, as distinguished from the European (including British) tradition of organizing a subject about a single "chair." The American pattern is to vest intra-departmental administrative authority in a chair*man*—who incidentally is not infrequently a woman—but for a limited term, commonly of five years. In principle, all full professors are fundamentally equals and there is a presumption that they will rotate in assuming departmental chairmanships though there is usually a selective factor other than purely random rotation.

The second principal structural innovation in the American system, relative to its European background, is the establishment of a graduate school which embodies both teaching and research in the pure disciplines. This is to say that the dual level structure, which in American terms we call graduate and undergraduate, was more firmly institutionalized under American conditions than under European. One might perhaps say that the British system—especially in Oxford and Cambridge—gave priority to the undergraduate level and only gradually institutionalized the functions of graduate study and research. On the continent of Europe however there is a sense, as Ben-David points out, in which all of the faculties of a continental university including the philosophical faculty were, in an approximation to the American sense, "professional" faculties.[5] Ben-David's suggestion regarding the German universities is that the faculty of Philosophy was in the first instance mainly a professional training facility for teachers in the high level secondary schools, the *Gymnasia*.

III

Let us now turn to the pattern aspect of the structure of the university. Looked at functionally, in terms of its place in a highly differentiated society taken as a whole, it is subject to certain distinctive circumstances. On the one hand as a teaching facility in the broadest relevant sense, the uni-

[4] Joseph Ben-David, *American Higher Education: Directions Old and New* (New York: McGraw-Hill, 1972).

[5] Joseph Ben-David, *Centers of Learning: Britain, France, Germany, United States* (New York: McGraw-Hill, 1977).

versity or more broadly higher education has become articulated with the age grading structure of the society. Though there are important exceptions and pressures to change, by and large the objects of the teaching function are persons in the pre-adult phase of their own personal development (if we mean by this prior to the assumption of full "career" status). The common designation for their status has come to be that of student. In a sense which is sufficiently evident, although it is not altogether anomalous for a retired professor like myself to say he continues to be a "student of higher education." As we generally think of it, students however are of two age grades: undergraduates following on the secondary school and graduate students in academic or professional schools. Platt and I have introduced the term "studentry" with special reference to the undergraduate phase because we did not wish to identify that phase with the usual reference to the term adolescence.[6]

In the age grading sequence, it is of course clear that higher education follows, for the typical individual who goes through the system, on the earlier stages of formal education which are ordinarily classified as elementary and secondary education. Preceding that, of course, is in turn the early socialization of the child centering in the family and informal neighborhood relations. Of course, informal "educational" influences continue to operate well beyond the beginning of formal education indeed within higher education.

Second, the university's primary concern is, as it is often put, intellectual matters. Again, Platt and I have related this primacy of intellectual matters to the value patterns which we have called those of underlying cognitive rationality.[7] These are to be distinguished in the first instance from instrumentally practical concerns which are dominant in the considerably largest proportion of the occupational system, whether they be the manufacturing or marketing of goods, cultivation of the soil, tending of animals, the functions of government at many levels, the applied professions like medicine and law. It seems quite clear that the faculties of arts and sciences constitute the structural core of the university complex. Not least important is the fact that undergraduate training is increasingly not tied to applied functions, but is regarded as a preliminary to applied professional training.

There are many problems about the relation of this cognitive complex to other fields in which other values predominate. One, however, particularly needs to be stressed here. This is that the implementation of cognitive values involves levels of advancement and of quality of achievement. The expectations for the acquisition of knowledge in good undergraduate colleges are clearly superior to those of elementary schools and indeed of secondary schools. One way to put it would be that the college student

---

[6] Parsons and Platt, *American University*, pp. 163–224.

[7] Ibid., pp. 33–102.

would be wasting his or her time if college work were exchanged for a return to elementary or even secondary school. What is true of these well known "levels of advancement" is true also in a different way of individual levels of attainment. One way of putting it is that there is an inherent competitive reference in the process of cognitive learning. Some succeed better than others, whatever the grounds of their capacity to succeed. There is therefore, from the social point of view, a selective dimension in the attainment of rising levels of intellectual advancement. Even though it has become a workable ideal that all members of an age cohort—with such exceptions as those of the mentally retarded—should complete secondary school, there has certainly been until now a presumption that admission to colleges should involve qualitative demonstration of capacity to do the work or as it is often put to "profit from the opportunity." Recent pressure for so called "open admissions" has raised very difficult questions in this connection.

There would, however, be rather little disagreement that attainment of the still more advanced levels requires special capacities. We could scarcely contemplate universalizing of the most advanced higher education. Thus, as myself an academic man who has had long experience of teaching both graduates and undergraduates, I simply cannot believe that "all students are created equal" in the sense of having equal intellectual capacity so that differentiation on the axis of excellence of intellectual achievement can be regarded as irrelevant or some kind of "bourgeois prejudice."

The implication of the above considerations is that an academic system is inherently a stratified system. This is true as between institutions, faculties, departments and within them, which inevitably vary on some kind of a scale of excellence of performance measured in the first instance in terms of cognitive variance. Here, however, I am concerned mainly with two other aspects of this stratification.

The first concerns stages in the life course as a function of the attainment of relevant capacities for cognitive and cognitive-related achievement. Within the system we call higher education, schematically, clearly, the lowest grade in this respect must be the undergraduate grade, which of course in turn is usually sub-graded by academic years. Thus, in American terms "upper classmen" are ranked higher than "lower classmen." The graduate study grade academic and professional must then be ranked above the undergraduate grade. For example, it is a common Harvard saying that many advanced undergraduates are "brighter" than graduate students.

Then, however, we come to an exceedingly important line. Some people who have been students, graduate and undergraduate, go on to become teachers and researchers in academic fields including of course the faculties of professional schools. I would strongly oppose the view that the completion of a degree program, undergraduate or graduate, implies a stopping point in the development of what we may call "cognitive competence." The extent to which individuals are capable of development beyond the points attained by the end of such a program certainly varies enormously and quite probably some of them never develop any farther. However, it would be folly to deny that experience gained in various post-training performances does not count. Therefore, there is a certain presumption that the experience of teaching, research and various other experiences contribute on the average to a substantial enhancement of such capacity. The implication of this is that the more senior cohorts, who are in the status of teachers and fully trained researchers, can claim superior competence to those who are still students. Superiority of competence is the general legitimizing base of superiority of status in the academic system. There are of course other factors such as the organizational exigencies of effective performance of the functions of the organization which would apply to any organization of comparable size and complexity.

We are all aware that in the recent disturbances, there has been a very pervasive attack on the stratification system of institutions of higher education, with the radical group pressing very hard in an egalitarian direction (in the most extreme form advocating the total abolition of any status differentials whatever). I am quite ready to argue that this is a utopian position and could never produce, if it were successfully institutionalized, an effectively functioning scheme of academic organization.

However that may be, the American academic system has come to be institutionalized in four primary strata of academic status. These are: 1) the status of undergraduate student; 2) graduate student; 3) junior faculty; and finally 4) senior faculty member. Of course many who have been undergraduate or graduate students go on to non-academic functions and the problem of their comparative status relative to those in faculty careers is a problem of a somewhat different order from that presently under consideration. Also, the size and complexity of academic organizations has come to be such that there has been a far reaching differentiation of what may be called administrative personnel and functions from the more purely academic. Departments of Buildings and Grounds, Financial Administration, and various others are indispensable parts of the academic scene. They cannot, in my opinion, be dispensed with and their role should be understood in terms of the theory of complex organization more generally.

Let me now turn to another particularly important aspect of structural pattern. Along with the common allegation that the main trend of structural change in modern societies has been rampant specialization, another common and related one has been that it has been bureaucratization. It is not uncommon to cite the university as an example of this. Contrary to this allegation I should like to maintain that, in its main structural pattern, specifically apart from the administrative aspect, the modern university is of quite a different structural type which I would like to call the *collegial association*. As Max Weber made very clear,[8] the main keynote of bureaucratic organization is the hierarchy of authority with the lines running from top to bottom, not horizontally. What I call the collegial association is not incompatible with stratification, but within a stratum the main principle is equality of status for those who occupy that kind of position. Thus, in the typical academic department colleagues of senior faculty status are equals of each other in principle. For certain purposes, all faculty members of the department are equals of each other for other purposes generally the junior members are not the equals of the senior members. Similarly, student groups or collegial groups have a status of peer equality *vis-à-vis* each other, but undergraduates and graduates are usually differentiated in this respect.

The relevant status of equality is not only incompatible with the bureaucratic pattern, but also with another common one in modern organization mainly that of market relationships. It is sometimes convenient to think of students as the "customers" who are in the market to purchase the service outputs of academic faculties. The student-teacher relationship, however, is sociologically of quite a different character from that of the buyer-seller relation in commercial markets. One of the striking indices of this is the concept of "admission." One is admitted to a given degree program or appointed to a given faculty status, one does not simply take advantage of the fact that the relevant services are offered on a market. This indicates, in my opinion, that there is an important phenomenon of the solidarity going with membership status which structures the expectations on both sides, for example, of the teaching relationship. This, incidentally, is characteristic of the professional-client relationship generally, far beyond the academic case.

Finally, the collegial association needs to be distinguished from what is generally called a democratic association. The point here is that collegial structures are compatible with stratification in a sense in which this is not applicable to the democratic association. Indeed, one of the main features of structural disturbance in the recent period has been the claim on the part of those in lower status grades that the university should indeed be treated as a democratic association involving the famous principle "one member, one vote."

There has been much talk in the discussion of academic problems about the institution of *tenure*. This is usually interpreted to mean permanent tenure or tenure without limit of time, subject only to organizational retirement policies. It seemed to Dr. Platt and myself, however, to make a great deal of sense to generalize the conception of tenure to include all four of the

---

[8] Max Weber, *Economy and Society,* ed. Guenther Roth and Claus Wittich (Totowa, N. J.: Bedminster, 1968; Vol. I, Section ii, "Legal Authority with a Bureaucratic Administrative Staff," pp. 217–226; first published in German in 1922).

principal grades of the core academic structure.[9] For the student, the important consideration is, as suggested above, that a student does not simply come and take advantage of the services a study program offers but has to be admitted to it. Then, if he is admitted, he is not to be severed from his membership status except for "cause." The cause may be inadequate academic performance or it may be some infraction of the institutional norms of the collectivity he has joined such as, for example, cheating on examinations. Subject to this qualification, however, he has "tenure" for the period necessary to complete the program for the pursuance of which he was originally admitted. This may be a standard period of years, as is common with undergraduate programs, or a much less standardized period as is common with PhD programs.

The junior faculty member, then, is as we say "appointed." The distinction between junior and senior status is largely that in the former case it is for a stated period of academic years, whereas (to repeat the formula) senior status is "without limit of time." What is common as between the four tenure statuses is associational membership with the implications for the nature of solidarity and treatment that such a category of membership carries with it.

For all four statuses the primary concern of academic organization is with intellectual performance governed as we have suggested in the first instance by the values of cognitive rationality. As a solidary community with its various subcommunities however, a university is never only what might be called a "knowledge factory." It has other functions. Thus, with special reference to the undergraduate college, Platt and I have strongly emphasized the importance of "socialization processes" which are in certain respects analogous to those carried on in the family.[10] This is to say that the student typically undergoes a transformation of character in the course of his student experience, only part of which can be directly related to the cognitive content of teaching and learning.

Thus, one primary aspect of the academic organization seen as a solidary community composed of a number of different types of subcommunities is that it provides its members with what is in certain respects a "protected environment" within which they carry on a pattern of life which is differentiated from those outside the solidary community in question. As we shall argue in the next section, these features of the academic community are of the greatest significance to the future of the societal communities of which universities have become such an important part.

One final point, the development of the system of higher education and the structural trends it has followed have introduced and accentuated one particular feature of modern society which should not be left without brief comment. In its earlier history, Western higher education rather generally

[9] Parsons, and Platt, *American University,* pp. 129–152.
[10] Ibid, pp. 163–202.

followed a strong pattern of segregation by sex. In its more recent phases, however, this has already changed greatly. The story is varied in different national systems, but in the United States co-education began to develop relatively early and has been greatly accelerated in the last generation. Within the recent period, it has been widely extended to what has been called co-residence, that is the sharing of residential units by students of both sexes. There has been a recent drive to increase the number of women in faculty status as well. This change surely has important implications for the kind of citizens who are being socialized through the higher educational system.

The academic version of what has above been referred to as the protected environment comes to focus on the much discussed institution of academic freedom. Because the academic system in general is especially concerned with cognitive matters, academic freedom has traditionally been interpreted to center on, as the old German phrasing had it, *Lehrfreiheit* and *Lernfreiheit,* or in English, "freedom to teach" and "freedom to learn." This is to say that whatever restrictions on intellectual freedom may apply outside the university they are less likely to be enforced within it when they concern what shall be taught, how it shall be taught, and how intellectual issues shall be discussed.

It is symptomatic of the disturbances of recent times, that not only has the university been subject to interference with academic freedom from outside, but also from inside. A particularly prominent issue has been the tendency of radical student minority groups to try to interfere with either the teaching of faculty members or with the freedom to speak of speakers from outside the university. A recent case and policy statement came in this respect from Yale University.[11]

Academic freedom in this sense is closely related to the rights of privacy enjoyed, for example, by the family and (subject to very broad restrictions) the rights of parents to have the main voice in the bringing up of their children. Tenure and academic freedom are the two principal distinctive institutional patterns of the academic world in the relevant respects.

IV

The latter 1960's going over to 1970 produced a world-wide set of disturbances in academic institutions from which those in the United States were by no means spared. If only to raise doubts about the common American explanation that the cause of these disturbances was the war in

[11] See the report of the Committee on Freedom of Expression at Yale (C. Vann Woodward, committee chairman), "Freedom of Expression at Yale," *American Association of University Professors Bulletin,* vol. 61, no. 4 (1975): 28–42.

Vietnam, it is worthwhile to call attention to the fact that they were indeed world-wide. It is difficult to believe that the disturbances in West Germany, Great Britain, and Japan were primarily protests against American involvement in the Vietnam War. I think we must look for deeper causes and for some inside the academic system, such factors as Vietnam seem to me more to be triggering occasions than the primary sources of the disturbance.

In the background, I should be inclined to place the very rapid expansion of the system of higher education and research which had gone on for a long period. Not only the scale of the system as a whole increased greatly and very rapidly, but also that of particular academic institutions. Many undergraduate students found themselves in an institutional setting which they not only shared with large numbers of peers (running into many thousands) but where undergraduates in particular had to share the attention of the faculty with graduate students and with the research interests which have burgeoned so conspicuously in the relevant period. It seems to me significant that the focus of the disturbances was among undergraduate students in the relatively high prestige colleges, whether part of larger universities or not. An important part of the picture was that the period since the end of the Second World War, in particular, was one of rapidly rising expectations of what was to be gained by particular student groups and including an immense broadening of the groups who were exposed to the expectations of higher education.

Naturally the explanation of these phenomena is a very complex matter indeed. It is not possible within the limits of this paper to attempt even a cursory treatment of the whole range. Instead of attempting that, I would like to call attention here to an aspect of the problem which has not figured in the more general discussion, at least in my country. This is the suggestion, which was developed by Gerald Platt and myself in our book,[12] that the system of higher education has been the subject of a cycle of inflationary and deflationary change which is in certain respects parallel to the cyclical changes which have taken place in modern economies. When I say parallel I mean specifically that, but not identical; a particularly important difference is that the strains and movements have not been in the monetary system but in the operation of other media which work in the general system of action and in the social system.

Though I am afraid that these media are unfamiliar to most of my readers, I cannot go without mentioning them. The first, operating at the level of the general system of action, we have called *intelligence*. In a special technical sense which we have defined in our book, the importance of intelligence in this meaning of the term derives directly from the cognitive emphasis of the whole enterprise of higher ducation. At the same time, however, the educational system is, as has just been noted, characterized

12 Parsons and Platt, *American University*, pp. 304–345.

by solidary groupings. It is essentially within such groupings that a second medium which we have called *influence* is of primary significance. Influence we take to be primarily of integrative significance in social systems and to have functions of regulating the allocation of an emphasis on rights and obligations among the membership of solidary social groupings.

We regard the expansion of the system, as has been true in economic cases, to have been accompanied by an increasing inflationary development. What inflation in this sense does, in economic as in other action systems, is to alter the terms of interchange so that by and large a given quantity of a medium of interchange is less effective in procuring quantities of desirable resources in exchange. The very fact, as Raymond Boudon has emphasized,[13] that much larger numbers have been participants in the academic system means that its output has become, relative to other good things in the society, less valuable than when it was monopolized by much smaller numbers. There is however a tendency for participants to accept the terms of exchange which had previously prevailed as "normal" and to feel disillusioned and disappointed when their value has declined.

Such an inflationary development can over time be cumulative and the strains involved in it become cumulatively more severe. Finally, some kind of a breaking point tends to be reached which produces a panic-like reaction. The classical example of this is the financial panic.[14]

We think that the student disturbances of the recent period were certainly at least in important part deflationary phenomena of a panic-like character. Students who previously had accepted the terms of participation in the academic enterprise more or less suddenly came to be disillusioned with it, attempted to withdraw on the one hand and on the other hand to change the terms of participation. There are two respects in which the parallel with deflationary movements in the economy stands out. The first is the susceptibility of wide ranges of the system to what may be called "contagion." For example, the great depression of the 1930's was initiated by widespread financial crises starting with the 1929 crash of the American stock market but spreading to Europe and indeed all over the world. We suggest that the effect of the Berkeley disturbance of 1964 was comparable to that of the Wall Street crash. It created an atmosphere of uneasiness in student populations over a very wide area and was followed by outbreaks in many different places which tended for a period to become cumulatively more serious.

The second parallel concerns the relative suddenness with which the disturbances ceased. In the case of the economy, financial panics have tended to be relatively short lived and to subside very rapidly. Often of course this change being importantly effected by deliberate measures of

---

[13] Raymond Boudon, "Crise Universitaire et participation," *Economies et sociétés*, vol. 4, no. 9 (1970).

[14] Neil J. Smelser, *Theory of Collective Behavior* (New York: Free Press, 1963).

intervention. At any rate in the case of student disturbances, 1970 was the last year of severe disturbances and since then there has been a surprisingly quiet atmosphere.

Since this perspective that the inflationary and deflationary movements are relevant to the academic situation is so unfamiliar, we will have to leave our exposition at that. I might suggest, however, that the perspective in which this whole paper has been placed, namely that the development of higher education is part of an educational revolution, was deliberately meant to draw a parallel with the Industrial Revolution. The so called trade or business cycle has been a primary feature of industrial economies ever since that period and, if the parallel is soundly drawn, there seems to be every reason to believe that comparable cycles will be found to operate in the system of higher education.

V

In conclusion, we may come to the fulfillment of the promise made in the title of this paper. Modern thinking about economic cycles has accustomed us to the use of the word recovery in relation to a deflationary or depression state of a modern economy. Looking back from the vantage point of the mid-1970's, it seems to me correct to say that there has been substantial recovery in the system of higher education (certainly in the United States) since the period from 1968 to 1970.[15] The main institutional patterns which have been outlined in Sections II and III above seem to have emerged intact with relatively few exceptions.[16] Above all, though the primacy of the values of cognitive rationality underwent a double challenge—on the one hand from the demand for politicization of the university and on the other hand from the demand to give primacy to expressive interests—on the whole this primacy has remained intact although probably greater scope has been given to both of the other types of concerns than was true previously.

One of the striking reinforcing factors has been the demand of undergraduate students for professional training and the discipline exercised by the professional schools through their control over the selection of candidates for admission to them. By and large, these schools have continued to enforce high standards of cognitive competence among their candidates.

Also, in the main, the stratification pattern of the educational system has not been greatly altered. The most important single point is that faculty status has not been destroyed in favor of a pattern of "participatory

[15] See Chapter 8 of this volume.

[16] See David Riesman and Verne A. Stadtman (eds.), *Academic Transformation: Seventeen Institutions under Pressure* (New York: McGraw-Hill, 1973).

democracy," in which students are treated as the complete equals of their teachers. Certainly there has been increased student participation in various aspects of what is popularly called "governance," but this has not, with a very few exceptions, extended to elimination of the lines of stratification which were outlined above. There have also been attacks on academic tenure and some on academic freedom, but they have not profoundly modified the structure.

If I am right that there has been, in a sense parallel to that of recovery from a deflationary phase in the economy, a substantial recovery of the system of higher education and research in modern societies (particularly the American), it seems to me that this provides substantial evidence that as a component of the structure of modern societies this system has come to be relatively firmly institutionalized and is unlikely to be profoundly altered in its main patterns in the course of further change, especially in the relatively near future. To use a familiar metaphor, we may say that the system has "weathered" the first major storm it encountered in its relatively recent phase of institutional development and the fact that it has weathered this storm is grounds for confidence that it will continue to develop. I think I should not take further space here to elaborate on these statements but should refer the reader to the last chapter in *The American University* [17] and to Chapter 18 of this volume. There are, however, two features of the impact of this fairly stably institutionalized structure on the larger society and action system about which I would like to say a brief word in conclusion.

If I am right that the academic system has been organized in the first instance about the institutionalization of the values of cognitive rationality, this means that a new level of the institutionalization of a set of components of culture has come to be a major part of the structure of modern societies, particularly that of the United States. For example, I may quote Daniel Bell in his well known judgment that the university has become strategically the most important sector of the society because it has developed and brought to bear on innumerable societal interests essentially a new factor in serious human affairs, namely to quote him "theoretical knowledge." [18]

It is by no means only those of Marxist persuasion who have contended in the past that the structural core of modern societies, since the Industrial Revolution, has lain in the economy. It seems to me that the whole utilitarian stance in social theory has tended to give primacy to the economy and that this has been shared by the economists growing out of the utilitarian tradition and the Marxian sociologists. If this is true, the rise to a new prominence of the cognitive complex means a profound shift of bal-

---

[17] Parsons and Platt, *American University*, pp. 346–388.

[18] Daniel Bell, *The Coming of Post-Industrial Society* (New York: Basic Books, 1973).

ance in the constitution of the society. Since cultural concerns stand higher in the cybernetic hierarchy of the system of human action, I do not hesitate to state the judgment that this shift constitutes fundamentally "an upgrading" of the level of organization of modern society. It means that the resources of an industrial economy are, to a far higher degree than before, at the disposal of culturally defined interests. It is for this reason that I have tended to feel that the term "capitalism" is no longer appropriate as the primary designation of the social system under which we live. On the other hand neither is it a socialist system in the usual sense of that term. If one includes both capitalism and socialism in the expression "industrial," perhaps it is legitimate to follow Bell in speaking of the beginning of "post-industrial society." [19]

The above considerations are not unconnected with another major theme upon which I should like to conclude. In Section III of this paper, I emphasized that the main institutional pattern of the system of higher education is not bureaucratic as many social critics of our time have asserted it to be. Nor is it an example of the market system, which has been central to the position of the economy, particularly in its "free enterprise" version. Finally, I have also asserted that the university should not be regarded, as the advocates of "participatory democracy" would like to have it, as a democratic association.

As compared to bureaucratic structure and market structure, I have characterized the university as primarily institutionalizing the pattern of collegial association. It seems to me that the growth of the university to the prominence which it has attained and its probable further growth means that far more than before we are entering the phase of a collegially associational type of social structure. This perspective in the history of social thought goes back particularly to the thinking of Emile Durkheim and among his works particularly to his first seminal book, *The Division of Labor in Society.*[20]

Associational emphases are, of course, by no means confined to the academic sphere. They are very prominent indeed in the governmental sphere particularly where direct democracy is modified by a variety of constitutional provisions such as in the United States which combines a separation of powers with a federal system. Such qualification of the pattern of direct democracy is in my opinion not possible without what is frequently referred to as a regime of law. This has become increasingly consolidated in American society, particularly through the special role assumed by courts of law, most conspicuously the Supreme Court.

I would like therefore to suggest that the rise to increased prominence of the university system is probably part of a larger process of structural

---

[19] Ibid.

[20] Emile Durkheim, *The Division of Labor in Society,* trans. George Simpson (New York: Free Press, 1964; first published in French in 1893).

development in modern societies which might be called progressively increasing "associationalizing." This is an outcome, provisionally at least, which is incompatible with two types of interpretations which have been highly prevalent in our time. The first of these is that market capitalism was progressively transformed into a bureaucratic society. The second is that the basis of effective social functioning of the modern system had been undermined and that we are facing a relatively early drastic decline. It seems to me that there is good evidence to support disagreement with both these interpretive positions and to suggest a third for which I think good evidence exists.

Additional References

BEN-DAVID, JOSEPH

"Organization, Social Control, and Cognitive Change in Science." In Joseph Ben-David and Terry Nichols Clark (eds.), *Culture and Its Creators: Essays in Honor of Edward Shils.* Chicago: University of Chicago Press, 1977, pp. 244–265.

Two special issues of *Daedalus,* Journal of the American Academy of Arts and Sciences, "American Higher Education: Toward an Uncertain Future," vol. 103, no. 4 (1974), and vol. 104, no. 1 (1975).

JENCKS, CHRISTOPHER, AND DAVID RIESMAN

The Academic Revolution. Garden City: Doubleday, 1968.

LADD, JR., EVERETT, AND SEYMOUR MARTIN LIPSET

The Divided Academy. New York: McGraw-Hill, 1975.

PARSONS, TALCOTT

"The Academic System: A Sociologist's View," *Public Interest,* no. 13 (Fall 1968):173–197; Special issue.

PARSONS, TALCOTT, AND GERALD M. PLATT

"Considerations on the American Academic System," *Minerva,* vol. 6, no. 4 (1968):497–523.

VEYSEY, LAURENCE R.

The Emergence of the American University. Chicago: University of Chicago Press, 1965.

6. Some Considerations on the Growth of the American System of Higher Education and Research

FEW WOULD CONTEST that by the usual standards of academic excellence the American system of higher education, has particularly during the present century, achieved a rather notable position, not merely of quantitative development but of qualitative level. It clearly differs, of course, from most European systems in that most of its institutions of higher education do not conform to a single national "plateau" standard; rather, there is an immense range, from a considerable number of institutions of an academic quality which compares favorably with the best in any country, through a bewildering variety of differing and, in terms of academic standards, lower-level institutions, until we get to the level of local community colleges, many of which have, perhaps unfairly, been referred to as slightly glorified secondary schools. Considering these qualitative differences, Raymond Boudon is probably correct in saying that the proportion of American students to population, in what is a rough and only approximately definite elite sector, is not very much different from that found in a number of European countries since the end of World War II.[1]

Nevertheless, there is a certain paradox in this development. The development we have in mind took off in the aftermath of the Civil War, just over a century ago, and gathered strength in two subsequent phases, namely, in the period which, starting in the 1890s, lasted until about the 1930s, and in the period following the end of World War II. The author

---

[1] Raymond Boudon, "Crise universitaire et participation," *Economies et sociétés* 4 (September 1970): 1670–1704.

happened to be an exchange student in Germany in the interim between the second and third phases, namely, in 1925. He well remembers a social occasion in the fall of 1925 in Heidelberg on which his dancing partner was curious about why he, an American, should have come to study in Germany. When I explained my interest about German culture and science, she said, condescendingly, "Oh, I understand—bei Ihnen gibt es wohl keine Wissenschaft." Even in 1925 this was scarcely a fair or competent judgment of the American academic scene, but it was much closer to being the truth then than it was later.

At any rate, as far as I personally was concerned, going to Germany rather than to an American graduate school in my own field—and this on top of a year in England at the London School of Economics—was probably an index of a certain "elitist" American attitude not uncommon at the time. This is to say that I had the usual view that European intellectual culture was superior to our own and that, in preparing myself for what at the time was a very vaguely defined career, I thought that extensive contact with that culture would be advantageous to me, not only for the specific benefit which I could derive from the studies, but also for the positive valuation attached to a European education.

This high evaluation of European culture stood at the time, as it has not ceased to do, in rather sharp contrast with the corresponding stereotypes about the "materialism" of American society and culture. It seems a special kind of paradox that this peculiarly materialistic culture, allegedly dominated by the pursuit of self-interest and profit, should have proved to be the place in which a distinguished university system grew up. Clearly, the roots of that system go back in certain respects to well before the Civil War, but there was a notable flowering in the period immediately following that war. Perhaps the appointment of Charles W. Eliot as president of Harvard in 1869 is as good a landmark as any. There were academic revivals throughout the older established universities—at Yale, Columbia, Princeton, and Pennsylvania—and in the notable new foundations, such as the Johns Hopkins University, Cornell, and the University of Chicago. The University of Michigan and the University of California, first at Berkeley, then at Los Angeles, and then Stanford University, also became important institutions.

This development rested on twin pillars. One was the land-grant policy, which was first enacted in the course of the Civil War and was overwhelmingly oriented to the training of young people in the practical arts of agriculture and mechanics. The other was the presence, even in the publicly supported institutions, of the "tradition" of liberal education. I think, for example, of the history of the University of Michigan, which early established a liberal-arts college, around which its distinguished complex of graduate and research institutions eventually grew up.

This development of American higher education also comprised a bewildering combination of public and private institutions and institutions with a variety of emphases. Eventually, however, a dominant type emerged.[2] This was the "full" university, centered on a faculty of arts and sciences, which in most cases had joint responsibility for teaching programs in a graduate school, on the one hand, and an undergraduate college, on the other. It became clear relatively early, however, that members of the faculties of such institutions would be expected to devote themselves to research objectives as a major function. This institutionalization of research as a primary academic function can be said to have gathered force in the early years of the present century. Finally, these universities did not confine themselves to the more purely academic functions at either the graduate or the undergraduate level but became, rather, the focal centers of a ring of schools of applied professional training, of which the three primary subcategories were law, medicine, and engineering; but the range substantially broadened in the course of the present century to include, for example, schools of business and public administration, education, and social welfare.

There is a certain sense in which this organization built on the traditions of European university organization. The preeminence, however, of the faculty of arts and sciences, and its relatively pure academic functions, was by and large an American development, not shared especially by the Continental institutions.[3] That the professional schools were included in the university complex we consider to be a notable feature of the development of this complex.[4] It should be noted, too, that faculties of arts and sciences usually came to include instruction and research in the whole range of intellectual disciplines, extending from mathematics and physics through the other natural sciences, the social sciences, and the humanities, and from time to time new disciplines were added to the traditional lists. Thus, economics became an established academic discipline in Great Britain in the late-nineteenth century and in this country at about the same time; sociology had a more tenuous hold in the beginning but has since become established; and psychology has experienced a phenomenal growth. An interesting case on the borderline of the social sciences and the hu-

[2] See Laurence R. Veysey, *The Emergence of the American University* (Chicago: University of Chicago Press, 1965).

[3] See Joseph Ben-David, *American Higher Education: Directions Old and New* (New York: McGraw-Hill, 1972).

[4] On certain considerations involving this development, see Talcott Parsons and Gerald M. Platt, *The American University* (Cambridge, Mass.: Harvard University Press, 1973); and Talcott Parsons, "The University 'Bundle': A Study of the Balance between Differentiation and Integration," in Neil J. Smelser and Gabriel Almond, eds., *Public Higher Education in California: Growth, Structural Change, and Conflict* (Berkeley, Calif.: University of California Press, 1974). Chap. 7 of this book.

manities is linguistics which became an established discipline only in quite recent years.

This upsurge of high-quality academic institutions, in which the development of universities, just sketched, was combined with a notable upgrading of a group of high-standard liberal-arts colleges which did not have graduate or professional schools, provided a base for the development of the larger system of higher education. Compared especially to European systems, the American had the additional feature of a much broader spread at somewhat varying levels of quality. The gradations have been continuous; that is, there has been no sharp break between elite and nonelite institutions. The hierarchy, furthermore, has not been a simple pyramid; for example, an undergraduate education in one of the better liberal-arts colleges has been fully equivalent to that offered in the undergraduate college of many major universities, though the liberal-arts colleges have not provided opportunity for graduate or professional study. Apart from this, however, there has been an enormous spread, also, with respect to the principal types of institutions. This has had a double significance for the system as a whole. In the first place, it has provided openings for some kind of higher education for an unusually large and rapidly increasing proportion of the relevant age cohorts. The American system has finally reached a stage where, even with recent cutbacks, more than 50 percent of the graduates of secondary schools go on to some kind of formal education beyond secondary school. The result has been a much broader educated base here than in most other countries.

The other particularly important advantage has been that the very extensive system of higher education has provided a job market for the people trained in the more central universities, notably in their graduate schools of arts and sciences. This market has been far more extensive here than in most European systems and has contributed to a general process of upgrading the academic standards of the system as a whole.

It would seem from these considerations that Boudon's point, which was made with special reference to the French system, is almost doubly relevant to the American.[5] There has been, that is to say, an immense quantitative increase, not merely in absolute but in relative sizes of institutions of higher education and in percentage involvements of the respective age cohorts. This has undoubtedly accentuated the phenomenon which Boudon stressed for the European systems, namely, the relative devaluation of the privilege of acquiring a higher education beyond the secondary school. To be a "college graduate" in the United States in the present generation confers nothing like the relative distinction it did when the grandparents of the recent graduates were young.

A particularly dramatic analysis of the way this situation has worked

[5] Boudon, "Crise universitaire et participation."

out has been presented in Neil Smelser's recently published monograph on public higher education in California.[6] California, in its policy for public higher education, tried to drive a "troika" of three "horses," namely, the university, the state colleges, and the community colleges. Smelser demonstrates vividly some of the strains which appeared when mere mortals attempted to manage this complex system.[7] For a time, however, it catered to virtually every interest. Thus the university sector, notably in the Berkeley and Los Angeles campuses, attained a very high level of academic distinction, particularly in research. The state colleges opened educational opportunity to a much wider sector of the age cohort than could have been admitted to the university. Finally, some higher education has been offered on a very large scale to still other sectors of the population through the community-college program.

How is one to explain this relatively sudden development of American institutions of higher learning, especially in view of the cliché that America is overwhelmingly materialistic? One very popular line of explanation must be rejected at the very start, as Max Weber, Merton, and other scholars have rejected it.[8] This is the notion that the development of knowledge, particularly in the sciences, which can be technologically applied, occurred in the first instance as a purely economic investment on the part of the business interests who expected to benefit from the technological results. After a fashion, this explanation fits with the establishment of the land-grant policy by the American Congress, and it fits in at certain later points as well; but it notably fails to fit with the high prestige that came to be accorded to "liberal education" and to pure rather than applied research.

The explanation I would like to outline is a different one—a multiple-factor explanation. It has to do with the fact that we have been dealing with a process of differentiation and other concomitant aspects of developmental change which cannot be reduced to a single set of paramount factors. We would like to suggest that there were two sets of factors in addition to the obvious economic interests. One of these lies in our own cultural background and can be focused in particular on the influence of

---

[6] Neil J. Smelser, "Growth, Structural Change, and Conflict in California Public Higher Education, 1950–1970," in Smelser and Almond, eds., *Public Higher Education in California*, pp. 9–141.

[7] Ibid.

[8] Max Weber, "Science as a Vocation," in H. H. Gerth and C. Wright Mills, eds., *From Max Weber: Essays in Sociology* (New York: Oxford University Press, 1946), pp. 129–56; and Max Weber, *The Protestant Ethic and the Spirit of Capitalism*, trans. T. Parsons (New York: Scribner's, 1930). See also Robert K. Merton, *Science, Technology, and Society in Seventeenth Century England* (New York: H. Fertig, 1970).

Puritanism or the Protestant-ethic tradition.[9] The other lies in the high prestige of European models of concern with culture.

The first of these two factors derives from an indigenous condition whose influence has already been subjected to an important analysis by Robert Merton, building on hints from Max Weber's work, and carried on in different respects by S. N. Eisenstadt and Joseph Ben-David.[10] It holds that a predisposition for rational intellectual culture was strongly present in the heritage of ascetic Protestantism which the founding fathers of the Colonial era brought to the shores of North America, notably to New England; but one should not forget that similar considerations were also important to the founders of Virginia.[11]

The second factor relates to the drive for upward mobility or success which has so strongly characterized American society almost from the beginning. Unquestionably, intellectual culture had very high prestige in Europe during the period of American history with which we are concerned. The very fact that American society was undergoing a new development of prosperity and economic productivity greatly enhanced the mutual attention Europeans and Americans paid to each other across the Atlantic. One manifestation of this attraction was intermarriage between wealthy American and aristocratic European families. Another important manifestation lay in American concern for the arts in the European style, which led to the foundation of a number of American museums, private collections, symphony orchestras, and the like by wealthy patrons. Finally, a third important manifestation was the large number of young Americans who went to Europe near the turn of the century to study, especially, though by no means exclusively, in the universities of Germany.

The first point, then, is to challenge the notion that the basic American cultural heritage, specifically that aspect of it relevant to the normative order, has been as materialistic as has so frequently been alleged. If Weber's position is historically correct, even to a moderate degree, the concern for economic productivity (with its many concomitants—notably profit) and the concern for morality and, indeed, for cognitive understanding have been by no means antithetical, or even totally unrelated, to each other. On the contrary, all of these features have common roots in a long cultural tradition of the West, certain directions of which reached a kind of culmination in Puritan England in the seventeenth century, producing an ethos

[9] See the extremely interesting analysis of this by Edward A. Tiryakian, "Neither Marx nor Durkheim—Perhaps Weber." *American Journal of Sociology* 81 (1975): 1–33.

[10] Merton, *Science, Technology, and Society.* Weber, *The Protestant Ethic and the Spirit of Capitalism;* see also the author's Introduction to this volume, pp. 13–31. S. N. Eisenstadt, ed., *The Protestant Ethic and Modernization: A Comparative View* (New York: Basic Books, 1968). Joseph Ben-David, *The Scientist's Role in Society: A Comparative Study* (Englewood Cliffs, N.J.: Prentice-Hall, 1971).

[11] See Perry Miller, *Errand into the Wilderness* (Cambridge, Mass.: Harvard University Press, 1964).

which was deeply ingrained in the early settlers of English-speaking North America.

This ethos was in certain respects the common background of the achievements of the "Anglo-Saxons" in economic productivity, in science and philosophy, and in certain aspects of the rational analysis of normative order, notably in the context of law. I think I should add that certain very central components of the modern pattern of individualism were also involved in this complex.[12]

The most important considerations on this point are that the primary cultural heritage of American society which centered on movements to the left of Anglican Protestantism throughout the Colonial period, and well down into the period of independence, was far from being, in the simple stereotypical sense, predominantly "materialistic." It seems to me open to grave doubt that even today this is the dominant meaning of institutionalized American orientations. I have long felt that the famous Protestant ethic, far from being dead, constitutes a continuing substratum of our national culture. I think Tiryakian makes a particularly important point in his contention that the Protestant ethic has been so pervasively institutionalized that it has come to form a kind of matrix that has selectively shaped the attitudes of the adherents of the other principal religious traditions that entered on the American scene in large numbers at rather late stages, namely, the tradition of Roman Catholicism, which does not greatly antedate the middle of the nineteenth century, and the tradition of Judaism, which, on anything like a mass basis, did not enter until near the end of the nineteenth century.[13]

The Protestant ethic in this sense could motivate—and, in my opinion, in historical fact has notably contributed to—both economic development and cognitive development. The record of British science in the crucial seventeenth century, including the foundation of the Royal Society, as

[12] As has been true of so many major contributions in the social sciences, Weber's analysis of the relation between the Protestant ethic and not only capitalism but other paramount features of modern "industrial" society has been the subject of extensive controversy, in the course of which many gross misinterpretations of his work have been made. We are now fortunate that three particularly competent and well-balanced surveys of literature on what has come to be called "the Protestant-ethic problem" are available in published form in English. The first of these is the one written by Dr. David Little in a bibliographical appendix to his notable study *Religion, Order, and Law* (New York: Harper Torchbooks, 1969). A second is the introduction by S. N. Eisenstadt to the volume entitled *Max Weber on Charisma and Institution Building* (Chicago: University of Chicago Press, 1968), pp. ix–lvi. The third one, by Benjamin Nelson, is Chapter 2, "Weber's Protestant Ethic: Its Origins, Wanderings and Foreseeable Futures," in Charles Y. Glock and Philip Hammond, eds., *Beyond the Classics?* (New York: Harper & Row, 1973). I would like to add another contribution to this list. This is the paper by Tiryakian, "Neither Marx nor Durkheim—Perhaps Weber." This paper is not, however, a survey of the literature, but the latter part of it on Weber contains an extremely insightful discussion of the Protestant-ethic problem in its relevance to the understanding of American society.

[13] Tiryakian, "Neither Marx nor Durkheim—Perhaps Weber."

analyzed in Merton's classic study, shows that as early as the first part of the American Colonial period the potentialities of the Protestant ethic for the promotion of science were already strong.[14] In this respect, then, there was not—as the common sense of today's intellectuals would often have it—a basic conflict between "materialistic" concern with economic productivity and "idealistic" dedication to intellectual productivity, particularly in the sciences and in the relevant branches of philosophy. Rather, both potentialities were built into the primary cultural heritage and have developed in response to differing circumstances in the environment of the cultural heritage.

One of the difficulties obscuring this point lies in the tendency to confuse the relationship between materialism and idealism with what, in this context, seems to be a secondary, though extremely important, distinction between concern for collective interest, on the one hand, and the pursuit of individual self-interest on the other. The relationship between the materialism-nonmaterialism dichotomy and the collectivism-individualism dichotomy clearly goes back to the Puritan heritage. Robert Bellah, in particular, stresses the extent to which the early Puritan settlers placed emphasis on the collective conception.[15] He quotes at length, for example, from the sermon delivered by John Winthrop on the evening before the landing in Massachusetts Bay in 1630. Quite clearly, Winthrop's emphasis was on the goal of setting up a truly Christian commonwealth on those barren shores, a conception which was otherwise phrased as establishing the "city on the hill." [16]

However, it is also well known that, certainly by the time of its Puritan phase, as distinguished from the original Calvinism, ascetic Protestantism had come to incorporate a very important individualistic component. In both England and the United States this component became increasingly prominent, certainly by the generation of the founding fathers of the republic if not before. The philosophical father of this aspect was John Locke, the primary ideologist, as it were, of the Glorious Revolution of 1688 in England and a major figure in the background of many intellectuals, both American and European.[17] One need perhaps mention only Thomas Jefferson and Benjamin Franklin among the founding fathers. Franklin is particularly important in this connection because of his role is creating a favorable cultural atmosphere for the pursuit of scientific interests. It might be remembered that Franklin was the most important

---

[14] Merton, *Science, Technology, and Society.*

[15] See Robert Bellah, *The Broken Covenant* (forthcoming).

[16] Cf. Miller, *Errand into the Wilderness.*

[17] John Locke, *The Second Treatise of Civil Government: An Essay Concerning the True Original Extent and End of Civil Government, and A Letter Concerning Toleration* (1690), edited with a revised introduction, by J. W. Gough (New York: McMillan, 1956).

founder of the American Philosophical Society, the oldest learned society in the United States.

It seems to me that the special salience of the syndrome of economic individualism—that is, the version of Utilitarian derivatives, which stressed and indeed glorified the rational pursuit of economic self-interest—is not in any simple sense attributable either to the Puritan tradition or to Locke's secularized version of it but rather to circumstances which developed in England and the United States mainly in the nineteenth century. Seen in this light, economic individualism can quite correctly be said to have served as the groundwork of the predominant ideology of what, following Alfred Marshall, we may call the "free enterprise" system—to avoid to some extent the connotations of the term "capitalism." [18]

With reference to the central problem of this essay, however, I should continue to insist that the development of economic individualism was not as such the central meaning of this kind of individualistic stance but was rather an ideologically exaggerated branch of the main cultural tradition. That this branch should not be permitted to stand alone seems to be made clear not only by its historical connections with the more collective emphasis but by the fact that certain of the cultural movements with which we are primarily concerned, though they are clearly individualistic in a certain emphasis, do not involve in quite the classical economic sense the rational pursuit of self-interest. This seems to be preeminently true of the commitment of motivation and careers to intellectual enterprises. This was an endemic feature of what I still think it is legitimate to consider a part of the main American cultural-normative tradition. Indeed, it is my view that the predominant trend has been toward a synthesis of the individualistic and the collective components. It seems to me that there has been a kind of a natural, ready-made synthesis, at least until very recently, in Great Britain. Most British economists and much ideology on the non-socialist side have strongly stressed the "rational pursuit of self-interest" in the best Utilitarian tradition,[19] but this emphasis has been strongly counteracted by a tradition of concern for the national collective welfare, even though the form it takes be imperialism, to say nothing of the welfare-state developments of more recent times. It seems probable that the tendency to bifurcation along these lines has in the American case been encouraged by lack of a nationalistic-aristocratic tradition of the British variety. In the absence of such a tradition, it has been easier to maximize the appeal to self-interest and to contribute to the ascendency of this syndrome in a quasiofficial ideological context.

---

[18] Alfred Marshall, *Principles of Economics*, 8th ed. (London: Macmillan, 1925).

[19] See Elie Halévy, *The Growth of Philosophic Radicalism*, trans. Mary Morris (New York: Macmillan, 1928); first published in French as *La Formation du radicalisme philosophique*, 3 vols. (Paris: F. Alcan, 1901–4). See also Lionel Robbins, *An Essay on the Nature and Significance of Economic Science*, 2nd ed. (London: Macmillan, 1935).

Certain tendencies to redress the balance have, at least, been conspicuous—in an intellectually limited sphere, to be sure—in the social sciences; we may note, for example, the development of the concept "institutionalized individualism." [20]

I shall return to this issue, but I should first like to introduce a hypothesis as to the nature of the process of social change out of which the American university system developed. As in other cases, a primary reference point for the beginning of analysis lies in the concept of a process of structural differentiation.[21] The differentiation I have in mind in the present case is not primarily one which has occurred within the traditional rubrics of distribution of collective organizations in the society, but somewhat cuts across them. I think the keynote is the differentiation between the two primary aspects of the instrumental-rational orientation, historically rooted in the Protestant ethic, which have just been discussed. What happened was a gradual process of differentiation of the more intellectual and cognitive orientational contexts from that of economic productivity. Business firms tended to become more and more definitely specialized as profit-oriented economic organizations. At the same time there grew up a societal "investment"—which was partly but by no means exclusively or predominantly financial—in the development of what we may call "cognitive production." This built on the general urge toward the universalization of education, which had started nearly a generation before the Civil War at the level of public elementary education and had then not only spread to increasingly larger proportions of the relevant age cohorts but had undergone a process of upgrading of educational quality to progressively higher levels.

It is mainly as a culminating stage in this upgrading process that the expansion of higher education, which is our primary concern in this paper, is to be seen historically. The structure of the system of economic enterprise has been such that a major development in these directions had to be, in the first instance, organizationally independent of economic enterprise. However important in-service training in industrial firms and industrial research organizations may have been, they could not become the main organizational sponsors and the main symbolic legitimizers of the complex of higher education and research.

[20] Though Bellah emphasizes his intention to stress this concept in his introduction to *The Broken Covenant,* the actual text of the book, as I have seen it, in fact fails to fulfill this promise. It seems to me a particularly crucial one for the appraisal of the issues with which Bellah is concerned.

[21] For the case of the Industrial Revolution, for example, see Neil J. Smelser, *Social Change in the Industrial Revolution* (London: Routledge & Kegan Paul, 1959), and David S. Landes, *The Unbound Prometheus: Technological Change and Industrial Development in Western Europe from 1750 to the Present* (London: Cambridge University Press, 1972).

Parallel considerations apply in a very interesting way to government. Unlike the situation in most of Europe, the main system of higher education here has received mixed government and private support and supervision. If anything, in the crucial phase of development of the university system, the private institutions tended to take the lead; but in the more recent period of growth, especially in the last fifteen years or so, massive support from public authority has been of central importance, in the first instance at the state level and secondarily at the local or community level, especially in the larger cities. It is very notable that, with minor exceptions, such as the three military academies, there is no such thing as a national university in the United States, in the sense of one established and basically controlled by the federal government. It is of course true that the federal government has intervened massively since World War II in the financial support of research and has gradually extended support for training programs in the sciences and the professions, such as medicine and engineering. By and large, however, the federal government has carefully avoided an openly directive role and has relied heavily on panels drawn from outside the government for evaluating proposals for research grants and training programs.

The circumstances in which government involvement in higher education and research developed favored a relatively decentralized system, one in which the teaching and research institutions, and the professional groups whose primary social location was within these institutions, enjoyed a considerable degree of autonomy. This means that there is a parallel between the process which led to the differentiation of the economic from the cognitive-intellectual concerns of the society, on the one hand, and the process which led to the differentiation of both from incorporation in the sphere of governmental function, on the other. At the same time, contrary to the tendency of many left-oriented interpreters to see government control around every corner of the winding way of academic development, these processes have not resulted in what is in any simple sense a government-sponsored or controlled system.

My contention, then, is that what has occurred in this country has been the development of what is, relatively speaking, a highly autonomous system. It is notable, of course, that the primary center of gravity of the research function has come to be located in the universities, not in organizationally separate research institutions on the model, say, of the Soviet Academy of Sciences. I have repeated this formula in print on a number of occasions,[22] but I think it has to be repeated once again in the present context. The most convenient reference is to the frequently expressed opinion of Daniel Bell, who belongs in a somewhat different sociological tradition from either Shils or myself, that the universities have come to be the most important sector of the American socal struc-

[22] See Parsons and Platt, *The American University*, esp. chap. 2, pp. 33–102.

ture. Bell goes on to say that the underlying reason for this is the development and mobilization of a new but crucially important resource in the operations of the society, namely, "theoretical knowledge." [23] I would here stress the term "theoretical." The important contributions of the educational system have mainly not been based in the old-fashioned practical-empiricist tradition but in the more theoretically oriented disciplines and subsectors of disciplines.

Our hypothesis was that the emergence of the higher-level cognitive complex in this context was the outcome of a process of differentiation— a process of differentiation occurring by and large between the two primary factors or orientational aspects of the underlying "rational" cultural tradition, namely, the one which was economically oriented, and the other which was cognitively oriented.

I agree with David Landes, in his analysis of the Industrial Revolution, that an essential component of such a process of differentiation is an impressive and quantitatively large payoff in advantage to those who have a "consumer's" interest in the process.[24] In the famous case of the British textile industry, which was the leader in the early Industrial Revolution, it was the massive cheapening of commercially acceptable cotton goods which constituted this payoff.

I would like to suggest that, for the development of the system of higher education, the payoff took the primary form of enhancement of prestige; this linked in with both the individual and the collective versions of the success orientation of American society. Prestige consisted, in this case, of the capacity of American groups to identify with the European models which were most important at the time and then to emulate and possibly even surpass them. In other words, a relatively massive increase in the availability of high-quality cognitive output was an essential condition of this process of differentiation, and the domestic consumers of this output were, on the whole, the prestige-hungry groups in the upper reaches of American society. They had become acutely conscious of the sense in which America's cultural status had come to be defined as inferior to that of the principal European nations, and they were, shall we say, desperately anxious at least to catch up, if not to excel. This consideration applied at the individual level and, in the relatively early stages, was particularly exemplified by the young American scholars who undertook, often at considerable personal sacrifice, studies at European universities in the late-nineteenth and early-twentieth centuries. At the collective level it was exemplified by the willingness of a notable generation of academic administrators to mobilize financial backing, much of which came from the business community, for the establishment of facilities for higher

---

[23] See Daniel Bell, *The Coming of Post-Industrial Society* (New York: Basic Books, 1973).

[24] Landes, *The Unbound Prometheus.*

education in which the research component came to be more and more strongly emphasized. Such figures as Eliot and Gilman and, in a slightly later generation, Harper and Nicholas Murray Butler, and also Andrew White at Cornell, were prototypes of this orientation.

I have the impression that these people were in a way representative of the business elite who, from the point of view of their personal careers, had not opted for a business role. Eliot is a striking example; he was the scion of a prominent Boston mechant family, who, instead of entering the family business, opted to become a scientist and, at the time of his appointment—at the age of thirty-five—to the presidency of Harvard, was an assistant professor of chemistry at MIT. The fascination of European culture was highly manifest in that generation of American upper-class young people. The James family was an interesting combination in that Henry moved permanently to England and became a prominent English literary figure, whereas William studied abroad, more in Germany than in England, and returned to the United States to become a leader in the development of American psychology and philosophy. Perhaps even the career of Henry Adams is relevant; although he never settled into an American academic career, the author of *Mont-Saint-Michel and Chartres* was surely one of the preeminent Americans of his generation to be deeply immersed in European high culture. My suggestion is, therefore, that without this reinforcement from the upper business groups and the willingness of some rather maverick members of those groups to devote their careers to this development, it probably could not have succeeded on anything like the scale that it did. In a certain sense it was a recapitulation of the involvement in European culture of a notable group of the founding fathers, among whom we have mentioned Franklin and Jefferson, both of whom undertook extremely important diplomatic missions in Europe in connection with the movement for American independence. Jacksonian Populism diminished this sensitivity of American society to aristocratically based European cultural influences, but the generation of the post-Civil War period revived that sensitivity at a crucial time from the point of view of the development of higher education and research.

This discussion of the process of differentiation suggests the relevance of three components of the paradigm of progressive social change with which I have worked.[25] These are adaptive upgrading, and value-generalization.

Adaptive upgrading refers to the meeting of the needs of what is, at the level of prestige and influence, analogous to a market demand. In the case of the Industrial Revolution it was quite literally a market demand;

[25] Cf. Talcott Parsons, "Comparative Studies and Evolutionary Change," in Ivan Vallier, ed., *Comparative Methods in Sociology* (Berkeley, Calif.: University of California Press, 1971), pp. 97–139. Also in *Social Systems and the Evolution of Action Theory* (New York: Free Press, 1977), Chap. 11.

in the case of the system of higher education, however, it seems to have been a hunger for the prestige which was derivable from some kind of identification with the standards of high European culture. As I have noted above, this hunger applied not only to the cognitive fields, but also to the arts, though perhaps, in American conditions, it was a little easier to institutionalize it in the predominantly cognitive fields of the sciences. This hunger was felt by the members of an increasingly affluent class, who in various ways were willing and able to provide financial support for the kinds of developments we have been talking about. On the liberal-education and research level, then, government involvement came a good deal later, and at a time when the practical technological payoff had become more prominent.

It is also interesting to observe the relation that developed between people identified with more or less established local "patriciates"—as in Boston, New York, Philadephia, and Baltimore—and some of the big "tycoons" of the new industrial development—the Rockefellers, Carnegies, and Mellons—who were, by comparison, *parvenus* and who had trouble in gaining full social acceptance even in the United States, to say nothing of European society. We suggest that their susceptibility to financial appeals for nonprofit causes, notably in the cultural area of the intellectual disciplines and the arts, was related to their *parvenu* status. After all, the Rockefellers and Carnegie established the first really large American philanthropic foundations, both of which have played a notable role in the development of the American academic system. The munificent gift of John D. Rockefeller, Sr., which made possible the founding of the University of Chicago is an outstanding symbol of this tendency. It is interestng that the Mellons, though they have supported such institutions as the Carnegie-Mellon Institute of Technology in Pittsburgh, have been more concerned with art. The fact that the late Andrew Mellon established the National Gallery of Art in Washington and donated to it his immensely impressive private collection of European paintings is a symbol of the adoption of the life-style of the higher reaches of European society by some American business leaders.

It is exceedingly important to note that in both the more definitely cognitive fields and in the arts there was a very strong emphasis on quality, The American academic founders of the new phase, men like Eliot, Gilman, White, and Harper, had an eye for academic excellence and tried to attract persons of great intellectual distinction to their faculties. Similar is Andrew Mellon's choice of Bernard Berenson and Sir Joseph—later Lord—Duveen as mediators in the transfer of ownership of important European art to the United States. We could multiply examples.

The American emphasis on quality in both the cognitive domain and the arts seems to be an example of the far from perfect but still impressive integration of cultural values with the prestige values which helped to motivate financial support. If we take the case of art, which provides a less controversial example than science, we can say that classical masterpieces of Renaissance or Dutch art are the ones which have commanded the highest prices where anything approaching a free market for such masterpieces has existed. The British National Gallery's acquisition of the famous *Cartoon* of Leonardo Da Vinci and the New York Metropolitan Museum's acquisition of Rembrandt's *Aristotle* at what were reported to be extremely high prices are cases in point.

Correspondingly, American standards of academic excellence have largely been modeled on the best of Europe, and the influx of European scholars, not unconnected with political disturbances in Europe, has contributed in a major way to this excellence.[26] Einstein's arrival of course somewhat preceded the migration forced by the Nazi movement, but in the physical sciences a very substantial number of European migrants were at least in a partial sense exiles, and to a lesser degree this was the case in other intellectual fields.

My suggestion is, therefore, that the initial payoff, outside the academic system itself, came from those socially elite elements who for complex reasons had a deep interest in identifying with and emulating the higher European cultural achievements. In the early stages of the expansion of the academic system this was a sufficiently extensive market to support the earlier take-off phases. In the later phases, however, other considerations have certainly played a role.

It may be of interest that I first met Edward Shils when I had a visiting appointment at the University of Chicago for the summer quarter of 1937. He organized an informal discussion group on matters of sociological theory during that quarter. As it happened, I was then engaged in reading the galley proofs of *The Structure of Social Action,* which appeared in the late fall of the same year.[27]

Whatever other merits *The Structure of Social Action* may or may not have had, it did constitute a major operation of international communication in theoretical sociology, above all through the prominence given in it to the work of Durkheim and Max Weber. It seems to me that the influence of both of these figures on American sociology had up to that time been minimal. One might almost put it that Durkheim had been badly misinterpreted, first, by social psychologists, as the group-mind theorist, and, second, by the anthropologists, as the armchair anthropologist. An extensive sympathetic account of the theoretical nature of his contributions

---

[26] See Donald Fleming and Bernard Bailyn, eds., *The Intellectual Migration: Europe and America, 1930–1960* (Cambridge, Mass.: Harvard University Press, 1969).

[27] Talcott Parsons, *The Structure of Social Action* (New York: McGraw-Hill, 1937).

had not really been provided by anyone in the English language. Weber, on the other hand, was virtually unknown in the English-speaking world; and, where he was known, it was in a narrow historical sense for his essay on *The Protestant Ethic and the Spirit of Capitalism*.[28] I think that it is correct to say that as a comparative sociologist he was virtually unknown in the mid-1930s, though Shils, as one of a few, had obviously thoroughly familiarized himself with Weber's work at that time.[29] Since that summer I have always considered Shils to be a major partner with myself in developing and communicating sociological theory at the high intellectual level of these two founders of the theoretical discipline and in subsequently being concerned with problems which had been to a very large extent shaped by their work. I think it fair to say that this use of certain European models had a major transformative effect on American sociological thinking and contributed importantly to raising the levels of theoretical sophistication in our discipline. In all probability I would not have undertaken my part of the venture had I not, as late as the mid-1920s, undertaken European study. And of the two countries in which I did study, namely, England and Germany, by far the more profound intellectual influences stemmed from the German experience, notably from the work of Max Weber. Though Weber had died five years before I went to Germany, Heidelberg, where I studied, had been his home for many years, and his intellectual influence was clearly dominant in the relevant part of the Heidelberg academic community.

In connection with the sociology of sociology, it will be remembered that in many places a major rationale for paying attention to this discipline was that it could form an intellectual groundwork for the field of social welfare and the emerging profession of social work. It seems to me a notable fact about the University of Chicago that these two sets of interests did not fuse there at all; instead, a sharp division took place in the face of the very notable development of social work in Chicago, connected above all with the name of Jane Addams. In the long run the University of Chicago department of sociology refused to have any close association with the social-work contingent in the pre-Weber/Durkheim phases of the development of sociology itself. It is perhaps worth noting also that when sociology finally came to Harvard as a recognized discipline, it for all practical puroposes replaced a modified program in the field of social work known as "social ethics." At Columbia, too, sociology was in its earlier days closely affiliated with social work, but by the time of Robert MacIver an essential separation had taken place; and in the influential phase of Columbia sociology just terminated, in which the dominant figures have been Robert Merton and Paul Lazersfeld, only very tenuous relations to

[28] Weber, *The Protestant Ethic.*

[29] Edward A. Shils, *The Intellectuals and the Powers, and Other Essays* (Chicago: University of Chicago Press, 1972).

social work existed, in spite of the fact that certain theoretical ideas influential in the social-work field had been originated largely by Merton and were further developed and popularized by certain of his students.[30]

As a final note, it may be remarked that Shils in the Chicago sociological community stood out in his graduate-student and early staff years as a kind of maverick, certainly in part because of his strong interest in Europe sociology; for the Chicago tradition had been overwhelmingly American in its intellectual background, in spite of its early emphasis on the work of Georg Simmel.[31]

Perhaps the considerations that I have sketchily presented and developed in this paper present at least the beginnings of an explanation of a very important institutional development in American society which the dominant ethos of American social science, which gives such heavy weight to economic considerations, has been unable, it seems to me, to explain satisfactorily. As Gerald Platt and I especially stressed in our recent book, *The American University,* and as I further developed in my contribution to the recent book edited by Smelser and Almond on higher education in California, there has never been any serious question of an organizational separation of the natural sciences—which, after all, have been the source of by far the most important technological payoffs—from the social sciences and the humanities. It is one of the primary features of what we have called the academic "bundle" that in the core arts and sciences sector of university organization, in spite of certain organizational variations, the whole range of intellectual disciplines—natural sciences, social sciences, and humanities—has been included.[32] If technological payoff had been as decisive a factor in the development of academic institutions as some have contended, it is hard to see why the natural sciences would not far more frequently have separated themselves off from the other disciplines in separate faculties—if not in separate institutions. We think the persistence of this aspect of what we have called the "bundle" is important evidence in favor of the kind of explanation of the process of institutionalization

[30] Cf. Robert K. Merton, "Social Structure and Anomie," in *Social Theory and Social Structure,* rev. ed. (New York: Free Press, 1957), pp. 131–60; also see, for example, Richard A. Cloward and Lloyd E. Ohlin, *Delinquency and Opportunity: A Theory of Delinquent Gangs* (New York: Free Press of Glencoe, 1961).

[31] English translations of a number of Simmel's essays appeared in the *American Journal of Sociology* in the years 1896–1906. Many of these essays and others have been reprinted in English in the following volumes: Robert E. Park and Ernest W. Burgess, eds., *Introduction to the Science of Sociology,* 2d ed. (Chicago: University of Chicago Press, 1924); Edgar F. Borgatta and Henry J. Meyer, eds., *Sociological Theory: Present Day Sociology from the Past* (New York: Knopf, 1956); and Kurt H. Wolff, ed., *Georg Simmel, 1858–1918: A Collection of Essays, with Translations and a Bibliography* (Columbus: Ohio State University Press, 1959).

[32] Cf. Parsons, "The University Bundle," in Smelser and Almond, eds., *Public Higher Education in California.* Chap. 7 of this book.

of a university system which I have put forward above. By and large, the sources of this spectrum of intellectual disciplines have been deeply embedded in the European model of intellectual culture which has played such an important role in the American development.

One particularly interesting case may be noted. Several American academic institutions have been primarily concerned with training in technological fields; these are the so-called "engineering schools." One of the most eminent of these is the Massachusetts Institute of Technology. On the hypothesis that technological payoff is the big factor in academic development, it seems to me that what has happened at MIT would be exceedingly difficult to explain. In the first place, MIT evolved broadly from a training school for applied engineers into one of the most distinguished institutions in the basic natural sciences underlying engineering. Its physicists, chemists, and, for example, microbiologists have been among the most famous in the relatively "pure" aspects of these disciplines. However, MIT did not remain a school of engineering and theoretical natural science; for more than a generation now, it has been progressively expanding into other fields. It is well known that it has one of the most distinguished departments of economics in the world, and it has supported distinguished work in various other social-science fields, such as the study of organizations and international relations. It has not established an independent department of sociology, but a great deal of important sociological work goes on at MIT. Its more recently established and perhaps most prestigious competitor, the California Institution of Technology, has followed a similar path and has recently been engaged in a definite campaign to strengthen its work in social science. Somewhat similar things are true of Carnegie-Mellon in Pittsburgh and other institutions which started as more or less specialized engineering schools.

When I have spoken of prestige, especially the prestige of certain sectors of European culture, I have definitely meant not to use this concept as indicating a crassly "materialistic" interest in the successful establishment of academic work in various fields. My own position is the direct contrary of this, since I contend that the economic importance of these cultural complexes has been a reflection of their levels and excellence and achievement in predominantly noneconomic contexts. At the extreme of the "pure" intellectual disciplines, the question of strictly economic applicability has been on the whole quite subordinate.[33]

[33] There is a famous story which may or may not be apocryphal—this hardly matters—that concerns the mood of the Harvard department of mathematics a generation and more ago where on some festive occasion a toast is said to have been drunk to the discipline of mathematics, and the toast ran, "To mathematics! May she never have any practical applications." It seems to me that this incident, whether it actually happened or not, may serve as a symbol of the kind of explanation I wish to put forward of the very big development of institutionalization in the academic world.

7. The University "Bundle":
A Study of the Balance Between
Differentiation and Integration

THIS PAPER GROWS OUT of a dialogue between Neil Smelser and myself about his study of the California state system of public higher education during the last twenty years. The university system in California has been conspicuous for its broad organizational syndrome—what Smelser calls the bundle. This syndrome has especially characterized the elite sector of the American system of higher education generally, concentrating on the "full" university. Smelser has expressed considerable skepticism about the viability of this syndrome, which he believes is largely responsible for the state of "functional overloading" and results from what he calls a "resistance to differentiation."

I am inclined to regard this functional overloading of the university as mainly a consequence of its extremely rapid growth, including a generous measure of inflationary pressure (see Chapter 7 of *The American University*). It seems substantially less likely that it results, as Smelser suggests, mainly from what he calls "resistance to differentiation." By this latter phrase he mainly refers to resistance to the separating out of the various components of what we are calling the bundle. He speaks especially of the possibilities of the organizational separation of teaching from research, and of the separation of what in California terms is called lower division teaching from the last two years of the undergraduate program. He does not, so far as I am aware, stress the undesirability of a continuing association between faculties of arts and sciences and professional faculties in the same universities.

From *Public Higher Education in California,* Neil J. Smelser and Gabriel Almond, eds. (Berkeley: University of California Press, 1974), pp. 275–299. Copyright © 1974 by The Regents of the University of California; reprinted by permission of the University of California Press.

There have also been external sources of overloading, especially of the faculty role, as well as of those internal to the university. I think here of the vast increase in interinstitutional communication and citizenship, through such media as conferences and the development of the activities and size of professional associations, especially though not exclusively in the disciplines. The typical elite university professor has indeed become a man who is subject to a multiplicity of demands.

It is very difficult to judge how much of this involvement should be regarded as excessive. A good deal of such involvement in the recent past probably should be. The main object of the present paper, however, is to argue what in a sense is the obverse case—namely, that great benefits accrue to the modern university system from the connectedness of the various components of the bundle.

The aim of the present paper is to probe more deeply into both the nature and the functional significance of the bundle. It thus constitutes a kind of epilogue to the book, *The American University,* on which I recently collaborated with Gerald Platt.[1]

It seems best to begin with an outline of the bundle. The first primary characteristic is the prominence in the typical high-level American university of a faculty of arts and sciences. Such a faculty is normally organized as a set of partially independent departments, each of which focuses on one of the well-recognized intellectual disciplines. Such faculties cover the range of these disciplines, which are conventionally grouped into three main categories—humanities, natural sciences, and social sciences. Although there are overlappings, this is a structural uniformity. Some units are organized for research and teaching on other bases than disciplines, but they are on the whole secondary to the main departmental structure.

In addition to their range of intellectual content, such faculties are multifunctional in another principal respect: they combine research and teaching. A highly conspicuous feature of the American university in its development during the present century has been the institutionalization of the research function as fundamental to the professional role. Research is no longer carried on by interested amateurs, but is highly professionalized. At the same time, most such professional research is not carried on in specialized research institutes outside the university, but as part of the academic professional's role within the university. The function most closely associated with research itself is graduate training of future members of the academic profession who typically will be researchers and teachers. An important part of this function is carried on through various modes of formal and informal apprenticeship.

Another prominent feature of the bundle is that the faculties of arts and sciences typically are engaged in general education, primarily at the under-

[1] Talcott Parsons and Gerald M. Platt, *The American University* (Cambridge: Harvard University Press, 1973).

graduate level. In part this undergraduate teaching has been oriented to certified qualifications for later occupational roles, but on the whole this has been declining in relative importance and is less prominent in the higher prestige institutions than the lower. Of course, one important function has been to qualify students for entry into both graduate school and post-graduate professional schools. The undergraduate college within the university was not displaced by graduate schools; rather, a kind of symbiosis has developed between the two. Organizational forms vary, but this is clearly a central pattern.

Another conspicuous feature of the American university is the absorption into the university of such professional schools as law, medicine, and engineering. These have increasingly become integral parts of the university, although they retain some autonomy. There has also been a notable development in recent decades of new professional schools in such fields as education, administration, and social work. The professional schools in general, and increasingly, have also institutionalized research as part of the professional role structure of their faculty members, and this in particular binds them to faculties of arts and sciences.

In addition to these formal, structural aspects of the bundle, there are two other important features. First, although there is no formal organizational component especially concerned with the function of supplying knowledge, competence, and cognitive standards to that diffuse group called intellectuals, there is no doubt of the universities' importance in an interchange with outside elements. Some members of university faculties can rightly be classified as intellectuals. The same term, however, can be applied to others, such as writers, journalists, politicians, artists, or generally interested citizens. Most of them are college graduates, and they are likely to be in close touch with currents of thought within the univesities. In the present century the universities have developed a central role in this context which did not exist to the same degree in the nineteenth century.

The final characteristic of the bundle is more highly formalized; namely, the existence of a ramified nexus of relationships, dealing with intellectual subject matters, which operate across the divisions into particular university units. Perhaps the most conspicuous aspect of this nexus is the set of national and international associations concerned with particular disciplines. Such associations started to develop at about the same time that the university structure was taking shape, in the latter nineteenth and early twentieth centuries. In addition to associations organized around particular disciplines, a considerable number were built on cross-disciplinary bases. The existence of this nexus means that the typical university faculty member is in rather intensive communication with colleagues outside his own institution, both within his own discipline and in wider relationships. For example, the members of such organizations as the National Academy of Sciences, the American Philosophical Society, and the American Academy of Arts and Sciences include not only representatives of a variety of disciplines and people attached to a variety of academic institutions, but a significant minority whose occupations are not academic.

Clearly, the bundle which constitutes the typical American university nexus has two primary aspects. It embodies a rather sharply differentiated institutionalization of functions that are concentrated on cognitive concerns more or less for their own sake. This is particularly true of research, at least in some sectors, and of graduate training of future academic professionals. The relatively high differentiation and consequent autonomy of this "core" complex, as Platt and I have called it, is both characteristic and relatively recent in the present state of development.

And there is also a complex set of concerns and interests that brings the university in contact with nonacademic sectors of the society. The two massively formal ones are the undergraduate college and the so-called professional schools. The great majority of college graduates will not become academic professionals, and the great majority of professional school graduates will not teach but practice. A substantial proportion, probably a considerable majority, of "intellectuals" are not academic professionals either, and this dual reference of the academic system is vital.

Some Theoretical Considerations

The remainder of this paper will be concerned with the parallels between the modern economy and the cognitive complex institutionalized in the modern university. It is an essential keynote that these two subsystems of action will not only be compared, but that they stand in a relation of developmental succession to each other. That is, the modern economy was largely a product of the Industrial Revolution, and some features of it became a primary storm center of social conflict and preoccupation of ideological discussions, centering notably about the role of labor and capital. The rise of the cognitive complex to a position of comparable centrality is a culminating consequence of the Educational Revolution, as we have called it. This, notably at the level of the role structure of higher education, has become a storm center of disturbance and a primary focus of ideological preoccupation centered on the status of cognitive standards, of the academic profession and of students. The shift has been from an adaptive level within the social system—the economy, to the adaptive level in the general system of action, with special stress on the *cultural* level.*

There are important structural differences in the economy between the units primarily concerned with the production of goods—manufacturing—

* On this background, see *The American University*.

and those primarily concerned with mediating economic to noneconomic sectors of the society—sales organizations. We suggest that there is a parallel distinction of organizational type in the cognitive complex. Research is the function most directly concerned with the production of new knowledge. Teaching, as a function, is more concerned with mediating the output of this knowledge to various categories of the population not equipped simply to take it as it emerges from the research process. Platt and I have developed a concept originating in a characteristic of professional schools which we apply to other mediating functions of the university. This is the concept of the *clinical focus,* the mobilization of revelant knowledge for the effective performance of some function other than the pursuit of knowledge itself. This concept is especially relevant in the field of medicine. Obviously the organization of knowledge in a clinical context is very different from that of intellectual disciplines.

The so-called science of medicine is not itself a discipline, but a body of knowledge put together for its relevance to the medical practitioner and drawn from many different disciplines. One reason why the intrinsically intimate relations between law and the social sciences have been hampered is that law is primarily a clinical discipline especially concerned with the settlement of cases, and its mode of organization cuts across that of the social science disciplines. There are parallel factors in the reorganization of knowledge appropriate to the undergraduate teaching functions and the output which is revelant to intellectuals.

Clinically relevant knowledge, however, is still subject to the fundamental cognitive canons of validity, although the standards of significance vary somewhat from the primarily cognitive focus. Cognitive interests have to be combined with noncognitive in this whole range of applied or articulated contexts. The valuation of health is not a cognitive interest, nor is the valuation of satisfactory settlement of disputes and maintenance of normative social order which are the double focus of law. Given the importance of the clinical contexts, what constitutes the social machinery of mediation betwen the core aspects of the academic system and these other partially, if not primarily, noncognitive contexts? The range of clinical foci are analogous to the problems of sales organization in the market systems.

In a second basic parallel to the economy, generalized symbolic media of interchange play a crucial part in the academic system—both internally and in its relations with the outside world—analogous to the economic role of money. Because knowledge is primarily focused in the cultural system, which is related to society at the level of the general system of action, Platt and I have given great prominence to *intelligence,* which we conceived as a generalized symbolic medium of interchange with functions comparable to those of money in the economy.[2] This unfamiliar use of

[2] *Ibid.,* chap. 2.

the concept of intelligence is distinct from its more common meaning as a trait of the individual personality.[3]

As a generalized medium of interchange we conceive intelligence as circulating. It can be acquired by individuals—for example, through learning, and it is spent as a resource which facilitates the solution of cognitively significant problems. It should, however, be clearly distinguished from knowledge, just as money should be distinguished from concrete commodities. The parallel to the point that money has no "value in use" also applies to intelligence. We may say that a person has more than the usual intelligence, but this should be understood as being parallel to the statement that a man has more wealth than others. In neither case is this category of "possession" a trait of his personality.

The cognitive enterprise in institutionalized at the social level, and a primary aspect of its institutionalization is the modern university with the bundle structure. As the social level the university and its subunits, as well as some of the interuniversity associations, constitute communities. Therefore, we have paid special attention to the generalized medium, at the social-system level, that is particularly concerned with the integrative functions centered on various kinds of community within the larger society.[4] This generalized medium we have called *influence,* and we have tried to combine the treatment of intelligence on the one hand, and influence on the other.

We conceive all generalized media, like money, to be contentless. The idea that money has no value in use, but only value as a medium of exchange, is very familiar from the work of the classical economists. Similarly, intelligence is not knowledge but the capacity to mobilize what it takes to produce or command knowledge and the other primary outputs and factors of the cognitive system. Intelligence can be converted into influence, and sometimes vice versa, through the *institutionalization* of cognitive functions in social organizations. So far as this occurs, cognitive excellence and cognitive achievement will acquire institutionalized *prestige* —the primary institutional way that influence as a medium acquires its legitimacy and justification. Those with prestige have access to influence, and through influence the capacity to persuade others of the merits of their positions on various matters. But we do not *conceive* influence to be intrinsically persuasive, as items of concrete information may be. It is, rather, a way of securing control over intrinsic persuaders, like information or commitments to action, and over factors of persuasiveness.

As a social structure, the university is differentiated by the relative primacy of cognitive functions, but within this conception it has all the primary features of an institutionalized complex. Cognitive function is

[3] *Ibid.,* see especially chap. 2 and the Technical Appendix.

[4] Talcott Parsons, *Politics and Social Structure* (New York: Free Press, 1969).

primarily anchored at the cultural level. For this reason, in our classification of social subsystems we placed the university in the "fiduciary" system. As an institutional complex, the university holds fiduciary responsibility for the maintenance, transmission, and development of knowledge in particular, and of cognitive functions and resources in general.

Finally, we should outline the units in the nexus of relationships where intelligence and influence have a combined relevance. First, there is intensity of concern. This is at its highest level for the academic professional as an individual, and for departments, faculties, universities, scholarly associations, and the like as collectivities. To become an academic professional is to accept a major stake in implementing the standards central to the cognitive function—a far greater stake than other occupational groups impose on their members, and the same applies *pari passu* to academically specialized collectivities.

Intensity in this sense may be regarded as the primary index of level of commitment to the values of cognitive rationality, the paramount value-pattern institutionalized in differentiated academic organizations. Among the manifestations of intense commitments in this direction are high valuation of knowledge and competence and high respect for the standards of cognitive validity and significance. It is, above all, in the intensity of their commitments to cognitive values that the special position of faculty members—especially senior faculty members—in the academic system is grounded. That commitment underlies the institutions of both tenure and academic freedom. The relative disadvantagedness of students in these respects is grounded in the recency of their involvement in the academic world and the fact that, for most of them, this involvement will be temporary and not—as it is for academic professionals—a career commitment.

The second unit is the extensive nexus within which the combined intelligence-influence medium can be effectively used, parallel to Adam Smith's famous idea of the "extent of the market." An important part of our argument rests on this nexus and the possibilities it opens up for the analogue of Smith's division of labor: namely, the differentiation of the components of the cognitive complex. These possibilities constitute a particularly important condition for a high level of the "gross cognitive product."

A fundamental theorem of modern sociology states that the unit of a social system always has multiple modes of participation, never a single mode. This means that an individual will be involved not in one role but in a plurality of roles. Thus, even if he is a specialist in cognitive functions, he will have other roles—familial ones, for example—in which the cognitive component is less salient. Hence it is important what modes of articulation occur, between the involvements of units in the cognitive complex in relationships where cognitive considerations are crucial and those other participations and interests where the cognitive component is less important.

Research as the Storm Center of Academic Disturbance

The prominence of the research function has played a great role in the development of the modern American university, particularly in recent years. Indeed, in one set of aspects, the recent phase of the educational revolution may be considered parallel to the Industrial Revolution. The primary social disturbances generated by the Industrial Revolution were focused on the status of labor, on the one hand as a role of a category of concrete human beings, and, on the other, as a factor of economic production. Out of these disturbances came a very powerful ideology, broadly called socialism, which gave birth to some extremely important social movements and had immense repercussions in the intellectual world. Its most influential version was formulated by Karl Marx.

Two key concepts of Marxist theory particularly relevant to the present problem—the *alienation* of labor and the *exploitation* of labor. (These have recently been greatly clarified by Anthony Giddens and Jeffrey Alexander.[5] Marx relied heavily on the general framework of utilitarian thought and also on some classical economic theorists, notably Ricardo. The alienation of labor consisted, above all, in the treatment of *labor power* as a commodity. The reasons for the exploitation of labor were that labor was the sole source of production (that is, the only important factor of production), but the laborer did not control the production process and did not own either the means of production or its resulting commodities.

Neither of these propositions is acceptable to the main currents of economic theory today. Labor is not, like commodities, a *product* of the process of economic production—that is, a category of output—but is a *factor* of production. Commodities—or *goods,* in recent usage—are now considered the result of a combination of production factors of which labor is only one element; the others are land, capital, and organization. Therefore, it is not theoretically legitimate to identify a category of economic output with a category of factor in a plural-factor process. The error goes

---

[5] Anthony Giddens, *Capitalism and Modern Social Theory* (Cambridge: Cambridge University Press, 1971), and Jeffrey Alexander, "The Transcendence of the Utilitarian Paradigm: An Essay on Marx, Durkheim, and Weber" (as yet unfinished Ph.D. dissertation, University of California, Berkeley). See also, Neil J. Smelser, *Social Change in the Industrial Revolution* (Chicago: University of Chicago Press, 1959).

back to Ricardo, who did not have an adequate analysis of the determinants of economic value or utility on the demand side of the supply-demand relationship. The discovery of the principle of marginal utility would later solve this problem.[6]

As Alexander [7] has shown, Marx treated the functioning of the capitalistic economy as wholly dominated by the play of economic interest, within the utilitarian framework of theoretical analysis. The development of capitalism, according to Marx, suppressed a crucial aspect of precapitalist society—what can perhaps legitimately be called *Gemeinschaft*. Marx repeatedly refers to the social character of labor and labor's alienation from its rightfully social character. But it can be argued that, from the point of view of the structure of society, the crucial event was that labor became a *mobile* factor of production. This was institutionalized especially in the separation of the context of economic production, the factory, from the kinship-oriented household. Most sociologists today regard this as a process of differentiation. Marx overwhelmingly regarded it as a process of destruction of the nexus of solidarities in which the worker had lived. [8]

In stating that research was the storm center of recent and current academic disturbance, we meant research as the spearhead of the differentiation of the cognitive complex relative to other sectors of the society, but particularly of the fiduciary subsystem in its special relation to culture. It is most closely analogous, in the economy, to that sector of differentiated "capitalistic" enterprise which grew prodigiously under the factory system. The clear primacy of economic orientation in the factory parallels the clear primacy of cognitive considerations in "pure" research, which has thus brought about complex repercussions on the other elements of both society and culture in which cognitive factors have been prominently involved.

In closer parallel to the industrial case in Marx's time are what Platt and I have called *cognitive standards of validity and significance*. This is *not* a category of cognitive output, but a primary *factor* in making qualitatively improved cognitive output possible. It occupies a similar position to that of labor as an economic factor of production. As such, it is an input to the cognitive system from the cultural complex, just as labor is an input to the economy from the fiduciary system of society. The cognitive output parallel to commodities is what we call knowledge, as a category of cultural objects, whereas commodities are a category mainly of physical objects evaluated for their economic utility. Cognitive standards are those,

---

[6] Cf. Joseph A. Schumpeter, *History of Economic Analysis,* edited from a manuscript by E. B. Schumpeter (New York: Oxford University Press, 1954).

[7] Alexander, *op. cit.* (n. 5, above).

[8] Robert Bellah, "Intellectual and Society in Japan," *Dedalus* (Spring 1972), pp. 89–115.

for the social sciences particularly, analyzed by Weber in his studies of the problem of objectivity in social science knowledge,[9] notably the "schema of proof" formalized by Von Schelting.[10] This set of standards is at the heart of the great controversy about value-free social science, or science in general, which parallels the famous controversy about the alienation of labor. The idea of value freedom in Weber's sense, discussed very specifically in *The American University,*[11] is widely judged a derogation of the dignity of culture in general. Nor is it far-fetched to say this parallels the conception of labor treated as a commodity. A factor in the generation of a category of outputs is being confused here with the outputs themselves. The confusion stems from the feeling that it is illegitimate to treat cognitive standards as a mobile resource clearly differentiated from other components in the production of knowledge, and to treat knowledge distinct from other components of culture.

There is then the tendency to impute to the modern cognitive world the idea that only firm adherence to these cognitive standards produces valid and significant knowledge. This notion is parallel to the famous labor theory of value, which alleged that labor alone created commodities. On the contrary, cognitive standards constitute *one* factor in the generation of knowledge and the other cognitive outputs. The other factors are first the *valuation,* based on cultural premises, of cognitive rationality, which is *not* identical with the substantive standards of cognitive validity and significance. Second, there is the *motivation* of researchers to solve strictly cognitive problems, which cannot be taken for granted as a simple function of the existence of the standards themselves. Finally, there are the *affective meanings* of cognitive pursuits, as compared to the other alternatives open to units in the social system. A special combination of all four sets of factors is needed to produce valid and significant knowledge—no one of them alone is *the* agent of its creation.

Current ideological controversy, then, concerns the alleged alienation of man's cultural heritage by subjecting it to the discipline of cognitive standards, a discipline analogous to the economic discipline of the labor factor. The same ideological controversies involve an idea of the *exploitation* of cultural standards by pressing them within the mold of this discipline, and the alleged suppression of alternative possibilities, notably in moral–political and expressive directions.

Such alienation is from a matrix parallel to that of *Gemeinschaft* as the alleged basis of the solidarity of precapitalist society. Because the

[9] Max Weber, "Objectivity in Social Science and Social Policy," in *Max Weber on the Methodology of the Social Science,* trans. and ed. Edward A. Shils and Henry A. Finch (New York: Free Press, 1949), chap. 2, pp. 50–112.

[10] Alexander von Schelting, Max Weber's *Wissenschaftslehre* (Tubingen: J. C. B. Mohr (P. Siebeck), 1934).

[11] Parsons and Platt, *op. cit.* (n. 1, above), chap. 2.

primary focus now has been transferred to the level of the general theory of action, rather than to that of the social system as such, the central concept of this matrix is probably an aspect of the cultural system, and was formulated in a famous and major concept of Weber's.

Weber called it *Gesinnungsethik,* as contrasted with *Verantwortung-sethik.* The latter is easily translated as "ethic of responsibility." *Gesin-nungethik* is difficult to translate appropriately—perhaps "ethic of sentiment" is adequate. Weber distinguished between these two types mainly with respect to their separate attitudes toward the consequences of decisions to act. What characterized *Gesinnungsethik.* Weber said, was the refusal to consider or take responsibility for consequences. Morally one was obligated to "do what was right" from the point of view of some pure and absolute standard, and to let it go at that. If the action in question had morally objectionable consequences, in Weber's religious terminology, the responsibility for them was God's, not man's. The ethic of responsibility, on the other hand, involves responsibility for consequences, even if indirect and unintended. The relevance to the present context lies in the fact that, in order to take responsibility for consequences, one must *know* what they are, and this knowledge is subject to the canons of *cognitive* validity and significance. The apostle of *Gesinnungsethik* can afford to be non- (if not anti-) intellectual, provided he is subjectively certain his position is right, but the apostle of the ethic of responsibility cannot afford this luxury. To act ethically he *must* be concerned with cognitive matters. This was Weber's own ethical position, and it was surely a very powerful motive for his pursuit of intellectual problems. Weber also felt great concern, in his extensive discussion and documentation, about the major role of *Gesinnungsethik* in social and cultural history.

It is quite clear that the ethic of responsibility postulates a much more highly differentiated cultural, social, and psychological orientation to problems of the moral legitimacy of action than does the ethic of *Gesinnung.* The apostle of the latter can merge moral–evaluative and expressive standards—my use of the term *sentiment* above is meant to suggest this—and either eliminate cognitive considerations altogether, or accept simplistic and cognitively dubious formulae. (Compare with Erikson's remarks, in his *Dædalus* paper on youth, about the "totalistic" stance of many young radicals today).[12]

Characteristically, radical and revolutionary movements postulate a "dedifferentiated" version of the main culture of our time. This was certainly true of the radical (Communist) wing of Marxian socialism—and certainly of Marx's economic theories—and we think it is also true of the radical opposition to the contemporary university system.

---

[12] Erik Erikson, "Reflections on the Dissent of Contemporary Youth," *Daedalus* (Winter 1970), pp. 154–176.

Formal Statement of the Correspondence Between Marxian Ideology and Contemporary Anti-University Ideology

In the previous section, I argued that there is a very striking formal similarity between the Marxian analysis of capitalism, both as economy and as society in the sense of *Gemeinschaft,* and the analysis (much less sharp and systematic than Marx's) by some New Left spokesmen of contemporary alienation, with special reference to the role of the cognitive complex. This formal similarity throws a bright light on the structure of felt strains and their symbolization in the current and recent academic situation. In sum, parallels are as follows:

First, the emergence by differentiation of the research complex from the more general matrix of cognitive concerns, especially teaching, seems analogous to the differentiation of factory production from those modes imbedded in relatively diffuse community settings, such as the peasant community and the town handicraft system. Second, the analogy to the role of factory labor is the use of clearly differentiated standards of cognitive validity and significance as the standards defining satisfactory research. From our formal analytical point of view, the use of these standards constitutes one of the primary factors in the generation of knowledge and other cognitive outputs.

This is a mode of implementing values of cognitive rationality which is directly parallel to economic rationality. Furthermore, as a formal factor in the genesis of knowledge, the use of cognitive standards occupies a place analogous to that of labor as a factor in economic production. Third, parallel to the sense in which Marx saw labor as alienated, we may speak of a more recent version of this concept as the alienation of the research-dominated intellectual worker from control of intellectual output and of the intellectual product itself. This extrusion from control allegedly subordinates the primacy of noncognitive factors to the interests of those who are bound by cognitive standards. As we have suggested, the matrix of this differentiation is what Weber called *Gesinnung.* Furthermore, the primary aspects of *Gesinnung* are a diffuse, undifferentiated combination of moral–evaluative and expressive concerns with "religious" concerns. This pattern clarifies what is often meant by *relevance* as a criterion of knowledge and cognitive procedures. From the point of view of dissident ideologists, relevant knowledge and its relevant pursuit would essentially subordinate cognitive considerations to moral–evaluative and expressive ones, thus turning the tables.

Fourth, as we have noted, interpreters of Marx [13] have laid great stress

[13] For example, see Giddens, *op cit.* (n. 5, above).

on the equation in Marxist thought of labor and commodities. There is, however, a theoretical difficulty in treating labor as a kind of commodity: in later post-Marxian economic theory, labor is a factor of production, whereas commodities are a category of economic output.

In the case of the cognitive complex, the parallel lies in the tendency to make absolute the relevance of purely cognitive standards by equating cognitive concerns specifically with knowledge, which is a kind of a scientistic orientation. The relationship is established by the concepts of economic rationality on the one hand and those of cognitive rationality on the other.[14] The *discipline* of these sets of rational standards is allegedly the focus of alienation in the two cases.

Fifth, the one-factor theory in the generation of relevant output is closely connected with these points. In Marxism, it is the famous "labor theory of value," the theoretical device for denying significance to the other factors of production and for equating labor and commodities. In the cognitive context there is a tendency to confuse what for Weber were the canons of the objectivity of knowledge, especially in social science, with the factors involved in the *social role* of the seeker after knowledge—the *Wissenschaftler,* in Weber's term, inadequately translated as scientist.[15] The factors in the scientist's role which are suppressed by this one-factor theory are the values of cognitive rationality itself; the motivations not only of the scientist but of the student to learn—that is, to engage in cognitive learning; and the affective meanings of the manifold alternatives in the commitment of action resources which relate cognitive to noncognitive considerations.[16] This is particularly crucial in the socialization of what Platt and I call the educated citizenry.

Sixth, there is also a close parallel to the Marxian theory of exploitation. Not only is the worker allegedly made into a kind of production machine by capitalism but the surplus value of his output is appropriated by his employer. The institutional mechanism through which this occurs is the ownership of the means of production and of the product by capitalists as their private property. All that is left to the worker in his disadvantaged, competitive position—disadvantaged because he owns neither the means of production nor the product—which only permits the subsistence of the workers and their reproduction, so that they will not be depleted in one generation. The institutional analogue of private property in the Marxian scheme is, in the dissident academic ideology, the control of cognitive resources by the academic profession, above all as institutionalized in tenure and academic freedom in a stratified manner. It is

[14] See Parsons and Platt, *op cit.* (n. 1, above), chap. 2.

[15] Max Weber, "Science as a Vocation," in *From Max Weber: Essays in Sociology* ed. H. H. Gerth and C. Wright Mills (New York: Oxford University Press, 1946). pp. 129–156.

[16] Parsons and Platt, *op cit.* (n. 1, above), chap. 4.

contended that the professional component, notably tenured senior faculty, have vis-à-vis students a monopoly of control through which they enforce the primacy of cognitive discipline on the academic community as a whole. The political component of the structure of the firm, in the Marxian account, parallels the stratification of the academic community into a superior component of faculty members and an inferior one of students. Students, it is alleged, are compelled by the competitive structure of the system to suppress their noncognitive interests in favor of rigorous cognitive discipline; and even here, control of the primary output of the process, notably knowledge, is appropriated by the superior class and put to uses about which the producers—partly in the role of students—have little, if any, decision-making power. I should link this with the frequent indictments of the university's "complicity" in the interests of the "establishment." It is also implied that students are "forced" to learn primarily in order to become, in their future occupational roles, instruments of the establishment.

The parallel does break down at one crucial point. The only possible analogy to the proletariat in Marxian thought is the student body. The proletariat, however, was treated as a class * in the sense of a transgenerational status group in which the typical individual inherited the manifold of opportunities open to him and would be expected to pass it on to his children. In this sense, of course, the student's status is not a class status, except in the sense that class influences the opportunity for higher education, but this is changing. The basic point, however, is that the status of student is a temporary one which has been overwhelmingly concentrated in one rather small sector of life, the postadolescent.

The consequences of this presumptively illegitimate subjection to cognitive discipline would have to be understood differently from the subjection to the discipline of capitalistic rationality. It would be a kind of diffuse and pervasive penetration of the culture as a whole with the values of cognitive rationality, and it would extend the exploitative subjection of the nonrational components—notably the moral–evaluative and expressive components—inculcated in student years, into the entire future lives of those concerned. It is somewhere along these lines that Marcuse's notion of the "repressive tolerance" of modern societies is to be interpreted. In the Marxian conception, even without tight monopolistic control, the institutionalization of private property in the hands of "capitalists" beats the "formally free" workers into an exploited proletariat. Similarly, even though the academic system is formally free in some respects, a repressive discipline is allegedly imposed on students, and if the socialization process is sufficiently effective, its consequences will permeate the whole of their future lives, and hence the society as a whole.

---

* That students do constitute a class in this sense has been asserted by some, for example Jerry Farber in *Student as Nigger*. For the reasons stated here, however, I cannot regard his position as acceptable.

Seventh is an aspect of the parallel that is particularly crucial to the problem of the bundle's significance. It will be remembered [17] that, in Marx's view, the division of labor was a primary aspect of the trap into which the worker fell to become the victim of alienation and exploitation. The principal reason for Marx's abhorrence of the division of labor was its relation to a system of *instrumental* interdependence in the market nexus. To be truly independent and free, the worker would have to escape this dependence on others. Expropriation from ownership of the means of production and of products was the index of this state of enslavement.

The bundle (with some modest extensions mentioned earlier) is the analogy in the cognitive world of the economic division of labor. One crucial property of the bundle is its high degree of *differentiation,* both of cognitive subject matter within the disciplines and of functions in relating cognitive content to various societal interests. This differentiated system is a highly integrated nexus analogous to the economic market system. The two important media of intelligence and influence constitute primary mechanisms of this integration. We have argued [18] that just as Adam Smith's concern with the "extent of the market" referred not only to the division of labor but to the conditions of productivity in the economy as a whole, so the extent of the bundle is not only a factor in promoting a high level of differentiatedness, but is also a major factor among the conditions of a high level of cognitive output for the cognitive complex as a whole. But this highly differentiated bundle creates a state of affairs which is analogous to the combination of a high division of labor with extensive markets. In such a state many plural units are interdependent, not specifically on the level of instrumental, but rather of cognitive–communicative, interdependence.

This point is important to the much discussed concept of relevance. As in all ideological discussions, the dissidents tend to make a sharp either–or dichotomy between relevant and irrelevant knowledge. But so essential is interdependence to the bundle that no such sharp dichotomy makes sense. This is illustrated by the relation between the relatively pure intellectual disciplines, on the one hand, and the clinical focus of the organization of knowledge and competence, on the other. For the purpose of relatively pure research, items and subbodies of knowledge have one sort of relevance to each other. For the purposes of clinical practice in the professions, they have another. Although these two sets are not incongruent, they are definitely differentiated. It is not cognitively legitimate to transfer from one context to the other without taking account of the differential contexts in which the various items are relevant.

[17] Giddens, *op cit.* (n. 5, above); and Ralf Dahrendorf, "On the Origin of Inequality Among Men," in *Social Inequality,* ed. A. Beteille (London: Penguin Modern Sociology Readings, 1969).

[18] Parsons and Platt, *op cit.* (n. 1, above), chap. 8.

In this connection, there is a very important sense in which the development of increasingly *theoretical* levels in the cognitive system have become focal to the storm center of cognitive disturbance. Daniel Bell has asserted the special importance, in the postindustrial society, of theoretical knowledge.[19] Theory is a level of cognitive generalization which produces relevance, in our sense, in a much wider range of contexts than those in which more specifically empirical statements of fact can be relevant. We think it significant that the prominence of the bundle at the organizational level of cognitive enterprises has roughly coincided in time with the rapidly increasing importance of theory in the culture of the cognitive system itself.

Differentiation and Dedifferentiation

Another very important aspect of the parallel we have been drawing has to do with levels of differentiation. The Marxian scheme of the economy suppressed several primary aspects of theoretical differentiation which subsequent economic theory has strongly emphasized. We would like to suggest a parallel in the understanding of the cognitive complex. For the economy there are three types of Marxian failure to recognize differentiations. As we have noted, the first is the differentiation between a factor of production and a category of economic output, as in the famous allegation that labor has become a commodity. The second is the differentiation between plural factors of production, which is denied by the theorem that labor alone is the source of production. The third is the failure to discriminate categories of economic output, notably goods and services. Although service belongs under the same rubric of output as goods, it is very clearly differentiated from goods. We should also clearly distinguish service as a category of output from labor as a factor of production. Service is a result of combining the labor factor with land, capital, and organization factors.

Much current ideology about the cognitive complex makes absolute cognitive standards as value-free, and identifies the primacy of cognitive standards with knowledge as output. We treat cognitive standards—that is, standards of validity and significance—as a *factor* in the development of cognitive outputs, not as a category of output in itself. Knowledge, however, is a category of output. Cognitive outputs are made possible, not by cognitive standards alone, but by the combination of cognitive standards with three other major factors: first, the values of cognitive rationality, which are different from standards of validity and significance; second, the

[19] Daniel Bell, "The Cultural Contradictions of Capitalism" *The Public Interest* 21 (Fall 1970), pp. 16–43.

person's motivation to cognitive learning, which is not a simple function of the existence of either values or standards or both together; and finally, the affective meanings of the alternatives contained in a manifold of possible social participation, which includes the devotion of personal and collective resources to cognitive concerns. We think it very important to note that there is not just one category of cognitive output, namely knowledge, but that there are others as well, particularly *competence*. Knowledge is an output to the cultural system and becomes incorporated in it as a type of cultural object. Competence, however, is an output to the personality system and is internalized as part of the personality structure.

The result of such analysis of factors, categories of outputs, and modes of relation between the sets makes it necessary to define some complex distinctions and interdependencies. Only in that way can we do justice to the complexity of the cognitive complex in its internal structure and its various modes of articulation with the noncognitive aspects of the action system.

We have been using Marxian ideology and the ideologies critical of the modern university system as a theoretical foil. It is not our purpose to judge the strength of either ideology in the process of social development. Rather, we have used the conceptual structure of these ideologies to illuminate the structural complexes of the organization of action with which they deal. Both ideologies postulate and advocate a far less differentiated system than the one already developed when the ideologies were promulgated, and which they have attacked as corrupt. We think we have been able to ascertain the precise points where differentiation is considered undesirable: notably, the plurality of factors in economic production and in cognitive output, and the differentiation of types of output.

Both ideologies want to replace the current differentiated structures with an idealized system in which both the differentiation and the alleged evils would be eliminated or at least greatly minimized. This would necessarily have a highly deflationary effect on the generalized media of interchange involved. Gregory Grossman, one of the principal authorities on the Soviet economy, speaks of the "demonetization" of the Soviet economy.[20] Another major consequence is to ignore some fundamental cost factors in economic production. As Marshall Goldman has shown, this particularly applies to land costs and capital costs.[21] It would seem to follow from our parallel that the implementation of the New Left ideology would have a highly deflationary effect on the media of intelligence and influence. It would also ignore the cost factors involved, particularly in motivation to cognitive learning and the values of cognitive rationality.

[20] Gregory Grossman, "The Politics of Economic Reforms: A Comment," *Survey* 70/71 (1969): 165–168.

[21] Marshall Goldman, *The Spoils of Progress: Environmental Pollution in the Soviet Union* (Cambridge, Mass.: MIT Press, 1972).

I would like here to emphasize that in *The American University* Platt and I laid great emphasis on the sense in which *all* generalized symbolic media of interchange are subject to inflationary and deflationary disturbance in ways which are strictly parallel to the comparable economic disturbances in which the monetary system is at the center. In particular we devoted a major chapter (the seventh) to inflationary and deflationary processes involving intelligence on the one hand and influence on the other as these two media are involved in the academic system. We have argued especially that, when viewed against the background of a long inflationary process, the recent student disturbances could be interpreted as in considerable part a deflationary crisis with respect to the media both of intelligence and of influence, with some relations to those of affect and value commitments.

It thus seems highly significant that movements dominated by Marxian ideology, especially more radical Communist ones, have not achieved political power in any of the highly industrialized societies. Their great successes have been in the underdeveloped world, which included Russia in 1917. We think there may be a parallel in the special appeal of the New Left ideology to youth and particularly to students. Because the socialization of youth has not yet been completed, they are analogous to an underdeveloped economy, and for them the ideological simplification has strong appeal.

The parallel between the Marxian diagnosis of capitalism and the recent dissident diagnosis of the educational revolution helps explain both the strikingly persistent use of Marxian themes and rhetoric by the New Left and the different emphases of the two ideologies. One sharp difference is the neglect of technical Marxist *economic* theories in contemporary discussion. Although there is a conspicuous nostalgia for the "working class," there is an equally conspicuous absence of any precise analysis of this nostalgia. As Erik Erikson notes, the New Left is content with asserting the common "dependency" of workers and students.[22] They speak of alienation, but in a different sense than Marx, discarding his special reference to the labor role in favor of fuzzy generalizations about personality. And there is also a subtly important difference between Marx's "exploitation" and contemporary "repressiveness." Finally, the value accents are inverted. Marxism defiantly asserted the value of "materialism," although qualified by the adjective "historical." Today, however, one prominent reason for the indictment of contemporary society is its materialistic character. Perhaps we can legitimately relate this inversion to the shift in concern from the economic to the cultural level.

Let us turn to the ways in which the development of "free enterprise"

---

[22] Erik Erikson, *op cit.* (n. 12, above).

economies has taken the historical course that has proved to be an alternative to Communist revolution. Because our interest has focused on labor, we suggest that the alternative has emerged mainly through the development of a complex system of *occupational* roles.

Two crucial points must be considered at the start. First, there has been a process of structural differentiation, between labor as a category of factor input and service as a category of economically valuable product output. Labor inputs have had to be combined with other economic factors to make them valuable. This has occurred primarily through the channels of socialization and formal education, which, *among other things,* have been processes of creating economic value. It is further significant that, although Marx confined the category *labor* to those roles specifically controlled by the owner of the firm, the occupational role has become a much wider category, including the institutionalized managerial functions and high-level professional functions as well as routine labor functions. The professional role-type particularly has become a kind of model prototype for the changing body of occupational roles. One aspect of this change, of course, has been the great proportionate reduction of the unskilled labor force. This has been accompanied by a rise in the level of qualifications for an increasing proportion of jobs. Occupational roles then, as forms of service, are performed in contexts of organization that have both political and community aspects. The associational structure of university faculties and departments, for example, is an important example of solidary social community. Furthermore, the academic community includes students in complex ways.

Parallel to their economic views, the dedifferentiating cultural revolution would minimize, if not destroy, the autonomy of the cognitive complex by incorporating it into a diffuse matrix of *Gesinnung.* But alternatively, this process of differentiation can be carried even further, uniting the patterns of integration into a differentiated structure that can bind them together. To achieve this, it is essential that cognitive standards be considered as a *factor* in cognitive output, and not a category of such output. That factor should then be treated, institutionally as well as theoretically, as one among a set of factors of cognitive output. Beyond that we would stress the development of competence as a learned and therefore internalized aspect of the individual personality, which can attain high levels of excellence only through a relatively prolonged and complex educational process.

We must also stress the importance of integrating the competent personality in a community-type societal nexus that is highly differentiated both internally and from other aspects of the society such as the economy and polity, and in which affect as a medium interchange plays a prominent part. The articulation of competence and the affectively controlled nexus of social community are we think, the principal answer to the charge that modern society and particularly its intellectual community is inherently alienative.

If this alternative to the cultural revolution is—as I personally believe —the probable way of the future, I scarcely mean to imply that the way will be smooth and harmonious. It is very likely that the prominence given to the cognitive complex—research and higher education—will continue to be a highly disturbing force in our society and culture. Therefore, its internal development and its complex relations to the rest of the society are likely to be turbulent. This has been true of all the great structural changes in the evolution of modern society.

The educational revolution is by no means complete. The complex developmental process will continue to involve many changes in structure, including changes in the composition of the bundle. Our use of ideological themes, however, and of the parallel between Marxist ideology and the current dissident attack on the cognitive complex, seem a useful way of highlighting some problems in the nature of the system that are vital to understanding the changes and tensions it has generated. But other approaches are also valid, and this essay is intended not as a program for action but as a paradigm of interpretation.

I referred to the work of Max Weber earlier. It is perhaps appropriate to conclude this discussion with a reference to the very much broader concept of the process of rationalization, which was a central preoccupation of Weber's work, particularly in his later years. Although his analysis was indeed different from Marx's, they can be linked through the concept of rationality. For Marx, the discipline of economic rationality, enforced on capitalists by the market and on workers by the capitalists, was a focal source of evil in the capitalist system. Robert Bellah, commenting on Marxism's strong appeal to Japanese intellectuals,[23] speaks of Marx's "nostalgia for *Gemeinschaft*."

On quite a different level, Weber was deeply disturbed by the process of rationalization, which produced what he called an "iron cage."[24] Weber had a different but comparable nostalgia for something akin to *Gemeinschaft*. But by Weber's time, the rationality factor in the organization of the economy had become one, albeit very prominent, instance within the much larger process of rationalization as a whole. Weber himself strongly emphasized the factor of *bureaucracy* in the structure of the economy and elsewhere in the society. He was also on the threshold of seeing the vast significance of the cognitive complex at the cultural levels, as well as the significance of social organization. In the half century and more

---

[23] Bellah, *op. cit.* (n. 8, above).

[24] Max Weber, *The Protestant Ethic and the Spirit of Capitalism*, trans. Talcott Parsons (London: George Allen and Unwin, 1930).

since Weber's death, however, the development at the cultural level has proliferated immensely.

Without that proliferation, the themes discussed in this paper would not have been as much at the center of contemporary preoccupation. I think it fair to say that we have been experiencing a sociocultural crisis comparable to the crisis that accompanied and followed the Industrial Revolution, which Neil Smelser has analyzed.[25] In my view, Weber, at the time of his premature death, was in the midst of working through some of the crucial problems arising from that vast social and cultural change, the educational revolution, and its ramifications through the entire society and culture. This essay will, I hope, prove a modest contribution to what, in the spirit of Weber, we may call both the value-free and the objective understanding of these changes.[26]

[25] Smelser, *op cit.* (n. 5, above).
[26] Neil J. Smelser, *Essays in Sociological Explanation* (Englewood Cliffs, N.J.: Prentice-Hall, 1968).

8. Stability and Change in the American University

JUST UNDER A YEAR ago there appeared under the auspices of the American Academy of Arts and Science's Assembly on University Goals and Governance a book entitled *The American University* which I co-authored with Gerald M. Platt.[1] Completed in the early summer of 1972, the book explicitly confined its major attention to the ideal type of the relatively elite, more or less "full" university characterized by the institutionalization of research functions, a graduate school of arts and sciences, an undergraduate college, and a ring of schools for training in the applied professions, the roster of which has varied somewhat from case to case. The authors of this book were acutely conscious that the ideal type on which they concentrated their attention did not stand alone, but was a pacesetting component of a very much larger and more ramified system. We thought, however, that its significance was of salient strategic importance for understanding the American system of higher education as a whole.

Substantive work on the book was terminated rather shortly after the subsiding of the era of worldwide disturbances in the university system of higher education. The academic year 1971–72, however, proved to be one of the most peaceful witnessed in a number of years, and if anything the calm has become more pronounced and deeper in the two years since the summer of 1972. The purpose of the present brief article is to assess what has come out of the period of turbulence, followed by one of renewed calm, in which the university system has been involved. This will of necessity be a rather limited attempt at appraisal, but I think certain things can be said.

[1] Talcott Parsons and Gerald M. Platt, *The American University* (Cambridge, Mass.: Harvard University Press, 1973).

Reprinted by permission of *Daedalus*, Journal of the American Academy of Arts and Sciences, Boston, Massachusetts. Fall 1974 (vol. 1), *American Higher Education: Toward an Uncertain Future.*

To what extent has the main structural and institutional core of the elite university remained intact through the vicissitudes through which it has passed, and how far has it been modified, and how substantially? The radical alternative to maintenance would be a fundamental revolution so that the university's resemblance to what existed in the early 1960s would be scarcely discernible today. It is our impression, on the basis not of a systematic study but of a somewhat impressionistic review of available evidence, that the integrity of the structural core has by and large survived without at least "revolutionary" alterations.

Evidence for this conclusion is based on three main sources. First, I have had personal experience of some degree of intensity in the decisive period in four institutions which in different ways fit the typological model of reference. The first is my own institution of Harvard, from which I formally retired a year ago but with which I have kept a certain amount of touch. The second is the University of Chicago, in which I served as a visiting professor for one quarter in the year 1971 and another in the fall quarter of 1972. The third is the University of Pennsylvania, where for 1973–74 I served as a part-time visiting professor on an appointment extending throughout the academic year. Finally, the fourth is Brown University, where in the spring semester of 1974 I had rather intimate associations occasioned mainly by delivering the Colver Lectures at the University. As my second source, I am greatly indebted to the book edited by David Riesman and Verne A. Stadtman entitled *Academic Transformation,* which reviews what has happened in the decisive era at 17 institutions.[2] By my admittedly crude classification, 10 of the 17 belong predominantly to the type with which Platt and I dealt in *The American University.*[3] Finally, the third source is unsystematic and miscellaneous reading and conversation about the situation at various institutions. Some of them are represented in the above lists, some of them are not.

In the final substantive chapter of *The American University,* Platt and I made a good deal of the multifunctional core which we called the "bundles," following a stimulus from Neil Smelser.[4] The university type with which we were concerned brought together a number of distinct functions. First among these is the inclusion in its personnel and curriculum of

[2] David Riesman and Verne A. Stadtman (eds), *Academic Transformation: Seventeen Institutions Under Pressure* (New York: McGraw-Hill, 1973).

[3] Parsons and Platt, *The American University;* the ten are University of California at Berkeley, Harvard, MIT, University of Michigan, University of Pennsylvania, Princeton, Rutgers, Stanford, University of Toronto, and University of Wisconsin. This classification is certainly true also of the two not included in the above list with which I have had personal contact, namely, University of Chicago and Brown, and also of three other notable ones not on either list, namely, Columbia, Cornell, and Yale. See Riesman and Stadtman, *Academic Transformation,* and Parsons and Platt, *The American University.*

[4] *Ibid.,* chap. 8.

virtually the whole range of the intellectual disciplines, usually classified in the tripartite rubrics of natural sciences, social sciences, and humanities. This, of course, is particularly the case for faculties of arts and sciences. A second function is the inclusion in the activities of such faculties both of teaching and of research. Unlike some other systems there has been no major American tendency to extrude the research function from the university. A third prominent function is that of the teaching of graduate students, destined for the most part to be academic professionals, as well as that of undergraduates—that is, the combination of a graduate school and an undergraduate college. Finally, the fourth function is the drawing close to the core university of the schools for training in the applied professions. The three classical instances are those of law, medicine, and engineering, but certain others have become increasingly prominent, such as business and public administration, education, and training in what are sometimes called the helping professions, such as social work. The exact list of professional schools varies from university to university; for example, it is minimal at Princeton. But when one looks at the elite university system as a whole, one cannot omit reference to this feature. The analytical problem is why these multifarious functions have remained together in a single bundle and have not come to be distributed among structurally separate and distinctive units.

Our first contention about the aftermath of the disturbances of the 1960s is that by and large this bundle has remained intact and has not been broken up into separate elements.[5] Its construction and strengthening were major features of university development from about the turn of the last century, and one striking outcome of the time of turmoil is that the structures built in this period have by and large survived. Along with other conditions in the society, such as financial support of at least minimal adequacy and political tolerance—though since 1971 there have been problems on both fronts—I should attribute this survival more than anything else to the involvement of relatively strongly professionalized faculties, the products of long and stringent processes of intellectual training either in graduate schools of arts and sciences, or in professional schools, or sometimes in both. The content of their training and their attitudes toward it have been strongly shaped by the values of cognitive rationality, as Platt and I have called them.[6]

It was an aspect of the disturbances of the 1960s that there were quite

[5] Talcott Parsons, "The University 'Bundle': A Study of the Balance Between Differentiation and Integration," in *Public Higher Education in California: Growth, Structural Change, and Conflict,* ed. Neil Smelser and Gabriel Almond (Berkeley: University of California Press, 1974).

[6] Platt and I have some new "hard" evidence for this continuity. The American Council on Education has kindly made available to us the data of a survey of faculty members collected in 1973. About one-third of the institutions in their sample were the same as those in our 1968 sample, and many of the questions used appeared on

strident movements advocating at least a major diminution in the prominence of cognitive values, if not something approaching their overturn.
These movements advocated change in two primary directions. The first of
them is perhaps best tagged by the term "relevance," which has meant,
above all, concern for political reform, and which was generally accompanied by an attack on the so-called doctrine of "value neutrality" in the
intellectual disciplines. Although it was most stridently advocated by certain groups of students, especially undergraduates, this concept was shared
to some extent by some faculty members. The second direction was that of
self-expression and a "freer" pattern of life with respect to which discipline in the intellectual sense was felt to be a hindrance. By and large, however, advocacy of these changes has subsided in the intervening period,
and I think it fair to say that though new forms of political involvement of
members of university communities have developed, and concern with
aesthetic expression has presumably increased, the dominant tone is still
a commitment to the primacy of intellectual and cognitive values.[7]

On the whole it seems fair to infer that the criteria for the evaluation of
candidates for faculty appointments at the very least show a prominent pattern of continuity with those before the disturbances of the 1960s. Similar
things can be said about the ethos of graduate and professional students.
My personal experience in four institutions also confirms the view that
the intellectual seriousness of a large proportion of graduate students has
not shown a substantial decline in favor of either or both of the other two
foci of concern. Indeed, on their part and on that of junior faculty members of my acquaintance, some intellectual work of the highest level that
I have encountered in a rather long teaching career has come to my attention within the relevant period. There are, of course, changes. One of them
is the phenomenon of "the new medical student" which was reported on by
Renée Fox of the Department of Sociology at the University of Pennsylvania in a recent unpublished paper. Professor Fox feels that, compared
to the medical students she studied about twenty years ago, a much larger
proportion of the current generation is seriously concerned with what she
calls the "existential" problems of medical practice and of their patients

---

both surveys. For the two highest prestige groups of institutions on our five-level
scale, the four most highly valued goals out of sixteen included were all primarily
expressions of cognitive values. These included teaching students to think clearly
and logically, to respect empirical evidence, and to achieve mastery of the content
of their discipline. On the four cognitive goals the percentages of respondents rank-
ing them highest ranged from well in the 80s to the high 60s. The highest of the
others who favored more noncognitive goals received priority from only 46 percent
of the respondents.

[7] See especially the annual report, dated April, 1974, of Edward H. Levi, President of the University of Chicago, entitled "The State of the University." Levi
makes the commitment of his university to intellectual excellence the primary keynote of this notable report.

as people. There is a considerable increase of interest in phenomena of suffering and death. It does not, however, follow that the current generation of medical students is less concerned with technical standards on the rational-cognitive side of medicine than were their predecessors. Somewhat similar things can be said about students in law schools, who tend to be more attracted by the possibilities of a public service orientation of law rather than with the standard corporate practice of a previous generation.

In faculties of arts and sciences there has been a good deal of talk about giving more attention to teaching, especially at the undergraduate level. Indeed, in his latest annual report, President Bok of Harvard made the introduction of a program for training in teaching by the Graduate School of Arts and Sciences his principal theme.[8] He felt it to be feasible and to be a serious obligation of the graduate school. I would think it likely that the Harvard example is not an isolated instance, and that an important movement in this direction will soon be underway. As in the medical case, however, it does not seem to me to be likely that there is a major trend, as many advocated during the disturbance, away from the professional concern of academic people with intellectual values and with research. My own expectation is that the main trend will be toward a synthesis of the two facets of the role of the academic profession rather than the serious downgrading of one and corresponding upgrading of the other.

This brings us to certain questions about the undergraduate college, both in the group of institutions with which Platt and I have been primarily concerned, and in a substantially wider group, especially the more or less elite liberal arts colleges. Students at the relatively elite colleges constituted the storm center of the disturbances we have been through, so it is not surprising that changes have been most prominent in this sector of the system of higher education. Indeed, I think substantial changes have already occurred and there are signs that at least some of them will stick. The most important of them can probably best be discussed under two headings which are categories of classical sociological significance. The first of these might perhaps be called authority structure, though this term does not cover the whole of what I have in mind. The second concerns sex composition at both the faculty and student levels.

In the first of these contexts the more radical sector of the movement of dissent carried a highly antinomian flavor. The extreme of this was the experimental establishment of what were sometimes called "free" universities, that is, some kind of collective process aimed at learning in which no status distinctions whatever were permitted between teachers and students or among students at different levels of competence. To my knowledge, none of these experimental attempts has proved to be stable and

[8] Derek C. Bok, "The President's Report, 1972–73" (Cambridge, Mass.: President's Office, Harvard University, January, 1974), multilithed.

come to be an institutionalized part of the system of higher education. On a less radical level, however, there was much talk about "student power" and a greater participation of students in various forms of academic decision-making. Two contexts of such decision-making may appropriately be distinguished: one in curricular matters, and the other in what has come to be called "governance." In the former, there has certainly been a trend toward broadening the areas of independent responsibility and initiative open to students, including undergraduate students. In many ways this has been an acceleration of a very long-term trend away from the rigid curricula prevalent before the days of the elective system. There has been, however, a substantial increase in opportunities for students to help in the design of their own curricula. Related to this has been a wave of objection to the older mechanisms of evaluation of student performance, notably the grading system. Detailed formal requirements have been considerably mitigated, and there are various other facets to the problem.

These, of course, are trends which did not originate in the 1960s, but go rather far back. I have the impression that even at the undergraduate level for both teachers and students the main outcome of the period of turbulence has left the principal intellectual standards intact, even though the organizational setting in which they are implemented has changed. The crucial points are whether or not either students or faculty members had turned decisively away from commitment to intellectual achievement and the disposition to reward, through whatever mechanisms, excellence in such achievement. I personally do not see the evidence that there have been any decisive changes in this respect.[9]

A major part in this continuity of the main ethos has presumably been

---

[9] The case of Brown University is a particularly interesting one. In 1969, largely under pressure from an undergraduate movement, the Brown faculty adopted what was called the "new curriculum," which introduced a very major step in the direction I have just spoken of. There were several facets to this change, but one abolished all distribution requirements, though those of concentration were retained; and another gave the student the option of being evaluated on a pass-fail basis, as it is usually called, in any or all courses. The program also greatly broadened the opportunities for students to design programs of study on their own initiative, though approval by a member of the faculty was still required if credit was to be given. Recently, as reported in the *New York Times*, there has been an atmosphere of student apathy in these matters, and the faculty did limit the proportion of courses where pass-fail grading would be permitted for any one student. The faculty in general has refused to repudiate the main idea of the new curriculum. Students, however, have become in some sense more "conservative" in their attitudes toward it. As shown in various documents about the situation, one of their concerns has been the acceptability of recommendations to admitting authorities in graduate and professional schools. I have the impression that the main intellectual climate of Brown has not been revolutionized away from the predisturbance standards. This brief account is based both on oral communications and on a set of documents, committee reports, and reports of officers of the university and the like, and articles in the alumni and student magazines which were made available to me. The *New York Times* article to which I referred was published on Sunday, February 24, 1974. I am particularly indebted to Professor Martin Martel of Brown University for making these materials available to me.

played by the relatively firm professionalization of academics in connection with their roles as members of faculties. In my opinion the continuing salience of the research function is of fundamental importance in this respect. The achievements which establish the reputations of the more elite members of the profession have rested above all in their contributions to the advancement of knowledge, and the intellectual quality and theoretical importance of these contributions. The most famous members of faculties are people with these kinds of achievements to their credit. Furthermore, the same ethos permeates the student level. I think first of graduate students and 'in particular' of the importance attributed to the dissertation. However, the same principle applies at the undergraduate level, particularly in the importance attributed to theses submitted by candidates for distinction. The prestige aspect of intellectual achievement becomes, it seems to me, increasingly important in proportion as the more authoritarian disciplinary constraints of previous stages of academic development have become less prominent. The continuing primacy of the cognitive focus also has a special order of importance. This concerns the maintenance of the structural distinctiveness of institutions of higher education vis-à-vis other structures in the society. In a politically pluralistic society it does not seem to make much sense for the university to transform itself into a protective base for movements of political reform, nor does it make much sense for it to transform itself into a glorified colony of artists. These are, of course, extreme formulae, but not unfair in the light of certain ideological movements.

It is convenient to use the relations of the sexes as a primary focus for the changes which have occurred most conspicuously at the undergraduate college level, but which have also permeated student life in graduate and professional schools and changed the character of faculties. It is, of course, a commonplace that there has been a great increase in the spread of co-education. An impressive number of institutions previously confined to students of one sex have introduced the admission of the other sex as well. This, of course, has been most prominent in the cases of what were previously all-male colleges like Yale, Princeton, and Dartmouth. A number of previously all-female colleges, however, though by no means all of them have done the same thing. For example, Smith, Mt. Holyoke, and Bryn Mawr have remained exclusively women's colleges. But even here cooperative arrangements with neighboring men's institutions have resulted in a great deal of coeducational instruction. In the background there are two particularly conspicuous innovations. One is the step from coeducation to what is frequently called "coresidence," that is, both sexes share the same basic residential facilities. Along with this has gone a very notable loosening of the so-called "parietal" regulations so that the behavior of men and women students has been increasingly treated as their private concern and not a proper subject for administrative regulation. This, of course, does not include the basic problems of maintaining order or, for example, controlling theft and other unpleasant disturbances of dormitory life. This is perhaps the most conspicuous area in which something like a revolution may be said to have occurred in the last decade or so on the American academic scene.

There has also been conspicuous pressure to increase the proportion of women in certain graduate schools, and especially at faculty levels. It is a notable fact of the larger society that the so-called "women's liberation movement" has not subsided along with the more general student disturbances, and pressure is coming from that movement and from government sources to increase women's participation at various levels. It has already made considerable headway.

This movement and its influence have been closely related to a more general egalitarianism, one major manifestation of which has been the pressure to increase the proportion of members of socially disadvantaged groups who are given the opportunity for quality higher education. This movement to increase the proportion of minority group members—notably blacks, but also, for example, so-called chicanos—in student bodies has been most prominent at the undergraduate college level, although by no means confined to that level. One example is the special program supported by several foundations for the training of black students in law in various prestigious law schools. One of the conditions in that particular program is a commitment on the part of the recipient to practice law in the South. The proportion of black lawyers practicing in southern communities has already been quite substantially increased by this program.[10]

This egalitarian trend, a society-wide phenomenon sparked by the civil rights movement of the early 1960s, has had very wide repercussions. In some of its more extreme manifestations it has produced the open admissions policy adopted by the city system of higher education in New York. The question of possible "discrimination in reverse" which was raised before the Supreme Court in a University of Washington Law School case still remains unsettled at the legal level. However, it is important that the movement and its consequent pressures have already substantially altered the composition of the student bodies of even the more elite units of the academic system, and of course not without rather severe disturbances in the process. Nevertheless, this also is in line with a long-term trend. A comparison of the composition of such student bodies by family origin will reveal that the process of "democratization" has been a continuing one.

The inclusion of such disadvantaged groups as blacks and chicanos in higher education has a certain parallel, though it is by no means exact, with

---

[10] Robert Spearman and Hugh Stevens, "A Step Toward Equal Justice: Programs to Increase Black Lawyers in the South, 1969–1973," An Evaluation Report to Carnegie Corporation of New York (New York: Carnegie Corporation, April, 1974, pamphlet).

the inclusion of Jews earlier in the present century. The more elite sectors of the system of higher education, though not in the political sense anti-Semitic, were notably restrictive at the level of both student admissions and faculty appointments with respect to Jewish participation, although somewhat less so with respect to other categories of what was then called the "new immigration," notably Roman Catholics from Ireland and eastern and southern Europe. In these respects there has clearly been a major transformation. Probably the Jews are very substantially overrepresented, relative to their proportionate numbers in the population generally, at almost all levels of the academic world, and by no means least in its more elite sectors. In the light of this previous history it does not seem likely that the egalitarian features of the recent trend will necessarily upset the core patterns of the academic community. The problem of changing participation of the sexes, however, raises a somewhat different set of issues.

Evidence from an as yet unpublished study of faculty members by Platt and myself at least suggests that the participation of women at faculty levels tends to involve a role pattern which is different from that of men.[11] It is our hunch, which we hope to examine carefully in the near future, that this is not a simple matter of "sexism," that is, of discrimination on grounds of sex, but that it may very well turn out to be at least partly a matter of sex-typed differences of preference and inclination. Two contexts will serve to illustrate such differences. In the first case, we find that women faculty members are by and large less concerned with commitments to research than their male counterparts of comparable training and appointment status and, correspondingly, are more concerned with teaching. Second, as between the two primary grades of teaching performed by members of faculties of arts and sciences, women faculty members are more concerned with undergraduate teaching than with graduate teaching. They tend to assume a kind of "caring" role vis-à-vis their students to a higher degree than their male counterparts.

If there is to be a major change in the sex composition of the academic profession, these differences and others comparable to them may in the longer run bring about considerable changes. I mention these straws of evidence simply to raise the problem of whether this will occur and in what form. It could turn out that undergraduate teaching would become a particularly feminine prerogative, but we cannot be sure. At any rate, there seems to be a warning against one of the stances of the women's liberation movement that there should be not merely identity of opportunity, but identity of formal result of career lines for members of the two sex groups.

I may come back for a moment to certain problems touching governance. First, with reference to student participation, there has been a sub-

---

[11] Talcott Parsons and Gerald M. Platt, "The American Academic Profession: A Pilot Study" (Cambridge, Mass.: Department of Sociology, Harvard University), multilith, 1968, out of print.

stantial increase in student representation on various decision-making bodies, notably various kinds of committees. In a minority of institutions this has extended to formal student participation in faculty appointments even at the senior level. However, it does not seem to me that there has been a major change of revolutionary proportions establishing essentially decision-making equality between faculty and students or otherwise radically altering the fourfold stratification scale I mentioned above in connection with the institution of tenure.[12] One way to put this estimate of probability is that the university is fundamentally a collegial, not a democratic, association. The formal equality in ultimate decision-making of all the participating members should not be regarded as an imperative of this type of social structure. Again, the primary focus of its difference from a democratic association lies in the commitments of the faculties to a career guided by values of cognitive rationality and aiming at maximal competence in their implementation. It is only where student prerogatives are protected by some kind of outside force that they have succeeded in upsetting the main outline of this balance, as for example, at the Free University of Berlin.

An apparently rather different issue concerns the problem of unionization and collective bargaining at faculty levels and in relation to academic administrations. A drive for unionization has indeed taken place, but it has had and is likely to have limited success. In particular it seems accurate to state that the elite core of the academic profession has not been engulfed by this drive, and that it has been most successful in those systems where mass teaching of undergraduate students is most prominent, such as the city system of New York. It has notably not succeeded in becoming established in the faculty of New York University.[13]

The drive toward unionization, if it goes far enough, would certainly introduce profound alterations into the social structure of the sectors of higher education affected. It is often put forward as an alternative to the institution of tenure. Judging by its consequences in industry and some sectors of governmental administration, however, it seems likely that it would shift the emphasis in the direction of prerogatives of seniority as distinguished from the connection between tenure and academic freedom. Unionized organizations very generally have been forced to accept a rather rigid system of seniority prerogatives which cannot be broken through in the name of excellence of individual achievement. This problem leaves a large question mark for the future of the academic world.

In conclusion, I would like to restate my impression that the core struc-

---

[12] In Parsons and Platt, *The American University*, chap. 3, we attempt to extend the concept of tenure from the senior level only to include three others: junior faculty, graduate students, and undergraduate students. I do not take space to explain this here, but the reader can find it fully discussed in the above reference.

[13] "World," *Saturday Review*, June 29, 1974.

tures of the more elite American university have by and large survived intact at a time when the storm of disturbance has conspicuously subsided and has remained calm for approximately three years. The question of whether it will remain so, of course, will require much more systematic and thorough testing than I have been able to subject it to. However, if it stands up to such testing, it seems to me that two primary conclusions may legitimately be drawn. The first of these, already stated above, is that on the whole the level of institutionalization of the main pattern which had been attained prior to the 1960s was relatively firm. There is no question that this framework has been subjected to severe pressures, but by and large it seems to have come out with relatively minimal alteration. Much of this alteration, moreover, is in directions for which there was a good deal of precedent in the developmental trends established well before the era of turbulence. I would hesitate to predict a future smoothness of development. It seems likely that the tensions involved in the development of the cognitive complex and its institutionalization in higher education will remain severe. It is far from impossible that comparable periods of disturbance await us in the future, and in future cases their consequences might be substantially more disruptive than the recent experience has proved to be. Nevertheless, I think it justified to claim that the establishment of the university system has constituted a major development of the structure of American society and culture and one which will not easily be pushed aside.

The other conclusion concerns the validity of the emphasis which Platt and I gave in our interpretation of what was at work in the disturbances themselves. Especially in the final substantive chapter of *The American University,* we stressed the concepts of inflation followed by deflationary crisis, using the model which had been developed in economic theory but applying it primarily to noneconomic components of the social and cultural system.[14] We interpreted a major feature of the disturbances to constitute a deflationary crisis in certain respects comparable to the financial panics which were common in advanced economies until certain orders of control had become established. We think, above all, that the relative rapidity with which disturbances have subsided, and the fact that the newly won stability has now lasted about three years are, at the very least, consistent with this interpretation. It is a point of view not commonly put forward by students of higher education, and we think it ought to be further developed and broadly considered in future research in this area.

[14] Parsons and Platt, *The American University,* chap. 8.

PART III
SOCIOLOGY OF RELIGION

Introduction to Part III

As NOTED IN the General Introduction, Part III contains five essays dealing with the boundary of the general system of action in the direction of the telic system of the human condition, as we have called it. In more familiar terms, these contributions all deal with problems in the "sociology" of religion; the quotation marks emphasize that if this word is interpreted in conventional terms its appropriateness in the present context is not to be taken for granted.

The first selection, Chapter 9, was, like Chapters 7 and 8 of *Social Systems and the Evolution of Action Theory*,[1] written for the *International Encyclopedia of the Social Sciences* (1968). It was meant to be a highly general essay in historical sociology, bringing together a whole range of considerations touching on the religious aspects and background of Western society, which have come to be intellectually important to me over the years. Many of these problems became paramount on my first reading of Weber's *The Protestant Ethic and the Spirit of Capitalism*,[2] which I translated into English and which has long been a major substantive anchor point. In the background also were Weber's panorama of comparative studies in the sociology of religion and his famous "Author's Introduction"[3] to the whole series, also included in my edition of *The Protestant Ethic,* although it was written many years later than that study. Whereas in this article I did not attempt to deal with comparative materials, the comparative perspective is never absent.

Taking, as I do, Weber's views on the Protestant ethic problem with great seriousness, I have felt it imperative to put the relevant considerations

---

[1] Talcott Parsons, *Social Systems and the Evolution of Action Theory* (New York: Free Press, 1977).

[2] Max Weber, *The Protestant Ethic and the Spirit of Capitalism,* trans. Talcott Parsons (New York: Scribner's, 1958; first published in German in 1904–1905), and in English 1930.

[3] Max Weber, "Author's Introduction," ibid., pp. 13–31; the "Author's Introduction" was published in 1920. See also Benjamin Nelson, "Max Weber's Author's Introduction (1920): A Master Clue to His Main Aims," *Sociological Inquiry,* vol. 44, no. 4 (1974): 269–277.

in as broad a historical perspective as possible, and Chapter 9, "Christianity," presents an essential part of my conclusions and recounts the salient facts on which they were based. Of course, the article expresses a point of view that will not prove acceptable to all historical and religious students of the field. I can only hope that the critic judging these conclusions will take as fully as possible into account their relevance to the theoretical problems that are involved not only in Part III but also in this whole volume of essays and beyond. Some but by no means all of these problems are discussed in the other essays included in Part III.

I hope, too, that readers will keep in mind that the relevant theoretical problems bear not only on religion and its relation to society and culture but also on many other empirical fields dealt with in the theory of action. For the reader who has read straight through this book and its predecessor, it should by now be evident that there are major, intrinsic connections between the phenomena of religion and those, for example, of the economy and of the polity. Thus, I do not in the least think that dealing with the problems of Part III implies the abandonment of my early interests in understanding the modern industrial economy and the relations between economic and sociological theory. Indeed, Chapters 9–13 are above all concerned with understanding what has been going on in modern, especially Western, society and with building a theoretical framework that among other things can enhance this understanding. I emphatically disagree with the contention of many authors that Weber's position has been refuted or that the Protestant ethic is dead.[4]

The second essay in Part III, a revisit to Durkheim's work on religion, illustrates the importance of theory for my own work in this field, which I

---

[4] The fate of Weber's famous Protestant ethic thesis would constitute an interesting study in the historical sociology of knowledge. Weber's study was first published in 1904–1905 (see notes 2 and 3 above). As early as 1930 I was told that Weber had been "definitively refuted." The reference was to the forthcoming book of H. M. Robertson, *Aspects of the Rise of Economic Individualism: A Criticism of Max Weber and His School* (Cambridge: At the University Press; New York: Wiley, 1933).

From time to time, other voices have been raised in the same vein. See Andrew Greeley, "The Protestant Ethic: Time for a Moratorium," *Sociological Analysis* vol. 25 (Spring 1964): 20–23; Daniel Bell, *The Coming of Post-Industrial Society* (New York: Basic Books, 1973); and David Riesman, *The Lonely Crowd* (New Haven: Yale University Press, 1950).

On the other hand, Little, Eisenstadt, Nelson, and myself maintain a sharply opposed view. See S. N. Eisenstadt (ed.), *The Protestant Ethic and Modernization: A Comparative View* (New York: Basic Books, 1968), pt. 1, "The Protestant Ethic Thesis in the Framework of Sociological Theory and of Weber's Work," pp. 3–63; David Little, *Religion, Order, and Law* (New York: Harper Torch books, 1969); and Benjamin Nelson. "Weber's Protestant Ethic: Its Origins, Wanderings, and Foreseeable Future" in Charles Y. Glock and Philip Hammond (eds.), *Beyond the Classics? Essays in the Scientific Study of Religion* (New York: Harper & Row, 1973), chap. 2. What accounts for the fact that the controversy has never been settled?

stressed previously in relation to Weber's work on very different empirical subject matters. Thus, Durkheim did not contribute much to the empirical understanding of Christianity or of Western religion more generally; rather, he devoted his main empirical attention in this field to the study of the religion of a primitive people, the aborigines of Australia. Nevertheless, I consider Weber and Durkheim to have been the two most important social theorists of their generation in the study of religion not because they dealt with the same empirical materials but because, dealing with widely different materials, they converged on what is, in highly important respects, a common theoretical framework for the analysis of religious phenomena.

Chapter 10, "Durkheim on Religion Revisited: Another Look at *The Elementary Forms of the Religious Life*," was written in response to request from Charles Y. Glock and Philip E. Hammond to contribute to the volume they were editing on the status of the sociology of religion since the work of certain classical students in this field. Accordingly, "Durkheim on Religion Revisited," was published in *Beyond the Classics?* (1973).

Among the many revisits I have made to the work of those whom I consider the classic authors in my field, this return to *The Elementary Forms of the Religious Life* [5] was one of the most fruitful. (I reread Durkheim's book, from cover to cover, in the original French—the English translation is passable but not distinguished.) Perhaps for present purposes it is sufficient to mention two principal points. In the Introduction to Part III of *Social Systems and the Evolution of Action Theory,* I mentioned the problematic character of the concept "society," about which I disagreed with Whitney Pope.[6] The best evidence that I could mobilize against Pope, in addition to Robert N. Bellah's Introduction,[7] came from *The Elementary Forms* itself. There it gradually became clear that the frame of reference in which Durkheim was attempting to analyze religion, even so "elementary" a religion as that of the Australians, was not society in the narrower analytical sense, which is part of a theory of social systems (the traditional meaning) but what I have been calling a general theory of action, with the human condition (discussed in Part IV, below), in the background.

[5] Emile Durkheim, *The Elementary Forms of the Religious Life,* trans. J. W. Swain (New York: Free Press, 1965; first published in French in 1912).

[6] Cf. Whitney Pope, "Classic on Classic: Parsons' Interpretation of Durkheim," *American Sociological Review,* vol. 38 (August 1973): 399–415; Talcott Parsons, "Commentary on 'Classic on Classic': Parsons' 'Interpretation of Durkheim' by Whitney Pope," ibid., vol. 40 (February 1975): 106–110; idem, "Commentary on 'De-Parsonizing Weber: A Critique of Parsons' Interpretation of Weber's Sociology by Cohen, Hazelrigg, and Pope," vol. 40 ibid., (October 1975): 666–669; and idem, "Reply to Cohen, Hazelrigg, and Pope," ibid., vol. 41 (April 1976): 361–364.

[7] Robert N. Bellah, "Introduction" to *Emile Durkheim On Morality and Society,* ed. Robert N. Bellah (Chicago: University of Chicago Press, 1973).

Of course, Durkheim did not have explicitly in mind all of the theoretical conceptualizations and distinctions I would now use. I in no way mean to suggest that he did. I mean, rather, that if one applies a general action scheme to interpret Durkheim's great work, many of his assertions, which are otherwise difficult to accept, can be seen to make sense. Examples are the meaning of numerous religious symbols, totems and others, that he discussed at such length, as well as many of the "psychological" aspects of ritual behavior—particularly, perhaps, the phenomenon he called "effervescence," which most definitely is not crowd behavior in the usual sense.[8]

The second main point that I mentioned in the General Introduction is essentially a corollary of the first. That is, if one takes Durkheim's concept of the social environment (*milieu social*)[9] as the focal meaning of "social" to him, this term can readily be interpreted in the more analytical sociological sense to designate the *internal environment* of the general system of action. This is to say, it is the primary environment in which human *individuals* act and to the circumstances of which they respond. There is here a notable convergence with Freud, who in his theory of *object relations,* which was particularly prominent in his later work, clearly was talking about social objects; among social objects he strongly emphasized persons other than the actor of reference and with whom the latter "interacted," as we say.[10]

The concept of the social environment was central to Durkheim from the beginning, thus being essential to his concept of *social facts.*[11] Its theoretical significance, however, became greatly extended in his later work, notably *The Elementary Forms.* I do not remember his giving any references to the work of his countryman Claude Bernard,[12] who introduced the concept of internal environment into physiology. Yet Durkheim was to my knowledge the first social scientist to introduce and develop this concept for *this* subject matter. Failure to appreciate what he was doing in this respect constitutes one of the main sources of the pervasive mis-

---

[8] Talcott Parsons, *The Structure of Social Action* (1937; reprint ed., New York: Free Press, 1949), chap. 11; and Bellah, "Introduction" to Durkheim, *On Morality and Society.*

[9] Emile Durkheim, *The Rules of Sociological Method,* trans. S. A. Solovay and J. H. Mueller, 8th ed. (New York: Free Press, 1964; first published in French in 1895).

[10] For a discussion on this point see Talcott Parsons, *Social Structure and Personality* (New York: Free Press, 1964), chap. 4, "Social Structure and the Development of Personality: Freud's Contribution to the Integration of Psychology and Sociology."

[11] Durkheim, *Sociological Method.*

[12] Claude Bernard, *An Introduction to the Study of Experimental Medicine,* trans. H. C. Greene (New York: Dover, 1957; first published in French in 1865).

understanding of Durkheim's work, for example, the egregious attribution to him of the "group mind fallacy." [13]

The other three papers in Part III belong together in the sense that they are all oriented to understanding the place of religion in modern industrial and postindustrial societies, especially the more or less contemporary United States. They are presented in the order in which they were written, a decision that has both advantages and disadvantages.

Chapter 11, "Belief, Unbelief, and Disbelief" was written for a conference on the "Culture of Unbelief" held under the auspices of the Vatican commission of that title, chaired by Franz Cardinal König. This essay was published in 1971 in *The Culture of Unbelief* edited by Rocco Caporale and Antonio Grumelli. Its focus is the phenomenon that has often been referred to as "secularization" in modern societies.

The article emphasizes a warning that departures from traditional patterns of religious belief in modern society should not too readily be interpreted to signify the loss of religious concern in favor of worldly or material interests. This emphasis is reflected in the distinction between unbelief and disbelief in the chapter title. Particularly important to me has been the Protestant pressure toward giving previously secular concerns religious meaning. I have interpreted these pressures as outgrowths of the stance of ascetic Protestantism, which Weber first clearly analyzed,[14] although they extend far beyond the field of economic affairs, as Weber formulated it in his concept of "the spirit of capitalism." It was especially important to me that my former collaborator in the teaching of the sociology of religion, Robert Bellah, played a key part in this conference and contributed two articles to the volume that issued from it.[15]

Chapter 12 is an article that I co-authored with Renée C. Fox and Victor M. Lidz. I was asked by the editor of *Social Research* to contribute a paper a special issue that was being planned on the subject of death. Since I had already collaborated on the same subject with Victor Lidz,[16] I asked the editor's permission to invite his collaboration, which was granted. Renée Fox then informed me she also had been asked to contribute to the same issue and wondered whether we might not join forces, which pleased Lidz and myself and was accepted by Arien Mack, the editor.

[13] See the quotation in Morris Ginsberg, "Introduction" to L. T. Hobhouse, *Sociology and Philosophy: A Centenary Collection of Essays and Articles,* ed. Morris Ginsberg (London: Bell, 1966); see also Talcott Parsons, "Review of L. T. Hobhouse, *Sociology and Philosophy,* in *Social Systems and the Evolution of Action Theory* (New York: Free Press, 1977), chap. 2.

[14] Weber, *Protestant Ethic.*

[15] Robert N. Bellah, "Religion and Social Science," in R. Caporale and A. Grumelli (eds.), *The Culture of Unbelief* (Berkeley: University of California Press, 1971), chap. 14.

[16] Talcott Parsons and Victor M. Lidz, "Death in American Society," in Edwin Schneidman (ed.), *Essays in Self-Destruction* (New York: Science House, 1967).

The three of us decided to focus our essay, "The 'Gift of Life' and Its Reciprocation," on the problem of attitudes toward death in the light of certain recent developments in biomedical research and practice, which could utilize Fox's intimate knowledge of these matters.[17] We tried, however, to put these developments in a broader setting on two levels. The more immediate of these was a consideration of the setting of medical practice and research in the society in relation to changes in ethical attitudes involved, and more generally in the background. In turn, we felt these developments could be related to a second level, that of the religio-cultural heritage.

The treatment of the last topic, which occupies the first part of the *Social Research* article for purposes of presentation, is related to Chapter 9, "Christianity." There is, however, an important difference of emphasis in that the latter selection relies largely on doctrinal precepts and ethical maxims in their relation to institutional structures, whereas the former, attempts a different order of analysis of the set of religious symbols related to the meaning of death. A third attempt to deal with the problem of death in our society, this time in the framework of human condition analysis, comprises Chapter 14 of Part IV.

Quite clearly, Chapter 12 could appropriately have been included in Part I of this collection. Its treatment of the religious background of the problems with which it deals seemed, however, from the point of view of the theory of action to be more innovative than that of the medical aspect. I am particularly grateful to my two collaborators for their permission to include this article in the present volume.

Chapter 13, "Religion in Postindustrial America: The Problem of Secularization," is in a sense a sequel to both Chapters 11 and 12. It is literally a sequel to the latter since it was also written at the request of Arien Mack and published in *Social Research* (1974). It is yet another of my attempts, of which doubtless there will be others, to deal with the main phenomena of religious developments in modern society as these are made understandable through use of the theoretical framework of the theory of action, supplemented by a still broader conception of the human condition (which is discussed more fully in Part IV). Perhaps Chapters 11–13 taken together, on the background of the general discussion of Christianity in Chapter 9 (and of course on the background of the rest of the volume and my other relevant writings), will give a better conception of the drift of these attempts than any one of them separately.[18]

[17] Renée C. Fox and Judith P. Swazey, *The Courage to Fail: A Social View of Organ Transplants and Dialysis* (Chicago: University of Chicago Press, 1974).

[18] In Chapter 10 (p. 216) reference is made to the "behavioral organism" as one primary subsystem, the adaptive, of the general system of action. The text is left unchanged since its original publication, but the reader should be aware of the substitution of the "behavioral" system in that formal position, a usage that is followed in Part IV of this volume. See *Social Systems and the Evolution of Action Theory,* p. 106, note 17, for the rationale of this change.

9. Christianity

THIS ARTICLE WILL deliberately focus on the particular problem of the importance of Christianity for the modern phase of the development of societies. This is, of course, only one combination of aspects of the almost infinitely complex phenomenon that is Christianity.

What social scientists call the modern type of society does not have multiple independent origins but has originated in one specific complex, within the area broadly called western Europe, and has been diffused from there, now even to areas with altogether non-Western culture, the first notable case being Japan. On the religious side the area of origin of modern societies has been Christian, with direct involvement, in decisive periods, of numerically small Jewish subcommunities and with largely hostile, although still culturally significant, interaction with the Islamic world.

The main carrier of the Christian traditions significant to modern society was its Western branch, which developed around the Roman papacy in the area inherited from the western Roman Empire. Apart from the sense in which Eastern Orthodoxy underlies the recent importance of Russia in the modern world, the Eastern branch cannot be said to have been a main center of modernizing innovation, in a sense comparable to the Western.

A somewhat parallel, although different and in many ways more complex, differentiation took place in the Reformation period, with the Protestant sector taking the lead in the relation of religion to modernization. This situation came to a head in the movement of "ascetic" Protestantism (as Max Weber called it) and particularly in its more individualistic and "liberal" branches, especially as they matured in Holland and England and were extended to the United States and the English-speaking British dominions. These processes, however, have been intimately involved in com-

From *International Encyclopedia of the Social Sciences,* David Sills, ed. Volume 2, pp. 425–447 (New York: The Macmillan Company and The Free Press, 1968). Copyright © 1968 by Crowell Collier and Macmillan, Inc. Reprinted with permission of the Publisher.

plex interactions both with Catholic Europe and with the nonascetic, especially Lutheran, branches of Protestant Europe.

This article will stress two primary themes. The first is the basic *continuity* of the evolutionary trend. This begins with the Israelitic and Greek cultural backgrounds of Christianity, each of which laid certain decisive foundations of the movement. It then continues through the establishment and survival of the early church, the establishment of the Western church and its differentiation from the Eastern, the very gradual institutionalization of the Christian society of the High Middle Ages, the transition into the Renaissance, and then the Reformation and the developments that led to modern society. I will place special emphasis on the Protestant branch in what follows, because I believe the major turning point in the development of modern society was not, as has so often been held, the industrial revolution of the late eighteenth century but rather the developments of the seventeenth century, which centered in Holland and England and, in a special way, in France, which, although profoundly involved in the Reformation, ended up as a Catholic power.

The second primary theme is the analytical *complexity* of the explanation of what has occurred and what may be projected. This article does not assert that Christianity as a religious movement "produced" modern society; rather it holds that Christianity contributed a crucial complex of factors, which, because of its own internal trends of "transformative" development and because of the great diversity of nonreligious conditions at various stages of the process and in various areas, operated very differently at different points in the developmental process.

Incorporating and synthesizing elements from both of its two main cultural forebears, the Israelitic and the Greek, and developing a new religious pattern of its own, the Christian movement crystallized a new pattern of values not only for the salvation of human souls but also for the nature of the societies in which men should live on earth. This pattern, the conception of a "kingdom" or, in Augustine's term, a "city" of men living according to the divine mandate on earth, became increasingly institutionalized through a long series of stages, which this article will attempt to sketch. Later it became the appropriate framework of societal values for the modern type of society.

Christianity, through the societal values it has legitimized, has been *one* principal factor in the evolutionary process that has led up to modern society. At every stage, however, the religious system and its values have stood in complex relations of interdependence with other factors, notably economic and political organization and interests, the underlying institutions of kinship and social stratification, and certain aspects of secular culture. Several times, as in the rise of monasticism and the Puritan "errand into the wilderness," the main innovative trend has been associated with the withdrawal of its carriers from the main societal arena, rather than with short-run acquisition of control over them. Indeed, in the larger perspective the power of religiously grounded values to shape secular life has depended on the increasing structural differentiation of religion from the organization of the secular society, as is indicated in the great weakening and eventual abolition of the long-standing institution of established churches.

Although the present article is confined to Christianity, it is written in the perspective of the comparative status of Christianity among the historic "world" religions, in their relations to the development of the societies in which they have originated and to which they have become diffused. (This perspective derives, more than from any other source, from the work of Max Weber.) Some centuries before the origin of Christianity, not only in the world of the eastern Mediterranean but eastward through India to east Asia, there had developed the varied system of "historic" religions, including Judaism, Hinduism-Buddhism, and Confucianism-Taoism. All of them in varying ways and degrees sharply accentuated the differentiation between the profane and the sacred, temporal existence and eternity, worldly and otherworldly, natural and supernatural. These great cultural movements redefined the problems of the meaning of human life both for the individual as a personality and for human societies. One main axis of the problems concerned the relative devaluation of the profane, the temporal or the natural. Should the interests of temporal life be renounced in favor of some conception of radical salvation? Was there to be religious legitimation of those temporal interests or even of human societies with their necessary natural and secular anchorage? How were the two basic references to be balanced in relation to each other?

The General Orientation and Setting

Christianity developed a very special pattern of solutions to these questions. It was second to no other religion in emphasizing the transcendental character of its conception of divinity. The God which the Christians inherited from the Hebrews was the creator-ruler God, the *sole* creator and governor of the world, which included the human condition generally—the condition of *all* peoples. Not only was Christianity a transcendental monotheism, but its theology focused specifically on the conception of a divinely ordained, active mission for man. God created man "in His own image" in order for man to "do His will" on earth. That will, in turn, ordained the performance of a great collective task that eventually was believed to consist essentially of the building of a society in the temporal world in accord with the divine plan. This conception of the God-man relationship greatly influenced the social world through the commitments of its adherents to remake that world in accord with the divine plan. It contrasted very sharply with some of the Oriental religions that motivated "adjustment to" the immanent order of the nonempirical universe.

This transcendental-activistic attitude alone, however, does not account for the broad societal impact of Christianity. It has also characterized Judaism and Islam, but neither of these great movements originated the makings of a modern society on its own. Judaism, after a brief period in a politically independent, "divinely ordained," small kingdom, was dispersed into small enclaves widely scattered over the civilized world and too small, politically powerless, and insulated to exert a major influence on very large-scale societal developments. Islam so directly fused religious leadership and the government of large-scale, rapidly expanding empires that it could not (as least within a short enough period of time) adequately control the institutional conditions of social change to channel them in the religiously indicated directions. Furthermore, the development of the religious orientation system itself was not "rationalized" and systematized in a manner comparable with the Christian.

The theme of human imperfection, in acute contrast with the transcendence and thus in some sense the glory of God, is sharply accented in Judaism and became the basis of the Christian doctrine of sin. Such imperfection, however, was inherently relative to the deep theme of the goodness of the divine creation, of which man, "created in God's image," was clearly the highest part. Then even such expressions as the "total depravity" of sinful man are not to be taken so literally as to imply no basic potential for religiously legitimized good. It is not the "things of this world" or of the "flesh" which are inherently evil but primarily man's willfulness, his presumptuousness in disobeying the divine commandments and in thinking he can do without divine guidance.

The other essential ingredient of Christianity came from Greek culture, which had distant relations to Hebraic culture but was predominantly independent of it in development and pattern. The institutional structure of Roman society had sufficiently fused with Hellenistic culture in the area in which Christianity originated, so that we can consider the parts played in the shaping of Christian theology by Greek philosophy and by the institutionalized individualism and law of the Roman polity to be of a piece. Greek culture provided a major *constitutive* component of Christian religious orientations, and early Roman imperial society provided both an environment in which the movement could spread and institutional components, notably a legal system, which were eventually absorbed by the Christian religious system and the church itself.

Particularly important to the Christian orientation to human society was the Greco-Roman conception of a universalistically defined system of order in the "nature" of the world. In its more cosmic references it underlay the Greek contributions to the beginnings of natural science. But it also had relevance to human relationships, and in this connection, especially among the Stoics, the ideal of human society came to involve the ordering of these relations in accord with the "order of nature." The fullest institutionalization of this universalistic conception came with the systematization of Roman law, which, by including both the *jus civilis* (which defined the rights and obligations of Roman citizens) and the *jus gentium* (which defined the relations among persons of a different civic or ethnic allegiance) in a single, coherent legal system, transcended the parochial particularism that characterized previous conceptions of social order. Furthermore, this transcendence implies that the basic bindingness of such an order must be defined in general terms and not in highly specific prescriptions and prohibitions as has been characteristic of many systems of religious law, such as those of Talmudic Judaism and Islam. This universalism of the secular normative order could then be matched with the universalism of religious evaluation, which was one of the crucial religious features of the Christian movement.

The marriage of Hebraic and Greco-Roman elements that produced Christianity involved a crucial differentiation of the new sociocultural entity from both parent sources. Judaism and Greek and Roman religion had been the religions of already established sociopolitical communities, the People of Israel and the city-states of the Greek and Roman worlds. To use the terms loosely, they had been "ethnic," "civic," or "national" religions. On the level of social structure it was decisive that Christianity arose as a sect within Judaism, at a time when Palestine was Hellenized and Romanized—certainly the members of the elite were culturally quite Hellenized. Since all sectarian movements have a separatist tendency, it was natural that early Christianity raised questions about how its differences from the rest of the Jewish community were relevant to the general Greco-Roman matrix. These questions reached a crux when St. Paul initiated the church's historic break with the traditional Jewish community by declaring that the observance of Jewish law had no bearing on a convert's status as a Christian. This status was to be based only on the individual's act of commitment to the church and the saving message of Jesus (Nock 1938). It seems that this development was occasioned by problems stemming from the very success of Paul's mission to the Gentiles —that is, by the fact that many Christians were essentially alien to the particularities of Jewish tradition.

Its break with the Jewish community gave the church freedom to develop and expand. This freedom was realistically important, particularly because of two main features of the society of the Roman Empire at that time, perhaps especially of its eastern half. First, under the pattern of order just noted, this society was predominantly individualistic in a sense matched by no other society of comparable scale until modern times. In spite of its many regional and ethnic particularities, Rome effected its governmental authority over an exceedingly wide area and maintained substantial peace and internal order for a considerable period. A primary factor in this stability was the highly universalistic system of law, with its quite generalized principles allowing very substantial freedom within its framework. It was a society in which considerable mobility for migration and settlement was feasible and in which the main urban centers, at least, were highly developed and cosmopolitan communities.

Second, the society was psychologically ready for the type of soteriological movement which Christianity represented. Within the Jewish community there had developed much interest in the salvation of the individual, in addition to the traditional primary focus on the destiny of the People of Israel, as recent research has particularly emphasized. Deutero-Isaiah emphasized the individual aspect, and the Christians were not the only sect within Judaism, as, for example, the Essenes show. Beyond the Jewish community there was also considerable ferment of this general character (Nock 1964). The Greek mysteries and various kinds of Oriental cults spread widely through the empire, for example, Mithraism and the Egyptian cult of Isis and Osiris, and schools of philosophy took on a quasi-religious, if not fully religious, character (Cumont 1910). All of these movements attracted individuals on terms ranging from the clientele of a simple cult to membership in relatively firmly structured associational groups.

The Early Movement—Doctrine and Organization

The church was the corporate vehicle of the implementation of a distinctive religious orientation. The God of the Christians was of course the God of Israel, in His transcendence as creator and ruler of the universe and as the One who defined man's mission on earth. Compared to the main lines of Judaism, however, there was a new centrality of the conditions of the salvation of the individual soul rather than of the fate of a community. The Saviour was not the Messiah—although partially identified with him —not a new Moses who would lead his people into a new Promised Land, but the bringer of eternal life to the souls of believers.

The critical thing was the Christ figure as the mediator between the divine and the human levels. As the conception of Christ became stabilized through its elucidation in terms of Neoplatonic philosophy, he was at the same time both divine and human; he was, as formalized in the Nicene Creed, of the *same*—not similar—substance as the Father. (For the importance of the *homousias* formula, see Lietzmann 1938.) But as mortal, as dying in the crucifixion, he was a man, sharing all the attributes of humanity. He was the "Word made Flesh."

The strict monotheism of Prophetic Judaism was thereby modified. God the Father had "begotten" his divine Son. The Son had the power to "save" the souls of men and they in turn could have access to this incomparable gift through faith, through commitment to him and his mission, not through belonging to the Chosen People. This conception in turn called for a third "aspect" of divinity, the Spirit which Christ emanated to the believers and by virtue of which they were reborn into eternal life. Hence the doctrine of the Trinity, which was at the same time one and three divine persons.

Against the background of Judaism the Christian doctrine can be seen to have preserved the transcendence of God, but at the same time broken the bond to the Chosen People as the sole basic vehicle of implementing the divine plan for man. The place of the People of Israel could be taken by the church, which by virtue of the role of the Holy Spirit could be conceived also as at once divine and human, the company of souls "in Christ," which after death were somehow in "eternity" but in this life on earth constituted a special sort of sacred association. Basically it could only be a collectivity grounded on belief, not an ethnic one (the "People"). This was the theological basis of a critical step of differentiation between the religious system and the main structure of secular society, without which the historic mission of Christianity could not have occurred.

It was crucial that constitutive symbolism of Christianity was built about the problem of death. The central validating event of Jesus' mission was the crucifixion. That he died was the symbol of his humanity; that he was resurrected was the symbol of his divinity. The relation of the church to the risen Christ constituted a crucial break with Judaic tradition in that its promise to men was not the reward of a worldly collectivity (the Chosen People) in a future "land of milk and honey," but the spiritual participation of the individual believer in "eternal life" and "in Christ." Through the sacrificial death of Jesus, death in general was for the believer not denied but transcended (Nock 1964). The granting of divine status to the mortal human being, to the flesh, and to worldly concerns was perhaps more firmly repudiated than in any other religious tradition. However, in being given the opportunity for salvation, man was called to participate in the world of the divine, in his purely spiritual capacity. Thus, the great Christian step was to spiritualize man while still retaining the legitimation of a mission for him in *this* world. By contrast, what may be called archaic religions went much further in the direction of divinizing the human—for example, by regarding the Egyptian pharaoh as a god. Indeed, the formula for the spiritualizing of man constituted the essential religious basis of the conception of the church.

Against the background of Hellenism the universalism of the conception of order in human relations in this world could be preserved. Even though the pagan society of imperial Rome could not be positively sanctioned, it could be negatively tolerated, as in the formula "render unto Caesar [a pagan emperor] the things that are Caesars," and Paul could be proud of his Roman citizenship. The articulation with the Christian theology, however, could go beyond the conception of an immanent order of nature to that of a potential new order which developed through the penetration of human society by the Divine Spirit through the agency of Christ and his church and the souls which had been elevated by their Christianization. There was here a new source of leverage over the world of secular human life, a basis, over the long run, of profound influence over it, the efficacy of which depended on many conditions, one of the most important of these being preservation of the basic Israelitic conceptual pattern that the mission of mankind was divinely ordained. The dimensions of this basic cultural orientation can be illuminated by its relation to four of the heresies that had to be combated well down into the Middle Ages.

The Gnostic heresy was perhaps most formidable in the eastern area in the early centuries. Derived from Neoplatonism and certain elements stemming from Persian and Egyptian cults, without the correctives of Hebrew and Roman empiricism and realism, it would have deprived Christianity of its leverage over the secular world by denying the reality of nature in favor of a realm of idealistic symbolization.

The major initial crisis, however, was over the Arian heresy, which in a certain sense was the obverse of the Gnostic heresy. It would essentially have denied the divinity of Christ by making him in substance only "similar" to the Father and thereby have deprived the church of the primary source of its leverage over the world. The church would have been at best divinely legitimized rather than "inspired." Without the Athanasian victory over Arianism it is hard to see how the church could have maintained its independence under the pressures of institutionalization as the state religion of the Roman Empire.

The Manichaean and the Donatist heresies were particularly important in the developments from Augustine to the High Middle Ages. The Manichaeans, to whom Augustine at one time belonged, would have destroyed the integration of the divine and human spheres, which was so crucial to the mission of Christ and the church, in favor of a basic metaphysical dualism that saw human life as an unending struggle between the forces of light and darkness. The Augustinian doctrine, on the contrary, saw the Christian task as not merely to defeat the forces of evil, but to organize and eventually include the lower and worldly elements in the higher. Although the secular world of his time was only negatively tolerated, Augustine affirmed the potential of Christianization for the "City of Man."

Finally, the Donatist heresy, although it had presented a major challenge even at the time of Augustine, came to a head at the time of Pope Gregory VII in the issue of the status of the clergy. It located the religious efficacy of priesthood not in the Holy Spirit as infused in the church but in the state of grace of the priest as an individual. Had it prevailed, it would have destroyed the fundamental *collective* character of the church, its capacity to serve as the agent of reorganization of secular life in the service of the religious ideal.

Thus, the early Christian church became clearly *differentiated* from *any* collective structure of the secular societies in which it originated and into which it spread. It thereby achieved a position of independence from all the structures of secular society, which was to prove of the utmost importance (Troeltsch 1912). As a collectivity itself, it embodied a type of structure that both favored its spread in the societies of the time and provided societies which had a considerable Christian population with a model for their change. Thus, in the Middle Ages the church was far more nearly modern in structure than was feudal society. Change came to be the modification of secular society to resemble the church, far more than the accommodation of the church to the secular patterns.

Forms of Christian Institutionalization

The Christian theological orientation provided the cultural grounding for establishment of the church as an association of believers committed through the faith and in a way that differentiated their status as church members from other elements of the status of the same people in the society in which they lived. The main patterns of institutionalization that the Christian church has assumed follow.

The first broad type is represented by the early church and in a considerably modified form by the many sectarian movements that have appeared throughout the history of Christianity. The common characteristic is the existence of the religious association of the Christian type as essentially a separate entity within a host society, without clearly stabilized relations to the rest of the society. It could, as the early church gradually did, move in the direction of establishment. It could also, like many pietistic sects, come to be stabilized in some kind of enclave within the society, under some kind of toleration—the Diaspora Jewish community is a model. Otherwise, it could fail to preserve its identity and could be dissolved or absorbed.

In the case of the early church the surrounding society was pagan. The church enjoyed a relatively high order of toleration, partly because in the earlier phases its members were relatively obscure people and were centered in the more impersonal urban communities. They supported themselves by work in the relatively ordinary ways; as Paul said, a man "must work that he may eat." This social situation was associated with the eschatological orientation of the early phase. Concern was overwhelmingly with eternal life and preparation for it. The Second Coming was, at least in a mythological sense (how literally is difficult to tell), paramount in Christian expectations and was to be associated with the Last Judgment and the end of the temporal world.

This orientation was repeatedly renewed, but most sects took positions short of this extreme dissociation from the environing society. In the first place, the society itself had become in some sense Christian; hence the differentiation was interpreted to mean that it was imperfectly so. Very broadly, we can say that the worldly "activism" that we have considered to be a major feature of the Christian movement generally has precluded full long-run stabilization in a sectarian status. An innovative movement within the Christian system would in the nature of the case be oriented to influencing the definition and structure of the system as such, including of course its relation to secular society. Many movements with a more or less sectarian origin have of course found a "niche"—for example, as religious orders within the Catholic system or as denominations within the Protestant.

The second primary type of Christian organization is the Catholic. This is interpreted in the sense of an established church, which is the "state" religion of a politically organized society. The critical difference here from other cases in which membership in the religious community coincides ideally with that in the secular is the *differentiation* of the church as a social collectivity from the secular political collectivity, the state in more or less the medieval sense. Church and state in this sense are distinct organizations. Their relations to each other, however, have necessarily been complex. Again very broadly, the Eastern Orthodox church, which took primary shape within the Byzantine political structure from Constantine on, was, as Harnack in particular has emphasized, oriented by the transcendental concerns of Christians. It therefore tended to be concerned eventually with its particular version of monasticism and to give the orders a kind of primacy over the secular priesthood, which did not exist for the Roman Catholic church. This in a sense gave by default a special position to the secular political authority, since there was no papal monarchy to match the secular. By contrast, the Roman papacy and secular priesthood gave the church a stronger organizational position, especially in the earlier phases, by contrast with the weak secular structures of the declining western Roman Empire.

Both were Catholic, especially in the sense of establishing a *sacramental* order, which gave the visible church a specifically transcendental character. The sacraments as the "power of the keys" were in fact the direct means of dispensing divine grace (Troeltsch 1912).

The third basic type is the Protestant. Here the break is fundamentally with the sacramental system, making the "true" church "invisible" and salvation dependent, from the human side, on faith alone. Again, there have been, in the broadest terms, two main forms of Protestantism. The first of these carried over the pattern of the established church from the Catholic versions, with its presumption of the coincidence of the religious and the secular political communities. This position carried with it the obligation of the enforcement, by ecclesiastical and political authorities in varying relations to each other, of doctrinal orthodoxy as a condition both of religiously acceptable standing and of secular citizenship.

The second type of Protestant orientation has basically differentiated the religious from the political systems, in a sense far more radical than that of the Constantinian church and its successors. It "privatized" religious adherence, introduced religious toleration, and eventually promoted denominational pluralism and the separation of church and state.

The special "sectarian" character of the early church was an essential condition of the church's institutionalization in the Roman Empire as differentiated from the secular "politically organized society." Moreover, of the two main versions of Catholicism, the Roman had the greater evolutionary potential because it could give a special, new meaning to the conception of the "City of Man," under the tutelary aegis of the church.

The shift to Protestantism essentially meant the abandonment of this tutelage with its special kind of religious paternalism. The Lutheran branch, however, had a sufficiently "inward" character, so that it entrusted the responsibilities for secular affairs to political authority in a manner somewhat similar to that of the Byzantine church and its Orthodox successor. The other main branch of Protestantism, the Calvinistic, was parallel to the Roman branch of Catholicism in developing in the activistic direction, placing the greatest emphasis up to that time on the conception of the kingdom of God *on earth*.

The Trend to Religious Establishment

The spread of Christianity did not fail to occasion considerable disturbances, including the wellknown persecutions of the Christians. However, the reign of the emperor Constantine the Great saw a consolidation of the social position of the movement. In 313 Constantine proclaimed full religious freedom for the Christians, in the Edict of Milan. He later took such an interest as to preside personally over the Council of Nicea (although perhaps partly for its political implications) and eventually was converted. By the end of the fourth century Emperor Constantine had established Christianity as the state religion of the Roman Empire.

When the church came to comprise a large sector of the upper class of the empire as well as the emperor and his court it was necessary to restructure the terms that had defined the distinction between Christians, who as such were free of the entanglements of the sinful world, and pagans, who constituted the secular society. By the third century, the spreading movement comprised a considerable proportion of the population of the Roman Empire and had begun to penetrate the higher social levels of the empire. The Roman upper groups may have been corrupt and pleasure-seeking, as legend of the Christian world has it to this day, but they were the carriers of the social responsibilities of their society, however badly they may have failed in their obligations. Clearly, not all of the upper-class converts to Christianity could withdraw from the secular world. Many of them, to be sure, did become anchorites. But some continued to be local magnates and even to hold imperial office.

The expansion of the church up to the critical period of the early fourth century was a slow and complex process. The basic role was evidently performed by the apostles, who as missionaries went from community to community to make converts. Among them, the original apostles, who had been the personal followers of Christ, were only the first of a continuing series. Where the apostles succeeded local associations were formed, which at first were highly informal. However, "teachers" and "deacons" soon appeared to assume certain differentiated functions in maintaining the doctrine and in carrying on the simple administrative tasks of the group. The oldest and largest churches, usually those located in communities that were particularly important in the secular society, became pre-eminent, and their officials assumed a special importance, especially in relation to the secular political order. Such pre-eminence soon became involved in the relations between the separate churches, and hence the offices of the leading churches became the points of crystallization for the episcopal organization of the church (Harnack 1902). It was natural that the emerging sacramental system and the administrative functions should become consolidated in the same office at both parish and episcopal levels.

This was a classic case of success threatening the deeper foundations of the values for which the original great commitments were made—not the last such case in Christian history. There is little doubt that this development presented the Christian church with an exceedingly severe temptation and that it partly succumbed. It succumbed much more fully in the eastern half of Christendom than in the western, a differentiation which became crucial in the development of the Western world and had much to do with the great schism of the eleventh century.

A most important feature of the Christian movement, as so far analyzed, was its establishment of *independence* from the ascriptive ethnic and lineage ties—whether Jewish or Greco-Roman—in which its predecessors had been involved. This was accomplished by combining a specifically religious orientation *and* a type of collective social organization of the religious community, which was in some respects as great an innovation as the constitutive religious symbolism itself. This independence was, however, notably threatened by the very success of the movement in reorganizing the religious constitution of the Roman Empire. The development of organized collective monasticism, as distinguished from individualistic anchoritism, was in important degree a response to this critical situation. This process—the major innovations being the work of St. Basil—resulted in a differentiation within the church that may be regarded as even more fundamental than that between clergy (administrators of the sacraments) and laity. This was the differentiation between the religious and the laity.

The religious, as members of the orders, became the elite of the church. Their withdrawal from the world, symbolized above all by the vows of poverty and chastity insured the independence from secular ties which had been so basic to the early church but which had become so much more difficult for most Christians to attain under the new conditions. The vow of obedience can be seen as assuring selective obedience to religious authority, specifically of the abbot, and hence protection against nonreligious influences and pressures.

In a sense this was a snobbish discrimination by "superior" Christians against "inferior" Christians. However, it differed crucially from the dualism of the early church in that the lay Christians were still Christians, not pagans, and were expected in principle to comprise practically the *whole* population of the relevant secular society, even though it took a long time to accomplish this. The pagan element had been religiously upgraded through its conversion by the Christian movement and had become eligible for *inclusion,* as a total society, in the category of Christian, at least potentially. Moreover, the society was not a small, precarious Chosen People in a vast sea of more powerful alien societies, but was the great Roman Empire, the secular organization of what then seemed to be practically the whole civilized world.

The conversion of Constantine was the event which symbolized concomitantly the enormous opportunity of the Christian church to shape the secular world and the equally enormous threat to its independence represented by its generalization to a great total population and by its conversion of the socially influential and responsible classes. The reality and importance of the threat is evidenced by the long series of conflicts between church and state and, more subtly and insidiously, the involvements of the clergy (and on occasion the orders) in the nexus of secular interests.

Formation of the Western Church

The next great stage of Christian history was associated with the differential fate of the two halves of the Roman Empire. In its original cultural constitution Christianity was much more Greek than Roman (Nock 1964; Jaeger 1961). It seems that it *could not* have arisen and grown to the level it attained had it been confined to the western half of the empire, since not only the Judaic but the Hellenistic component of its heritage was essential. Nevertheless, its greatest mission materialized not in its eastern "homeland," but in the west. One condition of this lay in the fact that, for a longer period, the west proved to be politically less stable than the east. At the same time, the west was the focus of both the ancient origin and the medieval resurgence of the distinctively Roman institutions of autonomous legal order; in both respects it developed much further than the Greek and the Byzantine elements indigenous to the east.

The decline of the Roman Empire was in the first instance that of the western empire. The eastern portion became highly stabilized, surviving the western by a full millennium. Even though its structure was gradually undermined, the sheer length of this survival is an extraordinary fact. In the west, however, the new crisis of the disorganization of the secular society (beginning with the removal of the capital from Rome to Constantinople) was associated with a great and many-sided surge of organization and innovation in the church.

The tendency for the two halves of the empire to split politically was related to a parallel tendency within the church. At the time of the Council of Nicea, the Arian faction derived its main support from the eastern segments of the church and the Athanasian faction from the western (Lietzmann 1936). In accord with this division, the east moved broadly toward political stabilization without major cultural innovation, whereas the west tended more to foster cultural innovations within the church and organization changes partly determined by them. Four principal trends crystallized within a relatively short period.

(1) The highest levels of theological formulation were greatly transformed by the figure whose doctrines, more than those of anyone else, shaped the distinctive nature of western Christianity, namely, St. Augustine. He lived and worked in western north Africa and wrote in Latin, not Greek. As Harnack so clearly put it (Harnack 1916; Vasil'ev 1917–1925), Augustine's conception of the "City of God" was, in one of its two main references, a potentiality for human life on earth. It was not confined to the realm of eternal life after death. Although the emphasis on the basic metaphysical dualism between divine and human, spirit and flesh, remained as sharp as in the Alexandrian theology and was even sharpened in certain respects, salvation was conceived to be not only *from* the sinfulness of the flesh but also *for* participation in the divine mission that God had ordained for Christian man in and through the church. The use of the concept of city is particularly significant in that it emphasized the continuity of the conception of the church with that of the polis. This was indeed part of the larger framework within which Augustine produced a new level of cultural generalization in the synthesis of the Christian soteriological message and the main patterns of classical culture. The main orientations of the Eastern

church remained at the level of theological concern established by the Alexandrine Fathers, whereas, with Augustine, the west began to build a new foundation, upon which grew the whole Western development, including both Scholasticism and the Reformation.

(2) We have noted that the monastic movement was first established in the east, emerging in close relation to the spread of Christianity, which culminated in its becoming the state religion of the empire. Basilian monasticism, which predominated in the Eastern church for many centuries, was overwhelmingly contemplative and devotional in its emphasis. But in the west there followed closely upon the theology of Augustine and certainly in connection with it a new turn in the monastic movement, starting with the establishment of the Benedictine order (Tufari 1965). The Benedictine Rule instituted a regime of secular useful work for its members, labor in agriculture and in crafts, as a religiously valued ascetic exercise— as Weber particularly noted. One might say that labor was no longer conceived as simply the "curse of Adam," but as an essential component of the most fully Christian way of life. It was patently connected with a synthesis of the transcendental focus of Christianity and the exigencies of Christian life in this world. Fostering this orientation, the Benedictine order was the first in a series of involvements by the monastic elements of the Western church with the problems, first, of firmly establishing the church in its relations with secular society and, second, of improving secular society itself from a Christian point of view.

(3) The west strongly consolidated the organizational structure of the church itself, with special reference to the position of the secular clergy and their control. In contrast to the Byzantine pattern, which placed the emperor religiously as well as politically above *any* bishop, the crucial factor in this development was the consolidation of the Roman papacy and the establishment of the primacy of the See of Rome and of the position of its bishop as the true head of the church in the west. Presumably the pope could not have assumed primacy had he been confronted with an emperor who claimed to be head of the church and was resident in the same city. But with the emperor a thousand miles away and Italy in a condition of relative political chaos, the elevation was possible. Of course, the traditions of Peter's mission to and martyrdom in Rome provided cultural legitimation for this crucial organizational change.

(4) Underlying this organizational consolidation were developments in the sacramental system, especially its extension to all the laity. The core sacrament, the Eucharist, formally ritualized the central constitutive symbolism of Christianity, the sacrificial death of Jesus and its transcendence. The Mass was the primary occasion upon which the communal solidarity of all members of the church was demonstrated at the parish level. (Weber [1921*a*] especially emphasized that the *common* participation in the Mass included all social classes.)

The sacramental system required a formally ordained, professional priesthood. The episcopal system organized the priesthood in a firm way, and papal monarchy had an opportunity to hold the territorially scattered bishops to a common organizational focus. These features of the organization of the church, which gradually became increasingly formalized and systematized through the development of canon law and administrative agencies, was particularly important because of the decentralized, segmented nature of the emerging feudal society. In the face of these tendencies the church in the west maintained a fundamental unity and a relatively bureaucratic structure.

What was new in the Western church was the idea that the church was not only ordained for the salvation of souls for eternity, but that it also had a mission for this world, to establish the kingdom of God on earth. In the first instance, this was to be realized in the monastic life, then in the church as a whole, and eventually in the whole of secular society. In contrast, the Eastern church had only one focus: eternity and the afterlife of the individual (Harnack 1916). Even when secular society had been Christianized (in the fourth-century sense), the true Christian was to live by the tenet "in but not of" it, almost in the Pauline sense. At the same time the church as organization had to come to terms with secular society, a fact particularly conspicuous at the parish level in the status of the priesthood as both married and virtually hereditary. At the highest social level the direct involvement of the church with government was indicative of a similar mode of accommodation. There was never an independent status of the church, with respect to secular society as a whole, comparable to that attained in the west. The Eastern church remained, in Harnack's striking phrase, "frozen" at the level of religious concern attained by Christianity generally in the third and fourth centuries under the influence of the theologians who had been Neoplatonists in philosophy. In these terms, a great turning point in the history of Christianity came in the west with the theology of Augustine.

The Medieval System and the Renaissance

The first culmination of the Western development was what Troeltsch called the "Christian society" of the High Middle Ages. This was partly preceded but also accompanied by a major development in monasticism, centering first in the Cluniac order, and by a new surge of energy and organizational reform in the church itself, especially during the papacy of Gregory VII, who had probably been a Cluniac monk himself. Certainly one of the most significant reforms was the formal institutionalization of clerical celibacy for the secular priesthood, which contributed greatly to the organizational independence of the church. However imperfect the enforcement of celibacy may have been, the policy meant that no priest—including bishops, who were often men of great power—could have *legitimate* heirs, so that clerical office could not become hereditary. This was particularly important, as Lea (1867) made clear, because the institution of aristocracy was becoming so central to secular society at that time.

Monasticism was also very much involved in the new theological developments, under the stimulus of Scholastic philosophy, especially within the Dominican order. Culminating in the *Summa theologica* of St. Thomas Aquinas, Scholasticism carried the integration of theology and philosophy a long step forward and, through the influence of the rediscovered texts of Aristotle, accomplished a new and more thorough incorporation of classical culture.

Greater involvement in the secular world was symbolized by the active building of churches, especially of cathedrals, all over Europe. This not only implied an increased concern for the lay Christian, providing better for his worship, but also gave him more opportunity to express his religious concern, since church building required immense efforts from whole communities. Great ecclesiastics competed for the services of architects; village stonemasons embellished the great piers of cathedrals with intricate carvings, and elaborate façades were peopled with sculptured figures, while painting and stained glass decorated interiors.

There was certainly a connection between these religious developments and the growth of urban communities. For example, the guilds, which were becoming ever more prominent in the secular organization of the cities, profited immensely in wealth and power from their part in building the cathedrals and great abbeys. Significantly, no less an authority than St. Thomas held the urban way of life more favorable to Christian virtue than the rural (Troeltsch 1912, p. 295 in vol. 1 of the 1960 edition)—an interesting contrast to some nineteenth-century religious views. A new level of concern for the laity was also shown in the increasing ecclesiastical emphasis on Christian charity, in which again monasticism, particularly the Franciscan movement, played the leading role. The material, as well as the spiritual, welfare of the economically disadvantaged Christian became more and more the concern of the church.

In growing measure the ecclesiastical development of the Middle Ages became Pan-European, at least from south to north. Italy, as the seat of the papacy, in many respects took the leading role, despite the fact that Scholasticism centered in Paris rather than in Rome; but in general the characteristic changes were as conspicuous north of the Alps as south. The Middle Ages developed a European society and culture far more than ever before, even at the height of Roman influence.

The medieval Christian system was hierarchical. At the top stood the members of the religious orders, who lived the fully religious life—with whatever lapses—and stored up "treasure in heaven" for the benefit of their less committed lay brethren. Not only did the orders exhibit an increasing concern for the world, both in church and in secular life, but also, in sharp contrast to Buddhist monasticism, this religious "upper class" was linked to the laity by an independent secular clergy that controlled the power of the keys.

The Christian laity were in religious terms all presumptive equals. Of course, one must recognize that at this stage there was no implication of secular, social or economic, equality. Not even slavery was morally condemned, although humane treatment of slaves was enjoined. Secular society was highly stratified, with rapidly crystallizing institutions of hereditary aristocracy. These changed gradually from predominantly feudal forms into territorial monarchies, with the monarchs heading the aristocratic classes. The mass of the common people were the tillers of the soil. However, European society differed from many others with a predominantly peasant base and an aristocratic elite in that, largely as a heritage of classical antiquity, corporately organized towns played a very important part. Their organization provided essential models and centers for the development of more egalitarian forms of political institutions and of law, as well as of guild industry and commerce. Crucially, their bourgeois citizens were neither aristocrats nor peasants, but an essentially independent middle class.

Medieval European societies were the first in history to have basic religious uniformity for a very large population as a whole. At the same time they fundamentally differentiated the religious organization, the church, from the secular structure, what in this special sense has been called the state. Thus, within the context of the total society, the church was able to maintain its structural independence. This fact, combined with its organizational features and relatively this-worldly orientation, enabled the church to exert an unprecedented influence on the process of social development.

Both culturally and socially there were certain inherent elements of instability in the medieval system which a certain contemporary romanticism is prone to obscure. On the whole, however, these seem to have involved openness to progressive change rather than a tendency to breakdown or societal regression. On the cultural side, the Scholastic system was shot through with tensions and controversies. Certainly, the emergence of nominalism as a major movement on the borderline between theology and philosophy was highly significant (McIlwain 1932; Southern 1953; Kristeller 1955; Huizinga 1919). In accord with Thomas' example in seeking confirmation from Aristotle there was a general turning to classical sources and models—for example, the humanistic concern with classical literature and the revival of interest in Roman law which, especially in relation to the place of canon law within the church, began early in the Middle Ages

(Gierke 1881). In fact, the high medieval culture merged almost imperceptibly into that of the Renaissance, however important certain dramatic advances may have been, such as those of Giotto and Masaccio in painting.

These processes of cultural elaboration and differentiation were grounded in the commitment of the Christian movement, especially accentuated in the west, to a genuine synthesis with classical culture. The critical development was the emergence of a differentiated system of secular culture more or less directly articulated with Christian orientations and, despite many tensions, legitimated in general by Christian values. Perhaps the most obvious field is that of art, where architecture was heavily oriented to the church and where painting, besides embellishing churches, dealt almost exclusively with religious subjects.

There was also instability in the relations between the church as organization and secular society. The imposition of clerical celibacy had been in one respect a measure to protect the autonomy of the church from overinvolvement in the responsibilities, as well as the perquisites and privileges, of secular affairs. The "investiture controversy" was typical of the structural difficulties at the feudal core of the system, because the bishops, as the principal officers of the church, were responsible for both its political and its property interests. But in feudal terms, the church as corporation could not simply "own" property or enjoy political "rights" in the modern sense. The church was so interwoven with the feudal system that, as property holder, it also became the lord with temporal political jurisdiction, a circumstance that gave rise to a basic question of allegiance: Where did it lie, with the church or the secular authority? In medieval terms, no clear answer was possible (Troeltsch 1912, chapter 2, parts 3 and 4).

Thus, there was an unstable oscillation between ecclesiastical subordination to secular authorities and the direct assumption of secular power by the church, as in the papal states and in a few ecclesiastical principalities north of the Alps. It was inevitable that religious and ecclesiastical problems became intertwined with secular politics, so that the tensions in one sphere fed into the other. This situation goes far to explain the fact that the Reformation stimulated a full break in the unity of western Christendom rather than a "reform" of the church in the more usual sense.

The whole spectrum of cultural development, however, from the spheres of philosophy closest to the theology of the church to the most secular aspects of arts, letters, and eventually science, steadily eroded the cultural foundations of the medieval system. Socially, the feudal core of the society receded in relative importance before the rise of the Italian city-states with their commerce and manufacturing, the growth of the free cities of the Holy Roman Empire north of the Alps from Switzerland to the Netherlands, and the establishment of truly national states, particularly France and England.

The Reformation and Its Aftermath

The Reformation was the culmination in the strictly religious sphere of the general trend of social and cultural change away from the medieval system and toward modernity. Although it was hostile to certain of the Renaissance achievements (e.g., in art), its basic continuity with the Renaissance is the more impressive fact, as evidenced in the close following of the Italian initiatives in science by Protestant scientists in Holland and England and the hostility of the Protestant north to many of the artistic innovations coming from Italy. It is not unimportant that the founder of the more "progressive" wing of the Protestant movement, Calvin, was trained in law as well as in theology. The Reformation became intimately related to the development of nationalism—vernacular translations of the Bible multiplied—and some Protestant areas advanced very rapidly in economic development.

Although its consequences and implications took long to unfold, the Reformation constituted both a truly fundamental innovation and an authentic evolutionary development from the medieval Catholic base. The aspect of greatest interest here concerns primarily the relation of the religious system to the secular society.

At the strictly religious level the crucial development was the upgrading of the Christian laity. This was effected by ending the individual's dependence on sacerdotal mediation. The individual soul stood in *immediate* relation to God through Christ (Bellah 1964). With respect to the ancient triad of functions the effect was to throw emphasis strongly away from the institutional forms of the "cure of souls" and of "casuistry." It opened the door to an altogether new emphasis on "conscience," which emerged particularly in the Calvinistic branch, once the more subjective concerns of Lutheranism had given way to concern with objective activism in secular callings. Although it is true that the basic status *differential* was eliminated, this did not imply any lowering in the evaluation of the clergy or of the system, within which statuses had been "equalized."

The upgrading is expressed in the basic Protestant doctrine of the *invisibility* of the true church. The visible social organization, the concrete church with its priests and sacraments, is *not* the mystical body of Christ; the latter exists only in the souls of those who by faith are its true members in the eyes of God. The visible church has become "secularized." But in the true visible church the layman has been placed on equal footing with the religious. If the layman truly gives his commitment of faith and accepts the divine grace, his status of sanctification is fully equal to that which had previously been reserved to the monk.

The radical implication was that it is not necessary, in order to be sanctified, to lead a way of life apart from the secular world and under a special discipline (Weber 1904–1905). Religious merit was in principle compatible with any ethically acceptable worldly "calling." Moreover, as Luther himself deliberately dramatized, it was compatible with marriage. Thus, the two crucial vows of poverty and chastity were no longer preconditions of the "truly" Christian life. The same fate for the vow of obedience was inevitable because, in the monastic state, obedience was owed to a human ecclesiastical authority, in the first instance to the abbot. The differentiation of church and state clearly meant that ecclesiastical authority could not govern conduct in secular callings and presumably not in any complete sense in marriage and family life. The legitimation of monastic separatism as the *one* pattern of the fully Christian life was thereby destroyed.

The change in the status of the sacraments as administered by the secular clergy was parallel. The direct relation of the individual's soul to God in seeking grace through faith precluded *any* humanly administered mechanism from intervention in God's dispensation of grace. The minister became basically a teacher, counselor, and leader of his congregation (Troeltsch 1912, chapter 3 in vol. 1 of the 1960 edition).

The human individual was no longer conceived as a unitary entity, whose secular or worldly life was inseparable from its spiritual state, but as encompassing a much sharper differentiation between the two components. The aspiration to gain sanctification would yet have consequences for conduct in the secular world, but the commitment of the religious would no longer be embodied in a way of life concretely different from that of the nonreligious. The same principle obtained in regard to the sacraments. No concrete acts of human beings could automatically dispense or withhold grace. The only source of grace was directly divine, and grace could come to the individual only through his private, subjective acceptance of it.

To understand the potential significance of this shift it is essential to reconsider the whole development since early Christianity. The early church and its membership constituted a precarious island of sanctification in a sea of paganism, the latter comprising the whole structure of the secular society. With the successful proselytization of the whole of Western society and Christianity's emergence as the official religion of the Roman Empire, the newly differentiated religious orders became the elite vanguard of the church. They preserved the central Christian orientation from secularization by absorption in an environment that was not fully Christian in the religious sense and led the movement to the upgrading of the whole lay population on Christian terms.

The Christian society of the High Middle Ages was a class-stratified religious society in that the visible church was endowed with a kind of fundamental guardianship, first and foremost over secular society—the position of the state in this connection being highly equivocal. Within the church there was a parallel guardianship of the laity by the clergy, both regular and secular. Since the Reformation was in the first instance a "revolution" within the church, its primary consequence was, as noted, the emancipation of the laity from this guardianship by the clergy. The implications for secular society, however, were implicit and could not fail to become salient unless the whole development were suppressed.

Although events moved much more rapidly during the Reformation than during the spread of Christianity in the ancient world, there is a significant similarity of pattern. Once a movement apparently so alien to the Roman ethos as Christianity was able to reach a position to bid for religious ascendancy in the empire, an alliance with secular authority was inevitable. In this case, it took the form of conversion of the legitimate Roman emperor and the eventual proclamation of the official status of Christianity. It would have made some, but perhaps not a fundamental, difference if a Christian military leader had gained political supremacy by conquest, as was typical in the spread of Islam. In either case the secularizing influence of political involvement would have operated. As noted, the primary response of the Christian church was to protect its independence, first, by the development of religious orders that had considerably more independence from secular society than the secular clergy, and, second, by retreating into the politically disorganized west, where the secular authority was relatively weak.

The parallel events in the Reformation involve Luther's alliance with the German princes. (In certain contexts Luther may be considered the Constantine of his day—in the sense of being a politicized churchman, not a converted emperor.) Had not this religious innovation, too, enlisted political power during its crucial period, it could never have succeeded. It could not have become cosolidated in strategic metropolitan centers and thus enjoyed the opportunity to spread into new areas. The price of this alliance, however, was a conservative turn—in the social sense—of the religious movement itself, exemplified by Luther's repressive attitude toward the peasant revolts and his general support of secular authoritarianism.

The developments of this period were the result of a complex combination of innovating and conservative elements at work. The princes were in fact pioneers in the construction of the national state, one of the institutional foundations of modern society. They were, however, at the same time markedly authoritarian in regard to independent movements within their jurisdictions. Luther's conservative position in economic affairs and especially affairs of political sovereignty vis-à-vis the subjects of the princes, accorded with this context. In an important sense, conservatism culminated in the Lutheran movement's acceptance of the Erastian principle that the political sovereign should also be the formal head of the church. Here, the development tended, as in Eastern Christianity, toward a symbiosis of church and state, severely compromising the religious potential for reconstructing the secular world. The parallel to the mystical, otherworldly orientation of Eastern monasticism was the Lutheran stress on "inwardness" of the Protestant Christian orientation, which also precluded undertaking major responsibilities in secular affairs. The truly Christian individual was to be primarily concerned with settling his accounts with God and hence relatively indifferent to the fate of secular affairs. The main responsibility for these affairs was to be left to a divinely ordained secular authority. Furthermore, the whole orientation was shot through with pessimistic convictions about the essential sinfulness of secular man, which would inevitably manifest itself in widespread unethical conduct, which could be checked only by a liberal resort to coercive measures on the part of the civil authorities (Troeltsch 1906; 1912, chapter 3, part 2 in vol. 1 of the 1960 edition). Although this conception was another version of the Christian society, it was not a very inspiring one from the viewpoint of secular idealism.

As must be expected of social movements directed toward such broad and generalized social change (Smelser 1962), Reformation Christianity has been characterized by a multiplicity of sectarian movements having a wide variety of orientational content and possibilities for influencing later social developments—as indeed has virtually every subsequent phase of Christianity. Some have been strongly chiliastic and sometimes antinomian and as such have generally failed to become permanently institutionalized —historically one of the most important was the Anabaptist movement (Cohn 1957; Knox 1950). Others have secured more or less stable interstitial positions (e.g., some of the Pietistic movements). Still others, like the two most important American movements, Mormonism and Christian Science, have been relatively close to the main line of ascetic Protestant development.

Ascetic Protestantism

The major Protestant alternative to the Lutheran development may be considered *the* main developmental line of Protestantism, if not of Christianity as a whole. Broadly, this started with the Calvinist wing of the Reformation. There is a striking parallel between this major differentiation within Protestantism and that between the eastern and western branches of the earlier church, even the geographical reference remaining stable in that the western was the more activistic branch. Indeed one might even suggest some significance in the fact of continuity with Rome; whereas Luther was a German monk steeped in Scholastic philosophy, Calvin was a Frenchman who had a predominantly lay education with special reference to law in the Roman tradition.

Asceticism within the Protestant framework had to be "this-worldly" in Weber's sense. Precisely by maintenance of the basic radical dualism between the transcendental and the "world" within that framework, the activistic potentials inherent in the whole Christian movement (and indeed back of it, in Judaism) were accentuated to a far higher degree than had been possible in the Catholic tradition. On the one hand, Calvinism, in common with the Lutheran branch, had emancipated secular society from ecclesiastical tutelage and put it "on its own"; on the other hand, the Calvinist version of the tensions between the divine mission and the human condition gave a far stronger anchorage to activistic orientations than did the Lutheran tendency toward resignation in the face of sin and divine Providence.

The Calvinist pattern centered on the conception, foreshadowed by Augustine but newly accentuated, of the holy community destined by divine mandate, but implemented by *human agency,* to bring into being a kingdom of God on earth (Miller 1956). This was from one aspect a collective orientation, but from another was perhaps the most radical expression of Christian individualism; at least it was an orientation to realistic possibilities of institutionalization in secular society rather than otherworldliness or antinomian expectations. Calvinism was, however, a developing religious system in a complex cultural and social environment, so that considerable time elapsed and many changes occurred before certain of the most important potentialities could emerge.

In the more immediate situation, the Reformation precipitated a critical period of conflict and reorganization in European society as a whole (Elton 1963)—to be sure, other factors were also involved, for example, the political impetus which led to and derived from the discoveries and extra-European expansion. The broad outcome of the tensions, which in secular terms operated mainly at the political level, was the creation of a northern European tier of predominantly Protestant communities. However, there were many crosscurrents in the political struggles, including those within the Protestant movement. The Catholic political bastions were Spain and the eastern Hapsburg domain, with disunited Italy being a continual battleground of interests. Northeastern Germany became solidly Protestant and with Scandinavia was the main focus of the institutionalization of Lutheranism. However, the most potent political unit of this system, the monarchy of Prussia, came to be dominated by a special version of Calvinism (Kayser 1961).

On the western wing, England, while also becoming, with her colonies in North America, the most important "mother" of institutionalized ascetic Protestantism, adopted in the Church of England the most nearly Catholic type of ecclesiastical organization of any Protestant church. France, after a bitter internal struggle in which the Protestant forces almost gained control, was carried by the most important Catholic victory during the wars of religion, but in a form which destroyed her religio-political "orthodoxy" and in some important respects paved the way for the French Revolution. Holland, in the heat of her struggle for independence from Spanish rule, was for a time the most Protestant of countries, only gradually to attenuate this characteristic in the subsequent period—a fact associated with the preservation, largely under French auspices, of the Catholicism of Flanders and of the German Rhineland, especially of its northern reaches.

The outcome of these complex restructurings, which was clear by the early eighteenth century, was politically inconclusive, but in one sense it was crucially decisive. The Reformation permanently broke the medieval form of the religious unity of western Christendom, and a Europe was created in which religious and political elements were interwoven in a very intricate, pluralistic fashion. Thus, in the mid-eighteenth century His Most Catholic Majesty, the king of France, could find himself first in an alliance negotiated by a cardinal with the Calvinist king of Prussia against the Hapsburgs and then in support of the very Protestant American colonies in their war of independence against the also Protestant British. After 1688 the danger of old-style political-Catholic domination of Britain was past. The position of Prussia made clear that there could be no Catholic reconquest of the eastern boundaries of the main European system—the Hapsburg monopoly was broken. Moreover, major societies of European origin and of predominantly ascetic Protestant orientation had been implanted overseas, beyond *any* basic control of the parent European system.

The main foundations of the ascetic Protestant religio-political system were laid in Holland and particularly in Great Britain (including Scotland) during the seventeenth century. The earlier version of the conception of the holy community was almost dramatically embodied in the Commonwealth under the Protectorate of Oliver Cromwell. Although this drastic political innovation lasted only a few years, like the Calvinist movement in France, it left indelible marks on the whole future of the country. The Restoration brought back the monarchy and aristocracy and consolidated the position of the Church of England, but by the time of the Settlement of 1688, religious toleration was assured and opportunity was opened for nonconformism to develop further—a Catholic restoration of the French type would surely have precluded a Methodist movement so soon after the Stuarts.

Besides the religious movement itself, this enormous "effervescence" crucially advanced the development of the British parliamentary system, which eventually extended into a political democracy. It greatly aided the consolidation of the characteristic features of the common law and hence the establishment of the foundations of the legal component of modern citizenship, the famous "rights of Englishmen" (Little 1963; Marshall 1934–1962). It also created a social environment more congenial to the development of science than any hitherto found in the west—the century and country of Cromwell were also those of Newton (Merton 1938). Finally, the very fact that the political emphases of the Cromwellian venture failed to gain ascendancy probably shifted the balance in favor of the economic emphases, which Weber elucidated in his famous analysis. All of these factors—admittedly combined with various others—had much to do with the fact that in the later eighteenth century it was Great Britain that fostered the momentous beginnings of the industrial revolution.

The foregoing summary is not meant to imply that the development in seventeenth-century England was either unitary or independent of non-Protestant antecedents. The depth of the internal division which was manifested politically in the English Civil War is clear. However, the Stuart Restoration did not become consolidated and a new unity was achieved after 1688 which broke the chronic tendency of the crown under the Stuarts to ally itself with Catholic powers and to threaten the Protestant succession. The main framework of the legal system was established, as was religious toleration. In the case of science, of course, the main foundations of the modern development had been laid in Renaissance Italy with Galileo as the most notable figure, but England provided a newly favorable cultural and social environment for the next main phase, with Newton as the great symbolic figure, and the establishment of the Royal Society as the organizational focus.

England was thus unique in the combination of cultural and social factors which led toward modernization. Its only close rival was Holland. Here, however, the efflorescence was briefer and somewhat less widespread —for example, there was less development in the fields of law and parliamentary institutions. Moreover, the insular position of England encouraged the development of a solidary national community and protected her more fully against the inhibiting and disruptive influences of the complex Continental situation, such as the military threats that would encourage a large standing army and restrictions of economic access to trade with immediately neighboring countries. In particular, England was in a strikingly advantageous position to extend her politico-economic influence beyond Europe, and this included religious as well as other types of development overseas.

On the cultural side, another extremely important difference seems to have been established, broadly, between predominantly Catholic and predominantly Protestant Europe. It has been emphasized above that the relation between Christianity and the more secular elements of culture, with their special roots in the classical heritage, presented problems of great significance. The Christian capacity to synthesize with these cultural movements, which in its terms have been primarily secular, has been one of its most important features.

The rise of early modern science, in its connections with philosophy, presented a new set of problems for the nature of this synthesis. Here the more ascetic branches of Protestantism seem to have been able to develop a relation with substantially less immediate and overt conflict than the more predominantly Catholic cultures—with the exception of what later came to be defined as the "fundamentalist" trends in Protestantism. The somewhat special relation between science and Puritanism in seventeenth-century England is a prominent case (Merton 1938), although the situation in Holland was similar in the same period.

By contrast, there seemed to be a greater conflict between science, and more generally the "intellectuals," and religion in the Catholic sphere. This came to a head in eighteenth-century France in the Enlightenment. By and large, the orientation of the Enlightenment was antireligious, which of course meant anti-Christian. Since the religious structure was Catholic, it was also anticlerical because of the central place of the clergy in the Catholic system. On the whole, the antireligious themes among persons committed to the secular intellectual disciplines have been much less prominent in Protestant areas, again especially those of ascetic Protestantism, although of course it has not been absent. This division still persists, especially between Continental European intellectuals and those of Anglo-American provenience. Thus, the resonance of Marxism has been notably weak in the latter area, which can almost certainly be associated with the militant anti-Christianism of the Marxists.

American Protestantism

There is an important sense in which the modernizing outcome of the European development of ascetic Protestantism occurred mainly in North America, although also in other places. In any case, the development there may serve to illustrate the second main subtype of Protestant institutionalization defined in the classification that was outlined above, namely, that characterized for a whole society by the "privatization" of organized religion and hence by the separation of church and state and the "spelling out" of religious toleration in a system of denominational pluralism, in which there is no distinction, as has persisted in England, between an established church and a set of "nonconformist" groups.

This development marks an important step in the general evolutionary trend of the Christian system from the "aspiration to Universal Brotherhood, to the institutionalization of Universal Otherhood" (Nelson 1949). The United States represents by far the largest scale of institutionalization of this type, and in addition, the fact of the American position of power and influence on the world scene, which has developed in the present century, gives this case a special empirical importance.

The case is, however, meant to deal with the realization of the "liberalizing" potentiality of Protestant development from a Calvinistic base, because of the special evolutionary significance of that trend in the total Christian picture. The role of this Protestant liberalism has been one of leading a trend, which could in turn be adopted by other groups, partly because of the generally modernizing developments in the respective societies, as in Scandinavia and much of Lutheran northern Germany and partly because of the impact of the "liberal" Protestant model which, for example, has certainly affected the development of the Catholic church.

Early Calvinism was predominantly collectivist in orientation. At the purely religious level it embodied the old Christian duality of spirit and flesh in the radical form of the doctrine of predestination. As interpreted in certain phases of Calvinism, this purported to categorize concrete human persons as either saved or damned, by divine decree, from eternity. Although the strict theological terms admitted of no visible signs of election, the social tendency was toward a certain kind of elitism, the rule of the presumptively elect over the presumptively damned, the reprobates. Nevertheless, this doctrine basically undermined the institution of aristocracy in the older European sense. There was never the slightest suggestion that God "predestined" persons to election by virtue of their ancestry; had there been, it would have been indefensible in theological terms. Moreover, the invisibility of the status of election raised the question of whether those who claimed it were not merely self-appointed.

Predestination tended continually to be confused with predeterminism and in this interpretation never could have been a genuinely Christian doctrine. It is one thing to assert that salvation comes to all men as a gift of God and that men are thus predestined to salvation. It is quite another to assert that some men are predestined to election and others to rejection. This latter interpretation was too radically in contradiction to the central conception of the mission of Christ to mediate the salvation of all humanity.

There is now clear evidence that the radical social elitism of original Calvinism should be regarded as characteristic only of an early phase of its development (Loubser 1965). In only two major cases has it actually lasted into the modern situation, namely, that of Prussia and that of the conservative wing of Dutch Calvinism in South Africa. In both the Prussian and the South African cases there was a crosscutting with religiously adventitious factors, which made anything like the relatively "pure" development of North American Christianity impossible. Both cases have in common an element of Christian militancy in facing a threatening environment on a frontier in such a way as to make their pattern of action religiously acceptable. Furthermore, in both cases the populations embodying the perceived threats were regarded as inferior by the bearers of the main tradition, namely, the Slavs on the eastern border of Germany and the "blacks" in South Africa.

American Protestant "fundamentalism" might be regarded as a third survival of "old Calvinism." In the South it has been intimately associated with racial segregation and the doctrine of the inferiority of the Negro. Like the South African and Prussian cases, it has been related to the frontier experience and indeed has recently been associated with the parts of the country where frontier traditions persist the most.

There can be little doubt, however, that the main line of development from the Calvinistic base has been a liberalizing one and, moreover, has not been predominantly secularizing in the sense of loss of religious commitment. Development along this main line has occurred in a number of nations, certainly in Holland and England, but most purely in the United States, with its earlier phases centering in Massachusetts.

As the general Protestant differentiation between the spiritual and secular components of an individual person matured, the predestination theology, with its categorization of total persons in temporal life as either sanctified or damned, became untenable. The basic Protestant tenet of salvation by faith then gained application to any individual who would make the commitment of faith. With this development, the conception of the church as in partnership with the political authority to enforce church discipline on the unregenerate also became untenable. The invisible church was a communion of souls in the faith, and the visible church of necessity became a voluntary association (Loubser 1964).

This development had gone so far by Independence that the provisions of the first amendment, separation of church and state and freedom of religion, were not seriously contested in the Constitutional Convention (Miller 1965). This fact was an index not of religious indifference, but of consensus on the religious principles involved. Another indication is that many local churches disapproved of taxation for support of the church well before it was held to be unconstitutional.

This article does *not* assert that on religious grounds alone the development that took place in America was inevitable. That, as contrasted with Dutch Calvinism in South Africa and, indeed, with much of American fundamentalism, it did take this direction was a function of a variety of social, economic, and political circumstances, some of which will be outlined. The crucial point here is that the religious system had the *potential* for this development, which was a religiously authentic and legitimate alternative. Its emergence, in stronger form than elsewhere, cannot be interpreted simply as the "rationalization" of a developing set of economic interests, as has so often been asserted.

This development was certainly favored by political decentralization, which predominated during the earlier phases of American society and gave wide scope for voluntary associations. The political structure also favored independent activity of the committed Christian in his calling— and not necessarily in any context of association—hence in that aspect of individualistic economic action associated with Max Weber's analysis of the relation between Protestantism and the development of capitalism. For a variety of reasons and under a variety of influences, America during the nineteenth century became in certain senses increasingly individualistic. However, this fact should not be placed outside the larger context of the conception of a holy community. The conception of the holy community was paramount among the early Protestant colonists, in Virginia as well as in New England (Miller 1956; 1959). As the scope of communication, trade, and common destiny grew the independent units tended to consolidate into a single community, a new "nation under God."

By the time of its establishment the new nation was religiously and politically pluralistic and was progressively developing increasing degrees of social and economic pluralism. Religiously, it went very far toward basing itself on the principle of voluntary association, a tendency that was virtually complete early in the nineteenth century. Although the exigencies that constrain political voluntarism are harsher, the trend was also toward a "free" polity more exposed to the hazards of populism than to those of traditional European authoritarianism.

The "individualism" of ascetic Protestantism should be understood in this context. It should be remembered that the Reformation eliminated the "two-world" system by virtue of which secular life in general and the secular callings of individuals in particular could not be valued equally with the "religious" callings. However, just as the religious calling and achievement of the individual in the monastic system occurred within the framework of the church, so the religiously critical performances of the Protestant layman in his calling occurred within the context of the holy community, which included *both* visible church and secular society, even though they were differentiated. Ascetic Protestant activism meant that "innerworldly" callings constituted the primary field for the individual to implement his religious commitments. The intensive activism of the general Christian commitment to regenerate (and hence upgrade) life was thereby channeled into achievement in worldly callings, among them, although by no means predominantly, business achievement.

This individualistic pattern bestowed the strong sanction of religious commitment on what is now often called achievement motivation and fostered the internalization of such motivation by typical individuals (Weber 1904–1905). It imbued the typical ascetic Protestant with a strong sense of responsibility for achievements in this-worldly callings, the obverse of which was the ambition to "succeed." This has not been primarily an anarchic individualism of impatience at all social restraint but an institutionalized individualism, the achievement of the individual ideally being a contribution to the building of the holy community. Thus, American individualism has been congruent with a prominent development of nationalism and the pervasive presence of many varieties of association, including much large-scale organization. What there is of the attempt to break down restraints in general—and there is a good deal—is more ideology than direct expression of the central cultural pattern.

American society has recently developed a trend that seems most important against the background of the historical trends sketched above. In its formative period the United States was an overwhelmingly Protestant society and one that developed its religious constitution in a liberal direction and toward a relatively advanced level of religious toleration. By immigration it acquired a large number of non-Protestants, so that by now about a quarter of the population is Roman Catholic and a very substantial number are Jewish. The change in the religious character of the immigrants culminated in the generation extending from about 1890 to World War I.

The crucial phenomenon is the *inclusion* of the non-Protestant groups in a national community which, though of course secular in government, still retains its religious character as a holy community in the transformed sense of a "nation under God." It has become a Judaeo-Christian ecumenical community having the positive form of religious toleration entailed in a denominational pluralism, which has been extended to all major groups in the population, including "secular humanists," who prefer to avoid involvement in organized denominational bodies (Herberg 1955; Parsons 1960). The important core of such groups is not the religiously "indifferent" who simply "backslide" in their religious principles, but the intellectuals who have severe reservations about commitment to any of the more traditional denominational positions. By contrast with much of Continental Europe, the American groups have generally not been characterized by militant atheism or anticlericalism.

We can thus speak of a near-consensus on a "civic" religion—perhaps somewhere near the boundary between theism and deism—expressed in such conceptions as "One Nation Under God" and "In God We Trust" (Bellah 1965). This in turn articulates with and legitimates the broad moral consensus on what I have called the pattern of institutionalized individualism, most massively expressed recently in the civil rights movement, which had the conspicuous backing of *all* the important religious groups as well as of the "humanists" and agnostics.

The religion of the churches, on the other hand, has been both voluntarized and privatized. More detailed belief systems, more specific observances, variations in ecclesiastical polity, and the extent of the individual's commitment to them are largely confined to the denominational level and its embodiment in the particular parish. Broadly, all of the groups that historically have belonged in the established church tradition—for which a Jewish equivalent may be discerned in Orthodox Judaism—have "accepted" this situation, some of course more enthusiastically than others.

This process has been interdependent, as suggested above, with a structural pluralizing in the society as a whole: residence, socioeconomic status, occupation, and political attachment have become increasingly dissociated from religious affiliation and from the ethnic components which have historically been so closely associated with religion. This process is by no means complete, and it is unlikely that a society will ever completely "privatize" ethnicity and religion. However, there can be little doubt that recent American developments have reached an altogether new level, certainly if scale is taken into account. The new American "secular city," as Harvey Cox (1965) has called it, despite all its complex strains, conflicts, and imperfections (which from *any* religio-ethical point of view are many and serious), has been legitimized as a genuine holy community in the ascetic Protestant sense. Yet, it has undergone a development that few of its Protestant forebears could have expected in its ecumenical aspect, having come to include all those who live under the God of Israel and of Jesus Christ. The newly pluralistic framework has come to be *institutionally* established, however incomplete the implementation of its grand pattern.

It seems justified to consider this another version of the institutionalization of what Troeltsch called a Christian society. To be sure, Troeltsch did not deal with it, or any European variant, as such, but seemed to contend that such a conception implied the institutionalization of an established church. With his dichotomy of church and sect, he seems not to have understood the most important unit of such a pluralistic system, the denomination, which is a voluntary religious association that is nevertheless accepted, both by its members and by others, as an institutionalized unit in the social order. Furthermore, it is not only a Christian society, but a Christian-Jewish-humanistic society, with its very important inclusion of elements from beyond strictly Christian boundaries.

The Modern Ecumenical Trend

If American society has produced the most highly developed version of the pluralistic ecumenical religious constitution that has so far appeared within a national framework, important developments have also continued in Europe. With the exception of the special fusion of Lutheran and Calvinistic elements in Prussia, perhaps the most obviously important movements have developed on a Lutheran base and have been more spiritual-cultural than organizational, from the point of view of the relation of religion to the secular society. However, they have already had a major impact on the contemporary situation.

Perhaps the most important reference point here is again the impact of the development of secular culture and, in particular, science. In the more western areas, the European terms, the two most important modes of coming to terms with science were the relatively full "synthesis" achieved, especially on an ascetic Protestant base—reaching a high point in the eighteenth century with Jonathan Edwards (Miller 1949)—and the anti-religious orientation and acceptance of the challenge associated with the Enlightenment.

In the more eastern sector, centering in Protestant Germany, one main base was the movement of idealistic philosophy. This was intimately associated with Protestant theological concerns and also brought such traditions into close contact with the Enlightenment and its romantic counterpart. Against the background of Kant and Hegel, the more rationalizing theology was best exemplified by Schleiermacher. This trend also involved the philosophical grounding of Marxism, which is more central European than western European in its main cultural foundation, although it linked with the Enlightenment in being strongly anti-Christian. The other major trend took its departure from the "subjectivism" of the Lutheran tradition. Its great landmark was the Christian existentialism of Kierkegaard, which in its cognitive structure stressed the limitations on rational philosophy that had been highlighted in the Kantian tradition. This general orientation has also been involved in the "neo-orthodox" movements in Protestant theology, starting with Karl Barth. In broadest terms, the existentialist movement seems to serve as a major counterfoil to the relatively empirical rationalism and the conception of a legally ordered pluralistic society, which have characterized the influence of ascetic Protestantism. It has figured in the revolt of both religious and secular intellectuals whose points of reference have ranged from the ascetic Protestant to the secular, at certain points even being based on Marxist philosophy.

This complex welter of cultural movements could not but become closely involved with the status of the Catholic position. Catholicism has, in its orientation to the secular society, comprised an immense range of different subtypes, from positions, in such areas as northern France and part of Germany and Belgium, that were very close to the Protestant to those, in southern Europe, that often preserved an antimodern traditionalism that was close to medieval.

Doctrinally, the Counter Reformation had hardened the Catholic position, not only against Protestantism but also against the movements of secular philosophy that began prominently in the seventeenth century. Until relatively recently we could therefore speak of the dominance of Neo-Thomism in the church. Although it certainly enhanced the activistic elements in Catholicism, the main concern of the Counter Reformation was to bolster the sacramental position of the church as the core of a Christian society. Hence, it operated to preserve a structural element that tended to be fundamentally premodern.

It can, however, be said that although all of these movements have been at work within the Catholic world, it has felt the impact of two of them especially strongly. On the one hand, the ascetic Protestant pattern of institutionalization of religion, in relation to secular society, has gone far to provide a model sharply different from the traditional Catholic pattern of the relation of church and state. This situation is, perhaps, best exemplified by the fact that the very large Catholic minority in the United States has come to accept the separation of church and state and its own position in the system of denominational pluralism; but this is by no means an isolated phenomenon. On the other hand, the impact of the more subjective-existentialist orientations has worked to attenuate the rigidity of the older Catholic conceptions of sacramental order in favor of what may be called a "spiritual individualism."

These cultural movements have been associated with institutional changes that have broadly followed the American pattern. Thus, although in only a few European countries have historic Christian churches been totally disestablished, only in the most conservative Catholic areas of southern Europe has the religious freedom of other groups, including the secular humanists, been severely restricted. For the most part, European society has become religiously pluralistic. Even Spain has recently shown signs of an incipient pluralization. The aristocracy, which has been a most important factor in bolstering religious conservatism everywhere, has been considerably more prominent in Europe than in America; but major changes have taken place in the present century, so that aristocracy no longer counts heavily in the more "modernized" countries.

Although the structural changes in European society have been retarded relative to the relevant aspects of American society they have been considerable. How far they have gone has to a certain extent been masked by such factors as the segmentation of Europe into a sizable number of national states, the political disturbances of the present century (especially the two world wars, which had their primary centers in Europe), and the political movements of fascism and communism.

Fascism has been predominantly a regressive phenomenon in the context of the evolutionary scheme developed in this article and is not likely to have left any major mark on the sociocultural constitutions of the societies in which it has figured prominently; it is not the basis of a new fundamental variant of Western society, although it has been a major source of disturbance, and has inflicted severe social injury.

The communist movement is quite another matter. It certainly should be classified as at least a quasi-religious movement that has certain strik-ing resemblances to Calvinism, both with respect to its mission as the agent of building an ideal secular society and with respect to the elitism of the two-class system, the party as the "vanguard" of the "proletariat" and the still socially unregenerate masses. Marxism is largely an offshoot of German idealistic philosophy and as such intimately associated with Protes-tantism. Indeed, the militant secularism of Marxism may be regarded as, in certain respects, the ideological accentuation of the importance of the kingdom of God on earth, or the "secular city"—God as the author of this great plan being replaced by the "dialectic of history." For these rea-sons it seems legitimate to treat the communist movement as part of the more general development of the relations between religiously grounded culture and the organization of secular society.

It is a striking fact that the communist movement has not—contrary to Marx's predictions—gained political ascendancy in any of the more ad-vanced industrial countries, either in Europe or outside it. Its first great success was in Russia, which was a semi-European power, substantially backward industrially as compared with western Europe, and the largest single area whose Christian history had been dominated by the Eastern Orthodox church. Communism in the Soviet Union—and in China—has certainly been intimately connected with the problem of moderniza-tion. Its spread to the "satellite" countries is of course a direct function of Soviet political control in eastern Europe. The communist movement there-fore cannot be regarded as a long-run basic alternative to the historic de-velopments of Christianity, although this judgment may not be possible to confirm—or disprove—for a considerable time. At any rate, the acute mutual antagonism between virtually all Christian denominations, perhaps particularly Roman Catholicism, and "atheistic communism" seems to have begun to subside somewhat.

Against this background the catalytic influence of the brief papal reign of John xxiii and the council, Vatican ii, which he called may well con-stitute a major breakthrough in the development of the Christian system, concerning the relation of the different branches to each other, of all of them to secular society and culture, and of Christianity to non-Christian religious movements and institutions. The fact that the initiative came from Rome seems to be particularly significant.

In the first place, this seems to indicate a further extension of the pat-tern of secular responsibility that the church had affirmed in the late nineteenth-century encyclicals on labor and related questions. Second, it seems to represent a major step in Catholic movement toward an ecumeni-cal position. It seems to represent very considerable mitigation of the relatively rigid position that has officially obtained ever since the Counter Reformation. In addition to this, the action taken by the council on the problem of relations to the Jews has gone far toward including them in a wider religious community going beyond Christian boundaries. In this respect the Catholic church as a whole has moved appreciably closer to the position that had been crystallizing in the United States, brought to a head especially in connection with the candidacy, election, assassination, and public mourning of John F. Kennedy, the first Roman Catholic to be president of the United States—indeed the first non-Protestant.

Third, the Vatican Council, along with parallel movements in Protestantism centering in the World Council of Churches, seems to represent a very important step in the direction of mitigating the exclusiveness of religious legitimation, even of the Judaeo-Christian complex, in favor of a still wider ecumenicism, which in particular has made overtures to the historic religious traditions of Asia. Pope Paul's VI's visit to the Holy Land could be interpreted in a purely Christian context, although its break with the tradition of remaining in Italy was striking, and it brought him necessarily into official contact with Jewish and Muslim groups. His visits to India and to the United Nations, however, must be interpreted as symbolic gestures in the broadest ecumenical context.

It thus seems justified to consider that Christianity is entering on a new phase, part of the trend to institutionalization of Christian values in secular society. The proper type of this society, broadly called modern society, is widely valued. This is not to say that modern society is acceptable to Christian ethics in all detail and without any critical reservation. Quite the contrary, like any other actually existing human society, it is shot through with elements of "evil," which range from the deplorable to the intolerable. Moreover, differences of evaluation within the Christian community have by no means disappeared, although they have been substantially mitigated.

There seems, however, to be emerging a consensus on a broad framework of the institutions of the morally acceptable society and on social problems to be solved. Thus, high standards in the economic, health, and education fields, certain fundamental patterns of equality, notably of citizenship and opportunity, and certain aspects of freedom and autonomy for individuals and associational groups are almost universally valued. Conversely, the widespread problems of illness and poverty, of exclusion from educational, occupational, and many other opportunities, and of destruction due to the use of physical violence are more widely recognized and protested against than ever.

Many of the intrasocietal and intersocial problems that distress the modern world owe much of their salience and form of statement to the processes of institutionalization of Christian values sketched above. The distress over them is not so much a measure of the irrelevance of the historic impact of Christianity as a measure of the incompleteness of institutionalization; a conception which implies that there has been in the past significant *relative* success. The magnitude of the tasks ahead often seems appalling, but they would not even have been defined as tasks if the attitudes of the earlier phases of Christian development still prevailed.

Bibliography

BELLAH, ROBERT N.   1964   Religious Evolution. *American Sociological Review* 29:358-374.

BELLAH, ROBERT N.   1965   Heritage and Choice in American Religion. Unpublished manuscript.

BLOCH, MARC   (1939-1940) 1961   *Feudal Society.* Univ. of Chicago Press. → First published as *La société féodale: La formation des liens de dépendence,* and *La société féodale: Les classes et le gouvernement des hommes.*

COHN, NORMAN   (1957) 1961   *The Pursuit of the Millennium: Revolutionary Messianism in Medieval and Reformation Europe and Its Bearing on Modern Totalitarian Movements.* 2d ed. New York: Harper.

COX, HARVEY   (1965) 1966   *The Secular City: Secularization and Urbanization in Theological Perspective.* New York: Macmillan.

CUMONT, FRANZ   (1910) 1956   *The Oriental Religions in Roman Paganism.* New York: Dover. → First published in German.

DUCKETT, E. S.   1938   *Monasticism.* Ann Arbor: Univ. of Michigan Press.

ELTON, GEOFFREY R.   (1963) 1964   *Reformation Europe.* Cleveland: World.

GIERKE, OTTO VON   (1881) 1958   *Political Theories of the Middle Age.* Cambridge Univ. Press. → First published as "Die publicistischen Lehren des Mittelalters," a section of Volume 3 of Gierke's *Das deutsche Genossenschaftsrecht.* Translated with a famous introduction by Frederic William Maitland.

HARNACK, ADOLF VON   (1902) 1908   *The Mission and Expansion of Christianity in the First Three Centuries.* 2 vols. 2d ed., rev. & enl. London: Williams & Norgate; New York Putnam. → First published in German. The first British edition was published as *The Expansion of Christianity in the First Three Centuries.* A paperback edition was published in 1962 by Harper.

HARNACK, ADOLF VON   1916   *Aus der Friedens- und Kriegsarbeit.* Giessen (Germany): Töpelmann. → See especially the essay on "Der Geist der morgenländischen Kirche im Unterschied von der abendländischen."

HERBERG, WILL   1955   *Protestant, Catholic, Jew: An Essay in American Religious Sociology.* Garden City, N.Y.: Doubleday.

HUIZINGA, JOHAN   (1919) 1924   *The Waning of the Middle Ages: A Study in the Forms of Life, Thought and Art in France and the Netherlands in the 14th and 15th Centuries.* London: Arnold. → First published in Dutch. A paperback edition was published in 1954 by Doubleday.

JAEGER, WERNER W.   1961   *Early Christianity and Greek Paideia.* Cambridge, Mass.: Belknap.

KAYSER, CHRISTINE   1961   Calvinism and German Political Life. Ph.D. dissertation, Harvard Univ.

KNOX, RONALD A.   1950   *Enthusiasm: A Chapter in the History of Religion;*

With Special Reference to the XVII and XVIII Centuries. New York: Oxford Univ. Press.

KRISTELLER, PAUL O. (1955) 1961 *Renaissance Thought: The Classic, Scholastic and Humanistic Strains.* Gloucester, Mass.: Smith. → First published as *The Classics and Renaissance Thought.* A paperback edition was published in 1963 by Harper.

LEA, HENRY C. (1867) 1957 *History of Sacerdotal Celibacy in the Christian Church.* New York: Russell. → First published as *An Historical Sketch of Sacerdotal Celibacy in the Christian Church.*

LIETZMANN, HANS (1932) 1952 *The Beginnings of the Christian Church.* History of the Early Church, Vol. 1. New York: Scribner. → First published in German as a separate work. A four-volume paperback edition was published by World in 1961 as *A History of the Early Church.*

LIETZMANN, HANS (1936) 1958 *The Founding of the Church Universal.* History of the Early Church, Vol. 2. 3d ed., rev. London: Butterworth. → First published in German as a separate work. A four-volume paperback edition was published by World in 1961 as *A History of the Early Church.*

LIETZMANN, HANS (1938) 1958 *From Constantine to Julian.* History of the Early Church, vol. 3. 2d ed., rev. London: Butterworth. → First published in German as a separate work. A four-volume paperback edition was published by World in 1961 as *A History of the Early Church.*

LITTLE, DAVID 1963 The Logic of Order: An Examination of the Sources of Puritan–Anglican Controversy and of Their Relations to Prevailing Legal Conceptions of Corporation in the Late 16th and Early 17th Century in England. Ph.D. dissertation, Harvard Univ.

LOUBSER, JOHANNES J. 1964 Puritanism and Religious Liberty: Change in the Normative Order in Massachusetts, 1630–1850. Ph.D. dissertation, Harvard Univ.

LOUBSER, JOHANNES J. 1965 Calvinism, Equality, and Inclusion: The Case of Afrikaner Calvinism. Unpublished manuscript.

McILWAIN, CHARLES H. (1932) 1959 *The Growth of Political Thought in the West, From the Greeks to the End of the Middle Ages.* New York: Macmillan.

MARSHALL, THOMAS H. (1934–1962) 1964 *Class, Citizenship, and Social Development: Essays.* Garden City, N.Y.: Doubleday. → A collection of articles and lectures first published in book form in England in 1963 under the title *Sociology at the Crossroads and Other Essays.* A paperback edition was published in 1965.

MERTON, ROBERT K. 1938 Science, Technology and Society in Seventeenth Century England. *Osiris* 4:360–632.

MILLER, PERRY 1949 *Jonathan Edwards.* New York: Sloane. → A paperback edition was published in 1959 by World.

MILLER, PERRY 1956 *Errand Into the Wilderness.* Cambridge, Mass.: Belknap. → A paperback edition was published in 1964 by Harper.

MILLER, PERRY (1959) 1965 *Orthodoxy in Massachusetts.* Gloucester, Mass.: Smith.

MILLER, PERRY 1965 *The Life of the Mind in America, From the Revolution to the Civil War.* New York: Harcourt.

NELSON, BENJAMIN N. 1949 *The Idea of Usury: From Tribal Brotherhood to Universal Otherhood.* Princeton Univ. Press.

NOCK, ARTHUR D. 1933 *Conversion: The Old and the New in Religion From Alexander the Great to Augustine of Hippo.* Oxford Univ. Press. → A paperback edition was published in 1963.

NOCK, ARTHUR D. 1938 *St. Paul.* London: Butterworth. → A paperback edition was published in 1963 by Harper.

NOCK, ARTHUR D. 1964 *Early Gentile Christianity and Its Hellenistic Background.* New York: Harper.

PARSONS, TALCOTT 1960 *Structure and Process in Modern Societies.* Glencoe, Ill.: Free Press. → See especially pages 295–321 on "Some Comments on the Pattern of Religious Organization in the United States."

SMELSER, NEIL J. (1962) 1963 *Theory of Collective Behavior.* London: Routledge; New York: Free Press.

SOUTHERN, RICHARD W. (1953) 1959 *The Making of the Middle Ages.* New Haven: Yale Univ. Press.

TROELTSCH, ERNST (1906) 1912 *Protestantism and Progress: A Historical Study of the Relation of Protestantism to the Modern World.* London: Williams & Norgate; New York: Putnam. → First published as *Die Bedeutung des Protestantismus für die Entstehung der modernen Welt.* A paperback edition was published in 1958 by Beacon.

TROELTSCH, ERNST (1912) 1931 *The Social Teaching of the Christian Churches.* New York: Macmillan. → First published as *Die Soziallehren der christlichen Kirchen und Gruppen.* A two-volume paperback edition was published in 1960 by Harper.

TUFARI, PAUL 1965 Authority and Affection in the Ascetic's Status Group: St. Basil's Definition of Monasticism. Ph.D. dissertation, Harvard Univ.

VASIL'EV, ALEKSANDR A. (1971–1925) 1928–1929 *History of the Byzantine Empire.* 2 vols. University of Wisconsin Studies in the Social Sciences and History, Nos. 13–14. Madison: Univ. of Wisconsin Press. → First published in Russian. Volume 1: *From Constantine the Great to the Epoch of the Crusades (A.D. 1081).* Volume 2: *From the Crusades to the Fall of the Empire (A.D. 1453).*

WEBER, MAX (1904–1905) 1930 *The Protestant Ethic and the Spirit of Capitalism.* Translated by Talcott Parsons, with a foreword by R. H. Tawney. London: Allen & Unwin; New York: Scribner. → First published in German. The 1930 edition has been reprinted frequently. A paperback edition was published in 1958 by Scribner.

WEBER, MAX (1921a) 1958 *The City.* Glencoe, Ill.: Free Press. → First published as *Die Stadt.*

WEBER, MAX (1921b) 1958 *The Religion of India: The Sociology of Hinduism and Buddhism.* Translated and edited by Hans H. Gerth and Don Martindale. Glencoe, Ill.: Free Press. → First published as *Hinduismus und Buddhismus,* Volume 2 of Weber's *Gesammelte Aufsätze zur Religionssoziologie.*

WEBER, MAX (1921c) 1952 *Ancient Judaism.* Glencoe, Ill.: Free Press. → First published as *Das antike Judentum,* Volume 3 of Weber's *Gesammelte Aufsätze zur Religionssoziologie.*

WEBER, MAX   (1922a) 1951   *The Religion of China: Confucianism and Taoism.* Glencoe, Ill.: Free Press. → First published as "Konfuzianismus und Taoismus" in Volume 1 of Weber's *Gesammelte Aufsätze zur Religionssoziologie.*

WEBER, MAX   (1922b) 1963   *The Sociology of Religion.* Boston: Beacon. → First published in German. A paperback edition was published in 1964.

10. Durkheim on Religion Revisited: Another Look at *The Elementary Forms of the Religious Life*

I

SINCE MORE THAN thirty years ago I wrote a long chapter (1937:640–96) on Durkheim's analysis of religion based mainly on the *Elementary Forms of the Religious Life* (Durkheim 1910), and I had only sporadically gone back to this focal book of Durkheim since then, it seemed that full rereading of the *Elementary Forms* was the best way to prepare myself to write a chapter in the frame of reference of the present book, namely: how do Durkheim's contributions in the field of religion look at the present time? It should be kept in mind that from the very beginning of his published work, Durkheim was deeply concerned with normative order as a fundamental constituent in the nature and structure of society. It was this emphasis on which I initially focused attention in my own first serious study of Durkheim's work. It seemed to me, and I think rightly at the time, that the *Elementary Forms* constituted the culmination for its author of a long and complex process of the deepening and clarification of his understanding of this very central problem area. Along the road, building on his analysis in the *Division of Labor in Society* (1893), Durkheim arrived at the full statement of the conception of internalization of moral norms in the personality of individuals and of the seminal conception of *anomie,* and I think very importantly of what I have called institutionalized individualism. Conspicuously, this last began with his analysis of the reasons why Protestants had higher suicide rates than Catholics.

From *Beyond the Classics?: Essays in the Scientific Study of Religion,* Charles Y. Glock and Phillip E. Hammond, eds. (New York: Harper & Row, 1973), pp. 156–180. Copyright © 1973 by Charles Y. Glock and Phillip E. Hammond. Reprinted by permission of the Publisher.

213

Looking back, I think I was somewhat ambivalent about two features of the *Elementary Forms*. The first was Durkheim's concentration on studying the religion of a single primitive society, indeed the most primitive about which he could find what he considered to be adequate evidence. The second was the stress he laid in the book on problems in the difficult boundary areas of epistemology and of the sociology of knowledge, which I had a certain feeling were being somewhat gratuitously "dragged in" to a study which I interpreted to be focused mainly in the sociology of religion.

As the background of a great deal that has happened to me intellectually in the long intervening period, I can say that I have come out of the rereading with a substantially altered perspective, an alteration which definitely enhances my appreciation of the greatness of the book. In the first place, stimulated along the way by Robert Bellah's (1959) significant paper, "Durkheim and History." I think I have come fully to understand the sense in which Durkheim had, by the time he wrote the *Elementary Forms,* come to be committed to a theory of evolution not merely of human societies in the analytical sense, but of the human condition generally. The choice of empirical material for the book and its main pattern of organization were clearly to a major degree determined by this commitment.

Second, I have come to see that the book is not primarily a study in the *sociology* of religion, but rather of the place of religion in human action generally. In the terms that I have used in recent years, it is couched primarily at the level of what I have called the general system of action, which includes the theory of the social system but also of cultural systems, personality systems, and of behavioral organisms. In a very important sense the last of these four references proved to be unexpectedly important in interpreting what Durkheim was doing. Above all, it makes much more intelligible the grounds for his concern with problems that I have called those of epistemology and the sociology of knowledge. Many of his formulations about the societal origins of the categories of the understanding, of space and time and the idea of force and, hence, causality that were unacceptable to me in earlier years are still unacceptable as adequate general statements, in the sense that I think the basic insights that he had can be reformulated in more acceptable terms. A very central shift of his, however, from the inherited traditions of the theory of knowledge was his placing of culture, including, of course, empirical knowledge, in a perspective which was only partly epistemological.

What I take to be his basic theorem is that human society and the cultural framework of the human condition, including knowledge, have evolved concomitantly from a common basis and, in relatively advanced stages of sociocultural development, have come to be differentiated from each other. This conception of common origin is very different indeed from a one-way conception of determinism, namely, that of society as an independently existing entity, determining the nature of the organization of knowledge. This, of course, has been the common sense of what might be called the vulgar sociology of knowledge, of which Durkheim most definitely was not a proponent.

Durkheim's position in epistemology was definitely Kantian, emphasizing the strong duality of the problems of sense data and their sources on the one hand, and the categorial structure of knowledge on the other hand. Indeed, in his conclusion Durkheim cites Kant's sound conviction that the grounding of cognitive knowledge and that of moral judgment should be treated as linked through the fact that they both concern universality of reference, as distinguished on the one hand from the data of the senses, and on the other from what he called the appetites. This is indeed the fundamental conceptual scheme of Durkheim's analysis: the duality on the one hand of the universal and the particular, on the other hand, the cross-cutting duality of the cognitive and moral references.

II

It is here that the famous distinction between the sacred and the profane enters in. I had earlier correctly understood, indeed it was very difficult to miss, that this distinction was in the religious context the equivalent of the distinction between moral authority and the utilitarian or instrumental pursuit of interests in the secular sphere. I did not, however, fully appreciate the lastmentioned implications of it, namely, the extent to which he identified the distinction in the moral sphere with that in the cognitive. At present, however, it seems correct to say that he thought of the category of the sacred as the synthesis or matrix of the other two primary categories of universality, namely, the categories of the understanding and the related cognitive rubrics and the category of the moral. This identification and the corresponding identification of the profane with *both* instrumental interests and sense data is by no means incompatible with a difference of relation of these pairs to social systems on the one hand and to the individual on the other. I take it that the really fundamental meaning of Durkheim's thesis of social origin is the evolutionary one that at sufficiently early stages, society and culture were undifferentiated from each other.

This brings us to another very central point, namely, Durkheim's assertion that sacred things are symbols, the meanings of which should not be interpreted in terms of their intrinsic properties. This, it will be remembered, was one of the main points of his, to me, devastating critiques of the theories of animism and naturism concerning religion. When, however, the question arose: symbols of what, Durkheim's tendency, disturbing to so many including myself, was to say symbols of society. In the usual received senses of the concept "society," this seemed very close to being nonsense. If, however, one looks at the problem in the evolutionary perspective and speaks of symbols of the grounding of human existence, which is always inherently, at least in major part, social, it seems a much more reasonable formula. I think that in both the cognitive and the moral contexts, Durkheim was essentially speaking of the basic framework of order, which must be assumed in order to make the phenomena of human life, with special emphasis on its social aspect, intelligible. Indeed, in the conclusion he speaks of a concentration in human society of the forces, I think it is fair to say, determining the functioning of living systems which is unique in the aspects of the universe we know. I should interpret this assertion in terms, which have become current since Durkheim's day, of the evolution in the direction of negative entropy of the organization of living systems, and the significance of the references lies in their revealing the fundamental conditions of this order of evolution. This interpretation gives a certain reasonableness to Robert Bellah's (1970) suggestion that we ought to speak of symbolic realism in the sense of abandoning the attempt, so prominent in Durkheim's case, but also in that of Freud, to interpret sacred and some other symbols as always representing something outside themselves.

III

In all these discussions on Durkheim's part there is a persistently recurring note, namely, the emphasis on separateness of the moral from the appetitive, of the categorial from the empirical, of the sacred from the profane. But second, there is the theme of the relation of categorial, moral, and sacred components to long-run concerns, as distinguished from day-to-day concerns, of the systems in which they form a part. It was this emphasis on a quite different time span which alerted me on my rereading to the very striking formal similarity between Durkheim's series of distinctions and the historic distinction in biological theory between those aspects of biological systems which are embodied in the *genetic* constitution of organisms as members of species and those which characterize the individual organisms. One formulation is the distinction between germ plasm and somatoplasm; another, genotype and plenotype; another, phylogenetic and ontogenetic references. The problem of separateness was fought out in the famous post-Darwinian controversies over the question of the inheritance of acquired characteristics with the negative view finally clearly prevailing.

Since what we have been calling behavioral organisms is an essential constituent of what we call action systems, it seems reasonable to assume that this dichotomy, which is fundamental to the understanding of all organisms, should also apply to the human organism in its role in action. If this is true, then why should not a closely related distinction be extended from the organic aspect of human action systems to the others? It seemed to me that many of Durkheim's discussions and observations were consistent with the view that this was one of the principal messages that he was trying to convey in his analysis.

In interpreting this it should be kept in mind that Durkheim was writing at a time when the social sciences, and sociology in particular, were fighting a strenuous battle against what has often been called biological reductionism. Durkheim's own, perhaps most important, single polemical opposition, namely, to Herbert Spencer, was part of that battle. Durkheim strenuously asserted that society was a "reality *sui generis.*" It is not an organism in the then current sense of the term "biological." Since that time, however, biological theory has undergone a profound process of change which in many respects, to much surprise, assimilates the understanding of the functioning of organisms far more closely to that of personality and social systems than had previously been thought reasonable. At least for the moment, the culmination of this change has been the development of the new genetics, with its conception of DNA as embodying, in its chemical structure as a very complex molecule, a code which can govern the reproduction of previous patterns of organization in living cells in the development of new cells. (Stern 1970, Stent 1970, Olby 1970). This extremely general feature of the operation of living systems is continued in many different respects, but above all with respect to genetic constitution, in the processes of bisexual reproduction.

Seen in this perspective, it has become increasingly clear that Durkheim's three separate categories could all be interpreted as pointing to, if not fully analyzing, the presence in the governing of human action processes of codes analogous in some respects to the genetic code. The parallel recent development of the science of linguistics has strongly reinforced this perspective in the intellectual atmosphere of our time. When one looks at Durkheim's discussions in this perspective, some very striking parallels in pattern of analysis emerge, of which I had been totally unaware in my readings in the 1930s.

Though in the realm of the sacred there are many particularized elements, I think we can correctly say that in Durkheim's conception beliefs about the sacred are organized in their core in terms of a cultural code, which is the primary focus of the stability of the complex action system. It is not, however, only a focus of stability, but also the locus of introducing variability, both in adaptation to changing conditions and of a sort which has evolutionary consequences. From this point of view, the culture may be conceived of as constituting a very major evolutionary emergent phenomenon which has enabled socially organized humans, who are culture bearers, to transcend many of the constraints of the more rigidly bounded life of organisms without culture. It is, of course, by now very well known that the mammalian brain, in its most highly developed form in the human organism, is the most fundamental organic bearer of the processes which make cultural communication and creativity possible.

Durkheim, of course, did not anticipate these developments in biology and linguistics, but he analyzed the phenomena of action systems in a frame of reference within which these phenomena fit in terms which are remarkably congruent with the theory which has developed in these other fields. It seems to me that this congruence places the significance of his views in a quite different light from that in which they appeared in terms of the initial impact of the *Elementary Forms* on the social science community, which we should remember was overwhelmingly unfavorable, especially in the English-speaking world.

IV

We may now turn to another set of themes that are closely related to those just reviewed. They are somewhat different but have another very interesting connection with biological thinking. It will be remembered that in Durkheim's whole discussion of religion and quite explicitly in his definition, the concept moral community appears very prominently. He defined religion, that is, as a set of beliefs and practices which unite those who adhere to and practice them in a *moral community,* which, he added, is called the church, a component of his definition which needs some comment. This emphasis on the moral community is, as I have already suggested, a major theme of Durkheim's work throughout his career, centering on his famous concept of the *conscience collective* in the connotation that *conscience* should be translated more nearly as conscience than as consciousness. His insights about the nature of this community, however, came to a certain kind of culmination in the *Elementary Forms,* building, of course, on his theory of internalization.

Closely related to the concept of moral community is that of the social environment of the individual, the *milieu social.* This figured in Durkheim's earliest attempts to define the problems of sociology, especially his early concept of social facts, to which he applied the Cartesian criteria of exteriority and constraint. This paradigm was formulated from the point of view of the acting individual in his relation to a social environment. The great break from the Cartesian tradition was not in the paradigm itself, but in the conception of *social* facts, within the conception that society is a "reality *sui generis.*" It is perfectly clear that Durkheim meant the term "reality" in this phrase as an object or set of them in the Cartesian sense.

There followed a great revolution in Durkheim's thinking which culminated in the insight about internalization and the meaning of constraint as constraint by moral authority. I had not, however, been fully aware of the extent to which the progression from the Cartesian conception of the facticity of the *mileu social* to the idea of constraint by moral authority was not simply progress from a more to a less elementary theoretical position but was the framework within which *both* conceptions came to be combined in a unique manner. The realization that this is the case has, I think, been basically dependent on the conception that much of Durkheim's thought was couched at the level of the general theory of action and not only of the social system.

The upshot is that I think it is quite clear Durkheim's conception of the *milieu social* should be interpreted as the internal environment of the system of action. The concept of the internal environment was of course introduced by the great French physiologist, Claude Bernard (1957), who was a contemporary of Durkheim's. W. B. Cannon's (1932) conception of *homeostasis,* is, of course, closely related. This, at a different level from that of the primary cultural codes, may be conceived as a focus of relative stability of human action systems. I stress here the level of action rather than, as Durkheim himself tended to do, society, if one interprets society or social systems to be a primary subsystem of action rather than action itself. The essential paradigm, complicated since Durkheim's early days, is that the *milieu social,* that is, the environment shared by the participants in the same society, is both a given, empirically present environment, which must be cognitively understood and instrumentally taken into account if, as one may put it in current terms, one is to act rationally. At the same time, however, those who act in relation to the same empirically given *milieu social* constitute a moral community, and this is the distinctive feature of what Durkheim calls society as a reality *sui generis* as distinguished from the predominantly physical environment which was the focus of the Cartesian tradition.

Indeed, this duality carried over from his earlier work provides the primary rationale of the inclusion of the two primary differentiated focuses of the normative components in human action as Durkheim saw them in the *Elementary Forms,* namely, the cognitive and the moral, which in his conclusion he so dramatically associated in his comment on Kant. To repeat, the essential thing is the inclusion of *both* references in the same formula, not the shift in interest from the cognitive to the moral.

Here, however, another very interesting problem arises. In his famous definition of religion, as I have noted, Durkheim said the moral community of which he was speaking could be called a church. Certainly, in the case of Australian Totemism there was no structural differentiation between the social community as a network of interlocking clans and whatever entity and subentities had religious significance, notably both the tribe and its constituent clans. In modern societies, however, with the differentiation and later the separation of church and state, it is by no means a simple and obvious question in what sense what is usually called secular society, if it is to be a society at all, should also be called a church. It seems to me that a major contribution to the solution to this problem has been made by Robert Bellah (1967) in his, I think, now famous paper, "American Civil Religion." In this paper Bellah showed that, precisely in the Durkheimian sense, the American societal community did indeed have a religion, with a relatively full panoply of beliefs and practices and that this could be considered both constitutive of and expressing the moral community which constituted the nation. It is not necessary for present purposes to spell out the details of Bellah's analysis, but it is quite clear that in some sense a belief in God and, therefore, the transcendental sanction of the nation as an entity is central to it, and he points out that after the tremendous national trauma of the Civil War and its culminating symbolic event, the assassination of Lincoln, a new note of martyrdom and sacrifice entered into the symbolization of the community, which brought the civil religion nearer to Christian patterns in that Lincoln was frequently conceived of as having died that the nation might live.

V

There is another striking resemblance to the conceptual structure of genetic theory in biology. In his chapter on the Australian idea of the soul, Durkheim sets forth the idea, which was well known to me and many others of his readers, that they believed in a theory of reincarnation. That is, an ancestral spirit which is conceived to remain for long periods in some sacred place (a water hole, a rock, or something of this sort), was conceived of as entering the body of a woman, and this event was interpreted as that of actual conception. Beliefs with respect to the male role in reproduction have been somewhat equivocal. All this is familiar, but what I had not remembered from previous reading was that it was not the *whole* of the ancestral spirit substance which became reincarnated in the newly conceived child, but a *part,* split off, as it were, from the main spirit substance. This splitting is not necessarily believed in by all of the Australian tribes, but Durkheim cites chapter and verse with respect to some.

This is highly suggestive of what you might call the logic of the germ plasm. The chromosomes themselves and, it is now clear at the molecular level, DNA are conceived of as dividing and reproducing themselves; in DNA the two helical components divide, in the chromosomes one unites with a matching chromosome from the other parent of the offspring. In either case, what goes into a daughter cell is not the *whole* of the genetic material but is, as it were, a fragment or a fraction which has been split off from a continuing stock of such material. In other words, the genetic heritage embodied in chromosomes and DNA molecules is not embodied in *any particular* mortal cell or organism but continues as the basis of continuity of the organic type, most familiarly, the species. That such a belief should turn up in a very primitive society and that Durkheim should see fit to emphasize it is to me a very striking development, which is strongly suggestive of the basic theoretical continuity between the biological sciences and the sciences of action.

Another very striking feature of the new theory of genetics has been, as was noted, the conception of a code which is biochemically embodied in the structure of the DNA molecule, which, of course, would vary according to species but with a basic continuity in the pattern of the code itself (Stent 1970). This code then is conceived of as being the template on which, by way of RNA, the enzymes which are, in turn, the agents of synthesis of other complex molecules are developed. We have noted that there is a striking logical resemblance of the conception of the genetic code in its function to the theory of linguistics, which again has developed enormously since the time when Durkheim wrote. Language, however, may be treated as, in certain respects, the prototype of what we have come to call culture, and, surely, the two primary cultural categories of Durkheim's concern in the *Elementary Forms,* namely, codes defining moral order and those defining cognitive structures, are, in certain fundamental respects, isomorphic with linguistic codes.

It was indeed suggested some twenty years ago by the biologist Alfred Emerson (1956), probably among others, that there is a fundamental functional equivalence between the gene, that is, the genetic constitution of species, and what Emerson called the symbol, which we might amplify as the codified culture of human action systems. In both cases they constitute the primary locus of the continuity of organizational type, transcending, in the case of the genes, the individual organism and its subunits down to cells and, in the case of action, individual organisms and personalities and, indeed, social systems. In these codes, both genetic and cultural, serving as templates, it is possible to synthesize, in the terminology of linguistics, messages or utterances, which can be individualized and particularized and yet carry the element of commonness, which in the language case is necessary for effective communication.

VI

We have seen that the religious component centering in the category of the sacred, the moral and the categorial or, for Kant, the a priori components of the cognitive system, constitute the grand triad of the fundamentals of a human action system as Durkheim worked them out in the *Elementary Forms*. In the terms I have been accustomed to using, these should be regarded as three primary focuses of the cultural system, namely, what I had called constitutive symbolization, moral-evaluative symbolization, and cognitive symbolization. They are then both institutionalized in societies in the analytical sense and internalized in personalities and behavioral organisms.

According to the theory of action, there should be a fourth central category at both the cultural and the other levels. At the cultural level it is what we have referred to as expressive symbolization, which links, in what loosely may be called socialpsychological terms, with the category of affect which I, contrary to much current usage, tend to identify as a generalized medium of interchange primarily anchored in the *social* system, but specifically mediating primary interchanges with both personality and cultural systems (Parsons 1970). Where does this stand in Durkheim's analysis?

It seems to me that there are several clues. It will be remembered that just as he contrasted sense data with the categorical component of knowledge, he contrasted what he called the appetites with the element of moral authority and order. "Appetite" is a term which was rather widely current in the psychology of Durkheim's time but has largely gone out of use.

There are, then, two other extremely important references. In his handling of the descriptive material about ritual in the Australian system, Durkheim continually emphasizes the phenomenon he calls effervescence, which is that participants in the rituals and significantly the collective rather than magical versions, that is, those which he would call religious, manifest states of high emotional excitement, of exultation, and, in certain connections such as funeral ceremonies, despair leading to self-mutilation of a rather serious character. We may suggest that for Durkheim this emotional excitement is both genuine in the psychological sense and socially ordered. In the latter context he emphasizes that the pattern of action and interaction is laid down in detail in the tradition of the tribe prescribing who should do what, in relation to whom, at what point in the time sequence. Thus, though the excitement is psychologically genuine, it is not a matter of spontaneous reaction to immediate stimuli. This meticulous ordering, of course, relates very much to the fact that the ritual actions are permeated with symbolic meanings, which refer in Durkheim's emphases in particular to the structure and situation of the social system.

We think that these three aspects of religious ritual may legitimately be identified with the structure of what we may call the affective complex at the general level of action. The symbolization, we would suggest, must be culturally ordered, and this, in turn, suggests that there must be a code aspect of expressive symbolism, which is parallel to that in the cognitive and the moral realms. This is perhaps most explicit in Durkheim's chapters (1912:book III, ch. 3, 4) on the mimetic and the representative rites. The articulation with the personality of the individual seems, above all, to be indicated in a phenomenon of effervescence, including a very important interpretation which Durkheim puts on the rites, and the psychological states of the participants. This is his interpretation that the rites do, in fact, not only reinforce, but generate what he explicitly calls "faith." He very specifically states that beliefs alone do not suffice but that the believer is only fully a believer if he translates the meaning of his beliefs into actions. It is in this connection that Durkheim states his famous aphorism about religion, *C'est de la vie sérieuse.*

The societal references are involved, it seems to me, at two levels. The first, which figures prominently in Durkheim's analysis, refers to the social content of at least a very large proportion of the symbolization. From a certain point of view, the totem animal or other species of object symbolically speaking is the clan, and frequently the participants in ceremonies, especially as later work has shown, feel themselves actually to be the mythical symbolic entities whose actions their ritual patterns represent (Bellah 1970: 20–50, Warner 1958). We may very broadly say that the closeness of this identification of ritual symbolism with societal content is, at least in part, an index of the primitiveness of the religious system Durkheim is analyzing.

The other principal societal reference is in the very conspicuous interpretation of Durkheim that a primary function of religious ritual is the reinforcement and, we might even indeed say the creation, of solidarity. Solidarity, of course, is a concept which figured very centrally in Durkheim's theoretical thinking from his first published writings until his death. There is, then, a certain linkage between faith and solidarity, because those who share a common faith constitute precisely in Durkheim's own formula a moral community, which, in the case of what we in the modern world would call a church, is primarily religious but is also a secular social system; whereas what we think of as secular society also has the kind of religious aspect which Bellah analyzed as the civil religion. It is a question of relative primacies, not of presence or absence.

With respect to the code aspect of the expressive-affective system, we think that there are some extremely significant emphases in Durkheim's treatment which he did not attempt to codify theoretically but which link with a good deal of comparative evidence. On the one hand, there are a good many references to the ritual significance of blood and the shedding of blood in ritual contexts. The most conspicuous in the Australian case concerns the initiation ceremony. There is, of course, a note of deliberately inflicted pain and hardship, but, at the same time, blood is clearly a sacred symbol. In a recent book David Schneider (1968) has analyzed the significance of the symbol of blood in the context of such expressions as "blood relations" in American kinship, and this would certainly apply much more widely. Anyone interested in comparative religion, then, to cite only one case which was surely in Durkheim's mind, cannot miss that significance in the Christian institution of the Eucharist, which is the central ritual of Christianity. The wine is explicitly declared to be the blood of Christ.

Schneider also strongly emphasizes the symbolic significance for kinship of sexual intercourse, which has a dual reference, namely, to the recreation and extension of the nexus of blood relationships, since it is through sexual intercourse that human procreation takes place and the children of a couple are related to each other and to both their parents in this symbolic sense by blood, though the incest taboo prevents the parents from being related in that way to each other.

It is striking here that first Durkheim calls attention to the general tendency of rituals of what he calls the positive cult to generate sexual excitement as part of the effervescence, and, second, he points out references to actual cases of ritual sexual intercourse which have the extremely interesting feature of being incestuous in terms of the Australian rules of exogamy. Presumably such incestuous relations, which generally do not involve members of nuclear families, are confined to the ritual context. The suggestion is that blood and sexual intercourse are both part of a symbolic complex in which the references which Durkheim calls those to faith on the one hand, to social solidarity on the other, are central. The intercourse of a married couple is the primary symbol of their very special solidarity. Their assumption of the burden of parenthood may be said to be a primary symbol of their faith, that is, in the societal future that extends beyond themselves and their personal interests.

There is a second very prominent theme of ritual symbolism, in this case involving the function of eating. On the one hand, Durkheim claims it is generally true that in all, in his sense, profane circumstances, the totem is taboo as a food source for the members of the clan of which it is a totem. This taboo, however, like that against clan incest, is ritually broken on certain specific occasions when there are ceremonial totemic meals. Again, this seems to be a very general theme in ritual systems. Thus, the standard Hebrew sacrifice to Jahweh was the burnt offerings of animals specifically in a context of edibility. In Christianity the second main component of the Eucharist is the mutual partaking of bread, and this is explicitly declared to be the body of Christ; but it also symbolizes membership in the church as an actual social collectivity. Finally, it can hardly escape notice that a very special symbol of family solidarity is the act of eating family meals together, very specifically heightened in significance on special occasions in our culture, such as Thanksgiving, Christmas, and birthdays of family members.

There are many things about this complex that are obscure, but it seems to me very likely that Durkheim, following particularly on the work of Robertson Smith and the study of sacrifice by his own associates Hubert and Mauss (1964), contributed notably to the beginning elucidation of a very general code of ritual symbolism, which is culturally expressive rather than primarily cognitive or moral, which is intimately concerned with the maintenance of levels of motivation in the individual, but which is also intimately connected with social solidarity. It is probably significant that these symbols relate very specifically to aspects of the organism, which is in a certain sense the common groundwork of all the other aspects of human action.

VII

With this, we think that Durkheim was at least well on the way to rounding out a highly generalized analysis of the principal system references and components of action. In so doing, he made great advances toward placing his conception of society and its solidarity in the kind of broader context which is necessary if many of the perspectives of misunderstanding through narrow interpretation, which have plagued the discussion over Durkheim's work for at least two generations now, should be overcome. It should be evident that we are convinced that this step to a higher theoretical level than the overwhelming proportion of the discussion over Durkheim, including my own earlier discussion, will lead to a much fuller integration of biological theory with the theory of human action than has existed for a very long time, indeed, since the break of the social sciences with the older, evolutionary biology.

I think it can correctly be said that Durkheim's initial focus was on society as such on the one hand and on the problem of normative order with respect to it on the other, which led him directly to the moral component, especially in his conception of moral authority. In the evolution of his thought which led to the *Elementary Forms* he not only, as it were, went behind his conception of the moral component in society, but he followed it to the levels of what Tillich (1952) called ultimate concerns, which were more or less explicitly religious. If, however, this was all that he had done, it might have constituted only a reversal of his original positivistic position and a return to a relatively conventional religious point of view, either that of the Judaism in which he was brought up or of the Catholicism which was the dominant explicit religion of France.

This, however, was not all that he did. First, he remained faithful to the emphases of the great positivistic tradition in by no means abandoning powerful stress on the significance of the cognitive component. He remained in a certain sense a Cartesian to the end but built his Cartesian frame of reference into a much wider paradigm of analysis. This appears in his consistent emphasis on the importance of the belief systems of his Australian subjects, however primitive and weird they may seem to the modern mind. Indeed, one can say unequivocally that placing, as he did, his great series of chapters on totemic beliefs before the chapters on ritual was a thoroughly considered decision on his part. He was never tempted by the kind of sociology of knowledge which would tend to make belief systems an altogether secondary function of other variables in the action system.

At the same time, however, he insisted on the centrality of the still further aspect of the more ultimate organization of an action system, namely, that expressed especially in ritual. This following up certain other developments in his earlier work, notably the conception of internalization and its relation to *anomie,* led him in a direction which would have included very close relations to psychology, namely, in those aspects which dealt with the nonrational. He did not go far along this path. For example, there is little evidence that he was very much aware of the beginnings of psychoanalysis. One must remember, however, that the first decade of the twentieth century saw only a very minimal dissemination of psychoanalytic ideas (A. Parsons 1956, 1969).[1] Nevertheless, Durkheim certainly in his analysis of ritual in its twin relations to faith on the one hand and solidarity on the other and the beginnings of the working out of the actual structure of symbolic codes made a very great contribution which can surely be integrated with those stemming from more technically psychological origins.

One may indeed perhaps say that, in line with many of the great traditions of Western thought, the most fundamental set of problems with which Durkheim was struggling concerned the conception of rationality and its limits. The problem was the nature of the cognitive component in human action, how was it related to noncognitive components, those ultimately involved in religious faith on one side, those involved in the motivations of human nature and the parameters of the human condition, all of these involving the question of the relation between rational, nonrational, and irrational aspects.

Certainly rereading the *Elementary Forms* strongly reinforces my conviction that Durkheim was one of the great contributors to the clarification of this very fundamental aspect of the human adventure. In the first instance, as a social scientist he had to have a very deep commitment, not only to the desirability of rationality, but to the feasibility of conducting studies by rational methods and producing verifiable results. At the same time, like his great contemporaries, especially Weber and Freud, he showed very deep sensitivity to the importance of the respects in which, shall we say, people as actors, as distinguished from people as scientists, could not

---

[1] The last chapter has been published in English translation as "Diffusion of Psychoanalytic Concepts" in A. Parsons (1969).

be rational beings in the traditional sense of the Enlightenment. He not only arrived at certain general conclusions in this sphere, but he made immense progress in clarifying the theoretical framework in which these problems will have to be approached in the coming phase of our cultural history.

VIII

This chapter as originally submitted failed to fulfill one major request of the editors of this volume, namely, to deal with the fate of the ideas about religion put forward by the author in question in the intellectual development subsequent to the time of his writing. It has not been possible in the time available for me to do the scholarly work necessary for a thorough review of this question comparable, for instance, to that done by Benjamin Nelson on the aftermath of Max Weber's study of the Protestant ethic. A somewhat impressionistic outline will, however, be presented.

In spite of a great deal of obtuseness figuring in the discussion of Weber's Protestant ethic thesis, it has clearly been a major focus of attention in a variety of fields of the study of religion and society. When this attention is combined with that given to the concept of charisma and, somewhat less, to the comparative studies in the sociology of religion, it can probably be said that Weber's influence has been the most important of any scholar of his generation in that branch of the study of religion which connected closely with sociological problems.

By comparison, the impact of Durkheim strictly in this field seems to have been rather meager. Very broadly, my own interpretation of this fact is essentially that intellectually Durkheim was too far ahead of his time and that, with very few exceptions, the social scientists, who are the only ones who have paid serious attention to Durkheim's work, have simply not been ready to appreciate the importance of the kinds of considerations which Durkheim put forward in the *Elementary Forms* and in some other writings as they have been reviewed in the body of this paper. It is perhaps not an entirely rash prediction to suggest the possibility of a rediscovery of Durkheim in the relatively near future which will give him a very different place in cultural and intellectual history than he has so far enjoyed.

There has been a very serious blocking over what Durkheim meant by the concept of society and its relation to the individual. In the field of religion this has been most obviously manifest in the interpretation that he spoke of religious entities, notably the concept of God, as simply symbolic representations of society, meaning by "society" a concrete, empirical entity. For a variety of reasons this interpretation has been substantively unacceptable to most modern social scientists. It has, however, been used positively, especially by anthropologists, through its relation to their use of Durkheim's conception of the social functions of religious ritual as serving to reinforce social solidarity. This point of view has, of course, above all been put forward by Radcliffe-Brown (1939) and carried on by a number of his students and followers. Notably, perhaps, E. E. Evans-Pritchard (1956), W. E. H. Stanner (1969), and W. Lloyd Warner, the latter not only in his book, *A Black Civilization* (1958), which dealt with an Australian tribe, but in his study of American quasireligious rituals as exemplified by the study of Newburyport, Massachusetts (1959). With the exception of Warner, this line of thought has been most conspicuous in British social anthropology. Theoretically, I think Stanner (1969) has gone beyond the others.

Somewhat different emphases have appeared in the French tradition which in certain respects have been mediated by Marcell Mauss (1954) and in the present generation especially by Claude Lévi-Strauss (1962, 1968). Lévi-Strauss's structuralism, I think, can be said to owe a great deal to Durkheim, and its implications extend into the religious field. I would think also that the very great generalization of this point of view by Jean Piaget, as summarized in his recent little book *Structuralism* (1970), clearly also owes a great deal to Durkheim. Again, this is a very general, theoretical point of view which only in part relates to the study of religion.

Preoccupation with the problem of the status of the concept of society has, however, seriously obscured a very central theme in Durkheim's thought which is very much concerned with religion. This is the idea he referred to as "the cult of the individual," as connected with organic solidarity in Western societies. His postulation of the nature of the collective system has so offended Western traditions of individualism, above all, those in the English-speaking world, that he has almost universally been interpreted to be the great denier of the essential reality and importance of the individual. This is, it seems to me, a profound misinterpretation. I have referred to Durkheim's basic conception in this area as one of institutionalized individualism in which a very special synthesis of individuality and social solidarity has been developed in the modern Western world. This theme was somewhat further developed by Mauss (1968) in a notable article that on the religious front has, to my knowledge, only been taken up by Robert Bellah. Few have realized to what an extent Bellah's (1967) very seminal conception of the civil religion is grounded in Durkheim's thinking. A much more extensive review of Bellah's relation to Durkheim in this and other respects is contained in his Introduction to the volume *Emile Durkheim on Morality and Society* (1973). Indeed, this Introduction, which became available to me only just as I was drafting this supplementary statement, makes it clear that Bellah stands virtually alone in not only the profoundity of his understanding of Durkheim's theoretical thinking, especially as it bears on the study of religion, but also in his positive use of Durkheim's insights in his own work. There are many points at which this becomes clear in the volume of Bellah's (1970) essays. It is particularly notable that the idea of the cult of the individual, but within the context of institutionalized individualism, is very central to Bellah's thinking.

Two other writers may be singled out for mention in this connection, though others might be. One, Kenneth Burke, is not a sociologist. I think here particularly of Burke's volume *The Rhetoric of Religion* (1961), but it is difficult to say how far Burke has been directly influenced by Durkheim. I would imagine not very much. There is, however, particularly in Burke's analysis of the symbolic content of Judaism and early Christianity in the essays of that volume, what seems to be a very definite convergence with the fully mature Durkheimian point of view in the *Elementary Forms*. Burke is one of the very few who have taken seriously the attempt to formulate what might be called a symbolic code as constitutive of basic religious orientations in the first case for the first three chapters of Genesis and in the second, in his analysis of the thought of St. Augustine. These seem to me to be specific studies which are directly in the line of development which Durkheim sketched out some sixty years ago.

Another very stimulating writer is Peter L. Berger, notably in his volume *Sacred Canopy* (1967). On the level of his analysis of religious symbol systems in the first four chapters of the book, it seems to me that Berger has developed a remarkably lucid picture which is basically very Durkheimian, though the extent to which, again, it is actually derived from Durkheim's influence remains unclear. Unfortunately, however, in the latter part of the book where Berger turns to the analysis of the process of secularization, he departs radically and, in my opinion, unfortunately from a Durkheimian perspective in what seems to be a kind of Neo-Marxian direction. The basic problem seems to be that he conceives of the world of the sacred as set totally over against the secular world, which to him is primarily focused on economic interest and the structure of markets. The all-important intermediate area of the solidarity of societal groups and communities is simply squeezed out, and, therefore, anything like a Durkheimian interpretation of the relation of religion to the nature and problems of modern society is radically precluded. Nevertheless, I think it can be said that Burke, who originated as a literary critic, and Berger, who is a sociologist specializing in religion, have been among those who have approached most closely to developing the lines of thought which Durkheim initiated. These books and the work of Bellah, which is as yet somewhat fragmentary, and also of such persons as Clifford Geertz (1968) seem to give a certain basis for the optimistic hope that the Durkheimian influence with special reference to religion has a fair prospect of coming into its own fairly soon.[2]

Bibliography

BELLAH, ROBERT N.
>   1959   Durkheim and History. *American Sociological Review*. Vol. 24, no. 4 (August), pp. 447–61.
>   1967   Civil Religion in America. *Daedalus* Vol. 96, no. 1 (Winter), pp. 1–21.
>   1970   *Beyond Belief: Essays on Religion in a Post-Traditional World.* New York: Harper & Row.
>   1973   Introduction to *Emile Durkheim on Morality and Society.* Heritage of Sociology Series. Chicago: University of Chicago Press.

BENDIX, REINHARD
>   1970   *Embattled Reason: Essays on Social Knowledge.* New York: Oxford University Press.

————, AND ROTH, GUENTHER
>   1971   *Scholarship and Partisanship: Essays on Max Weber,* Berkeley and Los Angeles, Calif.: University of California Press.

BERNARD, CLAUDE
>   1957   *An Introduction to the Study of Experimental Medicine.* Trans. H. C. Green. New York: Daler.

BURKE, KENNETH
>   1961   *The Rhetoric of Religion.* Boston: Beacon Press.

CANNON, W. B.
>   1932   *The Wisdom of the Body.* New York: Norton.

---

[2] How far the sociological profession still has to go in order to generalize such a level of appreciation of Durkheim's contributions is vividly illustrated by a chapter in a recent volume of essays by Reinhard Bendix and Guenther Roth (1971). In chapter 25 (written by Bendix), which is entitled "Two Sociological Traditions," a contrast is drawn between Weber and Durkheim with special reference to their respective contributions to the sociology of religion. Bendix is clearly one of the most culturally sophisticated of contemporary sociologists and a major contributor to the discipline in a number of fields. Yet the view of Durkheim which he presents, especially with respect to the field of religion, must be considered to be a caricature, not an interpretation. He accepts Durkheim's early statements of what I once called his "sociologistic positivism" at their face value, including the literal and naïve version of the view that God symbolizes society. This is to say that Bendix, as he put it in an earlier volume of essays (1970), treated Durkheim as a sociological reductionist, treating religion and various other phenomena as simple functions of an allegedly unproblematical entity called society—in a parallel fashion he there treated Freud as a biological reductionist—both in highly unfavorable contrast with Weber. The contrast of this picture of Durkheim with that presented by Bellah (Introduction to the Durkheim volume) and, if I may say so, in the body of the present essay, could hardly be sharper.

DURKHEIM, EMILE
  1893 *De la division du travail social*. Paris: Librarie Felix Alcan.
  tr. 1933 *On the Division of Labor in Society*. Trans. George Simpson. New York: Macmillan.
  1912 *Les formes élémentaires de la vie religieuse: Le système totemique*
  tr. 1915 *en Australie*. Paris: Librarie Felix Alcan. *The Elementary Forms of the Religious Life*. Trans. Joseph W. Swain. London: George Allen and Unwin.

EMERSON, ALFRED E.
  1956 Homeostasis and Comparison of Systems. In Roy R. Grinker, Sr., ed. *Toward a Unified Theory of Human Behavior: An Introduction to General Systems Theory*. New York: Basic Books, Inc.

EVANS-PRITCHARD, E. E.
  1956 *Nuer Religion*. Oxford: Clarendon Press.

GEERTZ, CLIFFORD
  1968 Religion as a Cultural System. In Donald R. Cutler, ed. *The Religious Situation*. Boston: Beacon Press.

HUBERT, HENRI, AND MAUSS, MARCEL
  1964 *Sacrifice: Its Nature and Function*. Trans. W. D. Halls. Chicago: University of Chicago Press.

LÉVI-STRAUSS, CLAUDE
  1962 *Totemism*. Boston: Beacon Press.
  1963 *Structural Anthropology*. New York: Basic Books, Inc.

MAUSS, MARCELL
  1954 *The Gift*. London: Cohen and West.
  1968 A Category of the Human Spirit. In Benjamin Nelson, ed. *Histories, Symbolic Logics, and Cultural Maps*. A special issue of *The Psycho-Analytic Review* Vol. 55, no. 3 (September), pp. 457–81.

NELSON, BENJAMIN
  1949 *The Idea of Usury*. Princeton, N.J.: Princeton University Press.

OLBY, ROBERT
  1970 Francis Crick, DNA, and the Central Dogma. *Daedalus* 99 (Fall): 938–87.

PARSONS, A.
  1956 La pénétration de la psychoanalyse en France et aux Etats Unis. Doctoral dissertation. Sorbonne.
  1969 *Belief, Magic and Anomie*. New York: The Free Press.

PARSONS, TALCOTT
  1937 *The Structure of Social Action*. New York: McGraw-Hill.
  1970 Some Problems of General Theory in Sociology. In John C. McKinney and Edward A. Tiryakian, eds. *Theoretical Sociology: Perspectives and Developments*. New York: Appleton-Century-Crofts.

PIAGET, JEAN
  1970 *Structuralism*. Trans. and ed. Chaninah Maschler. New York: Basic Books, Inc.

RADCLIFFE-BROWN, A. R.
  1939 *Taboo*. New York: Cambridge University Press.

1952   *Structure and Function in Primitive Society.* New York: The Free Press.

SCHNEIDER, DAVID M.

1968   *American Kinship: A Cultural Account.* Englewood Cliffs, N.J.: Prentice-Hall.

STANNER, W. E. H.

1969   *On Aboriginal Religion.* Melbourne: Oceania Monographs #11.

STENT, GUNTHER S.

1970   DNA. *Daedalus* 99 (Fall):909–37.

STERN, CURT

1970   The Continuity of Genetics. *Daedalus* 99 (Fall):882–908.

TILLICH, PAUL

1952   *The Courage to Be.* New Haven, Conn.: Yale University Press.

WARNER, W. L.

1958   *A Black Civilization: A Social Study of an Australian Tribe.* New York: Harper & Row, rev. ed.

1959   *The Living and the Dead: A Study of the Symbolic Life of Americans,* Vol. 5 in The Yankee City Series. New Haven, Conn.: Yale University Press.

11. Belief, Unbelief, and Disbelief

As a GENERAL COMMENTATOR on the Symposium on the Culture of Unbelief, there are two aspects of my position which should be made explicit at the outset. First, I am not a Roman Catholic, but a somewhat backsliding Protestant of Congregationalist background. Second, I am not a theologian, but a sociologist by profession. My commentary will not attempt a summary of the discussions—though the Agnelli Foundation has kindly made a copy of the transcript available to me—but rather will be critical in the sense of ranging about some of the principal issues which figured in the papers and discussions in my own terms, hoping in the process to help to define the situation for future stages of discussion and research in this field.

Belief, Disbelief, and Unbelief

The relevant context of the use of the terms "belief" and "unbelief" was of course religious. It does not seem useful here to attempt discussion of "What is religion?" in general terms. At certain points aspects of that question will arise and can be dealt with on those occasions. Since, however, the concept belief is so central, a brief commentary on it does seem to be in order. First a point of logic. In Western culture at least there has been a strong tendency to think in terms of dichotomies, often accentuated in their mutual exclusiveness by such expressions as "versus." Thus we have rational versus irrational, heredity versus environment, *Gemeinschaft* versus *Gesellschaft*.

If members of such dichotomous pairs are to be treated as types, however, they have frequently turned out, not only to admit of intermediate or

From *The Culture of Unbelief*, Rocco Caporale and Antonio Grumelli, eds. (Berkeley: University of California Press, 1971), pp. 207–245. Copyright © 1971 by The Regents of the University of California; reprinted by permission of the University of California Press.

mixed types, but to be resultants of a plurality of variables, so that study of the possible combinations of the component variables might at the typological level, yield, not a single dichotomous pair, but a larger "family" of possible types, which differ from each other, not on one, but on several dimensions.

I think—or "I believe"—that this is true of the concept of belief itself, at religious and at other levels. I might suggest that stating the problem in terms of belief-unbelief is already a start in this pluralistic direction in that the alternative to belief need not be simply disbelief but might be some way of avoiding being placed in the category either of believer or of disbeliever. The logic here is similar to that involved in the history of the concept of rationality and its antonyms. Namely, it was a major advance when rationality was contrasted not with irrationality but with nonrationality; there could be types which, though nonrational, were not irrational.

Certainly in the Western tradition, the concept of belief has a cognitive component. This is to say that however difficult this may be in practice, beliefs are capable of being stated in propositional form and then tested by standards of "truth" or cognitive validity. It is true that most propositions of religious belief are not subject to what we generally call empirical verification. But they still must, ideally, be tested by standards of conceptual clarity and precision, and logically correctness of inference.[1] The equivalent of the empirical component in science is the authenticity of the nonlogical components of religious belief, for example, revelation, or some kind of religious experience.

Another aspect of the problem, however, is brought out by the distinction which was discussed early in the conference, namely between what is meant by "belief *that* . . ." and "belief *in* . . ." In my view, it would not be appropriate to use the term belief in the latter context if there were *no* cognitive content involved, that is, if the action referred to were completely nonrational expression of emotions. The little word "in," however, suggests a noncognitive component which is not included in "that," which may be called commitment. The "believer in . . ." of course must, explicitly or implicitly, subscribe to cognitively formulable and in some sense testable propositions, but in addition to that, he commits himself to act (including experiencing) in ways which are, to put it in the mildest form, congruent with the cognitive components of his belief.

An important, perhaps the premier, example here is the Protestant doctrine, especially associated with Luther himself, of "salvation by faith alone." This is faith *in* the Christian God. The formula as such contains no reference to the cognitive set of beliefs, but it clearly implies them in the sense that faith is faith *in God;* with no cognitive conception of God the commitment would be meaningless. The alternative, for Luther, to salva-

---

[1] The aphorism of Tertullian, *"Credo quia absurdum est,"* could not prevail in Western religion.

tion by faith, was clearly that by works through the Catholic sacraments. The definition of these alternatives did not challenge the general strictly *theo*logical conceptions of God and his relations to man.

From the point of view of the Catholic Church of his time, Luther was a heretic. But his disbelief in the mission of the historical church and in the sacraments, was only one form of unbelief. Surely in many ways he was not only a believer in some vaguely general sense, but he was a believer in Christ and the Christian God. This is to say, he accepted much of the cognitive framework of the inherited tradition.

Professor Bellah has spoken of a strong cognitive bias in Christian religious tradition. That the emphasis on the cognitive component has been strong does not seem to be seriously open to doubt. That it has been a bias in the sense that over the long run it has distorted Western religious development is a question on which I prefer to withhold judgment. Prior to rendering a necessary basis for arriving at such a judgment, it seems to me more urgent to attempt to clarify the nature of the components, both cognitive and noncognitive, rational and nonrational, of religious orientation, and certain aspects of their relations to each other.

That there must be a major set of noncognitive components is a view which has been accepted in the introductory statements of this commentary and is indeed very widely accepted. This noncognitive component is, to my mind, what distinguishes religion both from philosophy on the one hand, and science on the other, both of which are intellectual disciplines. While theology may well be considered to be such a discipline, clearly religion is not. Durkheim's famous dictum about religion, *c'est de la vie sérieuse,* is one way of stating that difference and seems to be more or less adequately expressed in the term commitment which I have used above.

The Rational and Nonrational Components of Action

Bellah, in a paper presumably written almost immediately after the conference,[2] discusses explicitly the prominent role of the noncognitive and nonrational components of action in the work of the three great transformers of thinking about man and society in the generation of the turn of the century, namely Freud, Durkheim, and Max Weber. All three were prominently unbelievers in our sense though not unequivocally disbelievers, and all three were deeply concerned with religion. Bellah suggests that they were "symbolic reductionists" in that they granted a certain "reality" to religion, but held that the content of explicit beliefs must be taken to be the symbolic expression of something else.

[2] Robert Bellah, "Between Religion and Social Science," chapter 14 of *The Culture of Unbelief.*

It is in the realm of that "something else" that, according to Bellah, all three formulated the decisive noncognitive categories, namely in Freud's case the *unconscious,* in that of Durkheim, *society,* in a sense which in this context of usage clearly requires much interpretation, and in that of Weber, *charisma,* which also requires interpretation. Though these three formulations are by no means directly congruent with each other, they all constitute in some sense "residual categories" which are defined mainly by contrast with their antonyms, rather than positively.

In order to formulate a more adequate conceptual scheme it seems necessary to introduce at least two further distinctions in addition to that between the cognitive and the noncognitive. One touches the interpretation of the status of the noncognitive categories introduced by Freud and Weber, whereas the other concerns the interpretation of Durkheim's usage of society as a referent of such symbolism.

In the intellectual setting in which he introduced the concept of charisma, Weber had worked out what seems to the author a major clarification of certain aspects of the structure of the cognitive world. This occurred mainly in his famous essays on *Wissenschaftslehre* and eventuated in a special version of what is usually considered to be a "neo-Kantian" position. One aspect of it was the full extension of the cognitive paradigms, which had basically come to be established in the natural sciences, to what Weber called the *Kulturwissenschaften,* a category which included both the social sciences and the humanities. The second, however, was the introduction or clarification, in the area which Kant had left cognitively unstructured under the rubric of "practical reason," of a category of cognitive knowledge concerning values, and the underlying "problems of meaning" in reference to the human condition. Here Weber's contribution is the establishment of this category—of course he by no means stood alone—as a category of rational knowledge.[3]

This was the basis on which, in his classification of "types of action," Weber was able to introduce two rather than one rational type. Since the context was action rather than knowledge as such he called them *Zweckrationalität* (which I have translated as "instrumental") and *Wertrationalitat* ("value") respectively. From the beginning Weber's classification assumed that the rational types would be complemented by nonrational—not irrational—types. The duality on the rational side, however, strongly suggested the usefulness of a corresponding duality on the nonrational. In his actual classification Weber did indeed introduce two such categories, namely "affectual" and "traditional" action.

The line of distinction between the two rationalities of Weber's classification clearly concerns the direction of orientation, on the one hand downward to the empirically given conditions of human action, physical, biologi-

[3] Talcott Parsons, "The Sociology of Knowledge and the History of Ideas," unpublished.

cal and on certain levels even social and cultural and, on the other hand, upward toward the "grounds of meaning" of action and their modes of symbolization. In the paradigm we are outlining, this line of distinction should be extended onto the nonrational side. The nonrational category corresponding to instrumental rationality is that of the motivational components which are rooted in the biological nature of man, his needs and their affective modes of expression, modified as these have been from pure biologically inherited propensities, by various features of the processes of learning and socialization. Though the references of the term are highly complex and raise difficult theoretical problems, Weber's term "affectual," though perhaps not quite in the sense in which he defines it, is probably as good as any.[4]

The other category of the nonrational, like value-rationality, is a mode of orientation to the grounds and problems—in this sense interpreted in a largely noncognitive sense—of meaning. Here, curiously, Weber utilized the logic of the residual category in a special way, and placed here the concept "traditional," which was clearly nonrational, but oriented wholly to stability. He then introduced that of charisma as specifically a nonrational orientational force of innovation, but did not explicitly relate it to the types of action. Once, however, that it is seen that a typology of the components of action at the most general level should include their contribution to both stability and change and the balance between them, including the fact that Weber himself used the concept charisma outside the context of change,[5] charisma emerges as the appropriate concept in Weber's terms for the meaning-oriented category of the nonrational side.[6]

Seen in these terms, Freud's concept of the unconscious was definitely a residual category, originally formulated by contrast with the naïver ver-

---

[4] It will be noted that Durkheim also used this term. See the introduction in Emile Durkheim, *Elementary Forms of the Religious Life,* trans. Joseph Ward Swain (New York: The Free Press, 1965; first published in French in 1912).

[5] Cf. Talcott Parsons, *The Structure of Social Action* (New York: The Free Press, 1949). The distinction between the rational and nonrational components of *action* does not in any direct way concern the problem of "irrationality." Put slightly differently, the problem of irrationality does not reside in the nature of any of the components of action, but in their combination. Rationality is in one aspect a normative category. There are rational components of action because knowledge is so essentially involved with it. But rational action or deviation from its norms is always a function of the combination of all the components, including both rational and nonrational. Irrational action, then, is the outcome of tensions and conflicts within the organization of action, in which, it is essential to note, what at the more analytical level here have been called rational and nonrational components are involved on both sides (or several) of the tensions and conflicts. The exigencies of combination will of course vary according to the types of action, and their organization in systems, which are involved.

[6] For Durkheim perhaps the nearest equivalent was sentiment which appeared in his original definition of the collective conscience. See Emile Durkheim, *Division of Labor in Society,* trans. George Simpson (New York: The Free Press, 1964; first published in French in 1939, second edition with additional preface, 1902).

sions of the conception of rationality of action, at both cognitive and behavioral levels. This is not the place to follow through the complex developments of Freud's theoretical thinking. Originally, however, the content of the unconscious was overwhelmingly interpreted to be focused on instinct. This, however, proved to be unstable and Freud himself eventually placed the superego mainly in the unconscious and distinguished it from the id. The extent to which the superego was exhausted by its unconscious components and how it articulated with internalized culture more generally remained problematical, but in a rough sense it can clearly be said that Freud's distinction between id and superego paralleled that of Weber between affectual and charismatic components of action. Hence we may say that in both Weber and Freud the analytical basis for studying a nonrational aspect of religious orientation had been laid down in the great tradition of emerging social science.

Durkheim and the Moral Component of Society

For both Weber and Freud, the primary direct referent of their symbolic reductionism, as Bellah calls it, was values; references to the reality by virtue of which values were rendered meaningful, remained in different ways problematical for both. There is a major overlap in this focus with Durkheim's position, but the difference is of great significance for the problems of the symposium. Durkheim made a great deal of the thesis that sacred things were symbols, the referents of which should be sought out by research.

The basis on which he established the connection with society was the common attitude of moral respect. In his earlier work in areas quite other than the study of religion he had gradually come to give a special place to what we can now call the internalized and above all institutionalized structure of norms and values carrying what he called "moral authority." Indeed, when Durkheim presented his famous definition of religion in the *Elementary Forms of the Religious Life*,[7] he featured the crucial phrase "moral community." The normative regulation of secular life, for Durkheim, was interpretable in terms of Weber's value-rationality. The set of beliefs and practices which he called religious, constituted symbolic expressions of the same moral community.

Weber would emphasize the consensus on values which at least in considerable part derived from the belief system, including both the cog-

[7] In my translation into English it reads that, a religion is "an integrated (*solidaire*) system of beliefs and practices relative to sacred things, that is separate and taboo, which unite in one moral community called a church all those who adhere to it." Talcott Parsons, *The Structure of Social Action*, p. 412.

nitive component and that of commitment. Durkheim, on the other hand, did not really go beyond the existence, as institutionalized, of this moral community; Weber's was thus the deeper analysis. In stopping where he did, however, Durkheim brought to light—or to explicit attention—a most important concept which has flowered in Bellah's conception of the civil religion.[8] For Durkheim, the society was never only the community in which its members participated but was also, precisely to them, as well as to an outside observer, an object. As such the moral, and as another aspect the sacred, quality of it constituted one of its major constitutive properties.

In the French situation of his time Durkheim was a "laicist"; though of Jewish origin he was not a religiously practicing Jew and he belonged to the anticlerical left. These circumstances help to explain his views about the Church as that concept was included in his definition of religion. From his own normative point of view he repudiated two primary institutional developments of the Christian world. The one was that of the established Church, especially in the Roman Catholic form, but with differences in some Protestant cases, where the church, though established, was differentiated from the secular social order, with both the laity and the secular priesthood participating in both—members of religious orders, however, minimally in the secular world. The second is the institutional form which was first clearly developed in the United States but has increasingly become the dominant institutional form for the noncommunist Western world, namely denominational pluralism with religious freedom and toleration, and in the more logically developed cases, separation of church and state.

Such processes of differentiation, however, have been deeply grounded in the structure of predominantly Christian societies, with either Establishment constitutions or pluralistic ones, and doubtless further steps of differentiation are likely to occur, some of which will be suggested below. Hence we cannot accept Durkheim's identification of the societal moral community with a church. Bellah, however, has still been able to show, most clearly for the American case, that these differentiations are by no means incompatible with the societal community at the same time being secular and yet having a religious aspect. In that sense, of course, Durkheim was right.

Clearly these considerations are highly relevant to the discussions of the first day of the conference, which centered on Professor Luckmann's paper. In the course of those discussions there were many references to a Durkheimian point of view, which it is perhaps fair to say on the whole Professor Luckmann himself took. It is quite clear, however, that Durkheim did not have an adequate basis for the analysis of Luckmann's stage C, except perhaps rather vaguely in his analysis of the phenomena of collective effervescence.

[8] Robert Bellah, "Civil Rights in America," reprinted in William McLaughlin and Robert Bellah, eds., *Religion in America* (Boston: Houghton Mifflin, 1969).

The Concept of Secularization

The main Durkheimian position, however, sharply raises the question of the meaning of the concept of secularization about which something needs to be said before returning to the problems of belief, unbelief, and disbelief in the current sociocultural situation.

In this commentary and for many years, the general view which I have been espousing is that, in the socio-cultural sphere, and indeed also the psychological, what has come generally to be called "religion" stands at the highest level in the cybernetic hierarchy of the forces which, in the sense of defining the general directionality of human action among the possible alternatives permitted in the human condition, controls the processes of human action.[9] This is a view obviously shared with Max Weber, but also I think by Durkheim and Freud, though Freud has been widely interpreted to hold directly contrary views.

The question of secularization should be approached on this background. The term clearly refers, even etymologically, to concern with the world by contrast with the transcendent. It is clearly its claim to some kind of contact with the transcendent which is the hallmark of religion, whether the contact be conceived or felt as "knowledge of," as some noncognitive "experience of" or as being instrumental to the "will of" some transcendent entity. One suspects that all of these components, and probably others, are involved in an authentic religion, though in different combinations in different religions. It is in the nature of the case that there should, if the concept of transcendence is meaningful at all, be a sense of tension between the transcendent referent and the worldly. But just as there are various ways of experiencing or having contact with the transcendent, it is also true that the world is not to be conceived as a constant given entity, the properties of which are in no sense a function of human action and history.

If there is a generic meaning of the concept secularization it is probably a change, in this area of inherent tension, in the direction of a closer relation of the one to the other. The concept has, in the Western world and especially in religious circles, been widely interpreted to mean a one-way change, namely the sacrifice of religious claims, obligations and commitments, in favor of secular interests. The other possibility, however, should not be forgotten, namely that the secular order may change in the direction of closer approximation of the normative models provided by a religion, or by religion more generally. The tension seems to have been particularly

---

[9] It should be made clear that exercise of authority or power constitutes only *one* mode of control in the present sense, and in the context of this discussion, by no means the most important mode. There is an unfortunate tendency, which is by no means justified, to equate control with dominance and coercion.

pronounced in the Judeo-Christian religious tradition, or at least has been defined in ways familiar to most of us there. On the one hand, we have the conception of man as irrevocably sunk in "sin and death," whereas on the other hand we have the conception of man as created "in the image of God" and hence as the "lord of the Creation." Indeed the very center of the constitutive symbolism of Christianity would be meaningless without this duality—to put it in one way, if man were totally "lost" why should God make his "only begotten son" a *man* of flesh and blood in order to make human salvation possible? [10]

It was Weber, perhaps more than any other recent Western mind, who seriously began to explore the possibility that the second alternative should be taken seriously, namely of change in the world in the direction of institutionalization of religious values, though of course Troeltsch, in his conception of Christian Society, also moved in that direction abut the same time, and they both had many antecedents. Put in sociological terminology, there is the possibility that religious values should come to be institutionalized, by which we mean that such values come to be the focus of the definition of the situation for the conduct of members of secular societies, precisely in their secular roles. The processes by which this occurs are highly complex and would require an elaborate treatise to analyze at all fully. That it has in fact happened, however, seems to be indisputable. When it happens, however, tensions do not disappear, but come to be restructured; the world as such is in its very nature *never* the transcendently defined ideal.[11]

[10] On the general relations of moral order and original sin see Kenneth Burke, "The First Three Chapters of Genesis," in *The Rhetoric of Religion* (Boston: Beacon Press, 1961).

[11] In writing in the present context for what is, sociologically speaking mainly, though by no means wholly, a nontechnical readership, it is difficult to know how far to go in the exposition of underlying sociological frames of reference and paradigms. In part I am being deliberately paradoxical in attributing to the concept secularization what has often been held to be its opposite, namely not the loss of commitment to religious values and the like, but the institutionalization of such values, and other components of religious orientation in evolving cultural and social systems. This latter process, with which the remainder of the present paper is primarily concerned, has often, especially perhaps in religious circles, been held to constitute secularization in the former sense, though when seen in the larger perspective this turns out to be a misinterpretation. Such misinterpretations have, however, been extremely prevalent and have appeared repeatedly at various stages of the larger process.

Secularization in the second sense constitutes a dual process, on the one hand, of the differentiation of religious components from the secular—as in certain respects was the case for the differentiation of the Christian Church from both the Jewish ethnic community and the society of the Roman Empire. Such differentiation clearly involves a diminution of the religious value of the social and cultural components from which the newly emergent religious one becomes differentiated. Thus, while Roman society was in a certain sense quasi-sacred, for Christians it came to be, for the time being, entirely deprived of this quality.

Once this process has occurred, however, the questions which are crucial to us are not resolved by the process of differentiation alone, but concern a complex

The Institutionalization of Religious Values

It is by this path that a society—and in different ways its various sub-sectors—comes to be a moral community in Durkheim's sense, and hence acquires religious significance so that at least some of its institutions are, within certain limits of course, sacred things in the quite literal sense. If this is the case, then the totally concrete dichotomy between sacred and profane entities, transcendentally meaningful and worldly, becomes untenable. A particular human society, in different aspects, is both sacred and profane, both an embodiment (to use a specifically Christian image) of the transcendent and part of the secular world.

There is another of Durkheim's fundamental contributions the understanding of which is essential to our analysis. This lies in the implication of his decision to devote his basic analysis of religion and society to the case of the most primitive religion, as well as society, about which he thought there was adequate record, namely that of the Australian Aborigines. The fundamental contention is that there is no human society without religion. The two are concretely, though not analytically, indivisible. It follows that both the religious and the secular parts of the complex are involved in a

---

sequence of sequels which are, at various stages, contingent on inherently variable factors. In a very schematic way, the following seems to be the central one: The initial process of differentiation is very generally associated with sharp antagonisms between the newly emerging complex and that from which it is coming to be differentiated—thus early Christians versus both Jews and Romans, later, Protestants versus Catholic. If, however, the conditions for a successful process of institutionalization are present—which is by no means to be taken for granted—then three further modes of change must occur, in roughly the following temporal sequence, though clearly this is by no means rigid.

1. What will later be referred to as *inclusion*. By this I mean that the older order from which the new religious movement has come to be differentiated, will regain positive religious significance and be included within a broader sacred order. The medieval synthesis, as it has just been sketched, is a major case—secular society, the state in the medieval sense, came to be part of the same order as that of the Christian Church and incorporated many components of both Jewish and Roman institutions, e.g., both the Old Testament and Roman Law. The modern civil religions are cases of this phenomenon.

2. *Adaptive upgrading,* by which, in this context, I mean the reevaluation of the older, previously downgraded components to constitute assets from the point of view of the broader system. In the above case, the accord of a new positive religious value to secular life, as distinguished from the view that members of the segregated orders were the only groups which were in any real sense Christian, constitutes a massive phenomenon of upgrading.

3. *Value-generalization*. If both inclusion and upgrading, as outlined, are to be legitimized, this cannot take place literally in terms of the value-orientations of the religious movement which previously declared the excluded elements to be in principle illegitimate. There must be a restructuring of the valuation base at a more general level, according to which, in our example, both religious and laity are in some sense really Christian.

process of evolution and that this process always involves interdependence between them—and human personality as well.[12]

It is, I think, fully established that one major aspect of any process which can be called evolutionary is differentiation. In the course of such processes it is to be expected that both the religious and the secular aspects of both cultural and social systems should undergo differentiation within themselves and that there should be processes of differentiation between them. It is in this frame of reference that I should like to see the two-way aspects of what is frequently called the "process of secularization."

Where we of the Judeo-Christian tradition now stand on these matters is perhaps best made clear in terms of an exceedingly schematic sketch of the main historical stages by which we have arrived where we are.[13] First, the early Christian Church became differentiated, not only from the people of Israel, but from the society of the Roman Empire. The latter was defined as pagan, the former perhaps as sacred, but in a kind of a "quasi" sense. The great structural innovation, however, was the establishment of the Church as a religious association of individuals. In the early period, of course, in part buoyed by eschatological expectations, the church remained as aloof from both the Jewish community and Roman society as possible.

With the process of proselytization, however, this aloofness became decreasingly feasible. The process of growth ended with a dual change, namely first the acceptance of Christianity as the official religion of the Roman Empire and, within the Church itself, the differentiation between the religious orders and the laity (see Paolo Tufari, forthcoming Ph.D. dissertation, Harvard University). This development set the stage for the Catholic pattern which culminated in the Middle Ages. Another major development was the split between Eastern and Western churches, connected with the decline of the Western Empire. Our concern will be with the development of the West under the jurisdiction of the Roman papacy.

The medieval system, theologically defined above all by St. Thomas, interlarded, in ideal conception, a stratified church-state system—an internally stratified secular society (state in the medieval sense) and an internally stratified Church. In terms of the religious values the Church was clearly higher than the state. It was the field for the implementation of spiritual as distinguished from temporal commitments. But the significant new element, by contrast with the early Church, was the inclusion of the secular society, the state, as temporal arm in a Christian collective system. The layman then inherently came to play a dual role. He was a member of the church conceived as the "Body of Christ" but at the same time he

---

[12] See Robert Bellah, "Religious Evolution," reprinted in his *Beyond Belief,* and also my own *Societies: Comparative and Evolutionary Perspectives* (Englewood Cliffs, N.J.: Prentice Hall, 1966), chapter 3, on "Primitive Societies."

[13] See my article "Christianity," in David Sills, ed., *The International Encyclopedia of Social Sciences* (New York: Macmillan and the Free Press, 1968). Chapter 9 of this volume.

was a member of the secular social order. To mediate between them there developed the secular priesthood, precisely as distinguished from the religious orders. The former were implementing the Mission of Christ at one level down, as it were, in that they were both consecrated and members of the secular community, indeed its spiritual leaders.

This meant the basic moral and spiritual upgrading of secular society, on a basis which justified Troeltsch in calling it a "Christian Society," a designation which no Christian would have applied to the Roman Empire in the time before it became "Holy." At the same time the hierarchy relative to spiritual values was preserved in institutional structure at three levels. First, the priority, not in power but in legitimacy, of church over state. Second, within the church, in the priority of the still aloof religious orders over, not only the laity, but the mediating secular clergy. Third was the priority of the aristocracy, to which the medieval system certainly gave a fundamental moral sanction, over the common people. This sanction was predicated on the presumption of higher levels of spiritual and moral commitment on the part of aristocracies as compared with the populace.

This inclusion of secular society in the religiously legitimated system could not occur without profound theological changes from the early Fathers. It was Thomas who brought these to a culmination with the conception of a stratified Christian Order, in which spiritual and temporal, divine and human, Church and state were interlarded. The crucial point, however, was the religious legitimation of the secular order in a sense which could not be asserted of the early Christian view of pagan society. It was on this basis that medieval society could, in Durkheim's sense, be considered to constitute for Christians a "moral community" by virtue of its institutionalization of the sacred order.

From the Reformation to Ecumenicism

Grandly architectonic as it was, the medieval system proved not to be stable. The great crisis at the level of constitutive symbolism, and hence of belief, came with the Reformation. Whatever the causal factors leading up to it, Luther and other Reformers launched a fundamental attack on the Thomistic system. The crux of it of course concerned the status of the Church, especially through the sacramental system, as the machinery of salvation, and with it the status of the priesthood. The sacraments came to be by-passed by the direct relation of the individual believer to God through faith. The true church then became the invisible church of the faithful in communion with God, with no spiritual necessity for intermediary structures. The clergy then became spiritual guides and teachers but were deprived of the "power of the keys."

The reaction of the Church of course was to outlaw the Reformers as heretics and to assert the integrity of the "catholic" system more militantly than ever in what is usually called the counter-reformation. The full reestablishment of the older system was widely considered to be the sole condition on which Western Christendom could be viable. On the other side, the more radical Reformers maintained that the total destruction of Catholicism was equally essential from their point of view (some of my ancestors were in this category). Neither position, however, prevailed, but rather a quite different one. Many will still call it a dishonorable compromise, but I suggest another interpretation.

The first stage, signalized by the Peace of Westphalia, seemed to be one of resignation dictated by sheer exhaustion from the terrible costs of the Wars of Religion. But the formula *cuius regio, eius religio,* proved not only to be a formula of truce but also the beginning of consolidation and extension of a new process of differentiation and attendant related changes in the Western socio-religious system. First the coexistence within the same system of both Protestant and Catholic Principalities meant that there were common interests, for example, in maintaining peace or in promoting political alliances, which cut across the religious line. In the longer run, the effect of this was to confirm the differentiation between religious and secular collectivities by dissociating secular political interests from religious affiliation—as, for example, in the eighteenth-century political alliance between the France of Richelieu and the Prussia of Frederick the Great. It was not a terribly long step from there to the conception of the legitimacy of a pluralistic religious constitution internal to the principality, a step first taken in Holland and England after the Reformation. This of course is the origin of the system of denominational pluralism within the politically organized society, and hence of the differentiation between churches as primarily religious bodies and the moral community in Durkheim's sense, which is also in the civic sense a religious entity.

Eventually, through many conflicts and struggles, Protestantism and Catholicism have come to constitute differentiated sectors of the same ecumenical religious community. The inclusion of Jews in such a community was, again, not a very long step. There is a parallel with the growing tolerance, in democratic politics, of differing political parties, where choice among alternative party affiliations does not jeopardize the individual's status as a loyal citizen.

With this change in the underlying structure, gradually the definition of each of the plural denominational groups began to attenuate their initial tendency to define each other's members radically as disbelievers and often as heretics. Only in our own time, however, has the ecumenical movement reached the point where a new position is being widely institutionalized or approaching that status, namely where the individual is held to have a right to the religious adherence, including beliefs, of his own choice and, whatever the element of stratification in the religious system, that right includes recognition of the religious legitimacy of the adherents of other faiths. The great steps of our time have, of course, been those taken by the Roman Church with the Papacy of John XXIII and Vatican Council II, which he called into being.[14]

It is not, I think, too much to say that ecumenicism, however incomplete and, indeed, in certain respects precarious its institutionalization still is, represents a stage where belief can clearly no longer be assessed in terms of cognitive or nonrational (or both) commitment to one religious collectivity at the Church level. The contemporary Catholic, Protestant, or Jew may, with variations within his own broader faith, even for Catholics, be a believer in the wider societal moral community. This level he does not share in regard to specifics with those of other faiths. He has, however, as I have put it, come to respect the religious legitimacy of these other faiths. The test of this legitimacy is that he and the adherents of these other faiths recognize that they can belong in the same moral community—which may be a predominantly secular, politically organized society—and that this common belongingness means sharing a religious orientation at the level of civil religion. Hence we must speak of at least three references of the concept of believer, namely (1) full adherent of an established denominational religious body, usually though not always called a church; (2) the status of an adherent of another such denominational body (from the point of view of believers in (1) those in category (2) are clearly disbelievers, or at least unbelievers); (3) common membership in a moral community which is characterized by a civil religion. In this context members of both categories (1) and (2) can in common be believers.

The Enlightenment and Radical Secularism

Clearly, however, the complications do not stop here. As early as the seventeenth century, thought about man and society began to appear which

[14] In the United States, which has played a rather special part in these developments, the new ecumenicism was very sharply symbolized by the funeral of the assassinated President John F. Kennedy in November, 1963. This was particularly significant because Kennedy was the first Roman Catholic to be elected president of the United States. Since he was a faithful Catholic, the services were conducted in the Catholic Cathedral of Washington by the "parish priest" of the Kennedy family, Cardinal Cushing of Boston. The attendants at the funeral mass, however, were persons of all faiths, starting with the new president, Lyndon Johnson, very much a Protestant. Burial, finally, was in what Bellah calls the most sacred place of the American civil religion, the Arlington National Cemetery.

An almost equally symbolic event, which I personally attended, occurred in Boston, Kennedy's home city, two months later. This was a memorial Requiem Mass, held in the Cathedral of the Holy Cross in Boston with Cardinal Cushing officiating. What was new, however, was the fact that, as part of the service itself, the Mozart Requiem was played by the Boston Symphony Orchestra, a citadel of Boston Protestant "Brahmanism." It was the first time that the Boston Symphony had, as an orchestra, ever participated in a religious service. The ecumenical character of the occasion was further emphasized by the fact that the clergy of all faiths marched in the procession and sat in the sanctuary.

purported to be wholly secular, repudiating the entire religious tradition. Perhaps the earliest representative of the highest intellectual stature was Thomas Hobbes, who was an especially thoroughgoing materialist. This movement of secular thought gathered force and came to play a highly salient role in the Enlightenment of the eighteenth century, then underwent still further developments in the Positivism, especially of the nineteenth century, which are still reverberating.

This movement tended to repudiate traditional religion, Catholic, Protestant, or Jewish, specifically from the point of view of the status of the cognitive component of religious belief systems. Over part of the world of cultural sensitivity in the West, this movement led to a genuine polarization, perhaps most prominent in the secular anticlericalism which has been so prevalent in many predominantly Catholic countries.[15]

Positivism, of course, purported to make of empirical science the only valid mode of cognition accessible to man at all. Starting as early as Rousseau and certainly conspicuously with Comte and somewhat later Marx, though the belief component in the cognitive sense was purportedly held to the level of science, the commitments to action which were so prominent in these movements certainly came to include noncognitive components, as perhaps most vividly obvious in the connection of these rationalisms with the Romantic movement.

It is perhaps safe to say that a purely secular, positivistic counter-system to traditional Western religion reached a kind of apogee in the nineteenth century and then began to break down in a sense parallel to that in which the Protestant counter-system to Catholicism has broken down into ecumenicism, a process which of course required major modifications in the earlier Catholic system itself.[16]

Within the positivistic system, clearly the major modification is the abandonment of the closed materialistic determinism which was so prominent in intellectual circles over a long period, perhaps culminating in the later nineteenth century. The alternative could not, however, be philosophical idealism of the Hegelian variety, nor an idealism too closely Kantian. Many other participants in the conference are far more competent than I to assess the significance of a wide variety of these philosophical movements. Let me only say that for me personally, from the philosophical side, a particularly important figure was A. N. Whitehead.

The positivistic systems, to an important degree in the very process of transcending their scientism, reintroduced, in modified form, both nonempirical cognitive components and nonrational components into the picture. On the cognitive-rational side what was important was the reintroduction

---

[15] In this connection Weber spoke, with a certain awe, of the forms of "extreme rationalistic fanaticism" which appeared in the course of the French Revolution and in various connections during the nineteenth century. He clearly felt that such fanaticism was not a simple matter of cognitive beliefs alone.

[16] I am quite ready to acknowledge that the pattern of sequences outlined here, closely resembles that of the Hegelian-Marxian dialectic.

of components which are, to say the least, exceedingly difficult to treat as purely empirical. Perhaps the most conspicuous example is the dialectic of history of the Marxian system, which is a kind of restatement in secular-rationalistic terms of the Christian eschatological myth that, after the expulsion from Paradise (primitive communism), there have been many agonies of subjection to the sinful powers—both feudalism and capitalism —but that finally the, this time, *collective* savior, the proletariat, is born in the humblest of circumstances and mediates between the contemporary man and his sinful past, history, and is destined to bring about the imminent "second coming," the state of communism.

This intellectual (or symbolic) construction has occasioned problems of validation and indeed interpretation which are in important respects parallel to those confronted by the theologians of the Christian Church. It was suggested above that the early Church was confronted with not only one but two foils, namely, the historic, and clearly to it, sacred socio-religious community of the people of Israel, and the world of the gentiles, namely the rest of the population of the Roman Empire. Perhaps it is not too fantastic to suggest that the secular religion movement, culminating in Marxism, has faced, on the one hand, the partly "sacred" religio-moral community of capitalism, from which it has felt a special urgency to differentiate itself, but beyond that a much diffuser "pagan" world, namely that of the underdeveloped societies. Perhaps Moscow has become the "Rome" of one part of the new system, very clearly differentiated from the "Palestine" which might include the Rhineland, Paris, London, and New York.

In this context, however, events seem to have moved much faster than in the earlier developments. If the socialist movement was a kind of functional equivalent of the Reformation, in certain respects sanctifying the secular social world, then the ecumenical phase seems to have begun to develop with surprising rapidity. These conflicts and tensions are much farther from being resolved than are those having to do with Catholic-Protestant relations, or those of both Judaism and Jewry—though in the latter connection it should not be forgotten how recent the demise of Nazism is. Nevertheless the current difference in the Catholic case, especially since John XXIII, from the many pronouncements especially of Pius XII about "atheistic Communism," parallels in secular society the attentuation on the part of American political spokesmen of the not-so-distant past, of the virulent "cold war" ideological confrontation, the accusation, from the capitalist side that there is a communist conspiracy to conquer the world.

It may seem farfetched to set up the Communist movement, as the most politically effective outgrowth of Marxian theory and the socialist political movement, as a kind of culmination of the conception of the ideal of the totally secular sociocultural order. I think, however, that this view is defensible. Making allowances for the relevant differences in the stage of evolution of the Western system, the Communist societies are very closely comparable to those dominated by strict Calvinism, especially Calvin's own Geneva, John Knox' Scotland for a brief period, the apogee of Cromwell's ascendancy in England, and very early New England. The difference has not lain in the basic pattern, but in the level of secularity of the system idealized and subjected to drastic controls.

The new religio-secular ecumenicism is not, however, grounded only, or even mainly, in the intellectual confrontation between Christian theology, and Marxism, or other secularist, theory, but also in the emergence of emphasis on essentially noncognitive components. Perhaps because of my special intellectual standard, it seems to me—and I am happily in agreement with Bellah on this—that the especially important intellectual mediators have been Freud, Durkheim, and in somewhat different ways, Max Weber.

As I have already noted, the decisive factor was the emergence of the conception of the moral component, both in the structure of societies and in the personality and motivation of the individual. For Weber, it was exemplified above all by the internalization and institutionalization of the concept of the calling in ascetic Protestantism, and with it the new level of sanctification of secular callings. For Freud it centered on the concept of the superego and its intimate involvement with the unconscious. It was Durkheim, however, who most clearly and definitely saw and characterized the moral aspect of society, both as seen by its members as object, and as defining their orientations as participants. This, combined with Durkheim's conception of religious evolution, opened the door, as we have seen, to Bellah's fruitful conception of civil religion.[17]

This seems to me to be the main path by which what are often called "secular humanists" have been brought into the moral community of modern society, including the religious implications of its existence as such a community. Both the separation of church and state in the American tradition, and the inclusion of a lay component in full citizenship in continental Europe, seem to me to imply this. Many of these secularists never had any connection with Marxism; I have concentrated on Marxism because it is the most salient grand-scale antireligious (in the traditional sense) movement.

[17] In this respect, it has long seemed to me, Marxian theory has been notably ambivalent and vacillating. On the one hand materialism seemed to dictate a conception of the real forces of history as totally independent of any normative component. On the other hand the collective voluntarism of the socialist movement went far beyond extending opportunities for its members to satisfy their interests. On the contrary, it allegedly generated genuine solidarity and thereby imposed moral obligations on participants. In a sense, in between lay what Marx called the "relations of production" as distinguished from the "forces of production." The key component here was the system of legal norms, to which we may say Marxians have attributed a kind of semi- or pseudolegitimacy, as part, no doubt, of the more general semi-legitimacy of capitalism as referred to above.

In terms of the paradigm of contexts of belief and unbelief outlined above for the ecumenical process of inclusion, one can say that secular humanists in this sense are not even believers in the "faith of their own choice." At the level of the moral community and civic religion, however, they must be accorded the status of believers. At this level it may be suggested that disbelievers are the revolutionaries who basically challenge the moral legitimacy of modern societal communities, and commit themselves to their overthrow, and unbelievers those who, though not actively combating such communities, are alienated from them and seek to minimize participation.

From the point of view of the traditional Western religions, the most important epithet aimed in this direction has been "atheism." It is now relatively commonplace that preoccupation with this issue is at least partly an expression of Judeo-Christian religious parochialism since other advanced religions, notably Buddhism, have been said to be atheistic, but of course nonetheless religions for that reason. This, however, seems to be too simple an argument in the present context. A much more important point is the emergence, as defined explicitly as such, of the "civil religions" —the American is clearly one variant in a wider complex.

This is the result of a process of inclusion directly parallel to that sketched above in relation to ecumenicism. Durkheim's equation is here, as we have noted, decisive. Those who recognize and participate in a moral community may or may not, according to matters of definition, constitute a church, but they must share in what in some sense is a common religion. Conversely, those who share what can properly be called a religion must to some extent and in some respects, constitute a moral community.

The crucial point is that, in the development of modern societies and cultures, memberships have come to be pluralistic. There is not one moral community which is an undifferentiated unity after the manner of Rousseau, nor is there one true religion outside of which nonparticipants, or disbelievers, are cast into the "outer darkness." In its secular version Rousseauism led to exclusive nationalism and the Terror; in the religious versions, counter-Reformation Catholicism to the Inquisition, Calvinism to the execution of Servetus, and Communism to the great purges of Stalin's time.

Of course in this process it is highly significant that the great mediators, the three we have named (Freud, Durkheim, and Weber) and doubtless others, were neither believers in the traditional denominational senses, nor "principled atheists." Their roles have been more closely analogous to those of an Erasmus, a John Locke, a Thomas Jefferson, a Tocqueville, and indeed, if we stretch a point, a John XXIII.

The mediation process by which old dichotomous polarities have come to be mitigated, and new inclusions facilitated, in general has not only promoted new integrations, but has also opened new possibilities, which from many points of view have constituted versions of Pandora's box.

From the medieval point of view, the Reformation did this, and from that of even relatively ecumenical Christianity, the Enlightenment did it again.

The New Resurgence of the Nonrational

With all the salience in these previous phases of problems of the non-rational, notably in the case of faith in the Lutheran sense, and of both personality needs and collective urgencies in such fields as nationalism and other forms of community, the main line of Western religio-social restructuring has centered on the cognitive component of religious commitment or "belief in. . . ."

The new phenomenon in the present generation, as very much preoccupying the discussions of the symposium, for example, in Luckmann's stage C and in Bellah's oral statement and many comments on them, seems to me to be the emergence, perhaps for the first time in a comparable way since the early Christians before the Alexandrian Fathers, of the nature and significance of the nonrational components of religious systems and all their complex relations to the secular world.

There have, of course, been many outbreaks of the nonrational in Western religious history, such as perhaps the Children's Crusade, the Waldensian disturbances, and the Anabaptist outbreak in the early Reformation. There is, however, a sense in which the extension of the differentiation and inclusion process which we have been outlining, to the "sanctification" of a whole series of levels and aspects of secular society, starting with that of "worldly callings" in Weber's sense, has now reached something approximating an end of the line. There is indeed now a sense in which church religion has come to be largely privatized, but concomitantly religious or quasi-religious significance generalized to an immense range of what previously were defined as more or less purely secular concerns, such for example as racial equality and the elimination of poverty.

A particularly good indication of this end-of-the-line situation from the religious point of view is the fact that what, in its terms, has for nearly two centuries been defined as the most subversive cultural movement, namely materialistic rationalism, now seems to be in course of being brought "into the fold." Furthermore, from the societal point of view, perhaps it can be said that we are witnessing the last throes of the disappearing institutional legitimacy of aristocracy; the demand for inclusion of all human classes on a basis of some kind of fundamental equality has become irresistible.

From the point of view of the conventional criteria of progress, in spite of the turbulent vicissitudes of recent times, and the very present threats of engulfment by the Nazis, of victory of the Communist conspiracy or of mutual destruction in nuclear war, the story has been on the whole still one of progress, namely higher levels of welfare, of education, of health and longevity, of access, for the previously disadvantaged classes, to the good things previously monopolized by the privileged.

For partisans of the new movements of dissent and revolt, the refusal to be impressed by these achievements of modern society and the tendency to declare the latter to be basically corrupt indicates that the tensions underlying the current cleavages have taken a qualitatively new turn.[18] Far deeper than this, however, lies the problem of what in some sense is legitimacy. The questions are becoming such as "If now we have unprecedented facilities for attaining whatever goals are desired, how will the relevant goals be defined?" and second, "Among the goals professed in a liberal society, by what processes and criteria will priorities among them be set?"

The conflict over legitimacy, however, does not rage most fiercely over the failures of modern society with respect to these more or less classic problems of social justice—with perhaps the critical exception of commitment to the elimination of war, which I think has progressed considerably in recent decades. They come to focus, rather, on the legitimacy of areas of expressiveness in behavior, one major aspect of which, on the historic background, is a new permissiveness, in areas where highly restrictive codes have been institutionalized for many centuries.

In attempting to designate this focus we immediately run into terminological difficulties of the kind noted above. Probably the most widely acceptable term for the main thrust of the new striving for liberation is for affective concerns. These run all the way from the grossest levels of eroticism, and indeed aggression, to the most highly sublimated levels of love. Here, however, the critical thing is to remember that on the nonrational as well as the rational side of the action paradigm we have set forth, there is a dual, not a unitary reference. Only in one respect is everything expressive the same, namely by contrast with the nonexpressive.

We can then presume that, within the expressive rubric which is contrasted with the rationalism of the modern establishment, there is involved a charismatic component in Weber's sense, as well as permissiveness for the expression of nonrational motivational components. In Freud's terms, there may be superego as well as id components.

---

[18] The above negative evaluation of contemporary industrial society and its dangers for community were most fully expressed in the symposium by Bryan Wilson. As the transcript shows, I took rather sharp issue with his diagnosis of the situation, and I could have said a good deal more. There is, however, no doubt about the prevalence among intellectuals of these views, and probably of their strategic importance, whatever their status by standards of sociological correctness. In terms of the argument of this paper it might be said that they have the function of defining aspects of the world which can be religiously and morally condemned, thereby facilating the acceptance and eventually the sanctification of other worldly elements, some of which are now present, others in process of emergence, and others which will necessitate directed attempts to bring them about.

The New Religion of Secular Love

The current new movements, of the "Christening" of which Bellah so eloquently spoke, seem to have one very important kind of relation to early Christianity, namely their immense concern with the theme of love. So far as I can see, however, there are two especially prominent differences from the early Christian case, directly in this connection, and certain others on its boundaries.

First, the source of inspiration of reorientation is not seen in the same kind of theistic terms which linked Christianity with Judaism. In this connection probably another phenomenon of ecumenicism is important, namely, the increasing interest in and acceptance of the legitimacy of non-Western religions, notably those of the Hindu-Buddhist complex. It is of course well known that these have had a particularly strong appeal, often in seriously garbled form, in socially and culturally radical circles.[19]

Probably, however, the most important motivation for an avoidance of theism concerns the desire to emphasize the this-worldly location of the valued objects and interests. From one point of view, then, the new movement may be a kind of culmination of the trend of secularization we have traced which has sanctified, by inclusion, and moral upgrading component after component of what originally was conceived to be the world by contrast with the spiritual order.[20] If, as Weber stressed, the order of secular work could be so sanctified, why not the order of human love? The immediacy of this orientation pattern, however, is too oblivious to the need for a transcendent anchorage which must somehow include both affectively adequate symbolizations and some elements of cognitive belief. So far the dominant tone seems to be the repudiation of the inherited symbols and beliefs, but that may well prove to be temporary.

[19] An interesting and important index of this new trans-Western ecumenicism is the rapid decline of interest in Christian missions, both Catholic and Protestant. In the nineteenth century and the earlier part of the present one we quite literally believed in the urgency of converting the "Heathen Chinee," as the only half satirical phrase went. Now there is probably a disposition toward romantic overevaluation of exotic religions.

A related point is that we have had a strong modern tendency toward a cynical interpretation of the past, e.g., to the effect that the Europeans involved in the exploration and exploitation of the extra-European world were motivated only by concerns for money, profit and power, especially through slavery. That there were genuine religious concerns involved is, however, clear, not only in the American mythology about the settlement of New England, but also of Virginia—cf. Perry Miller, *Errand into the Wilderness* (Cambridge: Harvard University Press, 1956). Clearly very similar things were true of Catholic, Spanish, and French settlements; they were, in substantial part, missionary enterprises.

[20] With all due allowance for the basic differences, when a very central Christian aphorism is "For God so loved the world that He gave His only begotten Son . . . ." it is perhaps understandable that mere humans should "love the world."

The second central feature which is different from early Christianity is closely related. It is that the community of love is not felt to be properly defined as a separated entity concerned primarily with the afterworld (a *Heilsanstalt,* as Weber called it) but as an integral part of human society in the here and now. It is set apart only by the conflict between such movements, vague and relatively unorganized as they have been, and those elements of society which resist them and are unsympathetic to them. There is no clear equivalent of the Christian church's self-definition as separate and apart by virtue of its transcendental mission.

Though, as suggested, even expressive symbolization, to say nothing of belief systems, is still incipient, probably the master symbol has become that of community, that is, of secular collectivities in the organization and solidarity of which the dominant theme is the mutual love of the members. In the more radical versions, the ideal is that not only the national level of societies, but world society should become one vast concrete community of love. It seems to follow, to what Pareto called the "logic of the sentiments," that any other motivations and mechanisms of social control are inherently immoral and should not be accepted on any terms. This obviously is a Utopian ideal, certainly in Mannheim's sense, with a vengeance. It can, however, be said to be a legitimate sociocultural descendant of Christianity.

Objectively, so far, the trial institutionalization of the new religious orientation is confined to small, more or less self-isolated groups, which in some respects resemble the conventicles of early Protestantism. Whether or when it will crystallize into an organized mass movement depends on many factors, not the least of which is leadership. In the sense in which Luther and Calvin were the major prophets of the Reformation, Rousseau of the Enlightenment, and Marx of socialism, it does not seem that a major prophet of the new religion of love has yet appeared. Perhaps, in retrospect, Gandhi will appear as a kind of John the Baptist.

Moral Absolutism, Eroticism, and Aggression

The above two characteristics of the new, presumptively religious ferment help to explain, if their designation is correct, three aspects of the fermenting mix which are disturbing to those who are not themselves caught up in the ferment, but who are more disposed to be sympathetic with it than to condemn it out of hand. These are its tendency to moral absolutism, to forthright, indeed flamboyant eroticism, and to a seemingly new attitude of permissiveness toward or even legitimation of aggression and violence which seems difficult to reconcile with the stress on love.

The key to understanding these disturbing phenomena seems to me to lie in the phenomenon of regression and the understanding of it which has been attained in the last generation and more of the development of social science. The essential framework lies in the great principle of evolutionary biology, that "ontogeny repeats phylogeny," however complicated the empirical application of the principle may be. In terms closer to our own, the process of differentiation and its related processes, are critical to the evolution of human action systems, including their cultural, social, and personality and organic subsystems.

Regression then means that under pressure, a system will revert to patterns which have been dominant and appropriate in earlier stages of its development. Perhaps the most graphic demonstrations of the phenomenon have been provided in the field of psychopathology, especially through the insights of Freud. Fixation on and at particular levels of regression is the primary hallmark of psychopathological states, but the recognition and understanding of such fixations is the starting point of successful therapy. Therapy in turn is the first cousin of creativity. New creative developments in the personality or the cultural or social system are overwhelmingly associated with phases of regression.[21]

Throughout this paper I have stressed the importance of the moral aspect of the interface between the transcendental and the worldly references of the human condition, between religious commitments and coping with the given situation of action. What I here call moral absolutism is the product of dedifferentiation of the inherently pluralistic moral complexity of evolutionarily advanced social and cultural systems, to the point of fixation on what seems, under stress, to be the one essential moral commitment which not only must outrank others in a priority scale, but to which all others must unequivocally be subordinated, as presumptively the only way in which the treasured central value can be asserted and protected against abandonment.

The phenomenon itself is of course by no means new. It, in fact, characterizes charismatic movements rather generally, including early Christianity itself, the Reformation. Jacobinism, and Communist socialism. It is clear, however, that it generates severe conflicts in the course of developmental processes of the sort we have been analyzing, because of its incompatibility with the moral bases of structural pluralism. It challenges the legitimacy of the moral commitments of all elements in the system which will not give the demanded priority to the one absolutized value and hence escalates the conflict to the level of a value-conflict, which can be much more serious than the usual conflict of interests. Proverbially, religious wars are particularly bitterly fought.

This circumstance, combined with the centrality of the valuation of love in the new movement, helps to make understandable the complex set of relations among love and the erotic on the one hand, aggression and vio-

---

[21] An already classical explication of this phenomenon is presented in Erik Erikson's *Young Man Luther* (New York: W. W. Norton, 1962). See also his paper, "Reflections on the Dissent of Contemporary Youth," *Daedalus*, Winter 1970.

lence on the other. The involvement of religion with erotic themes is of course as old as the history of religion itself. Modern psychology and sociology, however, have made it possible to gain better analytic insight into the reasons for this interrelation than have previously been available. One such insight concerns the continuities between the erotic component in child care and its functions for socialization of the child, with the nature and function of genital eroticism for the adult.

In one sense the primordial solidarity is that between mother and child—as beautifully symbolized in the Renaissance Madonna theme. This is at the same time ideally a relation of mutual erotic gratification and of love. This critical feature is repeated at the adult level. There are many variants as a function of variations of kinship systems. The modern isolated nuclear family, however, precisely because in this case the family is highly differentiated from components of social structure with other functions, presents a particularly concentrated case of the relationship. Here, especially as analyzed by the social anthropologist David M. Schneider,[22] it becomes clear that sexual intercourse between spouses has become the primary cultural symbol of what Schneider calls their "diffuse enduring solidarity," which may well be translated as love, and not only as between themselves, but in their sharing of mutual responsibility for their children since they constitute the senior component in the family.

The incest taboo has an important bearing here, in that it draws a sharp line between the erotic relations of the married couple and, after early childhood, the prohibition of such relations between parents and children and between siblings.

I should postulate that love in a nonerotic sense must be the core concern of a religious movement in the sense suggested above. There is, however, at the same time the deeply rooted relation between eroticism and love, which in an important sense is a major bridge from organism to personality. Under the kinds of pressure which have been discussed, I should argue that there is a strong tendency to regression, in precisely the above sense, from the level of sublimated love, as Freud would have put it, to that of erotic attachment, and indeed a tendency to absolutize the significance of erotic experience. Especially as it occurs between two persons—autoeroticism is something else—it can seem to be almost the ultimate in genuine solidarity.

There are, however, two problems about a primarily erotic basis of the wider solidarities which, if we are to believe Durkheim, religions must involve. One concerns the regressive relations of the erotic complex in its significance for individual personality development. To give too great primacy to erotic relations in this sense is to skate on the edge of acting as a child and treating partners as children. The binding-in of the erotic com-

---

[22] David Schneider, *American Kinship: A Cultural Account* (Englewood Cliffs, N.J.: Prentice Hall, 1968).

ponent of motivation to adult capabilities and responsibilities is clearly a major function of the incest taboo.

The second problem derives from the fact that mutual erotic solidarity is bound to intimate bodily contact, by far most fully expressible in the diadic relation. Though group sex has certain attractions, its serving as a primary symbolization, even, of wider solidarities seems to be severely limited. Putting it simply, the wider the circle of erotic relations and the more casual that to any particular partner, the less is it possible for erotic experience to symbolize diffuse enduring solidarity. A full, culturally generalized language of love must be couched in terms of other media. Such languages have, by and large, been predominantly religious rather than carnal.

It seems to me that early Christianity solved the problem by drawing a very sharp line between religiously significant love and carnal appetites. The Pauline dictum "it is better to marry than to burn" was not exactly a glorification of conjugal love. The religious orders then, on their emergence, adopted full celibacy as a matter of principle and this was later extended to the secular priesthood.

Luther's marriage, however, in violation of his monastic vows and, significantly, to a former nun, was a symbolic act of new legitimation of the erotic complex and could not very well be interpreted, in the morally rigorous climate of early Protestantism, as simply "surrendering to the flesh." The fact that the institution of a married clergy was universalized in all branches of Protestantism is of course critical.

Various of the movements which led to the institutionalization of new sectors of religiously legitimate secular society have been accompanied by movements toward sexual liberation. This was true of the French revolution and also of the socialist movement. But where political freedoms and release from economic exploitation are felt to be the main stakes, neither love nor eroticism is likely to be central. In the current situation, however, I suggest that the institutionalization of love at some level of community has become central, and that regressive pressures operate strongly toward the erotic emphasis. These emphases, however, I also suggest, lead to unstable states because unsublimated erotic motivations do not form a sufficiently firm and generalized basis for solid attachments to ground a religiously legitimate and viable network of units and of moral community —remembering always that modern community must be pluralistic.

The early Christian pattern of radical segregation between love and the erotic component thus seems not to be viable nor, I should venture to say, even legitimate in the modern situation. At the very least the erotic relation of husband and wife, independently of the procreative function, must be legitimized, or it cannot function, in Schneider's phrase, as a primary symbol of diffuse enduring solidarity. What extensions beyond the conjugal relation may come to be legitimized I may perhaps be pardoned for not entering into here, not only because of the delicacy of the issues, but because this is already perhaps an overly long concluding paper. I do, however, think that there will be others.

The deepest reason why the early Christian pattern is not acceptable now, I hope has been made clear. This is that the new religious movement, which I feel will almost certainly prove to be largely Christian, cannot define itself as a separated collectivity outside of what has been called secular society, but must be defined as an integral part of the latter which hopes to permeate its moral and spiritual qualities. Not only the love component—which is not the same as the moral—of solidarities, but the erotic component, is too deeply intertwined in the texture of society, especially at the level of the interpersonal intimate relations which are coming to be so highly valued, for it to be extirpated. If, indeed, this extirpation were possible, which I doubt short of major convulsions, the price would be the postponement of any new community of love, probably for many centuries.

Finally, perhaps these considerations throw at least a little light on what to many of us seems to be the most irrational aspect of the new movements, namely the resurgence of aggression and violence. Important as these may be, a very large part of it seems to go beyond natural resentment or anger at being unjustly discriminated against, exploited, subordinated to dubiously, legitimate authority, blocked in pursuing legitimate goals, or simply not listened to. In making any such judgement of overdetermination it is of course essential to bear in mind that when we speak of the aggression and violence of the proponents of the new presumptively religious groups, they do not stand alone. There is also aggression and violence in other quarters, and there is little hope of disentangling who is guilty of aggression and who is understandably reacting aggressively.

Psychodynamically by now the interconnections between love and hate have become familiar. In one aspect they are the positive and negative sides, respectively, of the bonds of emotional significance of objects, in Freud's term of cathexis. As Freud put it, cathexis means an investment in relation to other persons—or groups as such—in social interaction, and failure of positive reciprocity can readily flip over into negativity, that is, hostility, hate, and aggression. The bitterness of family quarrels attests to this—far from it proving that the members do not in some sense love one another it is evidence that they do.

From this it seems to follow that he who makes a special commitment to love, by that very fact becomes especially vulnerable to hatred, where his expectations of reciprocation are frustrated. It takes an especially elevated level of love to transcend this dilemma, one which Christianity did in fact attain, but never succeeded in fully institutionalizing—it was most poignantly put in the injunction "love thine enemies."

Again, there is an enormous difference from early Christianity deriving from the fact that the current movements are so integrally involved with the affairs of secular society. When combined with moral absolutism, as it very generally is, the love-orientation disposes its proponents to aspire to political effectiveness, that is to power, which necessarily means coping with opposition at many levels. Where resort to violence, or confrontation, seems effective, the temptation is enormous. But in addition to the tempta- tion of tactical effectiveness there is the emotional seduction. If you can convincingly think of your opponent as really wicked he must deserve to be hated, not loved—and isn't the mere fact of his opposition almost suf- ficient proof of his wickedness?

In a situation where political stakes were very high, Gandhi's non- violent resistance movement achieved remarkable discipline in maintaining nonviolence, but when the British finally left India, there were disastrously violent clashes between Hindus and Muslims with many thousands killed. Perhaps one can suggest that in nonviolent movements aggression in the motivational sense is by no means generally absent. If the discipline of nonviolence is impaired, the aggressive component may easily break through into violent action and, short of that, of course verbal abuse and humiliation of opponents and the like may figure very prominently.

If, as many of us feel, there is enormous creative potential in the emerging religion of love, the danger of lapsing into aggression and vio- lence, along with that of moral absolutism, which are of course related to each other, seem to me more serious than the danger of regression into eroticism—or the related retreat into dependence on drugs. The point about the former two is the extent to which they serve as triggers to mobi- lize, not only legitimate opposition, in the sense of adherence to values somewhat different from those absolutized, or of defense of rights against violence or insult, but they release the irrational affective factors which lie back of the tensions inherent in such conflict situations, factors which in general in relation to creative movements operate repressively.

I may perhaps end this discussion on a Durkheimian note. The affec- tive-charismatic components of a religiously innovative movement are likely to be self-defeating and to lapse into some sort of antinomian anarchy if they are not somehow combined with the factors of the discipline which goes with moral order. I even venture to think that a substantial component of cognitive belief is an essential ingredient of the stabilization of religious innovation.

Conclusion

The basic structure of the belief-disbelief-unbelief problem in the con- temporary phase just sketched is the same as in the earlier phases. Two differences, however, complicate the too literal reference to precedents. The first is the overwhelmingly this-worldly orientation of the new religion of love, if I may consolidate a little the use of that term. The other is the salience, indeed primacy, in the movement of the nonrational components. Here there is a temptation, on the side of the proponents, to declare that problems of belief are totally irrelevant, and of opponents, that the movement is a simple case of disbelief in a sense which implies an obligation to combat it with the utmost vigor.

Deeply rooted cultural precedents predispose many in the West to the feeling that the only truly religious love is profoundly other worldly and must be sharply contrasted with any basis of worldly love, even though it is love of "thy neighbor." In the other context, far more than in the past, the reaction is against the rationality complex in very general terms. There is a crucial sense in which the most immediate antagonist is not the traditional organized religions, but the most secularized rationality systems, notably though perhaps ambivalently, Marxian socialism, but ramifying much more broadly into nonsocialist aspects of rationality, both in cultural systems and in social institutions, in the latter context, notably bureaucracy, but also clearly academic professionalism.

We have, however, argued that belief systems prominently involving cognitive components are essential ingredients in all religious systems which have a prospect of stabilization. For the principled antirationalist the construction of a viable cognitive belief system presents peculiar difficulties, which are not altogether unprecedented, but which become especially acute in these circumstances. I venture to suggest, however, that certain resources essential for this task are available, at least incipiently, in some of the social science sources which have been reviewed.[23] It is interesting to note that, from the point of view of the incipient religion, these sources are predominantly secular in a sense parallel to that in which the Greek intellectual tradition was secular from the point of view of the early Christian church. Clearly Freud, Durkheim, and Weber were not prophets of the religion of love any more than the Neoplatonists were prophets of Christianity, but what they, various of their successors, and others not associated with their names have done may well prove essential to the new movement. The fact that, in a profound sense, especially the latter two understood but rejected Marxian socialism, seems to me critical in this connection.

There has been much discussion of the role of youth, especially student youth, in this movement. This is, in my opinion, indeed crucial as a kind of spearhead, but this is not the place to go into the reasons why such appeals are so attractive to the contemporary student generation on a nearly worldwide basis. Social science, in my opinion, has progressed toward making such understanding possible.[24] It should, however, be clear that a

---

[23] Robert Bellah, chapter 14 of *The Culture of Unbelief*.

[24] Talcott Parsons and Gerald Platt, "Higher Education, Changing Socialization and Contemporary Student Dissent," in Matilda White Riley, et al., eds., *A Sociology of Stratification*, VIII of *Aging and Society* (New York: Russell Sage, 1972) and Erik Erikson, *Young Man Luther*.

student base is not a sufficient anchorage in the structure of societies for the institutionalization of a major religious pattern. Students remain students for only a few years, and they must face the dilemma of either relinquishing their legitimacy with relinquishment of student status, or extending the basis of legitimacy from the student phase to later phases in the life cycle. The slogan, "Never trust anyone over thirty" is a typical "chiliastic" aphorism which manifests a sentiment but cannot be stably institutionalized.

Each additional step in secularization, in the sense of the institutionalization of Christian patterns in the secular world, which we have traced adds a new set of complications to the belief-disbelief-unbelief problem. A most important point then needs to be emphasized. When the institutional resolution, inclusion, and upgrading has in fact occurred, the older patterns do not disappear, but continue to function, though in modified form, which often means in more restricted circumstances than before. Thus to go way back, Christianity did not extirpate Judaism, but the latter is now persisting ecumenically together with a wide variety of Christian churches and sects. Protestantism did not extirpate Catholicism, nor vice versa, and they not only coexist peacefully but have become integrated into a more general religious structure. Then, very recently, I suggest, rationalistic secularism has not only failed to extirpate church religion, but has gone far toward becoming included with it as a still broader religious framework, in which all the older religious groups—with some qualifications—survive.[25]

I see no reason why the general pattern of emergence of a movement, starting in acute conflict with its most immediate predecessor in the role of institutional establishment, moving to truce in that conflict on the pattern of *cuius regio, eius religio,* then eventually to the process of resolution by inclusion and upgrading, should not be repeated in the present case, as well as those which have gone before. I am sure that we are barely entering upon the phase of acute conflict, which we can only hope will not eventuate, for the next century, in a new cycle of wars of religion which might indeed be fatal to civilization, but most particularly to the religion of love, because, however partially justified their accusation of hypocrisy against their opponents may be, they simply cannot afford to let hatred and antagonism prevail over their central orientation. This factor and, among other things its cognitive understanding, plus of course the antiaggressive components of the whole great religious tradition of the Western world, give considerable hope that the sense of conflict will not be escalated to the point of the most serious threats of mutual destruction.

I have been so bold as to suggest that the contemporary situation, in

[25] Indeed, I look forward to the day when, in a Jewish, Catholic, or Protestant high ceremony like the Kennedy Memorial Mass, the Director of the Institute of Philosophy of the Soviet Academy of Sciences—a post which I interpret to be the equivalent of "Dean of the theological faculty of the religion of Marxism-Leninism" —will march in the procession and sit in the sanctuary as one of the assemblage of the clergy of all faiths.

which the problem of the meaning of unbelief has become so salient, may constitute both an end, and a turning point leading into a beginning, of a major cycle of human religious development. The key connecting symbol, which may, in Bellah's sense, be interpreted realistically as well as in the framework of symbolic reductionism, is clearly love. This was certainly the keynote of the Gospels, and has become so again today. The cycle, however, is not a simple return to the beginning, but a spiral, in the course of which much has happened, which, schematically, may be called the Christianization of the world.

Though in the current turbulent stage, it must be expected that conflict, confrontation, aggression, and hatred will be exceedingly prominent on both sides, the orientational content points to a pattern of resolution, which is inherently precarious in its initial stages, but which, if it materializes, may well usher in, not paradise, for this is not given to human societies, but a new phase of religious and social progress.

However important, on the one hand, insistence by the proponents of the new on their claims, at the risk of overreliance on moral absolutism and aggression, on the other hand by the defenders of the, after all not totally bankrupt, older values on their legitimacy—again at the risk of refusals to concede and insistence on discipline which will be interpreted as intolerably punitive—there is a basically solid foundation in Christian tradition for the resolution of these conflicts.

This frame of reference will necessarily, I think, apply on both sides of the conflict. There are, is seems to me, three main components of the essential orientation. The first is humility, in the historic Christian sense, which is inherently incompatible with moral absolutism, as the arrogation of the right to punish because the other has sinned and you are pure.[26] Note that I apply this on both sides—the proponents of love have no better moral right to punish their opponents than do those of the establishment. The second orientation may be called the sense of tragedy. Moral dichotomization into the "good guys" and the "bad guys" is proverbially unproductive. The nonrational sense, as well as the cognitive understanding, that the good are always engaged in a struggle with the evil elements within them, and that conversely the bad are always in some sense trying to overcome their evil motives, is an essential ingredient of resolution. Human history is not a morality play in which the good are rewarded and the evil punished, but a struggle for salvation, enlightenment, progress, or community in which many, indeed most, of the participants have been and are caught up in tragic conflicts and dilemmas. The third component, compassion seems almost to follow from the importance of the first two. If we love a person—or a group or a symbol—we must at the same time understand and empathize with his difficulties and his conflicts, including

---

[26] There are, of course, other bases of the legitimation of punishment. The arrogation referred to is a version of the Donatist heresy.

those which from our point of view are destructive of our values, and still love him, not only in the sense of particularized affection, but of giving him support for the implementation of the value of universalized love.

It seems to me that this was the basic message of Pope John XXIII. It was that Christian humility, a sense of tragedy, and compassion form the essential basis for a much greater extension of the regime of love than we have ever known before.

12. The "Gift of Life" and Its Reciprocation

Introduction

A FEW YEARS AGO, two of us (Parsons and Lidz) ventured to write a rather general article under the title "Death in American Society." [1] For the present venture we have been joined by Renée Fox, and the three of us have decided both to extend the analysis of the earlier article and to narrow the focus. The "extension" consists in going considerably deeper into the background of current American orientations toward death and its meaning in the Judeo-Christian religious tradition than was attempted in the earlier paper. The "narrowing" consists in trying to focus on the institutionalization in America of the promotion of health and the care of illness, with special reference to the medical profession and its ethical orientations.

This focus seems particularly appropriate since the most important empirical argument of the earlier paper concerned the distinction between the inevitability of the death of every person, marking the completion of a full "life course," and the "adventitious" components of the death complex. The latter includes two types of premature death: that brought about by "impersonal" causes—for the most part disease, but also accident—and that imposed by what is in some sense willful human action, such as "violence." It is often difficult to draw a line between accidental and violent death, but the analytical distinction is crucial.

The most dramatic consequence of recent developments in health care has been—and within somewhat more than a century in the "advanced"

[1] Talcott Parsons and Victor M. Lidz, "Death in American Society," in *Essays in Self-Destruction,* Edwin Shneidman, ed., New York (Science House, 1967).

From *Social Research,* vol. 39, no. 3 (October 1972), pp. 367–415. Co-authored with Renée C. Fox and Victor M. Lidz. Used by permission. *Social Research* is published by the Graduate Faculty of the New School for Social Research. (Reprinted in *Death in American Experience,* Arien Mack, ed. [New York: Schocken Books, 1973]).

societies—the doubling, if not slightly more, of life expectancy at birth. To a degree never before true, it has become customary for the aware individual to expect that he will live to complete a "normal" span of life and for parents, that their children, if born alive and healthy, will also do so. The differentiation of the inevitable from the adventitious aspects of death has focused a more powerful light than before on the component of inevitability. If so much is controllable by human action, one must ask, what does it mean that there is nevertheless an absolute limit to our control? This problem of meaning, of course, bears with special cogency on members of the medical profession because they are *par excellence* the institutionalized trustees of society's interest in the preservation of life.

We will note that there has been in recent years a significant increase in both medical and popular concern with the "existential" aspects of death and also suffering. Indeed, the volume which Dr. Shneidman edited—part of a rapidly growing literature—attests to this fact, as does the greatly enhanced concern of medical students and physicians themselves.

The earlier Parsons-Lidz article used as a foil a paper by Peter Berger in which he claimed that the "denial" of death was a basic aspect of the American outlook.[2] We still think we were right in refusing that interpretation. We now believe, however, that it is not necessary to make an either/or choice between "acceptance" and "denial"; we believe that, as in many cases involving underlying conflicts, what is often interpreted as denial is in reality a kind of "apathy"—i.e., being in a situation of not knowing quite what to say or do and thus minimizing overt expression or action. This may also be reinforced by the "stoical" component of the Puritan tradition. We shall attempt to show how certain features of the medical situation and medical ethics have involved this kind of conflict with this kind of result.

On the positive side, we wish to re-emphasize what we consider the fully established view—that it is biologically normal for all individual organisms to die. Death is now understood to be an important mechanism enhancing the adaptive flexibility of the species through the sacrifice of individuals; i.e., it makes certain that the bearers of newly emergent genetic patterns will rapidly succeed the bearers of older ones. Death may be even more critically important in contributing to cultural growth and flexibility than in supporting genetic change. Thus, we may regard death as a major contributor to the evolutionary enhancement of life, and thereby it becomes a significant part of the aggregate "gift of life" that all particular lives should end in death. That is why it cannot be a rational pursuit of modern medicine to try to end or even minimize the "inevitable" aspect of death.

Our approach will emphasize theoretical continuity between the organic

[2] Peter Berger and Richard Lieban, "Kulturelle Wertstruktur und Bestattungspraktiken in den Vereinigten Staaten," *Kölner Zeitschrift für Soziologie und Sozialpsychologie,* No. 2, 1960.

and the human socio-cultural levels, through the premise that the mortality of individuals has a positive functional significance for both human societies and the organic species. Beyond that, yet intimately related to it, is the fundamental distinction between, on the one hand, the "phenotypical" incorporation of genetic patterns in the lives of individual organisms and populations, and the genetic components themselves, and on the other hand, the modes and conditions of their preservation, implementation and development in the evolutionary sense. It is in this spirit that we devote our first substantive discussion to the field of *cultural* symbolization which in America bears on the problem of the meaning of death and, of course, its opposite, life. We think that the most important themes are found in the "constitutive symbolization" of the religious heritage.[3] To be sure, a substantial part of our contemporary population purports to "take no stock in religion." We feel, however, that the patterns of symbolization which we shall review have come to be constitutive of the *whole* culture by which we live, and that their relevance is by no means confined to the lives of self-consciously "religious" people. As social scientists we do not think that "science" in the usual sense has provided "functionally equivalent" symbolic patterns of orientation, though we think that the evidence just cited of the positive biological function of death and the recent enhancement of life expectancies is highly pertinent to our problem.

We shall be dealing with religious symbolism predominantly in the context of what has come to be called *myth*, in the sense used by Lévi-Strauss and Leach, and in another, related field, by Kenneth Burke and Northrop Frye.[4] We are not concerned with the problem of the historical veracity of the Books of Genesis and Exodus, or of the Four Gospels, but with clarifying the "structure," as Lévi-Strauss would put it, of certain of the themes expressed in such documents insofar as they bear on the problem of orientation to the death-life aspects of the human condition. Neither will we be concerned with the metaphysical question of the "existence of God." For us this belief is simply a basic element of the myth.

In addition, a principal theoretical emphasis has become much more salient than it was in the Parsons-Lidz paper, and has been especially emphasized by Fox in connection with her work with Judith Swazey on the

---

[3] Talcott Parsons, "Belief, Unbelief, and Disbelief," in Caporale and Grumelli, eds., *The Culture of Unbelief,* Berkeley (University of California Press, 1971), Chapter 12. Chapter 11 of this volume. See also Robert N. Bellah, *Beyond Belief: Essays on Religion in a Post-Traditional World,* New York (Harper and Row, 1970), and his paper, "Religion and Social Science," in Caporale and Grumelli, eds., *op cit.,* Chapter 14.

[4] Claude Lévi-Strauss, *Structural Anthropology,* New York (Basic Books, 1963). Edmund Leach's little book, *Genesis as Myth and Other Essays,* London (Jonathan Cape, 1971), has been of important substantive as well as methodological significance to us, as has Kenneth Burke's *The Rhetoric of Religion,* Boston (Beacon Press, 1961). See also Northrop Frye, "The Critical Path: An Essay on the Social Context of Literary Criticism," *Daedalus,* Spring 1970, pp. 268–342.

"existential" problems involved in organ transplants, which will be discussed below.[5] This is the theme of the importance of the *gift* and of gift-exchange, as it was classically introduced into social science literature—though not without antecedents—a generation ago by Marcel Mauss.[6] It will be remembered that Mauss stressed not only the ubiquity, in human cultures, of the theme of the *giving* of gifts, but also how this *giving* creates, for the recipients of gifts, an *obligation to reciprocate,* which on occasion can be onerous indeed.

In the following section of the paper it will be our principal thesis that in the Judeo-Christian tradition—and especially in the Christian phase—life, for the individual, is defined in the first instance as a *gift,* directly or indirectly, from God. It may be a niggardly gift, as with those born only to misery, want and suffering, or a munificent gift, as with those born with great talent and good fortune. Yet in both cases the gift of life creates an obligation to reciprocate. Our second main thesis will then be that the trend of religio-cultural development within this tradition has been toward defining the death of the individual, especially in the fullness of a complete life, as itself the gift which constitutes a full reciprocation of the original gift of life.

Not only may the obligation to reciprocate gifts be onerous, but the tragic view of the human condition has been in many vital respects structured about this onerousness. First, recipients must somehow be motivated to *try* to reciprocate: religiously, this commitment has, in our tradition, often been formulated as "faith." But the gifts, as we have noted, are by no means of equal value, and the sheer difficulties of reciprocation, except by "giving up," may be insurmountable. Particularly potent as a focus of tragedy is the fact that the fates of individuals are never neatly ordered in relation to those of the social collectivities in which they hold deeply meaningful membership. God is concerned not only with individuals but with "peoples" in the Old Testament sense. The problems of the beneficence or malevolence of God and of the shortcomings of individual human beings, religiously formulated as sin, are not to be neatly shoved aside by an equation of the reciprocity of gifts alone.

The Judeo-Christian Symbolization of Life and Death

To the social scientist, the sequence "life-death" strongly suggests the "life-cycle" or "life-course" of the individual, sometimes formulated as

---

[5] Renée C. Fox and Judith P. Swazey, *The Courage to Fail,* Chicago (University of Chicago Press, 1974).

[6] Marcel Mauss, *The Gift,* trans. by Ian Cunnison, Glencoe, Ill. (The Free Press, 1954).

"age"-grading or structure. But in alluding to this category, which includes both life and death, the social scientist almost automatically adds to the stimulus word "age," the words "and sex." With regard to individuals rather than species, these categories provide a frame of reference for analyzing the interface between the organic aspects of the human and the social, with the necessary relation to the cultural. "Age" connotes the passage through time of the individual, within the human-social matrix, from a beginning to an end. Since, however, individuals are mortal, the continuation of the socio-cultural system beyond the individual life-span depends on the mechanism of continuing replacement, through reproduction, of the passing generation. For man, as for almost all of the "higher" animal species, this mechanism is that of *bisexual* reproduction, with rather clearly differentiated biological roles for the two sexes in the reproductive process and, more problematically, differing roles at the social and cultural levels. "Age and sex" seem clearly to belong together in their biological and socio-cultural references. Sex is of course clearly dichotomously structured, while at first glance "age" may seem a linear continuum; but if one focusses on the terminal points of a clearly limited process, birth and death can also be treated as a dichotomous reference-base. Putting the two together we derive the familiar four-fold table of two dichotomous variables.

The myth of Genesis clearly embodies both variables, though in ways which are at one level somewhat contradictory. It is clear that God created man "as the Lord of the Creation" and "in His own image" to enjoy a very special status relative to the rest of the creation. In the first version, man is included with the animals in the formula "male and female created He them"; in the second, however, Adam was the sole human Creature, and when God saw that it "was not good for Adam to be alone," He created Eve out of Adam's rib so that they were of "one flesh and blood."

As Kenneth Burke [7] says, man, as the symbol-using animal, has the unique capacity of the "negative," i.e., he may not only assent, but also may say "no." There was one and only one prohibition imposed on Adam, and later Eve, in the Garden—namely that against "eating of the fruit of the tree of the knowledge of good and evil." Man, being even at that point what he was and is, defied that prohibition and, tempted by the serpent via Eve, "ate of the fruit." This was the mythical origin both of death—by divine decree at the point of expulsion from the Garden—and of sexual reproduction for humans, since in the Garden Eve was only companion to Adam, not sexual partner.

The symbolic implication of the Fall seems to have been a double one. On the one hand, the Fall was the simple result of disobedience to a divine command. On the other hand, having been told that if man disobeyed he would "surely die," it can be argued that Adam and Eve thought they

[7] *Op. cit.,* note 4.

could evade this consequence and presume to immortality, symbolized in the Garden by the "Tree of Life." It seems clear that "original sin" had this dual character—disobedience and the claim to an immortality which, since it was a divine prerogative, meant the claim to Godhead. The imposition of mortality on expulsion from the Garden indicates an emphatic divine insistence that man, as creature, was *not* divine.

At this stage the "gift" theme seems to be subordinate. To be sure, God gave life to Adam and Eve and enabled them to reproduce, through (in a sense) "compensating" them for their disobedience by giving them the "knowledge of good and evil." This knowledge has been interpreted by Leach [8] as comprising both knowledge of the inevitability of individual death, and knowledge of the "difference of the sexes," which can be further interpreted to mean the possibility of species survival beyond individual death through bisexual reproduction. Both must, in our view, be interpreted as at once good *and* evil. The evil side, besides death itself, is embodied in the famous curses by God during the expulsion from the Garden —for Eve, condemnation to childbearing in pain, for Adam, the need to subsist "by the sweat of his brow." Indeed, a major biblical interpretation has held that the whole of human life since the expulsion could be summed up in the formula "sin and death."

Another theme, however, appears in early Genesis, that of a *mediator*. As Leach suggests, even the serpent may be interpreted in this light. Just possibly, God "wanted" Adam and Eve to sin, or at least was not too angry that the serpent seduced them. Further along, Eve, as the symbolically prototypical woman, becomes a kind of mediator, a theme which much later becomes central in the figure of Mary, Mother of God.

Meanwhile, the great theme of most of the Old Testament is not the spiritual fate of individuals, but the fate of a religiously-sacred social community, the People of Israel. Symbolically, they end as Yahweh's *chosen* people—but not without many vicissitudes. In the first major phase, God was basically displeased with His highest creature and contemplated destroying His entire creation, but relented to save Noah and his extended family. In a way, He purified mankind by the flood, leaving only the descendents to Noah to inherit—this was the first "Covenant." Following this came a series of further decisions, the most notable of which were the Covenants with Abraham asserting that his descendents should become the chosen people, and later with Moses, in a sense the main mythical founder of Israel. Leach has circumstantially analyzed the many vicissitudes of this selection process by which the People of Israel are said to have become established as a religiously-grounded socio-political community.[9]

Moses, however, not only led the Exodus from Egypt and renewed the Covenant of Abraham, but also introduced the Law as a major innova-

[8] *Op. cit.,* note 4.
[9] Cf. "The Legitimacy of Solomon," in Leach, *op. cit.*

tion. This came to be constitutive of Judaism and, in a sense, of all its cultural derivatives. Throughout, little was heard of the "cure" of individual "souls," though such themes began to emerge in Hellenistic Judaism.

It should nevertheless be kept in mind that, not only by originally creating the human species but also by "choosing" Abraham and his "seed" and maintaining the Covenant with them, God gave his people the gift of corporate existence under divine sanction. This theme reappears later, in the conception of the Church of Christ and of a whole society as the "Kingdom of God on Earth." In the Old Testament, for the most part, both birth and death are treated within the framework of the sacred community, with the conception of death seen as "reception into the bosom of Abraham." The dead become honored ancestors of the living, with both incorporated in a time-extended, multi-generational community. As a background to the Christian phase, it is essential that the *permanence* of this community be assumed. There was no further divine threat to destroy it, as in the story of Noah; any further divine intervention would have to be different in character.

EARLY CHRISTIANITY

It is a big jump to the symbolism of the much later Christian development, but our primary concern is not with cultural history but with a symbolic complex. There is a crucial difference between the relation of God to Adam on the one hand and to Jesus on the other. God *created* Adam in His own image, but Jesus was "His only *begotten* Son." As just noted, we may infer that, by virtue of the series of covenants, God had committed Himself to the continuance of the human species, particularly but presumably not exclusively of His chosen people. His intervention in the human condition, therefore, had to be intervention in the affairs of humanity as "a going concern." Mary and the myth of the Annunciation is the symbolic focus of the divine recognition that "cooperation" with humanity is essential in order to carry out the grand plan. It is in this context that the very critical symbol, blood, becomes central, referring to the continuity of human generations which, of course, assumes the death of each individual together with the continuity of the population through sexual reproduction, what the Old Testament calls "begetting." The "blood" of Jesus had therefore both a divine and a human component, the latter being the blood of Mary.

Within the framework of the People of Israel, continuity was established in another way, through the role of Joseph as, in Leach's term, Jesus' "sociological father." Whatever the theological subtleties of the problem of the Virgin Birth may be, Jesus is forthrightly declared to be descended from Abraham through Isaac, and most especially to be of the

"House of David." This genealogy is *through Joseph* (Matthew, Ch. 1), and the emphasis on continuity in the sequence of generations is clearly another reference to "blood" as an essential symbol of Christianity.

Another crucial symbolic note is sounded in the Christ story. In Judaism, though Yahweh treated the people of Israel as His chosen people, protecting them and favoring them in many ways, His primary concern was with their obedience—that is, their observance of the Law He had imposed upon them. God was continually testing them, perhaps half expecting them to "betray" Him. The severity of the testing may be said to have culminated in the command to Abraham that he sacrifice his one fully "legitimate" son, Isaac. In Christianity, the new note is that of love, with its evident relations to the theme of giving. The crucial Gospel statement should perhaps be quoted in full: "For God so loved the world that he gave his only begotten son, that whosoever believeth in him should not perish, but have everlasting life. For God sent not his Son into the world to condemn the world, but that the world might be saved" (John, 3: 16, 17).

It will be noted that God is said to have loved not only his chosen people but "the world" as a whole. This universalistic note could of course have a double cultural derivation, from the Prophetic movement in Israel and from Hellenism. It is, in any case, fundamental to Christianity. Salvation was still basically contingent on faith—it was not to be open to "unbelievers," though the punitive tone of much of the Old Testament, as in the phrase "The Lord thy God is a Jealous God," is very much played down. Perhaps, above all, salvation was conceived as a gift *from* God, whereas earlier most of the giving had been the other way around, as "sacrifices" *to* God and obedience to His commandments.

In the New Testament there was a new conception of the relation between the "eternal" and temporal orders, the divine and the human. Through Mary's "Motherhood of God," the divine became human (John, Ch. 1). Jesus was taken to be both God and man at the same time. This view fundamentally altered the Judaic conception by making possible the upgrading of the status of humanity—"the world might be saved." [10] Again, in spite of certain tendencies within Hellenistic Judaism, I think we can correctly say that Judaism was not a religion of individual salvation in the sense that Christianity is. Burke has pointed out that the idea of a redeemer is implicit in the Genesis myth, and Leach has also emphasized the role of "mediators," but how the role of the redeemer should be conceived and in particular what the relation of this role to the fate of the People of Israel should be was still very much an open question.

Here it is crucial to note that the founding event of Christianity was mythologically the sacrificial *death* of Jesus by crucifixion. Christianity has

---

[10] See also John 1:12, "But as many as received him, to them he gave the power to become the sons of God."

traditionally held this to be a real death, and not, as was common in Greek mythology, the mere disappearance of a divine personage who had chosen to spend a certain amount of time on earth disguised as a mortal. Jesus really died on the cross and had to be "resurrected" in order to re-enter the divine sphere of eternal life. It is of course central that the meaning of Jesus' death was symbolized as *giving* His *blood*. Blood is what we may speak of as that *gift* of life which is above all centered in the conception of maternity. In the Christian myth Mary was the giver of life to Jesus, a specially symbolic case of the more general conception of a woman *giving* birth to her child. In ordinary usage the word "give" is not stressed in this expression, but we think it symbolically crucial. The human component of the blood of Christ, therefore, was a *gift* from Mary, who only in the more extravagant phases of Catholic symbolization has herself been considered divine. This human component, however, was combined with the divine component originating from the begetting of Jesus by His divine Father. In these circumstances Jesus' own death was relativized. The concept of death applied only to the human component, not to the divine. The symbol of blood is the primary focus of the unity of the divine and the human, the focus of the Christian conception of the transcending of death. Another meaning of the symbol, blood, which has Hebrew antecedents but was profoundly modified in the Christian phase, is reflected in the act of dying, which again was in an important sense voluntary on Jesus' part— that is, Jesus in a certain sense provoked the Roman authorities into crucifying Him. In the symbolism of the Last Supper, built into the basic sacramental ritual of Christianity, the Eucharist, there is not only the blood of Christ, symbolized by the wine, but also the "body" of Christ, symbolized by the bread. The body of Christ, meaning of course the risen Christ, came to be the symbol for the Church conceived as a supernatural entity embodying the Holy Spirit, which came to have the "power of the keys," the capacity to elevate the individual above the limitations of mortality and the other "Adamic" features of the human condition.

We do not think it too far-fetched to suggest that the Church was symbolically meant to "identify," in a sense not very different from the psycho-analytic-sociological sense, the ordinary human being with Christ. As a member of the Church, he became part of the "body of Christ" and thereby, *in dying* he became capable of *giving* his life, symbolized by blood, in a sense parallel to that in which Jesus gave His blood in the crucifixion. There seems to be a deep duality of meaning here: on the one hand, death is conceived to be deeply traumatic, symbolized by the suffering on the cross, and as much, a kind of "supreme sacrifice." On the other hand, the death of the individual can be conceived as not merely paving the way for his entrance into "heaven" but also as a sacrifice for the redemptive benefit of humanity in general. Quite apart from the metaphysical problems of what can possibly be meant by "survival" of the individual after death, this is a kind of positive sublimation of the grimly tragic view of the human condition as defined by the consequences of Adam's original sin. By the acceptance of the divine commandments and of Christ as the redeemer, man is not in principle totally expelled from the Garden to be dominated henceforth by "sin and death," but has the opportunity to participate in the divine order. He is thereby not in the Adamic sense *only* human. This represents a major upgrading of the religio-metaphysical status of man.

The collective reference has not been simply omitted here. It is through symbolic identification as part of the "body of Christ," i.e., the Church, that the individual can, even before death, participate in the "spiritual" as distinct from the "temporal" order. In a certain sense the old collectivity of the "people" became the model for a spiritual collectivity, membership in which was not by kinship but by faith, that is, acceptance of Christ. Yet Jesus was conceived not only as the "Son of God," but as "born of woman." His "body," though "mystical," was a means of mediating between divine and human.

Furthermore, this pattern seems to underlie a theme in Western religious history which has been emphasized repeatedly in the literature: this theme is that the biblical conception that God made man in His own image and lord of the creation eventually materialized as the conception of a "Kingdom of God on Earth." This in turn implied that human society and personality could be permeated with a divine spirit, and thus the gap between the divine order of things and "the things of this world" was narrowed. What we have called the relativizing of the meaning of death seems to be a central part of this pattern. This is a relativizing that centers on the conception that every individual's death is both a *sacrifice,* and a *gift.*

The individual's capacity to die in the role of a giver of gifts [11] is dependent on three earlier and crucially important gifts. The first is the gift given by God the Father of what is sometimes religiously called the "living Christ" to humanity—given, it should be noted, through the process of "begetting" (Christ, after all, was God's only begotten son). It is of great importance that the giving of this gift was motivated by "love" of the world. Again, this was a gift to humanity *from* God, not a sacrifice *to* God. The second gift was the gift of life as a human being to Jesus by Mary. The crucial symbolic focus of the Christian conception of the feminine role is that of "Mary, Mother of God," who has given the human component of the blood that is to be sacrificed for the redemption of humanity. The third basic gift is the sacrificial death of Jesus which has frequently been symbolized—for example, in the final chorus of Handel's *Messiah*—as the *giving of His blood* for our redemption. Within this

[11] Cf. Talcott Parsons, "Christianity," in *International Encyclopedia of the Social Sciences,* David L. Sills, ed., New York (The Macmillan Co. and The Free Press, 1968). Most explicit is the case of the soldier or martyr who, it is said, "gave his life for his country" or for a "cause." Chap. 9 of this volume.

framework, then, the death of the human individual can be conceived not only as a sacrifice *for* others, but also as a gift *to* others for the future of humanity.

The question now arises, what modifications of this predominantly Catholic vision should be introduced to take into account both Protestantism and more recent developments that are no longer predominantly Protestant? Before discussing the Protestant phase and what has followed it, let us sum up what seem to be the four principal steps in the development from the Book of Genesis to full-fledged medieval Catholicism.

1. It is clear that the original meaning of death was as punishment for the disobedience by Adam and Eve of the one prohibition imposed upon them in the Garden. Their sin, however, was not merely disobedience, but pretention to the status of divinity. Mortality being the *primary* evidence of non-divinity, the imposition of death and expulsion from the Garden was linked with the conception that this life should be burdened with travail.

2. With the development of the covenant relationship between Yahweh and His chosen people, death took on a new meaning. The biblical phrase is reception into "the bosom of Abraham," which we have interpreted to mean, in a sense parallel to the Chinese tradition, that the dead achieve the honorific status of ancestors in the transgenerational collectivity of "the people." This is an acceptance of mortality as part of the acceptance of the generalized human condition with all of its limitations but with a note of special valence in the concept of chosenness. The symbol of blood then emerges as a symbol of ethnic belongingness, not only in one generation, but in the continuity of successive generations. This in turn is linked with the special significance of the Law as divinely ordained through Moses.

3. In the original Christian system, a major step in differentiation took place. There was a relative dissociation from an ethnic community, with both the spiritual and temporal fates of the individual acquiring a new salience. Human life, however, is conceived as *given*. The primary symbol here is that of Jesus portrayed as the only *begotten* son of God the Father. God's begetting is quite different from the creation of Adam. It presumes the continuity of humanity and the human reproductive process. Mary gives Jesus the gift of life at the human level, and it is the synthesis of the divine and human elements, symbolized in the Annunciation, which qualifies Jesus to be the redeemer of mankind. Blood in this sense was neither wholly divine nor wholly human, but a special synthesis of the two which transcended the stark dichotomy of divine and human of the Book of Genesis.

4. It seems clear, then, that the primary symbolic effect of Jesus' sacrifice was the endowment of ordinary humans with the capacity to translate their lives into gifts that simultaneously express love for other human be-

ings (as "neighbors") and a love for God reciprocating God's love for "the world." These are the two fundamental commandments of the Gospel.

There is, therefore, a profound sense in which the sacrifice of Jesus on the cross becomes generalized so that all human deaths can be conceived as sacrifices. The element of sacrifice, however, emphasizes the negative, the cost side, of dying, which was so salient in the crucifixion because of Jesus' excruciating suffering. The positive side is the *gift* not by Mary of the particular human life of Jesus but to any living human person of *his* life. This seems to us to be the primary symbolic meaning of the Christian conception of the transcending of death. Death acquires a transbiological meaning because the paramount component of its meaning is the giving of life, at the end of a particular life, to God as an expression of love of God. This seems to symbolize the conception of a perpetuated solidarity between the bio-human level, symbolized by the blood of Mary, and the divine level, symbolized by the blood of Christ. In the ideal Christian death, one came to participate in the blood of Christ at a new level. This is the reciprocation of God's gift to mankind through Mary.

PROTESTANTISM

In the Catholic system this mutuality of giving as an expression of love was mediated by the sacramental system of the Church and from time to time fragmented by particularized absolutions. In the Protestant version, however, the sacramental system no longer had this power. The "power of the keys" was eliminated and the clergy became essentially spiritual leaders and teachers. Most important is that the life of perfection, the life which as a whole could be conceived to be both sacrifice and gift to God—namely, that of members of the religious orders—lost its special status, and every human being, layman and clergyman alike, was placed on the same level. We think, as Weber did, that this was basically an upgrading of the status of the laity rather than a downgrading of the status of the clergy. As Weber put it, "Every man was to become a monk." [12]

In one sense, the accent on life in this world was strengthened. This is seen in the Calvinist concept that it was man's mission to build the kingdom of God on earth. In this context the whole life of the individual was conceived as a unity. Its basic meaning was that of contribution to the building of the kingdom—that is, insofar as the individual lived up to religious expectations. His death then was *consummatory,* signalling the completion of the task for which he was placed in this world. This consummation, of course, required divine legitimation—i.e., through "faith"—but

[12] Cf. Talcott Parsons, "Christianity," *op. cit.*

it also meant that in a curious sense dying became a voluntary act. A sharp distinction was made between dying in the ordinary sense and being killed. This conception is beautifully symbolized in a phrase in the Episcopal funeral service, "His work is done." (Also: "Well done, thou good and faithful servant.")

The implementation of the divine plan for the world brings the individual into a special kind of partnership with God. One might say that it completes the transformation from the Genesis conception of a life of travail following expulsion from the Garden and its bitter ending in death to the conception of life in this world as an opportunity to serve as an instrument of the divine will in the great task of building the kingdom. It is in this sense that Protestantism has been permeated with an acceptance of worldly life as basically good, and acceptance of death as the natural and divinely ordained consummation for the individual, but not the society.

There is, however, an underlying conflict. This positive and, in a sense, optimistic conception of life and death is conditional on fulfillment of the divine mandate—actually *doing* God's will. And this cannot be guaranteed. What Burke calls the element of the negative, the capacity to disobey, is just as characteristic of modern man as it was of Adam. The problem of what is to happen to the inveterate sinner cannot be avoided, because it cannot be guaranteed that sinners will cease to exist. Hence the note of death as punishment and its symbolic aftermath is always counterposed to this positive Protestant conception. Furthermore, no *given* state of society can be considered to be *the* "good society." Individuals must combat not only their own sinfulness, but the collective phenomena blocking fulfillment of the "Kingdom."

Another negative aspect is the consequence of the psychological connections between love and hate and the parallel conflicts at the social level. What psychologists call aggression toward others generally involves a desire to injure them or see them suffer injury, and in more extreme forms to see them die, even to kill them. Such wishes are also often directed against the self and figure prominently in the urge to suicide. All this is clearly contrary to the interpretation of the death of an individual as consummatory. Furthermore, conflict, accompanied by hostile wishes, between social classes, ethnic groups and nations is not easily compatible with the conception of a society as approximating a "Kingdom of God on Earth." Considerations such as these seem to have something to do with the extent to which populations with a culture close to the Protestant model are prone to rather violent fluctuations between moods of optimism and benevolence, and pessimism, hostility, and guilt.

It seems to us that the same basic pattern has survived the secularization which has led to the abandonment of the traditional Judeo-Christian conceptions of the role of the transcendental God in relation to humanity.

The most conspicuous, though by no means only case, has been Marxian socialism, which—at least in its communist version—bears a great many resemblances to early Calvinism. Here the basic assignment is to contribute to the building of socialism. The view of the fate of the individual "soul" after death is clearly different from that of a theistic Protestantism; indeed, in some respects it is similar to Judaism.[13] But the basic pattern seems very similar—that is, acceptance of mortality and the other fundamental features of the human condition, and, therefore, a conception of the completion of life, in the ideal case giving death a consummatory meaning.

Recent movements suggest a shift from the emphasis on "work" in the "Protestant Ethic" sense to a communally-organized regime of love which, of course, links with the earlier Christian traditions of love at both the divine and the human levels. It is not clear just how these movements are going to crystalize, if at all, but one thing is almost certain, that they will share with Puritan Protestantism and Marxian socialism a religious sanctification of life in this world.

One other important point should not be neglected. The early Christians were eschatologically oriented to the idea of a second coming of Christ and with it the day of judgment and the end of the world as it had been known to people of their time. The saved would then enter a state of eternal life in a new paradise resembling in some respects the Garden of Eden, yet different from it. The idea of some kind of pre-existent paradise in which man once lived has reverberated through the centuries, perhaps most conspicuously in the idea of the state of nature that was so prevalent during the Enlightenment. Rousseau seems to be its most prominent single exponent. A pre-existent state of nature, however, has been dynamically linked with the conception of a terminal state where all the problems of the tragic human condition are conceived to have been resolved. This kind of utopia has been exceedingly prominent in the socialist movement, most notably in the vision of communism as the end state of the task of building socialist societies.

There seems to be evidence that very similar orientations characterize the movement that one of us has elsewhere [14] called the new "religion of love." Indeed, in its more extreme versions the suggestion is made that a regime of total love can be set up in the immediate future. It will, however, have to be a terrestrial regime which cannot conceive "the end of the world" as that phrase was meant by the early Christians. It could mean only the end of the evil parts of the world. We have the impression that a clear conception of the meaning of death has not yet emerged in these circles, but almost certainly there is a fantasy of immortality. Death, as it

[13] Perhaps the "bosom of Lenin" could be the equivalent of the "bosom of Abraham."

[14] Talcott Parsons, "Belief, Unbelief, and Disbelief," *op. cit.*

has been known since the abandonment of specifically Christian eschato-logical hopes, is somehow felt to be unreal and this conception may be attributed to the new versions of the centrality of previous human life.[15]

The Moral Basis of Modern Medical Ethics

THE PHYSICIAN'S INVOLVEMENT WITH PROBLEMS OF LIFE AND DEATH

If modern man has experienced the religious dimension of his life in the world as a gift from God, he turns in secular contexts to medical prac-titioners in order to gain expert assistance in preserving and enhancing his personal giftedness. In contemporary circumstances, the physician routinely takes part in the "giving" of birth, makes the first survey of the newborn's "gifts," including announcement of sex, and begins to prescribe for the preservation of its life. In the early years, when life is deemed fragile, the doctor is consulted frequently by responsible parents. Throughout mature life, the individual has the positive responsibility as well as freedom to seek a physician's aid whenever his gifts are endangered by disease or severe stress. Perhaps this obligation becomes especially strong when aging begins to enfeeble at least certain capacities. Unless death arrives suddenly and unexpectedly, medical treatment will ordinarily be involved, and in any case a physician will "pronounce" the death. Within the course of the in-dividual's life-cycle, the services of a physician are now often involved in many crucial transitions of life-stage and social status. Thus, medical ex-aminations, discussion, and prescriptive advice commonly accompany first entrance to school, the attainment of sexual maturity, enrollment in college, marriage, pregnancy and the birth of children, menopause, etc. Proper completion of such transitions in life status seems to require that a verifi-cation or determination of the giftedness of the individual be made by competent medical authority. Moreover, it is not unusual for relationships with a doctor to involve a diffuseness of concern for the welfare of the pa-tient's life that is quite unusual outside the sphere of intimate primary ties —otherwise approximated only perhaps by religious-confessional and some educational relationships.

Modern, scientifically rationalized medicine may thus be regarded as a special set of instrumentalities and procedures for protecting the "gift of life." Not only does it penetrate very deeply into the routine social proc-esses by which normal lives are constructed, but it is believed to act upon

[15] Perhaps the slogan, "Never trust anyone over thirty," may be interpreted as symbolizing the "denial of death," since those living from age thirty on must become progressively more aware that the time will come when they will die.

divinely given materials in circumstances of fragility, transformation, and danger. If the role of the physician involves not simply high status and honor but also a potential and frequently activated charisma of office, it derives these qualities from a fiduciary responsibility for maximizing those basic human gifts which individuals actually receive. In this respect the role of physician is closely related to that of teacher. In the context of the value patterns of instrumental activism that are institutionalized in modern society,[16] this specific type of responsibility constitutes a major normative structure in the articulations between religious premises and the secular social order.

The protection of the gifts of life involves practical efforts to control the causes of unnecessary and premature death. Despite this, the conditions under which particular deaths often occur represent the frustration of individuals' efforts to fulfill their personal roles in life. In a society that emphasizes occupational achievement as strongly as ours, this attitude toward death is perhaps especially poignantly felt when a promising individual dies in mid-career. The suffering and the disruption of the lives of others, generally family members, friends, and sometimes occupational associates, which usually accompany such a death must also be regarded as phenomena that hinder or reduce the realization of life potentials.[17] For many, the very prospect of death—especially in ways that symbolically touch upon powerful negative images in our culture, such as the degeneracy and loss of bodily control involved in cancer—produces horror that can substantially inhibit abilities to engage in many areas of social life. It is upon these reducible aspects or modalities of death that the life-enhancing efforts of modern medicine have tended to focus most sharply.[18]

Modern medicine can be distinguished from the practices with which most pre-modern societies have attempted to control the human impact of death by the strong specialization of its instrumentalities about the meliorable modalities of death. Modern medicine has tended to differentiate itself very sharply from religious, magical, and expressive means of orientation to the problems posed by death. It has tended not to deal directly with the existential issues of meaning raised by death. It does not claim to help patients deal with the "ultimate" problems associated with the eventual and sometimes imminent inevitability of their deaths. Rather, it has attempted to set such matters aside in order to develop specialized means of "treating" specific syndromes which are believed on scientific and empirical grounds to be "treatable."

---

[16] Talcott Parsons, *The System of Modern Societies,* Englewood Cliffs, N.J. (Prentice-Hall, 1971). See also Talcott Parsons and Gerald M. Platt, *The American University,* Cambridge, Mass. (Harvard University Press, 1973).

[17] Eric Lindemann, "Symptomatology and the Management of Acute Grief," in *American Journal of Psychiatry,* September, 1944, pp. 101–141.

[18] Here the concept of reducible death is an adaptation of the idea of adventitious death discussed in T. Parsons and V. Lidz, "Death in American Society," *op. cit.*

Historically, this instrumental focus of modern medicine has been a difficult achievement. In many respects—for example, the continued competition of Christian Science, widespread fears in society of medical violations of the body, common suspicions about efforts to "treat" mental disturbances—it remains a partial achievement. Perhaps substantial tension resulting from forces within religious, moral, and expressive culture, which even now tend to place some limitations upon the scope of practice and treatment, remains intrinsic even to specialized, modern medicine.

Indeed, there appear to be some very strong factors operating within the cultural and social organization of medicine that are profoundly interdependent with the limiting cultural forces. Perhaps we have explicated enough of the interrelations between religious orientations and the patterning of medical practice to make it a conveniently paradigmatic case. It should be clear that religious orientations toward the meanings of life and death have comprised an important historical source of the instrumental activism embodied in modern medical institutions. Synchronically, the instrumental activism of the general religious culture contributes both crucial legitimation and patterning of commitments toward sustaining the pragmatically activistic institutional forms that modern medicine has developed. Here, the religiously-grounded commitments provide important foundations for the role performances of both medical personnel and the patients and their families who must cooperate with the special types of treatment that can be legitimated within modern medicine. Thus the special legitimation and value-commitments required by modern medicine seem to depend on the existence of congruent religious orientations in the broader society.

Religious patterns condition the practice of medicine in at least one other principal respect. Physicians, nurses, and other medical personnel, as well as patients who are severely ill, are confronted by the phenomena of death in massive ways. People in these roles must often carry grave responsibilities and make extremely difficult decisions, while acting under the stresses generated by impending or probable death. In this difficult situation, and perhaps especially for those who must routinely confront it, a strong religious or philosophical faith seems essential to sustaining legitimate commitments to role performance. The very specificity and instrumentality of the proper performances, which do not permit the primary emphasis on treatment to be compromised by direct involvement of religious concerns—to say nothing of "spontaneous" emotional reactions—add to the extent to which certain *underlying* commitments must be profoundly *serious,* in the sense of Durkheim's definition of religion as belonging to "the serious life." [19] They must be serious enough to maintain their integrity even when denied direct expression.

[19] Emile Durkheim, *The Elementary Forms of the Religious Life,* London (George Allen and Unwin, 1915.

"SCIENTIFIC" MEDICINE AND THE "EXISTENTIAL" PROBLEM

A theoretical interpretation of the position of modern medicine must emphasize, then, both its comparative independence from direct or particularistic limitation by religion and its underlying dependence upon and penetration by religious culture.

What we now wish to examine is the comparable balance between independence and interdependence that characterizes the relations of medical orientations toward death with the general system of ethical beliefs in American culture. On the one hand, modern, scientific medical practice must operate independently of the diffuse processes of moral judgment in society. The physician's treatment of the patient is structured in terms of a professional exercise of applied science, not directly as a moral process of social control. The cooperative relation of physician and patient is often constricted, damaged, or undermined when the intrusion of diffusely moral judgment displaces instrumental calculation as the focus of treatment. Here, the modern physician's role contrasts sharply with that of the primitive witch-doctor or the archaic curer. There can be no presumption that the practitioner's efficacy is intrinsically bound up with the ways in which he exercises moral sanctions over the patient. Treatment is intrinsically technical and not dependent on moral judgment of the patient. On the other hand, the life-and-death responsibilities of the medical relationship impose strong moral exigencies upon all concerned just as inexorably as they raise religious problems. Hence, the treatment relationship must itself be controlled in terms of an autonomous ethical complex that is rationalized with respect to medical treatment that gives primacy to instrumental-technical calculation. Commitment to a specialized ethical system by physician, patient, and auxiliaries (e.g., the patient's family as well as nurses, aides, and hospital administrators) creates a crucial condition for stabilizing treatment relationships so as to offset the often severe and baffling stresses of uncertain diagnosis, treatment, and prognosis. Medical ethics have come to be rationalized so as to provide a set of categories of responsibility which can give general assurance that due care has been taken to protect the "gifts of life," whatever undesirable outcomes may ensue.

Although medical ethics require autonomy in adapting to the special moral problems of medical practice, they also require legitimation. And this can be gained only through integration with the general moral-evaluative system of the encompassing culture. In order to convey moral authority to specific medical practices and institutions, medical ethics must themselves be relatively congruent with the principles of the surrounding moral culture.[20] Moreover, the responsibilities and limits allocated to different ac-

---

[20] This conception of moral authority is developed out of Durkheim's usage in *Moral Education,* New York (The Free Press, 1956) and *The Elementary Forms of*

tors—e.g., doctors and patients—must not conflict too overtly with the expectations structured in other specialized sectors of the moral system.

Our frame of reference is here specifically cultural. Broadly, we conceive a moral-ethical system as transforming religiously grounded premises or "themes" into more specific moral prescriptions that provide authoritative bases for the organization of institutions and the planning of sequences of action.[21] Obversely, the same processes of transformation must come to terms with the moral problems generated by the various institutional operations affected by specific prescriptions. Moral-ethical functioning may be seen as simultaneously involving the "spelling out" of the complex practical implications of general religio-ethical principles and the reduction of these implications to certain consistent grounds of solution.[22] But problems of meaning are continually raised by the impact of specific principles on a variety of institutional situations and by the uncertainties which specific institutional situations bring to bear on a variety of ethical principles. Particular prescriptions generally draw upon a number of independent principles and have implications for a considerable range of interactive situations. Any equilibrium of consistency concerning specific ethical issues is apt to be shortlived, and problems of meaning are apt to reassert themselves with changes in institutional conditions or even in other specialized complexes of the moral system. Hence, despite the stability of many major structures of moral-evaluative culture over considerable periods of history, ethical order at the practical level must be a continually renewed achievement. Moreover, it must be achieved specifically at the cultural level, that is, through the abstract and generalized rationalization of interrelations among symbols, references, premises, principles, hypotheses, etc.

We interpret the religiously established theme of the great value of the divine "gift of life" as comprising a principal premise for medical ethics. Yet, it is important to recognize that it also comprises a premise for many other ethical complexes in our culture: police activity protects the "gift of life," educational activity serves to enhance the "gifts" of individuals, and automobile traffic is regulated with a view to restricting the loss of life— to cite only a few examples. However, as a general construct within the moral culture as a whole—although not necessarily in its bearing on medical ethics—the "gift of life" theme has not generally established an absolute principle of ethics. Thus, the general prescription of "give me liberty or give me death" has also been honored in American culture, and may even be said to have provided moral legitimation for conscription which has

---

the Religious Life, op. cit. See also V. Lidz, "Moral Authority," in J. Loubser, R. Baum, A. Effrat, and V. Lidz, eds., *Explorations in General Theory in the Social Sciences,* New York (The Free Press, 1976).

[21] *Ibid.*

[22] Professor Lon L. Fuller has shown that the institution of adjudication performs this function in settling legal conflicts. See his *Anatomy of the Law,* New York (New American Library, 1969).

obligated men to risk their lives when the national freedom was believed to be in danger. Yet the moral authority of the "gift of life" theme is not simply overridden in this case. Ideals associated with the "freedom" of society have exerted powerful symbolic meaning and moral authority in part because of the willingness of many individuals to die for them.[23] Moreover, particular freedoms which can be viewed as more costly in lives than beneficial to society—for example, the freedom of private citizens to carry handguns—are apt to lose much of their moral authority. We may expect that leadership in efforts to redefine the scope of such freedoms will often be exercised by individuals whose special moral responsibilities to protect lives have been stimulated by social conditions. For example, physicians who repair many gunshot wounds in emergency rooms of large city hospitals are apt to be proponents of stricter gun control laws. The theme of the dignity of life not only enters a variety of areas of moral discourse but does so in a complex array of combinations with other evaluative premises, such as that of freedom. We must now ask whether similar conditions apply to the functioning of the "gift of life" theme within the realm of medical ethics.

We may suggest that the major burden of the articulation of medical ethics within the broader moral-evaluative culture is carried by the principle of the dignity and importance of *divinely* [24] given human life. Within the broad manifold of human activities, medicine takes on its special moral authority and somewhat charismatic status—qualities apparently essential for effective treatment in many difficult situations—from its commitment to, and ability to implement, this crucial value. Medicine is continually engaged in an effort to increase the level of rationalization of its instrumental techniques for protecting health and life against a very broad range of threatening conditions and sentiments. Similarly, there are constantly on-going efforts to rationalize medical ethics as means for assuring the implementation of the basic commitment to preservation of the "gifts" of life, especially through the allocation of firm responsibilities for the care of individuals. The functional viability of modern medicine, then, may be seen to rest upon a crucial constraint on the system of medical ethics, namely, that a position of strong predominance must be given to the principle of the dignity of life. Other principles must be firmly relegated to secondary positions of importance.

The maintenance of this structural arrangement appears to be quite problematic in two respects. First, the institutional ordering of treatment relationships requires that attention be paid to other principles of value in medical ethics. For example, there must be considerable emphasis laid on

---

[23] Cf. Henri Hubert and Marcel Mauss, *Sacrifice: Its Nature and Function,* Chicago (University of Chicago (University of Chicago Press, 1964).

[24] Here, as above, we use the traditional religious terminology. Let us, however, repeat our view that the relevance of these themes is not confined to religious "believers." Atheists or agnostics would simply phrase them differently.

mutual respect between patient and physician, on honesty and fairness in communication, on limiting the costs of treatment to "reasonable" levels etc. In many situations, and perhaps especially when illness is severe and/or treatment technically difficult, attention to these themes may conflict with the maintenance of a superordinate orientation to the value of sustaining life. Secondly, there is a latent or potential conflict between medical ethics and other sectors of the moral-evaluative system in which the principle of preserving life is not directly given the same priority. Medical institutions, therefore, require ethical means of assuring that actors involved in medical situations, including patients and their families as well as medical personnel, will in fact act upon the normative priorities given in medical ethics rather than upon some others. This exigency exerts strong pressure toward giving medical ethics an autonomous and clearly bounded form vis-à-vis other complexes in the moral-evaluative system.

If we may speak in somewhat ideal-typical terms of a classical form of modern medical ethics, its principal structural features appear to be understandable as adaptations to the functional exigencies we have just highlighted. The structural core has been an absolutizing of the value of preserving life. Both the life of the individual patient and the physician's obligation to protect or save the patient's life have been taken as *divinely given*. The physician could then take the obligation to attempt to stave off the patient's death as an absolute prescription—a "Commandment"— having no explicit limitations. Only the insufficiencies of the physician's instrumental resources would limit his effort to combat the patient's death. There thus has been very strong ethical motivation to increase the technical capacities of the physician in order to better implement his obligation to save lives under ever more difficult circumstances. Indeed, it would seem that the extraordinary growth in technical capacity achieved by modern medicine should be explained by reference not only to the general prominence of the value pattern of "instrumental activism" in modern culture, but also to the way in which instrumental improvement has served to ease severe tensions within the system of medical ethics.

Orientation to the nearly absolute "commandment" to combat the death of his patient provided a very strong and clear definition of the situation [25] for the physician in several respects. It assured the physician that he could act in direct relation to a value of great importance without having to embroil himself in a broad range of difficult problems of meaning. It permitted, indeed required, that he pursue the "saving" of life at almost any cost, that is, by subordinating almost all other value considerations. This nearly absolute commitment to preserve life strongly insulated medical ethics from any ethical system or complex that did not place a commen-

---

[25] This is the technical usage of "definition of the situation" employed in Talcott Parsons, "Some Problems of General Theory in Sociology," in J. McKinney and E. Tiryakian, eds., *Theoretical Sociology*, New York (Appleton-Century-Crofts, 1970).

surate emphasis upon the value of preserving life, and thereby firmly grounded the autonomy of medical ethics. Finally, it offered a clear basis for disparaging any other ethical position, for it could reasonably be argued that no other position *really* respected the divine gift of life when hard choices had to be made.

Despite these impressive strengths, the classical ethics of modern medicine has contained some serious strains and weaknesses. One principal source of difficulty is that this ethical pattern allows little room for positive definitions of the significance and meaning of death. The primary meaning of death is structured to be seen as a medical defeat,[26] either for the physician personally or for the "state of the art" with which he is strongly identified. Especially when the circumstances are such that the physician is bound to "lose" many patients, he is placed under great personal strain. Empirical studies in hospitals have shown that there is a consequent tendency for physicians to be unable to give high levels of attention, emotional support, and careful treatment to their dying patients.[27] Often the attitude of the physician becomes extremely defensive just at the time when the dying patient and his family need assistance in managing the problems of adjustment to the impending death.[28] When the physician feels that he may have "caused" his patient to die by making a "mistake" in diagnosis or treatment, his burden of guilt (and perhaps fear of a legal suit or loss of professional standing) often severely restricts his capacity to treat and relate honestly to his patient.[29] Indeed, it seems that rather devious communication with the patient, often supported by other hospital personnel, is at least not infrequent under such circumstances. It also seems that many dying patients are better able than their physicians to orient themselves to the positive "consummatory" meanings of their impending deaths.[30] The physician may engage the patient in highly moralistic discourse, attempting to mobilize his "will to live" or his "fighting spirit" against death, even when death in the near future appears to be inevitable and the patient is

[26] Cf. Renée C. Fox and Judith P. Swazey, *The Courage to Fail, op. cit.*

[27] D. Sudnow, *Passing On*, Englewood Cliffs, N.J. (Prentice-Hall, 1967); Barney Glaser and Anselm Strauss, *Awareness of Dying*, Chicago (Aldine, 1965). Renée C. Fox, *Experiment Perilous*, New York (The Free Press, 1959) does not report the same conditions, or at least not in anything approaching the same degree. However, the patients in her study were gaining meaning for their deaths by being research subjects and, in dying, thereby contributing to the life of others in the future. This situation greatly affected their experiences of death as well as those of their physicians. Sudnow also reports conditions under which the stigmatization of dying patients by physicians and other hospital staff tended to bring about substantial relaxation of efforts to sustain the lives of dying patients. The strain also was manifest, e.g., in the "gallows humor" prevalent among the physicians.

[28] Elisabeth Kubler-Ross, *On Death and Dying*, New York (The Macmillan Company, 1969).

[29] Raymond Duff and August Hollingshead, *Sickness and Society*, New York (Random House, 1969).

[30] Kubler-Ross, *op. cit.*

more or less ready to accept his situation.[31] The physician may even make his continued close attention to the patient conditional upon a display of "fighting spirit" while the patient might prefer franker discussion of his prognosis. Treatment may be given more as a ritual commitment to the value of fighting death than out of rational expectation that it will help the patient. The patient's family—or indeed, the hospital—may be encouraged to make ill-afforded expenditures on such ritualistic treatment, while being discouraged from adapting their life circumstances—and especially their relationships with the patient—to the inevitable death.[32]

EXACERBATION OF STRAIN BY TECHNICAL ADVANCES

Some additional strains have been created by modern medicine's very high level of technical mastery, but these have become problematic for medical ethics only in relatively recent years. Despite the physician's "absolute" obligation to save lives and the givenness of the patient's life, the moral authority of the ethic is reinforced when the life being saved still holds much unrealized promise. Thus, medical treatment is generally undertaken with the greatest energy when at stake are the lives of children or adults "in the prime of life" or endowed with special talents or social responsibilities.[33] The physician's contribution to the patient's future fulfillment of promise or a calling comes to seem essential to the meaning of treatment. Under present conditions, however, it is not unusual that some of the most intensive and sophisticated treatment goes to aged patients dying from degenerative diseases. Often such patients can be kept alive only through massive artificial support, and have prognoses that do not permit realistic hopes of future fulfillment of a calling.[34] Sometimes treatment seems to contribute more to unwanted suffering than to preservation of the "gifts" of life. Under such conditions, severe problems of meaning are bound to arise within the classical framework of medical ethics, for the benefits of treatment are not obvious and the efforts to preserve life face comparatively rapid defeat.

The ethical focus on the obligation to defeat death through the mobilization of intense commitments and great quantities of medical resources has perhaps had some irrational effects on the development and allocation of medical resources. American medicine has become most clearly preeminent in providing the most intensive, most technically elaborate and

[31] Duff and Hollingshead, *op. cit.*

[32] *Ibid.*

[33] Note the way in which President Nixon so strongly emphasized that Governor Wallace must be assured the very "finest" treatment and care after he had been shot.

[34] The religious phrase, "His work is done," might function as one possible standard!

"modern," and least cost-conscious treatments for patients who are already engaged in well-defined struggles with death or debilitating diseases. In this situation, there is a strong tendency to demonstrate—again in a fashion having a strong ritual and religious quality—that "everything possible" is being done to aid the patient. Notably, this is the situation in which doctors speak of themselves as engaging in "heroics." Such medical activity clearly makes a potent statement about the valuation of individual lives, both within medicine and in the society at large. Nevertheless, the stress on such medical heroics has diverted attention and resources from public health measures that, in other societies, have preserved more lives at less cost—although leaving the physician with fewer "heroic" measures for the patient already struggling with death.

EMERGENCE OF NEW DEFINITIONS OF THE SITUATION

The strains we have just noted have been complemented by certain developments in medicine that tend to undermine the conception of the absolute givenness of human lives. One crucial area of change has concerned the understanding and definition of death as the "end" of life. Much attention has been given to the recent trend toward redefining death, so that brain function rather than breathing or heart function serves as the criterion of life. How this redefinition facilitates the transplantation of cadaver organs has gained much public notice. The broader background of this change is that a variety of recently perfected resuscitative and life-supporting techniques have confronted physicians with the routine experience of having large numbers of patients on the very border between life and death. Even early in their training, physicians now engage not merely in "saving" lives, but actually in bringing people back to life.[35] Large proportions of hospital patients lack, at least temporarily, the capacity to live but are "kept alive" artificially. Sometimes the decision to "allow" a patient to die by removing the artificial supports of life seems to be the most reasonable recourse, although it is a decision which physicians generally try to avoid. There are patients of whom it can reasonably be claimed that they have died more than once. Some transplant patients live only by virtue of the functioning of organs which were originally the "gifts" of another

---

[35] The process of technical advance brings an element of relativity into the conception of the "inevitability" of early death. As a striking example, one of us (Talcott Parsons) remembers years ago hearing, on the occasion of attending ward rounds at the Massachusetts General Hospital, Dr. Arlie Bock, who was the "visiting physician," tell that when he was a resident, he administered the first insulin given in that hospital to a patient in a diabetic coma. It was the first time that a patient in a diabetic coma had ever recovered in the whole history of the hospital. In a certain sense this was almost literally bringing her "back from death."

person.[36] Although these circumstances have been the result of gradual, incremental improvements in medical technique, they clearly raise some new and difficult questions about the meaning and medical significance of life and death.

The problematic nature of the boundary between life and death has also come to involve the origins of life in conception and birth. Both contraception and abortion have, of course, very long histories. Yet, recent improvements in technique, if complemented by mass campaigns for "birth control," will make possible an entirely new level of mastery not simply of numbers but also of inherited traits of those born into society. Indeed, if abortion becomes widespread, already foreseen developments in genetic counselling will permit very considerable control over the inborn "gifts" of babies, and perhaps even their distribution in society.[37] The ethical issues posed by birth control, and especially by the abortion of viable fetuses, however, are very difficult to resolve. Most attention has been given to the question of when, in the development from conception to birth, the fetus obtains the "gift of life" which makes it an autonomous being entitled to legal and moral protection. Perhaps more interesting in our present perspective is the disjunction between, on the one hand, the pro-abortion arguments that fetal life may be terminated in the interest of furthering the parents' mastery of their own life circumstances or the environment in which they will rear children and, on the other hand, the absolute valuation of life within classical medical ethics.

Two other developments seem also to bear stressfully on the absolute conception of the givenness of life. One is the emergence in recent years of surgical procedures, usually employed in conjunction with careful psychiatric analysis and treatment, for altering the sex of individuals.[38] Here, medical treatment is used to change the most diffuse and general of stable social identities that is ordinarily given with birth. The second concerns the treatment of individuals handicapped by markedly "subnormal" intelligence due to genetic causes. Together with increasing use of genetic counselling to minimize the number of births of such individuals, there has been a growing disinclination to place them in special institutions from birth or early childhood. Removing them from the general community may be interpreted as setting a certain boundary to the level of "giftedness" mini-

[36] Cf. Renée C. Fox, "A Sociological Perspective on Organ Transplantation and Hemodialysis," in *New Dimensions in Legal and Ethical Concepts for Human Research,* Annals, New York Academy of Sciences, 169 (January 2, 1970), pp. 406–428.

[37] It is an important feature of the process of differentiation under consideration here that an increasingly clear ethical distinction seems to be emerging between the moral status of contraception and that of abortion, at least beyond certain relatively early stages of pregnancy, although the boundary is not yet clearly defined. Even though the Catholic Church has so far refused to alter its historic position on either side, the change has gone very far indeed.

[38] See Harold Garfinkel's study of a transsexual in his *Studies in Ethnomethodology,* Englewood Cliffs, N.J. (Prentice-Hall, 1967).

mally characteristic of members of society. The tendency to reintegrate "subnormals" into the society, then, has the effect of somewhat blurring this boundary. Perhaps it is significant that persuasion of parents to keep their mentally handicapped children with the family has emphasized not only the benefits for the mental development of such children, but also the human pleasures and moral satisfaction to be gained by other members of the family.

That the increasing flux in definition of the boundaries of a human life has occurred at *both* ends of the "age" span seems to us to be particularly significant, as does the new possibility of deliberately changing biological sex identity. This seems to justify our focus, articulated at the beginning of this essay, on the "age and sex" frame of reference. Furthermore, the fact that there is a trend to include the mentally retarded in more normal social relationships is also very much related to the problem of the treatment of illegitimate children, especially by the institution of adoption.[39] Both of these developments relate to another of the main themes of our discussion of the religious background of the life-death complex, namely, that of the status of persons and groups gained through "inclusion" in significant collective entities, both temporal and spiritual; one may also add the current intensive preoccupation with the status of the "poor" and of various kinds of "minorities."

THE RESTRUCTURING OF MEDICAL ETHICS

The pressures on the classical form of modern medical ethics have by now become so powerful that there is a quite widespread feeling that the profession must undertake a very general re-examination of its morals. In some quarters, there is exasperation—almost despair—over the difficulty of the problems that must now be confronted. Yet, we think the process of re-examination is already underway and that the outline of a new ethic is becoming visible.

The emerging medical ethic may be termed "a relativized ethic" or, in Weber's sense, an ethic of responsibility.[40] While this newer ethic has major continuity with the absolute ethic in making the principle of protecting life its highest value-premise, it no longer treats this priority as an absolute. Instead, the physician is given positive responsibility for calculating rational articulations between this principle and other evaluative principles recognized in the ethical system, so that normative prescriptions can be flexibly adapted to ethically difficult situations. The physician is no longer

---

[39] Cf. Stephen B. Presser, "The Historical Background of the American Law of Adoption," *Journal of Family Law*, 1971.

[40] Max Weber, *From Max Weber: Essays in Sociological Theory*, New York (Oxford, 1947). See also Talcott Parsons and Gerald M. Platt, *The American University, op. cit.*, Chapter 5.

under an absolute commandment to preserve life, but may make a relatively free judgment—generally after consultation with colleagues, the patient, and the patient's family—about the extent to which treatment should be directed toward the preservation of life and the extent to which other ends should be given priority.

This form of ethics is more rational in that, by recognizing more explicitly the conditions under which direct struggle with death must be fruitless and even counter-productive in terms of other values, it permits fuller implementation of a broad range of ethical principles. At the same time, it allows firmer action to be taken with respect to a broad range of the modalities in which death is socially disruptive. A further impetus to adopting the ethic of responsibility is that it provides a stronger basis for dealing with the problems of meaning which recent medical developments have been generating. However, this ethic imposes some very serious responsibilities upon the physician. He no longer has the emotional support of an absolute which gives him clear prescriptive guidelines. He can no longer externalize the ethical grounds of his action through comparatively simple logical operations. Rather, he must bear personal responsibility for the specific ethical grounds of actions. He must subject issues of the practical valuation of life, suffering, death, departure from social ties, the fulfillment of "promise," etc., to personal examination. In order to act honestly, he must often engage patients and their families in dialogues on these disturbing issues at times when they are apt to be profoundly troubled themselves.[41] These obligations do not make for an easy calling.

Change in ethical orientation to death seems roughly to index the extent to which the ethic of responsibility has come to prevail. The relativized ethic provides a greatly enhanced basis for recognizing the consummatory meanings of death. The impending, inevitable death of a patient need not be taken as a defeat of treatment. The efforts of the physician may then—in a certain sense—facilitate the patient's death, supporting his sense of dignity and his ability to put his affairs in order,[42] encouraging a readjustment in his relations with his family, and meliorating the trying conditions of a death. These activities also aid the patient to employ his "gifts of life," but involve the mastery of death as social and psychological rather than physiological processes.

The relativized ethic also renders the boundaries of medical ethics more flexible in relation to other components of moral-evaluative culture. The physician must take more responsibility for admitting the medical significance of ethical considerations structured in other sectors of the moral system. The recognition of the consummatory significance of death is one

[41] Kubler-Ross, *op. cit.*

[42] We may recall the poignant words of Pope John XXIII when he clearly knew he was about to die, "My bags are packed, I am ready to go."

example of the new penetration of medical ethics by a religio-moral perspective having essentially non-medical origins.

Perhaps the most massive recent penetration of extra-medical considerations into medical ethics has been the acknowledgement, partly under political compulsion, that the distribution of medical care in our society must be rationalized to a greater extent in terms of "health rights" which citizens hold simply by virtue of membership in society.[43] Here, medicine is adapting its ethical system to moral considerations of a predominantly political and legal character. However, it is clear that the long-run effect should be a substantial upgrading in the quality of medical care available to the citizenry at large, especially to those in the lower economic classes. In terms of medical ethics, this change must be adjudged a great victory. One concomitant of this victory—in certain respects a cost and in others a benefit—will be the further projection of medical responsibilities into the realm of public discourse. When massive social planning for new systems of health care is undertaken, medical advice takes on a new importance in public affairs. The fiduciary responsibilities of the medical profession then come to include the task of providing expert leadership for the public's deliberation on health policy.

It would be a mistake, however, to regard this extension of the medical role in any simple sense as only political. At issue are many questions of value with moral and even religious dimensions. Reformulations of quite fundamental aspects of our societal value system are underway which constitute its generalization and upgrading, not abandonment. The meanings of life and death are so centrally at issue that the medical contribution to the discussion seems bound to be substantial. If the ethical reorientation we have discussed becomes consolidated in the medical profession and is projected into the realm of public deliberations, perhaps medicine will provide the leadership in some very interesting developments in modern normative culture.

Most important for the theme of this paper is the fact that the direction of this change opens new areas of freedom for defining a meaningful consummatory death as the reciprocation of the gift of life which the person received at his birth. In addition to the enormous contribution of the medical complex in differentiating the inevitable from the adventitious components of death, and to the very great diminution in the incidence of the latter, this change may not only help to enable the dying person to leave in the spirit of a giver of gifts, but also may enable members of the medical profession to facilitate this definition of impending death instead of blocking it. The ideal outcome would be a coincidence of the meaning of

[43] Cf. the conception of "social rights" developed in Talcott Parsons, "The Negro American," in his *Sociological Theory and Modern Society,* New York (The Free Press, 1967).

the words we have already quoted—"His work is done"—for the roles of both dying patient and physician. The patient is hopefully "ready to go," whereas the physician has not only done his best to "save" his patient's life, but has complemented these efforts by facilitating a dignified and meaningful death.

The "Existential" Problem of Death in Medical Perspective

For social scientists who conceive "society" in a restricted way, the foregoing discussion of the relation of life and death to medical ethics might seem to "stand on its own feet" without reference to the considerations of the earlier part of the paper. We believe, however, that the trends of change in medical ethics outlined above are inherently intertwined with the problems of the meaning of life and death. Furthermore, we believe that the structure of mythic themes which we selected from the Judeo-Christian religious tradition constitutes the best available framework for understanding these phenomena.

Over the course of the past ten to fifteen years, what might be called the religious dimension of modern American medicine—its relationship to the gifts of life and death and their consummatory meaning—has begun to be more overtly expressed. Although this existential aspect of medicine is an irreducible part of its deeper significance in a modern society, as in all others, until recently the strong instrumental focus of twentieth-century American medicine exerted a repressive influence on its outward manifestation. Various social control mechanisms existed in the medical profession that actively discouraged involvement with so-called philosophical issues. In the medical school climate of the 1950's,[44] for example, faculty virtually never raised questions with students like "what is death?" "why death?" or "in what deeper senses, if any, does death differ from life?" Even in situations conducive to such querying—notably, the anatomy laboratory, the autopsy, or in the face of students' early confrontation with terminally ill patients—instructors rarely initiated such discussions. And if a student made a timorous effort to do so, he was likely to be silenced by classmates and faculty alike with the quip, "that's too philosophical." Decoded, this meant "the matters of which you speak are not sufficiently rational, objective, scientific, or pragmatic to fall within the proper domain of medicine, or of

[44] These are direct, participant observations about American medical school milieux in the 1950's, made by one of us (Renéc Fox), in her role as field worker for a study of the education and socialization of medical students conducted during that period by the Columbia University Bureau of Applied Social Research. *The Student Physician,* edited by Robert K. Merton et al., Cambridge, Mass. (Harvard University Press, 1957), was a product of that investigation.

truly professional behavior." It was also characteristic of this decade that professionals were more inclined to speak euphemistically about the death of a patient—"he (she) expired," "passed on," or "was transferred to Ward X,"—than straightforwardly to state that death had occurred.

In sharp contrast to such medical attitudes in the 1950's (at least in academic milieux where new physicians were being trained and scientific research emphasized), the late 1960's and early 1970's appear very "philosophical," indeed. Currently, along with an increased social concern about the inadequacies and inequities in our system of delivering care, American medicine is publicly pondering more existential matters: problems of uncertainty, meaning, life and death, solidarity, and of intervention in the human condition. In fact, one might almost say that a certain amount of "radical chic" now accrues to engaging these topics, most particularly that of "death and dying."

There are those who contend that this discernible shift in the orientation of modern medicine is due to recent biomedical advances—actual and anticipated developments in genetics and genetic engineering, life support systems, birth technology, including asexual reproduction, the implantation of human, animal and artificial organs, behavior and thought control—and to the problems of decision-making and longer range consequences ensuing from them. Although we would not deny the important role that these scientific and technological events have played in making the moral and metaphysical concerns of modern medicine both more visible and legitimate, we would maintain that the greater interest in such issues is part of a broader and deeper process of cultural change in our society. It is not only in medicine, for example, that concern about the "quality of life," equity, human solidarity and societal community is manifesting itself. From an evolutionary perspective, both the scope and intensity of these preoccupations in American society at the present time suggest that we may be entering a new stage of advanced modernity.

As fundamental as any changes in the meta-ethics of ocntemporary medicine is the process by which conceptions of life and death, in relation to the physician's role responsibilities, are being reformulated. Reverence for the gift of life, and dedication both to its protection and prolongation are still basic value commitments of modern medicine. If anything, in recent years physicians have been more vocal than ever about their disinclination to "play God," as they themselves put it: that is, to arrogate to themselves the right to determine "who shall live and who shall die," by making more vigorous and continuing efforts to prevent the deaths and perpetuate the lives of some categories of patients over others. References to the Nazi medical war crimes as the ultimate sacrilege to which medicine can be brought are often made in such discussions. What is implied is that, because the role of physician centers on knowledge that pertains to life and death, unless great moral vigilance is continually exercised, the equivalent of original sin will again and again be committed. And in the collective extreme, this can become holocaust. There are evident relations between these medical concerns and the persistence of adventitious death in war and by other forms of violence as these concern a more general public.

Nevertheless, the profession of medicine has been steadily moving towards a less absolute position on what constitutes sanctity of life and the value of preserving it. Serious attempts are being made to distinguish vital processes which maintain the individual sheerly as a low-grade biological organism, from those which are essential to "humanness" and "person-hood." The new operational definition of death now in the process of being institutionalized in the medical profession and the larger society crystallizes this distinction. For, in defining death as the irreversible cessation of higher brain activity, it codifies the position that although the heart may beat and respiration continue (either naturally or by artificial means), without neocortical function and the cerebration that it makes possible, essentially *human* life does not exist. Thus, in the face of irreversible coma, the medical profession now seeks and is progressively obtaining justification for declaring a person dead, and for suspending life-sustaining efforts on his behalf. It is the opinion of the ethical scholar, Joseph Fletcher, that this redefinition of death represents a cardinal step in what he considers an at once needed and desirable evolution of medicine from an ethic based on the unconditional "sanctity of life" to one premised on the "quality of life." [45]

These changes seem to us, in general theoretical terms, to be interpretable as part of a more general process of "progressive social change." [46] As noted above, they constitute processes of differentiation, e.g., from the "absoluteness" of the physician's obligation to prolong life, to the opening up of several degrees of freedom in this area, with the consequence of imposing new burdens of decision on both physician and patient. There has been a process of upgrading, not only of the technical levels of medical service, but also of the opportunities to participate in a new "quality of life" for sick people and others, as well as a process of "value-generalization" by which the older formulae of the meaning of life and death are coming to be redefined.

Perhaps as a harbinger of these changes, more than thirty years ago one of us (Talcott Parsons) was startled, again at the Massachusetts General Hospital, by the sudden statement of an eminent senior surgeon, "no, human life is not sacred." At first blush this statement was wholly "mean-

[45] This analysis and opinion were offered by Dr. Fletcher in the course of a keynote address that he delivered at the National Conference on the Teaching of Medical Ethics, held at the Tarrytown Conference Center, Tarrytown, New York, on June 1–3, 1972. The conference was co-sponsored by the Institute of Society, Ethics and the Life Sciences and the Columbia University College of Physicians and Surgeons.

[46] Cf. Talcott Parsons, "Comparative Studies in Evolutionary Change," in Ivan Vallier, ed., *Comparative Methods in Sociology,* Berkeley (University of Calif. Press, 1971).

ingless." Fortunately, however, it was possible—knowing the background of the remark—to interpret its meaning. The speaker referred to a case which he had been discussing with his clinical clerkship group of medical students: it concerned an older woman for whom there was a "fighting chance" of gaining several years of good health and high "quality of life" if radical and dangerous surgery were to be performed, which at the same time there was a serious risk that the operation itself would be fatal. The alternative was a few more years of living in a gravely incapacitated state where only a low "quality of life" would be possible. The surgeon's statement was his way of asserting the moral justification of deliberately risking his patient's life in favor of the chance of a really meaningful terminal sector—i.e., a chance of a period of "high quality" life as against a longer, more certain period of "low quality" life.

THE BROADENING OF THE RANGE OF "CONCERN" FOR MEDICAL DECISIONS

At the same time that the medical profession is outspokenly reluctant to make such God-like decisions, it is also increasingly confronted with the inescapable obligation to use its "new controls over life and death in a responsible way." [47] One of the means by which medicine is dealing with this antimony is through broadening its patterns of professional collaboration. In medical amphitheatres throughout the country, and in many conferences on medical ethical issues, physicians are discussing these aspects of their life-and-death responsibilities with psychiatrists, social workers, ethicists, theologians, lawyers, and social scientists, among others. Often, these discussions turn around general principles and concepts, and *ex post facto* analyses of decisions about patients that have already taken place. But, especially in university-affiliated medical institutions, it is also becoming more common for such consultations to be sought while the physicians entrusted with a particular case are still deliberating about the most rational and humane course of action to take. Widening the orbit of colleagues whose advice they seek enlarges the range of expertise available to physicians, and provides them with intellectual and moral support from professional circles that are more than "strictly medical."

But perhaps the deepest significance of these more inclusive collegial patterns lies in their relationship to the closer integration with our main societal value system towards which the "new" medicine seems to be struggling.[48] Partly independently of the basic shifts in these values, e.g.,

[47] Joseph Fletcher, "Our Shameful Waste of Human Tissue: An Ethical Problem for the Living and the Dead," in Donald R. Cutler, ed., *The Religious Situation 1969*, Boston, Mass. (Beacon Press, 1969), p. 248.

[48] This clearly requires careful definition and analysis. Perhaps the best reference we can give is to Parsons and Platt, *op. cit.*, Chapter 2.

in the direction of their generalization, and partly as a consequence of them, medicine is now passing through a "time of troubles" and transition that centers on its growing capacity to sustain and abrogate life, its heightened tendency to raise questions of meaning, as well as of definition, about life and death, health and illness, and its greater concern with the equitable distribution of health care and scarce medical resources in our society. Through collaboration with other professionals, and also through the establishment of more collegial relations with patients and other consumers of health care, such as the families of patients, medicine seems to be reaching beyond the obtaining of counsel and consent on specific issues. A broader, more egalitarian moral consensus is being sought, that extends further than the "sacred trust" of traditional, one-to-one doctor-patient relationships, and the boundaries of what was previously defined as the medical professional community.[49]

ORGAN TRANSPLANTS AND THE GIFT COMPLEX

In our view, one of the therapeutic innovations that most dramatically exemplifies some of the overtly or covertly religious as well as moral problems with which modern medicine is grappling, is human organ transplantation.[50] For, central to transplantation is "the theme of the gift,"[51] a theme that we have shown to be fundamental to Judeo-Christian conceptions of life and death. With the possible exception of "giving birth," and to a lesser extent, donating blood, transplantation entails the most literal "gift of life" that a person can proffer or receive. The donor (a significant linguistic usage) contributes a vital part of his (her) body to a terminally ill, dying recipient, in order to save and maintain that other person's life. Because of the magnitude of this gift-exchange, and its symbolic, as well as biomedical implications, participating in a transplantation can be a transcendent experience for those involved, be it the live donor, the recipient, their relatives, the cadavar donor's family, or the members of the medical team. It may epitomize for them man's highest capacity to make the sacrificial gift of life-in-death, that is supreme love, commitment and communion. In this sense, regardless of how scientific the setting in which

[49] We conceive this, theoretically, to be a case of the complex which includes differentiation, upgrading, and the inclusion of new elements in the previously more restricted complex. We suggest that, in the recent phase, medicine is less inclined to "go it alone" without the help of other groups in the society. With respect to the changing structure within medicine itself, in the direction of a more ramified complex rather than a single diadic doctor-patient relationship, cf. Parsons and Platt, *op. cit.,* Chapter 5.

[50] This view of organ transplantation was first stated in R. C. Fox, "A Sociological Perspective on Organ Transplantation and Hemodialysis," *op. cit.* It is more fully developed in R. C. Fox and J. P. Swazey, *op. cit.*

[51] Marcel Mauss, *The Gift, op. cit.,* p. 66.

this transaction occurs may be, or how secularized the beliefs of those who take part in it, deep religious elements, some of them explicitly Christian, are at least latently present in the transplant situation.[52]

Nevertheless, here, as elsewhere, the properties of gift-exchange are such that transplantation confronts medicine and the larger society with a number of phenomena that are more troubling than transfiguring. To begin with, live-organ (kidney) transplantation involves both the donor and the medical team in an unprecedented act, whose morality is subject to question: the infliction of deliberate injury on a well person, in order to help another who is suffering from a fatal disease. However noble their motivation in performing major surgery on a healthy donor, the medical profession thereby compromises one of its basic, shall we say "absolute," ethical tenets: "to do no harm." [53]

Furthermore, under the circumstances in which live transplantations normally occur, the quality of consent obtained from the donor and recipient for this still experimental procedure is often strained. A family member is dying of renal disease, and his best chance for survival with a tolerable life is to be the recipient of a kidney from a relative whose tissue-type closely matches his own. No matter how scrupulously low-keyed and sensitive the medical team's process of screening candidates may be, the fact remains that, in this predicament, prospective donors are under very great inner and outer pressure to give an organ to their suffering relative who, in turn, is under extraordinary pressure to receive one. Thus, the norm of "voluntary informed consent" can only be imperfectly realized.

And what constitutes so-called healthy, positive motivation, either in life or in death for someone to donate a part of his body to a known or unknown other? Here, the medical profession has been brought face to face with the question of how much faith they collectively have in the altruistic principle, and how much belief in the desire and capacity of human beings to relate to one another as their "brothers' keepers" and as their "strangers' keepers," [54] which in Christian parlance may be phrased as "loving their neighbors."

Still another set of value-questions that transplantation has raised turns around the allocation of scarce resources. Who should be the beneficiaries

---

[52] So far, especially in the more radical transplant situations, the relations of living donor and recipient have been mainly "particularized," i.e., occurring between close relatives. In the case of cadaver donors, the identity of whom is concealed from the recipients and their families, the possibility has begun to emerge of something like "organ banks" in which organ "deposits" would be made, and withdrawals from them would be wholly impersonal—merely "equating" the functional capacity of organs with recipients' needs. How far such a development can go and what its consequences might be are problems on the fringe of the present discussion.

[53] This is perhaps to say that the striking increases in the potential to promote life at the same time imply risks and costs which may endanger life.

[54] Richard M. Titmuss, *The Gift Relationship: From Human Blood to Social Policy*, New York (Pantheon Books, 1971), *in passim*.

of the limited supply of human organs for transplantation that are made available through donation? What criteria of choice, if any, would be compatible with the highest value-commitments of our society? More fundamentally still, ought we to be expending so many material and immaterial resources for this kind of confrontation with terminal illness and death, when we might be investing them in the more universalistically life-giving purpose of providing good health care for our entire citizenry?

But perhaps the most chastening discovery that medicine has made about the gift relationship established by transplantation is that it can bind donor, recipient and kin to one another, emotionally and morally, in ways that are likely to be as fettering as they are liberating. Giving and receiving life in this form can lock the participants into an encompassing creditor-debtor relationship that blurs their separate identities, and diminishes their ability to reach out to others. Herein lies the potential tyranny of the human gift, its paradox, and perhaps its ultimate religious mystery. Organ transplantation suggests that the only perfect, truly redemptive gifts are *divine* ones. These are gifts of life and death from God, which constitute the at once sacred and flawed materials on which medicine acts: our essential humanity. The threat is to compromise the universalistic thrust of modern values.

Conclusion

We hope we have been able to draw certain lines of connection between some very ancient themes defining the human condition with reference to life and death, and some very immediate developments, with special reference to the orientations, functions and obligations of the contemporary medical profession.

Our primary theses are, first, that the problem of the meaning of death has been coming more and more explicitly to the fore in the recent development of our culture, and that a major focus of this salience has been in the medical world. Secondly we feel that, new as these developments are, they are not understandable except in reference to the great religious tradition of our culture, especially as expressed in the major constitutive "myths."

The theme of gift-exchange between God and man has been central to our analysis. In particular, we have emphasized the salience of the conception that human life is a gift from God. We have then, we think, been able to trace at least in outline the evolution of the conception that the death of the individual, at the close of a "full" life, not only *may* be, but in fact often *is,* interpreted as a reciprocal gift to God, the consummatory reciprocation of the gift of life. The emergence of this interpretation, we believe, has been enormously facilitated by medical control over the causes of adventitious death.

All of this has been occurring in the context of the development of a highly rationalized, technical, industrial society. "Scientific medicine" has been part and parcel of this society. The involvement, however, of the medical profession in the existential problems of the meaning of life and death, and at least its tentative movement in the direction of incorporating such a dimension, seems to us to be a striking example of the intimate interweaving of the more rationalistic and the more existential components in the development of modern society and culture. Far from there being a necessity to choose between the "scientific" attitude toward illness and health, life and death, and a "mystical" orientation, we hope that we have made a modest contribution to understanding the ways in which a synthesis of these two aspects of modern culture may be possible.

13. Religion in Postindustrial America: The Problem of Secularization

THE PRESENT PAPER is in some respects a sequel to "The 'Gift of Life' and Its Reciprocation," which appeared in the Autumn 1972 issue of *Social Research*.[1] I begin with the presentation and explication of a schematic paradigm of the symbolic structure of medieval Christianity, indicating the principal modifications that must be introduced to accommodate the development of Protestantism. I then turn to two major developments of the post-Reformation era: the process sometimes called secularization, and that which has led to the ecumenical movement of recent times. Within the framework of these two developments, I briefly discuss two phenomena that do not fit into what has traditionally been called religion: civil religion and Marxian socialism, which may be called a secularized religion. Finally, I consider the current religious situation, with special reference to the United States, and the appearance of what must be called post-Marxian themes in certain dissident social and cultural movements in the United States.

A Paradigm of Christian Symbolism

The figure on page 301 represents the main structure of Christian symbolism as found in the medieval Roman Catholic Church. It reflects some

[1] Talcott Parsons, Renée C. Fox, and Victor M. Lidz, "The 'Gift of Life' and Its Reciprocation," *Social Research*, XXXIX (Autumn 1972), 367–415. Chapter 12 of this volume. See also Talcott Parsons, "Belief, Unbelief, and Disbelief," in Rocco Caporale and Antonio Grumelli, eds., *The Culture of Unbelief* (Berkeley: University of California Press, 1971), pp. 207–245. Chapter 11 of this volume.

From *Social Research*, vol. 41 (Summer 1974), pp. 193–225. Used by permission. *Social Research* is published by the Graduate Faculty of the New School for Social Research.

The Human Condition as Symbolically Organized
About Age and Sex: The Christian Syndrome as Gift Complex

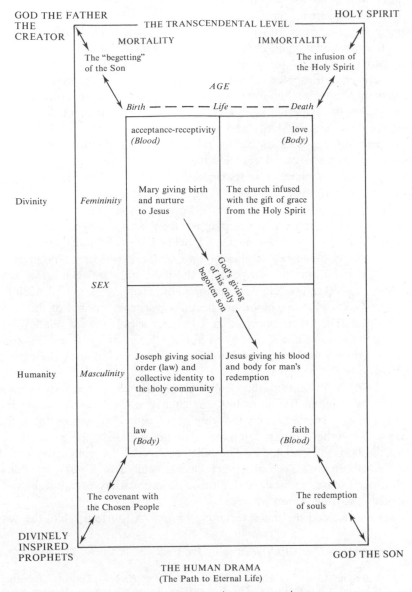

THE HUMAN DRAMA
(The Path to Eternal Life)

Conception/Birth / Receipt of the gift of life / Ego's life course / Dying in the faith / Reciprocation of the gift of life

of the ideas put forward in "The 'Gift of Life' and Its Reciprocation," in which my colleagues and I sought to explicate some aspects of the meaning of death in the Western religious tradition. We there adopted the concept of life as a gift, and utilized ideas of gift-giving and gift-exchange formulated a generation ago by Marcel Mauss.[2] The formulation of the paradigm was greatly facilitated by certain writings of Edmund Leach and Kenneth Burke as well as by the original biblical texts.[3]

The figure presents the two-level system of Christian symbolism: the temporal and the transcendental, or the secular and the sacred. In the figure, the inner rectangle, designated "The Human Level," is organized about two reference concept pairs. First is the one that has figured so prominently in anthropological and sociological thinking, namely, sex and age. It should be remembered that I am speaking in symbolic terms, though in some cases the symbolic figures are referred to in canonical documents with quite definite sex identity and sometimes with generation identity. In this respect the category of sex is relatively straightforward. For what social scientists have called age, I have substituted the life course as a whole with special reference to its beginning and its end, birth and death. The symbolization, then, has to do with certain relations between the cultural conceptions of what it means to be born and what it means to die.[4]

The second reference concept pair is taken from the symbolization of kinship relations as analyzed by David Schneider.[5] The most obvious of these symbols is blood, as habitually used in the expression "blood relationship." It is striking that in perhaps the most intimate relation of kinship, that of mother and child, a common bloodstream is not physiologically shared. Nevertheless, blood has become a primary symbol of this type of relatedness. The other concept that Schneider uses is that of relationship in law, organized not about blood but about what is in some sense a contract. The prototypical empirical kinship case is the relation of the parties in a marriage.

In religion as in kinship, the symbol blood plays a central part. This is true in many religious traditions but particularly in Christianity, where the blood of Christ is symbolized by the wine in the central Christian ritual, the eucharist. The other primary component of the eucharist, the bread, symbolizes the body of Christ. In "The 'Gift of Life,'" my colleagues and I argued that body as a symbol is very closely related to a relation of law in Schneider's sense, and indeed this turns up in a variety of cultural traditions other than the American.

I have structured the inner rectangle to yield a fourfold table, the two

[2] Marcel Mauss, *The Gift,* translated by Ian Cunnison (Glencoe, Ill.: Free Press, 1954).

[3] See Edmund Leach, *Genesis as Myth and Other Essays* (London: Jonathan Cape, 1969), and Kenneth Burke, *The Rhetoric of Religion* (Boston: Beacon Press, 1961).

[4] Cf. Matilda W. Riley, Marilyn Johnson, and Ann Foner, eds., *Aging and Society,* Vol. III: *A Sociology of Age Stratification* (New York: Russell Sage Foundation, 1972).

[5] David M. Schneider, *American Kinship: A Cultural Account* (Englewood Cliffs, N.J.: Prentice-Hall, 1968).

dichotomized dimensions of which are (in the vertical axis) femininity and masculinity, and (in the horizontal axis) birth and death—that is, the old categories of sex and age in the appropriate modifications as just explained. In New Testament tradition, three of the four cells are related to symbolic individuals, and they are related to each other and to other human beings through a gift relationship. The fourth I think of as symbolizing the church, which, in the words of the eucharist, constitutes the mystical body of Christ. The two left cells are what Leach would call the "sociological" parents of Jesus, of whom, in the religiously symbolic sense, clearly the more important is Mary, the "Mother of God." Leach, however, aptly refers to Joseph as Jesus's "sociological" father. Symbolically, the figure of Joseph seems to represent continuity between the Christian group and the Jewish community within which Christianity arose. Thus, in the gospel according to Matthew, there is an elaborate genealogy which traces Joseph's descent from the patriarchs and prophets and strongly asserts his belonging—and therefore his sociological son Jesus's belonging—to the "House of David." This in turn we may associate with the continuity in some sense of the Jewish law, despite the profound alteration of the meaning of that law by Jesus and Paul.

It will be noted that Mary is depicted as *giving* birth and nurture to Jesus. Jesus himself, then, having been given birth by a human mother, in his sacrificial death on the cross is symbolized as *giving* his blood and body for man's redemption. Finally, the church is conceived as infused with the gift of grace from the Holy Spirit.

Whereas the vertical axis of the inner rectangle is conceived in terms of the sex dichotomy, the horizontal axis is concerned with a dichotomized version of the age variable, focusing on the two extreme points of the life course, birth and death. From this point of view, it is highly symbolic that in a certain sense the founding act of Christianity was Jesus's sacrificial death. The church, then particularly in the Catholic tradition, was conceived as the agency through which the transcending of death and the achievement of eternal life could come about.

The other two primary reference symbols—namely, blood and body— are depicted as characterizing the diagonals of the inner rectangle. Blood is involved not only in Jesus's sacrifice but also in his relation as blood child to Mary. It therefore symbolizes both a religious event and a terrestrial kinship. The other diagonal axis is associated with the symbol of body, but interestingly in both cases not specifically an individual's body but corporate bodies. If my interpretation is correct, the relatively secular community that has been sanctified through its relation to the heritage of Israel is a necessary substratum for the religion. This, in turn, is related to the church as the mystical body of Christ with all its well known meanings. Here the gift theme appears again in the concept of grace as the instrument of human salvation.

The outer rectangle in the figure is designated "The Transcendental Level." At three of its corners I have placed the three persons of the Trinity. The concept of God the Father, which is placed at the upper left corner, gained a new meaning in Christianity in contrast to Judaism through the symbolic act of God's "begetting" a son, Jesus, through the human woman Mary. This act of begetting is quite different from that of creation as portrayed in Genesis. God created Adam and Eve, but he begat Jesus. Among other things, begetting symbolizes the continuity of the human species, which began with an act of creation.

The second main act of God in the drama of salvation was the "giving of his only begotten son" for the redemption of mankind. The upper right corner represents the concept of the Holy Spirit, which has a special relationship to the church and the gift of grace. The lower right corner is the locus of God the Son, the personal agent of redemption.

The lower left corner does not involve a person of the Trinity but rather the Christian inheritance from the Jewish tradition. I have focused it about the divinely inspired patriarchs and prophets, notably Moses and David, as establishing a particularly sanctified human community, the "Chosen People." It will be remembered that the concept of the covenant, which was central to the Old Testament, was carried over into Christianity in various forms and is particularly important in the Puritan branch of Protestantism.

Finally, at the bottom of the figure, outside either rectangle, is a schematic notation about the human drama that I have labeled "The Path to Eternal Life." The duality is present in the spiritual conception of Jesus and his actual physical birth. Jesus, standing in a certain symbolic sense for mankind, was by that set of circumstances the receiver of what I have called the gift of life. According to Mauss, the acceptance of a gift calls for its reciprocation. Part of that reciprocation is living a religiously acceptable life, the consummation of which is dying in the faith, which completes the reciprocation of the gift.

The paradigm omits reference to two particularly important features of the Catholic system. The first is the sacraments. Besides the eucharist, already mentioned, the church instituted several other sacraments, notably penance, baptism, marriage, and extreme unction. The sacraments were considered to be consequences of the gift of grace coming to the church through Jesus's sacrifice and through the Holy Spirit. The church claimed a monopoly of the legitimate use of the sacraments. It became its policy, contrary to practices of early Christianity, that the sacraments could be administered only by ordained priests deriving their authority through apostolic succession from St. Peter, whose direct successor as the head of the church was the bishop of Rome, the pope.

A second important feature omitted from the paradigm is the religious order, whose members took vows of perpetual devotion to the religious life. Although in early Christianity there were individual anchorites, collective monasticism did not develop until the third century. Members of the religious orders, the regular clergy, were the true "upper class" of the church, with—to pursue the metaphor—the secular clergy serving as a kind of middle class and the laity constituting, religiously speaking, the unprivileged "masses."

There has been a remarkable stability in the main Catholic pattern down to the present day. Mention should be made, however, of two important developments. After the outbreak of the Reformation, which will be discussed presently, the Catholic Church reacted by tightening discipline, particularly over the clergy, and by more strictly defining the sacramental system. For the laity it insisted on full doctrinal conformity and maintenance of prescribed religious practices. The spirit of this Counter Reformation is embodied in the Society of Jesus, founded by St. Ignatius Loyola in 1540. From the start, the Jesuits were militant servants of the papacy rather than monks absorbed in devotional exercises.

The second important development is a much more recent one. In a sense, the main pattern of the Counter Reformation endured into the present century: only a century ago, in 1870, Pius IX promulgated the doctrine of papal infallibility. The recent period, however, has seen increased participation of the Roman Catholic Church in what has come to be called the ecumenical movement. The brief papacy of John XXIII and the Second Vatican Council precipitated a critical situation within the church. For example, there has been since then a vastly increased demand for the termination of the requirement of celibacy for the secular clergy, and there have been many resignations from the priesthood over this issue.

Changes Introduced by the Protestant Movement

The Reformation revolutionized the religious constitution of Europe. Although the outcome was long uncertain, by the Peace of Westphalia (1648) it had become evident that the change was irreversible. There would never again be religious unity in Western Europe under the aegis of the Roman Church.

Of the many religious changes introduced by Protestantism, perhaps the most significant was the elimination of the conception of the sacraments as the actual quasi-magical operation of divine grace. In Max Weber's terms, this deprived the church—that is, in its Protestant version—of the status of a *Gnadenanstalt*.[6] The church was no longer the mediator of the

---

[6] Max Weber, "Basic Sociological Terms," in his *Economy and Society*, edited by Guenther Roth and Claus Wittich (New York: Bedminster Press, 1968).

mystical-transcendental transactions between God and man. For Protestantism the so-called visible church became essentially an association of believers with a common interest in fulfilling the conditions for salvation prescribed in the Bible, including especially cognitive understanding of those conditions. The clergy were no longer manipulators of divine grace but became teachers, leaders of congregations, missionaries to the lay public exhorting it to commitment to and steadfastness in the faith. To be sure, the sacraments were maintained, but with profoundly altered meaning. They became merely symbolic affirmations of faith and commitment to the Christian message. In its modified form the eucharist remained the central ritual. But marriage, for example, increasingly lost its sacramental quality, a loss which underlay later toleration of divorce.

Another important change was the elimination of the religious orders in favor of a kind of democracy of all Christians. With this went the famous shift, beginning in Luther's own writings, of which Max Weber made so much in his essay *The Protestant Ethic and the Spirit of Capitalism*[7]—the shift to the view that religious obligations in the fullest sense could be discharged by laymen and specifically in lay occupations (*Berufe*) rather than by clergy in segregated monastic communities. Associated with this shift was the legitimation of clerical marriage. This was dramatically symbolized by Luther's own decision to marry in violation of his monastic vows and by the fact that the woman he married was a former nun.

This change has often been interpreted as reflecting a relaxation of standards of religious rigor. Indeed, this is the beginning of a line of argument about secularization of which I shall have more to say below, and it represents one—possibly the prevalent—view. There has, however, been another interpretation of the change. This is to the effect that the change was not primarily a downgrading (religiously speaking) of the clergy, both regular and secular, but rather an upgrading of the laity. Luther's marriage, from this point of view, symbolized his conviction that the fully religious life could be lived in the ordinary status of the lay citizen and not only as a monk or priest. Weber quotes a religious notable of the period, Sebastian Franck, to the effect that, as a consequence of the Reformation, "every man was expected to be in essence a monk." [8]

The Reformation was an exceedingly complex religiosocial movement. Weber, nevertheless, suggests that it can be divided into two principal branches, the Lutheran and the Calvinist. The Lutheran branch represented the more inward, spiritualistic interpretation of emancipation from the institutionally "objective" Catholic Church. Its primary concern was with the soul of the individual Christian believer. The Calvinist branch, on the other hand, emphasized the Christian community as a corporate entity, a

---

[7] Max Weber, *The Protestant Ethic and the Spirit of Capitalism*, translated by Talcott Parsons (New York: Charles Scribner's Sons, 1958).

[8] Weber, *The Protestant Ethic and the Spirit of Capitalism*, p. 121.

fully legitimized descendant of the early and medieval churches and the bearer of the main Christian heritage. Calvinism prevailed in northwestern Europe, notably in Holland and Great Britain, and eventually in North America. It also had a profound impact on France. Calvin himself was a Frenchman, and in the religious wars of the seventeenth century the Calvinist party only narrowly missed achieving political control of France.

Protestant rulers, like Catholic, initially assumed that their subjects would adhere to their religion. Indeed, *cuius regio eius religio* was the formula by which the Peace of Westphalia brought at least a provisional end to the wars of religion. Before that, however, notably in Holland and England, limited religious toleration had developed. In England, nonconformist sects existed beside the established Anglican Church. Although religious uniformity was enforced within several of the English-speaking American colonies, as was the case in Massachusetts, different colonies were of different religious persuasions, so the thirteen colonies taken together presented a picture of religious pluralism.

Generally speaking, what might be called the liberal tendency of Protestant development within the original Calvinist framework has prevailed. This is true of England and Holland, although the Church of England has never been disestablished and as late as the 1870s only those who subscribed to the Thirty-nine Articles, the official creed of the Church of England, were eligible for membership in the universities of Oxford and Cambridge, whether as students or teachers. Only the United States insisted on a thoroughgoing separation of church and state. The First Amendment to the Constitution forbade Congress to "establish religion" or "to interfere with the free exercise thereof." The United States thus became the leader in the movement toward religious toleration and denominational pluralism. This first occurred on a substantial scale within the Protestant movement itself. Only later, with the advent of large bodies of Roman Catholic immigrants, first from Ireland and then from continental Europe, did there arise an important problem as to the status of Catholics. Still later, the status of considerable numbers of religious Jews presented a problem. The outcome has been a denominationally pluralistic and increasingly ecumenical religious situation in both Western Europe and America. The situation in Communist-controlled countries is, of course, different.

The Problem of Secularization

From one point of view, the development just sketched constituted an individualization or "privatization" of the religious situation. Religious freedom, of course, included the freedom to abstain from formal religious participation, and I think it can be said that increasing numbers from all three religious backgrounds have taken this course. We might therefore add to the three—Protestants, Catholics, and Jews—a fourth category, secular humanists.

In view of the sociocultural background, this individualization does not, however, represent the whole story. Nor is the story fully told in the usual sense of the term "secularization" as used even by so sensitive a student as Peter L. Berger.[9] The key to the complexities of that concept lies not so much at the level of individual belief and religious practice as in what has happened to the various societies as corporate entities with the privatization of religion and abstention from traditional religious organizations.

An extremely important clue is to be found in Robert Bellah's conception, put forward a decade ago, of what he called the civil religion.[10] Bellah's analysis of this concept constitutes a landmark in the understanding of the American religious situation, for civil religion seems to represent one of the two primary alternatives confronting modern Protestantism.

Ascetic Protestantism always affirmed that the primary field for action prompted by authentic religious impulse was the secular world. Indeed, the collective aim of the Puritan movement was the establishment of the kingdom of God on earth. From the point of view of earlier Christian tradition, this would seem to be almost by definition an impossible task. The Puritans' sustained commitment to this goal, however, testifies to their belief that success of some sort was possible. And, in fact, with the establishment of an independent American republic, there was something of a conviction in elite circles that a major part at least of this extraordinary task had been accomplished.

Well before the achievement of independence, the development of American Protestantism had clearly taken an individualistic direction. The most important consequence was the establishment of the voluntary principle with respect to the more formal aspects of religious obligation, notably church membership. This in turn was closely associated with the high development of religious toleration and the conception of colonial society as denominationally pluralistic. The constitutional provision for the separation of church and state merely ratified the existing situation.

These developments seem to me to have constituted a differentiation between levels of religious significance. The process referred to above as individualization had rendered untenable the old coincidence of the individual's concern with personal salvation and the collective concept of the church as a social entity—a *Gnadenanstalt,* in Weber's sense. In Puritan doctrine, however, the great task was the collective one of constructing the kingdom of God on earth. It is my view that the roots of the civil religion in America lie in the attempt to validate the legitimacy of the Puritans' claim to have achieved a measure of success. The "new nation," as Lipset

[9] Peter L. Berger, *The Sacred Canopy* (Garden City, N.Y.: Doubleday, 1967).
[10] Robert N. Bellah, *Beyond Belief: Essays on Religion in a Post-Traditional World* (New York: Harper & Row, 1970).

called it, was interpreted from the very first canonical document, the Declaration of Independence, to be a sacred entity.[11]

The development of the civil religion was a way by which two crucial themes of American cultural and social history could be combined. One of these was secularization in the usual sense which denied traditional denominational bodies any official status. The new society became a secular society in which religion was relegated to the private sphere. The other theme is no less important: the building of the kingdom of God on earth. The establishment of the new American nation was a culmination of this process. The very facts of independence and a new constitution "conceived in liberty and dedicated to the proposition that all men are created equal" were developments that could not fail to carry with them a religious dimension. This took a form that was relatively consistent with traditional Christian conceptions and definitions, and it is this that is the core of what Bellah calls the American civil religion. There was no radical break with the primary religious heritage, though there was a careful avoidance of any attempt to define the new civil religion as Christian in a specifically dogmatic sense. Bellah documents, for example, how the many official statements—notably presidential inaugural addresses—that use the term "God" or various synonyms such as "Supreme Being" carefully avoid reference to Christ.

This civil religion must be sharply contrasted with the religious outcome of the French Revolution. French society had developed under a particularly stringent form of monarchical absolutism. Furthermore, the Catholic Church in France was extremely conservative. Thus the general background of presumptive religious freedom that had been so important to the development of the American colonies during the eighteenth century was missing in Catholic monarchical France. In making a sharp break with the past, the French revolutionary movement not only bitterly opposed the monarchy but was also strongly anticlerical. The civil religion deliberately established by the French revolutionaries—worship of the Supreme Being —was, as Bellah points out, very different from that which developed in America. Its conflict with traditional French Catholicism was acute indeed.

The most influential thinker in the background of the French Revolution was Rousseau. Rousseau contrasted in the sharpest possible way a romantically conceived state of nature with a completely unitary civil society. The central mechanism of this unitary entity was the General Will, which in principle had to be shared in by the whole population of citizens. There was no place for the political pluralism that was so characteristic of American society. The very radicalism of the French model of a revolutionary society proved fatal to the maintenance of its integrity. After the Terror, a reaction set in that brought a succession of regimes not easily identified with the revolutionary ideal. These culminated in the Empire of

[11] Seymour M. Lipset, *The First New Nation* (New York: Basic Books, 1963).

Napoleon I and, after his fall, in the Bourbon restoration. France did develop a certain type of bourgeois society somewhat similar to England's. However, throughout the nineteenth century and well into the present one, French society remained deeply divided between the revolutionary tradition, republican and militantly anticlerical, and the conservative tradition based on the monarchy, the army, and the Catholic Church. In a sense, nineteenth-century France provided the most extreme pattern of the internal conflicts that were general throughout Europe.

The most important politicocultural movement to emerge in Europe after the French Revolution was socialism, whose ideological leadership was provided by Karl Marx. Marx was a German who spent the most important part of his productive life as an exile in London. Lipset has shrewdly observed that Marx's economic data were derived from English developments while his political ideas were shaped by developments in France.[12] In the second half of the nineteenth century, Marxism became a "secular religion." As such, it could claim a direct cultural descent from the thought of Rousseau and the traditions of the French Revolution. Furthermore, given the essential disestablishment of the traditional Christian churches, Marxism was the most important alternative to the American version of the civil religion.

Let us start with the striking resemblance between Marxism and traditional Christian doctrine. From its earliest beginnings to the Protestant Reformation, Christianity conceived of secular society as inherently depraved. Only through divine intervention could men be quite literally saved, that is, rescued from the sin and death that were the natural condition of temporal man. This view was profoundly altered by Calvinism and other influences. Because American Protestants believed they had succeeded in setting up a truly Christian commonwealth, it was impossible to accept the traditional Christian view of the utter corruption of secular society. Any nondenominational religious orientation that could survive in this situation had to give a positive sanction to the newly institutionalized social order.

The situation in Europe as a result of the French Revolution was very different. The Revolution had pursued a highly romanticized conception of an ideal society characterized by the total absence of individual self-interest. With the ebbing of the revolutionary élan, however, the maintenance of this ideal proved to be impossible, and society reverted to a state of Rousseauian corruption in which self-interest figured very prominently indeed. In the revolutionary tradition there remained the memory of the Revolution's short-lived victory over the evils of corrupt society, and

[12] Seymour M. Lipset, personal communication. For a more general discussion of Marx, see Seymour M. Lipset, "Issues in Social Class Analysis," in his *Revolution and Counterrevolution,* rev. ed. (Garden City, N.Y.: Doubleday Anchor Books, 1970), and Reinhard Bendix and Seymour M. Lipset, "Karl Marx's Theory of Social Classes," in Bendix and Lipset, eds., *Class, Status and Power,* 2nd ed. (New York: Free Press, 1966), pp. 6–11.

some of those who were deeply imbued with that tradition maintained that only revolution could eliminate the corruption of traditional society.

The French revolutionaries had located the corruption of the old regime in the monarchy, aristocracy, and church. With the vast weakening of monarchies and aristocracies in the course of the nineteenth century, and with the development of the fruits of the Industrial Revolution, Marxists found the source of the trouble in the system of economic organization—capitalism. Correspondingly, the saving element could no longer, at least initially, be the people as a whole, as in the main French revolutionary tradition, but had to be that part of the people who were allegedly uncorrupted by the capitalist system. This pointed rather obviously to the exploited and—in the Marxian sense—alienated working class.

The Marxian secular religion and, more broadly, the socialist movement generally took on an eschatological orientation very similar to that of traditional Christianity. Men of good will were condemned to suffer the humiliations and deprivations of a corrupt society until such time as the revolution could occur. With the revolution would come liberation, that "leap into freedom" from the coercion and slavery of capitalism. The socialist movement thus not only resembled the main Christian tradition in its pessimistic diagnosis of the contemporary secular world, but was characterized by a very similar pattern of eschatological hope. The new society was to be brought about not by a last judgment but by a political revolution. And the revolution was to be brought about not by the second coming of an individual savior but by the intervention of a collective savior—the proletariat.

The fundamental changes in the religious constitution of Western society which culminated in the later eighteenth century thus did not lead to the destruction of the influence of religion but rather to the development of two strikingly important new types and levels of religion. The antagonism between them finally came to something of a head in the present century with the Russian Revolution. There was, of course, considerable tension before then, but it has been particularly acute in the more than fifty years since that event. The vicissitudes have been many and complex, notably complicated by the rise of Nazi Germany in the 1930s with its common threat to both the West and the Soviet Union. This produced in the Second World War what in certain respects was an unnatural alliance between the Soviet Union and the Western democracies, paralleling in some ways the eighteenth-century alliance between Catholic France and Protestant Prussia which underlay the basic religious changes of that period.

In any case, I think it is legitimate to interpret what has often been called the "cold war" as in a very important aspect constituting a set of wars of religion which are not without their relation to the wars of religion that followed the Reformation. Although the tensions remain very strong, there seems some reason to believe that the most acute phase of this particular polarization of the Western world has begun to come to an end. The primary task of the rest of this paper is to outline a diagnosis of the implications of this changed situation for a phase of religious development onto which we have barely begun to enter.

Some Aspects of the Contemporary Situation

The two syndromes reviewed in the preceding section may in my opinion properly be called civil religions in Bellah's sense. In the American case, the civil religion was from the beginning part of the constitutive structure of the new nation. It can be considered a direct and legitimate descendant of the orientation of the Puritan colonists, particularly as their position has been presented and analyzed in the work of Perry Miller.[13]

Marxian socialism was originally the civil religion of an alienated opposition movement. In this respect, it clearly resembled early Christianity before it became the official religion of the Roman Empire. The resemblance is even closer if we consider, not the Empire as a whole, but only the Jewish community, which by the time of the appearance of Christianity was already a diaspora. Although Christianity was at first a sect within Judaism, Paul's denial of the relevance of the Jewish community and the law made it into a revolutionary movement relative to its Israelitic background.[14]

For considerably more than half a century Marxism was a movement in stark opposition to the institutionalized regimes of the Western world in which it arose. The Russian Revolution created a situation in certain respects comparable to that of Christianity after Constantine, though with extraordinary complications that cannot be entered into here. In the non-Communist world, which includes countries with strong traditions of democratic socialism like Great Britain and the Scandinavian countries, Marxian socialism must still be regarded as in a certain rather fundamental sense alienated from the main institutionalized social structure.

When we come to the recent contemporary and short-run prospective situation in the Western non-Communist world, and particularly the United States, I think it is legitimate to speak of a fundamentally new phase in the development of the Western religious tradition.[15] The most salient feature

[13] Perry Miller, *Errand into the Wilderness* (Cambridge: Harvard University Press, 1956).

[14] Talcott Parsons, "Christianity," in David L. Sills, ed., *International Encyclopedia of the Social Sciences* (New York: Macmillan and Free Press, 1968), II, 425–447. See also Arthur D. Nock, *St. Paul* (New York: Harper & Bros., 1938). Chapter 9 of this volume.

[15] The following statement is a revised version of the material presented in the last section of my article "Belief, Unbelief and Disbelief."

of this situation is the emergence of a movement that resembles early Christianity in its emphasis on the theme of love. Although this theme has never been absent from the older branches of Christianity, both Catholic and Protestant, there are several things that are new about the contemporary movement. In the first place, it is clearly focused at a this-worldly rather than a transcendental level. Its field of application and institutionalization is clearly what Christian tradition defines as secular society. In this respect it is a legitimate heir of the versions of Protestantism that attempted to establish a kingdom of God on earth and of both versions of the modern civil religion to which I have referred.

Second, it is, in a sense that was not true of the Christian predecessor movements, relatively nontheistic. I use this term as a conscious alternative to "atheistic." This theme certainly has something to do with the this-worldliness of the movement, since there is in it no equivalent to the gospel conception expressed in the famous statement "In my Father's house are many mansions." In this statement, of course, the Father's house has generally been interpreted to refer to heaven, that is, the other world which the redeemed souls of the dead would enter and in which they would enjoy eternal life. In the new religion of love, if I may use that term, there is no "Father's house" separable from this world—that is, the concrete human condition—to be entered only after death. Indeed, a major problem for this new orientation is the interpretation of the meaning of death, about which I will have something to say before I conclude.

The nontheistic feature of the new religious tendency permits its followers to seek a rapprochement with some of the great Oriental religions, notably those in the Hindu-Buddhist tradition. Many proponents of the contemporary counterculture have been fascinated by these Oriental religions, and both Hinduism and Buddhism—certainly the classical Brahminism that historically underlies both of them—are devoid of the specific kind of theism that has characterized the Judeo-Christian and, of course, the Islamic traditions.

A rather prominent part in the new religious movements has been taken by people involved in the so-called counterculture. This movement is strongly colored by a sense of alienation from much of the current industrial and even incipiently postindustrial society. In this respect it resembles some of the movements deriving from the influence of Rousseau in the Enlightenment and after the French Revolution, and also the movement of Marxian socialism within the developing industrial society.

Proponents of the counterculture have made much use of Marxian rhetoric, especially with respect to the class struggle and the upgrading of disadvantaged sectors of society in the name of egalitarian values. I think, however, that there is in the counterculture a major shift of emphasis from the kind of relatively orthodox Marxism that was most influential in establishing the Communist states in Eastern Europe, especially the Soviet

Union. Perhaps the most important difference is that in the newer movements it is difficult to impute a clear doctrine of historical materialism. One wing of the Neo-Marxian movement is almost obsessively concerned with the alleged power of the capitalist system,[16] but other wings use the Marxian rhetoric to express their alienation from the established institutional order. With their more or less revolutionary stance, they tend to grasp at almost any way of expressing this alienation. As a conceptual system, however, their position can only dubiously be called Marxist in the traditional sense.

Common to all the radical traditions, from Rousseau on, has been the idealization of a state of relatively spontaneous community solidarity. Although Marx's principal works were written before that of Tönnies, the latter's formulation of the concept *Gemeinschaft* has been exceedingly important to the relevant discussions.[17] Marxists, with their eschatological orientation, have always drawn a sharp dichotomy between the capitalist system, with its economic and power interests, and communism, with its spontaneous solidarity, projecting the realization of communism into the future. The new movements also idealize a society free of economic and power interests, free of coercion and even of rationally oriented discipline, achieving spontaneous solidarity in ways often governed by the imperative of love. There is probably more of a disposition, however, to see the realizability of such a society in the present or the quite immediate future. Furthermore, that society is even less institutionalized than the classical Marxian conception of the communist utopia. The more radical elements of the counterculture come very close to principled anarchism.

In the United States and other countries, there have been numerous attempts to set up what in a sense are experimental living groups, or communes, organized on this kind of ideal basis.[18] There seem to be three important points about the commune movement which pose certain problems about the institutionalization of a larger and more successful movement of religiously oriented change. The first is the fact that communes have established such order as they have only for rather small numbers of people, usually living in a state of considerable segregation from the mainstream of modern society. Many of them have avoided urban communities and established themselves in rural areas where they can cultivate extremely

[16] See Herbert Gintis, "Radical Analysis of Welfare Economics and Individual Development," *Quarterly Journal of Economics,* LXXXVI (November 1972), 572–599.

[17] Ferdinand Tönnies, *Community and Society,* translated and edited by Charles P. Loomis (New York: Harper & Row, 1963).

[18] On communes, see Rosabeth Kanter, *Commitment and Community: Communes and Utopias in Sociological Perspective* (Cambridge: Harvard University Press, 1972) and *Communes: Social Organization of the Collective Life* (New York: Harper & Row, 1973). See also Jesse R. Pitts, "Survey Essay on Communes," *Contemporary Sociology,* II (July 1973), 351–359.

simple life styles. I have the impression, though I do not think the field has been quite adequately surveyed, that the rate of failure is extremely high in such groups. They have been organized on widely varying principles; some, for example, have insisted on mutual sexual access of all members to each other, notably those of opposite sex, while others have permitted relatively exclusive sexual relations confined to particular pairs. There are also variations in the degree to which individual participants are required to give up all personal property or personal claim to money earned outside the commune to the common needs of the commune. Perhaps the most striking structural development, however, seems to be that a disproportionate number of those communes that have achieved a certain stability and viability have accepted a quasi-dictatorial pattern of leadership on the part of one dominant leader. It seems that the achievement of a fully participatory democracy on the part of the members is very rare and difficult. It should also be kept in mind that, relative to the total population, commune memberships have been highly selective. They have consisted primarily of young people of about college or more-or-less immediately post-college ages. They conspicuously lack the middle- and older-aged components which any general population necessarily includes. There have been small children involved with a wide variety of arrangements for their belongingness and care. I have the impression that the fate of children in the commune constitutes a very difficult problem, and that there have been many failures in this respect.

To have any chance of influencing the religious orientation of a large proportion of the population, a movement of religious innovation will have to meet conditions that have not been met by the small-scale communal experiments I have very briefly referred to. What can be said about the kinds of conditions that will be necessary and the prospect of their actualization?

In the "effervescent" phase of the modern New Left countercultural movement, there has been a very strong stress on the liberation of the erotic component and its generalization outside the conventional marriage context. Janet Giele has suggested that an important process of differentiation has indeed been occurring among the relatively new generations as part of the "sexual revolution." [19] The principal new note seems to be the establishment, within the participant groups, of the legitimacy of overt heterosexual relations before and even outside of marriage, provided that two conditions are fulfilled. The clearer one is that the parties should have, as Dr. Giele puts it, "affection for each other," that is to say, that their erotic relationship should not be confined to the generation of organic pleasure. Closely linked to this and a very important item but somewhat

[19] Janet Zollinger Giele, "Changes in the Modern Family: Their Impact on Sex Roles," *American Journal of Orthopsychiatry*, XLI (October 1971), 757–766.

more vaguely felt is the criterion of a certain commitment to relative durability of the relationship. Casual one-night stands are not given a very high mark for legitimacy.

I would like to attempt to carry the analysis one step further by introducing the important concept "affect." Affect may be defined as a generalized symbolic medium of interchange at the level of the general system of action.[20] I use the concept in a sense closely related to Freud's use of it in his *Interpretation of Dreams,*[21] but—in a way not suggested by Freud— anchored at what I would technically call the level of the social system. This is to say, it is a medium particularly functioning in the area of mediating relations of solidarity. Freud quite correctly emphasized in his own analysis its bearing on the relation of sexual partners, especially importantly in marriage. I would carry this forward to the views of David Schneider of sexual intercourse as a primary *symbol* and not the primary bond of the solidarity of marriage partners. Seen in this context, affect is not in the first instance primarily a psychological medium but rather one whose primary functional significance is social and cultural.

Its relation to eroticism seems to me to be that of a generalized medium to what I have sometimes called its security base. A ready example is the role of certain precious metals as a security base for money. At certain stages gold functions both as a commodity and as a form of money. It is a boundary entity from this point of view. But in modern systems only the tiniest fraction of the actual circulating medium of exchange consists of gold. On the other hand, until at least very recently, a "gold standard" meant the interchangeability of nonmetalic money with gold. This is by and large no longer the case. I suggest that in at all diffuse and enduring relations of human solidarity which involve an erotic element the situation is similar to that of the involvement of gold in a monetary system. Where, that is to say, there is an erotic component, the organic aspect is not the only meaning of erotic pleasure; it is also a symbol of a nonerotic aspect of the relationship, the one that Janet Giele calls affection. As I have pointed out elsewhere,[22] mutual erotic attraction has one particularly severe limitation as the basis of the kind of solidarity that can involve large numbers of people over long periods of time—in which I would include specifically transgenerational periods. This derives from the simple fact that erotic stimulation is a matter of organic body relatedness and requires access to the body of the partner. This is clearly most readily attainable in

[20] See Talcott Parsons and Gerald M. Platt, *The American University* (Cambridge: Harvard University Press, 1973), especially chaps. 4 and 8.

[21] Sigmund Freud, *The Interpretation of Dreams,* Vols. IV–V of the *Standard Edition of the Complete Psychological Works of Sigmund Freud,* translated by James Strachey in collaboration with Anna Freud (London: The Hogarth Press and the Institute of Psychoanalysis, 1958). See also Talcott Parsons, *"The Interpretation of Dreams* by Sigmund Freud," *Daedalus,* CIII (Winter 1974), 91–96.

[22] Parsons, "Belief, Unbelief and Disbelief."

the dyadic relationship of which the prototype has become marriage. Some approximation to its meaningfulness can be attained in wider groups—"group sex," for example, has developed certain attractions. The group in such a case, however, cannot be a very extensive one because of the inherent limitations on the universalization of bodily contact among large numbers of people, and the attenuation of solidary relationships.

Given these considerations, I think it follows that some transcending of the consideration of erotic pleasure in defining the mediation and bonding of solidarity is a fundamental functional imperative for large communities. Freud provided a psychological reference for this transformation in his famous concept of sublimation. The main purport of this crucial concept is that what in its genetic origin may have been a purely erotic basis of attachment can be and frequently is transformed to a level of generality that omits the erotic component or reduces it to purely symbolic status. In this statement I mean the term "symbolic" to signify something that is expressively meaningful but, as such, does not play a determinative role.

It seems to me that what in a religious or quasi-religious context we tend to refer to as love can be interpreted in more technical sociological jargon as a bond of solidarity between persons as individuals and involving their mutual identity as members of a collective entity which is mediated not by accessibility to mutual erotic pleasure but by a more generalized accessibility to an "attitudinal" entity, which I call affect. Without some such mechanism I cannot see how secularized "love solidarity" of large communities can be sociologically possible. It seems to me it is clearly impossible if the positive condition is mutual erotic concern of every member with every other.

Such solidarity, of course, involves multiple levels in the general system of action. Affect as I understand it, since it is a medium at the general level of action, is not specifically internal to the social system, but mediates between the social system and the other components of the general system, notably the personality of the individual on the one side, and the cultural system on the other. Insofar then as the new religious tendency wishes to make the pattern of mutual love salient, I think it is particularly bound to the effective operation of the medium of affect. It should, however, be kept clearly in mind that affect in my present sense is a *medium* of interchange and not the primary bond of solidarity itself. I mean this in a sense parallel to that in which money is a medium operating in a market system of economic exchange. But such solidarity as participants in such a market system are able to achieve is not a function only of their monetary dealings and the interests associated with them.

The question therefore arises of what other than affect—or love—is a functional requirement of the viability and stability of large-scale community structures characterized at the social system level by the kind of solidarity which the proponents of the love doctrine clearly have in mind.

I raise this question on the assumption that the Puritan pattern has in fact prevailed in the sense that spiritual solidarity—which may be defined as religiously motivated love—cannot be projected into a transcendental world, but must somehow be defined and institutionalized as part of the empirically given system of human action—social, cultural, psychological, and otherwise. In that sense, but only in that sense, it must be a "secular" phenomenon.

I think the key term here is "institutionalization." One way of stating what I have in mind involves the familiar concept "spontaneity." By its radical proponents, spontaneity seems to connote the "giving" of oneself in what I define as a love relationship without any expectation of reciprocity of any sort. To be "pure" such giving should indeed be explicitly defined as independent of any expectations of reciprocity. In marginal human conditions instances of this type surely do occur. Yet I think we are entitled to be highly skeptical that they can be stabilized and generalized to constitute a major movement that can shape civilizational futures. The reciprocity of giving, however, cannot be posited only on the giving relationship itself with no pattern of the definition of mutual obligation and no supplementation by other factors in the determination of social relationships.

In the Christian tradition, the love of Christians for one another and for the church was considered not to be totally spontaneous but a matter of obligation. Fulfillment of this obligation was a condition of acceptability in the church and in the religious orders as a full Christian, and failure in fulfillment of this obligation defined unacceptable behavior. In other words, one could not love or not love according to momentary whim; religiously acceptable love had to have the quality of diffuseness and enduringness of which Schneider speaks in the context of modern marriage. The regulation and in a certain sense assurance of such reciprocity seems to me the only basis on which involvement of a generalized medium of the character which I assert to be that of affect is functionally significant.

For the regime of love to be stable, it must institutionalize the expectation of both diffuse and enduring ties. This in my opinion transforms it from a matter of simple encounter between persons into a nexus of solidarity in the institutionalized sociological sense of that term.

Solidarity in this sense, however, is *never* a function of a single variable, but always involves a combination of essential factors. I conceive these factors to operate at both the level of the general system of action and that of the social system. At the level of general action, in addition to affective attraction itself, I feel that absolute necessities are, first, the kind of personal motivational commitment that, following Freud, I call the cathexis of social objects, and second, a component transcending the mutual attraction of individuals for each other, affirming allegiance to a much more broadly defined order which I would define as a moral order. Without attachment beyond the level of motivational self-interest to other objects and without commitment to participate in a moral order, a community that uses the primary symbol of love cannot be an authentically stable community. If these components, other than what are sometimes thought of as affective ties taken alone, are essential to the stabilization of a love-dominated community at the general action level, namely, the cathexis of objects and the commitment to a moral order, there is a further set of such conditions at the social system level. The two most important of these I conceive to be, first, responsiveness to appropriate leadership initiative in defining the obligations, rights, and tasks of any such collectivity, including those applicable to its nonleader members, and second, what I have called the valuation or the commitment to valued association, which I consider to be a specification of a commitment to a moral order.[23] Hence I very specifically assert the Durkheimian position that not only is a religious entity a moral community but it must for viability extend this community aspect to meet the exigencies of stability on a social level.[24]

Finally, I would also include in this set of conditions that there should be an adequate rational component. Many of the counterculture people who have functioned as the spearhead of the movements I have been discussing have stood in sharp reaction against the whole rationalistic cognitive tradition of Western society. In my view this reaction has been pressed too far; if what they advocate were in fact fully implemented, it would produce a drastically unstable orientation.[25] There must be a major component of rationality at at least two levels in a viable "religion of love." The first of these must be at the level of belief in the more or less traditional religious sense. It is not possible to have a system of spontaneous sentiments which are not regulated by the cognitive discipline of beliefs. Beliefs, of course, need not be rigid as they have been in some religious systems. On the other hand, the cognitive questions about who we are, where we belong in the universe, what we are doing and expected to do, cannot be left without any cognitive response. It is clearly not sufficient to say that people should "do their own thing" in the sense of whatever they have a momentary impulse to do.

This component of rationalization, however, must extend beyond the cultural level to the social. The general purport of such a requirement is that persons who share what is in some sense a common religious orientation—for example, as defined by mutual love—must have some cognitively intelligible definition of what this entails with respect to their own conduct and their expectations of reciprocal conduct from each other and from others with whom they interact. This seems to me to be a profound mean-

---

[23] See the categories developed in "Technical Appendix: Some General Theoretical Paradigms," in Parsons and Platt, *The American University*, pp. 423–447.

[24] Emile Durkheim, *The Elementary Forms of the Religious Life*, translated by Joseph W. Swain (New York: Free Press, 1965).

[25] See David Martin, "The Naked Person," *Encounter*, XL (June 1973), 12–20.

ing of Durkheim's dictum that a religion constitutes not only a moral community but one which may be called, as he put it, a "church." A church is an institutionalized social organization of human participants. To be a viable collective entity it must have rules—rules that can be communicated and understood in cognitive terms. It cannot be a community within which "anything goes," and this way of putting it has not only moral but also cognitive implications.

The Expressive Revolution

It is altogether possible that a new religious movement of far-reaching importance will follow the kinds of beginnings I have sketched above. If this does occur, it will be a major aspect of what I would call the expressive revolution. It would result in a tilting of the previous balance between the rational-cognitive components of our cultural orientation and the modes of its institutionalization in favor of the affective-expressive emphasis relative to the cognitive-rationalistic emphasis. As such, it would inevitably include a value change, but not a drastically revolutionary repudiation of the society's previous value system. The primary change would be in the relative standing of different components of the inherited value system.

One way of formulating this point is in terms of an interpretation of the frequent allegation that the Protestant ethic is dead.[26] In my opinion the Protestant ethic is far from dead. It continues to inform our orientations to a very important sector of life today as it did in the past. We do value systematic rational work in "callings," and we do so out of what is at some level a religious background. In my opinion the instrumental apparatus of modern society could not function without a generous component of this kind of evaluation. This, however, is not to say that systematic rational work is the only thing we value. In a certain sense we have always valued solidary human relationships, community in some sense, and love relationships. I suggest that the expressive revolution is bringing about an enhanced valuation of this latter set of components of the value system.

The counterculture version, with its exclusive emphasis on pure expressiveness and pure love and glorification of the totally autonomous self, seems to me to be definitely not viable as a cultural and social phenomenon. But to say this is not to say that the counterculture is not a symptom of a profound change which is already under way. Indeed, I think it is.

There is a negative as well as a positive sense in which the counterculture may be interpreted as a harbinger. This is that it is a reaction against certain aspects of the rationalistic and utilitarian individualism of the recent phases of development of American society and industrial societies generally. This reaction has been spearheaded particularly in the student move-

[26] This has been most recently asserted with no qualifications in Daniel Bell, *The Coming of Post-Industrial Society* (New York: Basic Books, 1973).

ment of recent years, but if it is confined to the student generation it cannot take hold as a major transformation of the cultural-religious situation of the society as what we might call a new version of the civil religion. For that to happen it must involve a much broader band of the age structure than the student population.

The Watergate scandal and the whole complex of activities associated with the Nixon administration which have so preoccupied the American public in the last year or two represent the kind of individualistic corruption well suited to serve as the negative target of a movement of resuscitation. I think this movement must point in the direction of a lessening of the stress on self-interest in the traditional utilitarian sense, of a strong reinforcement of the affective solidarity—that is, love—of individuals for each other, and of revival of the sense of collective solidarity which was an essential part of the original Puritan ideal.

A further important point needs to be made about the contemporary situation. Certainly for American conditions I would add to the other non-affective components of a viable new religious movement that it should fit with a pluralistic social ethic and social structure and should not manifest the monolithic characteristics either of the community characterized in Rousseau's thinking by the General Will or the community posited by Marxian socialism. There is a certain sense in which this condition is both over- and underemphasized in the counterculture.[27] One might say that in such circles there is an utter horror of any requirements of doctrinal conformity, although pragmatically within such groups severe pressures to peer conformity often actually operate. To have a serious chance to be widely institutionalized, such a movement in my opinion must be in some basic sense compatible with continued allegiance to Catholic, Protestant, and Jewish religious commitments, to secular humanism, and also to a tentative and exploratory set of allegiances to Oriental religions, notably in the Hindu-Buddhist complex. This religious pluralism, or extended ecumenism, if the term is appropriate, seems to me the only possible system that would be congruent with the structural pluralism of American society and the relation of that to its emerging pattern of individualism.

Let me make a very brief comment on this emerging pattern. I have in a number of places referred to the conception of "institutionalized individualism" by deliberate contrast with the utilitarian version. In the pattern of institutionalized individualism the keynote is not the direct utilitarian conception of "the rational pursuit of self-interest" but a much broader conception of the self-fulfillment of the individual in a social setting in which the aspect of solidarity, as I have discussed it, figures at least as prominently as does that of self-interest in the utilitarian sense. I have a profound conviction that, unlike the Marxian solution to the problems of

---

[27] See Robert K. Merton, "Insiders and Outsiders: A Chapter in the Sociology of Knowledge," *American Journal of Sociology,* LVIII (July 1972), 9–47; reprinted in Robert K. Merton *The Sociology of Science,* edited by Norman W. Storer (Chicago: University of Chicago Press, 1973).

industrial society, the sacrifice of individualism is not indicated, is not necessary, and would be particularly inappropriate to American conditions. Specifically, I think that the kinds of restrictions on individual freedom, particularly in the cultural sphere, which have been conspicuously manifested in the Soviet Union, even very recently, constitute a danger of a quite different kind from the one that I think is developing in this society. That is to say, I expect that the new religion of love will manifest a strong individualistic emphasis, that people will love as individuals, and that they will form attachments of love to other objects also with a very high valence attached to the individuality of the object.

The above is about as circumstantial an account as is yet feasible of the kind of movement that I think has already occurred in an incipient form and has a chance of very significant further development in the American situation. I would emphasize its basic continuity with the American civil religion as this has been outlined by Bellah, but I would also emphasize the emergence of new emphases and new components into salience. Finally, however, I wish to insist very strongly that "love is not enough." If the movement is to be viable and to have a major transforming effect on the culture and society, it must incorporate conditions other than the mutual love of participants.

To recapitulate what I said above, the new religious movement will have to have a political component in the sense of adequately effective leadership. Second, there will have to be a commitment widely shared in the movement to a pattern of moral order to what I have called "valued association." Third, and by no means least important, there will have to be a cognitive-rational component—that is to say, at the religious level a belief system and at the level of moral implication a rationally defensible ethic. This, in my opinion, will articulate with the famous Protestant ethic, but will not be identical with the version that has been historically operative and has attracted the greatest attention. Let me repeat, however, that I do not for a moment think that the Protestant ethic is dead.

Finally, I am very strongly of the opinion that the new religion, precisely because it will be in a certain historic sense a secular religion, must achieve, if it is to be viable, a special and new level of integration with the secular society in which it comes to be institutionalized. This requirement clearly includes integration with the rational-technological aspect of that society, which is said by so many proponents of the counterculture to be an intolerable feature of modern industrial society. To me it is inconceivable that modern industrial society is to be abolished. It can be modified and transformed, but I would follow Marx's profound insight in saying that the "productive forces" which have created an industrial society will remain indispensable to human welfare and it is the most drastically fatal kind of romanticism to advocate their destruction.

PART IV

THE HUMAN CONDITION

Introduction to Part IV

AFTER WHAT HAS BEEN SAID in the General Introduction and other introductory discussions, the Introduction to Part IV can be brief. The pièce de résistance is clearly Chapter 15, "A Paradigm of the Human Condition." It seemed best to give this selection the place of honor as the final chapter of the book especially since more than any other chapter it looks toward the future of the development of this kind of theory. It did, however, seem appropriate also to include in Part IV Chapter 14, "Death in the Western World," because this essay is so closely related to the paradigm. Indeed, as was noted in the General Introduction, "Death in the Western World" was written for the new *Encyclopedia of Bioethics* immediately after the completion of the first draft of "A Paradigm of the Human Condition." Readers with a specially strong theoretical interest may well prefer to read Chapter 14 after the more general Chapter 15. One of the great virtues of books, as distinguished from aural communications, is freedom to choose the order in which to pay attention to component parts.

The only other point about Chapter 14 that needs to be made here is to remind the reader that it is the third in a series of attempts by me to deal with the problem of the meaning of death in modern society (as noted in the Introduction to Part III). The first was the paper, in collaboration with Victor M. Lidz, entitled "Death in American Society";[1] the second, Chapter 12 of the present volume, "The 'Gift of Life' and Its Reciprocation," was written with Renée C. Fox and Victor Lidz. In contrast, I am the sole author of Chapter 14, which differs from its predecessors in two important respects. The first is the much more developed and explicit use of a Kantian philosophical framework—a direct consequence of the work I had done earlier on Chapter 15, the relevance of which to the theme of Chapter 14 seemed overwhelmingly clear. The second difference is also a consequence of the theoretical developments that so far have culminated in Chapter 15; namely, greater clarification of the relations between the treatment of certain problems at the level of action and at that of the or-

[1] Talcott Parsons and Victor M. Lidz, "Death in American Society," in Edwin Schneidman (ed.), *Essays in Self-Destruction* (New York: Science House, 1967).

ganic system, a clarification that is particularly important for understanding the problem of human reaction to human deaths. After all, it is in the first instance the human *organism* that dies. The fate of the personality is, philosophically and theologically, far more problematical. It was considerations such as these that led me to put greater stress than before on the biological normality of death and thus to raise serious questions about the tenability of the common thesis that American culture is prominently characterized by the "denial of death."

Turning now to Chapter 15, it is important to note that the initiation of the line of thought that eventuated in this essay (which has not been published elsewhere) was the hunch that the four-function paradigm, with which I had been working for about twenty years, could provide an analytical framework whereby the human action system could be placed *relative* to other features of the world with which we humans necessarily have occasion to deal. This idea crystallized in the academic quiet of the summer of 1974. As it took shape, I drafted a brief memorandum, which I sent to a few people with whom I had had close intellectual associations. Among them were the colleagues with whom I had worked in the previous academic year at the University of Pennsylvania—Renée Fox, Victor Lidz, Harold Bershady, and Willy de Craemer. On my rejoining this faculty in the fall of 1974, we decided to organize a small discussion group on this general topic, and we met regularly during the academic years 1974–1975 and 1975–1976. In the spring term of 1976, we were joined by Charles Bosk. The group also had one meeting with A. Hunter Dupree and two with Hildred Geertz and Clifford Geertz. "Rump" meetings, held when Fox and de Craemer were abroad, including a notable one with Robert N. Bellah, also took place in the fall of 1976. We plan to publish a collaborative volume as soon as feasible, but in the meantime the group has kindly given me permission to publish the draft of a general statement, which I prepared in the summer of 1976 and have substantially revised in 1977, in the present volume. Its indebtedness to them should be evident.[2]

The hunch I mentioned had an initial payoff and the basic paradigm (Figure 1 of Chapter 15) crystallized early enough so that it could be included in the memorandum of the summer of 1974. As is clear from the essays included in Parts I–III of this volume and the introductory materials that accompany them, there had been a long buildup to this breakthrough. The key was the conception that all the principal components of the human

---

[2] The title of the project, the analysis of the human condition, was also agreed upon by the Philadelphia group. It is of course a rather widely used term, for example, Hannah Arendt, *The Human Condition* (Chicago: University of Chicago Press, 1970). We, however, above all had in mind its earlier use by André Malraux as the title of his famous novel *La Condition humaine* (Paris: Gallimard, 1933). Unfortunately, in our opinion, the English translation is entitled *Man's Fate*, H. M. Chevalier (New York: Modern Library, 1934). We think the original French title is much more appropriate.

condition could be fitted into a cybernetic hierarchy. The most important single clue to the place of the action system lay in the relation of the sciences dealing with action to the other sciences. It seemed clear that the classification that has come to be institutionalized in modern academic organization as comprising the physical, the biological, and the social sciences could be used to differentiate three of the four functional subsystems of the human condition for theoretical purposes.

The physical and the organic world obviously constitute, in the technical, scientific sense, environments of human life and activities. Since Durkheim, however, it has become common to speak of the social environment of the *action* of the human individual.[3] By this path of reasoning I arrived at the ideas that human experience could be divided into three primary categories and that all three could be conceived to constitute environments. The idea of the order of their hierarchical relations was by this reasoning already established. It thus seemed to make eminent sense to treat the physical world as the adaptive subsystem since it is above all, in its meaning for humans, the ultimate source of the conditional resources on which we depend (energy, materials, etc.). The organic world, then, is not only an environment of action but also the organizational base of human action since all human individuals are living organisms, belonging to a distinctive organic species. No action system dissociated from living human or similar organisms indeed seems conceivable. Hence, it also stands to reason that these components are, from the human point of view, integrated with each other principally in and through the system of action, in the technical sense of our usage.

This left the pattern-maintenance cell unspecified in content, but there was a very obvious candidate for the place. This problem concerns the rationale behind placing a set of essays in the sociology of religion in Part III of this volume, immediately preceding the treatment of the human condition. Certainly, since writing *The Structure of Social Action*,[4] I have been seriously concerned with the status of the category "nonempirical reality." That such a category has to make scientific sense was a clear inference from my own analysis of the methodological difficulties of the several varieties of positivism. Substantively, the special influence on my position was Weber's work on the sociology of religion.[5] Recognition of such a concept as a residual category is surely better than denial of its relevance altogether, but as in the case of the parallel category of "nonrational" to leave it at that is less than satisfactory.

With respect to its cognitively accessible "existential" aspects, which

---

[3] See the Introduction to Part III and see also Chapter 10 of this volume.

[4] Talcott Parsons, *The Structure of Social Action* (1937; reprint ed., New York: Free Press, 1949).

[5] Max Weber, *Gesammelte Aufsätze zur Religionssoziologie* (Tübingen: Mohr, 1921), 3 vols.

surely are less than exhaustive of the category, placing it in the pattern-maintenance cell of a functional paradigm seemed to be an important step in theoretical specification and clarification.

That there was a preliminary acceptable fit of this placement in the more general paradigm was agreed on by the Philadelphia discussion group; hence, the provisional designation of the P–M subsystem of the human condition as telic. In addition, in the meeting mentioned earlier, this conceptualization proved stimulating to Robert Bellah in its potential for further theoretical development in his field of special interest, the sociology of religion.

This central paradigm remained of focal significance to the Philadelphia group for the two academic years in which we met regularly. There were wide-ranging discussions touching on many phases of the intricate problems, scientific and philosophical, and it was only on the basis of these discussions that I felt myself in a position further to elaborate upon the implications of the paradigm.

In the sense of formal theory construction these steps followed the same pattern that had proved fruitful on two less generalized levels, namely, first that of the social system and second that of the general system of action. Two main steps in this development involved formalization. They followed the same formal models that had been used in the Technical Appendix of *The American University* for the social system and the general system of action, respectively.[6] The first is presented in Figure 4 of Chapter 15, "Media and Their Normative Contexts." It suggests the designation of four such media, each anchored in one of the four functional systems, on the analogy of money, political power, influence, and value-commitments in the social system. Associated with each medium, on a one-to-one basis, are what have been called a "category of orientation," on the one hand, and a "standard of evaluation," on the other. I shall not anticipate the discussion of Chapter 15 by enumerating these twelve conceptions here. It will be noted, however, that one of the suggested media is health, which is anchored in the organic system (see the Introduction to Part I and see Chapter 3).

The second formal step beyond Figure 1 was the development of categories to designate what is involved in each of the six sets of double interchanges that are posited as taking place among the four primary subsystems of the type of functionally differentiated systems we have been dealing with. It is clear that since we have confined the phenomenon of symbolic level expression and understanding of meaning to the action system, our previous restriction to "generalized *symbolic* media of interchange" could

[6] Talcott Parsons and Gerald M. Platt, in collaboration with Neil J. Smelser, *The American University* (Cambridge, Mass.: Harvard University Press, 1973), "Technical Appendix: Some General Theoretical Paradigms," pp. 423–447.

not be adhered to for the human condition; this problem is further discussed in Chapter 15. Again, I shall not anticipate the discussion to follow by further elucidation here. The interchange set is presented in Figure 5 of the essay.

Carrying formalization as far as these two steps have attempted to do is surely a kind of theoretical tour de force. Since this is a first attempt in a very unfamiliar area, so far as systematization is concerned it cannot be but exceedingly tentative. It seems to me, however, that only when such an attempt is made and the targets thereby set up systematically shot at—so that some will fall down but maybe some will stand fast—can a solid basis be established from which to judge whether formalization of this sort is theoretically fruitful or not, and if so how it can be carried out. Such "shooting at" is of course expected to lead to revision not only in the particular categories proposed but also in the more general structure of the conceptual scheme into which they have been fitted.

It goes without saying that substantively most of the categories proposed are already familiar. This is exemplified by the borrowing of three central concepts from Kant.[7] What is new is not so much the categories themselves as the way in which they have been ordered relative to each other. It also goes without saying that such sense as the proposals advanced in Chapter 15 make is attributable to long experience in working with similar problems for other systems (in my case, most notably the social system and the general system of action) and long discussions of many of the problems with my colleagues.

The final section of Chapter 15 attempts to use the outline that has been worked out to try to clarify some very general problems in the theoretical analysis of human action and interests. The two sets of problems I have chosen to discuss are, first, the very old and pervasive matter of the relations between the cognitive aspect of human orientation and what has often been called the affective aspect. Put a little differently, it is the problem of the relation between the rational and nonrational. The second problem area concerns the broader, transsocial significance of the old sociological concept pair of age and sex not only as these appear as dimensions of human social organization but also as they help to link the latter with the organic realm, as well as with the telic (in our terms), in that they play such a prominent part in so many cases of religious symbolism.

Most generally, however, I hope the reader will treat Chapter 15 as it is meant—a highly tentative first attempt. He can expect a further set of

---

[7] Set forth in Immanuel Kant's three critiques: *The Critique of Pure Reason*, trans. N. K. Smith (New York: Humanities Press, 1950); *The Critique of Practical Reason*, trans. and ed. L. W. Beck (Chicago: University of Chicago Press, 1950); and *The Critique of Judgment*, trans. J. C. Meredith (Oxford: Clarendon, 1964). The three critiques were first published in German in 1781, 1788, and 1790, respectively.

developments over the name not of one but of several authors. But this will certainly constitute at best one further set of steps in the development of the implications of an idea. If there is anything seriously important in the idea, its repercussions, including criticism of it, should be expected to be felt for a long time to come.

14. Death in the Western World

THAT THE DEATH of every known human individual has been one of the central facts of life so long as there has been any human awareness of the human condition does not mean that, being so well known, it is not problematical. On the contrary, like history, it has needed to be redefined and newly analyzed, virtually with every generation. However, as has also been the case with history, with the advancement of knowledge later reinterpretations may have some advantages over earlier.

I start from the proposition that if we are to speak of the death of individuals, we need some conceptualization, beyond common sense, of what a human individual, or "person," is. First, I do not propose to discuss the meaning of the deaths of members of other species, insects, elephants, or dogs, but only of human individuals. Second, I propose to confine discussion to individual persons and not to examine societies, civilizations, or races in this sense.

I

Within these limitations I should like to start with the statement that the human individual is a synthesized *combination* of a living organism and a "personality system," conceived and analyzed at the level of "action" in the sense in which I and various others have used that term.[1] In older terminology, he is a combination of a "body" and a "mind." The concept of a personality as *analytically* distinguished from an organism is no more mystical than is that of a "culture" as distinguished from the human population (of organisms) who are its "bearers." The primary criterion of per-

---

[1] Talcott Parsons, *Social Systems and the Evolution of Action Theory* (New York: Free Press, 1977).

---

sonality, as distinguished from the organism, is an organization in terms of symbols and their meaningful relations to each other and to persons. In the process of evolution, personalities should be regarded as emergent from the organic level, as are cultural systems in a different, though related way.

Human individuals, seen in their organic aspect, come into being through bisexual reproduction—and birth—as do all the higher organisms. They then go through a more or less well defined life course and eventually die. The most important single difference among such individual organisms is the duration of their lives, but for each species there is a maximum span: for humans, it is somewhere between ninety and one hundred years. In this sense death is universal, the only question being "at what age?" Within these limits the circumstances of both life and death vary enormously.

It seems that these considerations have an immediate bearing on one of the current controversies about death, namely, the frequent allegation that American society—and some say others—attempts to "deny death." [2] Insofar as this is the case (and I am skeptical), the contention has to be in the face of a vast body of biological knowledge. If any biological proposition can be regarded as firmly established, it is that, for sexually reproducing species, the mortality of individual, "phenotypical" organisms is completely normal. Indeed, mortality could not have evolved if it did not have positive survival value *for the species,* unless evolutionary theory is completely wrong. This fact will be a baseline for our whole analysis.

The human individual is not only a living organism but also a special kind of organism who uses symbols, notably linguistic ones. He learns symbolic meanings, communicates with others and with himself through them as media, and regulates his behavior, his thought, and his feelings in symbolic terms. I call the individual in this aspect an *actor.* Is an actor "born"? Clearly not in the sense in which an organism is. However, part of the development of the human child is a gradual and complicated process, which has sometimes been called *socialization,* whereby the personality becomes formed. The learning of patterns of relation to others, of language, and of structured ways of handling one's own action in relation to the environment is the center of this process.

Does a personality, then, also die? Because the symbiosis between organism and personality is so close, just as no personality in the human sense can be conceived to develop independently of a living child organism, so it is reasonable to believe that no human personality can be conceived

[2] See Peter Berger and Richard Liban, "Kulturelle Wertstruktur und Bestattungspraktiken in den Vereinigten Staaten," *Kölner Zeitschrift fur Soziologie und Social Psychologie,* no. 2 (1960); and Robert Fulton in collaboration with Robert Bendiksen (eds.), *Death and Identity* (rev. ed.). (Bowie, Md.: Charles Press, 1976), especially the articles by Robert J. Lifton, "The Sense of Immortality: On Death and the Continuity of Life" (pp. 19–34), and by Erik Lindemann, "Symptomatology and Management of Acute Grief" (pp. 210–221).

as such to survive the death of the same organism, in the organic sense of death. With respect to causation, however, if the personality is an empirical reality, it certainly influences what happens to the organism, the person's "body," as well as vice versa. The extreme case is suicide, which surely can seldom be explained by purely somatic processes, without any "motives" being involved, as often can a death from cancer. But more generally there is every reason to believe that there are "psychic" factors in many deaths, all manner of illnesses, and various other organic events.

It is firmly established that the viability of the individual organism, human and nonhuman, is self-limiting. Thus, even in the absence of un-favorable environmental conditions, in the course of the "aging" process, there will occur gradual impairment of various organic capacities, until some combination of these impairments proves fatal. Organic death can be staved off by medical measures but cannot be totally prevented. There seems every reason to believe, but there is less clear-cut evidence on this point, that the same is in principle true of the action-personality component of the individual. This means that, with aging, various components of that complex entity lose the necessary capacities to maintain its balances, which eventually will lead to a breakdown. The cases in which there is virtual cessation of personality function without organic death are suggestive in this sense. More generally, if, as I strongly believe, the phenomena of mental illness are real and not merely epiphenomena of organic processes, then it stands to reason that some of them can be severe enough to eventu-ate in personality death, partly independent of organic death.

We have already noted that at the organic level the human individual does not stand alone but is part of an intergenerational chain of indefinite, though not infinite, durability, most notably the species. The individual organism dies, but if he/she reproduces, the "line" continues into future generations. This intergenerational continuity is as much a fact of life as are individual births and deaths.

There is a direct parallel on the action side: An individual personality is "generated" in symbiosis with a growing individual human organism and dies with that organism. But the individual personality is embedded in transindividual action systems, at two levels, social systems (most notably, whole societies) and cultural systems. There is a close analogy between these two and the relation between somatoplasm and germ plasm on the organic side, both of which are "carried" by the individual organism. Thus, the sociocultural "matrix" in which the individual personality is embedded is in an important sense the counterpart of the population-species matrix in which the individual organism is embedded.

At the organic level the individual organism dies, but the species con-tinues, "life goes on." Also, the individual personality dies, but the society and cultural system, of which in life he was a part, also "goes on." I strongly suspect that this parallel is more than simple analogy.

What is organic death? It is of course a many-faceted thing, but as Freud and many others have said, it is in one principal aspect the "return to the inorganic" state. At this level the human body, as that of other organisms, is made up of inorganic materials but *organized* in quite special ways. When that organization breaks down, the constituent materials are no longer part of a living organism but come to be assimilated to the inorganic environment. In a certain sense this insight has been ancient religious lore; witness the Gospel, "Dust thou art, to dust thou shalt return."

Is the death of a personality to be simply assimilated to this organic paradigm? Most positivists and materialists would say, yes. This answer, however, has not been accepted by the majority in most human societies and cultures. From such very primitive peoples as the Australian aborigines, especially as their religion was analyzed by Durkheim,[3] to the most sophisticated of the world religions, there have persisted beliefs in the existence of an individual soul, which can be conceived both to antedate and to survive the individual organism or body, though the ideas of preexistence and of survival have not always coexisted in any given culture. The literature of cultural anthropology and of comparative religion can supply many instances.[4] The issue of the individuality of this nonorganic component of the human individual, outside its symbiosis with the living organism, is also a basis of variability.

II

Western civilization has had a historical background in which the dominant religious influence has been that of Christianity. Science has in recent times been the major focus of interpretation of the nonorganic component. Let us then try to outline the main Christian patterns of orientation and indicate modifications of the old materialistic-religious dichotomy that seem to be dictated by the emergence of a complex of disciplines dealing with human problems at the level of action.

In collaboration with Renée Fox and Victor Lidz I have presented an analysis of the Christian orientation to death.[5] There is no doubt of the predominance of a duality of levels in the Christian paradigm of the human condition, the levels of the spiritual and the temporal, as one formula states it. There is a striking resemblance between this duality and that in the

[3] Emile Durkheim, *The Elementary Forms of the Religious Life,* trans. J. W. Swain (New York: Free Press, 1965; first published in French in 1912).

[4] See Robert N. Bellah, "Religious Evolution," *American Sociological Review* (1961): 358–374, reprinted in idem, *Beyond Belief: Essays on Religion in a Post-Industrial World* (New York: Harper & Row, 1970), pp. 20–50.

[5] Talcott Parsons, Renée C. Fox, and Victor M. Lidz, "The 'Gift of Life' and Its Reciprocation," *Social Research,* vol. 39, no. 3 (1972): 367–415. Chap. 12 of this book.

organic world between species and individual organism, as well as between the former and that in the action world between individual personality and sociocultural system. The Christian paradigm, however, seems to bracket the human condition within a still broader dichotomy. On the one hand, there is the material-temporal world, of which one religious symbol is "dust" as cited earlier. On the other, there is the spiritual world of "eternal life," which is the location of things divine, not human. The individual soul is conceived as in some sense an "emanation" from this second "world."

We attempted,[6] relying heavily on biblical documentation, to interpret this syndrome in terms of Marcel Mauss's paradigm of the gift and its reciprocation.[7] Seen in this way, the life of the individual is a gift from God, and like other gifts it creates expectations of reciprocation. Living "in the faith" is part of the reciprocation but, more important for us, dying in the faith completes the cycle. It is surely notable that our ordinary language is permeated with references to giving in this connection. Thus, a woman is said to *give* birth to a child and we often say that in dying a person *"gives* up the ghost."

The language of giving also permeates the transcendental level of symbolism in the Christian context. Thus, Mary, like any other woman, *gave* birth to Jesus. God also *gave* his "only begotten Son" for the redemption of humankind. Finally, Jesus, in the Crucifixion and thus the Eucharist, *gave* his blood for the same purpose. By the doctrine of reciprocation mankind assumes, it may be said, three principal obligations, namely to "accept" the human condition as ordained by divine will, i.e., the gift of life, to live in the faith, and to die in the faith. If these conditions are fulfilled, salvation is the reward.

One further point should be stressed: the way in which the symbiosis of the organic and the action level of the human condition is symbolized in this Christian complex (that is, through the sacralization of the family, which is the primary social organization having to do with human reproduction, birth and death, health and illness, and their relations). The focus here is the Holy Family, with even the Trinity having certain family-like characteristics: witness God the Father and God the Son. It may further be noted that the two most important Christian seasonal festivals "celebrate" the birth of Jesus—Christmas—and commemorate his death— namely, Easter, though with the doctrine of resurrection, commemoration also becomes celebration.

Christianity, in its Catholic form, has institutionalized a special duality in the human societies and cultures in which it has existed; namely, in medieval terms, that between church and state. These institutional complexes

[6] Ibid.

[7] Marcel Mauss, *The Gift: Forms and Functions of Exchange in Archaic Societies* New York: Free Press, 1954; first published in French in 1925).

have very closely corresponded to the duality, within the individual between soul and body, with the church having custody, as it were, of the soul.
A major change, however, occurred with the Protestant Reformation. This
particular version of Christian dualism was "collapsed" in that the sacraments no longer mediated (for Protestants) between God and man; no
priesthood held the "power of the keys"; and withdrawal from the "world"
into monasteries was abolished.

The primary consequence of this collapsing was not, as it has often been
interpreted, so much the secularization of the religious component of society as it was the sacralization of secular society, making it the forum for
the religious life, notably, though by no means exclusively, through work
in a "calling" (as Weber held).[8]

Though Calvin, in his doctrine of predestination, attempted to remove
salvation altogether from human control, this doctrine could not survive
the cooling of the "effervescence" of the Reformation itself. Thus, later
versions of Protestantism all accepted some version of the bearing of the
individual's moral or attitudinal (faith) merit on salvation. Such control
as there was, however, was no longer vested in an ecclesiastical organization but was left to the individual, thus immensely increasing his religious
and moral responsibility.

The Reformation as such did not fundamentally alter the meaning of
death in human societies. The collapse of the Catholic version of duality,
however, put great pressure on the received doctrine of salvation. Hence,
the promise of a *personal* afterlife in "heaven," especially if this were conceived to be "eternal," which must be taken to mean altogether outside the
framework of time, became increasingly difficult to accept. The doctrine
of eternal punishment in some kind of "hell" has proved even more difficult to uphold.

The conception of a "higher" level of reality, a "supernatural" world,
did not in any immediate sense give way; yet, it became increasingly hard
to "visualize" it by simple extrapolation from this-worldly experience. Indeed, a fundamental challenge did emerge as part of the penumbra of the
rise of modern science, which by the eighteenth century had produced a
philosophy of scientific "materialism." The primary form of this was a
"monism" of the physical world. There was, at that time, little "scientific"
analysis of the world of action, or even of the organic world, and there
was a tendency to regard the physical universe as unchanging and hence
eternal. Death then was simple, namely, in Freud's formula, the "return
to the inorganic" state, which implies a complete negation of the conception of "eternal life" since the physical, inorganic world is by definition the
antithesis of life in any sense.[9]

---

[8] Max Weber, *The Protestant Ethic and the Spirit of Capitalism,* trans. T. Parsons
(New York: Scribner's, 1930; first published in German in 1904–1905).

[9] Sigmund Freud, *Beyond the Pleasure Principle,* in vol. 18 of *The Standard
Edition of the Complete Psychological Works of Sigmund Freud* (London: Hogarth

III

The development of science has over time changed these matters. The sciences of organic life underwent their first great efflorescence in the nineteenth century and have gone much further in the present one. Moreover, a conception of evolutionary change came to be at the very center of biological thought, crystallizing in the work of Darwin.[10] This development laid the foundations for the view of the biological normality of death.

A second and more recent development was the maturing of what we have been calling the sciences of *action*. These of course have deep roots in humanistic tradition, but only in recent times can a cluster of generalizing sciences be said to have branched off from the humanistic "trunk." Indeed, these disciplines may well not yet have had their "Darwin," though I am inclined to think that the Durkheim-Weber-Freud combination comes close to filling such a role. It seems that a conception of evolutionary change, articulating with the organic theory, has also become an integral part of this scientific movement.

There is also a parallel in that not only has this development of the action disciplines produced a useful conception of the human personality as analytically distinguished from the organism but also it has created an intellectual framework within which the mortality of this personality can be understood to be normal. Moreover, this personality, as entity, can be seen to develop, live, and die within a matrix that is analogous to the physico-organic species matrix of the individual organism. Seen in terms of the nature of societies and cultures, the death of individual persons is presumably just as normal as is that of individual organisms. Of course, again, this action matrix is conceived as evolving, in a sense parallel to organic evolution.

Not least important of the developments of science, finally, was the altered conception of the physical universe in recent times. First, there occurred the relativization of our knowledge of the physical world to the conditions of human observation of it, most saliently put in the ways in which Einstein's theory of relativity modified the previous assumptions of the absolute, empirical givenness of physical nature in Newtonian tradition.[11] Second, evolutionary ideas were extended to the physical cosmos. If one adds the physical to the organic and the action field one comes to the conclusion that for modern man the *whole* of empirical reality is in certain

---

Press and the Institute of Psychoanalysis, 1955; first published in German in 1920), pp. 7–66.

[10] Charles Darwin, *On the Origin of Species by Means of Natural Selection, or The Preservation of Favored Races in the Struggle for Life* (London: Murray, 1859).

[11] See Alfred N. Whitehead, *Science and the Modern World* (New York: Macmillan, 1925).

senses conceived to be relative to a human perspective and to be involved in evolutionary changes.

There is a parallel problem of relativization on the other side of the bracketing framework of the human condition. In the philosophical wake of Christian theology, as it were, there has been an energetic search for the conceptualization of the "metaphysical" *absolute*. In the context of the present analysis it seems that this can be likened to the search for the equally absolute, universal laws of physical nature. This quest, too, has been subjected to severe strain as a result of the altered conception of the human condition since the Reformation and has tended to break down in a comparable sense.

IV

Coming late in the crucial eighteenth century, the work of Immanuel Kant seems to me to have been the turning point away from *both* physical absolutism and metaphysical absolutism.[12] Thus, Kant fundamentally accepted the reality of the physical universe, as humanly known, but at the same time in a sense relativized our knowledge of it to the categories of the understanding, which are grounded not in our direct "experience" of physical reality but in something "transcending" this. At the same time, Kant relativized our conceptions of transcendental reality—the existence of which, note, he by no means denied—Kant was no materialist—to something closer to the human condition. Indeed, it may be suggested that, for "substantive" propositions about the absolute, Kant substituted a "procedural" conception.

Kant introduced the conception that what "pure" and "practical" reason can accomplish is to provide *formal,* as distinguished from *substantive,* categorization for human orientation in the relevant problem areas. For the empirical world it was above all the categories of the understanding and for the practical world (in his special sense) it was the categorical imperative which produced the formal structures.

That Kant's formalism in this sense is related to the use of procedural norms and considerations by others is indicated by his own explicit discussion of different kinds of *laws* in these connections. Thus, he held the categories of understanding to be essential to establishing laws for the

---

[12] Immanuel Kant, *The Critique of Pure Reason,* trans. N. K. Smith (New York: Macmillan, 1929); idem, *The Critique of Practical Reason,* trans. L. W. Beck (Chicago: University of Chicago Press, 1950); and *The Critique of Judgment,* trans. J. C. Meredith (Oxford: Clarendon, 1964). Originally published in German in 1781, 1788, and 1790, respectively.

physical world; whereas in his definition of the categorical imperative he specifically referred to a maxim as having to have the force of "the principle of a general act of *legislation* [*Gesetzgebung*]." [13] Surely, if procedural norms figure prominently anywhere in modern societies, it is in their legal systems.

It is further essential to realize that Kant did not leave the empirical and practical orders in a simple, yawning dichotomy relative to each other. In *The Critique of Judgment,*[14] the role he assigned to "esthetic judgment," as he called it, is explicitly that of *mediating,* from the human point of view, between the necessities of the empirical world and the freedom of the world of morality. It is notable that in this connection he spoke of both the "purposiveness" (*Zweckmässigkeit*) of nature and of individual self-interest, indeed pleasure (*Lust*—the same word used by Freud),[15] as well as of judgment as the mode of synthesizing the two.

Though Kant denied the possibility of reliable knowledge of the absolute, he insisted that, in all three of the spheres analyzed in his critiques, human orientation depends on a *transcendental* component, which is more than the simply "given" experience of either the "external" reality in question, of the source of human freedom, or, indeed, in the case of *The Critique of Judgment,* of the individual's own "subjectivity."

In his combination of relativizing and of yet insisting on the indispensability of recognizing a transcendental component of human orientation to the human condition, Kant explicitly included the belief in personal immortality, in the sense of eternal life, in his list, along with belief in the existence of God, beliefs that he maintained could not rationally be proved. Of course, this completely vitiated the fundamentalist (Catholic or Protestant) view of the meaning of death and, along with it, that of life.

At the same time, by contrast with scientific materialism, it is crucial in this connection that Kant did not collapse the difference of levels between the physical and what we may perhaps call the "telic" realm. He was, in this sense, neither a materialist nor an idealist but recognized the indispensability of both references and attempted to connect them with each other. Yet the way in which he proceeded to do so entailed complex redefinitions of received views throughout.

With respect to the bearing of Kant's philosophy and its influence through subsequent culture on the problem of the meaning of death, there are two primary, interconnected contexts to consider. The first concerns the intermediate zone *between* the realm of the material and that of the transcendental, in Kant's sense, which he tried in a tentative but very significant way to bridge in *The Critique of Judgment.* The second concerns above all the boundary relations between the sphere of action and that

[13] Kant, *Critique of Practical Reason.*
[14] Kant, *Critique of Judgment.*
[15] Freud, *Beyond the Pleasure Principle.*

aspect of the transcendental realm that Kant attempted to categorize in *The Critique of Practical Reason.*

With reference to the former context, we previously outlined the immense process of development, including differentiation, of the corpus of scientific knowledge, which has occurred roughly since Kant's time. The salient events of that development, from the present point of view, have been the development of biological knowledge and that of systematic, theoretical knowledge in the field of human action, as distinguished from the humanistic tradition. Within each of these spheres, then, there has appeared a crucial line of differentiation. In the organic this is the differentiation between the individual, phenotypical organism and the transgenerational, organic system (prototypically the species). The parallel differentiation within the action sphere is that between the individual as personality and the sociocultural matrix in which he is embedded. The two components of individuality meet in a special symbiosis to constitute a "person." This whole differentiated structure of the human condition may be said to have evolved, in our cultural system, since Kant wrote; nevertheless, it is congruent with, and in part anticipated and influenced by, the Kantian framework.

V

In certain respects the structure of the reality postulated between the two Kantian boundaries may be said to be symmetrical, coming to focus on the human individual. But there is one respect in which it is profoundly asymmetrical. This we may state in cybernetic terms; namely, in certain respects organic life can "control" components of the physical world and, in turn, human action systems can in a similar sense control the organic, in the first instance the human body. However, the source of organic energy is physical and that of personality, organic. From this point of view, the transcendental structure of "reason" in Kant's "practical" reference is the apex of the cybernetic hierarchy, so far as it involves the human condition. Kant's "relativism," then, may be interpreted to mean that he saw no reason to postulate an "absolute" reality that is humanly knowable, in either direction, but restricted his postulation to what we have called "procedural" forms.

It seems unnecessary to dwell on the problem of the meaning of purely organic death, which is adequately defined as "return to the inorganic state," except for one major point, of which presently. Some materialists still maintain that this is the only important meaning of death for human beings in modern societies. The proponents of this view, however, can scarcely claim to have the field to themselves [16] since the other direction of the cybernetic series must clearly be taken into account. Their view of the ultimate fate of the individual human being as organism—in an *analytical sense*—may well be correct, but we have argued all along that this creature is not *only* an organism but also a personality. What of *his* fate?

Certainly, incorporation in a "great chain of being," in Lovejoy's sense,[17] in either or both of these aspects can give meaning to a temporally limited life and hence to the termination of that life, long after the individual's death. One may surmise that the prominence of ancestral cults is especially marked in societies in which cultural status and social status have tended to be fused. In modern societies, however, they have come to be largely differentiated, especially through the externalization of cultural outputs in writing and printing and in works of art. Neither Kant nor Max Weber was, to my knowledge, one of my biological ancestors, yet I can consider both to have been cultural ancestors in whose line I feel honored to stand. To me, their lives, though limited in temporal duration, were profoundly meaningful; without them my own life would have been greatly impoverished.

I have argued that it was a primary contribution of Kant in his analysis of the relation of the human knower to "external reality," which for him was in the first instance that of the physical world, to refuse to reduce the relation to a simple "mirroring" of that reality in human consciousness, a view which would have erased an essential boundary between the human and the nonhuman worlds. If Kant was right in this position, it seems to me that there are parallels to his fundamental distinction between the sensory and the categorial components of human empirical knowledge on two levels. The first of these levels is the distinction between the phenotypical aspect of the higher organisms and the genotypical aspect, which is primarily visible only at the level of aggregates, notably the species. The second is the distinction between the human personality, in the action sense, and the larger action systems in which he is embedded, namely the social and cultural systems. With respect to the duality of components and the relations of these components to each other, it seems to me that there is a striking isomorphism. In all three cases the one component—sensory, phenotypical, individual—is temporally limited in its existence, whereas the other component, which is necessary to give the former meaning, is, in Kant's own term, "transcendental" by comparison. Surely such considerations have some bearing on the problem of the meaning of individual death in the human case.

---

[16] For a discussion of this view see the Introduction to William McLaughlin and Robert N. Bellah (eds.), *Religion in America* (Boston: Houghton Mifflin, 1969).

[17] Arthur O. Lovejoy, *The Great Chain of Being: A Study in the History of an Idea* (Cambridge, Mass.: Harvard University Press, 1961; first published in 1936).

If we accept Kant's fundamental position, which in essentials I do, then his skepticism about absolutes must apply on *both* sides of the fundamental dichotomy. Modern biology certainly must be classed as knowledge of the empirical world in his sense. Hence, the strictures he applied to physical knowledge must apply to it as well and, indeed, to our scientific knowledge of human action. In his famous terminology, there is no demonstrable knowledge of the *Ding an sich* in *any* scientific field.

We have continually stressed that, precisely in empirical terms, organic death is completely normal. We have, and according to Kant presumably can have, no knowledge of the survival of any organic entity after death except through the process of organic reproduction, through which the genetic heritage does indeed survive. Kant, however, would equally deny that such survival can be excluded on empirical grounds. This circumstance has an obvious bearing on the Christian doctrine of resurrection of the body. *If* resurrection is meant in a literal, biological sense—and I am aware that this is by no means universally accepted—then the implication is clearly that this phenomenon can never be proved but it can be speculated about and it can be a matter of faith. If, however, it is maintained as dogma, with the implication that it can be either scientifically or philosophically proved, the answer must be negative.

When we turn to the action-personality component of the personality, for partly obverse reasons much the same implications seem to be indicated. Just as there is no *Ding an sich* that is knowable in the empirical realm, there is none in the metaphysical realm. Clearly, the "eternal life" of the individual soul belongs in this category, and the existence of such entities cannot be intellectually proved. However, Kant would insist that they cannot be *disproved* either. Thus, like resurrected bodies, they can be speculated about and believed in as matters of *faith,* which is different.

Among the victims of Kant's skepticism, or as we have called it relativization, is belief in the cognitive *necessity* of belief in survival of human individuality after death. We have stressed that this skepticism applies to the survival of both of the two components of the human individual with which this analysis began and hence obviously to their combination, without dissolution of that combination. These strictures apply with special cogency to the Christian conception of the entry into eternal life, if (as we stated earlier) by this is meant literally timelessness rather than indefinite duration.

All this needs to be seen in the context of what we have called Kant's procedural position. His skepticism both closed and opened doors. It of course undermined the traditional specificities of received, to say nothing of enforced, beliefs. By the same token, by contrast with scientific materialism, it opened the door not merely to *one* alternative to received Christian dogma but to a multiplicity of them.

The grounding of this door opening process lies in Kant's conception of *freedom* as the central feature of what he called "practical reason." [18] In essence, the human "will," as he called it, can no more be bound by a set of metaphysical dogmas than can man's active intellect be bound by alleged inherent necessities of the empirical, relevant *Ding an sich*. This doctrine of freedom, among other things, opens the door to Western receptivity to other, notably Oriental, religious traditions. Thus, Buddhist tradition, on the whole by contrast with Christian, stresses not the theme of individuality except for *this* terrestrial life but rather the desirability of absorbtion, after death, into an impersonal, eternal matrix (as opposed to a personal eternal life). The recent vogue of Oriental religion in Western circles suggests that this possibility has become meaningful here.

VI

It has been common to interpret the constraints on absolute human freedom, which Kant dealt with under the heading of *transcendental* matters, as creations of the "human mind" in something like an empirical sense. Thus, at least secondary interpreters of the work of Claude Lévi-Strauss [19] and of Noam Chomsky [20] often use this phraseology in speaking of the structure of culture, on the one hand, and the deep structures of language, on the other. In my opinion this phrasing is open to serious misinterpretation in that "mind" may be held to mean the structure of the human personality, or of some related collective entity, in an *empirical* sense. Clearly, nothing could be further from the Kantian position. Both the human personality and human collectivities—and presumably languages—are empirical objects, "phenomena" in Kant's sense. They cannot possibly be used to ground transcendental ordering in *any* of these contexts.

We would like to state the matter differently. The transcendental framework of human "consciousness," in Kant's sense, is part of the *human condition* but it is not an *object* of human knowledge. It is, rather, in Kant's favorite phrase, an a priori set of conditions of human knowledge and orientation more generally. Nevertheless, it constitutes a set of constraints, perhaps in a sense close to Durkheim's,[21] on what can be humanly *meaningful*. Thus, the categories of the understanding are by no means "arbitrary conventions" with which scientists operate in trying to establish cognitively intelligible order in the phenomena they study but which they can

---

[18] Kant, *Critique of Practical Reason.*

[19] Claude Lévi-Strauss, *Structural Anthropology* (New York: Basic Books, 1963; first published in French).

[20] Noam Chomsky, *Syntactic Structures* (The Hague: Mouton, 1957).

[21] Emile Durkheim, *Sociology and Philosophy,* trans. D. F. Pocock (New York: Free Press, 1974).

alter at will. Similarly, Kant would hold that the categorical imperative is not an arbitrary, culture-bound convention of *one* possible ethical position but is grounded in the human condition itself. I think it is good Kantian doctrine that, only with recognition of the binding qualities of these conditions of meaningfulness, is the basic freedom of the human will itself a meaningful concept. This is a very different position indeed from the contention that the basic organization accessible to human experience is "imposed" by the empirical "human mind."

The developments in science that we have sketched in this essay have elaborated the system of constraints on human freedom, with which Kant dealt as transcendental. In one sense, any person is "free" to deny death—for instance, to "pretend" that a deceased love object is still alive—but this is not meaningful behavior; indeed, it may be in a strict sense pathological. In general, I would class the normality of death, on both the above levels, among the constraints that have been derived from the *combination* of transcendental and empirical factors and which it has thus become "irrational" to "deny."

Kant's sphere of freedom includes the freedom to speculate and to believe. In particular, this is the freedom to symbolize and to mythologize, to construct "representations," individual or collective, that fill the gaps left open by the indeterminacies of both our empirical knowledge and our grasp of transcendental or telic reality. One thing that Kant did was to deprive beliefs in both these areas of the apodictic certainty that had been claimed for them in the received cultural tradition.

This leaves us in the position that the problem of the meaning of death in Western tradition has, from a position of relative closure defined by the Christian syndrome, been opened up in its recent phase. Above all, there is a new freedom, for individuals and sociocultural movements, to try their hand at innovative definitions and conceptions. At the same time, the "viability" of these innovations is subject to the transcendental, as well as the empirical, constraints of the human condition, with which we have been concerned.

It is perhaps relevant, in interpreting the human phenomenon more generally, to refer to the statement of the late Arthur D. Nock, one of the most distinguished students of religion of his generation, that, to his (very extensive) knowledge, no religion had *ever* claimed to be able to "beat death." [22]

This open, in a sense "individualistic," situation with respect to the meaning of death—and of course the life of the individual—is of a piece with the general situation in the modern world, which has seen a pervasive undermining of older certainties and authorities in favor of a variety of

[22] Arthur D. Nock, *Conversion: The Old and the New in Religion from Alexander the Great to Augustine of Hippo* (New York: Oxford University Press, 1961; first published in 1933).

enhanced freedoms and autonomies.[23] Perhaps one need only mention the institutionalization of political democracy and of intellectual freedom, especially in the academic world, and also some of the newer freedoms in the realm of more personal conduct. These have by no means become universal, and there are many pessimists about their future. They have certainly encountered formidable resistance, especially on the part of groups that contend their acceptance means the end of all meaningful order in human life. I, for one, however, cannot see that they are so dangerous that it is likely that in our time, or that of our childrens' children, this main trend will be reversed.

It may be noted that one of Kant's principal emphases in this connection was on the pattern of *universalism*.[24] Not only was the category of causality, for example, to be regarded as of universal relevance in the empirical world, but also the categorical imperative was formulated in parallel terms. If a single keynote of the main trend of the development of modern civilization could be selected, I think it would be the trend toward cultural universalism. The interpretation of this principle involves many complexities. Yet it seems to be an essential conclusion that its universalizability is one of the central conditions of freedom.

This leaves the problem of the meaning of death in Western civilization in what, to many, must appear to be a strangely unsatisfactory state. It seems to come down to the proposition that the meaning of death is that, in the human condition, it cannot have any apodictically certain meaning without abridgment of the essential human freedom of thought, experience, and imagination. Within limits, its meaning, as it is thought about, experienced for the case of others, and anticipated for oneself, must be autonomously interpreted. Is this, however, pure negativism or nihilism?

I think not: This openness is not the same as declaring death, and of course with it individual life, to be meaningless. If this were the case, the human condition as a whole would have to be negatively valued, as indeed it has been in some quarters for many centuries. Kant's views of the purposiveness of nature and its connection with human pleasure, however, seem to indicate that positive acceptance of being human, with all its uncertainties and limitations, is not in the least incompatible with acceptance of both cognitive and attitudinal openness, which in one aspect is uncertainty, about many of the most essential features of the state of being human.

So far as Western society is concerned, I think the tolerability of this relatively open definition of the situation is associated with the "activistic" strain in our values, the attitude that human life is a challenging undertaking that in some respects may be treated as an adventure—by contrast with a view that treats human life as a matter of passively enduring an externally imposed fate. Even though Western religion has sometimes stressed

[23] See Bellah, "Religious Evolution."
[24] Kant, *Critique of Practical Reason.*

man's extreme dependency on God, and indeed the sinfulness of asserting independence, on the whole the activistic strain has been dominant. If this is the case, it seems that men can face their deaths and those of others in the spirit that, whatever this unknown future may portend, they can enter upon it with good courage.

VII

So far as it is accessible to cognitive understanding at all, the meaning of death for individual human beings must be approached in the framework of the human condition as a whole. It must include both the relevant scientific and philosophical understanding and must attempt to synthesize them. Finally, it must, as clearly as possible, recognize and take account of the limits of our scientific as well as our philosophical understanding.

We have contended that the development of modern science has so changed the picture as to require revision of many of the received features of Christian tradition, both Catholic and Protestant. This development of science took place in three great stages marked by the synthesis of physical science in the seventeenth century, that of biological science in the nineteenth, and that of the action sciences in the nineteenth to twentieth.

The most important generalizations seem to be the following. First, the human individual constitutes a unique symbiotic synthesis of two main components, a living organism and a living personality. Second, both components seem to be *inherently* limited in duration of life, and we have no knowledge which indicates that their symbiosis can be in any radical sense dissociated. Third, the individualized entity *both* is embedded in and derives in some sense from a transgenerational matrix which, seen in relation to individual mortality, has indefinite but not infinite durability.

From this point of view, death, or the limited temporal duration of the individual life course, must be regarded as one of the facts of life that is as inexorable as the need to eat and breathe in order to live. In this sense, death is completely normal, to the point that its "denial" must be regarded as pathological. Moreover, this normality includes the consideration that, from an evolutionary point of view, which we have contended is basic to *all* modern science, death must be regarded as having high survival value, organically at least to the species, actionwise to the future of the sociocultural system. These scientific considerations are not trivial, or conventional, or culture-bound but are *fundamental*.

There is a parallel set of considerations on the philosophical side. For purposes of elucidating this aspect of the problem complex I have used Kant's framework as presented in his three critiques. On the one hand, this orientation is critical in that it challenges the contention that absolute knowledge is demonstrable in *any* of the three aspects of the human condition. Thus, any conception like that of the ontological essence of nature, the idea of God, or the notion of the eternal life of the human soul are categorized as *Dinge an sich,* which in principle are not demonstrable by rational cognitive procedures.

At the same time, Kant insisted, and I follow him here, on the cognitive necessity of assuming a transcendental component, a set of categories in each of the three realms, that is not reducible to the status of humanly available inputs from either the empirical or the absolute telic references of the human condition. We have interpreted this to mean that human orientation must be relativized to the human condition not treated as dogmatically fixed in the nature of things.

The consequence of this relativization that we have particularly emphasized is that it creates a new openness for orientations, which men are free to exploit by speculation and to commit themselves in faith but with reference to which they cannot claim what Kant called apodictic certainty. At the same time, we again insist with Kant that this openness must be qualified by the continuing subjection of human life to the constraints of the transcendental aspects of the human condition, which presumably cannot be altered by human action.

If this is a correct account of the situation, it is not surprising that there is a great deal of bafflement, anxiety, and indeed downright confusion in contemporary attitudes and opinions in this area. I think that in its broad lines what I have presented is indeed an accurate diagnosis of the situation, but it would certainly be too much to claim that such an orientation is fully institutionalized.

It can be said to be most firmly established at philosophical levels and those of rather abstract scientific theory. Even there, however, there is still much controversy and anything like full consensus seems to be far off. Yet I still maintain that the development, say, from the medieval Catholic synthesis, is the *main line.* The grounds for this belief rest on the conviction that no equally basic alternative is available in the main cultural tradition and that this broad orientation is the most congenial to "reasonable men" in our situation. So far as fundamentals are concerned, I am afraid that, within the limitations of this essay, it will be necessary to leave it at that.

It may help, however, to mitigate the impression of extreme abstractness if in closing I very briefly discuss three empirical points. First, though scientific evidence has established the fact of the inevitability of death with increasing clarity, this does not mean that the *experience* of death by human populations may not change with changing circumstances. Thus, Victor Lidz and I have distinguished between inevitable death and "adventitious" death—that is "premature" relative to the full life span and in principle preventable by human action.[25] Within the last century and a half or so, this latter category of deaths has decreased enormously. The proportion of persons in modern populations over sixty-five has thus increased greatly, as has the expectancy of life at birth to seventy-two in 1975 in the United States. This clearly means that a greatly increased proportion of modern humans live out a full life course. Perhaps precisely because of this change, premature deaths from diseases, wars, accidents, or natural disasters like earthquakes have become more, rather than less, disturbing events than they were previously.

Moreover, persons who live to a ripe old age will experience an inevitably larger number of deaths of persons important to them. These will be in decreasing number the deaths of persons younger than themselves, notably their own children, but increasingly those of their parents and whole ranges of persons of an older generation such as teachers, senior occupational associates, and public figures. (During this writing, for example, I learned of the death of Mao Tse-tung, certainly a figure of worldwide significance.) Quite clearly, these demographic changes have a strong effect on the balance of experience and expectation of the deaths of significant others and on anticipation of one's own death.

Second, one of the centrally important aspects of a process of change in orientation of the sort described should be the appearance of signs of the differentiation of attitudes and conceptions in the relevant area. As Fox, Lidz, and I [26] have pointed out, there has indeed been such a process of differentiation, which seems not yet to be completed, with respect to both ends of the life cycle. With respect to the beginning, there is the controversy over abortion. However this controversy may eventually be resolved, it seems unlikely that public attitudes will go back to the traditional positions of either no abortions in any circumstances or only abortions that are strictly necessary to save the life of the mother. The interesting feature of this controversy is that it has entailed attempts to specify the point at which the life of a human *person,* as distinct from the human *organism* at conception, begins.

Concomitant with this has been an attempt at redefinition of death. So far the most important approach has been to draw a line *within* the organic sector between what has been called "brain death," in which irreversible changes have taken place, destroying the functioning of the central nervous system, and what has been called "metabolic death," in which above all heartbeat and respiration have ceased. The problem has been highlighted by the capacity of "artificial" measures, say, mechanical respirators, to keep persons "alive" for long periods despite the fact that brain function

[25] See Talcott Parsons and Victor M. Lidz, "Death in American Society," in Edwin Schneidman (ed.), *Essays in Self-Destruction* (New York: Science House, 1967).

[26] Parsons, Fox, and Lidz, "The 'Gift of Life.'" Chap. 12 of this book.

has irreversibly ceased. The point of major interest here is the connection of brain function with the personality level of individuality. Hence, an organism that continues to "live" at *only* the metabolic level may be said to be dead as a person. We would expect still further elaborations of these themes in the future.

Third, we may make a few remarks about the significance for our problem of Freud's most mature theoretical statement.[27] It will be remembered that in his last major theoretical work, Freud rather drastically revised his views on the nature of anxiety, coming to focus on the expectation of the loss of an "object." By "object" Freud meant a human individual standing in an emotionally significant relation to the person of reference. To the child, of course, his parents become "lost objects" as he grows up in that their significance to him as growing child is inevitably "lost." The ultimate loss of a concrete human person as object (of cathexis, Freud said) is the death of that person. To have "grown away" from one's parents is one thing but to experience their actual deaths is another. Freud's own account of the impact on him of his father's death is a particularly relevant case in point.[28]

Equally clearly, an individual's own death, in anticipation, can be subsumed under the category of object loss, particularly in view of Freud's theory of narcissism,[29] by which he meant the individual's cathexis of his own self as a love object.

Anxiety, however, is neither the actual experience of object loss nor is it, according to Freud, the fear of it. It is an anticipatory orientation in which the actor's own emotional security is particularly involved. It is a field of rather free play of fantasy as to what might be the consequences of an anticipated or merely possible event.

Given the hypothesis, to which I subscribe, that in our scientifically oriented civilization there is widespread acceptance of death—meant as the antithesis of its denial—I see no reason why this should eliminate or even substantially reduce *anxiety* about death, both that of others and one's own. Indeed, in speaking earlier about the impact of demographic changes in the incidence of death, I suggested that in certain circumstances the level of anxiety may be expected to increase rather than the reverse.

It seems that the frequent assertions that our society is characterized by pervasive denial of death may often be interpreted as calling attention to widespread anxiety about death, which I submit is *not* the same thing. There can be no doubt that in most cases death is, in experience and in anticipation, a traumatic event. Fantasies, in such circumstances, are often

[27] Sigmund Freud, *Inhibitions, Symptoms, and Anxiety,* vol. 20 of *Standard Edition* (1959; first published in German in 1926), pp. 77–178.

[28] See Sigmund Freud, *The Origins of Psychoanalysis: Letters to Wilhelm Fliess, Drafts and Notes, 1887–1902* (New York: Basic Books, 1954).

[29] Freud, *Inhibitions, Symptoms, and Anxiety.*

marked by unrealism. But the prevalence of such phenomena does not constitute a distortion of the basic cultural framework within which we moderns orient ourselves to the meaning of death.

Indeed, in my opinion, this and the two preceding illustrations serve to enhance the importance of clarification at the theoretical and philosophical levels, to which the bulk of this essay has been devoted. Clarification is essential if we are to understand such problems as the shifts in attitudes toward various age groups in modern society, particularly older persons, the relatively sudden eruption of dissatisfaction with traditional modes of conceptualizing the beginning and the termination of human lives, and allegations about the pervasive denial of death, which is often interpreted as a kind of failure of "intestinal fortitude." However important recent movements for increasing expression of emotional interests and the like, ours remains a culture to which its cognitive framework is of paramount significance. It is as a contribution to the understanding of this framework and its meaning, in an area that is emotionally highly sensitive, that I would like this essay to be evaluated.

Additional References

BURKE, KENNETH
> The Rhetoric of Religion: Studies in Logology. Boston: Beacon, 1961.

DURKHEIM, ÉMILE
> The Division of Labor in Society. New York: Free Press, 1960; first published in French in 1893.

FREUD, SIGMUND
> The Ego and the Id. In vol. 19 of The Standard Edition of the Complete Psychological Works of Sigmund Freud. London: Hogarth; New York: Macmillan, 1961; first published in German in 1923. Pp. 12–63.

FREUD, SIGMUND
> "The Future of an Illusion." In vol. 21 of The Standard Edition of the Complete Psychological Works of Sigmund Freud. London: Hogarth; New York: Macmillan, 1961; first published in German in 1927. Pp. 5–58.

HENDERSON, LAWRENCE JOSEPH
> The Fitness of the Environment: An Inquiry into the Biological Significance of the Properties of Matter. New York: Macmillan, 1913. Boston: Beacon (paperback), 1958.

HENDERSON, LAWRENCE JOSEPH
> The Order of Nature: An Essay. Cambridge, Mass.: Harvard University Press, 1935.

HENDERSON, LAWRENCE JOSEPH
> Pareto's General Sociology: A Physiologist's Interpretation. Cambridge, Mass.: Harvard University Press, 1935.

LEACH, EDMUND

    Genesis as Myth and Other Essays. London: Jonathan Cape, 1969.

MONOD, JACQUES

    Chance and Necessity. New York: Random House, 1972.

WARNER, W. LLOYD

    The Living and the Dead: A Study of the Symbolic Life of Americans. Westport, Conn.: Greenwood, 1975; first published in 1959.

WEBER, MAX

    The Sociology of Religion. Boston: Beacon, 1963; first published in German in 1922.

15. A Paradigm of the Human Condition

I. Introduction

THE PRESENT CHAPTER takes up formally the task of working out an outline analysis of the system we have, in various introductory discussions, called that of the *human condition*. It is hardly necessary to reiterate that this chapter is meant to be primarily a *theoretical* attempt rather than an addition to the voluminous philosophical and in the humanistic sense critical literature. In other words, it is meant to be strictly comparable to previous attempts to conceptualize the social system and the general system of action and to articulate them.

For the present purpose it is essential to say something about the intellectual background of this venture. In the course of the development of the theory of action there has, as long as I have been involved with it, never been any lack of awareness that what came to be called the *general system of action* does not stand alone among the objects of cognitive understand-

---

Written with the collaboration of Harold Bershady, Willy de Craemer, Renée C. Fox, and Victor M. Lidz.

A greatly respected friend, who has read the manuscript of this chapter, and who is a practitioner of one of the natural sciences, has advised against the use of the word "Paradigm," both in the title of this chapter, and at many points in the course of it. His ground is that the concept has become so controversial around the work of Thomas Kuhn (*The Structure of Scientific Revolutions*, 2nd ed.; Chicago: University of Chicago Press, 1970) that some readers are likely to interpret the author's position as taking sides in those controversies rather than in terms of his own conceptions. On the other hand, equally valued commentators, including two of the original "Human Condition" discussion group, have advised retaining its use. As is evident, I have taken the advice of the latter group, which included introducing a note such as this.

I have, for a good many years, since shortly after the publication of the Kuhn book, been very much aware of his position and the widespread interest it has aroused. But neither my own position, nor that of my colleagues, has, in any important way, been determined by Kuhn or the controversies over him. In fact, long before the human condition project began, I had been regularly

ing with which human investigation is occupied. In particular, there have been two classes of objects which, it became increasingly clear, in some sense stood on the boundaries of the system of action. Since the concepts of boundary definition and boundary maintenance had become crucial to the theory, there did not seem to be any logical reason why the same order of conceptualization should not be attempted at and beyond such boundaries, as had proved to be so important to analysis within the system of action, especially in analytically discriminating the primary subsystems of the latter from each other (e.g., social and cultural systems).

One of these two salient boundaries of action is that vis-à-vis living organisms. The status of this boundary had been a major concern of mine even before I became committed to a career in social science. A kind of theoretical jolt, however, occurred when, as noted in the General Introduction, Charles Lidz and Victor Lidz submitted to me their essay on what they called the "behavioral system," with its proposal that this term should be substituted for my term "behavioral organism," defined as the adaptive subsystem of the general system of action.[1] They made a cogent case, which persuaded me that the organism as an analytical category should be entirely excluded from the system of action—except, of course, for zones of interpenetration—and that the system of cognitive organization at symbolic levels should be treated as an essential part of action.

This development necessitated a thoroughgoing reconsideration of the boundary between action and the organic world. We were of course very much aware that most psychologists had refused to make much of the distinction, many of them defining psychology simply as the study of "the behavior of organisms." We, on the other hand, had come more and more clearly to draw an essential line that, following Durkheim, Weber, Freud, Piaget, G. H. Mead, and others, emphasizes the distinctiveness of the involvement of *symbolic processes* in what in other respects could quite correctly be called human "behavior." In this connection I consider Freud's

---

speaking of the "four-function paradigm" in a sense with which readers of my work will surely be familiar. The term is used here simply to refer to an attempt at conceptually formal statement of the primary elements of a theoretical scheme and their relations to each other. Indeed, if my memory does not deceive me, one of my first sensitizations to the term came from Robert Merton's presentation of his outline of a "Paradigm for Functional Analysis" (in *Social Theory and Social Structure*, rev. ed.; New York: Free Press, 1957, pp. 50–55), which was well before the publication of Kuhn's book. (My first published formulation of the four-function scheme or paradigm was in *Working Papers in the Theory of Action*, with R. F. Bales and Edward Shils; New York: Free Press, 1953, Chaps. II and III.)

[1] Charles Lidz and Victor Lidz, "The Psychology of Intelligence of Jean Piaget and Its Place in the Theory of Action," in J. Loubser, R. Baum, A. Effrat, and V. Lidz (eds.), *Explorations in General Theory in Social Science: Essays in Honor of Talcott Parsons* (New York: Free Press, 1976), chap. 8.

insistence on the distinction between "organic" and "psychic" (discussed in Chapter 4 of this volume) exceedingly important.

There can be no question of the enormous importance, for the understanding of human action, of its interrelations with organic systems. In turn, these interrelations cannot be understood without theoretical understanding of the organic side, just as the human implications, for example, of organic evolution, cannot be adequately grasped without a corresponding understanding of the action system. Indeed, it may be said that less harm has been done by social scientists "biologizing" action phenomena directly than by their failure to attempt the requisite theoretical understanding of the organic level as well as that of action, with behavior standing in between.

At any rate, in the period leading up to my memorandum of the summer of 1974 a great deal of attention was paid, as has already been recounted, to biological theory. The resulting better understanding of biology, including some of its more recent developments, paved the way for the attempt to include both the organic and the action level in a single, at least partly integrated, conceptual scheme, a "theory of living systems." A very general paradigm such as that presented in this chapter can of course develop only a broad outline of the interrelation we have in mind. The view we hold, however, is that any serious and competent contribution to this problem is better than its simple neglect.[2]

The second major boundary of the system of action, which has concerned me and many other sociologists and cultural theorists, lies, cybernetically speaking, in the other direction. Since *The Structure of Social Action*[3] I have been cognizant of these problems, but earlier I adopted the relatively cautious policy of referring to it in terms of a residual category, namely, cognitively as "nonempirical." From the beginning, however, I meant this formula to mark off my own position quite decisively from a positivistic position that implies that *only* empirical science is a source of valid understanding of the human condition. I think it fair to say that on such positivistic premises Weber's sociology of religion[4] would not make sense.

In gradually working toward giving some coherent structure to this

---

[2] An essentially programmatic statement on this point that I wrote with A. Hunter Dupree is "The Relations between Biological and Socio-Cultural Theory," which appears in Talcott Parsons, *Social Systems and the Evolution of Action Theory* (New York: Free Press, 1977), chap. 5.

[3] Talcott Parsons, *The Structure of Social Action* (1937; reprint ed., New York: Free Press, 1949).

[4] Max Weber, *The Sociology of Religion,* transl. by E. Fischoff (Boston: Beacon, 1963; first published in German in 1922); idem, see also *The Religion of India: The Sociology of Hinduism and Buddhism,* trans. and ed. Hans H. Gerth and Don Martindale (New York: Free Press, 1958; first published in German in 1916–1917); idem, *The Religion of China: Confucianism and Taoism,* transl. and ed. by H. H. Gerth (New York: Free Press, 1951; first published in German in 1915); and idem, *Ancient Judaism,* transl. and ed. by H. H. Gerth and D. Martindale (New York: Free Press, 1952; first published in German in 1917–1919).

residual category I have been especially influenced by repeated revisits to Weber's work. The crucial problem was that: in his extensive discussions of what he called the "problems of meaning," Weber stressed a diversity of "orientations" that have been adopted in different religious systems in response to such problems. Various interpreters of Weber have contended that these variations were for Weber essentially random, but the better I came to know Weber's work, the less acceptable was this interpretation. As relevant considerations I may point to two positions Weber strongly stressed.[5] The first was the contention that original Calvinism and early Buddhism can be treated as polar opposites of each other in the range of variations of possibly meaningful religious orientations. The second was the significance he attributed to the two dichotomies he used for characterizing types of orientation—on the one hand, that between asceticism and mysticism and, on the other, that between "innerworldly" and "otherworldly" orientations. The last two dichotomies can easily generate a fourfold table. At any rate, such considerations convinced me that Weber was feeling his way toward a structural classification of types of religious orientations and that had he lived a few more years he would very likely have promulgated one (Weber died at age fifty-six).

Besides this type of mulling over of some of the implications of Weber's position, a decisive influence on my thinking in this area was a revisit to Kant that was stimulated by discussions of the Pennsylvania group. Thus, though Kant was skeptical of what is meant by "metaphysics," one could certainly interpret his position in the following way. In *The Critique of Pure Reason,* Kant clearly did not treat space and time or the categories of understanding as being themselves in the ordinary, empirical sense objects of knowledge, as phenomena, but rather held them to constitute what in his sense was a "transcendental" framework in terms of which empirical knowledge is made possible.[6] He used essentially the same kind of reasoning in *The Critique of Practical Reason* [7] and in *The Critique of Judgment,*[8] attempting to abstract out in these two spheres, as well, the transcendental framework of "assumptions," or whatever they are called, by virtue of which valid judgments are possible. It may be noted that in the first of these contexts Kant, unlike Hume,[9] did not ask *whether* valid empirical knowledge is possible but stated that we *have* valid knowledge and, given this fact, the question is *how* is this possible?

Kant clearly thought in terms of dual levels: the sense data of empirical

---

[5] Weber, *Sociology of Religion.*

[6] Immanuel Kant, *The Critique of Pare Reason,* trans. N. K. Smith (New York: Macmillan, 1929; first published in German in 1781).

[7] Immanuel Kant, *The Critique of Practical Reason,* trans. and ed. L. W. Beck (Chicago: University of Chicago Press, 1950; first published in German in 1788).

[8] Immanuel Kant, *The Critique of Judgment,* trans. J. C. Meredith (Oxford: Clarendon, 1964; first published in German 1790).

[9] David Hume, *A Treatise of Human Nature,* ed. L. A. Selby-Bigge (Oxford: Clarendon, 1958; first published in 1739–1740).

knowledge and the categories of the understanding; the "problems" of practical ethics and the "categorical imperative"; esthetic "experience" and the canons of judgment. There seems to be a striking parallel between his version of duality and the linguist's "deep structures" and "surface struc- tures," the biologist's "genotypes" and "phenotypes", the cyberneticist's "high on information" and "high on energy," and indeed the sociologist's "values," or "institutional patterns," and "interests." We therefore suggest that the first term in each of these pairs be used to designate a *meta-* structure, which is not as such a property of the phenomena (also Kant's term) under consideration but is rather an *a priori* set of conditions without which the phenomena in question could not be conceived in an orderly manner. We consider that this point of view is not open to the traditional objections usually implied in the term "metaphysical." The fact that Weber was thoroughly steeped in Kantian thought helps, in this regard, to make Weber's ideas intelligible.

In the context, above all, of the idea of cybernetic hierarchy, which has become increasingly salient in this line of theorizing, it has seemed appro- priate to designate the "system" that is beyond the boundary of the action system in this direction as the *telic* system of the human condition. In using this modification of the Aristotelian term "teleology," which has been so thoroughly excoriated by the partisans of positivistic views, we have been particularly encouraged by the related use of such modifications by two eminent scientists of contiguous generations. The first is the physiolo- gist Lawrence J. Henderson, who in his notable book *The Order of Nature* took the view that the Aristotelian problem, if it may be called such, could not be expunged from the thinking of *modern* science.[10] The second is the contemporary biologist Ernst Mayr, who for his own purposes introduced another modification, *teleonymy,*[11] which clearly belongs in the same lin- guistic family. Subsequently, we will have more to say about both Hender- son's and Mayr's conceptions.

Clearly, we think of the telic system, standing as it does in our treat- ment in a relation of cybernetic superordination to the action system, as having to do especially with religion. It is primarily in the religious context that throughout so much of cultural history belief in some kind of "reality" of the nonempirical world has figured prominently. With full recognition of the philosophical difficulties of defining the nature of that reality we wish to affirm our sharing the age-old belief in its existence.

For many purposes, of course, it is not necessary to go beyond this; we can content ourselves with the bare statement that "something is there." But for some of our purposes this statement of self-denial will not suffice. This consideration is linked with the fact, just outlined, that at least

[10] Lawrence J. Henderson, *The Order of Nature: An Essay* (Cambridge, Mass.: Harvard University Press, 1917).

[11] Ernst Mayr, "Teleological and Teleonomic: A New Analysis," in Marx War- tovsky (ed.), *Method and Metaphysics: Methodological and Historical Essays in the Natural and Social Sciences* (Leiden: E. J. Brill, 1974), pp. 78–104.

for Kant the existence of the *meta-* reality must be taken into consideration in positively structured ways. Kantian epistemology without giving content to the categories would surely be a poor thing, as would Chomsky's linguistics [12] be, if he insisted that the existence of deep structures must be assumed but that nothing more can be said of them. We thus wish to contend both that the assumption of this *meta-* world must be assumed notably with respect to religion and that the attempt must be made, in the course of theoretical work, to give it relevant specific content. What this content is to be will depend on the exigencies of theory construction as their relevance to the problems develops.

The reader will have noted that we have so far dealt with two of the broad traditional areas of scientific theorizing, the organic world and the world of action, and with the nonempirical, telic world, as we call it. But what of that which is usually called the "physical" world? Some would not distinguish the physical from the organic world or vice versa, but not such prominent biologists as Henderson,[13] Mayr,[14] or Luria.[15] I think the physical realm must be treated as a world in its own right, differentiated from the organic, or from the "biosphere" as it is often called. Furthermore, the physical world is clearly part of the human condition in that it constitutes an essential component of the environment of man, as both organism and actor. Indeed, man himself *is* in one principal aspect a physico-chemical system and this aspect is in certain respects continuous with the others.

In attempting to clarify the status of the physical world, notably in relation to the organic, I have found Henderson's two small and rather early books, *The Fitness of the Environment* (1912) and *The Order of Nature* (1917), especially helpful.[16] Henderson made clear in the latter book that he considered that we must presume that a "teleological" aspect, as he phrased it, must be taken into account in theoretical treatment of even the physical world; thus, the very popular idea of "mechanism" is not by itself adequate. Henderson rested his view above all on the conception, which he elaborated at considerable length, that one of the principal properties of the physical world is *order*. Another word he used frequently—one nearly synonymous with order—was *organization*.[17] I shall not pursue

---

[12] Noam Chomsky, *Language and Mind* (New York: Harcourt, Brace, 1968).

[13] Henderson, *Order of Nature*.

[14] Ernst Mayr, *Populations, Species, and Evolution* (Cambridge, Mass.: Harvard University Press, 1970).

[15] Salvador Edward Luria, *Life: The Unfinished Experiment* (New York: Scribner's, 1973).

[16] Lawrence J. Henderson, *The Fitness of the Environment: An Inquiry into the Biological Significance of the Properties of Matter* (New York: Macmillan, 1913); and idem, *Order of Nature*.

[17] It seems reasonable to relate Henderson's contention here to a famous statement by Albert Einstein to the effect that "the eternal mystery of the world is its comprehensibility" (*Out of My Later Years* [Westport, Conn.: Greenwood Press], p. 61).

This statement of Einstein is of such critical importance to my general argument that I enlisted the help of an Einstein expert to track down the exact wording of his statement in German, and in the authorized English translation, with some indication of its context. This information was kindly supplied to me by Professor Gerald Holton, a physicist and historian of science who has specially studied Einstein. The German text, written by Einstein himself, of the decisive formula, is: *Das ewig Unbegreifliche an der Welt ist ihre Begreiflichkeit,* which is immediately followed by an illuminating reference to Kant: *Dass die Setzung einer realen Aussenwelt ohne jene Begreiflichkeit sinnlos wäre, ist eine der grossen Erkenntnisse Emmanuel Kants.*

The fuller German text in the article "Physik und Realität," which includes the above two statements and the paragraph preceding them, is as follows:

Der zweite Schritt liegt darin, dass wir jenem Begriff des körperlichen Objektes in unserem (unsere Erwartungen bestimmenden) Denken von den jenen Begriff veranlassenden Sinnesempfindungen weitgehend unabhängige Bedeutung zuschreiben. Dies meinen wir, wenn wir dem körperlichen Objekt "reale Existenz" zuschreiben. Die Berechtigung dieser Setzung liegt einzig darin, dass wir mit Hilfe derartiger Begriffe und zwischen ihnen gesetzter gedanklicher Relationen uns in dem Gewirre der Sinnes-Empfindungen zurecht zu finden vermögen. Damit hängt es zusammen, dass jene Begriffe und Relationen—obgleich freie Setzungen des Denkens—uns fester und unabänderlicher erscheinen als das einselne Sinnenerlebnis, dessen Charakter der Illusion oder Hallucination gegenüber doch nie vollkommen gesichert erscheint. Anderesits aber haben jene Begriffe und Relationen, insbesondere die Setzung Objekte, überhaupt einer "realen Welt" nur insewoit Berechtigung, als sie mit Sinneserlebnissen verknüpft sind, zwischen welchen sie, gedankliche Verknüpfungen schaffen.

Dass die Gesamtheit der Sinnen-Erlebnisse so beschaffen ist, dass sie durch das Denken (Operieren mit Begriffen und Schaffung und Anwendung bestimmter funktioneller Verknüpfungen zwischen diesen sowie Zuordnung der Sinneserlebnisse zu den Begriffen) geordnet werden können ist eine Tatsache, über die wir nur staunen, die wir aber niemals werden begreifen können. Man kann sagen: *Das ewig Unbegreifliche an der Welt ist ihre Begreiflichkeit.* Dass die Setzung einer realen Aussenwelt ohne jene Begreiflichkeit sinnlos wäre, ist eine der grossen Erkenntnisse Emanuel Kants.

Journal of the Franklin Institute
(Vol. 221, No. 3, March 1936), pp. 314–315.

A somewhat fuller excerpt from the English translation, which includes the three paragraphs preceding the German excerpt and the one which follows it, is also presented:

On the stage of our subconscious mind appear in colorful succession sense experiences, memory pictures of them, representations and feelings. In contrast to psychology, physics treats directly only of sense experiences and of the "understanding" of their connection. But even the concept of the "real external world" of everyday thinking rests exclusively on sense impressions.

Now we must first remark that the differentiation between sense impressions and representations is not possible; or, at least it is not possible with absolute certainty. With the discussion of this problem, which affects also the notion of reality, we will not concern ourselves but we shall take the existence of sense experiences as given, that is to say as psychic experiences of a special kind.

I believe that the first step in the setting of a "real external world" is the formation of the concept of bodily objects and of bodily objects of various kinds. Out of the multitude of our sense experiences we take, mentally and arbitrarily, certain repeatedly occurring complexes of sense impression (partly in conjunction with sense impressions which are interpreted as signs for sense experiences of others), and we attribute to them a meaning—the meaning of the bodily object. Considered logically this concept is not identical with the totality of sense impressions referred to; but it is an arbitrary creation of the human (or animal) mind. On the other hand, the concept owes its meaning and its justification exclusively to the totality of the sense impressions which we associate with it.

The second step is to be found in the fact that, in our thinking (which determines our expectation), we attribute to this concept of the bodily object a significance, which is to a high degree independent of the sense impression which

Henderson's argument here but shall assume that it represents a scientifically respectable point of view the acceptance of which does not vitiate the thought of a nonspecialist in physical science.

In *The Fitness of the Environment,* Henderson discussed those features of the physico-chemical environment that are especially important as conditions on which living organisms depend. These include the temperatures on the surface of the earth; the atmosphere, with its composition of gases; the prominence of water, with its special properties; and above all the circulation of both air and water and the continual interchanges between

---

originally gives rise to it. This is what we mean when we attribute to the bodily object "a real existence." The justification of such a setting rests exclusively on the fact that, by means of such concepts and mental relations between them, we are able to orient ourselves in the labyrinth of sense impressions. These notions and relations, although free statements of our thoughts, appear to us as stronger and more unalterable than the individual sense experience itself, the character of which as anything other than the result of an illusion or hallucination is never completely guaranteed. On the other hand, these concepts and relations, and indeed the setting of real objects and, generally speaking, the existence of "the real world," have justification only in so far as they are connected with sense impressions between which they form a mental connection.

The very fact that the totality of our sense experiences is such that by means of thinking (operations with concepts, and the creation and use of definite functional relations between them, and the coordination of sense experiences to these concepts) it can be put in order, this fact is one which leaves us in awe, but which we shall never understand. One may say *"the eternal mystery of the world is its comprehensibility."* It is one of the great realizations of Immanuel Kant that the setting up of a real external world would be senseless without this comprehensibility.

In speaking here concerning "comprehensibility," the expression is used in its most modest sense. It implies: the production of some sort of order among sense impressions, this order being produced by the creation of general concepts, relations between these concepts, and by relations between the concepts and sense experience, these relations being determined in any possible manner. *It is in this sense that the world of our sense experiences is comprehensible. The fact that it is comprehensible is a miracle.*

Journal of the Franklin Institute
(Vol. 221, No. 3, March 1936), pp. 349–351.

It will be noted that, in the critical phrasing, the translation misses the sharp German juxtaposition of *Unbegreifliche* and *Begreiflichkeit* and that the translator uses quotation marks, whereas Einstein did not. It should also be noted that the sentence which precedes the critical statement ends, in translation, with "understand." The German is *begreifen.* Thus, Einstein in his native language rang the changes three times on the word *begreifen,* whereas the translator used its nearest English equivalent, "understand," only once. Furthermore, Einstein's reference to Kant in the very next sentence is notable, and is usually not mentioned when his statement is quoted.

As Holton writes, "The basic achievement of Einstein's theory was not to preserve hallowed, traditional conceptions of mechanisms; it was not to produce a logically and tightly structured sequence of thought; it was not to build on a beautiful and pedagogically persuasive experiment. Rather, the basic achievement of the theory was that, at the cost of sacrificing all these, it gave us a new unity in the understanding of nature" (Gerald Holton, *Thematic Origins of Scientific Thought: Kepler to Einstein* [Cambridge, Mass.: Harvard University Press, 1973], p. 329).

them, based on the solubility in water of the gases of the atmosphere.[18] Within this set of conditions then, Henderson especially emphasized the importance for life of the plenitude and accessibility of three chemical elements; hydrogen, oxygen, and carbon.[19] Their importance lies in the high degree to which these elements can enter numerous complex combinations, producing exceedingly varied compounds with diverse properties, which are "emergent" relative to simpler compounds. These elements include all the constituents of water, and in the form of free oxygen and of carbon dioxide, represent the most important components of the atmosphere to life.

It is not fortuitous that hydrogen, oxygen, and carbon are the prime concern of so-called organic chemistry. Henderson argued that they make a special order of complexity possible, which at the biochemical level is one of the especially important features of living organisms.

It is of great interest here that Henderson discussed two other primary properties of organisms besides complexity. The first, *metabolism,* is related to the three elements in that the basic chemical process of metabolism is oxydation, which requires carbon and other substances that, in combining with oxygen produce organically usable energy. The other substances that are important are to a high degree organic compounds. The second additional property he discussed was *regulation,* which relates to the fact that the equilibrium that is maintained through metabolic processes of interchange with the environment is not itself the same as the equilibrium of the environmental system but is unique to the organism. This distinctiveness can be maintained only if the organism possesses regulatory mechanisms that operate in particular ways.

It seems significant that Henderson as a physiologist was concerned primarily with the individual organism. Perhaps it is for this reason that he did not include a fourth distinctive property of living systems, namely, ordered patterning and transmission of a genetic heritage. If this property is added to the three Henderson discussed, the basis seems to be given of a very direct comparison, in functional terms, between the organic and the action "world" as we have been calling them. More of that later.

The main relevance of Henderson's analysis to the present discussion, however, is that his account established a basis for treating the physical world not as something altogether foreign to the worlds of organic life

---

[18] As I wrote this chapter (summer 1977), the public was being newly alerted to the importance of these conditions by the landing of the Viking nodule on Mars and the interest of scientists in whether that planet possesses the necessary conditions for even elementary (microbiotic) life.

[19] It was known even when Henderson wrote *The Fitness of the Environment* (1913) that the table of the chemical elements applied to the physical universe as a whole, not just to the earth or solar system. In his Introduction to Lawrence J. Henderson, *The Fitness of the Environment* (Boston: Beacon, 1958), George Wald suggested, without explanation, that a fourth element, nitrogen, should be added to Henderson's three.

and of action but as something maintaining relatively clear and specific relations to them.

II. The Main Outline of the Paradigm

All students of human action have long been aware of the importance to human beings of the physical world, the organic world, and, though its status has been more controversial, the "transempirical" (telic) world, besides that of action itself in our technical sense. What is new in the present venture is the attempt to put their relations to action and to each other into a more systematic framework.

It will be no surprise to followers of the theory of action that the framework chosen for this effort is the familiar scheme of four functional categories that we have been using in a variety of ways for more than twenty years. If there proves to be a good fit between this scheme and the criterial properties and relations of the four systems, or worlds as we have called them, then the use of the four-function paradigm in this context rather than signaling lack of originality has a very important advantage: Its fit should enable us to systematize these properties and their relationships much more effectively than would be the case if a different paradigm were to be employed. This of course is because so many of the properties and relationships of action systems have already been worked out in these terms; thus, there is one sense but only one in which the presentation of a four-function paradigm of the human condition is derived essentially by an extension of the paradigm of the general system of action.

Figure 1 is the simplest version of the paradigm. It designates only the proposed functional placing of the four primary categories and the two dichotomous variables, from the cross-classification of which the designations of the four cells are derived. In interpreting what we have done it is essential to keep in mind that in speaking in the sense we do of the human condition we explicitly assume an anthropocentric point of view. Accordingly, the paradigm categorizes the world accessible to human experience in terms of the *meanings* to human beings of its various parts and aspects.

Figure 1 General Paradigm of the Human Condition

	Instrumental	Consummatory	
Internal (to human condition) L	Telic System	Action System	I
External A	Physico-Chemical System	Human Organic System	G

Since we are engaged in constructing scientific theory, the paradigm itself must be judged in terms of its *cognitive* meanings as a "contribution to knowledge" put forward by one set of human beings for consideration and evaluation by others who may be interested in it.

Thus, the "point of view of the observer," which has come to be of such importance in the modern philosophy of science, all the way from Einstein's theory of relativity to contemporary social theory, must relate to the human system of action.[20] The first problem, then, is where this viewpoint is to be located in the paradigm. We have decided to locate it in the integrative cell, which it seems to us makes excellent sense. It is, after all, human minds that integrate the various components of knowledge or other aspects of the human experience of the other three categories of "worlds" in the human condition to form some kind of meaningful whole. A meaningful whole in this sense, however, must be expressible in *symbolic* terms. This criterion excludes the organic world in our sense from the point of view of the observer (or actor). This is not at all to say that human actors do not have authentic experience of their own and other organisms but, if it is experience in the technical sense, it is part of action, or it is "psychic" as Freud put it.[21]

If the preceding argument is acceptable, it seems to follow that *relative to* this integrative position of the action system, the physical world should be placed in the adaptive position. The physical world is the ultimate source of the generalized resources on which all living systems on the earth depend, and it provides the ultimate conditions of their functioning. The above summary of Henderson's analysis of the fitness of the physical environment states the considerations that are essential to the placement of this "world" in the paradigm of the human condition.[22]

If we take seriously the cybernetic hierarchy, which has been discussed so much in related work,[23] this consideration almost by itself solves the problem of where to place the organic system since cybernetically organic systems control aspects of the physical system probably by way of (Henderson's) "regulation" and in turn are in certain respects controlled by

---

[20] Lewis A. Coser, "Sociology of Knowledge," in David L. Sills (ed.), *International Encyclopedia of the Social Sciences* (New York: Free Press and Macmillan, 1968), 8:428–45.

[21] Even what the translators of Freud—James Strachey and Anna Freud—have called the "instincts" (*Triebe*) are not organic phenomena but are rather what he called "representatives" of organic processes to the psyche. Sigmund Freud, *Three Essays on the Theory of Sexuality,* vol. 7 of *The Standard Edition of the Complete Psychological Works of Sigmund Freud* (London: Hogarth Press and the Institute of Psychoanalysis, 1961; first published in German in 1905), p. 168.

[22] Henderson, *Fitness of the Environment.*

[23] Norbert Weiner, *Cybernetics: Or Control and Communication in the Animal and the Machine* (New York: Wiley, 1948); see also Karl W. Deutsch, *The Nerves of Government: Models of Political Communication and Control* (New York: Free Press, 1967).

action systems. Thus, organic illness may be regarded in one aspect as a breakdown in such mechanisms of control at either level or both. This of course is to say that the organic system is to be placed in the goal-attainment cell of the paradigm. There is a gratifying correspondence between this placement and Mayr's emphasis in his discussions of teleonymy [24] on the relation of that property of organic systems to goal-striving.

If we are to confine ourselves to four functional subsystems of the human condition and are now left with one, the telic, unassigned, its placement can be decided by deductive logic alone. There is, however, a positive rationale for placing it in the pattern-maintenance cell. First, the whole logic of our earlier discussion of the telic system asserts that in cybernetic terms this system is superordinate to the action system; if the latter is to occupy the integrative position, then the only position consonant with that criterion is that of pattern-maintenance. Besides, this placement seems to fit the criterion of "latency" in the sense that whatever content may be imputed to the telic system is not overtly manifest at the action level but has to be defined, as it were, through processes of action, including cognitive processes. The telic system may also be said to be relevant to the function we have long called "tension management"; thus, there are problems of orientation in relation to telic considerations that arouse strong emotions in human beings. The problems of suffering and of evil as Weber deals with them are examples.[25]

Though it is logically prior, discussion of the two coordinates on which the paradigm is built has been postponed until placement of the "worlds" in the four cells had been examined. This seems justified since our presentation does not pretend to be an exercise in formal logic. It is, however, logically essential that intelligible meaning be given to these two coordinates for the human condition case—meaning that will justify treating it as a special case of the more general four-function paradigm.

In the latter, the vertical axis by convention is treated as representing *internal–external* relations. In recent diagramming practice, the internal has comprised the upper row; the external, the lower. In interpreting this configuration for the present context we should keep in mind that the paradigm is formulated relative to the action point of view; therefore, the action system should be treated as internal. If this be granted, then there is no difficulty, at least since Descartes,[26] in treating the physical world as external to action. After all, that consideration is central to the subject-object relationship as Descartes formulated it.

[24] Mayr, "Teleological and Teleonomic."

[25] Max Weber, "Religious Rejections of the World and Their Directions," in *From Max Weber: Essays in Sociology,* ed. and trans. H. H. Gerth and C. Wright Mills (New York: Oxford University Press, 1946), chap. 13.

[26] René Descartes, *Discourse on Method,* trans. Laurence J. Lafleur (New York: Liberal Arts Press, 1954; first published in French in 1637).

The other category classified as external would then be the organic world, or the biosphere. Although, as Comte held,[27] biological science has followed physical in order of development, it makes sense to argue that the organic world is the second most readily amenable to scientific study. Furthermore, it surely is not a matter of chance that the sciences of action did not develop notably until after the biological sciences, with the partial exception of economics (which among the former group is most like physical science).

If the action system should, for the reasons we have stated, be treated as internal to the human condition, then so it seems should the telic system. Our suggestion is that the centrally important boundary line between the external and the internal is defined by the criterion of meaning at the symbolic level. Clearly, Mayr, in his discussion of teleonymy, understood this concept in a sense much broader than that of symbolic process,[28] and Henderson, in his discussion of the fitness of the environment, never suggested that this category include symbolic meaning.[29] So far, the physical and biological sciences have systematically excluded the level of symbolic meaning from the empirical systems they conceive. This leaves us with the result that only man has language and, more important, culture in our sense.

We suggest that consequently only man among known living systems has telic problems in the sense in which we have defined that concept. This we think is because they are problems of an order that do not arise unless the capacity to learn and use symbols and their meanings already exists. We would relate this argument to Marshall Edelson's [30] interpretation of Freud that dreaming presupposes language and we would compare it with such evolutionary breakthroughs as bisexual reproduction. Thus, species at an evolutionary level more primitive than that of bisexually reproducing species have no functional need of strict differentiation between germ plasm and somatoplasm.

It is in this sense that we consider telic problems, and hence the telic system, to be internal to the human condition. As we have said, only human beings bother about what we call telic problems. It seems to follow that if human action is subject to the rational form of cognitive understanding, then there can be no cogent reason why the telic area should be excluded from this possibility of rationally apprehending. On the contrary, it is our view that *all* of the essential modes of human action orientation are relevant to man as actor's orientation to all of the environments to which, in the human condition, he is exposed.

[27] Auguste Comte, *Cours de philosophie positive,* 4th ed., 6 vols. (Paris: Baillère, 1877; first published in 1830–1842).

[28] Mayr, "Teleological and Teleonomic."

[29] Henderson, *Fitness of the Environment.*

[30] Marshall Edelson, "Language and Dreams: The Interpretation of Dreams Revisited," *Psychoanalytic Study of the Child,* vol. 27 (1972): 203–282.

If the external–internal axis is closer to that of space in its physical meaning, the axis labeled *instrumental–consummatory* is more closely related to time. An original prototype of this was the means-end relationship, with the clear proviso that the application of the means *must precede* the attainment of the end. The formulation of this rule for an instrumental-consummatory relationship is meant to generalize beyond the rational interest case, especially to include nonrational cases. The present problem is whether a further step of generalization can be accomplished that would comprise the principal aspects of the human condition other than action itself.[31]

It may be recalled that long ago, in discussing the action frame of reference, I examined the distinction between "means" and "conditions" of action.[32] The criterion of the distinction, which is essentially analytical, concerned whether or not these "external" entities were subject to the control of the actor. By this criterion, from the point of view of the action system, means as well as conditions are to be found in both the physical and the organic system of the human condition as well as in the action system itself. Their relation to action or in action can in this context be called instrumental in the sense of the four-function paradigm.

It should be remembered that in a more concrete sense *any* object of significance to human actors may be given any one of these types of meaning. Hence, physical objects often can be given consummatory meanings (e.g., artifacts, most especially perhaps works of art or food objects), and the same is true of organic objects. Certainly, many phenomena of nature (e.g., the proverbial sunset) have such meanings. At the same time, we would suggest that physical objects are most likely to have purely instrumental meanings, and this can occur with least strain, organic objects perhaps come next. Most obviously, human individuals and collectivities are among empirical objects least susceptible of being treated as wholly instrumental.

The bearing of these points on many previous and contemporary evaluative and ideological controversies will not be missed. Perhaps mention should be made of the Marxist dogma about the capitalistic treatment of human labor as a "commodity," [33] which is almost synonymous with a purely instrumentally significant object. (To mention this view is not to subscribe to it.) The relation of this axis to Kant's famous categorical imperative of *moral* action is also evident.[34] This is not the place to enter into an extended discussion of the relations between the Kantian imperative and Marxist doctrine. Our intention is simply to point out the irrelevance

[31] Dean Robert Gerstein, "A Note on the Continuity of Parsonian Action Theory," *Sociological Inquiry*, vol. 45, no. 4 (1975): 11–15.

[32] Parsons, *Structure of Social Action*, chap. 2.

[33] Alexander D. Lindsay, *Karl Marx's Capital: An Introductory Essay* (New York: Oxford University Press, 1925).

[34] Kant, *Critique of Practical Reason*.

of this doctrine to the theme of instrumental–consummatory problems for our frame of reference.

We maintained earlier that symbolic meanings constitute the essential dividing line between action systems and organic systems. We thus consider that Mayr's concept of teleonymy is more general than that of the means-end relationship and includes nonsymbolic organic level "strivings" that may be interpreted to be "subcultural." [35] Perhaps Edward C. Tolman's famous category of "Purposive Behavior in Animals and Men" [36] comes close to Mayr's teleonymy although Mayr would presumably object to the word "purpose." It would seem broadly correct to use "teleonymy" as a criterion of the distinction between the organic and the physical world in the sense that the physical world is not teleonomic even though it is "organized" in Henderson's usage.

Finally, what of locating the telic system on the instrumental side of this dichotomy? To some this must appear as almost a final reductio ad absurdum. Does not the telic category define the "chief end of man"? I think that the clue to the answer to this question lies in the word "define" in the preceding sentence. It seems correct to say that telic considerations do in fact *define* man's end and various other things, but this is not the same as saying that they *constitute* it. The point is that the *analytical* distinction between the action system and the telic system implies that there is a sense in which "telic systems do not act," which is parallel not only to that in which do physical systems not act but also to that in which they are not, as we have just said, teleonomic.

The principal reason, if it may be claimed to be such, for this judgment is that we conceive empirical living systems to be "bracketed" from two directions. The first direction encompasses the physical conditions of the environment and of the constitution of organisms and of human actors. The second direction is constituted by the telic conditions of organic and human existence, the transcendental, nonempirical, or *meta-* conditions, whichever phrasing is more appropriate. These conditions stand in a relation of cybernetic hierarchy to each other; indeed, we consider this cybernetic order to be the most important single axis of the directionality of evolution in the human condition at large, including the evolution of the physical cosmos, of organic life, and of the phenomena of human action.[37] From the *human* point of view, however, to which we have attempted consistently to adhere, the phenomena of cybernetic ordering and of evolution *must* be considered to be limited within a finite conception of a "universe." And, if the universe is to be considered "two-ended," not "one-ended" and thus "circular," there must be two, not one, *kinds* of limiting conceptions of "order,"

[35] Mayr, "Teleological and Teleonomic."

[36] Edward C. Tolman, *Purposive Behavior in Animals and Men* (New York: Appleton Century, 1932).

[37] Perhaps the most general appropriate term is "organization" in something like Henderson's sense (see Henderson, *Order of Nature,* pp. 73 ff.). Wiener stresses negative entropy.

as it were, or put a little differently of "conditions." Both of these limits must be considered to be sources of some kinds of 'inputs" to the human condition relevant to some kinds of human "experience," and both of them the destinations of some kinds of "outputs" from the human condition, that is, at the least of "meaningful" orientation.[38]

It does not seem appropriate here to pursue the discussion of these admittedly deep-ranging problems. It seems better to pass immediately to the presentation of our suggestions for further specific structuring of the paradigm of the human condition. Only when what we have to offer in such respects is before the reader will it be profitable to come back, but in the present chapter very briefly, to such considerations.

III. The Metatheoretical Framework

How are not only the structural but also the dynamic or processual relations within the human condition system to be described and analyzed? Since we are adopting an action point of reference, this means in particular how are the relations of the action system to the other three systems to be conceived? We can, however, hardly have a complete processual paradigm without also considering the relations of the organic to the physical system, the physical to the telic, and the organic to the telic. Nevertheless, it will be easier to take the first set of three, which involves the system of action, first.

There is one obvious difference from our previous work. In discussing such relations *within* the action system we have treated the mechanisms of interrelation as symbolic on *both* sides of each pair. Clearly, this practice has to be modified for the analysis of the human condition. For the first set of three, if our position is to be upheld, there can be symbolic mediation on only *one* side of the relationship; for the second set of three, the symbolic relation must be excluded altogether (in a sense subsequently to be explicated).

We have already maintained that human "orientation" to the world takes the form of treating the world, including that of action itself, as composed of entities that have symbolically apprehendable *meaning* to

---

[38] This problem of defining the sense in which the telic system must be conceived not to "act" first arose for me in an acute, substantively theoretical sense in the period shortly after publication of Talcott Parsons and Edward A. Shils (eds.), *Toward a General Theory of Action* (Cambridge, Mass.: Harvard University Press, 1951). At that time an asymmetry of the subsystems there treated became evident, with the contention that, unlike personalities and social systems, a cultural system did not act. I now think that this attribute should have been imputed to the telic system, not the cultural system as a subsystem of action. This issue has been discussed with great theoretical acumen by Victor M. Lidz, "The Functioning of Secular Moral Culture" (Doctoral dissertation, Harvard University, 1976).

human actors. We therefore think it appropriate to call these entities "objects" and to speak of the relevant mode of relationship as a subject-object relationship.

1. In the history of Western thought the prototype of such a relationship has usually been called "cognitive," the relation of a *knowing* subject to an object *known*. The classical statement of this was of course made by Descartes.[39] The great controversies in Western epistemology have been over the question of what contributes, and how, to knowledge of the "external world" as Descartes called it. Empiricists, usually using such phrases as "sense impressions," have stressed the contribution from *outside* the knowing subject; some, like Hume,[40] have denied the existence of any other component. Kant, however, insisted that there is another contribution, from the "categories of the understanding," which has be to conceived as *combining* with sense data.[41] The Kantian formula for empirical knowledge thus meets the formal requirement of a *two-way* relationship, symbolic or otherwise, between subject and object.

We think it is legitimate to adopt the Kantian account of *knowing* as the prototype of a mode of relation between human actors and worlds outside the action system as well as objects within it. From the human actor side, the feature of the human action system that is most crucial to the possibility of acquiring knowledge is that such systems are characterized by the possession of *language*. In this sense language is not itself a form of knowledge but a *medium* through which knowledge may be acquired from an indefinite range of categories of objects and communicated to and about objects. From this point of view, in the general sense of information theory, an object is an aspect of a relational nexus about which cognitively meaningful information can be acquired and communicated by human actors. Thus, among other things, in order to be "known" an object must be or have been "observed." "Have been" implies that knowledge of an object can be communicated by the use of language from an observer to another actor who has not observed that object.

As we suggested previously, we think that the cognitive mode of orientation, though in the human sense it is as old as language, first acquired formal status as the cultural phenomenon *science,* in the case of knowledge of the physical world; concentration on it was typical of all the great epistemologists of the seventeenth and eighteenth centuries. This is probably because physical objects do not react to their human knowers in the same sense that other humans, as well as more generally the higher living organisms, do. Apparently, then, other modes of orientation than the cognitive play a relatively more important part in relation to nonphysical objects.

2. Two of these are of immediate concern here. The first of them was

[39] Descartes, *Discourse on Method.*
[40] Hume, *Treatise of Human Nature.*
[41] Kant, *Critique of Pure Reason.*

perhaps classically formulated for modern culture by Freud, and it is appropriate to use his term *cathexis*.[42] It is significant that especially in his later work Freud explicitly used the word "object" in this context. The context clearly had to do with emotional or affective as distinguished from cognitive meaning, and Freud had primarily in mind human individuals although he did not exclude human collectivities or nonhuman objects.[43] (Animals also serve widely as symbols in human culture.)

We hold that the subject–object relationship in this sense has in one (for us) crucial respect essentially the same structure as in the cognitive case, namely, the *duality* that makes it possible for the relation to be conceived as *two*-way not *one*-way. In cathecting an object, a human actor receives something from the object and also gives something to it; both of these components have linguistic meaning from the action point of view. This relation is thus in the same sense constructed from components that come from *both* sides as in the cognitive case.

We must further point out that probably without exception human relations to objects have *both* cognitive and cathectic components. The relation between these components varies as a matter of relative primacy not of presence or absence.

It also seems reasonable to suppose that there is a certain priority in actors' cathectic relations, outside the sphere of action itself, to organisms as distinguished from physical objects. The "energy" that Freud contended is used in establishing and maintaining cathexes, *libido,* has its principal source [44] in the organism, and certain features of the organism, in particular the erogenous zones, acquire *symbolic* meanings in the "construction" of objects for cathexis.[45] This is not at all to say that only organisms are cathected, as symbolically or otherwise significant. All classes of objects are cathected, but there is a priority in this relation of the organic, parallel to that in relation to cognition of the physical.

3. The problem of categorizing the relation of actors to the telic sys-

[42] Sigmund Freud, *The Ego and the Id,* in vol. 19 of *Standard Edition* (1961; first published in German in 1923), pp. 12–16.

[43] Talcott Parsons and Edward A. Shils, with the assistance of James Olds, "Values, Motives, and Systems of Action," in Parsons and Shils (eds.), *Toward a General Theory of Action,* Part 2, pp. 47–243.

[44] This is a very tricky problem about which there has been much confusion. When we speak of the "source" of motivational or affective energy as used by the human personality, we most definitely do *not* imply that Freud's *libido* should be conceived as itself to be a form of organic energy but rather that one especially important "source" of such energy, in the sense of a factor essential for it, is what Freud called the "flow of stimulation" from the organism to the *psyche,* to use his term. The old confusion caused by the use of "instinct" as a translation of Freud's *Trieb* favors the interpretation that instinct or libido is a form of organic energy for Freud. Rather, libido is a complex, combinatorial phenomenon in the psyche or personality, of which energy from the organism is *one* component. I hope all readers of this chapter will keep this point *very* clearly in mind. If they do not, they will be in grave danger of misinterpreting much of the argument.

[45] Sigmund Freud, *New Introductory Lectures on Psycho-Analysis,* in vol. 22 of *Standard Edition* (1964; first published in German in 1933); pp. 5–182.

tem is of a somewhat different order from that of categorizing this relation to the other two systems although I should insist that there are still essential common features. Foremost of these features is surely that this relation takes the form of constructing meanings at the symbolic level, which are in principle formulable and communicable in linguistic terms. Although in this sense "transcencental" entities are often symbolized by human actors as themselves 'actors," such as gods, this is no more the "true" nature of such entities than is personification of the "forces of nature."

We would also hold that such a subject-object relation should be expected to maintain a duality of structure comparable to that which characterizes the other two relations we have discussed. In this case, however, we may suggest that the levels should be treated as reversed. The type case perhaps is that of Kant's categories of the understanding. He himself used the term "transcendental" to characterize their status in relation to empirical knowledge. Here the human actor, in this case a philosopher like Kant, can come to understand the necessity and role of such categories but *he* does not "determine" them. They come to human knowledge from "outside," in a sense parallel to that in which sense data come from the "external world." Thus, the human actor is a kind of middle man, the "combiner."

As in other connections, I should like here to attempt to generalize from the epistemological case to others. The general proposition is that for each of the modes of human orientation there is a *meta-* level that is concerned with "conditions" or "assumptions" that are necessary in order for an orientation to be meaningful, to "make sense." As was noted earlier, it seems to me that in the two critiques that followed *The Critique of Pure Reason* Kant followed essentially the same pattern of analysis that he had laid down in the latter. Assuming the basic duality of which we have been speaking and assuming also that human experience is available or given in both other sectors as sense data are in that of empirical cognition, he sought to clarify and define the transcendental component for each of the others. Clearly, the other spheres are sufficiently different both from that of pure reason and from each other so that *three* not one or two rubrics were necessary.

The more familiar of the other two spheres is that of "practical reason." It is quite clear that in Kant's treatment this is the sphere we ordinarily think of as that of *morality*. In terms of our paradigm it is the sphere of meaningful relations among human actors, in other words, part of the general system of action. The equivalent of the categories of the understanding in the epistemological sphere Kant found in his famous categorical imperative, which in a certain sense may be interpreted as a modernization of the Golden Rule of Christianity.

This position of Kant's is clearly of central importance to the general theory of action. We hold that it is the locus of the most fundamental underlying premises or assumptions of *social* ordering at the human level. It should explicitly be defined not as the *data* of moral problems but as the *transcendental normative conditions of the ordering of such data.* This Kantian philosophical position clearly underlies both Durkheim's and Weber's treatment of the moral component of societies, especially modern societies.

The Critique of Judgment, then, dealt with what Kant himself called the sphere of esthetic judgment. We may relate this sphere to the goal-attainment cell of the paradigm of transcendental components, which has a particularly important bearing on human orientation to the organic sphere, including the human body itself. This sphere encompasses tele-onomic aspects in a variety of connections, particularly of birth and death but also of "pleasure."

Finally, there is according to our paradigm a fourth sphere of transcendental ordering to which Kant did not devote a special critique. We think it has particularly to do with religion. It seems possible that Kant, as a good child of the Enlightenment, was sufficiently skeptical in this sphere so that he did not venture to say anything positive but rested content with stating his famous denial of the *provability* of the existence of God. There is, however, a logical gap here that demands to be filled.

It is also relevant that in the paradigm the place of this category is the *Latency* cell. We may interpret this to mean that this aspect of the transcendental order does not enter explicitly into the human condition in the same sense that the other three aspects do. However, such empirical studies as those of both Durkheim [46] and Weber,[47] and to a lesser extent Freud,[48] demonstrated the importance of religion in human action systems. Both of the former struggled to define the religious component more specifically. It therefore does not seem to be merely "naive metaphysics" to work on the assumption that there must be "something there" in the sense of a potential, cognitively understandable set of objects, along with objects of cognitive, moral, and esthetic experience.[49]

Robert N. Bellah made an important suggestion in this connection.[50] He objected to the tendency of the "great agnostics" of the turn of the last century generation to insist that religious symbols must "symbolize some-

[46] Emile Durkheim, *The Elementary Forms of the Religious Life,* trans. Joseph Ward Swain (New York: Free Press, 1965; first published in French in 1912).

[47] Weber, *Sociology of Religion.*

[48] Sigmund Freud, *Moses and Monotheism: Three Essays,* in vol. 23 of *Standard Edition* (1964; first published in German in 1939).

[49] Perhaps this is where Kant's category of the "transcendent," as distinguished from the "transcendental," should be placed.

[50] Robert N. Bellah, "Between Religion and Social Science," in Rocco Caporale and Antonio Grumelli (eds.), *The Culture of Unbelief* (Berkeley: University of California Press, 1971), chap. 14.

thing," that is, have referents that are empirically knowable objects within the human condition. The most famous example is Durkheim's contention that God symbolizes "society," to be sure in a highly ambiguous meaning of that word.[51] As an alternative, Bellah suggested the idea of "symbolic realism," according to which the meaning of the symbols should be regarded as "immanent" in themselves rather than to be found in referential objects outside of them.[52] We would suggest that if the above analysis is acceptable, Bellah's idea of symbolic realism should apply to *one component* of the symbol, namely, its "particularized" but not to its transcendental—again in Kant's sense—component. We may reiterate that the two components lie at different levels. What we are here calling the "particularized" component of religious symbols is comparable to the sense data of empirical knowledge not to the categories; to the phonetic particulars of linguistic utterances not to the deep structures; to the organic phenotype not to the genotype; and indeed to the interest structure of human societies not to their institutional patterning.

Turning now to the relationship pairs that do not directly involve the action system, we may first make an important point that follows from what has been said earlier. To be sure, in none of these three systems is symbolic meaning substantively involved in the *processes* of interrelation as conceived here, and as we have postulated that it is on *both* sides within the action system. Furthermore, it is involved on *one* side in those human condition relationships that involve the action system, as we have just reviewed them. We are, however, as we have insisted from the beginning, dealing with the human condition from an anthropocentric point of view so that in *this* context we are *giving* symbolic meaning to the phenomena we are discussing. What we are *not* doing is to impute the apprehension and communication of meaning at this level *to the objects* that we are considering. We do not attempt to interpret what they are and do from their own "subjective point of view," as Weber called it.[53]

The most familiar of the three relational nexus is that between the physical and the organic system. This is clearly a two-way relationship in our interchange sense. From the point of view of the study of organisms this is usually formulated in the statement that the organism is an "open" system involved in continual interchange with its physical environment and, for our purposes confined to animals. Thus, especially for the higher organisms there is a continual output of heat, through skin and lungs, balanced by internal oxydation.[54] Oxygen is absorbed from the air and carbon

[51] See Robert N. Bellah's Introduction to his edition of Emile Durkheim, *On Morality and Society* (Chicago: University of Chicago Press, 1973).

[52] Bellah, "Between Religion and Social Science."

[53] Max Weber, *Economy and Society,* ed. Guenther Roth and Claus Wittich (Totowa: Bedminster, 1968, "Basic Sociological Terms;" first published in German in 1922), 1: 3–62.

[54] Walter B. Cannon, *The Wisdom of the Body* (New York: Norton, 1932).

dioxide extruded to the environment. Nutritional materials are ingested from the environment and waste products returned to the environment. All this is exceedingly familiar. The same of course is true, with the appropriate empirical differences, of plants.

That there is in some sense a "mutuality" of adaptation is a less familiar idea. It has, however, been stated in Henderson's conception of the fitness of the environment, to which we have referred frequently. The environment does not merely "condition" the functioning of living systems in random ways; the relation is *selective* on *both* sides. Not least important, there is a set of physico-chemical components that is internally part of any given living organism. Life, from this point of view, is a mode of the *organization* of the physical world, and not every set of physical components is equally favorable to different kinds of living organizations.

From the human action point of view, then, there is a variety of meanings of the organic-physical relationship. The core of these meanings is to be found in the biological and physical sciences, but this knowledge has come to be applied in innumerable ways (which need not be gone into here).

A second example of a relationship not involving action is that between the telic and the physical. Looked at in terms of human orientations, both systems are outside the system of action and hence the ingredients of their human meanings have to "come" through the channels that were reviewed earlier. The relation itself, however, includes the grounds of what is often spoken of as "cosmological" problems for man. For example, what is the meaning of the enormous development of astronomical knowledge in the twentieth century? The physical universe is now understood to be of an extensity beyond the wildest dreams of Copernicus and Newton. Another example is that of the meaning of death. Various people, including Freud (his view of the "death instinct"), have defined organic death as the assimilation—in a sense, the "return"—of the living organism to the inorganic, that is, physical, state.[55] This phenomenon clearly has human meaning not only in a scientific sense but also in a religious sense, as do certain cosmological problems.

Finally, the third relational category not involving action directly is that of the telic to the organic. This encompasses what are in one sense the "facts of life," namely facts about man as organism. These of course include birth and death, human reproduction, and the differentiation of humans by age and sex. Scientific knowledge about these facts of life must, as in the case of the physical world, rest on inputs from outside the action system, both "data" and cognitive categories. Similarly, the religious meanings of these facts must be built upon certain categories of human experience and upon the constitutive structures of the religious meaning of the human

[55] Sigmund Freud, *Beyond the Pleasure Principle*, in vol. 18 of *Standard Edition* (1955; first published in German in 1920), pp. 7–66.

condition and its vicissitudes. The primary category of meaning at this point seems to be neither cognitive meaning nor religious meaning but a dimension of orientation that is often referred to as "feeling." Perhaps, indeed, this is an appropriate place to make use of the much discussed concept of *affect*. In order to avoid certain connotations of the contrast between "pleasure" and "pain" perhaps an appropriate characterization of the dichotomy is "euphoric-disphoric." I further suggest that this is the primary field of relevance of Kant's canons of "judgment" that he himself qualified by the adjective "esthetic" [56] although he also used the word later adopted by Freud—*Lust*.[57] Finally, it must not be forgotten that *all* of the categories in this scheme are analytical not concrete.

We may now undertake another step in formal categorization, again using the theoretical model provided by the elaboration of the four-function scheme for analysis of the general system of action and its subsystems. This step concerns not the designation of systems and subsystems and the characterization of their structural relations to each other but the conceptual framework with which we approach the analysis of the dynamics of their interrelations. This conceptual scheme may be regarded as an extension of the pattern of regulation that Henderson attributed to all organic systems.[58] Parts II and III of this chapter attempted, by reviewing the principal substantive relations, to prepare the way for this formalization.

In building up a conceptual armory adequate for coping with the analytical problems we wish next to work out, there is a further particularly important item, namely, cybernetic theory, associated especially with Norbert Wiener.[59] Wiener's relevant work came a full generation after Henderson's—Wiener's book *Cybernetics* was published in 1948. Then, whereas Henderson's work above all concerned the boundary relations between physical and organic systems, that of Wiener may be said to be applicable to the whole range of science, from physics to the theory of action and very much including biology.[60]

Most discussions of Wiener confine their attention to the two complementary categories of energy and information and their relations to each other. This topic is indeed central, but it should not be forgotten that in his most general statement, Wiener added and related to the other two a third category, the familiar *matter*. This addition gives a much more comprehensive basis for our purposes than the first two alone.

There can be no doubt of the significance for our purposes of the

[56] Kant, *Critique of Judgment*.

[57] Freud, *Beyond the Pleasure Principle*.

[58] Henderson, *Fitness of the Environment*.

[59] Wiener, *Cybernetics*.

[60] In the following discussion, we shall rely on Wiener's work, as well as on Henderson's two relevant books, *The Fitness of the Environment* and *The Order of Nature*.

energy-information relationship. The central proposition is well known, namely, that under properly defined conditions a system high in energy but low in information can be effectively controlled by a system with the obverse characteristics—that is, one low in energy but high in information. Thus, for example, a thermostat that has been "set" can control, with the use of minimal physical energy, the temperature of an enclosed space by turning a heating apparatus on and off when the temperature deviates slightly from the set value, the thermostat of course being high on information, the heating apparatus high on energy.

Wiener's first explorations were in the organic field, especially its physiological branch, so it is clear that the control processes in such systems by high information subsystems could be brought under Henderson's category of regulation, among the three organic categories with which Henderson dealt. From the point of view of this amateur biologist, there seem to be three principal such levels of regulation applying to the individual organism: that through enzymes and the like at the intracellular level; that through hormones and other components in the bloodstream at the total organism level; and that through the nervous system, especially in regulating the behavior of an organism in relation to its environment. In addition, we should note again that at the level of populations and species the genes also involve, quite explicitly in the work of the microgeneticists, informational control processes.

It seems clear that in the preceding respects the Wiener scheme has in common with that of Henderson the ordering of a set of relationships both within the organic sphere and between it and the physical. Some common themes may be seen to be that a living organism is conceived to be a physico-chemical system that is unique in at least two respects. First, it is a specially *organized* system that is characterized by a pattern of internal order different from that of its environment—a conception with which Henderson was fully familiar. Second, this difference implies that the organism has boundaries vis-à-vis its environment, and the differential states within and outside the boundaries are maintained by "mechanisms" that Henderson characterized as involving "regulation" and that would certainly, in Wiener's terms, involve information controlling energy.

On the background of both analyses, there is, however, a further problem. Put in Wiener's terms, the question is whether it is only the properties of the physical matter that composes subsystems at the physico-chemical level that account for the capacities differentiating them from other such systems to regulate internal order and to maintain boundaries? For this to happen, matter must through some kind of chemical or other processes be caused to produce energy. Henderson gave a precise account of how for organic life this process of energy production from matter occurs through oxydation, generally the chemical combination of carbon compounds with oxygen, which produces among other things carbon dioxide.

The carbon compounds may in a sense be regarded as the fuel necessary to produce organic energy.

There are, however, two further aspects of the problem. First, if the distinctiveness of the organism is to persist for any appreciable time, the supply of fuel in this sense initially present within its boundaries will not suffice. This fuel is consumed in the course of what Henderson called "metabolic" processes, and if these are to continue the fuel must be replaced by inputs from the environment, as well as potentially toxic products of metabolism, like carbon dioxide disposed of. Thus, physico-chemically speaking, an organism must be an *open* system engaged in continual interchanges with its environment. Second, if the oxydation process that produces organically useful energy is to meet the conditions of continuing functioning of the organism, it cannot consist of oxydation at random, like setting fire to a pile of dry wood. It must be a *controlled* process of oxydation, which means that the fuel must be especially processed after its input to the organism and the conditions under which it is "burned" meticulously regulated. At any rate, in the higher organisms this occurs through the ATP complex,[61] the biochemistry of which has come to be understood only since Henderson's day.

It is at this point that Wiener's scheme makes contact with the category of "complexity," which from a different point of view figures prominently in Henderson's. Oxydation, as the process for the organic world necessary to transform matter into energy, is the focal center of the ramified cluster of chemical substances and processes that are characteristic of living systems, of which in turn the propertics of carbon constitute the center. Of course, oxydation also plays a role in the biochemistry of proteins, enzymes, hormones, RNA, DNA, and many other substances that have become familiar in the biology of recent generations.

It would be unsuitable to leave this discussion of Wiener without referring to a striking statement of his toward the end of *Cybernetics*.[62] To wit, when he first concerned himself with matters physiological, the almost universal disposition was to regard the organism primarily as a "heat engine" and to state the relevant biochemical problems accordingly. By the time he wrote *Cybernetics,* however, matters had greatly changed and the primary disposition among physiologists had come to be to regard the organism above all as an information processing system. This is a striking change indeed and surely one that fits the design of the present intellectual enterprise.

It also seems to be entirely clear that the importance of the relations that Wiener set forth between systems high in energy and those high in information clearly applies to the action level. For long we have grounded

[61] J. D. Watson, *Molecular Biology of the Gene,* 2d ed. (New York: W. A. Benjamin, 1970).

[62] Wiener, *Cybernetics,* pp. 53–54.

much of our analysis, for example, of the ways in which social organization is controlled by cultural symbol systems and at the individual level motivational energy is controlled by nonenergic factors deriving from the internalization of objects and from information received from the external environment, in this point of view.

In the latter context one particularly striking and highly relevant example may be given. In *The Ego and the Id* (written twenty-seven years before the publication of Wiener's *Cybernetics*), Freud, in discussing the relations between these two structural subsystems of the human personality, introduced the metaphor of a horse and its human rider.[63] The id, which of course has the role of the horse, is obviously much stronger than the ego, its human rider, and in any contest of sheer strength would easily win (surely, greater strength can be read "higher in energy"). Yet if the horse is "broken in" (read "socialized") and the rider sufficiently skilled, the rider can in certain respects control the behavior of the horse—where it takes the rider, at what pace, etc. (again surely, had Freud known Wiener's work, he would have agreed that in Wiener's sense a human rider can be "higher in information" than a horse.) In the context of the common tendency today to interpret Freud as an instinctive reductionist, his use of this metaphor seems particularly important.

Throughout this discussion we have construed Wiener's categories as applicable throughout the range of the hierarchy among the four functional subsystems *even* at the level of the human condition. If this interpretation is correct, it clearly must signify that the three basic concepts must be meant in a sense more general than that in their fields of original usage and must be capable of further specification to particular areas.

Let us take energy first. It seems clear that Wiener's original reference was to energy in the physical sense, heat, for example. He applied this model, however, without hesitation to organic phenomena. But from the evidence we have reviewed, especially in the work of Henderson, *among* physical or physico-chemical processes of the production of energy, which we presume in some sense to constitute its transformation from matter, the energizing of living systems is not just physical energizing in general but is rather a special setting in which that process can take place. The most striking case is that of the ATP complex, which to my knowledge Wiener does not mention and Henderson could not have known about.

The question then arises whether organic energy is the same thing as physical energy. The whole logic of the position we have been working from and on would suggest *no!* for the answer, but this is not to deny continuity.

The central point of the relevant logic is that any functionally essential component of structure and process must be conceived as having been produced by a combination of components and factors deriving from the

[63] Freud, *The Ego and the Id.*

next lower level of organization of relevant systems. This point seems to be made crystal clear by Henderson.[64] The concept of physical energy in all its forms simply cannot be adopted unchanged at the organic level. It seems that to become organic, physical energy must undergo a transformation that must be combinatorial in nature—presumably, the development of chemical compounds from the combination of chemical elements is the prototype at this level.

Then, whatever the immense ramifications within the organic sphere, we think one of the most important inferences from Freud's work has to be that in the transition from the organic level to that of the psychic, as he himself called it, there occurs another transformative and combinatorial change. If this interpretation is correct, then Freud's conception of libido cannot legitimately be interpreted as organic energy in *any* form, that of instinct or otherwise. One of its components is clearly the "flow of stimulation" from the organism, which Freud stressed,[65] but this is only *one* of the components. I submit (and will try to substantiate later) that among the other principal ones are symbolic meanings at the human level. Somewhat similar considerations should be relevant at the other boundary line, that between the human action level and the telic. I shall postpone discussion of these problems until a further treatment of the telic system in its relation to that of action has been presented. After all, also, these problems were outside the range of interest of such authorities as Henderson and Wiener.

It is somewhat more unorthodox to suggest that a similar relativizing needs to be applied to the concept "matter" since that has so widely been assumed, at least outside the discipline of physics, to be a physical absolute. Our cue to formulating a suggestion in this direction may raise the problem of what should be meant by the *internal environment* of an organism even of a given species. From one point of view, particularly as analyzed by Henderson and Walter B. Cannon,[66] a mammalian organism *is,* for example, a physico-chemical system, encompassing many chemical components and physical features in common with the external environment but surely in a pattern of *organization* different from the latter except for other organisms of the same species and genus. Is it not reasonable to suggest that in a sense relevant to Wiener's usage of the concept "matter," this organized physico-chemical system may be construed to constitute a new kind of matter relative to the table of the chemical elements, all of which can be identified outside any living system! This seems to be true in particular from the point of view of considering the conditions of the generation of energy. If the conception of organic as distinguished from physical energy makes any sense, its base in matter must be the whole

[64] Henderson, *Order of Nature* and *Fitness of the Environment.*
[65] Freud, *The Ego and the Id.*
[66] Cannon, *Wisdom of the Body.*

organized biological system not just a set of chemical elements that have properties of a form that is not dependent on their relations within any system of living organization.

If this line of argument makes any scientific sense with reference to the much controverted boundary between physical and organic systems, as defined for the humanly significant world, it is difficult not to raise the question of the relevance of these kinds of considerations to the next primary boundary in the cybernetic series we have postulated, namely, that between the organic and the action level. (It is not irrelevant to note that with respect to the other boundary there are still those who stoutly maintain a position of biological mechanism whereby living organisms are simply physical systems without anything special about them.)[67]

If we are nearly right that what we have called the human action system should be treated as a newly emergent level in the evolution of living systems, then there is every reason to believe that it also has evolved an internal environment, or a set of them, that should be distinguished from and related to the external environments of the same system. To my knowledge, it was first Durkheim, thinking in the Cartesian tradition, who endowed this environment with objective status, or "facticity," from the point of view of the human individual who acted in relation to it. He did so by calling the empirical component of the knowledge of this environment *facts* and labeling the entity about which these constituted knowledge the *milieu social*. Earlier I discussed the interpretation of Durkheim's view —that it constitutes the postulation of an environment internal to the general system of action.[68]

If I suggest now, which I do in all seriousness, that Durkheim's position may, in terms congruent with the position of Wiener, be interpreted to mean there is here a new order of *matter* in Wiener's sense of the term, I shall doubtless be greeted with the expression "ridiculous." The critic will go on to say that "everybody knows" that matter is a category of the physical world and it can only cause confusion to attribute it to phenomena of human action, which I myself contend consists mainly of symbolic meanings (the very antithesis of things physical).

This commonsense view, however, overlooks one set of problems, namely, whether Wiener's triad of fundamental categories (matter, energy, and information) does in fact apply to the whole range of phenomena accessible to understanding by science. That they are not confined to what is usually called the physical level but extend to the biological has already been made quite clear from Wiener's own discussions, unless one is to exempt matter from this extension. It must also apply to the level of action, or is libido after all just another term for physical energy (like heat

[67] Jacques Loeb, *The Mechanistic Conception of Life* (Cambridge, Mass.: Harvard University Press, 1964).

[68] See Chapter 10 of the present volume.

or electricity) and Freud, so far as he contributed to understanding human action, essentially a physicist? I have yet to encounter a plausible attempt to deduce the psychoanalytic theory of personality from the general laws of physics!

If the case for relativizing the concepts of matter and energy as Wiener used them for purposes of cybernetic theory is a good one along the lines just discussed, that for information seems to be very clear. The step from the level of microbiology to human action systems is by most standards rather a long one. Yet a social scientist cannot but be struck by the fact that microgeneticists themselves directly use the "language of language" in their own writing. DNA (Deoxyribonucleic acid) and its operation comes to be understood in terms of a genetic code. The *codon,* a succession of three adjacent genes on the DNA molecule, is a sentence, with the three items serving as subject, verb, and predicate. Then the information embodied in the codon is transcribed onto RNA and finally through enzyme action is "translated" into the synthesis of a protein.[69] Surely, this is turning the tables on the physical or mechanistic reductionists with a vengeance! It is taking the model of human language, which is about as nonmaterial as you can get according to the philosophy of science of the last two centuries, and applying it to the organization of chemical processes in the most technical sense. Ernst Haeckel [70] and his like must be revolving with great rapidity in their graves. Is this science, or have people who call themselves scientists simply gone mad?

If this is the intellectual climate of microbiology, which has the reputation of being very hard science indeed, it does not seem too difficult to defend the view that symbolic meanings have something to do with the structure of human personality and that personality is not reducible to an epiphenomenon of the biochemical processes of the brain. Furthermore, we should note again that for Wiener himself the relevance of the concept "information" did not stop at the organic level but covered all the realms of science.

The most striking set of cases among physical systems of course is certain human artifacts. Thus, one of Wiener's favorite examples of a cybernetic control mechanism in a physical system was the "governor" built into a steam engine, a more "mechanical" case than the thermostat. This, however, extends above all into the field of communication technology, especially the telephone, radio, and television fields. Here the humanly significant functions of such technologies have to do with the processing and transmission of information, precisely in Wiener's technical sense of that term.

[69] Gunther S. Stent, "DNA," in Gerald Holton (ed.), *The Twentieth-Century Sciences* (New York: Norton, 1972), pp. 198–226.

[70] Ernst Haeckel, *The Evolution of Man: A Popular Exposition of the Principal Points of Human Ontogeny and Phylogeny* (New York: Appleton, 1886).

Perhaps, however, the most striking example is the modern computer. For present purposes the most important point is that a computer is in the strictest sense a physical system that operates electronically rather than mechanically. Of course there is no evidence that operable computers have spontaneously evolved in strictly *physical* nature. Those we know are human artifacts manufactured according to human design. If there is an analogue in nature it is clearly the brain of the higher organisms, especially the human brain, but this is not in the usual sense a physical phenomenon; rather, it is very definitely a phenomenon of the organic system.

Nevertheless, we have no reason to assume that some of the factors that make computers possible are not present in the physical world independent of human agency. We should not forget that for Henderson "organization," which for him was closely related to the concept "system," was an essential feature of the order of nature generally, including its physical aspect. There is every reason to think that Wiener also shared this view. Indeed, it may be appropriate to close this phase of the discussion by recalling the famous statement of Einstein that the most incomprehensible thing about nature is its comprehensibility for human understanding.[71] Einstein was thinking mainly of physical nature, and if the category of information has strictly nothing to do with the "nature of nature," it would be difficult to make sense of Einstein's dictum.

IV. The Structural Paradigm Elaborated

On the basis of the preceding disquisitions, we now feel prepared to introduce the next step in our program of formalization of the analytical essentials of our paradigm of the human condition. This is graphically summarized in Figure 2, which follows a format identical with those previously worked out for the social system and the general system of action.[72] Figure 2 constitutes the extension of the four-function analysis of Figure 1 by applying the logic of its analysis again to each of the four primary subsystems of the human condition: the action system, the human organic system, the physico-chemical system, and the telic system. The result is a sixteenfold table, with each of the previous four categories redivided into four.

It may be noted that Figure 2 was not included in the first unpublished draft of this chapter for a very simple reason; namely, at the time that draft was written it had not yet proved possible sufficiently to work out the

[71] Cf. fn. 17.

[72] Talcott Parsons and Gerald M. Platt, in collaboration with Neil J. Smelser, *The American University* (Cambridge, Mass.: Harvard University Press, 1973), "Technical Appendix: Some General Theoretical Paradigms," figs. A2 and A6.

Figure 2 Structure of the Human Condition as System

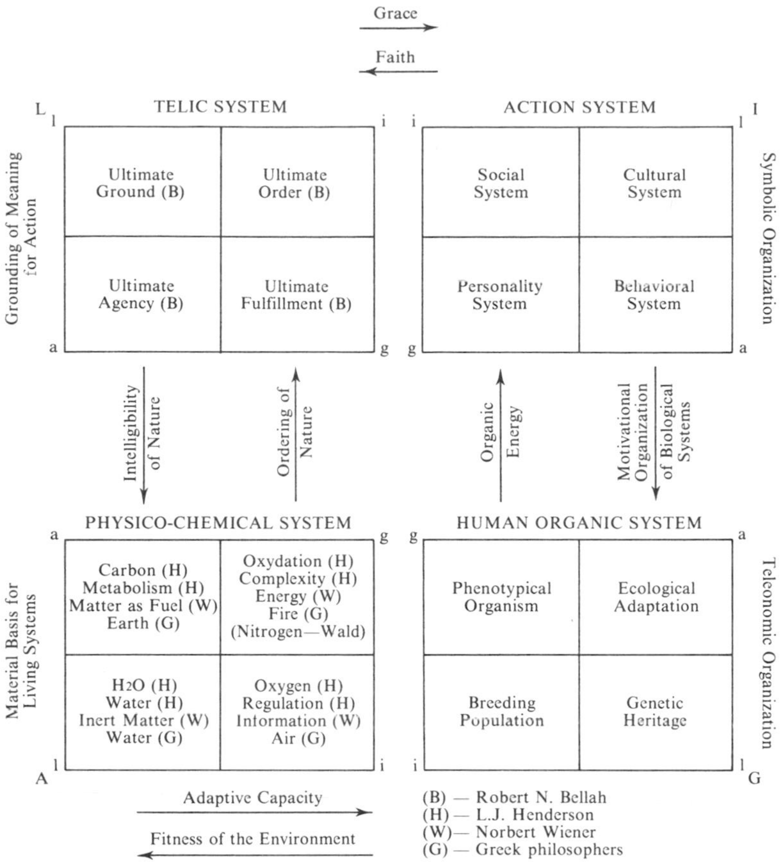

analytical problems to feel confident that the categories inserted into each of the twelve boxes outside the four of the action system itself made sufficient theoretical sense to justify their publication. Needless to say, the formulations have gone through a series of modifications and Figure 2 is necessarily highly tentative.

For two reasons we have treated the human action system as the primary point of reference. The first is the mundane reason that it marks the intellectual path by which the formulation of the larger conceptual scheme has been reached. There is something to be said, as investigative policy, for proceeding from the relatively well known to the unknown rather than vice versa. The second reason, however, is that, as we stated at the beginning of the chapter, we conceive the human condition as a version of whatever universe may in some sense be knowable and which is quite specifically and self-consciously formulated and organized from the perspective of its significance to human beings and indeed relatively contemporary ones. From this point of view it is the system of action that constitutes the necessary reference base for such an enterprise. Whatever the possibilities, for instance, through transcendental meditation, of transcending this reference base, we have not attempted to do so but have quite consciously used the perspective of the sciences developed by twentieth-century Western human beings in the cultural tradition of that civilization. The action system is, in our opinion, the most sophisticated cognitive framework within which this perspective has yet been formulated. We therefore write and speak as human actors within that framework and attempt to relate ourselves to the rest of the human condition on the assumption that in the relevant sense this is "what we are."

The breakdown of the general system of action into four functional subsystems has a long history in our work and need not be considered problematical for present purposes. The reader should, however, be reminded that we have abandoned the earlier usage of treating the "behavioral organism" as the adaptive subsystem of the general system of action and have substituted for it the "behavioral system" as that conception has been worked out by Lidz and Lidz.[73] Let us, then, essay an entry into the less familiar territory by discussing the place and breakdown analytically of the organic system, especially relative to that of action. First, we have labeled it the *human* organic system, as distinguished from such common designations as the biosphere, which as such have no specific reference to things human. Our question is, in what does this "world" consist from a human perspective? Entering on the consideration of this question, then, an initial point of reference must be that "I," that is, any human actor, am at the same time an actor in our analytical sense *and* a living organism of the species *Homo sapiens*. As organism, my identity is not specified by being human alone, but within that rubric I belong (anatomically) to one of two sex categories and have a fairly definite place in a structure of age and succession of generations. At higher levels of aggregation, I may be identified as belonging to an ethnic group, a territorial-residential group, and various others.

To say that the individual of reference "is human" is thus not only to characterize a unique organism but also to place that organism in a larger biological context. To say that organically speaking "I am human" is to assert membership in a particular organic species that most notably is characterized by a highly specific genetic heritage, one not shared by any other species to say nothing of living organisms in general. Surely, our microgeneticist friends, because they have been absorbed in studies of *E. coli*, do not assert that since this species has been so useful to their research there is no difference between it and other species of living organisms, especially *Homo sapiens*, of which all microbiologists are phenotypical exemplars.

---

[73] Lidz and Lidz, "The Psychology of Intelligence of Jean Piaget."

Figure 3   The Phenotypical Human Organism

Genetic Heritage	Regulation
Metabolism	Complexity

L ⌐ ¬ I
A ⌐ ¬ G

Since we have stressed the importance of Henderson's functional categories applied to the individual phenotypical organism, it is important to give the reader a place to fit them into our formal scheme. This is at the level of differentiated breakdown immediately beyond that presented in Figure 2 and shown here as Figure 3, which is a further specification of the G–cell of Figure 2. Seen in this way metabolism may be treated as involved primarily in the adaptive functioning of the individual organism and in regulation in the integrative functioning. It seems also, as noted in an earlier discussion, that Henderson's regulation is primarily informational in Wiener's sense. Metabolism, then, is the process by which organic energy is produced. In *The Fitness of the Environment,* however, Henderson also related metabolism to his third category, which he called "complexity." This stands on a somewhat different level from the other two, but it has seemed most appropriate to place it in the G–cell of Figure 3. Complexity stands for the biochemical potential of providing the base for a very wide variety of organic functions. Finally, we noted previously that Henderson, as a physiologist, did not even mention the genetic heritage, which, however, is to be found not only in the species but also in every phenotypical member of it, indeed in every cell of the body.

As a phenotypical, individual, human organism, the human being is as such a member not only of his species, which differs from all others although it has many things in common with others, but also of narrower collective groups of human organisms, notably that recently important category "population." In particular, we consider it highly important that a human society, as that concept has come to be defined by a number of action theory sociologists, should organically speaking be regarded as the social organization of a population in the biological sense.

This is a particularly significant node of articulation for our purposes because there is a striking matching of the biologist's criteria of what for him are the primary collective units and the sociologist's criteria of a human society. Thus, Mayr [74] listed three criteria of a species: (1) that it is a "reproductive community" usually not interbreeding with other species; (2) that it is an "ecological community" whose members are not spread

[74] Mayr, *Populations, Species, and Evolution.*

randomly in physical location but are concentrated in a defined "habitat," which of course may be shared with other species; and, most important, (3) that its members share a common gene pool. Since a population in the biological sense is a segmentary subunit of a species, the same criteria apply to it.

A human society, then, (1) has a definable membership, mainly, though not always wholly, recruited by organic reproduction; (2) it maintains control—vis-à-vis other societies—of a definite territorial area; and (3) as a system of action it is characterized by a common cultural heritage, usually, though not invariably, including a common language.[75] It is clear that since there is only one human species but many societies, the organic membership base of a society is a population.

Constitutive of the human species and its populations, in common with all other species down to the humble *E. coli,* is a gene pool, or genetic heritage. The members of a human society, as constituting a population, stand in some kind of relation to other human populations organized to constitute other societies. At the level of significance for action these relationships may be highly complex like trade relations at economic levels, political relations, and cultural relations. At the same time, any society and its members stand in exceedingly complex relations to numerous other species. This is to say that they are part of what biologists call one or more ecosystems. Organically, probably the most basic relationship is human dependence, along with all other animals, on the plant world for food materials or, indirectly so far as he consumes animal foods, on the food animal's utilization of plants. Other organisms also have many meanings to human beings—from our love of horses and dogs to our hostile feeling toward mosquitoes and other "pests," though we seldom pay much attention to beneficent insects, to say nothing of bacteria, whereas the bacterial agents of infectious diseases are among the prime "enemies" of mankind.

For our purposes, the most illuminating treatment of the relations between the organic and the physical world is Henderson's, which is of course crucially supplemented by Wiener, with the significance of both depending on the common background in knowledge of the physical as well as organic worlds. It is essential for us, however, to note that the special importance of Henderson and Wiener rests in their *focusing* of certain elements of the more general fund of biological and physico-chemical knowledge on problem areas relevant to the conditions on which organic life depends and through it the human condition.

Here Henderson's "fitness" analysis presented a special breakdown of specific features of the physical world, which was the natural starting point. The primary reference of course is his review of the properties of water and evaluation of their significance for living systems. For its place in the

[75] Talcott Parsons, *The Evolution of Societies,* ed. with an introduction by, Jackson Toby (Englewood Cliffs: Prentice-Hall, 1977).

physical environment of human as of all other forms of organic life, water is thus the natural pattern-maintenance base.

Henderson could not have stressed more strongly the theme of the stabilizing effects of such a water focused environment, its chemical inertness, the predominance of its liquid form, its high specific heat, its circulation, etc. Yet, one of its two chemical components, hydrogen, is among the most combustible of elements—witness the disasters accompanying attempts to use hydrogen gas to lift balloons. It is presumably this extreme combustibility, certainly in the presence of free oxygen, which cannot be eliminated from the earth's atmosphere, that accounts for the fact that the primary energy source of organic life on the earth is not the oxydation of hydrogen but that of carbon and its compounds (in many of which to be sure hydrogen has a place). This, then, is the locus on the environmental side of Henderson's special category of complexity. Carbon may be regarded as the chemical base of organically utilizable energy production; whereas hydrogen must be "controlled" either by its "impoundment" in water or by its involvement in more complex organic compounds. Since oxydation is the basic chemical source of organic energy, there must be a balance maintained between the chemical constituents of this process, carbon compounds and oxygen, and the waste products resulting from the process, carbon dioxide and, for the higher animal, urine.

This set of conditions provides a kind of functional "ground plan" for the existence of organic, including human, life. It will be seen that the formulation of the paradigm is quite explicitly from the human organic perspective, not in any sense a generalized paradigm of the nature of the physical world. This arrangement, however, seems to be congruent with Wiener's categorization. Thus, we suggest, as outlined previously, that his category of matter should be treated as common between the L– and the A–cell of the paradigm and that the distinction between its two significant "forms" for our purposes should be made between water, with its property of chemical inertness, and what we have called "fuel," which Henderson clearly centered in carbon and its compounds. If this sector of the chemical environment were chemically as inert as water, presumably there would be no organic life. The outcome of the oxydation process, then, is energy, I think without question in the technical sense of Wiener's use of that concept. Finally, however, this outcome, in the setting of fitness, does not occur in the "free" setting of the environmental world, as in the numerous cases of uncontrolled fires, but in a highly controlled way inside the organism. Chemically this process primarily involves balancing oxygen utilization, fuel, and the production and disposal of energy and carbon dioxide. Henderson called this process regulation, and surely it involves in Wiener's sense the control, by informational mechanisms, of higher energy systems and their background in matter. Considering the complexity and the unfamiliarity of this way of ordering our knowledge of the physico-chemical environment of organic systems, it seems to us that our attempt at formalization, with the aid of Henderson and Wiener, has produced a scheme that somehow makes sense and is more than a mere figment of the imagination. But the reader must judge!

Henderson and Wiener can surely be considered to be among the most intellectually respectable "meta-scientists" of the present century; hence, reliance on them can constitute an "appeal to authority," in Pareto's term,[76] made at little risk to an author's intellectual reputation. Reference to pre-Socratic Greek philosophy may, however, be a different matter, opening the door to the accusation of wild speculation. However that may be, there was set forth in that cultural milieu, more than twenty-five centuries ago, a set of designations and a classification of the elements of nature. To readers of college textbooks in the history of philosophy this is familiar as the set earth, air, fire, and water. The obvious point of connection with the preceding discussion is Henderson's consideration of the importance of water. It should be remembered that the pre-Socratics were thinking and writing from a "human" point of view.[77] Of course, man as organic species is indissolubly bound up with the rest of the organic world, and Henderson made it clear that without water not only would man not exist but also there would be no life on planet earth at all.

Earth, then, in a symbolic sense may be thought of as referring to the utilizable resources of the planet, with the one central exception of oxygen, which may be assigned to the category "air" in the pre-Socratic scheme. There is at least an implication that carbon compounds and oxygen do not stand on quite the same level with reference to the production of energy through oxydation, but there is some sense in which the former may belong, in Wiener's sense, more closely to the category of matter, the latter more to that of information. This kind of problem will have to be left to those more knowledgeable about chemistry than ourselves. Finally, placing the pre-Socratic "fire" in the G–cell surely makes sense if the inclusion of this scheme in any way makes sense.[78]

The adaptive cell of Figure 2 thus becomes rather complex through combining three sets of categories: (1) those derived from Henderson's work and in this case from *both* sides of his "fitness" relationship; namely, the categories that are primarily designations of functional significance for organic life and the categories designating the centrally important chemical

[76] Vilfredo Pareto, *Trattato di sociologia generale,* A. Livingston, ed., and A. Bongiorno and A. Livingston, transl. (Florence: Barbera, 1916). Published in English as *The Mind and Society* (New York: Harcourt, Brace, 1935).

[77] W. K. C. Guthrie, "Pre-Socratic Philosophy," in *The Encyclopedia of Philosophy* (New York: Macmillan and Free Press, 1967), 6:441–446.

[78] Of such attempts as the present one, Dr. Johnson's famous observation may be adapted, to the effect that as in the case he used of the woman preaching, the surprising thing is not the perfection of the fit with our scheme but the fact that a plausible case can be made for *any* fit.

elements and compounds for organic life. I have even ventured to enter in the G–cell George Wald's suggestion that Henderson should have added nitrogen to his original list of three chemical elements.[79] If this element belongs, it indeed should be juxtaposed to complexity.

Next, (2) I have included Wiener's categories in addition to Henderson's. The rationale for so doing lies in the fact that the relation between these two sets of categorizations constituted the main logical framework of the preceding analysis. Either both have to be included and related to each other or the whole analysis must be thrown out. Finally, (3) as somewhat more than speculative curiosity, I have included the four symbols (as I think we should call them) of the philosophy of nature of the pre-Socratic philosophers. It seems to me that the sense in which these symbols may be said to fit has a genuine bearing on the structure of the general scheme for analyzing the human condition, to which this chapter is devoted.

Since now, in a tentative way, three of the four primary subsystems of the human condition have been lined up in terms of certain of their interrelations, it may be appropriate to pause to evaluate any discernible relational patterns. As we go up the cybernetic control hierarchy, we proceed to increasingly higher levels of "organization," if this term may be used, which in Wiener's scheme would be called the increase of *negative entropy*. We may recall that Henderson used the term "organization" to characterize certain features of the physico-chemical world as such. But he maintained not that this physical world is in general and as such a "fit" environment for living systems but rather that certain special features within it, of elements and compounds and their properties, which can form the basis for a selective and distinctive mode of *organization* which is most certainly not randomly distributed within the physical world, have the property of fitness. It is only when such a new level of organization has been attained— presumably through an evolutionary process—that such concepts as metabolism and regulation in Henderson's sense begin to make sense. In Wiener's terms this step is clearly associated with a new involvement of information in the control of high energy systems.

As noted earlier, it is particularly striking to us that the connections of information with meaning at the linguistic level have so deeply penetrated the thinking of microgeneticists. Accordingly, once self-perpetuating living species appear, biologists speak of the codification and translation of information, through strictly biochemical mechanisms, in the operation of the genes.[80]

If this kind of conceptualization is not gross misinterpretation in the attempt to explicate the boundary relationships between physico-chemical and organic systems, then surely such concepts must be relevant to under-

[79] Wald, Introduction to Henderson, *Fitness of the Environment* (1958 ed.).
[80] Stent, "DNA."

standing the relations that obtain at the boundary between the levels of organic life and of action, which we also interpret to constitute a transition from one level of organization to another. Yet, it is surprising how prevalent the view is, even among contemporary intellectuals, that human action is, to use a common phrase, simply "the behavior of organisms," meaning behavior in the strict behavioristic-reductionist sense (that is, an epiphenomenon of essentially physiological processes). It will of course be incumbent on us to counter this reductionist view, but I think it better to postpone this attempt until a fuller view of the human condition system as a whole is before us (see Part VI of this chapter).

Figure 2 portrays one other primary subsystem that has not yet received even cursory explication. This is in part because in one sense it is the most problematical of the subsystems and, as previously stated, I have long been hesitant about venturing into this, for a self-proclaimed scientist, admittedly dangerous intellectual territory. Yet after recounting the vicissitudes of dealing from the present point of view with the territories of the hard sciences, I wonder how much more complicated the understanding of this material will prove than has been the case for the other, allegedly more intelligible areas.

However that may be, a particularly important clue to the continuity between the problems faced here and those encountered elsewhere in the paradigm lies in Weber's frequent reference to "problems of meaning," [81] which expression he of course meant in the context of meaning to an actor from the subjective point of view (*Verstehen*). Nevertheless, it is not unreasonable to relate this usage in turn to the category of information in Wiener's scheme, for if information does not have meaning in the sense that messages need to be interpreted, what does the category signify at all? We already suggested that human language constitutes a link between the generality of Wiener's concept and the applications of the term to many phenomena at the level of human action.

Weber used the phrase "problems of meaning" especially in the context of religion, and we have adopted it for purposes of explicating the telic system. Before undertaking that task, let us consider Weber's famous definition of sociology: "Eine Wissenschaft, welche soziales Handeln deutend verstehen und dadurch in seinem Ablauf und seinen Wirkungen ursächlich erklären will." [82] I have thought it best to quote Weber's own German version in full. In *The Structure of Social Action* I translated this definition as follows: "A science which attempts the interpretive understanding of the subjective meanings of human actions (to the actors) and thereby to arrive at a causal explanation of them." [83]

---

[81] Weber, *Sociology of Religion.*

[82] Max Weber, *Wirtschaft und Gesellschaft,* ed. Johannes Winelmann (Tübingen: Mohr, 1956), 1:1.

[83] Parsons, *Structure of Social Action,* p. 641.

There has been much comment on the dual reference in this definition —to both "interpretive understanding" and "causal explanation." Some critics, especially German, have contended that they are strictly incompatible. Especially in view of the discussion of this chapter, with its emphasis on Wiener's conceptions, it seems to me that an interpretation is indicated in the light of which they are indeed compatible. Whereas Weber confined his conceptualization to the level we call human action (including its bordering on the telic system), we include the whole of the human condition. Accordingly, we suggest that the idea of causal explanation applies to the perspective of a downward view along the cybernetic hierarchy, whereas the interpretation of meaning is formulated from the perspective of an upward view. In this suggestion we set interpreting information and understanding meanings as broadly equivalent; causal explanation, on the other hand, is looked at in terms that Wiener would classify as involving matter and energy, with the qualifications of those concepts we discussed previously.

It seems to me Weber was right in introducing a special adjective in relation to meaning in his definition: "subjective." It is only at the level of action that we can speak of an *actor* in our technical sense, that is, as one whose intentions or subjective meanings can be an object of study, however important the transitions may be in the field of animal behavior (and also of prelinguistic human infantile behavior).

Very much on a Weberian background, to be sure, the four categories used to fill the four boxes of the telic system here were suggested by Robert Bellah in their present arrangement.[84] The most important common word is *ultimate,* which was immediately derived from the work of Paul Tillich, who defined religion as dealing with matters of "ultimate concern" [85] (to human beings of course). The concept in some way involves the boundary that human actors are up against, with their finite resources for dealing with problems of meaning, which they cannot transcend in terms of those resources alone.

This, however, does not mean that man can have no meaningful orientation, cognitive or otherwise, in the face of ultimate problems in this sense. Indeed, we have already suggested that Weber himself, far from accepting that human cognitive orientation in this context has to be random, which is another name for meaningless, acknowledged that the possibilities can be meaningfully structured. Figure 2–L is a tentative framework for a scheme of such meanings.

It seems clear that a central reference point for the outline is the "problem of salvation" in its historic religious sense. This, in my inter-

[84] Bellah made this suggestion in a discussion with members of the Philadelphia group in October 1976, and he has given his kind permission to introduce these categories here (he has not yet used the set in any publication over his own name).

[85] Paul Tillich, *The Courage to Be* (New Haven: Yale University Press, 1952).

pretation, is the reference of the formula "ultimate fulfillment" in the G–cell. This formula is clearly meant to be anthropocentric in that it posits meaningfulness from the perspective of the concrete human individual. Of course, it is at the same time meant to avoid any *particular,* culture-bound conception of what salvation or ultimate fulfillment may be.

Clearly, salvation or ultimate fulfillment in this sense cannot mean simply human welfare but must have a transcendental reference. The other three categories may be considered modes of spelling out that implication. First, if the conception of "agency" is meaningful, to be "ultimate" in the currently relevant sense, the agent cannot be either a "human" or a "natural" entity but must have, in accord with our whole line of argument, "transcendental" credentials. Thus, in Christian symbolism, as outlined in Chapter 12 of this volume, the agent of salvation is the God-Man, Jesus Christ, who very explicitly is not conceived as just an ordinary man. Back of him stands God the Father, who is obviously much less only human (if human at all). Presumably for paradigmatic purposes, the latter is the ultimate agent.

If there is such a thing as a "world" of ultimate entities at all, even in relation to the humble human world, it must have meanings or indeed functions, that go beyond the salvation or fulfillment of human individuals as such; restriction to such meanings would hardly make sense. In line with the kind of perspective that has run all through this analysis, surely such other meanings must in some sense involve notions of order. The notion of order and its negatives such as disorder, chaos, and disorganization has surely been a central focus of human orientation along the whole spectrum of the human condition—from the order of nature in Henderson's sense, through the order of human society, to some idea of a divinely or transcendentally meaningful basis of order.

Something of this sort seems to me to be what Bellah had in mind in suggesting that the integrative cell of the telic system paradigm be labeled "ultimate order." [86] The penumbra of meaning of the concept order is, however, I think sufficiently well known so that the reader will not be surprised that according to Bellah even ultimate order cannot be considered to be ultimately ultimate; there must be one more step in the cybernetic hierarchy to what he calls "ultimate ground." This conception is also familiar in the history of religion and of philosophy so its introduction need not be surprising, and it does seem to fit our paradigmatic needs as the place to speak of the meaningfulness of a conception of what is ultimately ultimate.

It may be noted that throughout the long journey up the cybernetic scale Wiener's category of information has shown a special affinity for the integrative position in the four-function paradigm. There has been a special "dialectic" relation, as it were, between the adaptive and integrative

[86] Robert N. Bellah, personal communication, August 1977.

categories in the paradigm, on which we have commented especially in connection with the problem of the relationship between the internal and the external environment of both organic and action systems. It is suggestive that the problem of the relation between conceptions of ultimate agency, on the one hand, and those of ultimate order, on the other, which has figured prominently in the history of religion, may have certain affinities with this problem area at scientific levels.

Finally, a remark may be added about Wiener's scheme. We have stressed that he dealt with three, not only two, major categories of the constitution of systems, in his case clearly those accessible to scientific analysis. Cybernetically speaking, "matter" is the more ultimate "ground"; energy stands at a higher cybernetic level; and information stands still higher. We placed these categories in the a-, g-, and i-cells, respectively, of the physical world paradigm, and also suggested that they are by no means of only physical or physico-chemical significance but that their relevance covers the whole of the human condition.

If this be the case, the logic of our analysis indicates that there ought to be a fourth category. Just as Henderson as a physiologist concerned primarily with the individual phenotypical organism tended to ignore (by taking for granted) the genetic component of the organic system, so Wiener as a mathematician concerned primarily with the broad world of natural science tended to ignore the problematical character of the epistemological foundations of scientific knowledge. It may well be that Wiener's threefold scheme needs to be supplemented by a fourth category of "ground," of the general character of Kant's categories of the understanding,[87] which is essential to our knowledge of the whole empirical world, including the physical, but not as such reducible to empirical considerations. It seems that the meaningfulness of some such conception would round out the symmetry of our four-function paradigm at each of the four primary levels of organization postulated in the paradigm of the human condition.

One final remark: There seems to be, in this regard, a duality in the meaning of the term "ground." In one connection it was stated that matter was the "ground" for Wiener; in the other, the epistemological grounding of knowledge. Bellah's "ultimate ground" clearly belongs in the latter category. The possible meaning of this duality will bear further thought.

V. Media of Interchange, Categories of Orientation, and Standards of Evaluation

We wish to outline the three sets of concepts set forth in Figure 4, most but not all of which have figured in the preceding discussion, and attempt

[87] Kant, *Critique of Pure Reason.*

Figure 4 Media and Their Normative Contexts

	Media	Categories of Orientation	Standards of Evaluation
L	Transcendental Ordering	Transcendentality	Critique (Kant)
I	Symbolic Meaning	Generativity	Interpretation *(Verstehen)*
G	Health	Teleonymy	Diagnosis
A	Empirical Ordering	Causality	Adequacy of Explanation

Symbols for media: L: (T); I: (M); G: (H); A: (E)

a formal classificatory ordering of their relationships to each other. The theoretical model goes back to the generalized symbolic media of interchange as these were first worked out for the social system and then generalized to the general system of action. It will be remembered that in each of the above cases a list of four such media was presented, with the contention that each medium could be considered to be anchored in one of the four primary functional subsystems of the larger system in question (money in the economy; power in the polity; influence in the societal community; and value-commitments in the fiduciary system).[88]

To these lists of media, then, were related two other sets of four concepts. The first additional set was, for the social system, called "value-principles"; again the economic case served as a model, namely, in the use by economic theorists of the principle of utility. The other three concepts, in the same functional order as previously, were (collective) effectiveness, solidarity, and integrity. The final set of four formulated the standards by which appropriate use of the medium to regulate the allocation of resources and rewards in the relevant functional context could be justified. The economic case here was the "solvency" of the economic unit; the political, the level of "compliance" with binding collective decisions; the integrative, the level of "consensus" attained with reference to communal processes; and the fiduciary, the level of "pattern-consistency" by which particularized value-commitments could be guided.[89]

In approaching the comparable set to be presented here for the human

[88] Parsons and Platt, *American University,* "Technical Appendix," figs. A4 and A12.

[89] It seems unnecessary to present an outline of the parallel categories worked out for the general system of action. The interested reader is referred to ibid., fig. A12 but is warned that a few important modifications will be introduced in forthcoming publications.

condition considered as a system, the first point to be made is that at the human condition level media of interchange, so far as they exist, cannot always be symbolic because symbolic phenomena and relationships are confined to the human action level. Therefore, the only symbolic media must be those that emanate from the human action system in interchange with the other three. The reciprocal media, as inputs to the action system, cannot themselves consist of symbols with their meanings but must somehow be capable of being equated with—that is, made meaningful in terms of—symbols. In Part IV we reviewed the three categories of this one-way symbolic relation and need not repeat it here. We should, however, emphasize that this condition applies to the relation of action to the telic system, as well as to the other two.

In judging Figure 4 and the explication of its proposed content, the reader should bear very much in mind the tentativeness of the proposal. To our knowledge this is the first at all comparable attempt to work out an ordering of these materials and there is no reason to believe that such a first effort will prove to be in any sense definitive. Our justification for imposing this scheme on the reader is simply the familiar one that it is better to try, accepting the risk of error and the probable need for future revision, than never to try at all.

Of the three categories of concepts set forth in Figure 4, the most strategic for our purposes seems to be that of media. As we argued earlier, all of what we call media at the human condition level cannot be called symbolic in the same sense that those internal to the system of action are. Nevertheless, we still argue that the other three words in the original formula—"generalized," "interchange," and "media"—all remain applicable. Let us start with the concept medium. It is surely tautologous to say that the function of a medium is to mediate, but this statement calls attention to an important set of problems. Specifically, the phenomena with which we are concerned are shot through with differences that under certain circumstances lead to the development of conflicts. If these conflicts occur within systems for the functioning of which there is some basis of interest, then there is a problem of whether and how such systems can be integrated in the sense of coordination among the parts and avoidance or toning down of conflict, which is disruptive to functioning. Controlling potential conflict, furthermore, is only one aspect of integration. Another, especially important one is extension of the range of coordinated or organized interrelations among parts.

Our first proposition is that in systems to some degree integrated in this sense there are certain mechanisms or principles that in a significant way account for such levels of integration as exist, along with "coping with" phenomena that tend or threaten to disturb the state of integration. At the action level certain such mechanisms are sufficiently distinctive so that we can identify and characterize them as separate entities such as money or power. In the case of organisms there are equally distinctive entities, for example, genes, neural mechanisms, hormones, and enzymes. In the physical world there is a presumption that these mechanisms are not concretely distinguishable but must be given the status of principles or the patterns of order found in the phenomena. However, as Henderson's treatment of the concept of organization in the physical world made clear,[90] they are nevertheless essential to the understanding of physical phenomena by science.

We thus suggest three classes of media in our sense. Those operating in the action system can properly be called symbolic. Those operating in organic systems are concretely distinct substances or processes that have identifiable functions in the operation of systematic processes. Apparently, those in the physical world are not observably so distinct, but they may be abstracted from the observed nature of physical systems and are necessary to rendering intelligible the phenomena of such systems.[90a]

The concept of a medium to us implies that it establishes relations between or among diverse and variant phenomena, tendencies, and so on. If this is the case, media must be able to relate to these entities beyond simply dissolving into their diversity. This property of a medium, namely, its capacity to transcend and thereby relate, diverse things, may be called its *generality,* which varies by levels of generalization. Logical generalization is one primary mode of this. At the symbolic level, a sum of money can be said to stand for and hence mean a variety of more concrete things in terms of their economic value. Money can thus serve as a medium of integration of a market nexus in which a variety of specific goods and services is integrated by being made comparable through money prices and therefore exchangeable. Hence, it can be said that a medium is general and can serve to facilitate interchanges. Indeed, interchanges are in a sense the mechanisms by which a medium can perform its integrative functions.

Let us now review our proposals for the identification and characterization of media operating at the level of the human condition. The most obviously central one is that anchored in the action system itself; it must have to do with language, which is the most generalized vehicle for the acquisition and communication of symbolic meaning and which for our purposes is the most distinctive human capacity that defines what we mean by action. It seems best, however, not to treat language itself as the medium but to place it in a position analogous to that of property in relation to money or authority in relation to power. One feature of our usage favors this decision, namely, that what "circulates," what is acquired and passed on through communication, is not what we ordinarily call language but is rather symbolic meanings or perhaps information (I think the latter con-

[90] Henderson, *Order of Nature.*
[90a] See Einstein's statement, cited and discussed in note 17 above.

cept is too general). Therefore, I propose that symbolic meanings, or meanings for short, should be treated as the medium anchored in the action system.

Symbolic meanings exhibit all the features that classical economists attributed to money. The meanings of words, phrases, and sentences are not objects of the external world in the usual sense (e.g., they cannot be consumed) but they are essential components of knowledge about such objects and can convey feelings about objects. Symbolic meanings circulate in the sense that they can be transmitted from one actor to another. They can also be externalized, or embodied in physical objects, of which the most familiar form is the written or printed word. Externalization in this sense is analogous to the saving of money in that, by the properties of both media, symbolic meanings are exempted from certain conditions of perishability in immediate situations to which most other classes of objects are subject.

Finally, there is reason to believe that symbolic meanings have another property that is vital to the social and action media: The supply of meanings available in a given culture at a given time need not be assumed to be fixed; rather, it is capable of increase or improvement by human action just as money can be increased through credit creation. It seems reasonable to suppose that what is called "creative writing" may well be an instance of this phenomenon as may well also be scientific "discovery."

Another reason for the choice of symbolic meanings rather than language itself as the medium is that by no means all such meanings in human action systems are conveyed in linguistic form. The arts other than literature (painting, sculpture, architecture, and music) all use predominantly nonlinguistic media, as it is usually put. Mathematics and symbolic logic, on the other hand, should presumably be considered to be specializations of ordinary language since they use primarily visual symbols that are components or forms of writing.

It seems best in the interest of clarity of exposition to follow the discussion of each medium by that of the other two entries in the same row of Figure 4, which are in the columns headed, respectively, "Categories of Orientation" and "Standards of Evaluation." The first designation is meant to indicate what in principle is the major functional problem area in which the medium operates; whereas the second designates the standards that are appropriate to evaluation of the consequences of employing the medium in a given context and manner. Comparing Figure 4 with Figures A4 and A12 of *The American University* [91] will make clear that in the series from the social system through the general system of action to the human condition system, the categories used as column headings each time have been located, in the transition from one to the next, at one step higher in level of generality. Thus, patterns of meaning are more general

[91] Parsons and Platt, *American University,* "Technical Appendix."

than value-principles, and foci of orientation are still more general. Similarly, value-standards are more general than coordination standards, and standards of evaluation (in the present context) still more general.

The entry in the integrative row in the middle column, on the same level a symbolic meaning as medium, is the term "generativity," obviously borrowed from Chomsky's usage in linguistics.[92] It comprises the operation of the rules of transformation by which what Chomsky has labeled deep structures are connected to surface structures to generate meanings in the form of concrete sentences, which then can be meaningfully communicated. Chomsky in particular emphasizes that the possibilities of formulating new meanings by utilizing the resources of a language are indefinitely great. This property seems clearly to relate to the general property of media noted earlier; namely, the supply of the medium is not fixed but is capable of expansion (in this case by human action). We think there is every reason to believe that the concept generativity is applicable to nonverbal forms of meaningful symbolization.

In the third column, headed "standards of evaluation," we have placed in the same row the term "interpretation." The most familiar case is that of the standards by which it is judged whether a linguistic utterance makes sense or not—what in fact it means. This judgment may be that the utterance is ambiguous and does not convey any one precise meaning but can be read in two or more ways that are both meaningful, or we may dismiss an utterance as nonsensical. Again, we do not see any good reason why the same kind of standards should not be applicable to nonverbal symbolizations. An important point is that very generally meanings are "translatable" not only from one language to another but also, for example, from language to music and vice versa. It may further be noted that the term "interpretation" is prominently used in psychoanalytic practice in a sense that appears consistent with its use here. The relevance of this term to Weber's category of *Verstehen* is evident.[93]

It is probably best to turn next to the adaptive medium, which is the most familiar of the remaining three. This medium is of course a mode of talking about empirical knowledge or knowing. We should be clear about the special ways in which this familiar phenomenon is relevant here. We have tried to make it fully clear that the media at the human condition level other than symbolic meanings themselves cannot be symbolic. Therefore, the medium cannot be empirical knowledge itself since that is a symbolic entity par excellence. This is one reason why we have used the word "ordering" to designate this medium.

What we are trying to capture is the orderliness that is imputed through the *relation* of knower and objects known to, in the first instance, the physi-

---

[92] Noam Chomsky, *Syntactic Structures* (The Hague: Mouton, 1957).
[93] Weber, *Economy and Society*.

cal world, by virtue of which, to quote Einstein again, it is "intelligible" to human minds.[94] Since Kant, we *know*, rather than surmise, that knowledge of the physical world requires more than the "given data" of the external world, notably the categories of the understanding, which are not as such data in Kant's sense.

The ordering that we have in mind comes about in the interrelations between human knowers and manipulators and the world of physical objects. Above all, it would be an egregious example of the empiricist fallacy to assert that human physical knowledge is simply an input from the physical world to the human mind. Knowledge is a combinatorial resultant to which the input from the objects contributes only one set of factors. It would seem to be the implication of both Einstein's and Henderson's positions that the input from external objects is not random but ordered and that this element of order is accessible to human minds through the structure of the human condition.

There are many points from which evidence for such a view may be mobilized. Perhaps the most familiar to many of us nonspecialists concerns the status of the concept of entropy. I take it that the state of maximum entropy in the physical universe as a whole would be the negation of any component of order in the phenomena themselves. But clearly the practice of physical scientists is not to argue that maximum entropy is the empirically verifiable state of the physical world as a whole or its predominant "tendency"; it is, rather, the concept of a limiting state.[95]

"Ordering" in the present usage may be thought of as circulating in the sense that both within the physical system and in its relations to the other subsystems of the human condition the kind and distribution of order is continually undergoing transformation. I wonder whether it would be considered too far-fetched to suggest that the parallel to the property of action system media, that they have "value in exchange" but not in "use," lies in the fact that order in the physical world has to be "abstracted" from the phenomena of concern rather than being immediately, i.e. "empirically," evident. Finally, there seems to be much opinion that the relevant order is not a fixed quantity but is subject to change through various processes including growth. This possibility is a central concern in theories of evolution, in cosmology, in the organic world, and in the world of human action.

For paradigmatic purposes, as we stated earlier, we have located the physical world in the adaptive cell and accordingly designate empirical ordering as the medium anchored in this system. We have, however, done this in a way not meant to declare that the kinds of considerations just reviewed are irrelevant to either the organic world or that of human action.

[94] See fn. 17.

[95] David Layzer, "The Arrow of Time," *Scientific American,* vol. 233, no. 6 (1975): 56–69.

On the contrary, we would generalize these basic orientations to all objects of empirical, scientific knowledge.

The relevant principle seems to be that there are certain constant features of the process of ordering in the relations of human actors to objects that have empirical significance to them. These features are, for objects we call physical, most nearly sufficient to take into account for this case. For the other classes of objects, however, it is necessary to take further features into account such as those related to health for living organisms and to symbolic meanings for action systems. Put somewhat differently, it must be kept in mind that the categorizations of systems and relevant concepts we use are *all* analytically abstract. Thus, the preceding sentence on this page is a physical object consisting of black marks on white paper; the former are interpreted to be letters in the English alphabet grouped in what we call words, with spaces between them, punctuation marks, etc. This physical object is not a living organism but it does have meaning for persons who know the English language, which other types of physical objects do not.

The corresponding focus of orientation we designate *causality*. This selects one of Kant's categories of the understanding [96] as crucial for present purposes. From the anthropocentric point of view that this analysis takes, this choice implies that the primary function of the process of ordering with which we are concerned is one type of cognitively significant orientation, namely, to make accessible understanding of the "causes" of the phenomena of concern. The corresponding standard of judgment, then, is *adequacy of explanation*. These components clearly cannot be inputs to the actor from the physical or other scientifically observed world itself alone but must come from other parts of the human condition.

We suggest that empirical ordering as process and medium may be considered to be an expression of capacity for causal understanding, the end result of which should be adequate explanation. In a parallel way, the development of symbolic meaning is an expression of capacity for generativity, the result of proper use of which is meaningful interpretation. But just as the meaningfulness of interpretations is possible only as evaluated by proper standards, so the adequacy of an explanation implies evaluation by determinable standards.

On carefully rereading the discussion of the suggestion that the medium for the adaptive system in Figures 2 and 4 should be the concept of "empirical ordering" in the above sense, certain doubts come up. Rather than attempt to revise at this point—just before going to press—it seems best to state these doubts and leave the issues for future consideration.

The case for symbolic meanings as the I–medium seems quite straightforward. The obvious reason for this is that the action system is itself constituted by symbols and their meanings. There may, however, be a

[96] Kant, *Critique of Pure Reason*.

problem of whether the medium concept is too general. Presumably, the same cannot be said of the physical world, if one maintains the basic distinction between the nature of that world and knowledge about it. The question is whether the concept "ordering" is not *too* anthropocentric, as presuming the inclusion of what we call the physical system not only in the human condition but also in the system of action itself. The problem surely comes to focus in the cognitive field, in other words, that of the epistemological problem in the traditional sense.

For those who, like myself, approach this area in Kantian perspective, it is tempting to adopt Kant's own distinction between the sense data emanating from the external world and the categories of the understanding, which are of transcendental grounding. The difficulty here seems to be the tendency, in much of the tradition of Kant interpretation, to assess sense data as random and to place the whole onus of ordering on the categories. This tendency has, for instance, seemed to me to feed into that of certain phenomenologists, in the tradition of Alfred Schütz, to interpret scientific theory in general as "fictional," in their case of course attributing "reality" to "subjective experience" rather than to external objects.[97]

I propose that it is possible to draw a line of differentiation relative to the Kantian dichotomy. A suggestion in that direction is Henderson's conception of the *order* of or in nature; another is the implication of Einstein's remark about the intelligibility of nature. If this line of thought is followed up, it would indicate that there is the possibility of salvaging the concept of empirical ordering without either identifying it with categorial "idealism" or falling into the fallacy of Humean empiricism. If there exist possibilities in this direction, they may well turn out to have their parallels on the subjective side of the subject-object dichotomy and hence to mitigate the pressure of exposure to the stark dilemma of Schütz: Either ignore the reality of subjective experience or treat all scientific theory as fiction!

As a possible move in the empirical direction I am reminded of the relevance of a suggestion made by Victor Lidz.[98] According to him, the place of water, as Henderson presented it as the "foundation" as it were of the fitness of the environment for organic life, had some of the features of a generalized medium in our sense. In our discussion we compared water with money. Thus, water, being chemically inert, does not "disappear" into compounds, just as money is not as such consumed. A very wide range of chemical substances is soluble in water, as commodities are "convertible" into money, and especially because of the predominance of the liquid phase water circulates all over the earth, including the atmosphere and organisms. If it were only gaseous, this element would circulate too readily; if solid, not readily enough. Like money, water has what

[97] See Alfred Schütz, *Collected Papers,* 3rd ed. (The Hague: Nijhoff, 1971).

[98] Victor M. Lidz, personal communication, June 1977.

is in a sense a controlled circulation. It will be noted that water is not just "the environment" in general for Henderson but a special feature of the terrestrial environment of organisms.[99] Similarly, money is not *the* economically valuable item of the environment of action in general but a special part of that environment.

Perhaps following such a line of reasoning it will be possible to work out adequate conceptions of media that are essential to the human condition system as a whole but are not integral to the action system. Similar considerations seem pari passu to be relevant to the status of the concept "transcendental ordering," to be discussed presently.

The suggestions for the G row of Figure 4 will very likely seem strange at first glance to most readers. It will be remembered that in Figure 1 the organic world was placed in the G position. On being asked recently to write an article on the concepts of health and disease from a sociological perspective (included in this volume as Chapter 3), I thought of the fact that traditionally these concepts have been anchored in the organism, and the idea came to mind that it might make sense to think of health as a medium on the *model* of the media previously developed within the action system but in this case located in the human condition system. (Chapter 3 explores this possibility with on the whole positive conclusions.)

Given the assumption of anchorage in the organism, this way of looking at health has the appeal of establishing a basis for linking the conceptions of organic, or somatic, and mental health. On the hypothesis that health, as a medium, circulates in the sense just considered, one could speak of the state of health of the personality, linked to, but not part of, the organism, as part of the action system, in a sense parallel to speaking of the economic position of a family (even though a family is not primarily an economic collectivity). In the other direction, toward the physical world, then, one could think of health as an agent that operates in regulating the selection of appropriate inputs from the physical environment. Clearly, this usage necessitates modifications of current conceptions of health as a trait of the individual organism. There is a parallel here to Platt and my use of the concept intelligence as a medium rather than as a psychological trait of the individual.[100]

Health in this meaning clearly cannot be a symbolic entity; thus, the question has to be faced of the sense in which it can have value in exchange but not in use. As in other cases I think that the clue to the answer is the concept's generality. It is true that references are made in medical circles to healthy and diseased organs or even tissues, but the concept health refers mainly to the state of the individual as a whole, and organs, tissues, or complexes are thought of as examples of or contributors to states of good or ill health.

[99] Henderson, *Fitness of the Environment.*
[100] See Parsons and Platt, *American University,* chap. 2.

Health thus conceived also seems to meet the other principal criteria of a medium. First, it may be conceived to circulate insofar as it can be acquired from one or more of its environments, through other persons, notably those engaged in health services. Second, health can be spent in that many human activities are at the expense of health, temporarily at least, and some habits of life may be definitely injurious to health. A balance of input and output is necessary for the maintenance of a state of health.

The preceding considerations indicate that the rates of income and expenditure of health may not be constant and that it is possible to save or even to hoard one's store of health.[101] Health is also used as a measure of organic well-being and this usage has been extended to the personality system. Finally, as in the other two cases discussed, there is no reason to believe that a person's state of health is a fixed quantity unsusceptible to improvement by a variety of measures. It is not subject, that is, to a zero-sum condition.

This seems to be the appropriate point to call attention to one highly important line of analytical division that runs through both the system of action and the organic system. The occasion is that by and large the concept health in a human context—and we think it should be extended to plants and nonhuman animals—is confined to the individual human being as organism and/or personality. There has even been talk of "sick" societies, but this usage does not seem appropriate.[102] It is striking, though, that speaking of health is a way of integrating the organic, action, and physical aspects of the individual. Social systems and cultural systems, on the other hand, are not confined to particular individuals but are collective in reference, as are populations, species, and genotypes.

[101] The possibility of "hoarding health" is more than suggested by certain current tendencies in discussion of health problems. There seems in the late 1970s to be a movement toward "health absolutism," the postulation of health as the "ultimate" value to which all others allegedly should be subordinated, the result of which is a "health Puritanism." The label "injurious to your health," conspicuously invoked for the case of cigarette smoking, seems to have become a generalized negative symbol. Such things are to be avoided at all costs, even formally forbidden, without any reference to a "cost-benefit" balance. This is of course a classic instance of opting for *Gesinnungsethik* in preference to *Verantwortungsethik* in Weber's classic formulation or what I have called "value-absolutism," that is, the dominance of *one* value. A conspicuous recent instance is John H. Knowles, "The Responsibility of the Individual," *Daedalus*, vol. 106, no. 1 (1977): 57–80. Knowles's sentiment is clearly that not only cigarette smoking but probably also most (if not all) use of alcohol, and he suggests even a good deal of sex are "injurious to health" and should be viewed with great suspicion, if not actually banned. Another, closely related manifestation of this trend is the widespread campaign, certainly emanating largely from medical circles, to the effect that anything even remotely related to cancer should, without further ado, be regarded with the greatest suspicion and probably formally banned. The reaction of a medical layman is, "Doesn't the ordinary citizen have any rights to take risks with his own health?" The reply of the health absolutists is a resounding, "No!"

[102] R. H. Tawney, *The Acquisitive Society* (New York: Harcourt, 1920).

There is a direct parallel within the organic world in the distinction between phenotype and genotype, to which we have called attention a number of times. May we suggest that the situation for the physical and telic systems is different. Both of these are treated, especially cybernetically, as limiting systems of the human condition. There is no category more specifically conditional to human life than the physical, and none more specifically, well, telic than the telic—hence our use of the term. This suggests that although the line between individuality and collectivity runs *through* the action system and the organic system, it runs *between* the physical and telic systems. Thus, in the cognitive sphere, empirical knowledge is relatively particularized, whereas the categories of the understanding are highly generalized.

To return to the category of health, as the corresponding category of orientation we have employed Mayr's concept of teleonomy.[103] This concept, like that of health, is rooted in the organic system, and it does not carry any connotations of symbolic meaning. The relation between a medium and a unit's capacity is also strongly emphasized here. Health may be said to be a form of teleonomic capacity. In Chapter 3 of this volume, I pointed out its relation to the conception, in medical tradition, of the *vis medicatrix naturae*.[104] This is in turn a case par excellence of the occurrence of self-regulatory properties of living systems, both organisms and action systems, which Cannon[105] and others have emphasized.

Finally, to designate the corresponding standard of evaluation, we have chosen the medical term "diagnosis." This choice obviously matches the use of the term health to designate the medium, with one possible qualification that does not appear to be serious. Specifically, we mean evaluation to include the positive as well as the negative, which is indeed medical usage.[106] The usage to designate ill health or illness is, however, sufficiently prominent so that this caution seems called for.

Last, we come to the problem of the designations for the medium and the other concepts anchored in the telic system. For the medium, it has seemed best to emphasize the parallel with the physical system and thus to use the term "ordering" with reference to both. Ordering alone, however, is insufficient; hence, having qualified its use in the physical case by "empirical" we propose to qualify it for the telic case by "transcendental," specifically in the sense used by Kant, as explained earlier.

An additional point is that we do *not* conceive this to be a symbolic medium for the same reason that we denied this quality to empirical ordering and to health. Transcendental ordering may, however, be regarded as

[103] Mayr, "Teleological and Teleonomic."

[104] See Chapter 3 of this volume.

[105] Cannon, *Wisdom of the Body*.

[106] Thus, I have had a physician report to me after a checkup "I find you to be in good health."

the capacity within the framework of the human condition to order the relations between thinking and feeling human beings and the telic problems that impinge on their lives and the limits within which these lives are lived. Let me reiterate the earlier reference, in this connection, to Weber's thought [107] and my conviction that Weber was far from content with the state of this problem area and that, had he lived a few years longer, he probably would have arrived at a positive intellectual ordering in this area far beyond the statements he did in fact arrive at.

Designating transcendental ordering as a medium in our sense is of course far from presenting a typology of *substantive* ordering in this area. If, however, we accept the necessity of this step, it should help in our search for the proper statement of the relevant substantive problems. This is meant in the sense in which major contributions to the science of linguistics do *not* in themselves constitute solutions of the scientific or philosophical—or indeed esthetic—problems that authors attempt to solve by the *use* of language; nevertheless, knowing better how languages operate should clarify thinking in such areas.

We suggest that transcendental ordering may be conceived to circulate in essentially the same sense as other media. This would apply *within* the telic system if the different kinds of telic problems can provide opportunity for a kind of consistency of orientation, both logical and affective, which is parallel to Einstein's conviction of the intelligibility of physical nature. Had Weber in fact achieved a better ordering in the field of what he called the "problems of meaning," it would have involved circulation in our sense between the telic system and the action system. Finally, it seems a notable fact about Kant's epistemological schema that *both* sets of components, the sense data and the categories, are outside the action system; they are both inputs to the human knower. Insofar as they are both derived from objects, both are equally inaccessible to human beings. This seems to be the meaning of Kant's insistence that we cannot have full or direct knowledge of the *Ding an sich,* the "thing in itself." [108] What we construct as an object of human knowledge is not the thing in itself but a humanly built combination of components that is not identifiable with it.

If telic or transcendental ordering circulates in this sense, it surely functions as a measure of value in the sense of making otherwise diverse things comparable. What is a philosophy of life, *Weltanschauung,* but a rendering comparable of orientations that would otherwise be incomparable? Cognitive and religious innovation, among other forms, should also convince us that the "quantity" of transcendental ordering cannot be spoken of as fixed. Surely, both cognitive innovation through discovery and originality of thought and religious innovation seem to indicate the unacceptability of a static view in such matters. Indeed, Weber's famous

[107] Weber, "Religious Rejections of the World."
[108] Kant, *Critique of Pure Reason.*

category of *charisma* may be regarded as an attempt to designate, if not very fully to analyze, the innovative aspects in this area.[109]

The use of the term "transcendentality" for the category of orientation in this context seems almost tautologous. What is relevant is the idea that transcendental ordering as a medium should be conceived as a form of transcendentality or as a capacity, as we have discussed that relation in connection with health as teleonomic capacity.

Finally, the introduction in the column of evaluative standards of the term "critique" should, in the light of previous discussion, be almost self-explanatory. The term is used in Kant's sense, and the relevance of the three critiques that Kant authored is the main substantive point.[110]

VI. Mediated Interchange Sets

Let us now turn to a still further effort at formalization, namely, the attempt to designate the relevant categories of interchange among the four subsystems of the human condition. The anthropocentric point of view from which this undertaking is attempted should be kept in mind here as elsewhere. Such interchange categories can most conveniently be interpreted as forms of the media reviewed in Part V or as categories of exchangeables that are controlled by such media in the sense in which, given a market structure, a specific sum of money controls access to possession of certain goods and services.

We must start with a simple logical point: In any set of four entities there are *six* relational pairs, consisting of the relations of each of the four to each of the other three. The diagrammatic representation of this point is a square, with four sides and two diagonals, as shown in Figure A1 of *The American University*, all on a horizontal plane, as in Figures A3 and A7 of that book.[111] There is one difference, however. It has seemed best to place the L–I interchange at the top, the L–A and I–G interchanges just below, and the A–G interchange next lowest. At the bottom, then, will be found the two diagonal sets. This arrangement is, of course, purely conventional.

Each of the six sets consists of four categories, making twenty-four categories in all. Each set of four in turn is divided into two pairs labeled, respectively, "products" and "factors."

The logic of this format was first worked out by Neil Smelser and

---

[109] Weber, *Economy and Society,* "The Types of Legitimate Domination," pp. 212–301.

[110] Kant, *Critique of Pure Reason, Critique of Practical Reason,* and *Critique of Judgment.*

[111] Parsons and Platt, *American University,* "Technical Appendix."

myself to represent the interchanges between the economy and the other three primary subsystems of society.[112] Each subsystem was conceived to transmit one category of product *to* each of the three others and to receive one *from* each of the others, and correspondingly with factors. The model from which this scheme was worked out was that of the shares of income and the factors of production as these are conceptualized in economic theory. The fourth item in each set was treated as a special case.

In the geometric representation, the product pair is placed on the outside of the diagram—or, for the diagonals, on the top—and the factor pair on the inside—or bottom for the diagonals. In the horizontal representation it is always products on top, factors on the bottom. Finally, a letter on the right side of each interchange set identifies the relevant medium, as these were included at the bottom of Figure 2 of this chapter. The categories selected are set forth in Figure 5.

A primary aspect of the circulation of the media, as discussed in Part V is that in any given interchange between two functional subsystems, *each* of the two media circulates in *both* directions. One of these movements is in the factor interchange; the other, in the product interchange. Only with this dual directionality of media interchange is a structural differentiation between factor level and product level supportable. The prototypical case, in terms of which Smelser and I initially developed the paradigm, is the interchange between economy—with the firm as unit—and the family household; we allocated the latter to the fiduciary (pattern-maintenance) system.[113] The household is a source of labor, a factor of production, which by employment becomes available to the firm as a unit of the economy. In reciprocation the firm pays the household a money wage. This money, which is a product of household activity in that it has been earned by one or more household members, is then returned to the economy (not usually the specific employing firm) in exchange for goods in what is usually called the consumers' market. Both labor as factor and goods as consumable products have been treated (Economy and Society) as governed by value-commitments.

For purposes of explication it seems best not simply to "go around the clock" and then to the diagonals but to take the sets in a rough order of ready understandability. Probably the best to start with is the A–G relationship, that between the physical and organic worlds. As the factor output from the physical to the organic we have entered Henderson's category "fitness of the environment." What the environment does for organic life is to provide the conditions in which living organisms of many kinds can effectively function. The reverse output, from organic to physical, seems to be the place for the well-known concept of adaptive capacity.

[112] Talcott Parsons and Neil J. Smelser, *Economy and Society* (New York: Free Press, 1956).
[113] Ibid.

Figure 5   Categories of Interchange for the Human Condition

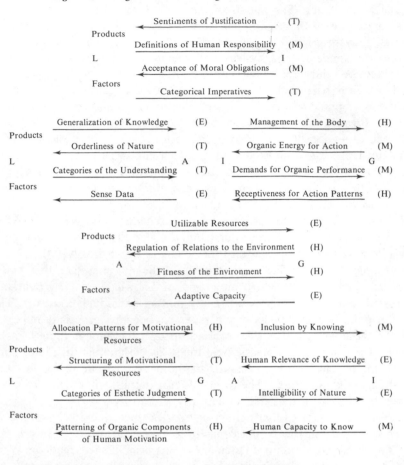

Symbols for media: L: (T); I: (M); G: (H); A: (E)

The reciprocity of the two creates some kind of symbiotic balance, on the planet earth at least, between organic life and physical environment.

Shifting, then, from the factor level to that of products, the environment provides resources necessary for living organisms such as, for animals, oxygen, nutritional materials, and media for motility (water or land surface) in or on which the animal can swim or run. The presence of life regulates and thereby modifies the environment, sometimes but by no means always in a polluting manner.[114] The whole set simply formulates the main aspects of the ways in which organisms, in relationship with their physical environments, function as what have often been called open systems.

[114] René Dubos, *A God Within* (New York: Scribner's, 1972).

Perhaps the most readily understandable interchange set is that between L and A, which is the primary locus of the epistemological problem as we reviewed it earlier. The famous Kantian position seems to fit directly in the factor pair in that the output from the physical world to the transcendental may properly be categorized as sense data, whereas the reverse, from transcendental to physical, consists in the categories of the understanding. We must remember that we are not dealing with knowledge itself, which is part of the action system, but with factors in knowledge as humanly imputed to other sectors of the human condition.

In formulating the product interchange categories for this case it seemed to us appropriate to go to the more concrete level of the analysis of knowledge, as contrasted with Kant's famous pair. The output from L to A in those terms would then be the *generalization* of knowledge; that from A to L would be the orderliness of nature as we previously discussed that conception. It seems that because of the strong cognitive orientation of modern Western culture, the two interchange sets just reviewed are highly familiar and readily understandable. For this reason it may be advisable next to take up the third interchange, which involves the physical world, namely, A–I. Since I is the locus of the action system, this involves not so much the ultimate components of knowledge as the relation of knowledge to human action, especially human individuals as actors. Thus, at this point our anthropocentric perspective becomes especially important.

In these terms it seems appropriate to take the famous remark of Einstein, which we have quoted several times, as designating the factor output from the physical world, or nature, to the action system, using the phrase "intelligibility of nature." The reverse factor output, from action to nature, may then be called the "human capacity to know."

When it comes to the product categories, then, the more obvious one seems to be, from I to A, not capacity to know but the "human *relevance* of knowledge." One famous statement of this principle was made by Weber, in his methodological writings, when he anchored the concept of relevance by the use of the term "values".[115] That question may be left open.

The reverse output, from nature to action, raises another set of problems. We have called this product "inclusion by knowing." The term "inclusion" is used in a technical sense (as explicated in Chapter 11 of this book). The essential point is that nature, by coming to be humanly known, comes to be in a crucial sense part of the system of action rather than only part of the external world "out there." Briefly, I should like to suggest that this may be taken to mean that, though nature is indeed out there, *knowledge* of it becomes part of the *internal environment* of action, with all the very important implications of such a status. Put a little differently,

---

[115] Max Weber, *The Methodology of the Social Sciences,* trans. and ed. Edward A. Shils and Henry A. Finch (New York: Free Press, 1969). The essays contained in this volume were first published in German in 1904, 1905, and 1917.

knowledge of nature is a "social fact" in Durkheim's strict meaning of that concept.[116]

The reader will have noted two things about the preceding explication of the interchange categories. First, in formal terms all three sets that have been discussed so far involve the adaptive subsystem of the human condition, which in Figure 1 was labeled the "physical system." Second, the three sets all deal substantively with knowledge and its problems, that is, with the cognitive complex.

At least one link between these commonalities, which we have already discussed briefly, is the fact that in the development of modern science, knowledge of the physical world was the first to develop and has in an important sense remained prototypical. We have, however, already stated emphatically that science is not to be confined to the physical sciences but is to be extended to the other two major categories, which Comte called the biological and the social; [117] the latter we are calling the "sciences of action."

The possible contradiction between defining the adaptive subsystem as physical and treating knowledge as referring to the two categories of living systems as well must be resolved by treating the categories of *both* the physical world and knowledge as *analytical abstractions*. It is highly relevant for the present context that we have elsewhere treated knowledge, or "cognitive symbolization," as belonging to the adaptive subsystem of the *cultural* system,[118] which we treat in turn as a subsystem of the general system of action. Thus, the physical and cultural systems are *both* adaptive subsystems; however, one is outside, the other inside, the system of action. We referred to this phenomenon in speaking of knowledge as included in the action system, as being part of the internal environment of action for human actors.

This leaves three further sets of interchanges, but since the A-centered cluster involves all four functional foci, the others cannot have any one functional reference in common. I propose to discuss them in the first instance by using G, the organic system, as my point of reference. If one discusses all three interchanges involving G, there is an important set of formal consequences: One of the sets overlaps with the cluster of physical-cognitive interchanges (A–G), whereas the set L–I does not belong in either cluster. We shall comment on the significance of these formalisms presently; first we shall explicate the G cluster and then that of the L–I interchange.

To introduce this discussion we may remark that the G–A interchange, from the point of view of organic systems, concerns the nonliving sources

[116] Emile Durkheim, *The Rules of Sociological Method,* trans. Sarah A. Solovay and John H. Mueller, ed. George E. G. Catlin, 8th ed. (New York: Free Press, 1964; first published in French in 1895).

[117] Comte, *Cours de philosophie positive.*

[118] See Parsons and Platt, *American University,* p. 17.

of resources essential for organic life in the physical environment, characterized by Henderson as fit, which is the obverse of organismic adaptation to that environment. Turning next to G–I, we note that the postulated factor output to the organic system from that of action is phrased as "demands for organic performance." [119] The return is then labeled "receptiveness for action patterns." The corresponding product interchange, which, it should be remembered, is at a more concrete level than that of factors, involves the output of organic energy to the personality, and the corresponding return, "management of the body," on the part of the actor.

This interchange, taken as a whole, is exceedingly important for our general theoretical position. This is that, parallel to the sense outlined earlier in which knowledge comes to be included in the action system and thereby to constitute part of its internal environment, by virtue of the interchange under discussion (G–I), for the human actor the body comes to be *included* with what we call the personality to constitute what we call the human individual.

To us the seminal theorist of this crucial relationship was Freud. Along with the many facilities that the human organism provides to the human actor (e.g., the motor system for dealing with the environment; the brain for cognitive functions), the organism is the primary source of the *energy* that to use Freud's own term "drives" (*treibt*) the human actor as a functioning unit of the general system of action. On the *action* side of the boundary, Freud [120] categorized the available energy as *libido,* which, according to the usage of most translators of Freud, can be considered to work through a cluster of instincts. It should, however, be remembered that Freud explicitly located his "instincts" at the "psychic"—to us *action* —level, not the organic. This crucial relationship is further analyzed in Part VII.

This phenomenon of inclusion is as crucial to the nature of the human condition as is that of *knowledge* of the Cartesian external world in another direction. The integration of the human actor in what we call an *individual,* of which a phenotypical living organism is a completely constitutive part, is perhaps the central feature of individuality in our sense. This integration is directly parallel to two others. The first is the integration of organic life with the physical world in the symbiosis, as we have called it, of living organisms adapted to a fit physical environment. The second is the integration, of which Durkheim was the great seminal theorist, of the human actor—as "individual"—in social and cultural systems at the human action level, an integration that involves interpretation of the I–L interchange. [121]

---

[119] It is worth noting that this formulation was arrived at in self-conscious parallel with that of "interest-demands" as a factor output from the societal community to the polity in the interchange paradigm for the social system (ibid., fig. A3).

[120] Freud, *The Ego and the Id.*

[121] Bellah, Introduction to Durkheim, *On Morality and Society.*

The particular process of inclusion (G–I) that is so central to Freud's theoretical work is a product of a process of differentiation that has occurred in the course of organic evolution and by virtue of which the human species has acquired its distinctiveness in the zoological world. The focus of this differentiation has been the emergence of the capacity to create and use *symbols*. As organized about symbolic structures and processes, this process of differentiation has resulted in the establishment of a system of *action* in the technical sense of that term.[122] The articulation of the human action system with human organisms, however, has operated mainly through what we have called the personality, which, with the organism of the same individual, must achieve a special state of integration with each other.[123] It is this state of integration that we label inclusion. Note that Freud, speaking from the action side of the differentiation, which with reference to personality he called "psychic," spoke specifically of *symbols* that mediate the relationship between organism and personality at the boundary, notably of course the erogenous zones, precisely as having symbolic meaning.[124]

Before entering into an explication of I–L interchanges, it is essential first to say something about the G–L interchange. Whereas the G–I inter-

---

[122] Since there has been so much discussion of sociology recently, it is well to try to make the relations of Edward O. Wilson's work to the present discussion as clear as possible. As I understand it—and I have read his book—Wilson is writing definitely as a biologist but of course of a far more general basis than human biology; after all, he made his reputation mainly in the study of social insects. He is interested in human social problems and in the social sciences so-called, but he does not have a clearly articulated conception of a theory of action and its distinctively human relevance. See Edward O. Wilson, *Sociobiology: The New Synthesis* (Cambridge, Mass.: Belknap Press of Harvard University Press, 1975).

The analysis presented in this chapter deals rather extensively with what we have called the organic level of the organization of living systems, specifically, the human case. However, it does so with the aim of articulating the organic with the physico-chemical system, with reference to which we have relied particularly on the work of Lawrence J. Henderson, and especially with the system of human action in our technical sense. In order to do this it is necessary to have adequate conceptualization on *both* sides. I have, for example, in my analysis of Freud's treatment of the articulation of the symbolic meanings of the erogenous zones below attempted to be as accurate as possible about the relevant facts of human biology, but in addition to that I have introduced a formal paradigm of components of linguistic meaning. The organic and action levels are then articulated with each other through the use of a *common* functional paradigm. Though this overlaps somewhat with Wilson's analysis, the chapter clearly is not an essay in sociobiology in his sense.

[123] Adrian Hayes suggested in a personal communication (July 1977) a modification of the G set in Figure 2: Substitute in the a–cell "behavioral organism" in place of "ecological Adaptation." The suggestion was made after the final draft of the chapter was written. It appeals to me, but there has not been time to consider its merits carefully so I have let the previous decision stand. This may serve as an example of the *tentativeness* of a good many of the formulations included in a theoretical enterprise like the present chapter.

[124] Freud, *The Ego and the Id*; see also Marshall Edelson, "Toward a Study of Interpretation in Psychoanalysis," in Loubser et al. (eds.), *Explorations in General Theory in Social Science,* 2: Chap. 6.

change deals with the ways in which the organism articulates with the action system in terms of mutuality of substantive functional interdependence, the G–L interchange is in this sense nonsubstantive. It deals with the grounding, in our anthropocentric perspective, of the normative conditions of the meaningfulness of organic life as part of the world of human experience and especially of the life of human beings as organisms, including their mortality. The best keynote, perhaps, is our reliance once more on Kant. Parallel to the sense in which we incorporated Kant's categories of the understanding in the L–A interchange, we have incorporated his canons of esthetic *judgment* in the present one.

We shall soon see that we have also made use of his third transcendental focus in the L–I interchange: the categorical imperative of moral order. The difference may be said to lie in that the moral order focuses above all on human individuals as actors as well as in their collective relations with each other; whereas esthetic judgment focuses on the human individual as organism. Both are analytically essential and complement each other when seen in the context of the human condition as a whole.

For a framework of such judgments to be meaningful, there must be available, in some way, parallel to the cognitive significance of sense data, experience of what may be called the organic sources of human motivation. Such experience must be capable of somehow being authenticated in a sense parallel to that in which the cognitive significance of sense data can be validated, verified, and ordered. It should be recalled that, as in the case of knowledge, these are humanly understandable conditions of authentic experience in this context. Thus, we maintain that the authenticity of experience, in the meaning we have given to both of these terms, is for human security just as much in need of transcendental grounding as is the validity of empirical knowledge.[125]

The combinatorial product of this process, applicable to the organism, then, may be called "patterns for (the structuring of) motivational resources"; we think of the obverse output, from organism to telic system, as *actual* structuring of such motivational resources in allocative patterns.

Underlying the present discussion is a problem that should be made explicit. It concerns the relation between the anthropocentric point of view and the reality of nonaction components of the human condition. The problem is that at the anthropocentric level "motivation" enters into more complex courses of action, organized in symbolic terms and subject to "voluntary" selection and choice. A line of distinction must, however, be drawn between this level and that possible for organisms as differentiated from actors. Presumably, human experience of motivational drives rooted in the organism is filtered through the symbolic structures of action and

[125] Lionel Trilling, *Sincerity and Authenticity* (Cambridge, Mass.: Harvard University Press, 1972).

is no more immediately accessible to socialized humans than is direct cognition of the external world. There is thus a sense in which human attitudes toward such drives are partly projected from an action point of view; whereas the problem of how directly they can be felt, uncomplicated by modifications from action sources, remains moot.

Many practitioners of cognitive enterprise tend to allege that our knowledge of the external world is directly "given" by the "nature" of that world and that humanly formulated "theory" unless inferred by the strictest rules of *induction alone* is distortion. However, there is an equally, indeed recently even more prominent, tendency to maintain that humans have directly authentic experience of organically grounded motivation and that to "free" such authentic motivation from alleged distortions it is necessary merely to brush away the symbolic structuring of human action systems. In this sense, if Hume be the great apostle of cognitive empiricism,[126] then Rousseau must be identified as the apostle of direct motivational "experience";[127] Schütz [128] stands in this prophetic line. Both extremes are equally unacceptable to an unreconstructed Kantian like myself.

What, then, is to be said about the last of the six interchanges, that between L and I, or the telic and action systems? To start we may note again that as in the cases of the other two interchanges involving the telic system, we have taken a Kantian transcendental component to define the *factor* output from the telic system, this time to action. This is the famous categorical imperative, the nature and role of which constitute the principal concern of *The Critique of Practical Reason.* The most significant point for the present discussion is the strong *moral* emphasis of Kant's thinking in this context. Indeed, there seems to be a striking resemblance in this connection between Kant and Durkheim. The reciprocal factor output category, from action to telic, we have designated "acceptance of moral obligations," which is a decidedly Durkheimian phrasing.[129]

The product interchange, then, incorporates the relevant derivatives of the combination of these two, plus of course the human perspective. From the point of view of telic contribution, we have suggested "definitions of human (moral) responsibility" and, reciprocally, from the action system we have designated the relevant output as "sentiments of justification." This formula includes both the positive and the negative. This is to say that in the light of their perception of transcendental imperatives, human actors may feel either justified (e.g., in Luther's sense of "justification by

---

[126] Hume, *Treatise of Human Nature.*

[127] Jean Jacques Rousseau, *Emile, or Treatise on Education,* trans. B. Foxly (London: Dent, 1969; first published in French in 1762).

[128] Schütz, *Collected Papers.*

[129] Emile Durkheim, "The Determination of Moral Facts," *Sociology and Philosophy,* trans. D. F. Pocock (New York: Free Press, 1970; first published in French in 1924), pp. 35–62.

faith") [130] or the negative, unjustified (i.e., guilty, sinful, and their variants).

VII. Structural Coordinates of Living Systems: The Articulation of Action and Human Biology

If we look back at the core structure of our suggested paradigm of the human condition as formulated in Figure 2, two lines of general patterning stand out. First, the line between what in the general, four-function schema were defined as the internal and external components defines not only what we have called our anthropocentric point of reference but also the line between the two categories of living systems that we have discussed: the action system and the organic system. Second, followers of the use of this schema will have noted that the sixteenfold version shown in Figure 2 follows the format originally presented in *The American University*.[131]

Figure 6   Symbolic Components of Human Personality as a System of Meanings

COMPONENTS OF GRAMMATICAL MEANING	
Subject	Verb
Modifier	Predicate

(Identity) in Meaning

COMPONENTS OF SOCIAL ROLE STRUCTURE	
Mother	Father
Son	Daughter

(Superego) Social Object System

EROGENOUS ZONES	
Mouth (Anus)	Penis
Vagina	Breast

(Id) Reservoir of Libido

SENSORY CHANNELS	
Touch	Taste (Smell)
Hearing	Vision

(Ego) Sensory Experience

The words in parentheses under each of the four sets are the ones previously used to identify the functional subsystems of the personality within the structural paradigm of the general system of action. The L designation is taken from Erikson, the others from Freud. How these concepts are to be related to those presented here remains to be worked out.

[130] Max Weber, "Luther's Conception of the Calling," *The Protestant Ethic and the Spirit of Capitalism,* trans. Talcott Parsons (New York: Scribner's, 1958; first published in German in 1904 1905), pp. 79–92.

[131] Parsons and Platt, *American University,* "Technical Appendix," figs. A2 and A6.

We have grouped the four subparadigms around a circle, as it were, with, in each case, the g subsystem at the inside corner and the l subsystem at the outside corner and the other subsets arranged accordingly.

For the two categories of living systems, then, we have strongly emphasized what is the "matching" similarity between an "individual" and a "collective" component as, on occasion, we have labeled them. For the organic system, the individual component involves the phenotypical organism, which stands in direct relation to the environment external to the system; whereas the collective component involves the genotype and such collective entities as populations and species. On the action side of the boundary, the individual component comprises the behavioral system and the personality; the collective component comprises the social and cultural systems. Finally, the logical consequence of the format itself is to *juxtapose* in the vertical axis the two sets of individual components but not their collective counterparts. I suggest that these formal relationships constitute a syndrome with considerable theoretical significance.

Precisely from our anthropocentric point of view, the problem of the meaning of this juxtaposition comes to focus with reference to the relation between the individual phenotypical organism and the individual actor as behavioral system and as personality. Together, we have proposed, these come to constitute a human individual or person. Thus, to be formal once more, we suggest that it is not theoretically fortuitous or arbitrary that we have arranged our paradigm in the format, from top to bottom, of L–I; A–G; then A–G; and L–I (instead of L–I; A–G; then L–I; and A–G again). The deeper theoretical grounding of the rationale of the arrangement we have used remains to be further clarified, but for the present I propose to give it the benefit of the doubt.

In the context of the potential theoretical significance of the preceding considerations, I would like to devote this last section of a long chapter to a closer examination of the interrelations of the human organism and the human individual as actor, specifically on the personality side, leaning particularly on Freud's conceptualization. As a further part of the context of this analysis, however, I should like to relate this analysis to certain features of the other axis of the main paradigm, which in the most general terms we have called the instrumental-consummatory. We have already suggested that there is an affinity between Wiener's concept of information and the integrative subsystems of these functional paradigms. As we stated in our explication of the A–cell of Figure 2, these questions are undoubtedly complex, but there seems to be little doubt that in some sense the A–cell is more closely related to matter-energy and the I–cell to information. From certain points of view it makes sense for the physical system to focus energy in the G–cell.

Whatever the case may be for the suborganic levels, when we get to the organic there seems to be no doubt of the validation of a syndrome.

Thus, however energy may be produced, to be utilizable in the system of reference it has to be transformed, controlled, and we may say channeled through the operation of mechanisms that Henderson called "regulatory" and Wiener called "informational." All this at the organic level. But what of the impingement of this process on the human actor, who in one primary aspect is a personality system?

That man has an unusual, organically grounded capacity to process information is surely evidenced by the special status of the human brain among central nervous systems. There are also two other patently significant features of the human organism that are especially relevant to man's instrumental capacities. The first of these is provided by the human hands and arms, as generalized, all-purpose tools, and the second by the capacity to use brain, vocal chords, lips, tongue, and oral cavity to produce speech, a conveyor of information par excellence, which requires auditory reception of sound-encoded information, of course through a brain. From the point of view of organic evolution, all three of these are closely linked with the achievement by man of the erect posture. As Edward O. Wilson says, man is the only true biped! [132]

But what of the sources and processing of "action-energy" or as it is often called affect or "motivation"? We think that, although a large part of the answer has been contributed by Freud's later analysis of the human personality,[133] its significance has been greatly obscured by difficulties of interpretation, especially the tendency to view Freud in a biologically reductionist frame of reference as an instinct theorist. We suggest that the present human condition frame of reference makes it possible both to clear up various of these difficulties and to extend and round out Freud's analysis. This is what the present section of this chapter proposes to attempt to do.

Freud a number of times spoke of the ego, by which in this context he meant the self-conscious, personal self, as "beset" by influences or forces from three directions. The first of these directions he characterized as a "flow of stimulation" coming to the actor from his own body, the organism. This is simply a category of energy. The second we may call "information," coming from what Freud, like Descartes before him, called the "external world." This area of course also involves bodily organs, namely, the organs of sense. The third source of besetting, then, is the social environment, built into the personality as the superego through the internalization or the "introjection" of "parental function," as Freud put it in his most careful statements.[134]

[132] Wilson, *Sociobiology.*

[133] Freud, *The Ego and the Id;* see also idem, *Inhibitions, Symptoms, and Anxiety,* in vol. 20 of *Standard Edition* (1959; first published in German in 1926), pp. 77–178.

[134] The following discussion refers to Freud's mature theoretical writings, from *Three Essays on the Theory of Sexuality,* in vol. 7 of *Standard Edition* (1953; first published in German in 1905), pp. 123–243, to *Inhibitions, Symptoms, and Anxiety.*

It is notable that the organic source of what Freud called the flow of stimulation was left anatomically unspecific, whereas he clearly indicated that stimuli from the external world come through specific organs of sense. It seems justified to interpret the flow of stimulation as the input to the personality of organic energy. But if this be assumed, what happens to the energy? It eventually forms the content of what Freud called the "reservoir of libido." But the flow of stimulation is not itself libido; rather, it is an essential factor in the generation of the latter. Beyond that Freud described libido as governed by the "pleasure principle"; [135] nevertheless, he made no reference to pleasure in speaking of the flow of stimulation, and libidinal pleasure was related in certain specific ways to a set of bodily organs, the erogenous zones. It has been common to interpret their significance as lying primarily in the fact that their stimulation, for example, by touch, generates *organic* pleasure and that search for this kind of pleasure is the goal of erotic activity.

But whatever the nature and role of such physiological mechanisms, this line of argument totally ignores a set of dimensions that certainly had prime significance for Freud. The central point is that the erogenous zones become symbols that have meanings to human actors even though those meanings are for the most part unconscious (specifically in Freud's sense). If this line of argument is pursued, then the questions arise of what is the structure of this erogenous complex as a symbolic complex and what functions it serves in the personality.

Five such zones figured in Freud's discussion: the mouth, the anus, the woman's breasts, the penis, and the vagina. They have in common that they can all be pleasurably stimulated by touch, caress, etc. Moreover, all are organs of the body through which specific types of interchanges with the environment take place. So far as these interchanges are primarily organic in significance they fall into two sets—metabolic and reproductive—that are linked in critical ways. Of course, the mouth, anus, and breasts have primarily metabolic significance; the penis and vagina, reproductive. In the organic aspect, it is further notable that with some exceptions these zones are all associated with metabolic input *and* output processes. It is thus sometimes forgotten that the mouth, or more generally the oral complex, is an excretory organ in that it is the channel for the extrusion of carbon dioxide, a waste product of the metabolic process, which if retained in the body in large quantities would be highly toxic. Then of course there is the association of the genitals of both sexes with the excretion of the other most important waste product of the metabolic process, urine, the retention of which, as in cases of renal failure, can also be fatal. The penis, the anus, and the breasts, however, seem to be organs only of biologically important output. We must mention that the oral region, as the locus of the organs of speech, has more than metabolic or re-

[135] Freud, *Beyond the Pleasure Principle.*

productive significance, indeed, its significance in this respect is primarily for the action level.

If the erogenous zones are considered as a set, there is the notable fact that only mouth and anus are common to *all* living human organisms. The genitals are differentiated by sex, and only females have breasts in the relevant sense. Furthermore, the erogenous zones are conspicuous markers of age-generation relationships. Boys have penises at birth, and their testicles normally descend just prior to birth. Girls do not develop breasts until adolescence. The significance of the vagina as a part of the reproductive system is signaled by the onset of menstruation; prior to menarche the vagina seems "only" to be a urinary organ.

The preceding review may seem an unduly laborious account of commonly known facts of life, but if we are to grasp the *meanings* of these facts for a symbolic system, then the patterns of their order must be meticulously clarified. The striking feature of the pattern from the present point of view, which concerns the *linkage* of the organic and action components of individuality, is that biologically speaking these components have a *dual* reference. First, they refer to certain basic conditions of living on the part of the human individual as organism; this aspect concerns the metabolic complex.[136] The second reference is to reproduction and the succession of generations. It seems evident that Freud was attempting to interpret this latter complex of meaning in his references to the life and death instincts. The meaning structure in *both* contexts, however, refers to man as organism not actor.[137]

Let us now attempt to take a still further step toward treating the erogenous zones systematically as a set. As we noted, Freud dealt with five, but it is surely legitimate to raise the question whether reduction to four is not meaningful. If so, there is the possibility that the set of four may have four-function significance in the requisite frame of reference. We think that this is the case. The obvious step of reduction is to consolidate mouth and anus. They have a common reference to the alimentary aspect of metabolism in that they constitute the two ends of the alimentary canal. Also, as excretory organ, the anus should be differentiated from the genitals in that its output is not as such a product of the metabolic process but consists of the rejects of the alimentary process, which are very different in physiological significance from urine and carbon dioxide. This difference is widely expressed in the derogatory meaning of feces in much linguistic

---

[136] It is striking that in mammals, although the respiratory and alimentary apparatuses, are fully developed during gestation, they go into operation only at birth and that occurs very suddenly. The fetus is supplied with oxygen and carbon dioxide is removed through the placenta and hence the maternal organism; the fetus is nourished and urine removed also through the placenta. Thus, metabolically speaking for mammals birth is the establishment of independence in a radical sense.

[137] Freud, *Beyond the Pleasure Principle.*

usage. It is also probably revealing that the anus is not a locus of significant input except as a substitute vagina in certain sexual practices.

If, then, we carry out this consolidation, the remaining four zones fall into two clearly marked pairs: mouth and breast as concerned with metabolism and with the feeding not of humans generally but only of infants, on the one hand, and male and female genitals, concerned with reproduction, on the other. Given the dependency status of human offspring it seems legitimate to treat femininity as the internal aspect of the human condition, organically speaking, and masculinity, symbolized by the penis, as the external aspect. Noted that the mouth is common to both sexes and also to all ages. For a variety of formal theoretical reasons, finally, it seems correct to locate the two pairs on the diagonals of the fourfold paradigm. This is presented as the adaptive subsystem of Figure 6, which as a whole is one mode of formulation of a structural paradigm of the human personality system.

It should be kept clearly in mind that the entries in these boxes are *not* persons in roles or individual organisms but human organs *as symbols*.

As a next step it seems best to take up briefly Freud's second direction of "besetment" of the human personality, or the ego, namely, that from the external world through the senses.[138] The traditional schema refers to the five senses, vision, hearing, taste, smell, and touch. What of connections between this list and that of the erogenous zones? Clearly, the alimentary complex most directly involves taste and probably smell. The feeding of infants is obviously a central task of the mother role, and very early the taste of food becomes important to the child. Smell is early associated, certainly by adults and presumably by children, with the urinary and fecal excretions but of course also with food and other items. Hearing becomes highly significant by the time of language learning; yet surely quite early an infant includes the probability of being heard among the meanings of crying, and sounds made by adults acquire various kinds of meanings for the child. In Freud's context of thinking, a particularly important kind of relevance of visualization is that the symbols of dreams are predominantly visual.

For purposes of personality theory can the senses be systematically ordered? Here the problem of number arises again. I suggest that taste and smell can be consolidated because of their common involvement with the oral complex and through it with alimentary-metabolic functions. The four categories remaining can then be ordered in a clear cybernetic hierarchy that is often characterized as the range from proximal to distal in the order touch, taste, hearing, and vision. This ordered set is presented as the relevant G subsystem of the personality in Figure 6.

In the generation of a reservoir of libido, we are now in a position to

[138] Freud, *The Ego and the Id.*

speak of a combinatorial process. We have two orders of inputs from outside the personality, the flow of stimulation from the organism, surely a category of energy, and the stimuli to the senses, surely a category of information in Wiener's meaning. Certain features, not of one organism but of human organisms, in some sense experienced by a human child, they acquire symbolic meanings in the course of that experience, through which they come to be organized and generalized. In the present context we are concerned primarily with the energy aspect, affect or libido, whereas the more informational aspect should be treated more in the context of the behavioral system. Nevertheless, it is essential to include information in the former case, just as we include energy or affect in the latter but of course in different proportions.

This is by no means the end of the theoretical story since we know that Freud [139] spoke of a third direction from which the ego is "beset." Before taking that up, however, it will be helpful to try to consolidate certain aspects of the involvement of the first two. It seems essential to Freud's theory of child development that from the very beginning he postulated a duality of coordinated inputs from the human environment: food and the stimulation of the capacity for erotic pleasure. The former is obviously in the first instance of organically metabolic significance; the latter, more specifically psychological.

These operate through two sensory channels, namely, the pleasurable aspect of the ingestion of food through taste, that of the contact of mouth and breast, and more generally the pleasure of being cuddled by a maternal person through touch. Our way of arranging subsystem G of Figure 6 suggests the hypothesis that touch has the more powerful and immediately consummatory significance and hence greater leverage capacity for socialization. It may well be the prototype of what Freud meant by the pleasure principle. [140]

A further property of pleasure in this context is noteworthy. In our technical terms of pattern-variable analysis, pleasure may be said to be functionally diffuse. It therefore should be in a certain sense generalizable to a variety of contexts. If the mouth, in the feeding experience of the neonate, has primacy as an erogenous zone, the pleasure felt in the oral area may be generalized in other areas. This is suggested by the fact that the pleasure of being breastfed is not confined to the oral area but includes the broader pleasure of being held and cuddled. [141]

The interplay between taste and touch in relation, on the one hand, to the organic facts of life, notably, the nutritional needs of the infant, and the establishment of a relation of social solidarity between the infant and

---

[139] Ibid.

[140] Freud, *Beyond the Pleasure Principle*.

[141] Alice S. Rossi, "A Biosocial Perspective on Parenting," *Daedalus*, vol. 106, no. 2 (1977): 1–31.

the agent of nurturant care, on the other, is, I think, the essence of the famous oral phase of the socialization process as laid out by Freud. In one perspective this can be stated as the relation between two modes of dependency; that is, the dependency of the infant for its metabolic needs on adult human care and what is often called its emotional dependency on a nurturant (*not* nutritive) relationship with another human being, "normally," in spite of all the controversies, the child's mother.

It appears possible to state the purport of this transition or transformation in terms of a general theoretical formula that we have used repeatedly: the establishment, for the living entity under consideration, of a relation to an *internal environment* (in this case of an action system). We wish this to be considered in strict analogy to the transition of matter from the status of part of the physico-system only to that of part of the living organism. It seems that here, as in the other case, it requires informational inputs to bring about the shift and that in the case of the oral socialization of human infants the focus of this input process is nurturant maternal care at the human action level. Again, whatever the organic antecedents, for present purposes the critical point is that this care has *symbolic* meaning, initially to the maternal agent but in due course also to the infant.

Put in a more general *action* frame of reference, this meaning concerns the *inclusion* of the infant in an action level *social collectivity,* with all the connotations of these crucial concepts. For the child this is his first social environment in Durkheim's sense.

The conception of oral eroticism, specifically in its relevance to the understanding of infantile psychological development, is one of Freud's central contributions to the theoretical understanding of the *psyche,* in Freud's own term, *as distinguished from the organism.* Also central to Freud's theory is his linkage of infantile eroticism with that of adults at genital levels. As just noted, the bridge is the symbolic meaning, to the infant, of the pleasurable character of maternal nurturant care, which need not be delivered by the child's biological mother nor need the primary channel of operation be breastfeeding. However the intricacies of these relationships may be worked out, the organ pair of mouth and breast have clearly acquired this meaning in human psychology, and they are linked, through the common erotic dimension, with the pleasure of genital eroticism as experienced by adult members of both sexes in the act of sexual intercourse, which involves the second pair of erogenous zones.

Furthermore, though Freud did not succeed in fully working out the links among organism, individual psyche, and structure of the social environment, his basic views are in accord with the relevant social facts as these have come to be better understood since Freud's day. Thus, at the level of social structure in action terms, a special relation between the very young infant and his own mother (or mother surrogate) seems to be established as a structural universal in human societies. A further universal consists in the fact that such a dyad always has some socially structured relation of solidarity to one or more adult males in the society. This statement is carefully worded to avoid the implication that the nuclear family is universal, but it may be interpreted to mean that the structural components of the nuclear family are universal given the additional fact that children are always identified as belonging to one or the other of two sex categories.[142]

We suggest that the fact that in the foregoing sense every human child "has a mother" (or is born into a social situation in which most children have mothers) is, along with the association of pleasure with nurturant care, the focus of the mechanisms of transformation whereby a mechanism of provision for metabolic survival functions becomes the template for development of a relationship at the human action level that gives meaning to two components. The first mechanism is the two-generation feature of relations among human persons, namely, the child and the adult agent of nurturant care, including a particularistic relationship between them. The second mechanism depends on the fact that *one* party to this relationship is identified by another feature, her belonging to one sex, anatomically by having breasts, which can be the source of food for the infant; at the same time it is crucial that this person, not only her breasts, is the agent of nurturant care.

According to psychoanalytic theory a highly complex set of events occurs between the completion of the oral phase and the development of the oedipal transition. For present purposes, however, I propose to pass over those intermediate phases because they are less important to the argument than the end situations. Though the erogenous zones are organs, not persons in roles, they do constitute reference points for the categorization of persons as belonging to one of two generation categories and one of two sex categories. We have suggested that in the oral phase, at the level of symbolic meanings, the transition from the organic reference to the action-social reference has been made for the parent-child differentiation but not yet for that of sex.

It seems that the main significance of the oedipal transition is to be located here; it is the focus of the set of socialization mechanisms through which the identity and concurrently the role structure of sex differentiation are added to the categories of age or generation to constitute a fourfold reference scheme, which constitutes a transformation frrom the scheme of the organic level to that of the social role level.

At the same time, it seems to be here that the high significance of the category of masculinity should be emphasized since it is, precisely from the point of view of meaning to the child, the *new* thing by virtue of differentiating the sexes; heretofore, only adult femininity has been identified with "parental." Now the category of masculine must be relativized. The

---

[142] Terence S. Turner, "Family Structure and Socialization," in Loubser et al. (eds.), *Explorations in General Theory in Social Science,* chap. 19.

primary focus of this problem area is the significance of the penis as the *symbol* that provides the link between the organic and the action level in this particular context.

There is an important sense in which, from the child's point of view, because of the dyadic structure of the all-important collectivity shared with the mother the farher is *excluded* from his/her world of significant persons. The oedipal problem can be stated, then, as that of the process by which the father comes to be *included*. This problem should be stated in sufficiently general form to cover the shift for children of both sexes. Furthermore, it can be assumed that the inclusion of the father, specifically as distinguished from the mother by virtue of his role, is the basis on which the child's own identity by sex has to become established.

There is, to be sure, a simple anatomical sense in which this process makes the girl's newly acquired sex role residual. By far the most distinctive anatomical characteristic of the mother is her breasts, but the daughter as child lacks these, and as we suggested the reproductive significance of the girl's vagina is not evident. The male child, however, has a visible penis and shares this characteristic with his father. Presumably, children of both sexes can and generally do, in the preoedipal period, discover (most commonly through masturbation) that the genitals can be an organ of erotic pleasure. Hence, through this channel the genitals can be brought within the orbit of the erotic complex.

The most important set of considerations, however, concerns not eroticism, oral or genital, but role structure. The oedipal period is indeed, for children of both sexes, the period of the renunciation, through repression as Freud maintained, of erotic pleasures especially perhaps through diffuse, affectionate bodily contact. We may perhaps reuse the residual argument and suggest that, again from the child's point of view, the father is the residual parent—hence the necessity for his inclusion and the fact that this process is problematical. Furthermore, in modern urban society, the father's as opposed to the mother's functions tend to be performed away from home (e.g., in factory or office) and to be of a character difficult for children to understand.

There seems to be no reason why Freud's late theory of anxiety [143] as fear of object loss should not be generalized to include anxiety about what a newly included object or one in the process of inclusion will turn out to be like and to mean. That young couples approaching marriage should feel high anxiety is almost a commonplace. Hence, I suggest that the castration anxiety of the boy, which Freud emphasized so strongly, should largely be interpreted to center on the *character* of the father and prospectively what it will mean for the boy himself to grow up to be a man. Indeed, this last point can go far to explain why girls do not share that anxiety; not only does the girl not have a penis to lose but also she does

---

[143] Freud, *Inhibitions, Symptoms, and Anxiety.*

not have to face the problem of what it would mean to her if she had one. Her prospective role as an adult is much more tangible to her through identification by sex with her mother.

Also, just at this point, the girl has less reason for anxiety than her brother because she does not face so serious a renunciation, namely through change in her relation to her mother. The famous desire of the oedipal boy to displace his father in relation to his mother is compatible with the hypothesis about anxiety over change in the relationship. Both sexes of course must face the relative renunciation of childhood eroticism precisely, I think, as a *symbol* of solidarity with the mother. It is also highly significant that the proportion of children's activity outside the small circle of fellow members of the household rapidly increases in this stage. Furthermore, I have often emphasized that I do not think it fortuitous that in all societies with formal educational systems, the school age is placed somewhere near six years, very soon after the oedipal period. Going to school involves the child much more seriously and responsibly outside the family circle than before.[144]

It is a notable fact that with the repression of infantile eroticism the food complex, mediated by the sense of taste, reemerges as a primary symbolic focus yet not as the symbol of the solidarity of mother and oral child but as that of the household (in modern society mainly the nuclear family). Commensality, eating meals together, not only serves the metabolic needs of family members but also has ritual and symbolic significance. Furthermore, special family occasions like birthdays, Thanksgiving, and Christmas are celebrated with ritualized dinners. It is surely significant that the mother of the family normally stands at the center of this food complex. In the dwelling the kitchen is primarily her domain, and it is held highly desirable for her to cook well.[145] Finally, children are generally excluded from the parental bedroom, especially if there is any question of a "primal scene", whereas the family table is specifically for *all* members of the family.

The most important point, however, is that the generational and sex roles are *not,* as the erogenous zones are, organs of human bodies but are role components of the structure of human societies, which is quite different. What occurs in the socialization process from birth through the oedipal transition is not just organic maturation, although this is part of the concrete phenomenon, but also *transformation,* in the sense of

---

[144] On the oedipal problem generally, in addition to Turner, "Family Structure and Socialization," see Anne Parsons, "Is the Oedipus Complex Universal? The Jones-Malinowski Controversy Revisited," in her *Belief, Magic, and Anomie* (New York Free Press, 1969), chap. 1. See also Ruth Lidz and Theodore Lidz, "Male Menstruation: A Ritual Alternative to the Oedipal Transition," *International Journal of Psycho-Analysis* (1977).

[145] Mary Douglas, "Deciphering a Meal," *Daedalus,* vol. 101, no. 1 (1972): 61–81.

Chomsky's theory of linguistics, from one level to another.[146] In the world of living systems, this process leads from the status of *organism only* to that of *member* of a social collectivity within a system of action in our fullest technical sense of that term.

Indeed, I think it is legitimate to say that, from the point of view of what psychoanalysts call the genetic development of the child, the erogenous zones as symbols, not as the outlets of "instincts" in the traditional biopsychological sense, constitute "deep structures," which are not themselves "modes of action" but which enable the socialized human being to generate an indefinite variety of such modes, the latter being meaningful at the level of concrete action. The "rules of transformation" in this case are the modes of connection that can insure a "healthy" environmental development for the child through socialization. This view seems to be consistent with Freud's placing the erotic complex, among his structural subsystems of the personality, in the id. Indeed, there is an interesting correspondence of terminology between the psychoanalytic discussions of "depth" psychology and the linguistics term "deep structures."[147] One common feature of both is "unconsciousness." Thus, the ordinary, "healthy," and unanalyzed action person is unaware of the nature and importance of the erotic complex, which is part of his personality, as the ordinary, "competent speaker" of a language is unaware of the nature and role of the deep structures of that language. For that matter, so is the ordinary, healthy human unaware of the complex processes and factors by which his metabolic functions operate.

If the A subsystem of Figure 6 is a paradigm of the deep structures of the human personality, from the point of view of the transformation of organic energy and its availability for utilization in action, the I subsystem may be regarded as the minimal framework of a grammar of the surface structures of human *social* action. It is crucially important to emphasize the word "social" in this statement. The four centrally important erogenous zones thus *cannot* be the organs of any *one* phenotypical organism; similarly, the four social role components *cannot* be the roles of the same acting individual. In both cases the items that are symbolized incorporate both sexes and two adjacent generations in the succession of generations. *Indeed, it is the common reference of both sets to bisexuality and to the succession of generations that is the basis of their congruence with each other.* Without these two common sets of meanings, the process of transformation of which we have spoken presumably could not take place. If this were the case, clearly not only Figure 6 but also the developed master paradigm of this chapter, Figure 2, would have to be discarded.

Inspection of Figure 6 will show that maternal function is the primary common element of the two subsets A and I. At the erogenous zone level

---

[146] Chomsky, *Syntactic Structures.*
[147] Ibid.

it is breasts, which are the symbol of nurturant care; whereas at the social role level, "mother" is the common designation for a role in the family as a social collectivity. Both categories, that is, are placed in the *integrative* role, with all the implications for function involved in that placement. One way of translating this implication is to say that at the organic level, as symbolized by feeding the child, the mother integrates the organic functions of the two biological parents; a child is the consequence of sexual intercourse and requires nurturant care to survive. At the social role level, the mother most directly integrates the role of father, as more involved in extrafamilial relations than herself, and of sons, who, if not already, will prospectively be so involved. If these categories are interpreted as role components and not concrete role types, no "male chauvinist" inferences need be drawn since so long as there are families or family-like social structures, the primary functions will have to be differentiated from each other, whatever the allocation of persons to them. As it is the mode of integration between the organic and the action level that has been the primary theme of this section, the analysis certainly leaves a good deal of leeway for variation, which Terence S. Turner makes clear.[148] Yet, so long as women bear the children and assume a somewhat greater degree of responsibility in early child care, it seems that organic structure and the structure of human social organization cannot stand in random relations of variation to each other.

Of course the oedipal transition is by no means the end of the story. So as not to become involved in a discussion of variations of kinship structures at this point, I shall confine these brief remarks to the Western situation. It has already been noted that the postoedipal child soon goes to school, and from then on has a progressively broadening and deepening involvement outside the natal family. After what Freud called the period of latency, there comes the major reorganization of libidinal structures that we have come to label "adolescence." [149] Structuring their orientations around incest rules, adolescents of both sexes tend to develop erotic attachments to *agemates* of opposite sex *outside* the natal family. There is thus the *double* shift in what Freud called "object-choice" to an agemate (not a parental generation person) and to a nonfamily member. In addition, for girls there is change in the sex of the principal object from the mother to a male.[150]

Turner's searching analysis of the problem of the universality of the nuclear family [151] enables us to say with some confidence that these four

[148] Turner, "Family Structure and Socialization."

[149] Sigmund Freud, *Introductory Lectures on Psycho-Analysis,* vols. 15 and 16 of *Standard Edition* (1961 and 1963; first published in German in 1916–1917).

[150] For a recent survey and analysis of how the problem of incest rules stands see David M. Schneider, "The Meaning of Incest," *Journal of Polynesian Society,* 1976.

[151] Turner, "Family Structure and Socialization."

role components constitute a universal template of the development of social role structures generally, which is not in any usual sense culture-bound. It is by virtue of this fact, which Robert F. Bales and I suggested for the more restricted thesis about the significance of the nuclear family a long time ago,[152] that a successful mode of articulation has evolved between the human level of organic structure and that of the system of action, or, put a little differently, that it has been possible for an action system to evolve at all from the organic level of evolution. In this sense, David M. Schneider is right that Western society, with its high differentiation of the nuclear family from other social structures, has presented, especially in its American but not excluding its early twentieth-century Viennese version, a particularly favorable set of cases for studying the essentials of human kinship and its relation to personality development.[153]

As my final word on this topic, I may repeat that it is not only important but *absolutely essential* for the reader to be clear that the preceding analysis is *not* an analysis of the individual phenotypical organism as it is articulated with the individual human personality or psyche. Very differently, it is an analysis of the articulation of the *human organic system with the human action system,* as wholes. This is *not* the same thing. I think that a great deal of the difficulty over interpreting Freud as a biological reductionist stems from the implicit assumption of this position of theoretical individualism; the personality is treated simply as an "expansion" of the phenotypical organism. Thus, to drive the point home, of the three category sets around which we have organized this discussion, only that of the sensory channels can be dealt with in terms of *any* one individual either as organism or as actor. The other two, the erogenous zones and the components of kinship role structure, both require reference to plural individuals who must be related to one another in a structural set that includes populations and species, on one side, and societies and cultures, on the other. The same applies to the fourth set, linguistic meaning, to a brief discussion of which we now turn.[154]

---

[152] See Talcott Parsons and Robert F. Bales, in collaboration with James Olds, Morris Zelditch, and Philip E. Slater *Family, Socialization, and Interaction Process* (New York: Free Press, 1955).

[153] David M. Schneider, *American Kinship: A Cultural Account* (Englewood Cliffs: Prentice-Hall, 1968).

[154] It should be quite clear that this discussion of Freud's theory of human personality in relation to certain features of the human organic system must not be construed as a "reversion to biological determinism" with respect either to my own position or to my interpretation of Freud. I maintain strongly the position stated in Chapter 4 of this volume that Freud's discussion of *psychic* phenomena, which he always carefully distinguished from organic, belongs at the level of the system of action not at that of the organic system. He thus defined "instincts" (not his word but his translators') as "representatives *to the psyche* of organic drives." Furthermore, he quite definitely treated the place of the erogenous zones in the organization of the personality as *symbolic,* and symbolic meaning is not a category of organic structure. The sensory channels, then, have an organic reference of a different

By the conception that has underlain not only the present chapter but also the whole of this volume, what we call an action system, is characterized by and organized about symbols and their concatenated relationships of meaning. Furthermore, the distinctively human vehicle for the expression, communication, and interpretation of meaning is language. It therefore has seemed appropriate to treat certain fundamentals of the meaning structure embodied in language as the pattern-maintenance "base" of a human personality specifically treated as a system of action. In line, however, with the emphatic statement of the last paragraph, it is essential to emphasize that though, to use Chomsky's phrase, competence in at least one language is an essential attribute of the normal human being,[155] language as such is most definitely a *transindividual* phenomenon. "Possession" of language is an attribute of action *systems* that transcends individuals and is centered in the cultural sector but also is deeply involved in the social sector as the speech community. It is well known that there is no record of any individual "feral" child having wholly "on his own" developed a language. From this point of view, being competent in a language is as essential a criterion of an individual's being humanly "alive" as is his being possessed of a normally functioning central nervous system. Thus, aphasia in the extreme case is a kind of "language death" not dissimilar to "brain death."

From very ancient tradition, considerably refined by modern linguistic science, a simple paradigm of the most fundamental components of the grammatical structure of meaning has emerged; this paradigm is set forth in the L box of Figure 6. The context of the paradigm portrays the minimal components that make an ordinary sentence meaningful.

The primary reference base should clearly be the subject, which implies a speaker or communicator whose meaning is embodied in the sentence. This subject must then in the first instance be related to a predicate, which is what the sentence is "about." Subject and predicate, however, do not simple relate themselves to each other; rather, their relation must be sig-

---

sort, as channels of input of information to the personality. See Figure 6 of this chapter.

The other two sets of categories that have been discussed, the components of kinship role structure and the components of linguistic meaning, are not organic in *any* sense but belong at the level of action. Thus, this discussion is an attempt to clarify the *articulation* of the human personality, as a system of action, with the human organic system. Earlier, in discussing the articulation of the organic system with the physico-chemical environment, we examined Henderson's conception of the fitness of that environment for the emergence and development of organic life. In a parallel sense we might speak of the fitness of the human organic environment for the emergence of an action system. In neither case is the position reductionistic nor is it a denial of the relevance of the "lower" level of organization (physico-chemical in the one case, organic in the other) for general understanding of the higher (organic and action, respectively).

[155] Noam Chomsky, *Reflections on Language* (New York: Pantheon, 1975).

nified, or we might say mediated, by a verb element. This conception of mediation is clearly of integrative significance in our sense.

The three components subject–verb–predicate can of course form a minimal sentence, but the potential for communication of information is enormously enhanced if a fourth component grammatically different from the other three is added—namely, one or more examples of the class known as modifiers, of which a familiar member is the adjective. Modifiers may be conceived to adapt the meaning system to the more complex environment outside the immediate intentions of the speaker.

It should be quite clear that this set of grammatical components is not the deep structure of language in Chomsky's sense but a long-established framework for analyzing what Chomsky calls surface structures. In this respect they are parallel to the components of the role structure of human kinship as set forth in the I–cell of Figure 6 and discussed earlier.

The connections between the acquisition of language and the process of socialization as previously discussed are fairly well known. The first main stage of language learning begins toward the end of the first year of life. It is of course *spoken,* not written, language. Language acquisition goes on for a considerable period, perhaps nearing a kind of completion only at the oedipal period. It is, I think, highly significant that the beginning of language learning presupposes the consolidation of the oral inclusion discussed in this section and that the primary agent of early language teaching is typically the mother. Edelson puts forward the interesting view that dreaming presupposes the acquisition of language;[156] prelinguistic infants do not dream because they have not yet learned to manipulate symbols at the linguistic level. This observation connects with another highly significant one of Freud's, namely, that the primary symbols that figure in dreams are *visual.* Is there a contradiction with the fact that the child first learns spoken language? Freud thought not and explained that auditory symbolization, through its relation to language, imposes a logical ordering on the relations among such symbols that is incompatible with the expressive needs that find their outlet in dreams. Touch and taste presumably do not offer sufficient scope to carry the burden of dream symbolism; yet of the two higher sensory modes of symbolization, the auditory is not primary because it is blocked by its relation to language.

We have already noted that the learning of written language (i.e., learning to read and write) occurs mainly *following* the oedipal transition. This surely cannot be fortuitous or culture bound in the vulgar sense. It seems to be one of a good many cases in which "ontogeny repeats phylogeny" in living systems, both organic and action systems. There are thus many societies that have spoken language but no written language although no case is known of a literate society with no spoken language. Though

---

[156] Edelson, "Language and Dreams."

deaf-mute children can, by special methods, be taught to read and write, surely it is normal for the child first to learn to speak and only when this competence is rather advanced to add the visual to the auditory medium.

I ended the earlier draft of this chapter by pointing out very briefly that what on the basis of sociological usage I have called the "age-sex" frame of reference has proved to be applicable not only to the study of sexually reproducing organic species, where the phenotypical individual is mortal, and to human kinship structures but also to the study of religious symbols. My personal involvement in the last of the three areas is above all based on the Christian case as set forth in the two articles included in the present volume as Chapters 12 and 13.

Chapter 12, which was written collaboratively with Renée Fox and Victor Lidz, is an attempt to fit Christian symbolism into the conception of gift exchange as worked out by Marcel Mauss,[157] especially in its relation to Christian conceptions of the meaning of death. We stressed the scriptural formula that "God *gave* His only begotten Son" for man's redemption. Furthermore, we were struck by the expression that a woman *gives* birth to a child; thus, in the narrative version of the Nativity, Mary (conceived as a human woman) *gives* birth to Jesus. Hence, the ordinary human individual and Jesus have in common that they are recipients of the "gift of life" and thus, by Mauss's formula, have incurred the obligation to reciprocate the gift.

In Figure 1 of Chapter 13, which I wrote about a year after Chapter 12, I attempted to formalize this symbolic structure. To do so required making a distinction between two levels, the human and the divine, or transcendental, as I called it. In the latter were placed the three persons of the Christian Trinity, the relation between Father and Son clearly suggesting human kinship symbolism. In the human level paradigm were placed the protagonists of the Christian drama of the birth and Crucifixion of Christ as the agent of salvation.

When I undertook the revision of the present chapter I had, since writing the first draft, worked out the paradigm presented here as Figure 6. Only in the course of actually undertaking the revision did I go back, in a mood of adequate theoretical seriousness, and *directly compare* the new Figure 6 with Figure 1 of Chapter 13. Of course, I was fully aware that both used the age-sex frame of reference, but I was astonished to realize that in their formal relations the two levels in each case were, with appropriate consideration of *particular* symbols, structurally identical. This is to say that the transcendental level paradigm of the Christian symbol system is isomorphic with the I–cell paradigm of Figure 6 in the present

[157] Marcel Mauss, *The Gift: Forms and Functions of Exchange in Archaic Societies,* trans. Ian Cunnison (New York: Free Press, 1954; first published in French in 1925).

chapter and that the human level paradigm of Chapter 13 is isomorphic with the A–cell paradigm of Figure 6, that ordering the relations of the erogenous zones *as symbols*.

To spell out this convergence, a little, Mary, as the "Mother of God," is, like the organic vagina, placed in the L–cell; whereas in the upper level paradigm God the Father is placed in the same cell as, in the kinship components table, is the human father, as *role* player. Thus, in both cases, sexes are reversed. Then, in the human level paradigm, the human Jesus, who died on the cross and "gave his body and his blood for human redemption," is placed in the G–cell. This position is occupied by the penis in the erogenous zone table, which may shed light on the Catholic church's insistence on the masculinity of Jesus (as symbol) and through him of the priesthood.

Then, on the other axis, in the case of the I–cell of the human paradigm, the religious version designates the Church, as infused with the "gift of grace"; the erogenous zone paradigm places the breast(s) in this category. Surely, the prevalence of such expressions as "Mother Church" lends potential significance to this association. On the transcendental level, the I category becomes the Holy Spirit. It will be noted that this is the only person of the Trinity the sex of which is not designated in theology. We suggest that there is a kind of latent femininity implied. However that may be, surely at the human level of religious social organization the Church has become a collective organization (indeed the first) in which the individual comes to be included most generally and significantly through infant baptism. Possibly also, the Holy Spirit is the locus in the doctrine of the Trinity where, without designation by sex, the "Divine Mother" who has figured so prominently in the history of religions has found a place.

From the point of view of relatively immediate symbolic interpretation, the relation of the two pairs of A–cells to each other is clearly the most problematical. Some suggestions, however, come from the sense in which, in the I–cell of Figure 6, the daughter role is treated as residual. If there is some plausibility in treating the Holy Spirit as a mother figure in the transcendental paradigm, then the conspicuous fact is that the Trinity leaves the daughter role unfilled, not only unnamed as such. I have ventured to suggest in Chapter 12 that this role might be filled by referring to the divinely inspired prophets who in biblical terms are not, like Jesus, half divine but though human are true dispensers of "the Word." One might say, by contrast with the special mission of the Son from the Father, they carry on the divine infusion of the human from the transcendental world more routinely.

It seems appropriate to identify in this cell for the human level the inherited "holy community" of the people of Israel as the counterpart, but not in the role of, the Christian church. In Jewish tradition this community is especially identified with the role of law in regulating human intercourse; indeed, such is in a sense the great historic contribution of Judaism.[158]

In Figure 1 of Chapter 13 we have included, along with this, a reference to the New Testament figure of Joseph. There has, of course been century-long speculation about the dual paternity of Jesus, one neat resolution of which problem is Edmund R. Leach's proposal that Joseph should be considered to be Jesus' "sociological" father.[159] Here, however, I would like to suggest that the primary symbolic function of the Joseph figure is to establish Jesus as the legitimate heir of the kings of Israel, of the "House of David." His genealogy in this account is explicitly traced through Joseph not Mary.

Finally, in Chapters 12 and 13, a good deal is made of the importance of the two symbols blood and body as they crystallized in Christian tradition. The symbolic climax is the formula of the Eucharist, the master ritual certainly of Catholic Christianity, that Jesus, in dying on the Cross, gave his body and his blood for the redemption of mankind. The bread of course symbolizes the body of Christ and the wine the blood of Christ.

Obviously, these symbols cannot be construed to be a literally scientific set of biological categories. First, isn't blood part of the body? Clearly not symbolically, on which level the two are separated. Second, perhaps the prototype at human kinship levels of close blood relationships is that between a mother and her own child, but biologically they do not share a common bloodstream, even in utero, etc.

It is further significant that in the religious paradigm the dual uses of each of these symbols are placed at diagonally opposite corners of the paradigm: "blood" at L and G, "body" at I and A. I am inclined to relate this placement to the special theoretical import of the diagonal relations, namely, integration and adaptation, on the one hand, and pattern-maintenance and goal-attainment, on the other, which has been noted a good many times. It does not, however, seem appropriate to pursue these problems further here; nevertheless, they are very much on the agenda for future work.

There is an additional problem of interpretation that should be mentioned at this point, although I shall not attempt to resolve it. The reader will have noted that the placing of God the Father in the transcendental set of Figure 1, Chapter 13, does not fully agree with the categorization of the telic system in Figure 2 of the present chapter. There is a discrepancy if the Christian conception of God the Father is construed to be an instance of the category "ultimate agency" as formulated by Bellah [160] and adopted for the telic system in this chapter.

---

158 Weber, *Ancient Judaism.*

159 Edmund R. Leach, *Genesis as Myth and Other Essays* (London: Jonathan Cape, 1969).

160 Robert N. Bellah, personal communication, August 1977.

These two examples indicate that this venture into the problems of religious symbolism is fraught with difficulty. It does not, however, seem that this is adequate ground on which to dismiss the isomorphism just discussed between symbolic structures linking the organic and action levels, on the one hand, and those linking the level of the action system with that of the telic system, on the other, as "fruitless speculation."

One of the problems that will have to be faced in evaluating the significance of this isomorphism is culture-boundedness: The only religious example analyzed in this book is that of Christianity. Thus, are our findings culture-bound and, if so, in what ways? Without being in the position here to go into that problem, I suggest that there is a parallel with the problems of the universality of the nuclear family and of the oedipal complex as those problems were dealt with in earlier discussions. We need a Terence Turner to review the evidence for the universality of the symbolic *components* of Christianity. I suspect that a likely outcome of such a review would be that of course Christianity is not universal; yet, a core set of the *symbolic components* of Christianity may well turn out to be, that is, from the point of view of the human condition as it is the subject of analysis in this chapter.

If, with the modifications that are to be expected, this core set of symbolic meanings indeed proves universal, the implications for the unification of our knowledge of the human condition would surely be immense. Such a schema would provide well-ordered linkages across two of the four "round-the-clock" gaps in the human condition paradigm, making theoretical sense of the relations of three of the four primary subsystems to each other.

We think that this chapter has presented considerable evidence for the establishment of humanly meaningful linkage across one of the two remaining gaps, namely, that between the physico-chemical world and organic life, relying heavily on the work of Henderson and Wiener. We maintain that in the great tradition of philosophical epistemology above all and also in other traditions there is much known that can help to bridge the gap between the physical world and the telic system, especially using Kant's epistemology as a point of reference. We also think that there is reasonable ground for understanding at least in part the nature of the diagonal relationships in our paradigm.

On this note of relative and cautious intellectual optimism, but still definitely optimism, it seems appropriate to bring this long and complicated, but I hope not confused, analysis to a close. The present close, however, is also the beginning of a new phase of exploration of these problems.

Bibliography of Talcott Parsons

1928 "Capitalism" in Recent German Literature: Sombart and Weber, I. *Journal of Political Economy*, vol. 36:641–661.

1929 "Capitalism" in Recent German Literature: Sombart and Weber, II. *Journal of Political Economy*, vol. 37:31–51.

1930 Max Weber, *The Protestant Ethic and the Spirit of Capitalism* (translated by Talcott Parsons). London: Allen & Unwin; New York: Scribner's.

1931 Wants and Activities in Marshall. *Quarterly Journal of Economics*, vol. 46:101–140.

1932 Economics and Sociology: Marshall in Relation to the Thought of His Time. *Quarterly Journal of Economics*, vol. 46:316–347.

1933 Malthus. *Encyclopedia of the Social Sciences*, vol. 10:68–69.
Pareto. *Encyclopedia of the Social Sciences*, vol. 11:576–578.

1934 Some Reflections on "The Nature and Significance of Economics." *Quarterly Journal of Economics*, vol. 48:511–545.
Society. *Encyclopedia of the Social Sciences*, vol. 14:225–231.
Sociological Elements in Economic Thought, I. *Quarterly Journal of Economics*, vol. 49:414–453.

1935 Sociological Elements in Economic Thought, II. *Quarterly Journal of Economics*, vol. 49:645–667.
The Place of Ultimate Values in Sociological Theory. *International Journal of Ethics*, vol. 45:282–316.
H. M. Robertson on Max Weber and His School. *Journal of Political Economy*, vol. 43:688–696.

1936 Pareto's Central Analytical Scheme. *Journal of Social Philosophy*, vol. 1:244–262.
On Certain Sociological Elements in Professor Taussig's Thought. *Explorations in Economics: Notes and Essays Contributed in Honor*

NOTE: A few foreign-language works, translations, and editions of Talcott Parsons's writings are listed in these pages, but the bulk of them is not. We hope to compile a separate list for those.

of F. W. Taussig, Jacob Viner (ed.). New York: McGraw-Hill. Pp. 352–379.

1937   *The Structure of Social Action.* New York: McGraw-Hill. Reprint edition, 1949.

Education and the Professions. *International Journal of Ethics,* vol. 47: 365–369.

1938   The Role of Theory in Social Research. *American Sociological Review,* vol. 3:13–20. Address presented to the 1937 annual institute of the Society for Social Research at the University of Chicago.

The Role of Ideas in Social Action. *American Sociological Review,* vol. 3:653–664. Address written for a session on the problem of ideologies at the 1937 annual meeting of the American Sociological Society. Reprinted in *Essays in Sociological Theory* (1949).

1939   The Professions and Social Structure. *Social Forces,* vol. 17:457–467. Address written for the 1938 annual meeting of the American Sociological Society. Reprinted in *Essays in Sociological Theory* (1949).

Comte. *Journal of Unified Science,* vol. 9:77–83.

1940   Analytical Approach to the Theory of Social Stratification. *American Journal of Sociology,* vol. 45:841–862. Reprinted in *Essays in Sociological Theory* (1949).

Motivation of Economic Activities. *Canadian Journal of Economics and Political Science,* vol. 6:187–203. Public lecture at the University of Toronto. Reprinted in *Essays in Sociological Theory* (1949) and in *Human Relations in Administration: The Sociology of Organization,* Robert Dubin (ed.).

1942   Max Weber and the Contemporary Political Crisis. *Review of Politics,* vol. 4:61–76, 155–172.

The Sociology of Modern Anti-Semitism. *Jews in a Gentile World,* J. Graeber and Stuart Henderson Britt (eds.). New York: Macmillan. Pp. 101–122.

Age and Sex in the Social Structure of the United States. *American Sociological Review,* vol. 7:604–616. Address presented to the 1941 annual meeting of the American Sociological Society. Reprinted in *Essays in Sociological Theory* (1949); in *Sociological Analysis,* Logan Wilson and William Kolb (eds.), and in *Personality in Nature, Society, and Culture,* Clyde Kluckhohn and Henry A. Murray (eds.).

Propaganda and Social Control. *Psychiatry,* vol. 5 (no. 4):551–572. Reprinted in *Essays in Sociological Theory* (1949).

Democracy and the Social Structure in Pre-Nazi Germany. *Journal of Legal and Political Sociology,* vol. 1:96–114. Reprinted in *Essays in Sociological Theory,* revised edition (1954).

Some Sociological Aspects of the Fascist Movements. *Social Forces,* vol. 21 (no. 2):138–147. Presidential address presented at the 1942 annual meeting of the Eastern Sociological Society. Reprinted in *Essays in Sociological Theory,* revised edition (1954).

1943   The Kinship System of the Contemporary United States. *American*

Anthropologist, vol. 45:22–38. Reprinted in *Essays in Sociological Theory* (1949).

1944   The Theoretical Development of the Sociology of Religion. *Journal of the History of Ideas*, vol. 5:176–190. Reprinted in *Essays in Sociological Theory* (1949) and in *Ideas in Cultural Perspective*, Philip Wiener and Aaron Noland (eds.). New Brunswick: Rutgers University Press, 1962.

1945   The Present Position and Prospects of Systematic Theory in Sociology. *Twentieth Century Sociology*, Georges Gurvitch and Wilbert E. Moore (eds.). New York: Philosophical Library. Reprinted in *Essays in Sociological Theory* (1949).

The Problem of Controlled Institutional Change: An Essay on Applied Social Science. *Psychiatry*, vol. 8:79–101. Prepared as an appendix the the *Report on the Conference on Germany after World War II*. Reprinted in *Essays in Sociological Theory* (1949).

Racial and Religious Differences as Factors in Group Tensions. *Unity and Difference in the Modern World*, Louis Finkelstein et al. (eds.). New York: Conference on Science, Philosophy, and Religion in Their Relation to the Democratic Way of Life.

1946   The Science Legislation and the Role of the Social Sciences. *American Sociological Review*, vol. 11 (no. 6):653–666.

Population and Social Structure. *Japan's Prospect*, Douglas G. Haring (ed.). Cambridge, Mass.: Harvard University Press. Pp. 87–114. (This book was published by the staff of the Harvard School for Overseas Administration.) Reprinted in *Essays in Sociological Theory*, revised edition (1954).

Certain Primary Sources and Patterns of Aggression in the Social Structure of the Western World. *Psychiatry*, vol. 10:167–181. Reprinted in *Essays in Sociological Theory* (1949) and as "The Structure of Group Hostility," in *Crisis and Continuity in World Politics* (2d ed.), G. Lanyi and W. McWilliams (eds.). New York: Random House, 1973. Pp. 220–223.

Some Aspects of the Relations between Social Science and Ethics. *Social Science*, vol. 22:23–217. Address presented to the 1946 annual meeting of the American Association for the Advancement of Science.

1947   Science Legislation and the Social Sciences. *Bulletin of Atomic Scientists* (January). Reprinted in *Political Science Quarterly*, vol. 62 (no. 2).

Max Weber: The Theory of Social and Economic Organization (co-edited and translated with A. M. Henderson). Oxford University Press. Introduction by T. Parsons. (The Introduction was reprinted in *Essays in Sociological Theory*, first edition, 1949.) Reprinted by The Free Press (1957).

1948   Sociology, 1941–1946 (co-authored with Bernard Barber). *American Journal of Sociology*, vol. 53:245–257.

The Position of Sociological Theory. *American Sociological Review*, vol.

13, 156–171. Address presented to the 1947 annual meeting of the American Sociological Society. Reprinted in *Essays in Sociological Theory* (1949).

1949 *Essays in Sociological Theory Pure and Applied.* New York: Free Press. Revised edition 1954.

The Rise and Decline of Economic Man. *Journal of General Education,* vol. 4:47–53.

Social Classes and Class Conflict in the Light of Recent Sociological Theory. *American Economic Review,* vol. 39:16–26. Address presented to the 1948 annual meeting of the American Economics Association. Reprinted in *Essays in Sociological Theory,* revised edition (1954).

The Structure of Social Action (reprint edition). New York: Free Press.

1950 The Prospects of Sociological Theory. *American Sociological Review,* vol. 15 (no. 1):3–16. Presidential address presented to the 1949 annual meeting of the American Sociological Society. Reprinted in *Essays in Sociological Theory,* revised edition (1954).

Psychoanalysis and the Social Structure. *Psychoanalytic Quarterly,* vol. 19:371–384. Substance of this paper was presented at the 1948 annual meeting of the American Psychoanalytic Association. Reprinted in *Essays in Sociological Theory,* revised edition (1954).

The Social Environment of the Educational Process. *Centennial.* Washington, D.C.: American Association for the Advancement of Science. Pp. 36–40. Address presented to the AAAS Centennial Celebration (September 1948).

1951 *The Social System.* New York: Free Press.

Toward a General Theory of Action. Editor and contributor with Edward A. Shils et al. Cambridge, Mass.: Harvard University Press. Reprinted, Harper Torchbooks, 1962.

Graduate Training in Social Relations at Harvard. *Journal of General Education,* vol. 5:149–157.

Illness and the Role of the Physician: A Sociological Perspective. *American Journal of Orthopsychiatry,* vol. 21:452–460. Address presented to the 1951 annual meeting of the American Orthopsychiatry Association. Reprinted in *Personality in Nature, Society, and Culture* (2d ed.), Clyde Kluckhohn, Henry A. Murray, and David M. Schneider (eds.). New York: Knopf, 1953.

1952 The Superego and the Theory of Social Systems. *Psychiatry,* vol. 15: 15–25. Substance of this paper was presented at the 1951 meeting of the Psychoanalytic Section of the American Psychiatric Association. Reprinted in *Social Structure and Personality* (1964) and in *Working Papers in the Theory of Action* (2d ed.), Talcott Parsons, Robert F. Bales, and Edward A. Shils (eds.). New York: Free Press, 1953 and 1967.

Religious Perspectives in College Teaching: Sociology and Social Psychology. *Religious Perspectives in College Teaching,* Hoxie N. Fairchild (ed.). New York: Ronald Press, Pp. 286–337.

A Sociologist Looks at the Legal Profession. *Conference on the Profession of Law and Legal Education,* Conference Series Number II. Chicago: Law School, University of Chicago. Pp. 49–63. Address presented to the Fiftieth Anniversary Celebration of the University of Chicago Law School (December 1952). Reprinted in *Essays in Sociological Theory* (1954).

1953   *Working Papers in the Theory of Action* (in collaboration with Robert F. Bales and Edward A. Shils). New York: Free Press. Reprint edition 1967.

Psychoanalysis and Social Science with Special Reference to the Oedipus Problem. *Twenty Years of Psychoanalysis,* Franz Alexander and Helen Ross (eds.). New York: Norton. Pp. 186–215. Substance of this paper was presented to the Twentieth Anniversary Celebration of the Institute for Psychoanalysis (October 1952).

A Revised Analytical Approach to the Theory of Social Stratification. *Class, Status, and Power: A Reader in Social Stratification,* Reinhard Bendix and Seymour M. Lipset (eds.). New York: Free Press. Pp. 92–129. Reprinted in *Essays in Sociological Theory* (1954).

Illness, Therapy, and the Modern Urban American Family (co-authored with Renée C. Fox). *Journal of Social Issues,* vol. 8:31–44. Reprinted in *Patients, Physicians, and Illness,* E. Gartly Jaco (ed.). New York: Free Press, 1958.

Some Comments on the State of the General Theory of Action. *American Sociological Review,* vol. 18 (no. 6):618–631.

1954   The Father Symbol: An Appraisal in the Light of Psychoanalytic and Sociological Theory. *Symbols and Values: An Initial Study,* Bryson, Finkelstein, MacIver, and McKeon (eds.). New York: Harper & Row. Pp. 523–544. Substance of this paper was presented to the 1952 annual meeting of the American Psychological Association. Reprinted in *Social Structure and Personality* (1964).

Essays in Sociological Theory (rev. ed.). New York: Free Press.

Psychology and Sociology. *For a Science of Social Man,* John P. Gillin (ed.). New York: Macmillan. Pp. 67–102.

The Incest Taboo in Relation to Social Structure and the Socialization of the Child. *British Journal of Sociology,* vol. 5 (no. 2):101–117.

1955   *Family, Socialization, and Interaction Process* (co-authored with Robert F. Bales, James Olds, Morris Zelditch, and Philip E. Slater. New York: Free Press.

"McCarthyism" and American Social Tension: A Sociologist's View. *Yale Review,* 226–245. Reprinted as "Social Strains in America," in *The New American Right,* Daniel Bell (ed.). New York: Criterion Books.

1956   *Economy and Society* (co-authored with Neil J. Smelser). London: Routledge & Kegan Paul; New York: Free Press.

Éléments pour une theorie de l'action (translated, with an introduction, by François Bourricaud). Paris: Plon.

A Sociological Approach to the Theory of Organizations, I. *Administra-*

tive Science Quarterly (June):63–85. Reprinted in *Structure and Process in Modern Society* (1960).

A Sociological Approach to the Theory of Organizations, II. *Administrative Science Quarterly* (September):225–239. Reprinted in *Structure and Process in Modern Society* (1960).

1957   The Distribution of Power in American Society. *World Politics*, vol. 10 (October):123–143. Reprinted in *Structure and Process in Modern Society* (1960).

Malinowski and the Theory of Social Systems. *Man and Culture*, Raymond Firth (ed.). London Routledge & Kegan Paul.

Man in His Social Environment—As Viewed by Modern Social Science. *Centennial Review of Arts and Sciences*, vol. 1, (no. 1):50–69.

The Mental Hospital as a Type of Organization. *The Patient and the Mental Hospital*, Milton Greenblatt, Daniel J. Levinson, and Richard H. Williams (eds.). New York: Free Press.

Réflexions sur les organisations religieuses aux Etats-Unis. *Archives de la sociologie des religions* (January–June):21–36.

Sociologia di dittatura. Bologna: Il Molino.

La teoría de la acción. *Boletín del Instituto de Sociología*, vol. 10 (no. 1):1–68.

1958   Authority, Legitimation, and Political Action. *Authority*, C. J. Friedrich (ed.). Cambridge, Mass.: Harvard University Press. Reprinted in *Structure and Process in Modern Society* (1960).

The Definitions of Health and Illness in the Light of American Values and Social Structure. *Patients, Physicians, and Illness*, E. Gartly Jaco (ed.). New York: Free Press. Reprinted in *Social Structure and Personality* (1964). Translated into German as "Definition von Gesundheit und Krankheit im Lichte der Wertbegriffe und der sozialen Struktur Amerikas."

Social Structure and the Development of Personality. *Psychiatry* (November): 321–340. Reprinted in *Social Structure and Personality* (1964).

General Theory in Sociology. *Sociology Today*, Robert K. Merton, Leonard Broom, and Leonard S. Cottrell, Jr. (eds.). New York: Basic Books.

Some Ingredients of a General Theory of Formal Organization. *Administrative Theory in Education*, Andrew W. Halpin (ed.). Chicago: Midwest Administration Center, University of Chicago. Reprinted in *Structure and Process in Modern Society* (1960).

Some Reflections on the Institutional Framework of Economic Development. *The Challenge of Development: A Symposium*. Jerusalem: Hebrew University. Reprinted in *Structure and Process in Modern Society* (1960).

Some Trends of Change in American Society: Their Bearing on Medical Education. *Journal of the American Medical Association*, vol. 167 (no. 1):31–36. Reprinted in *Structure and Process in Modern Society* (1960).

The Pattern of Religious Organization in the United States. *Dædalus*

(Summer):65–85. Reprinted in *Structure and Process in Modern Society* (1960).

The Concepts of Culture and of Social System (co-authored with A. L. Kroeber). *American Sociological Review* (October):582. Reprinted in *Ideas of Culture: Sources and Uses,* Frederick Gamst and Edward Norbeck (eds.). New York: Holt, Rinehart & Winston, 1976.

A Short Account of My Intellectual Development. *Alpha Kappa Deltan.* Claremont: Pomona College. Pp. 3–12.

1959   An Approach to Psychological Theory in Terms of the Theory of Action. *Psychology: A Study of a Science,* Sigmund Koch (ed.). New York: McGraw-Hill. Vol. 3:612–711.

The Principal Structures of Community: A Sociological View. *Community,* C. J. Friedrich (ed.). New York: Liberal Arts Press. Reprinted in *Structure and Process in Modern Society* (1960).

"Voting" and the Equilibrium of the American Political System. *American Voting Behavior,* Eugene Burdick and Arthur Brodbeck (eds.). New York: Free Press.

Comment on "American Intellectuals: Their Politics and Status." *Dædalus,* vol. 88 (no. 3):493–495.

Durkheim's Contribution to the Theory of Integration of Social Systems. *Emile Durkheim, 1858–1917: A Collection of Essays, with Translation and a Bibliography,* Kurt H. Wolff (ed.). Columbus: Ohio State University Press, 1959.

Implications of the Study ("Book Selection and Retention in California Public and School Libraries," by Marjorie Fiske). *The Climate of Book Selection,* a symposium of the University of California School of Librarianship. Berkeley: University of California Press.

Some Problems Confronting Sociology as a Profession. *American Sociological Review,* vol. 24 (no. 4):547–559.

The School Class as a Social System. *Harvard Educational Review,* (Fall). Reprinted in *Social Structure and Personality* (1964) and in *Education, Economy, and Society,* A. H. Halsey, Jean Floud, and Arnold C. Anderson (eds.). New York: Free Press, 1961. Also reprinted in *Socialization and Schools,* Reprint Series No 1, compiled from the *Harvard Educational Review,* 1972:69–90.

An Approach to the Sociology of Knowledge. *Proceedings of the Fourth World Congress of Sociology* (Milan, Italy), vol. 4:25–49.

1960   Mental Illness and "Spiritual Malaise": The Roles of the Psychiatrist and of the Minister of Religion. *The Ministry and Mental Health,* Hans Hofmann (ed.). New York: Association Press. Reprinted in *Social Structure and Personality* (1964).

Structure and Process in Modern Society. (A collection of essays.) New York: Free Press.

In memoriam: "Clyde Kluckhohn, 1905–1960." *American Sociological Review* (August).

Commentary on *The Mass Media and the Structure of American Society* (co-authored with Winston White). *Journal of Social Issues,* vol. 16, (no. 3):67–77.

Pattern Variables Revisited: A Response to Professor Dubin's Stimulus. *American Sociological Review* (August).

Toward a Healthy Maturity. *Journal of Health and Human Behavior,* vol. 1 (Fall):163–173. Reprinted in *Social Structure and Personality* (1964).

Social Structure and Political Orientation: A review of *Political Man,* by Seymour M. Lipset, and *The Politics of Mass Society,* by William Kornhauser, *World Politics,* vol. 13 (October):112–128.

Review of *Max Weber: An Intellectual Portrait,* by Reinhard Bendix. *American Sociological Review* (October).

The Physician in a Changing Society. *What's New,* no. 220:11–12.

1961   *Theories of Society* (two vols.) (co-edited with Edward Shils, Kaspar D. Naegele, and Jesse R. Pitts). New York: Free Press.

Some Principal Characteristics of Industrial Societies. *The Transformation of Russian Society since 1861,* C. E. Black (ed.). Cambridge, Mass.: Harvard University Press. Reprinted in *Structure and Process in Modern Society* (1960).

The Link between Character and Society (co-authored with Winston White). *Culture and Social Character,* S. M. Lipset and Leo Lowenthal (eds.). New York: Free Press. Reprinted in *Social Structure and Personality* (1964).

The Contribution of Psychoanalysis to the Social Sciences. *Science and Psychoanalysis,* vol. 4.

The Cultural Background of American Religious Organization. *Proceedings of the Conference on Science, Philosophy and Religion.*

The Point of View of the Author. *The Social Theories of Talcott Parsons,* Max Black (ed.). Englewood Cliffs: Prentice-Hall.

The Problem of International Community. *International Politics and Foreign Policy,* James N. Rosenau (ed.). New York: Free Press.

Polarization of the World and International Order. *Preventing World War III,* Q. Wright, W. M. Evan, and M. Deutsch (eds.). New York: Simon & Schuster. Also in the *Berkeley Journal of Sociology* (1961).

Some Considerations on the Theory of Social Change. *Rural Sociology,* vol. 26 (no. 3).

A Sociologist's View. *Values and Ideals of American Youth,* Eli Ginzberg (ed.). New York: Columbia University Press.

Comment on "Preface to a Metatheoretical Framework for Sociology," by Llewellyn Gross. *American Journal of Sociology,* vol. 68 (no. 2): 136–140.

In memoriam: "Alfred L. Kroeber, 1876–1960." *American Journal of Sociology,* vol. 67 (no. 6):616–617.

Comment on "Images of Man and the Sociology of Religion," by William Kolb. *Journal for the Scientific Study of Religion* (October).

Discussion of Trends Revealed by the 1960 Census of Population. *Proceedings of the American Statistical Association Section on Social Statistics.* American Statistical Association.

Clyde Kluckhohn, Anthropologist. *Science,* vol. 144 (no. 3464):1584.

1962   Foreword to *Herbert Spencer: The Study of Sociology*. Ann Arbor: University of Michigan Press (paperback).

In memoriam: "Clyde Kluckhohn, 1905–1960" co-authored with Evon Z. Vogt). *American Anthropologist*, vol. 64 (no. 1), pt. I:140–161. Reprinted as the Introduction to a new edition of Clyde Kluckhohn, *Navajo Witchcraft*. Boston: Beacon, 1962.

Comment on "The Oversocialized Conception of Man," by Dennis Wrong. *Psychoanalysis and Psychoanalytic Review*, (Summer).

Review of *Law and Social Process*, by Hurst. *Journal of the History of Ideas*, vol. 23 (no. 4):558–565.

The Aging in American Society. *Law and Contemporary Problems*, vol. 27 (no. 1):22–35.

The Law and Social Control. *Law and Sociology*, William M. Evan (ed.). New York: Free Press.

In memoriam: "Richard Henry Tawney, 1880–1962." *American Sociological Review* (December).

Review of *Reason in Society: Five Types of Decision and Their Social Conditions*, by Paul Diesing. *Industrial and Labor Relations Review*, vol. 16 (no. 4):630–631.

La struttura dell' azione sociale (introduction by Gianfranco Poggi). Bologna: Il Molino. Translation of *The Structure of Social Action* (1937).

Considerazione teoriche intorno alla sociologia della medicina. Estratto dai *Quaderni di sociologia*, vol. 11 (no. 3):243–279.

The Cultural Background of American Religious Organization. *Ethics and Bigness: Scientific, Academic, Religious, Political, and Military*, Harlan Cleveland and Harold D. Lasswell (eds.). New York: Conference on Science, Philosophy, and Religion in Their Relation to the Democratic Way of Life. Pp. 141–167.

Youth in the Context of American Society. *Dædalus* (Winter):97–123. Reprinted in Social Structure and Personality (1964) and in *Youth: Change and Challenge*, Erik H. Erikson (ed.). New York: Basic Books, 1963.

1963   Introduction to Max Weber, *The Sociology of Religion* (translated by Ephraim Fischoff from *Wirtschaft und Gesellschaft*). Boston: Beacon.

Social Strains in America: A Postscript (1962). *The Radical Right*, Daniel Bell (ed.). Garden City: Doubleday.

Christianity and Modern Industrial Society. *Sociological Theory, Values, and Sociocultural Change: Essays in Honor of Pitirim A. Sorokin*, Edward A. Tiryakian (ed.). New York: Free Press. Pp. 33–70.

Social Change and Medical Organization in the United States: A Sociological Perspective. *Annals of the American Academy of Political and Social Science*, vol. 346:22–33.

On the Concept of Influence (with rejoinder to comments). *Public Opinion Quarterly* (Spring). Reprinted in *Sociological Theory and Modern Society* (1967).

On the Concept of Political Power. *Proceedings of the American Philosophical Society*, vol. 107 (no. 3):232–262. Reprinted in *Socio-*

logical Theory and Modern Society (1967). Translated into Italian as "Il concetto di potere politico," I. *Il Politico* (University of Pavia), vol. 28 (no. 3):614–636. "Il concetto di potere politico, II. Ibid. (no. 4):830–955.

Death in American Society (co-authored with Victor M. Lidz). *American Behavioral Scientist* (May): 1963. Reprinted in *Essays in Self-Destruction*, Edwin Schneidman (ed.). New York: Science House, 1967.

Old Age as Consummatory Phase. *Gerontologist*, vol. 3 (no. 2):53–54.

1964 Some Theoretical Considerations Bearing on the Field of Medical Sociology. Written for a symposium that did not take place. Published in *Social Structure and Personality* (1964).

Social Structure and Personality. (A collection of essays.) New York: Free Press.

The Ideas of Systems, Causal Explanation, and Cybernetic Control in Social Science. *Cause and Effect*, Daniel Lerner (ed.). New York: Free Press. Address presented at the Fourth Hayden Colloquium, Massachusetts Institute of Technology (1964).

Evolutionary Universals in Society. *American Sociological Review*, vol. 29 (no. 3):339–357. Translated into German as "Evolutionare Universalien der Gesellschaft." Reprinted in *Essays on Modernization of Underdeveloped Societies*, A. R. Desai (ed.). Bombay: Thacker. Pp. 560–588.

Max Weber, 1864–1964. *American Sociological Review*, vol. 30 (no. 2): 171–175.

Sociological Theory. *Encyclopedia Britannica*.

Some Reflections on the Place of Force in Social Process. *Internal War: Basic Problems and Approaches*, Harry Eckstein (ed.). New York: Free Press.

Levels of Organization and the Mediation of Social Interaction. *Sociological Inquiry* (Spring):207–220.

Die Juengsten Entwicklungen in Der Strukturell-Funksionalem Theorie. *Koeiner Zeitschrift fuer Soziologie und Sozialpsychologie*. Pp. 30–49. (English version in Haring *Festschrift*.)

Youth in the Context of American Society. *Man in a World at Work*, Henry Borow (ed.). Boston: Houghton Mifflin. Modified version of an article previously written for *Dædalus* (1961).

Unity and Diversity in the Modern Intellectual Disciplines: The Role of the Social Sciences. *Dædalus* (Winter) 1965:39–65.

La Theorie de la société. *Les Etudes philosophiques, perspectives sur la philosophie nord-américaine*, vol. 3 (no. 4):537–547.

Commentary. *Crane Review*, vol. 7 (no. 2):92–97. Address presented to the First Crane Conference on the Ministry (October 1963).

1965 An American's Impression of Sociology in the Soviet Union. *American Sociological Review*, vol. 30 (no. 1):121–125.

Full Citizenship for the Negro American? *Dædalus* (November). Reprinted in *The Negro American*, Talcott Parsons and Kenneth Clark (eds.). Boston: Houghton Mifflin, 1966.

Changing Family Patterns in American Society. *The American Family in Crisis.* Forest Hospital, Des Plaines, Ill.: Forest Hospital Publications. Vol. 3:4–10.

Max Weber, 1864–1964. *American Sociological Review,* vol. 30 (no. 2): 171–175.

Evaluation and Objectivity in the Social Sciences: An Interpretation of Max Weber's Contributions: *International Journal of the Social Sciences.* Reprinted in *Sociological Theory and Modern Society* and in *Max Weber and Sociology Today,* K. Morris (trans.). New York: Harper & Row, 1971. This address presented to the Weber Centennial (April 1964) was published first in German (*Wertgebundenheit und Objektivität in den Sozialwissenschaften:* Eine Interpretation der Beiträge Max Webers) in *Max Weber und die Soziologie Heute,* Otto Stammer (ed.). Tübingen: Mohr. Pp. 39–64.

1966   *Societies: Evolutionary and Comparative Perspectives.* Englewood Cliffs: Prentice-Hall.

The Political Aspect of Social Structure and Process. *Varieties of Political Theory,* David Easton (ed.). Englewood Cliffs: Prentice-Hall.

The Negro American (co-edited with Kenneth Clark). Boston: Houghton Mifflin.

Die Bedeutung der Polarisierung fur das Sozialsystem: Die Hautfarbe als Polarisierungsproblem. *Militanter Humanismus,* Alphons Silbermann (ed.). Frankfurt: Fischer.

1967   The Nature of American Pluralism. *Religion and Public Education,* Theodore Sizer (ed.). Boston: Houghton Mifflin.

Social Science and Theology. *America and the Future of Theology,* William A. Beardslee (ed.). Philadelphia: Westminster.

Sociological Theory and Modern Society. New York: Free Press.

Death in American Society (co-authored with Victor M. Lidz). *Essays in Self-Destruction,* Edwin Shneidman (ed.). New York: Science House.

Comment on "An Economist Looks at the Future of Sociology," by Kenneth Boulding *et al.* vol. 1 (no. 2).

Working Papers in the Theory of Action (reprint edition) (in collaboration with Robert F. Bales and Edward A. Shils). New York: Free Press.

1968   Components and Types of Formal Organization. *Comparative Administrative Theory,* Preston P. LeBreton (ed.). Seattle: University of Washington Press.

Comment on "The Future of the Nineteenth Century Idea of a University," by Sir Eric Ashby. *Minerva* (Spring).

American Sociology (A collection of essays edited by Talcott Parsons.) New York: Basic Books.

Commentary on "Religion as a Cultural System," by Clifford Geertz. *The Religious Situation: 1968,* Donald R. Cutler (ed.). Boston: Beacon.

Christianity. Emile Durkheim. Interaction: Social Interaction. Vilfredo Pareto: Contributions to Economics. Professions. Systems Analysis: Social Systems. Utilitarians: Social Thought. *International Encyclope-*

dia of the Social Sciences, David L. Sills (ed.). New York: Macmillan and Free Press.

The Position of Identity in the General Theory of Action. *The Self in Social Interaction,* Chad Gordon and Kenneth J. Gergen (eds.). New York: Wiley.

The American Academic Profession: A Pilot Study (co-authored with Gerald M. Platt). Cambridge, Mass.: multilith (out of print).

The Academic System: A Sociologist's View. *Public Interest* (special issue), no. 13 (Fall).

On the Concept of Value-Commitments. *Sociological Inquiry,* vol. 38 (no. 2). Reprinted in *Politics and Social Structure.* New York: Free Press, 1969.

Cooley and the Problem of Internalization. *Cooley and Sociological Analysis,* Albert J. Reiss, Jr. (ed.). Ann Arbor: University of Michigan Press.

Sociocultural Pressures and Expectations. (A paper presented to the American Psychiatric Association.) *Psychiatric Research Reports* (February).

Order as a Sociological Problem. *The Concept of Order,* Paul G. Kuntz (ed.). Seattle: University of Washington Press.

The Problem of Polarization on the Axis of Color. *Color and Race,* John Hope Franklin (ed.). Boston: Houghton Mifflin.

Considerations on the American Academic System (co-authored with Gerald M. Platt). *Minerva,* vol. 6 (no. 4).

Law and Sociology: A Promising Courtship? *The Path of the Law from 1967,* Harvard Law School Sesquicentennial Papers, Arthur E. Sutherland (ed.). Cambridge, Mass.: Harvard University Press.

The Disciplines as a Differentiating Force (co-authored with Norman Storer). *The Foundations of Access to Knowledge,* Edward B. Montgomery (ed.). Syracuse: Division of Summer Sessions, Syracuse University.

1969   Research with Human Subjects and the "Professional Complex." *Dædalus* (Spring). Chapter 2 of this volume.

Politics and Social Structure. New York: Free Press.

On Stinchcombe's Conceptualization of Power Phenomena: A Review of *Constructing Social Theories,* by Arthur L. Stinchcombe. *Sociological Inquiry* (May):226–231.

1970   Some Problems of General Theory in Sociology. *Theoretical Sociology: Perspectives and Developments,* John C. McKinney and Edward A. Tiryakian (eds.). New York: Appleton-Century-Crofts.

Age, Social Structure, and Socialization in Higher Education (co-authored with Gerald M. Platt). *Sociology of Education,* vol. 43 (no. 1).

Decision-Making in the Academic System: Influence and Power Exchange (co-authored with Gerald M. Platt). *The State of the University: Authority and Change,* Carlos E. Kruytbosch and Sheldon L. Messinger (eds.). Beverly Hills: Sage Publications.

Theory in the Humanities and Sociology. *Dædalus,* vol. 99 (no. 2).

The Impact of Technology on Culture and Emerging New Modes of Behavior. *International Social Science Journal,* vol. 22 (no. 4).

Equality and Inequality in Modern Society, or Social Stratification Revisited. *Sociological Inquiry,* vol. 40 (Spring):13–72.

On Building Social Systems Theory: A Personal History. *Dædalus,* vol. 99 (no. 4). Reprinted in *The 20th Century Sciences: Studies in the Biography of Ideas,* Gerald Holton (ed.). New York: Norton, 1972.

Some Considerations on the Comparative Sociology of Education. *The Social Sciences and the Comparative Study of Educational Systems,* Joseph Fischer (ed.). Scranton: International Textbook.

1971   *The System of Modern Societies.* Englewood Cliffs: Prentice-Hall. Companion volume to *Societies: Evolutionary and Comparative Perspectives* (1966).

Kinship and the Associational Aspects of Social Structure. *Kinship and Culture,* Francis L. K. Hsu (ed.). Chicago: Aldine.

Comparative Studies and Evolutionary Change. *Comparative Methods in Sociology,* Ivan Vallier (ed.). Berkeley: University of California Press. Pp. 97–139.

The Normal American Family. *Readings on the Sociology of the Family,* Bert N. Adams and Thomas Weirath (eds.). Chicago: Markham. Pp. 53–66. Reprinted from *Man and Civilization: The Family's Search for Survival,* Farber, Mustacchi, and Wilson, New York: McGraw-Hill, 1965.

Belief, Unbelief, and Disbelief. *The Culture of Unbelief: Studies and Proceedings from the First International Symposium on Belief,* Rocco Caporale and Antonio Grumelli (ed.). Berkeley: University of California Press. Pp. 207–245. Chapter 11 of this volume.

1972   Higher Education as a Theoretical Focus. *Institutions and Social Exchange: The Sociologies of Talcott Parsons and George C. Homans,* Richard Simpson and Herman Turk (eds.). Indianapolis: Bobbs-Merrill.

Higher Education, Changing Socialization, and Contemporary Student Dissent (co-authored with Gerald M. Platt). *Aging and Society, vol. 3: A Sociology of Age Stratification,* Matilda W. Riley, Marilyn E. Johnson, Anne Foner. New York: Russell Sage.

Commentary on "Structural-Functionalism, Exchange Theory and the New Political Economy: Institutionalization as a Theoretical Linkage." by Terry Clark. *Sociological Inquiry,* vol. 42 (nos. 3–4):299–308.

Readings on Premodern Societies (co-edited with Victor M. Lidz). Englewood Cliffs: Prentice-Hall.

Field Theory and Systems Theory: With Special Reference to the Relations Between Psychological and Social Systems. *Modern Psychiatry and Clinical Research: Essays in Honor of Roy R. Grinker, Sr.,* Daniel Offer and Daniel X. Freedman (eds.). New York: Basic Books.

The Action Frame of Reference and the General Theory of Action Systems. *Classic Contributions to Social Psychology: Readings with Commentary,* Edwin P. Hollander and Raymond G. Hunt (eds.). New York: Oxford University Press. Pp. 168–176. Slightly abridged from *The Social System.* New York: Free Press, 1951. Pp. 3–11, 15–19.

The "Gift of Life" and Its Reciprocation (co-authored with Renée C. Fox and Victor M. Lidz). *Social Research*, vol. 39 (no. 3):367–415. Reprinted in *Death in American Experience*, Arien Mack (ed.). New York: Schocken, 1973. Pp. 1–49. Chapter 12 of this volume.

Review of *Scholarship and Partisanship*, by Reinhard Bendix and Guenther Roth. *Contemporary Sociology*, vol. 1 (no. 3):200–203.

Culture and Social System Revisited. *Social Science Quarterly*, (September):253–266. Reprinted in *The Idea of Culture in the Social Sciences*, Louis Schneider and Charles Bonjean (eds.). Cambridge: At the University Press, 1973. Pp. 33–46.

1973 Durkheim on Religion Revisited: Another Look at *The Elementary Forms of the Religious Life. Beyond the Classics? Essays in the Scientific Study of Religion*, Charles Y. Glock and Phillip E. Hammond (eds.). New York: Harper Torchbooks. Pp. 156–180. Chapter 10 of this volume.

The American University (co-authored with Gerald M. Platt and in collaboration with Neil J. Smelser). Cambridge, Mass.: Harvard University Press.

Clyde Kluckhohn and the Integration of Social Science. *Culture and Life: Essays in Memory of Clyde Kluckhohn*, Walter W. Taylor, John L. Fischer, and Evon Z. Vogt (eds.). Carbondale: Southern Illinois University Press. Pp. 30–57.

Review of *A Critique of Max Weber's Philosophy of Social Science*, by W. G. Runciman. *Political Science Quarterly*.

The Bellah Case: Man and God in Princeton, New Jersey. *Commonweal*, vol. 98 (no. 11):256–259.

Religious Symbolization and Death. *Changing Perspectives in the Scientific Study of Religion*, Allan Eister (ed.). New York: Wiley-Interscience.

Some Reflections on Post-Industrial Society. *Japanese Sociological Review*, vol. 24 (no. 2):109–113. Address presented to the Japan Sociological Association (September 1973).

The Problem of Balancing Rational Efficiency with Communal Solidarity in Modern Society. *International Symposium on "New Problems of Advanced Societies."* Tokyo: Japan Economic Research Institute. Pp. 9–14.

The Social Concept of the Present Civilization. *Tribuna Medica*, (September):19–20.

Review of *Sociology and Philosophy*, by L. T. Hobhouse. *Sociological Inquiry*, vol. 43 (no. 1):85–87.

Review of *Capitalism and Modern Societal Theory: An Analysis of the Writings of Marx, Durkheim, and Max Weber*, by Anthony Giddens. *American Political Science Review*, vol. 67 (no. 4):1358–1360.

1974 The University "Bundle": A Study of the Balance Between Differentiation and Integration. *Public Higher Education in California: Growth, Structural Change, and Conflict*, Neil J. Smelser and Gabriel Almond (eds.). Berkeley: University of California Press. Chapter 7 of this volume.

Review of *A God Within,* by Rene Dubos. *Commonweal,* vol. 100 (no. 2):42–44.

The Institutional Function in Organization Theory. *Organization and Administrative Sciences,* vol. 5 (no. 1):3–16. Address presented at the Comparative Administrative Research Institute, Kent State University (May 1974).

Sigmund Freud: *The Interpretation of Dreams. Dædalus* (special issue), vol. 103 (no. 1):91–96. Chapter 4 of this volume.

The Life and Work of Emile Durkheim. Emile Durkheim, *Sociology and Philosophy* (reprint ed.). New York: Free Press. Pp. xliii–lxx.

Review of *Ideology and Social Knowledge,* by Harold J. Bershady. *Sociological Inquiry,* vol. 44 (no. 3):215–221. Reprinted as part of Chapter 6 in *Social Systems and the Evolution of Action Theory* (1977).

Review of *Social Organization: A General Systems and Role Theory Perspective,* by Alvin L. Bertrand. *Social Forces,* vol. 53 (no. 1):126–127.

Comment on "Current Folklore in the Criticisms of Parsonian Action Theory," by Turner and Beeghley. *Sociological Inquiry,* vol. 44 (no. 1):55–58.

1975   Pareto's Approach to the Construction of a Theory of the Social Systems. Rome: Accademia Nazionale dei Lincei. Address presented at the International Conference on Vilfredo Pareto (October 1973).

The Present Status of "Structural-Functional" Theory. *The Idea of Social Structure,* Lewis A. Coser (ed.). New York: Harcourt Brace Jovanovich. Reprinted in *Social Systems and the Evolution of Action Theory* (1977). Chapter 4.

The Sick Role and the Role of the Physician Reconsidered. *Millbank Memorial Fund Quarterly,* vol. 53 (no. 3):257–278. Reprinted in *Action Theory and the Human Condition* (1978). Chapter 1 of this volume.

Social Structure and the Symbolic Media of Interchange. *Approaches to the Study of Social Structure,* Peter M. Blau (ed.). New York: Free Press. Reprinted in *Social Systems and the Evolution of Action Theory* (1977). Chapter 9 of that volume.

Some Theoretical Considerations on the Nature and Trends of Ethnicity. *Ethnicity: Theory and Experience,* Nathan Glazer and Daniel P. Moynihan (eds.). Cambridge, Mass.: Harvard University Press. Reprinted in *Social Systems and the Evolution of Action Theory* (1977). Chapter 13.

Commentary on "Classic on Classic: Parsons' Interpretation of Durkheim," by Whitney Pope, and "Moral Freedom through Understanding in Durkheim," by Jere Cohen. *American Sociological Review,* vol. 40 (no. 1):106–110.

Commentary on "De-Parsonizing Weber: A Critique of Parsons' Interpretation of Weber's Sociology," by Cohen, Hazelrigg, and Pope. *American Sociological Review,* vol. 40 (no. 5):666–669.

Commentary on "A Radical Analysis of Welfare Economics and Individual Development," by Herbert Gintis. *Quarterly Journal of Economics,* vol. 89:280–290.

Comment on "Parsons as a Symbolic Interactionist," by Jonathan Turner, *Sociological Inquiry,* vol. 45 (no. 1):62–65.

1976 Some Considerations on the Growth of the American System of Higher Education and Research. *Culture and Its Creators: Essays in Honor of Edward Shils,* T. N. Clark and J. Ben-David (eds.). Chicago: University of Chicago Press. Reprinted in *Action Theory and the Human Condition* (1978).

The Sociology and Economics of Clarence E. Ayers. *Science and Ceremony: The Institutional Economics of Clarence E. Ayers,* Culbertson and Breit (eds.). Austin: University of Texas Press.

Social Stratification. Professions. *Enciclopedia italiana,* Vincenzo Cappelletti (ed.). Rome.

Reply to Cohen, Hazelrigg, and Pope, with Special Reference to Their Statement "On the Divergence of Weber and Durkheim: A Critique of Parsons' Convergence Thesis." *American Sociological Review,* vol. 41 (no. 2):361–364.

A Few Considerations on the Place of Rationality in Modern Culture and Society. *Revue européenne des sciences sociales et cahiers Vilfredo Pareto* (special issue), vol. 14, (nos. 38–39).

Vico and History. *Social Research,* vol. 43 (no. 4):881–885.

Social Science: The Public Disenchantment. *American Scholar,* (Autumn):580–581.

Faculty Teaching Goals, 1968–1973 (co-authored with Gerald M. Platt and Rita Kirshstein). *Social Problems,* vol. 24 (no. 2):298–307.

1977 *The Evolution of Societies* (edited, with an introduction, by Jackson Toby). Englewood Cliffs: Prentice-Hall.

Social Systems and the Evolution of Action Theory. New York: Free Press.

A 1974 Retrospective Perspective: Alfred Schütz, Talcott Parsons, *Zur Theorie Sozialen Handelns, Ein Briefwechsel,* Herausgegeben und Eingeleitet von Walter M. Sprondel. Frankfurt am Main: Surkamp Verlag.

Comment on Burger's Critique: A Reply to Thomas Burger, "Talcott Parsons, the Problem of Order in Society, and the Program of an Analytical Sociology," both in *American Journal of Sociology,* vol. 83, (no. 2):335–339 and 320–334.

Two Cases of Social Deviance: Addiction to Heroin, Addiction to Power (co-authored with Dean R. Gerstein). *Deviance and Social Change,* Edwin Sagarin (ed.). Beverly Hills, Calif.: Sage Publications.

Forth-
coming

The Future of the University. *Vestes* (Australian journal). Reprinted in *Action Theory and the Human Condition* (1978). Chapter 5 of this volume.

Action, Symbols, and Cybernetic Controls. *Towards the Sociology of Symbolic Structures,* Ino Rossi (ed.).

Health and Disease: A Sociological and Action Perspective. Death in the Western World. *Encyclopedia of Bioethics.* New York: Free Press. Reprinted in *Action Theory and the Human Condition* (1978). Chapters 3 and 14 of this volume.

Law as an Intellectual "Stepchild." *Sociological Inquiry,* vol. 47 (nos. 3–4) (1978).

Epilogue to *The Doctor-Patient Relationship,* Eugene B. Gallagher (ed.). 1978.

The Symbolic Environment of the Economy (Japanese translation). *Contemporary Economics,* a journal.

Index